CONDITIONAL LOGIC IN EXPERT SYSTEMS

CONDITIONAL LOGIC IN EXPERT SYSTEMS

Edited by

I. R. GOODMAN
Naval Ocean Systems Center
San Diego, California
U.S.A.

M. M. GUPTA
Intelligent Systems Research Laboratory
College of Engineering
University of Saskatchewan
Saskatoon, Canada

H. T. NGUYEN
Department of Mathematical Sciences
New Mexico State University
Las Cruces, New Mexico
U.S.A.

G. S. ROGERS
Department of Mathematical Sciences
New Mexico State University
Las Cruces, New Mexico
U.S.A.

1991

NORTH-HOLLAND
AMSTERDAM • NEW YORK • OXFORD • TOKYO

ELSEVIER SCIENCE PUBLISHERS B.V.
Sara Burgerhartstraat 25
P.O. Box 211, 1000 AE Amsterdam, The Netherlands

Distributors for the United States and Canada:
ELSEVIER SCIENCE PUBLISHING COMPANY INC.
655 Avenue of the Americas
New York, N.Y. 10010, U.S.A.

Library of Congress Cataloging-in-Publication Data

Conditional logic in expert systems / edited by I.R. Goodman ... [et al.].
p. cm.
Includes bibliographical references.
ISBN 0-444-88819-5
1. Expert systems (Computer science) 2. Logic, Symbolic and mathematical. I. Goodman, Irwin R.
QA76.76.E95C6644 1991
006.3'3--dc20 91-8635
CIP

ISBN: 0 444 88819 5

Printed in The Netherlands

PREFACE

The concept of information is essential in everyday decision making processes. As humans, our perception of information generally suffices and our brain proceeds to the making of decisions. Yet over and beyond mere philosophical reasons, there is a real need to develop an artificial language to represent information and to model human reasoning in this era of automation within an information based society.

In its most general sense, information is a hard concept to capture mathematically. One companion of information is the concept of probability; but, to many people, probability and information are conjoined like the "chicken and the egg". Nevertheless, it has been customary to represent uncertain knowledge via probability measures. But, as Richard Bellman emphasized (Bellman, 1978), this should not be taken to mean that uncertainty is always probability. (Details of references in this preface can be found in the references of the contributed papers.) This aspect is more apparent in the various domains of Artificial Intelligence. In fact, when observations (data) cannot be obtained in exact form but the simple events form a partition of the sample space, belief functions or random set specifications can be used in place of pointwise probability distributions. And, when information is expressed in some natural language, the concept of fuzziness seems to be most appropriate in modeling imprecision and subjectivity of word meanings.

In one view of information, knowledge or data is always *conditional* and probability is no exception. Thus, mathematically, one needs to model *conditional information* first and then *reasoning processes* based on that. In other words, one needs to develop a language in which facts, rules, and inference procedures based on conditional information can be represented and manipulated. This is one logical view of knowledge representation and inference for decision making by machines.

This edited volume is a collection of articles devoted to the investigation of various basic aspects of *conditional logics* in precisely this spirit. The articles by Dubois and Prade, Hestir, Nguyen and Rogers, Goodman, Gupta and Qi, Smets, and Thoma relate to belief functions and fuzzy logics. Those by Calabrese, Goodman, Walker, Nguyen and Rogers, Dubois and Prade, and Spies are centered on the newly developed theory of measure-free conditioning. This deeper examination of conditional logics was reactivated around 1987 (Calabrese) sparked by the interest in AI, as exemplified by a logic of conditionals (Adams, 1975) and popularized in Pearl's book on probabilistic reasoning (Pearl, 1988; see also Neapolitan, 1990).

By conditional logics, we mean mathematical logics of implicative propositions in uncertain environments. There has been some duplication of effort in the scattered works touching pieces of this topic and traceable back to Boole (1854). The corner stone is the mathematical concept of conditional events (measure-free). Although conditional probability seems to be sufficient for most statistical analysis of random phenomena, logicians and "subjective probabilists" had trouble with this concept; various difficulties were noted by Koopman (1940), Copeland (1941), De Finetti (1964), Schay (1968), Adams (1975), and Hailperin (1976). Suprisingly, these works seem to be independent of one another, suggesting that this topic lacks a recognized home. A comprehensive theory of conditional events and their associated logics will soon appear as a companion to this edited volume (Goodman, Nguyen, and Walker, "Conditional Inference and Logic for Intelligent Systems: A Theory of Measure-Free Conditioning".)

Many of the articles in the present volume are detailed discussions of topics presented at The SIAM Annual Meeting, San Diego, CA, July 1989, The Third IFSA Congress, Seattle, WA, August, 1989, and The First International Symposium on Uncertainty Modeling and Analysis, College Park, MD, December, 1990. We extend our thanks to all contributors.

We would also like to thank N. Batle and J. Miro for courtesies extended to H. Nguyen during a Fulbright Professor (Specialist Exchange) Program at Palma de Mallorca in December, 1987.

I.R. Goodman, M.M. Gupta, H.T. Nguyen, G.S. Rogers

LIST OF CONTRIBUTORS

Calabrese, P.	Naval Ocean Systems Center, Code 421, San Diego, CA, 92152-5000, USA
Dubois, D.	Institut de Recherche en Informatique de Toulouse. Université Paul Sabatier, 118 Route de Narbonne, 31062-Toulouse, France
Goodman, I.R.	Naval Ocean System Center, Code 421, San Diego, CA, 92152-5000, USA
Gupta, M.M.	Intelligent Systems Research Laboratory, College of Engineering, University of Saskatchewan, Saskatoon, Saskatchewan, S7N0W0, Canada
Hestir, K.	Department of Mathematical Sciences, New Mexico State University, Las Cruces, NM, 88003, USA
Nguyen, H.T.	Department of Mathematical Sciences, New Mexico State University, Las Cruces, NM, 88003, USA
Prade, H.	Institut de Recherche en Informatique de Toulouse, Université Paul Sabatier, 118 Route de Narbonne, 31062-Toulouse, France
Qi, J.	Intelligent Systems Research Laboratory, College of Engineering, University of Saskatchewan, Saskatoon, Saskatchewan, S7N0W0, Canada
Rogers, G.S.	Department of Mathematical Sciences, New Mexico State University, Las Cruces, NM, 88003, USA
Smets, P.	IRIDIA, Université Libre de Bruxelles, 50 Av. F. Roosevelt, CP 194-6, 1050 Brussels, Belgium
Spies, M.	IBM German Science Center, Institute for Knowledge-based Systems, Schlosstrasse 70, d-7000, Stuggart, Germany
Thoma, H.M.	CIBA-GEIGY Corporation, 556 Morris Avenue, Summit, NJ, 07901, USA
Walker, E.A.	Department of Mathematical Sciences, New Mexico State University, Las Cruces, NM, 88003, USA

CONTENTS

Conditional Logic in Expert Systems
I.R. Goodman, M.M. Gupta, H.T. Nguyen and G.S. Rogers (editors)
Elsevier Science Publishers B.V. (North-Holland), 1991

ALGEBRAIC AND PROBABILISTIC BASES FOR FUZZY SETS AND THE DEVELOPMENT OF FUZZY CONDITIONING

I.R. Goodman

Code 421, Command & Control Department
Naval Ocean Systems Center
San Diego, CA 92152-5000

Abstract. This paper first develops an extension of the Negoita-Ralescu Representation Theorem for fuzzy sets in terms of flou sets relative to operators and partitionings. It then reviews in some detail both the random set/random variable basis for fuzzy sets, as well as the foundation of conditional event algebras. Both of these areas are tied together, first in the form of conditional event indicator functions, and then through the development of conditioning fuzzy sets. Specificially, it is shown that the structure of conditional event algebra as proposed here drives the structure for fuzzy conditioning, resulting in conditional fuzzy sets being necessarily of a simple form relative to their membership functions to a given marginal. It is seen that with this approach, a full calculus of operations, extending that of ordinary conditional events, is obtained.

Keywords. Fuzzy sets, membership functions, flou sets, conditional fuzzy sets, random sets, partitionings, conditional event algebra.

1. Introduction.

Even after twenty-five years following Zadeh's introduction of fuzzy sets (1965), controversy still persists in this arena of uncertainty modeling: 1. Should one choose a fuzzy set or probability approach to a particular problem at hand? 2. Can objective criteria be set up for comparing and contrasting fuzzy sets and probability? 3. What, exactly, are the relations between the two approaches and can they be reconciled with each other? 4. Can an analogue of conditioning in probability be established for fuzzy sets, especially in light of the newly-developed area of conditional event algebra (Goodman & Nguyen, (1988), Goodman, Nguyen, Walker (1991))?

The first question still remains an open issue to this day. An approach to answering the second one has been done through the use of game theory, as proposed by Lindley (1982) and reconsidered by Goodman, Nguyen & Rogers (1991). As for question three, previously Goodman (1981), Höhle (1982), and Goodman & Nguyen (1985), among others, initiated work on relating directly fuzzy sets and probability through random set theory. In another direction, Negoita & Ralescu have considered the relationship between fuzzy sets and certain collections of nested ordinary sets (or "flou" sets) (1975), while Gaines has considered both fuzzy sets and probability logic from a common algebraic framework (1978). (See Goodman & Nguyen (1985, Chapter 7) for a more thorough history of attempts at connecting fuzzy sets with probability.) The last question has been addressed by a number of individuals. E.g., Mattila (1986), Sembi & Mamdani (1979), and Yager (1983) consider extensions and modifications of ordinary material implication, while Zadeh (1978), Nguyen (1978), Hisdal (1978), Bouchon (1987), and Goodman & Stein (1989) approached fuzzy conditioning with at least some concept of conditional probability relative to ordinary sets in mind.

A common theme underlies the above issues and their responses: there is a real need to, once and for all, establish a unifying approach to fuzzy sets, their algebraic or syntactic bases, and their internal and external relations to probability. Recently, conditioning in probability has been re-examined and it has been demonstrated that a firm algebraic basis -- in addition to the usual numerically-oriented approach -- can be derived for conditioning. (See Schay (1968), Adams (1975), Calabrese (1987), and Goodman, Nguyen, & Walker (1991), as well as the work of Dubois & Prade (1990).) Thus,it would also be desirable to be able to extend the above work to fuzzy sets based on firm logical considerations.

The purpose of this paper is twofold: First, to develop a sound algebraic basis for fuzzy sets, based upon the fundamental work of Negoita & Ralescu (1975). This will serve as a lead-in to the probability basis for fuzzy sets. In short, flou sets -- and a new alternative, but equivalent, representation in the form of ordered partitionings -- are proposed as the natural candidates for the syntactic foundations of fuzzy sets, underlying the semantic evaluations: fuzzy set membership functions. However, the scope here is a limited one and the very generalized set theory encompassing fuzzy sets in the form of categories and pseudotopoi will not be treated here. (See, e.g., Barr (1989), Eytan (1981), Pitts (1982), Goguen (1974), and Stout (1984).)

In addition, extensions of the Stone Representation Theorem to fuzzy sets as, e.g., treated in Glas (1984) and Belluce (1986) will not be considered. The second goal of this paper is to be able to apply the basic algebraic and probabilistic foundations for fuzzy sets to the development of conditioning and related concepts.

This paper consists of eight additional sections. In section 2 the basic spaces are considred: partitioning, flou, and membership function spaces and their bijections. In section 3 a standard procedure is reviewed for inducing isomorphisms from bijections relative to the base spaces. Section 4 develops operations isomorphic to fuzzy set membership operations, including cartesian products, sums, intersections, unions, complements, functional and inverse functional transforms, among others. A similar development for partitioning sets is given in section 5. Section 6 reviews briefly conditioning of ordinary sets and establishes a connection with three-valued fuzzy set membership functions as a special case of finite-valued membership functions. In section 7, logical models for fuzzy sets are characterized. In turn, external probabilities of fuzzy set membership functions are determined. These are especially useful as a rationale for single figures-of-merit for fuzzy sets -- analogous to the moments of cdf's. In a direction opposite to section 7, the underlying probability basis for fuzzy sets is summarized in section 8. The focus here is the uniform randomization of flou sets and partitioning sets, as well as their isomorphic relations to the class of membership functions. (A third connection between probability and fuzzy sets is given briefly at the end of sect. 4 via cdf's as formal fuzzy set membership functions.) Finally, in section 9 conditional fuzzy sets are defined, based upon random set considerations as developed in the previous sections. A full calculus of operations and relations is derived, extending all of the previous results obtained for ordinary conditional events to fuzzy sets.

2. Fundamental Spaces and Bijective Mappings.

Throughout the remaining paper denote the unit interval $[0, 1] = \{t : 0 \le t \le 1\}$ by u. Also, let SET denote the collection of all well-defined sets and consider the operators Part, Flou, Mem:SET $\rightarrow$ SET and mappings on SET, ϕ, ψ, where for all $X \in$ SET, $\phi(X) : \text{Flou}(X) \rightarrow \text{Mem}(X)$ and $\psi(X) : \text{Part}(X) \rightarrow \text{Flou}(X)$.

$\text{Part}(X) \overset{d}{=}$ set of all *ordered disjoint nonvacuous exhaustive partitionings* q of X, where typically (2.1)

$$q = (q_t)_{t \in J_q}, \quad \emptyset \neq J_q \subseteq u \; ; \; q_t \in \mathcal{P}(X); \; q_s \cap q_t = \emptyset, \; s \neq t; \; \bigcup_{t \in J_q} q_t = X. \tag{2.2}$$

$\text{Flou}(X) \overset{d}{=}$ set of all *flou sets* (see originally Gentilhomme (1968)) a of X, where typically (2.3)

$$a = (a_t)_{t \in u}, \; X = a_0 \supseteq a_s \supseteq a_t \supseteq a_1 \supseteq \emptyset; \; \bigcap_{t \in J} a_t = a_{\sup(J)}, \; \text{all } J \subseteq u; \; 0 \le s \le t \le 1 \tag{2.4}$$

arbitrary real. The right hand side relation is continuity from above.

$$\text{Mem}(X) \overset{d}{=} \text{set of all } \textit{fuzzy set membership functions } f \text{ of } X$$

$$= u^X = \{f : f : X \rightarrow u\} \, , \tag{2.5}$$

including all ordinary set indicator functions $g : X \rightarrow \{0, 1\}$.

$\phi(X) : \text{Flou}(X) \rightarrow \text{Mem}(X)$, the *fundamental membership mapping* is defined for any

$a \in \mathrm{Flou}(X)$, $\phi(X)(a) : X \to u$, where for all $x \in X$,

$$\phi(X)(a)(x) \overset{d}{=} \sup\{t : t \in u \ \& \ x \in a_t\}. \tag{2.6}$$

$\psi(X) : \mathrm{Part}(X) \to \mathrm{Flou}(X)$ is the *fundamental fuzzy set forming mapping*, where for any $q \in \mathrm{Part}(X)$ and any $t \in u$,

$$(\psi(X)(q))_t \overset{d}{=} \cup\{q_s : s \in J_q \ \& \ t \leq s \leq 1\}. \tag{2.7}$$

All of this leads to

Theorem 2.1. For each $X \in \mathrm{SET}$, $\phi(X)$ is a bijection, with inverse $\phi(X)^{-1}$: $\mathrm{Mem}(X) \to \mathrm{Flou}(X)$ given for any $f \in \mathrm{Mem}(X)$ as $\phi(X)^{-1}(f) \in \mathrm{Flou}(X)$, where for all $t \in u$,

$$(\phi(X)^{-1}(f))_t \overset{d}{=} f^{-1}[t, 1] = \{x : x \in X \ \& \ 1 \geq f(x) \tag{2.8}$$

the tth*-level* (or *cut*) *set* of f. Note also that for all $x \in X$, the supremum in eq. (2.6) is always achieved, so that

$$x \in a_{\phi(X)(a)(x)}, \quad \text{all } x \in X. \tag{2.9}$$

Proof: Though Negoita & Ralescu (1975) have developed a representation theorem with a slightly different form, for purposes of completeness, a full proof for the present version will be presented here.

Obviously, $\phi(X)$ is well-defined. For any $f \in \mathrm{Mem}(X)$, define $\phi(X)^{-1}(f)$ as in (2.8). Clearly, from the basic properties of inverse functions, $\phi(X)^{-1}(f)$ satisfies property left hand side of (2.4). For the right hand side of (2.4) let $J \subseteq u$ arbitrary (nonvacuous). Then, for any $x \in X$, $x \in \cap\{f^{-1}[t, 1] : t \in J\}$ iff $f(x) \geq J$ iff $f(x) \geq \sup(J)$ iff $x \in f^{-1}[\sup(J), 1]$. Thus, (2.4) is satisfied and $\phi(X)^{-1}(f) \in \mathrm{Flou}(X)$. In turn, for any $x \in X$, $\phi(X)(\phi(X)^{-1}(f))(x) = \sup\{t : t \in u \ \& \ x \in f^{-1}[t, 1]\}$ $= \sup\{t : t \in u \ \& \ t \leq f(x)\} = f(x)$, implying that $\phi(X)$ is surjective with $\phi(X)^{-1}$ being a candidate for its inverse. Next, let $a \in \mathrm{Flou}(X)$ arbitrary and for any $t \in u$,

$$\begin{aligned}(\phi(X)^{-1}(\phi(X)(a)))_t &= \phi(X)(a)^{-1}[t, 1] = \{x : x \in X \ \& \ \phi(X)(a)(x) \geq t\} \\ &= \{x : x \in X \ \& \ \sup\{s : s \in u \ \& \ x \in a_s\} \geq t\}.\end{aligned} \tag{2.10}$$

Now, if $x \in a_t$, then clearly $\sup\{s : s \in u \ \& \ x \in a_s\} \geq t$. Conversely, if the $\sup \geq t$, then letting $J_x \overset{d}{=} \{s : s \in u \ \& \ x \in a_s\}$, by RHS (2.4) property,

$x \in \cap\{a_s : s \in J_x\} = a_{\sup(J_x)}$ with $\sup(J_x) \geq t$, whence $x \in a_{\sup(J_x)} \subseteq a_t$.

Thus, for all $t \in u$, $x \in a_t$ iff $\sup\{s : s \in u \ \&\ x \in a_s\} \geq t$; all $x \in X$. (2.11)

Combining (2.10) and (2.11) shows

$$(\phi(X)^{-1}(\phi(X)(a)))_t = \{x : x \in a_t\} = a_t, \tag{2.12}$$

verifying that for all $a \in \mathrm{Flou}(X)$,

$$\phi(X)^{-1}(\phi(X)(a)) = a. \tag{2.13}$$

It is readily seen that (2.13) is sufficient to show that $\phi(X)$ is injective. Since $\phi(X)$ was also shown to be surjective, the above shows that it is bijective. Finally, (2.13) also shows (2.9) directly. ■

Theorem 2.2. $\psi(X)$ is a bijection with inverse $\psi(X)^{-1} : \mathrm{Flou}(X) \to \mathrm{Part}(X)$, given for any $a \in \mathrm{Flou}(X)$ as $\psi(X)^{-1}(a) \in \mathrm{Part}(X)$, with index set

$$J_{\psi(X)^{-1}(a)} = \{t : t \in u \ \&\ a_t - a_{t^+} \neq \emptyset\}, \tag{2.14}$$

where

$$a_{t^+} = \cup\{a_s : t < s \leq 1\},\ t \in u, \tag{2.15}$$

and where for all $t \in J_{\psi(X)^{-1}(a)}$, i.e., $a_t - a_{t^+} \neq \emptyset$,

$$(\psi(X)^{-1}(a))_t \overset{d}{=} a_t - a_{t^+}, \tag{2.16}$$

with the convention that

$$a_{1^+} = \cup_{\emptyset}\{a_s\} = \emptyset. \tag{2.17}$$

Proof: First, note that for any $q \in \mathrm{Part}(X)$, and hence $\psi(X)(q) \in \mathrm{Flou}(X)$: For all $0 \leq s \leq t \leq 1$,

$$\begin{aligned}(\psi(X)(q))_0 = \cup\{q_s : s \in J_q\} = X \ ;\ (\psi(X)(q))_s &= \cup\{q_r : r \in J_q, s \leq r\} \\ &\supseteq \cup\{q_r : r \in J_q, t \leq r\} = (\psi(X)(q))_t,\end{aligned} \tag{2.18}$$

verifying the left hand side of (2.4). For any $K \subseteq u$, let $x \in (\psi(X)(q))_{\sup(K)}$. Thus, there exists $s \in J_q$ with $s \geq \sup(K)$ such that $x \in q_s$. Hence, for each $t \in K$, there exists $s \in J_q$ with $s > \sup(K)$ and $x \in q_s$. Hence,

$$x \in (\psi(X)(q))_{\sup(K)} \subseteq \bigcap_{t \in K} \bigcup_{t \leq s \leq 1} q_s = \bigcap_{t \in K} (\psi(X)(q))_t \tag{2.19}$$

Conversely, let $x \in \bigcap_{t \in K} (\psi(X)(q))_t$. Since q is a partitioning of X, there is a unique $t_o \in J_q$ such that $x \in q_{t_o}$. Thus, $x \in \bigcap_{t \in K} (\psi(X)(q))_t$ becomes: for all $t \in K$, $x \in (\psi(X)(q))_t$, so that for each $t \in K$, there is an $s \in J_q$ with $t \leq s$, $x \in q_s = q_{t_o}$, noting that $t_o \geq K$. Hence

$$x \in q_{t_o} \subseteq \bigcup_{s\in[\sup(K),1]\cap J_q} (q_s) = (\psi(X)(q))_{\sup(K)} \tag{2.20}$$

Combining (2.19) and (2.20) shows the right hand side of (2.4) holding. Hence (2.4) completely holds and $\psi(X)(q) \in \text{Flou}(X)$. Hence, $\psi(X) : \text{Part}(X) \to \text{Flou}(X)$ is a well-defined mapping.

Next, consider the mapping $\phi(X)\circ\psi(X) : \text{Part}(X) \to \text{Mem}(X)$ which is also well-defined since ϕ and ψ are. For any $f \in \text{Mem}(X)$, consider the partitioning

$$q(f) = ((q(f))_s)_{s\in J_r} \; ; \; J_f \overset{d}{=} \text{range}(f) = \{f(x) : x \in X\} \; ; \; (q(f))_s \overset{d}{=} f^{-1}(s), \tag{2.21}$$

for all $s \in J_f$. Then, for all $x \in X$, using (2.21),

$$\phi(X)(\psi(X)(q(f)))(x) = \sup\{t : t \in u \;\&\; x \in \bigcup_{(s\in J_f, t\leq s)} f^{-1}(s)\}$$

$$= \sup\{t : t \in u \;\&\; x \in f^{-1}[t, 1]\} = f(x), \tag{2.22}$$

showing $\phi(X)\circ\psi(X)$ is surjective with

$$(\phi(X)\circ\psi(X))(q(f)) = f, \text{ all } f \in \text{Mem}(X). \tag{2.23}$$

next, for each $q \in \text{Part}(X)$, define $f_q \in \text{Mem}(X)$ by, for all $x \in X$,

$$f_q(x) \overset{d}{=} s, \text{ for that unique } s \in J_q \text{ for which } x \in q_s \tag{2.24}$$

Clearly, (2.24) is equivalent to the relation

$$f_q^{-1}(s) = q_s \, , \text{ all } s \in J_q. \tag{2.25}$$

Note, using the notation of (2.21), $J_{f_q} = \text{range}(f_q) = J_q$, and since for all $s \in J_{f_q}$, (2.25) shows $(q(f_q))_s = f_q^{-1}(s) = q_s$, then one has

$$a(f_q) = q. \tag{2.26}$$

Finally, replacing f by f_q in (2.23), using (2.26), shows that

$$(\phi(X)\circ\psi(X))(q) = f_q. \tag{2.27}$$

In turn, (2.27) shows that $\phi(X)\circ\psi(X)$ is also injective. Hence, by the previously established property of being surjective, $\phi(X)\circ\psi(X)$ is bijective.

Next, (2.23) in conjunction with the bijectivity of $\phi(X)\circ\psi(X)$ shows

$$\psi(X)^{-1}\circ\phi(X)^{-1}(f) = (\phi(X)\circ\psi(X))^{-1}(f) = q(f). \tag{2.28}$$

Then, letting $a \in \text{Flou}(X)$ arbitrary and choosing $f = \phi(X)(a)$ in (2.28), since by Theorem 2.1, $\phi(X)^{-1}(\phi(X)(a)) = a$, one obtains

$$\psi(X)^{-1}(a) = q(\phi(X)(a)), \tag{2.29}$$

where by (2.21)

$$J_{q(\phi(X)(a))} = \text{range}(\phi(X)(a)) = \{\sup\{t : t \in u \ \& \ x \in a_t\} : x \in X), \tag{2.30}$$

and for each $t \in J_{q(\phi(X)(a))}$, by (2.24),

$$(q(\phi(X)(a)))_t = (\phi(X)(a))^{-1}(t). \tag{2.31}$$

But, Theorem 2.1 shows

$$a_t = (\phi(X)(a))^{-1}[t, 1] \tag{2.32}$$

and

$$a_{t^+} = \bigcup_{t<s\leq 1} a_s = \bigcup_{t<s\leq 1} (\phi(X)(a))^{-1}[s,1]$$
$$= (\phi(X)(a))^{-1}\Big(\bigcup_{t<s\leq 1} [s, 1]\Big) = (\phi(X)(a))^{-1}(t,1]. \tag{2.33}$$

Combining (2.29)-(2.33), shows for all $t \in J_{\psi(X)^{-1}(a)}$,

$$(\psi(X)^{-1}(a))_t = (\phi(X)(a))^{-1}(t) = (\phi(X)(a))^{-1}[t, 1] - (\phi(X)(a))^{-1}(t, 1]$$
$$= a_t - a_{t^+}, \text{ matching eq. (2.16).} \tag{2.34}$$

Finally, by (2.29) and (2.31),

$$a_t - a_{t^+} = (\phi(X)(a))^{-1}(t) \neq \emptyset \ \text{ iff } \ t \in \text{range}(\phi(X)(a)) = J_{q(\phi(X)(a))}. \tag{2.35}$$

Eq. (2.35) shows (2.14). ■

The proof technique of Theorem 2.2 leads immediately to

Corollary 2.1. $\phi(X)\circ\psi(X) : \text{Part}(X) \to \text{Mem}(X)$ is a bijection, where $\phi(X)\circ\psi(X)$ can be expressed as in eqs. (2.27) and (2.24), with inverse $(\phi(X)\circ\psi(X))^{-1}$: $\text{Mem}(X) \to \text{Part}(X)$, which can be expressed, using (2.23) as

$$(\phi(X)\circ\psi(X))^{-1}(f) = \psi(X)^{-1}\circ\phi(X)^{-1}(f) = q(f). \tag{2.36}$$

■

Summarizing, the following diagram of bijections holds:

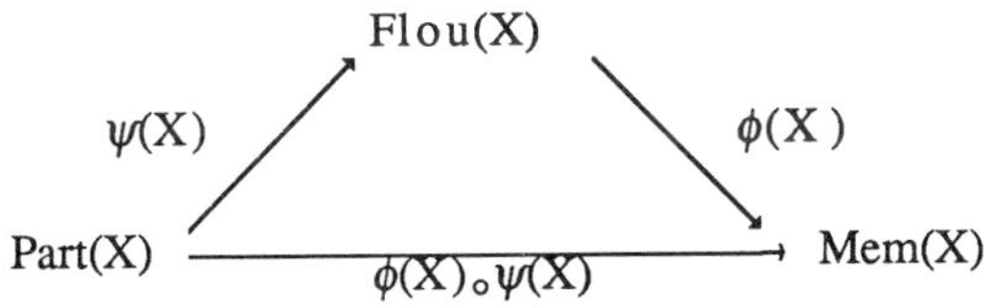

Figure 2.1. Summary of bijections for Mem(X), Flou(X), Part(X).

The basic relationships are, omitting the (X) notation for ϕ, ψ, for all $q = (q_t)_{t\in J_q} \in \text{Part}(X)$, $a = (a_t)_{t\in u} \in \text{Flou}(X)$, $f \in \text{Mem}(X)$, and all $t \in u$, $x \in X$:

$$\left.\begin{array}{l}\phi(a)(x) = \sup\{t : t \in u \ \&\ x \in a_t\};\ (\phi^{-1}(f))_t = f^{-1}[t,1];\ (\psi(q))_t = \cup\{q_s : s \in J_q, t \le s \le 1\};\\ J_{\psi^{-1}(a)} = \{t : t \in u \ \&\ a_t - a_{t^+} \ne \emptyset\};\ (\psi^{-1}(a))_t = a_t - a_{t^+},\ \text{all } t \in J_{\psi^{-1}(a)};\end{array}\right\}$$

$$\left.\begin{array}{l}(\phi\circ\psi)(q)(x) = f_q(x) = s \ \text{(for that unique } s \in J_q, \text{ where } x \in q_s);\ J_{(\phi\circ\psi)^{-1}(f)} = \\ \text{range}(f);\ \ ((\phi\circ\psi)^{-1}(f))_s = f^{-1}(s),\ \text{all } s \in \text{range}(f).\end{array}\right\} \quad (2.37)$$

3. Isomorphisms among Operations over the Fundamental Spaces: Introduction.

First note the following general constructive procedure:
Let $(X, *)$ be a given space with operation $*$ over X which could be n-ary as $* : X^n \to X$ and let Y be any other (nonvacuous) set such that $\tau : X \to Y$ is a bijection. Then, define (n-ary) operation $\tau(*) : Y^n \to Y$ by

$$\tau(*)(y_1,...,y_n) \overset{d}{=} \tau(*(\tau^{-1}(y_1),...,\tau^{-1}(y_n))),\ \text{all } y_1,...,y_n \in Y, \quad (3.1)$$

i.e.,
$$\tau(*) \overset{d}{=} \tau\circ *\circ\tau^{-1}\ \text{(n-ary)}; \quad (3.2)$$

so that τ and $*$ commute through $\tau(*)$:

$$\tau(*(x_1,...,x_n)) = \tau(*)(\tau(x_1),...,\tau(x_n)),\ \text{all } x_1,...,x_n \in X, \quad (3.3)$$

i.e., $(X, *)$ and $(Y, \tau(*))$ are *isomorphic through* τ. (A similar construction holds when τ^{-1} is replaced by, say, $\eta : Y \to X$ throughout eqs. (3.1)-(3.3).) Call $(Y, \tau(*))$ *the space induced isomorphically by bijection* τ.

We will apply the above procedure several times throughout the paper to determine the natural isomorphic counterparts among operators defined over Part(X), Flou(X), and Mem(X), *based on the traditional Zadeh and Zadeh-extended operators and relations with respect to Mem(X).* (See, e.g., the standard text by Dubois & Prade (1980) for background on these operators.) Specifically, the operators and relations to be considered here are: 1, cartesian products and their specialization to intersections; 2, cartesian sums and their specialization to unions; 3, subset relations; 4, complement operator; 5, attribute tranforms/functional extension principle; 6, inverse attribute transforms; 7, modifiers -- intensifiers and extensifiers. Conditioning, an important eighth type of operator will be considered separately in later sections, especially sections 6 and 10.

First, a brief note on the notation: Unless otherwise specified, $X, Y, Z, X_1, X_2, ..., X_n, Y_1, ..., Y_n \in$ SET arbitrary but fixed for any arbitrary but fixed positive integer n.

$T : X \to Y$ is any mapping and $T^{-1} : \mathcal{P}(Y) \to \mathcal{P}(X)$ is its inverse mapping, where $\mathcal{P}(\ )$ denotes the power class of $(\ )$ or the class of all (ordinary) subsets of $(\ )$.

$T_n : \times_{j=1}^{n} X_j \to Y$ is arbitrary as is $H : u \to u$ (recalling that u denotes the unit interval). Also, choose any continuous n-copula, i.e., cdf of an n by 1 r.v. representing the joint behavior of n one-dimensional marginal r.v.'s which are distributed uniformly over u. Thus, cop is the cdf for $\underline{\mathcal{U}} = (\mathcal{U}_1, ..., \mathcal{U}_n)$, where $\mathcal{U}_j : \Lambda \to u$, $j = 1, ..., n$, relative to some fixed probability space $(\Lambda, \mathcal{A}, p)$. Dually, denote the DeMorgan transform $1\text{-cop}(1 - (\ ),...,1 - (\ ))$ (n-ary operation) by cocop (cocopula). (See Schweizer & Sklar (1983) for general background.) In particular, note Zadeh's original copula min, as well as prod and minsum(only, 2-copulas) $\text{minsum}(s, t) \overset{d}{=} \max(s + t - 1, 0)$, all $s, t \in u$, as well as a wide variety of other examples as given in Goodman & Nguyen (1985, sect. 2.3.6). Three important examples of cocopulas are Zadeh's original max and probsum, and maxsum, where $\text{probsum}(s, t) \overset{d}{=} 1 - ((1 - s)\cdot(1 - t))$ and $\text{maxsum}(s, t) \overset{d}{=} \min(s + t - 1, 0)$ (the latter being only a 2-copula). (Again, see references above for further details.)

Also, let $f^{(1)}, f^{(2)}, f \in \text{Mem}(X)$, $g \in \text{Mem}(Y)$, and $f_j \in \text{Mem}(X_j)$, $j = 1, ..., n$ all arbitrary fixed. Use the multivariable notation

$$\underline{f} \overset{d}{=} (f_1,...,f_n) \text{ (n arguments) } ; \ \underline{X} \overset{d}{=} (X_1,...,X_n) \ ; \ \times\underline{X} \overset{d}{=} \times_{j=1}^{n} X_j \ ; \ \underline{x} \overset{d}{=} (x_1,...,x_n) \in \times\underline{X},$$

i.e., $x_j \in X_j$, $j = 1, ..., n$; $\underline{f}(\underline{x}) \overset{d}{=} (f_1(x_1),...,f_n(x_n))$; for any $\underline{t} \overset{d}{=} (t_1,...,t_n) \in u^n$, $\text{cop}(\underline{t}) \overset{d}{=} \text{cop}(t_1,...,t_n)$. When $X = X_1 = .. = X_n$, $\underline{f}(x) \overset{d}{=} (f_1(x),...,f_n(x))$, $x \in X$.

The seven types of Zadeh -- and related -- fuzzy set operations and relations defined through the membership functions to be considered here are in summary:

(1) cartesian product of $\underline{f}$ wrt cop $\overset{d}{=} \times_{cop}(\underline{f}) \in \text{Mem}(\times\underline{X})$, (3.4)

$$\times_{cop}(\underline{f}) \overset{d}{=} \text{cop}(\underline{f}(\underline{x})) , \text{ all } \underline{x} \in \underline{X}. \tag{3.5}$$

In particular, for $X = X_1 = .. = X_n$,

$$\text{intersection of } \underline{f} \text{ wrt cop} \overset{d}{=} \cap_{cop}(\underline{f}) \in \text{Mem}(X), \tag{3.6}$$

$$\cap_{cop}(\underline{f})(x) \overset{d}{=} \text{cop}(\underline{f}(x)), \text{ all } x \in X. \tag{3.7}$$

(2) cartesian sum of $\underline{f}$ wrt cocop $\overset{d}{=} \dagger_{cocop}(\underline{f}) \in Mem(\times\underline{X})$ (3.8)

$$\dagger_{cocop}(\underline{f})(\underline{x}) \overset{d}{=} cocop(\underline{f}(\underline{x})), \text{ all } \underline{x} \in \underline{X}. \quad (3.9)$$

In particular, for $X = X_1 = .. = X_n$,

$$\text{union of } \underline{f} \text{ wrt cocop} \overset{d}{=} \cup_{cocop}(\underline{f}) \in Mem(X), \quad (3.10)$$

$$\cup_{cocop}(\underline{f})(x) \overset{d}{=} cocop(\underline{f}(x)), \text{ all } x \in X. \quad (3.11)$$

(3) $f^{(1)}$ is in subset relation to $f^{(2)}$ iff, by def. , $f^{(1)} \le f^{(2)}$ over X. (3.12)

(4) complement of $f \overset{d}{=} f' \overset{d}{=} 1 - f \in Mem(X)$ (3.13)

(5) T-attribute transform of $f \overset{d}{=} T(f) \in Mem(Y)$, (3.14)

$$T(f)(y) \overset{d}{=} \sup(f(T^{-1}(y))) = \sup_{x \in T^{-1}(y)} f(x) = \sup_{T(x)=y} f(x), \text{ all } y \in Y. \quad (3.15)$$

In particular, for $X = \times\underline{X}$,

$$\text{T-attribute transform of } \underline{f} \text{ wrt cop} \overset{d}{=} \mathbf{T}_{cop}(\underline{f}) \in Mem(Y), \quad (3.16)$$

$$\mathbf{T}_{cop}(\underline{f})(y) \overset{d}{=} \sup(\times_{cop}(\underline{f})(T^{-1}(y))) = \sup_{\underline{x} \in T^{-1}(y)} (\times_{cop}(\underline{f})(\underline{x})). \quad (3.17)$$

(6) T^{-1}-attribute transform of $g \overset{d}{=} T^{-1}(g) \in Mem(X)$, (3.18)

$$T^{-1}(g) \overset{d}{=} g_{\circ}T, \text{ i.e., } T^{-1}(g)(x) = g(T(X))), \text{ all } x \in X. \quad (3.19)$$

(7) H-modifier of $f \overset{d}{=} H_{\circ}f$, i.e., $(H_{\circ}f)(x) = H(f(x))$, all $x \in X$. (3.20)

Note that though (6) and (7) look similar in form, (6) is the composition of the membership function on another (T), while (7) is the composition of a function (H, necessarily over u) on the membership function.

The next section constructs the isomorphic counterparts of the above over Flou(X).

4. Construction of Operations over Flou Spaces Isomorphic to Those over Fuzzy Set Membership Function Spaces.

Negoita & Ralescu (1975) and Ralescu (1979) were among the first to develop a full isomorphism between fuzzy set membership functions over a set endowed with Zadeh's original operations min for intersection or cartesian product and max for union or cartesian sum and flou (as nested collections of) sets with component-wise intersections and unions -- but not complements nor other operations. (This work extended the earlier work of Gentilhomme (1968) who introduced finite collections of nested sets as "flou" sets to explain multiple logic concepts through the use of ordinary sets, indeed without referring at all to Zadeh's still earlier pioneering effort (1965).) Radecki (1977) also considered independently a similar situation, emphasizing the level set forms of the nested sets relative to given membership functions.

In this section all of the above work is extended to include the seven types of operations and relations introduced in section 3. The resulting isomorphism from the procedure of section 3 applied to Theorem 2.1 show why it is natural to employ Flou(X) as the algebraic basis for fuzzy sets. In addition to the notation introduced in the previous section, denote $\underline{a} \overset{d}{=} (a^{(1)},...,a^{(n)}) \in \mathrm{Flou}(\underline{X}) \overset{d}{=} (\mathrm{Flou}(X_1),...,\mathrm{Flou}(X_n))$, when $a^{(j)} \in \mathrm{Flou}(X_j)$, $j = 1,...,n$ arbitrary. Similarly, denote $\underline{b} \overset{d}{=} (b^{(1)},...,b^{(n)}) \in \mathrm{Flou}(Y)$, when $b^{(j)} \in \mathrm{Flou}(Y_j)$, $j = 1,...,n$. Also $a \in \mathrm{Flou}(X)$ and $b \in \mathrm{Flou}(Y)$ are typical elements; $\phi(\underline{a}) \overset{d}{=} (\phi(a^{(1)}),...,\phi(a^{(n)}))$ (n arguments); for any $\underline{t} \in u^n$, $\times a_{\underline{s}} \overset{d}{=} a^{(1)}_{s_1} \times .. \times a^{(n)}_{s_n}$, etc. For clarity, bold face is used on some operations:

(1) cartesian product of $\underline{a}$ wrt cop $\overset{d}{=} \times_{cop}(\underline{a}) \in \mathrm{Flou}(\times\underline{X})$, (4.1)

$$(\times_{cop}(\underline{a}))_t \overset{d}{=} (\phi^{-1}(\times_{cop}(\phi(\underline{a}))))_t = (\times_{cop}(\phi(\underline{a})))^{-1}[t, 1]$$

$$= \bigcup_{\substack{\text{over all } \underline{s} \in u^n, \\ cop(\underline{s})=t}} (\times a_{\underline{s}}), \tag{4.2}$$

for all $t \in u$. Intersection becomes for $X = X_1 =..= X_n$,

$$\cap_{cop}(\underline{a}) \in \mathrm{Flou}(X);\ (\cap_{cop}(\underline{a}))_t = \bigcup_{\substack{\text{over all } \underline{s} \in u^n, \\ cop(\underline{s})=t}} (\cap\, a_{\underline{s}}),\ \text{all } t \in u. \tag{4.3}$$

For the special case cop = min, note the reductions of (4.2) and (4.3)

$$(\times_{min}(\underline{a}))_t = \mathop{\times}_{j=1}^{n} a^{(j)}_t;\ (\cap_{min}(\underline{a}))_t = \bigcap_{j=1}^{n} a^{(j)}_t,\quad \text{all } t \in u. \tag{4.4}$$

(2) cartesian sum of $\underline{a}$ wrt cocop $\overset{d}{=} \dagger_{cocop}(\underline{a}) \in \mathrm{Flou}(\times\underline{X})$, (4.5)
where analogous to the cartesian product case in (4.2),

$$(\dagger_{cocop}(\underline{a}))_t = \bigcup_{\substack{\text{over all } \underline{s} \in u^n, \\ cocop(\underline{s})=t}} (\times\, a_{\underline{s}}),\quad \text{for all } t \in u. \tag{4.6}$$

Union becomes for $X = X_1 = .. = X_n$,

$$\cup_{cocop}(\underline{a}) \in Flou(X);\ (\cup_{cocop}(\underline{a}))_t = \bigcup_{\substack{\text{over all } \underline{s} \in u^n,\\ cocop(\underline{s})=t}} (\cup\, \underline{a}_{\underline{s}}),\ t \in u. \tag{4.7}$$

For the special case cocop = max, note the reductions of (4.6) and (4.7)

$$(\dagger_{max}(\underline{a}))_t = \overset{n}{\underset{j=1}{\dagger}} a_t^{(j)} \overset{d}{=} (\overset{n}{\underset{j=1}{\times}} a_t^{(j)\prime})';\ (\cup_{max}(\underline{a}))_t = \bigcup_{j=1}^{n} a_t^{(j)},\ t \in u. \tag{4.8}$$

(3) For any $a^{(j)} \in Flou(X)$, j = 1, 2, it easily follows that

$$a^{(1)} \le a^{(2)} \text{ iff } \phi(a^{(1)}) \le \phi(a^{(2)}) \text{ over } X \text{ iff } a^{(1)} \subseteq a^{(2)}. \tag{4.9}$$

(4) $a' \in Flou(X)$ is given by , for all $t \in u$,

$$a'_t = (\phi^{-1}(\phi(a)'))_t = (1 - \phi(a))^{-1}[t, 1] = \{x : x \in X \ \&\ \phi(a)(x) \le 1 - t\}$$
$$= X - \phi(a)^{-1}(1 - t, 1] = X - a_{(1-t)^+} \tag{4.10}$$

where

$$a_{(1-t)^+} = \phi(a)^{-1}(1 - t, 1] = \bigcup_{1-t<s\le1} \phi(a)^{-1}[s, 1] = \bigcup_{1-t<s\le1} a_s. \tag{4.11}$$

(5) $T(a) \in Flou(T(X))$, where for all $t \in u$,

$$(T(a))_t = (\phi^{-1}(T(\phi(a))))_t = (T(\phi(a)))^{-1}[t, 1]$$
$$= \{y : y \in Y \ \&\ \sup\{s : s \in u \ \&\ y \in T(a_s)\} \ge t\}. \tag{4.12}$$

Define

$$T(a) \overset{d}{=} (T(a_t))_{t\in u}. \tag{4.13}$$

Now, $T(a) \in Flou(T(X))$. *Proof*: First, the left hand side of (2.4) can be verified directly. As for the right hand side of (2.4): Let $J \subseteq u$, $y \in \bigcap_{s\in J} T(a_s)$. Hence, $y = T(x)$ for some $x \in a_s$, all s U J, implying $y \in T(\bigcap_{s\in J} a_s) = T(a_{sup(J)})$, using r.h.s. (2.4) property of a itself. Conversely, if $y \in T(a_{sup(J)})$, there exists $x \in a_{sup(J)}$ with $y = T(x)$. But, $a_{sup(J)} = \bigcap_{s\in J} a_s$, so that $y = T(x)$, $x \in a_s$, all $s \in J$, implying $y \in \bigcap_{s\in J} T(a_s)$. Hence, r.h.s. (2.4) holds and thus $T(a) \in Flou(X)$.

Next, applying Theorem 2.1 to T(a), shows for all $t \in u$,

$$(T(a))_t = \{y : y \in Y \ \&\ \phi(T(a))(y) \ge t\} = (\phi(T(a)))^{-1}[t, 1] = T(a_t), \tag{4.14}$$

i.e., using (4.13),

$$T(a) = T(a). \tag{4.15}$$

In particular, the multiargument case where $X = \times\underline{X}$ becomes

$$T_{cop}(\underline{a}) = T(\times_{cop}(\underline{a})). \tag{4.16}$$

(6) For all $t \in u$,

$$(T^{-1}(b))_t = (\phi^{-1}(T^{-1}(\phi(b))))_t = (\phi(b)_\circ T)^{-1}[t, 1] = T^{-1}(\phi(b)^{-1}[t, 1]) = T^{-1}(b_t). \tag{4.17}$$

(4.17) shows

$$T^{-1}(b) = T^{-1}(b) = (T^{-1}(b_t))_{t\in u}. \tag{4.18}$$

(7) The H-modifier of a is determined as

$$H_\circ a = \phi^{-1}(H_\circ\phi(a)) \in \text{Flou}(X), \tag{4.19}$$

where for all $t \in u$,

$$(H_\circ a)_t = (\phi^{-1}(H_\circ\phi(a)))_t = (H_\circ\phi(a))^{-1}[t, 1] = (H_\circ\phi(a))^{-1}[t, 1] = \phi(a)^{-1}(H^{-1}[t, 1]). \tag{4.20}$$

If H is monotone increasing with $H(0) = 0$ and $H(1) = 1$, then (4.20) becomes

$$(H_\circ a)_t = \phi(a)^{-1}[H^{-1}(t), 1] = a_{H^{-1}(t)}, \quad \text{all } t \in u, \tag{4.21}$$

whence

$$H_\circ a = a_{H^{-1}}. \tag{4.22}$$

On the other hand, if H is monotone decreasing with H(0) 1 and $H(1) = 0$, then (4.20) becomes

$$(H_\circ a)_t = \phi(a)^{-1}[0, H^{-1}(t)] = X \dashv \phi(a)^{-1}(H^{-1}(t), 1] = X \dashv a_{H^{-1}(t)^+}. \tag{4.23}$$

Summarizing the above results:

Theorem 4.1. Let * refer to any of the seven types of operations and relations defined for Mem(X) (or Mem(×X̲)) in section 3, eqs. (3.4)-(3.20). Let $\phi^{-1}(*)$ refer to the corresponding seven types of operations and relations given for Flou(X) (or related spaces) in this section, eqs. (4.1)-(4.23). Then (using the X form for generality), $\phi : (\text{Flou}(X); \phi^{-1}(*)) \to (\text{Mem}(X); *)$ is a surjective isomorphism.

Proof: Immediate consequence of the constructive procedure of section 3 for τ^{-1} replaced by ϕ (and τ by ϕ^{-1}), relative to the bijection ϕ as shown in Theorem 2.1.

■

In another direction, recall the concept of the sup norm of a fuzzy set membership function (see e.g. Goodman & Nguyen (1985, section 3.3)):

$$\|\ \| : \text{Mem}(X) \to u \ ; \ \|f\| \overset{d}{=} \sup_{x\in X} f(x). \tag{4.24}$$

Then,

$$\|\phi^{-1}(f)\| \overset{d}{=} \sup\{t : t \in u \ \& \ \phi^{-1}(f)_t = f^{-1}[t, 1]$$

$= \sup\{t : t \in u \ \&\ t \leq f(x), \text{ for some } x \in X\} = \|f\|, \text{ all } f \in \mathrm{Mem}(X),$ (4.25)

so that

$$\|\phi(a)\| = \|a\|, \text{ all } a \in \mathrm{Flou}(X), \tag{4.26}$$

showing the invariance of $\|\ \|$ wrt ϕ. Similar remarks hold for trace norms, where a fuzzy intersection relative to a fixed membership function is used.

As a final segment to this section, suppose we restrict Mem(X) to Dist($\mathbb{R}$), the class of all cumulative probability distribution functions (cdf's) over the real line $\mathbb{R}$ (recalling that a cdf F is characterized as $F : \mathbb{R} \to u$ being nondecreasing, continuous from the right with $F(-\infty) = 0$ and $F(+\infty) = 1$). Also, define Ant($\mathbb{R}$) as the class of all anti-distribution functions G over u in the sense that $G : u \to \mathbb{R}$ is any nondecreasing, continuous from the left function with (abusing notation relative to the domains of use) $G(0) = -\infty$ and $G(1) = +\infty$. Also, recall the pseudoinverse of cdf F as given by

$$F^{\square}(t) \stackrel{d}{=} \inf F^{-1}[t, 1], \text{ all } t \in u, \tag{4.27}$$

with the usual properties such as $F_{\circ}F^{\square}{}_{\circ}F = F$ and $F^{\square}{}_{\circ}F_{\circ}F^{\square} = F^{\square}$, etc. (See e.g., Goodman & Nguyen (1985, pp. 121 et passim).) Dually, define for each $G \in \mathrm{Ant}(\mathbb{R})$, G^{Δ} and $\tau(G)$, where

$$G^{\Delta}(x) \stackrel{d}{=} \sup G^{-1}(-\infty, x], \text{ all } x \in X;\ \tau(G) \stackrel{d}{=} ([G(s), +\infty))_{s \in u}, \tag{4.28}$$

and let the range(τ) be denoted as Pseu($\mathbb{R}$). Then, it follows that for all $F \in \mathrm{Dist}(\mathbb{R})$, $G \in \mathrm{Ant}(\mathbb{R})$,

$$F^{\square\Delta} = F \ ;\ G^{\Delta\square} = G\,, \tag{4.29}$$

and hence $(\ )^{\Delta} : \mathrm{Ant}(\mathbb{R}) \to \mathrm{Dist}(\mathbb{R})$ and $(\ )^{\square} : \mathrm{Dist}(\mathbb{R}) \to \mathrm{Ant}(\mathbb{R})$ are well-defined inverse bijections of each other. It also follows for any $F \in \mathrm{Dist}(\mathbb{R})$ that

$$\phi^{-1}(F) = ((\phi^{-1}(F))_t)_{t \in u}\ ;\ (\phi^{-1}(F))_t = F^{-1}[t, 1] = [F^{\square}(t), +\infty) = (\tau(F^{\square}))(t), \tag{4.30}$$

and for any $G \in \mathrm{Ant}(\mathbb{R})$,

$$\phi(\tau(G)) = G^{\Delta}. \tag{4.31}$$

The above can all be summarized by the following diagram of bijections:

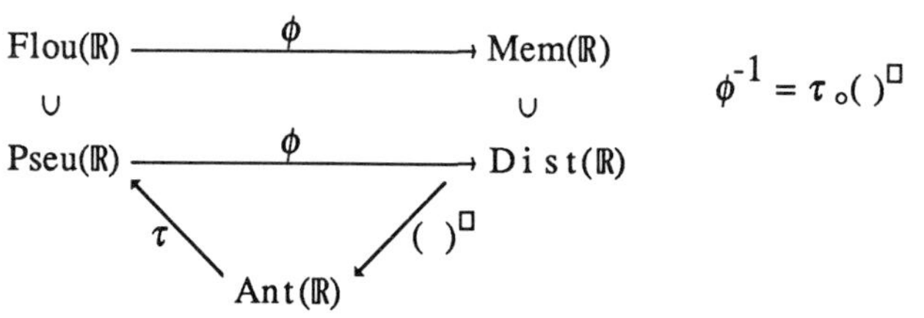

Figure 4.1. Summary of bijections involving cdf's as membership functions.

All of the above can be generalized to $\mathbb{R}^n$ with suitable modifications. In addition, the construction technique of section 3, as applied in the earlier part of this section to developing the bijections among Mem(X) and Flou(X) into isomorphisms is valid here as a special case, showing a basic connection between probability (via cdf's) and fuzzy sets.

5. Construction of Operations over Partitioning Spaces Isomorphic to Those over Fuzzy Set Membership Function Spaces.

In addition to the previous notation introduced, denote $\underline{q} \stackrel{d}{=} (q^{(1)},\ldots,q^{(n)})$ where $q^{(j)} \in \mathrm{Part}(X_j)$ is arbitrary, $j = 1,\ldots,n$. Similarly, denote $(\phi\circ\psi)(\underline{q}) \stackrel{d}{=} (\phi(\psi(q^{(1)})),\ldots,\phi(\psi(q^{(n)})))$, noting $\underline{q} \in \mathrm{Part}(\underline{X}) \stackrel{d}{=} (\mathrm{Part}(X_1),\ldots,\mathrm{Part}(X_n))$ while $(\phi\circ\psi)(\underline{q}) \in \mathrm{Mem}(\underline{X})$, etc.

By use of the isomorphism construction technique discussed in section 3, where now $\tau^{-1} = \phi\circ\psi$ and X is replaced by Mem(X), while Y is replaced by Part(X), the following counterparts are obtained for the seven basic membership operations and relations:

(1) cartesian product of $\underline{q}$ wrt cop $\stackrel{d}{=} \times_{cop}(\underline{q}) \in \mathrm{Part}(\times\underline{X})$, (5.1)

where

$$\times_{cop}(\underline{q}) = (\phi\circ\psi)^{-1}(\phi\circ\psi)^{-1}(\times_{cop}(\phi\circ\psi)(\underline{q})) \tag{5.2}$$

with index set

$$J_{\times_{cop}(\underline{q})} = \mathrm{range}(\times_{cop}(\phi\circ\psi)(\underline{q})) = \mathop{\times_{cop}}_{j=1}^{n}(J_{q^{(j)}}). \tag{5.3}$$

For each $t \in u$,

$$(\dagger_{cocop}(\underline{q}))_t = ((\phi\circ\psi)^{-1}(\dagger_{cocop}((\phi\circ\psi)(\underline{q}))))_t = \bigcup_{\substack{\text{over all}\\ \underline{s}\in J_{\dagger_{cocop}(\underline{q})},\\ cocop(\underline{s})=t}} \left(\mathop{\times}_{j=1}^{n} q^{(j)}_{s_j}\right) \tag{5.4}$$

with similar forms holding for "intersections".

(2) cartesian sum of $\underline{q}$ wrt cocop $\stackrel{d}{=} \dagger_{cocop}(\underline{q}) \in \mathrm{Part}(\times\underline{X})$ (5.5)

has index set

$$J_{\dagger_{cocop}(\underline{q})} = \overset{n}{\underset{j=1}{\dagger_{cocop}}}(J_{q^{(j)}}). \tag{5.6}$$

For all $t \in u$,

$$(\dagger_{cocop}(\underline{q}))_t = ((\phi\circ\psi)^{-1}(\dagger_{cocop}((\phi\circ\psi)(\underline{q}))))_t = \bigcup_{\substack{\text{over all} \\ \underline{s} \in J_{\dagger_{cocop}(\underline{q})}, \\ cocop(\underline{s})=t}} (\overset{n}{\underset{j=1}{\times}} q^{(j)}_{s_j}), \tag{5.7}$$

with similar forms holding for "unions".

(3) For any $q^{(1)}, q^{(2)} \in \text{Part}(X)$, $q^{(1)} \le q^{(2)}$

$$\text{iff } (\phi\circ\psi)(q^{(1)}) \underset{\text{over } X}{\le} (\phi\circ\psi)(q^{(2)}). \tag{5.8}$$

Then it can be shown that

$$\left.\begin{array}{l} q^{(1)} \le q^{(2)} \text{ iff } q^{(2)} \text{ is a refinement of } q^{(1)}, \text{ i.e., for each } s \in J_{q^{(1)}} \\ \text{there exists } I_s \subseteq J_{q^{(2)}} \text{ with } s \le I_s \;\&\; q^{(1)}_s = \bigcup_{t \in I_s} q^{(2)}_t. \end{array}\right\} \tag{5.9}$$

(4) For all $q \in \text{Part}(X)$, $q' = (\phi\circ\psi)^{-1}(((\phi\circ\psi)(q))')$, (5.10)
with index set

$$J_{q'} = \text{rang}(((\phi\circ\psi)(q))') = 1 - J_q = \{1 - t : t \in J_q\}. \tag{5.11}$$

For all $t \in u$

$$(q')_t = (((\phi\circ\psi)(q))^{-1}(t))'$$
$$= \{x : x \in X \;\&\; f_q(x) = 1 - t\}\} = f_q^{-1}(1 - t) = q_{1-t}. \tag{5.12}$$

(5) T-attribute transform of $q = \mathbf{T}(q) = (\phi\circ\psi)^{-1}(\mathbf{T}((\phi\circ\psi)(q))) \in \text{Part}(\mathbf{T}(X))$ (5.13)
with index set

$$J_{\mathbf{T}(q)} = \text{range}(\mathbf{T}((\phi\circ\psi)(q)))$$
$$= \text{range}\,(\mathbf{T}(f_q)) = \{\sup\{s : s \in J_q \;\&\; y \in \mathbf{T}(q_s)\} : y \in Y\}, \tag{5.14}$$

For all $t \in u$,

$$(\mathbf{T}(q))_t = (\mathbf{T}((\phi\circ\psi)(q))^{-1}(t) = (\mathbf{T}(f_q))^{-1}(t)$$
$$= \{y : y \in Y \;\&\; \sup\{s : s \in J_q, y \in \mathbf{T}(q_s)\} = t\}. \tag{5.15}$$

(6) T^{-1}-attribute transform of $q = (T^{-1}(q))_t = (\phi_\circ\psi)^{-1}(T^{-1}((\phi_\circ\psi)(q)))$,

(5.16)

with index set

$$J_{T^{-1}(q)} = \text{range}(T^{-1}((\phi_\circ\psi)(q))) = \text{range}(T^{-1}(f_q)) = \text{range}(f_q{}_\circ T)$$

$$= \{s : s \in J_q \ \&\ T^{-1}(q_s) \neq \emptyset\}.$$

(5.17)

For all $t \in u$,

$$(T^{-1}(q))_t = ((\phi_\circ\psi)^{-1}(T^{-1}((\phi_\circ\psi)(q))))_t$$

$$= (T^{-1}(f_q))^{-1}(t) = (f_q{}_\circ T)^{-1}(t)$$

$$= T^{-1}(f_q^{-1}(t)) = T^{-1}(q_t).$$

(5.18)

(7) H-modifier for $q = H_\circ q = (\phi_\circ\psi)^{-1}(H_\circ f_q)$,

(5.19)

with index set

$$J_{H_\circ q} = \text{range}(H_\circ f_q) = H(J_q).$$

(5.20)

For all $t \in u$,

$$(H_\circ q)_t = ((\phi_\circ\psi)^{-1}(H_\circ f_q))_t = (H_\circ f_q)^{-1}(t) = f_q^{-1}(H^{-1}(t)) = q_{H^{-1}(t)} = \bigcup_{s \in H^{-1}(t) \cap J_q} (q_s).$$

(5.21)

Summarizing the above results:

Theorem 5.1. Let $*$ refer to any of the seven types of operations and relations defined for Mem(X) (or Mem(x$\underline{X}$)) in section 3, eqs. (3.4)-(3.20). Let $(\phi^\circ\psi)^{-1}(*)$ refer to the corresponding seven types of operations and relations given for Part(X) (or related spaces) in this section, eqs. (5.1)-(5.21). Then (using the X form for generality), $\phi_\circ\psi : (\text{Part(X)}; (\phi_\circ\psi)^{-1}(*)) \to \text{Mem(X)}; *)$ is a surjective isomorphism.

Proof: Immediate consequence of the constructive procedure of section 3 for τ^{-1} replaced by $\phi_\circ\psi$ (and τ by $(\phi_\circ\psi)^{-1}$), relative to the bijection $\phi_\circ\psi$ as shown in Theorem 2.2. ■

<u>Remarks</u>. In summary, the following diagram holds, superseding Figure 2.1:

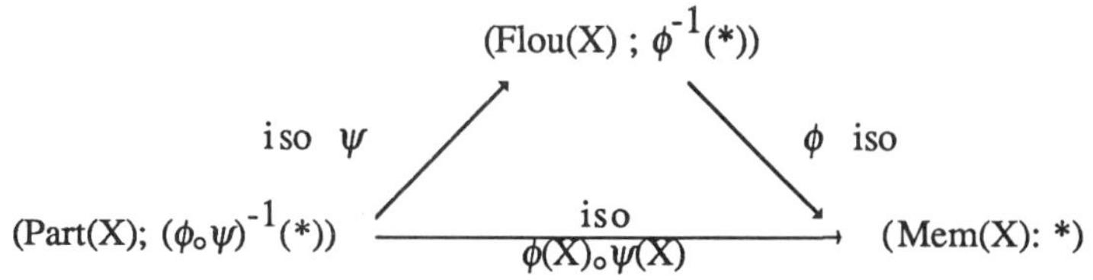

Figure 5.1. Summary of isomorphisms among Mem(X), Flou(X), Part(X).

Thus, the initial Zadeh operations and relations defined over Mem(X), the usual semantically or numerically-oriented space representing fuzzy set membership functions, can be isomorphically represented by *both* counterparts over Flou(X) and those over Part(X). The last two spaces in light of Theorems 4.1 and 5.1 can be considered to be the natural syntactic or algebraic structures representing fuzzy sets. Of course, a number of other operations and relations could have been considered, but the above seven seems to be a reasonable demonstration of the natural relations among the spaces. (Conditioning will be treated later as a special type of operation.)

The next section considers the important special case of finite-valued membership functions and the corresponding flou and partitioning sets, together with some relationships with conditional events, as previously developed for ordinary (i.e., non-fuzzy) events and sets.

6. Finite-Valued Fuzzy Set Membership Functions and Relations with Conditional and Unconditional Sets

In this section we specialize some of the previous results for the general case to the setting where only finite-valued membership functions are considered and relate this to conditional event algebra for the three-valued subcase.

In particular, let $f \in \mathrm{Mem}(X)$ be such that it is arbitrary fixed with

$$\mathrm{range}(f) = \{t_j : j = 1,\dots,m\} \; ; \quad 0 \le t_1 < t_2 < .. < t_m \le 1,$$
(6.1)

for some arbitrarily fixed positive integer m and real t_j. It follows that the corresponding flou set is from Theorem 2.1

$$\phi^{-1}(f) = ((\phi^{-1}(f))_s)_{s\in u} \tag{6.2}$$

where now

$$(\phi^{-1}(f))_s = f^{-1}[s,1] = \begin{cases} \emptyset, \text{ if } t_m < s \le 1; \\ f^{-1}\{t_{j+1}, t_{j+2}, \ldots, t_m\} \\ f^{-1}(t_{j+1}) \cup f^{-1}(t_{j+2}) \cup \ldots \cup f^{-1}(t_m), \\ \text{if } t_j < s \le t_{j+1},\ j=1,2,\ldots,m-1; \\ X, \text{ if } 0 \le s \le t_1. \end{cases} \tag{6.3}$$

The corresponding partitioning set is from Theorem 2.2

$$(\phi\circ\psi)^{-1}(f) = (((\phi\circ\psi)^{-1}(F))_s)_{s\in J_{(\phi\circ\psi)^{-1}(f)}} \tag{6.4}$$

where from (2.37)

$$((\phi\circ\psi)^{-1}(f))_s = f^{-1}(s),\ s \in J_{(\phi\circ\psi)^{-1}(f)}, \tag{6.5}$$

where index set

$$J_{(\phi\circ\psi)^{-1}(f)} = \text{range}(f) \tag{6.6}$$

given in (6.1).

It is clear by inspection that any finite partitioning $q = (q_s)_{s\in J_q} \in \text{Part}(X)$ arises from some finite-valued f. (See also the proof of Theorem 2.2.) Similar remarks hold for the correspondences of finite flou sets, i.e. flou sets with only a finite number of distinct component sets, and finite-valued membership functions. Summarizing:

Theorem 6.0. Theorems 2.1 and 2.2 remain valid when the bijections ϕ, ψ, and $\phi\circ\psi$ are all restricted to the classes of finite-valued elements -- in the above senses -- of their domains. Indeed, in light of Theorems 4.1 and 5.1, these bijections are actually isomorphisms when so restricted. ■

Next, let us treat in some detail two particular subcases of finite-valued membership functions and a modified third subcase.

First, consider single-valued, or equivalently, *constant*, membership functions and their corresponding flou and partitioning sets: For any constant c in u, use the standard identification with $c : X \to u$, where

$$c(x) = c(\text{constant}), \text{ all } x \in X, \tag{6.7}$$

is used. Denote the class of all such functions as

$$\text{Mem}_1(X) \overset{d}{=} \{c : c : X \to u,\ c \in u\}. \tag{6.8}$$

The corresponding flou set is easily seen to be

$$\phi^{-1}(c) = ((\phi^{-1}(c))_s)_{s\in u}, \tag{6.9}$$

where for all $s \in u$,

$$(\phi_{-1}(c))_s = c^{-1}[s, 1] = \begin{cases} X, & \text{if } 0 \le s \le c, \\ \emptyset, & \text{if } c < s \le 1. \end{cases} \tag{6.10}$$

Denote the class of all such flou sets as

$$\mathrm{Flou}_1(X) \overset{d}{=} \{\phi^{-1}(c) : c \in u\}. \tag{6.11}$$

Next, the corresponding partitioning set to c is

$$(\phi_\circ\psi)^{-1}(c) = (((\phi_\circ\psi)^{-1}(c))_s)_{s\in J_{(\phi_\circ\psi)^{-1}(c)}} \tag{6.12}$$

where

$$J_{(\phi_\circ\psi)^{-1}(c)} = \mathrm{range}(c) = \{c\};\ ((\phi_\circ\psi)^{-1}(c))_c = c^{-1}(c) = X. \tag{6.13}$$

That is,

$$(\phi_\circ\psi)^{-1}(c) = \{X\} \text{ (with index value c)}. \tag{6.14}$$

Denote the class of all such partitioning sets as

$$\mathrm{Part}_1(X) \overset{d}{=} \{(\phi_\circ\psi)^{-1}(c) : c \in u\}. \tag{6.15}$$

Next, consider membership functions which can have possibly two values 0 or 1, i.e., the class of all ordinary set membership, or equivalently, *indicator*, functions $1_A : X \to \{0, 1\} \in \mathrm{Mem}(X)$, where the standard relation holds for any ordinary subset A of X

$$1_A(x) \overset{d}{=} \begin{cases} 1, & \text{if } x \in A, \\ 0, & \text{if } x \in A'. \end{cases} \tag{6.16}$$

Corresponding to any 1_A, $A \in \mathcal{P}(X)$, the flou and partitioning sets are:

$$\phi^{-1}(1_A) = ((\phi^{-1}(1_A))_s)_{s\in u}, \tag{6.17}$$

where

$$(\phi^{-1}(1_A))_s = 1_A^{-1}[s, 1] = \begin{cases} X, & \text{if } s = 0 \\ A, & \text{if } 0 < s \le 1. \end{cases} \tag{6.18}$$

$$(\phi_\circ\psi)^{-1}(1_A) = (((\phi_\circ\psi)^{-1}(1_A))_s)_{s\in J_{(\phi_\circ\psi)^{-1}(1_A)}}; \tag{6.19}$$

index set

$$J_{(\phi_\circ\psi)^{-1}(1_A)} = \mathrm{range}(1_A) = \{0, 1\}, \tag{6.20}$$

unless

$$A = X, \text{ implying } J_{(\phi\circ\psi)^{-1}(1_X)} = \{1\}; \text{ or } A = \emptyset, \text{ implying } J_{(\phi\circ\psi)^{-1}(1_\emptyset)} = \{0\}. \tag{6.21}$$

For $A \in \mathscr{P}(X)$ in general again,

$$((\phi\circ\psi)^{-1}(1_A))_0 = 1_A^{-1}(0) = A' \; ; \; ((\phi\circ\psi)^{-1}(1_A))_1 = 1_A^{-1}(1) = A. \tag{6.22}$$

The special cases $A = X$ and $A = \emptyset$ yield

$$(\phi\circ\psi)^{-1}(1_X) = \{X\} \text{ (with index val. 1)}; \; (\phi\circ\psi)^{-1}(1_\emptyset) = \{X\} \text{ (with index val. 0)}. \tag{6.23}$$

Denote the above class of membership functions with values in $\{0, 1\}$ as $M_2(X)$ with the corresponding flou class as $Flou_2(X)$ and the corresponding partitioning set class as $Part_2(X)$.

Next, consider any fixed $t \in u$ and define the class

$$Mem_{t,3}(X) \overset{d}{=} \{0, t, 1\}^X = \{f : f \in Mem(X) \;\&\; range(f) \subseteq \{0, t, 1\}\}. \tag{6.24}$$

In turn, define the union

$$Mem_3(X) \overset{d}{=} \bigcup_{t\in u} Mem_{t,3}(X), \tag{6.25}$$

noting from (6.24),

$$Mem_{0,3}(X) = Mem_{1,3}(X) = \{0, 1\}^X = Mem_2(X). \tag{6.26}$$

For any $t \in u$ and any $f_t \in Mem_{t,3}(X)$, the corresponding flou and partitioning sets are:

$$\phi^{-1}(f_t) = ((\phi^{-1}(f_t))_s)_{s\in u}, \tag{6.27}$$

$$(\phi^{-1}(f_t))_s = f_t^{-1}[s, 1] = \begin{cases} X, \text{ if } s = 0 \\ f_t^{-1}(t) \cup f_t^{-1}(1), \text{ if } 0 < s \le t, \\ f_t^{-1}(1), \text{ if } s = 1. \end{cases} \tag{6.28}$$

$$(\phi\circ\psi)^{-1}(f_t) = (((\phi\circ\psi)^{-1}(F_t))_s)_{s\in J_{(\phi\circ\psi)^{-1}(f_t)}}, \tag{6.29}$$

with index set

$$J_{(\phi\circ\psi)^{-1}(f_t)} = range(f_t) = \{0, t, 1\}, \tag{6.30}$$

and for $s \in \{0, t, 1\}$

$$((\phi\circ\psi)^{-1}(f_t))_s = f_t^{-1}(s) = \begin{cases} f_t^{-1}(0), & \text{if } s = 0 \\ f_t^{-1}(t), & \text{if } s = t \\ f_t^{-1}(1), & \text{if } s = 1. \end{cases} \tag{6.31}$$

Next, let $q = (q_0, q_t, q_1)$ be any ordered partitioning of X where any one or two of the component q_s may possibly be vacuous. Denote $\text{Part}^{(3)}(X)$ as the class of all such ordered partitionings of X. In turn, for each $q \in \text{Part}^{(3)}(X)$, define the class

$$a_t(q) \overset{d}{=} \{f : f \in \text{Mem}_3(X) \text{ \& for all } s \in \{0, t, 1\}, \text{ if } q_s \neq \emptyset, \text{ then } f(x) = s, \text{ for all } x \in q_s;\ t \in u\}. \tag{6.32}$$

In a related direction, for any sets $A, B \in \mathscr{P}(X)$, and any $t \in u$, define one natural extension of the ordinary set indicator function given in eq. (6.16) to three values as (using ∨ for max, ∧ for min, etc.) $1_{(A|B)_t}$,

$$1_{(A|B)_t}(x) \overset{d}{=} 1_{A\cap B}(x) \vee 1_{B'}(x)\cdot t = \begin{cases} 1, & \text{if } x \in A \cap B, \\ 0, & \text{if } x \in B - A, \\ u, & \text{if } x \in B'. \end{cases} \tag{6.33}$$

Finally, define the function $1_{(A|B)}$ as

$$1_{(A|B)}(x) \overset{d}{=} 1_{A\cap B}(x) \vee 1_{B'}(x)\cdot u = \begin{cases} 1, & \text{if } x \in A \cap B, \\ 0, & \text{if } x \in B - A, \\ u, & \text{if } x \in B'. \end{cases} \tag{6.34}$$

$1_{(A|B)}$ is the standard *conditional event* (or conditional set) *indicator function*, as first developed independently by Schay (1968) and DeFinetti (1974). More on this topic later; summarizing the above relations:

Theorem 6.1. The following relations hold among the special cases of Mem(X), Flou(X), and Part(X) considered above:

(i)
$$\left.\begin{matrix} \text{Mem}_1(X) \\ \text{Mem}_2(X) \subseteq \text{Mem}_{t,3}(X) \end{matrix}\right\} \subseteq \text{Mem}_3(X) \subseteq \text{Mem}(X), \tag{6.35}$$

with the same relations holding in (6.35) when Mem is replaced by Flou and Part.

(ii) $(\text{Part}_j(X); (\phi\circ\psi)^{-1}(*))$, $(\text{Flou}_j(X); \phi^{-1}(*))$, and $(\text{Mem}_j(X); *)$ are all isomorphic relative to the appropriate restrictions for ψ, ϕ, and $\phi\circ\psi$ as given in Theorems 4.1 and 5.1 and summarized in Figure 5.1, when: j = 1, as given in (6.7)-(6.15); j = 2, as given in (6.16)-(6.23); and $j = (t, 3)$, as given in (6.24)-(6.31).

(iii) For all $A, B \in P(X)$, one can make the natural identification

$$1_{(A|B)} = \{1_{(A|B)_t} : t \in u\}. \tag{6.36}$$

Since also

$$\mathrm{Mem}_{t,3}(X) = \bigcup_{q \in \mathrm{Part}^{(3)}(X)} (a_t(q)), \tag{6.37}$$

one also has the identifications

$$\mathrm{Mem}_3(X) = \bigcup_{\substack{q \in \mathrm{Part}^{(3)}(X) \\ t \in u}} (a_t(q)) = \{1_{(A|B)} : A, B \in \mathcal{P}(X)\}. \tag{6.38}$$

Proof: Straightforward from the definitions. ■

Brief overview of conditional event indicator functions and conditional events.

With the basic tie-in between conditional even indicator functions and three-valued fuzzy set membership functions pointed out, a short summary of the development of conditional events and their indicator functions will be presented. (See Goodman (1987), Goodman & Nguyen (1988, 1991), and Goodman, Nguyen, Walker (1991) for general background.)

In the following, unconditional events or sets are indicated by A, B, C, D, .. which, in place of the concrete situation (via direct considerations or use of the Stone Representation Theorem), where they are all subsets of X forming a boolean algebra which is a subclass of P(X), one can consider them to form an abstract boolean algebra R or events or propositions. In this case, the operators are: conjunction $\cdot$ (replacing the more concrete $\cap$); disjunction $\vee$ (replacing the more concrete $\cup$); complement or negation $(\ )'$ (which for simplicity is denoted by the same symbol as in the concrete case); $\leq$ (replacing the more concrete $\subseteq$); $<$ (replacing the more concrete $\subset$); 1 (replacing the more concrete X); 0 (replacing the more concrete $\emptyset$); material/logical implication $\Rightarrow$ given as $B \Rightarrow A \stackrel{d}{=} B' \vee A$ (replacing the more concrete $B' \cap A$); material/logical equivalence $\Leftrightarrow$ given as

$$B \Leftrightarrow A \stackrel{d}{=} (B \Rightarrow A)\cdot(A \Rightarrow B) = AB \vee A'B' = (A + B)',$$

dropping the conjunction notation $\cdot$ when no ambiguity arises, where $A + B \stackrel{d}{=} A'B \vee AB'$, etc.

Conditional events arise in order to provide a systematic/rigorous way to deal with arbitrary logical combinations of implicative statements relative to all probability evaluations, when it is appropriate to interpret the probability evaluations of each separate implicative statement as a conditional probability in the natural sense. For example, suppose one wants to obtain the probability p((if B then A) or (if D then C)), where the evaluations p(if B then A) = p(A|B) (=p(AB)/p(B), assuming p(B) > 0) and p(if D then C) = p(C|D) hold. No current standard approach exists in the numerically-oriented field of conditional probability (including Renyi's comprehensive extension (1970)) whereby the implicatives "if B then A" and "if D then C" can be given meaning, independent of the particular probability p being used. This is so that these expressions can be combined with other expressions, in conditional or unconditional form, analogous to the way the unconditionals A, B, C, D, .. can all be manipulated and combined, compatible with all probability evaluations. Certainly, a "natural" candidate for such an interpretation is material implication, so that in the above example one would obtain by the usual Poincaré expansion

$$\begin{aligned} p((\text{if B then A}) \text{ or } (\text{if D then C})) &= p((B \Rightarrow A) \vee (D \Rightarrow C)) = p(B' \vee A \vee D' \vee C) \\ &= p(B') + p(A) + p(D') + p(C) - p(B'A) - p(B'D') - p(B'C) \\ &\quad - p(AD') - p(AC) - p(D'C) + p(B'AD') + p(B'AC) + p(B'D'C) \\ &\quad + p(AD'C) - p(B'AD'C). \end{aligned} \tag{6.39}$$

However, the main drawback to the above approach is that *material implication is inconsistent with conditional probability as its probability evaluation* since it can be readily shown: [Author's note: this and all subsequent results can be found in the above reference Goodman, Nguyen, Walker (1991) or in Goodman (1991) in detail; for the most part, these references will not be repeated here.]

$$p(B \Rightarrow A) = a - p(B) + p(AB) = p(A|B) + (p(A'|B)\cdot p(B')) \geq p(A|B), \tag{6.40}$$

provided p(B) > 0, where in general strict inequality holds above. Indeed, Lewis (1976) showed that in general *there is no function* $g : R^2 \to R$ *(boolean or otherwise!) such that equality could hold in a modified version of (6.40), where* $\Rightarrow$ *is replaced by* g, i.e.,

$$\text{For all } g : R^2 \to R, \text{ it is not true that } p(g(A, B)) = p(A|B), \text{ all } A, B \in R. \tag{6.41}$$

Thus, the search for syntactic or algebraic interpretations of implicatives compatible with all conditional probability evaluations, if at all possible must lie in functions $g : R^2 \to S$, where $S \not\subseteq R$. Of course, if all of the antecedents of the implicatives present are identical, then no real problem arises and the search for algebraic representations of "conditional events" g(A, B) = (A|B) is avoided. For example, in the original example, if antecedents B = D, then it is indeed natural to compute in effect

$$p((\text{if B then A}) \text{ or } (\text{if B then C})) = p((A|B0 \vee (C|B)) = p((A \vee C|B)) = p(A \vee C|B), \tag{6.42}$$

provided $p(B) > 0$, where in the standard approach to conditional probability, the middle two expressions would not be used. However, when the antecedents are not all identical, in general it would seem that one should seek a common denominator-like antecedent so that the technique provided through the example in (6.42) could be employed. It will be seen later that this is an equivalent viable approach to the basic problem, but that the "common denominator" is not trivial.

While it was stated previously that the direction of conditional probability is away from the algebraic, a relative handful of researchers have seriously considered this problem at one time or another. This list includes: Boole (1854, Chpt. et passim), Hailperin's restatement and rigorizing of Boole's ideas using the modern approach of Chevalley-Uzkov algebraic fractions; Mazurkiewicz' original use of principal ideal cosets (in a boolean algebra) to represent conditional events (1956), Copeland's futile attempts (seen now in light of Lewis' "triviality" result cited above)(1950, 1956) at forcing, in effect, conditional events to be in the original boolean algebra R; DeFinetti's efforts, including the defining of conditional event indicator functions (as in (6.34)) (1974) independent of all others; Schay's proposal for conditional event indicator functions (1968), independently coinciding with DeFinetti, but also for the first time, developing a full calculus of operations and relations for conditional events; Adams (1975) proposing operations for conditional events that independently coincided with Schay, but gave no interpretation for the conditional events themselves!; Calabrese (1987), also independently of all others, first proposing that conditional events should be interpreted as partial deduct equivalence classes, and in turn developed as Schay before him, a full calculus of operations and relations coinciding for the most part with Schay's results; and also recently, among others, Bruno & Gilio (1985) bringing forth the basic issue of combining implicatives compatible with conditional probability and proposing, in part, a calculus of operations.

All of this lead the author and colleague (H.T. Nguyen) to inquire if there is any unified approach to the basic problem which does not rely upon ad hoc formulations for both the form conditional events must take as well as their operations extending the usual boolean ones for the unconditional case. Certainly, the indicator function approach of Schay and DeFinetti was plausible, but Schay (being the only one of the pair attempting to develop operations and relations) did not justify the choice of his operations. Similarly, Calabrese provided a rationale for his choice of the structure of conditional events, but other than empirical appeal, none for his operations and relations. The others mentioned in the list above did not attepmt to develop operations among conditional events with differing antecedents, except for Adams' formal proposals previously indicated.

The results of this inquiry lead to the following, which provided a new calculus of operations and relations for conditional events, while at the same time justified and related the previous work of most of those mentioned above:

Call any $g : R^2 \to S$ a *feasible candidate for being a conditional even forming function* iff $S = \text{range}(g)$ and

$$g(A, B) = g(AB, B); \text{ if } g(A, B) = g(C, D), \text{ then } AB = CD \ \& \ B = D, \text{ for all } A, B, C, D \in R, \tag{6.43}$$

noting that when the above holds, then for all prob. $p : R \to u$,

$$p(g(A, B)) = p(A \mid B),\ p(B) > 0;\ \text{all } A, B \in R, \tag{6.44}$$

is well-defined. Also, define the *natural mapping* $\text{nat} : R^2 \to R$, where for $A, B \in R$,

$$\text{nat}(A, B) \overset{d}{=} R\cdot B' \vee AB \overset{d}{=} \{x\cdot B' \vee AB : x \in R\} = \{y : y \in R \ \& \ AB \le y \le B \Rightarrow A\} = \{y : y \in R \ \& \ yB = AB\}, \tag{6.45}$$

the *principal ideal coset generated by* B' with residue AB, noting that for each fixed B, $\text{nat}(\cdot, B) : R \to R/RB'$ is a homomorphism, where for any $A \in R$,

$$\text{nat}(A, B) \in \text{nat}(\cdot, B)(R) = \{\text{nat}(A, B) : A \in R\} = R/RB', \tag{6.46}$$

the *boolean quotient algebra* with the usual coset operations $\cdot, \vee, (\ )'$

$$\text{nat}(A, B)' = \text{nat}(A', B)\ ;\ \text{nat}(A, B)*\text{nat}(C, B) = \text{nat}(A*C, B),\quad * = \cdot, \vee, +, \text{ all } A, B, C \in R. \tag{6.47}$$

Denote

$$\tilde{R} \overset{d}{=} \text{range}(\text{nat}) = \{\text{nat}(A, B) : A, B \in R\} = \bigcup_{B \in R} R/RB' \subseteq \mathcal{P}(R), \tag{6.48}$$

the class of all principal ideal cosets of R.

Theorem 6.2. Structure of conditional events.

(i) nat is a feasible candidate for being a conditional event forming function.

(ii) If $g : R^2 \to S$ is any feasible candidate for being a conditional event forming function, then g is globally isomorphic to nat. That is, there is a bijection $\kappa : S \to \tilde{R}$, where $\kappa \circ g = \text{nat}$ and for each $B \in R$, $\kappa_B : S_B \to R/R\cdot B'$ is a bijection, and hence, an isomorphism through the same technique as in the beginning of section 3 inducing an algebraic structure on S via R/RB', where

$$S_B \overset{d}{=} \text{range}(g(\cdot, B)) = \{g(A, B) : A \in R\} \tag{6.49}$$

and

$$\kappa_B(g(A, B)) \overset{d}{=} \kappa(g(A, B)) = \text{nat}(A, B), \text{ all } A \in R \tag{6.50}$$

■

Remarks. Theorem 6.2 justifies the choice for conditional event forming function to be nat, so that from now on, define

$$(A|B) \overset{d}{=} \text{nat}(A, B), \text{ all } A, B \in R; \ (R|R) \overset{d}{=} \tilde{R} = \{(A|B) : A, B \in R\}, \tag{6.51}$$

and note, via (6.44), any prob. $p : R \to u$ extends consistently to $p : (R|R) \to u$, where

$$p((A|B)) = p(A|B), \text{ all } (A|B) \in (R|R), \quad p(B) > 0. \tag{6.51'}$$

It can be shown that the algebraic fraction approach of Hailperin and the partial logical deduct approach of Calabrese, both cited earlier, are, in fact, equivalent to the form nat.

Note the division of conditional events into 5 distinct classes:

(I) *Unconditional events in conditional form*:
Since it follows readily that one can identify

$$(A|1) = A, \text{ all } A \in R, \text{ whence } R \subseteq (R|R) \subseteq \mathcal{P}(R), \tag{6.52}$$

call all such conditional events unconditional ones, noting the probability assignment, via (6.44) becomes here simply

$$p((A|1)) = p(A). \tag{6.53}$$

(II) *The indeterminate conditional event*:

$$(A|0) = (0|0) = R, \text{ all } A \in R, \tag{6.54}$$

noting

$$p((0|0)) \text{ not defined.} \tag{6.55}$$

(III) *Unity-type conditional events*: Call the class of all such events $\mathcal{U}$

For all $B \in R$, $B \neq 0$, $(1|B) = (B|B) = RB' \vee B = R \vee B = \{x : x \in R \ \& \ x \geq B\}$,

(6.56)

the *principal filter of* R *generated by* B, noting the probability evaluation

$$p((B|B)) = p(B|B) = 1. \tag{6.57}$$

(IV) *Zero-type conditional events*: Call the class of all such events $\mathcal{Z}$

$$\text{For all } B \in R, B \neq 0, (0|B) = (B'|B) = RB' = \{xB' : x \in R\}, \tag{6.58}$$

the *principal ideal of* R generated by B', noting the probability evaluation

$$p((O|B)) = p((B'|B)) = p(0|B) = 0. \tag{6.59}$$

(V) *Proper conditional events*:

$$\text{For all } 0 < A < B < 1, A, B \in R, (A|B) = RB' \vee AB, \tag{6.59'}$$

with probability evaluation

$$0 < p((A|B)) = p(A|B) < 1. \tag{6.60}$$

Note also the basic properties for all $(A|B), (C|D) \in (R|R)$, from (6.43):

$$(A|B) = (AB|B) \;\&\; (A|B) = (C|D) \text{ iff } AB = CD \;\&\; B = D. \tag{6.61}$$

Returning to the conditional event indicator function given in (6.34), note that by its very definition and use of eqs. (6.38) and (6.61), where now the concrete case of $R \subseteq P(X)$ holds, it follows that $Mem_3(X)$ (with the modification that $P(X)$ in its characterization in (6.38) is replaced by R) and $(R|R)$ are bijective through the relation

$$1_{(A|B)} \mapsto (A|B), \text{ all } A, B \in R. \tag{6.62}$$

Finally, it should be remarked that the conditional event indicator function takes on the following forms relative to each of the 5 types of conditional events:

(I) Unconditional events: $1_{(A|1)} = 1_A \in Mem_2(X)$. (6.63)

(II) Indeterminate event: $1_{(0|0)} = u(\text{const.}) = Mem_1(X)$ (via (6.36)). (6.64)

(III) Unity-type conditional event: $\text{range}(1_{(B|B)}) = \{u, 1\}, 0 < B < 1$. (6.65)

(IV) Zero-type conditional event: $\text{range}(1_{(0|B)}) = \{0, u\}, 0 < B < 1$. (6.66)

(V) Proper conditional events: $\text{range}(1_{(A|B)}) = \{0, u, 1\}$.

The next theorem motivates the choice of operations and relations over $(R|R)$ to be determined:

Theorem 6.3. Characterization of monotonicity of conditional probabilities, ordering of conditional event indicator functions and zero and unity values.

As before, let $R \subseteq \mathcal{P}(X)$ be a fixed boolean algebra of sets. In addition, suppose (needed only for probability part) R is atomic. For any $(A|B), (C|D) \in (R|R)$, but not indeterminate:

(i) If $(A|B)$ is not zero-type and $(C|D)$ is not unity type (certainly satisfied if both are proper), then the following three statements are equivalent:

(I) $1_{(A|B)} \leq 1_{(C|D)}$ point-wise over X.

(II) $AB \leq CD \;\&\; C'D \leq A'B$ (i.e. $B \Rightarrow A \leq D \Rightarrow C$).

(III) For all prob. $p : R \to u$, with $p(B), p(D) > 0$, $p(A|B) \leq p(C|D)$.

(ii) $(A|B)$ is of zero-type iff $1_{(A|B)} \leq u$ over X (wrt order $0 \leq u \leq 1$) iff for all prob. $p : R \to u$ with $p(B) > 0, p(A|B) = 0$.

(iii) $(A|B)$ is of unity-type iff $1_{(A|B)} \geq u$ over X iff for all prob. $p : R \to u$ with $p(B) > 0, p(A|B) = 1$. ■

Consider next the standard *functional image extensions* of an arbitrary function, say,

$f : Y^n \to Z$ to the power class level $\hat{f} : \mathcal{P}(Y)^n \to \mathcal{P}(Z)$, where

$$\text{for all } \mathcal{A}_j \in \mathcal{P}(Y),\ \hat{f}(\mathcal{A}_1,\ldots,\mathcal{A}_n) \overset{d}{=} \{f(x_1,\ldots,x_n) : x_j \in \mathcal{A}_j, j = 1,\ldots,n\}. \tag{6.67}$$

If $\mathcal{Q} \subseteq \mathcal{P}(Y)^n$ and $\mathcal{R} \subseteq \mathcal{P}(Z)$ are subclasses of interest, it is important to determine whether the restriction of $\hat{f}$ to $\mathcal{Q}$ is closed wrt to $\mathcal{R}$, i.e., range($\hat{f}$ restrict. to $\mathcal{Q}$) $\subseteq \mathcal{R}$. In particular, for the problem at hand, $Y = Z = R$, f is any n-ary boolean function over $\mathcal{R}$, $\mathcal{Q} = (R|R)^n$, and $\mathcal{R} = (R|R)$. It is fortuitous that in this case closure indeed does hold, as the following theorem states, where for simplicity the hat $(\hat{\ })$ notation is omitted:

Theorem 6.4. Functionally-image extended boolean operations and relations over (R|R).

For all $A, B, C, D, A_j, B_j \in R$, $j = 1,\ldots,n$:

(i) All functionally-imaged extended boolean operations over R to being over (R|R) are closed and computable for $n = 1$ and 2 as:

$$(A|B)' \overset{d}{=} \{x' : x \in (A|B)\} = (A'|B);\quad (A|B)\cdot(C|D)$$
$$\overset{d}{=} \{x\cdot y : x \in (A|B), y \in (C|D)\} = (ABCD|r_2); \tag{6.68}$$

$$(A|B) \vee (C|D) \overset{d}{=} \{x \vee y : x \in (A|B), y \in (C|D)\} = (AB \vee CD|q_2); \tag{6.69}$$

$$(A|B) + (C|D) \overset{d}{=} \{x + y : x \in (A|B), y \in (C|D)\} = (AB + CD|s_2); \tag{6.70}$$

$$(C|D) \Rightarrow (A|B) \overset{d}{=} \{y \Rightarrow x : x \in (A|B), y \in (C|D)\}$$
$$= (C|D)' \vee (A|B) = (C'D \vee AB|t_2); \tag{6.71}$$

$$(C|D) \Leftrightarrow (A|B) \overset{d}{=} \{y \Leftrightarrow x : x \in (A|B), y \in (C|D)\}$$
$$= ((C|D) \Rightarrow (A|B))\cdot((A|B) \Rightarrow (C|D)) = ((A|B) + (C|D))' = (AB \Leftrightarrow CD|s_2), \tag{6.72}$$

where

$$r_2 \overset{d}{=} A'B \vee C'D \vee BD = A'B \vee C'D \vee ABCD;$$
$$q_2 \overset{d}{=} AB \vee CD \vee BD = AB \vee CD \vee A'BC'D;$$
$$s_2 \overset{d}{=} BD;\quad t_2 \overset{d}{=} C'D \vee AB \vee BD = C'D \vee AB \vee A'BCD. \tag{6.73}$$

(ii) Part (i) above can be extended the same way to arbitrary n, yielding the closed forms for $\cdot$, $\vee$, $+$:

$$(A_1|B_1)\cdot..\cdot(A_n|B_n) = (A_1B_1\cdot..\cdot A_nB_n|r_n);\ r_n \overset{d}{=} A_1'B_1 \vee..\vee A_n'B_n \vee (A_1B_1\cdot..\cdot A_nB_n); \tag{6.74}$$

$$(A_1|B_1) \vee..\vee (A_n|B_n) = (A_1B_1 \vee..\vee A_nB_n|q_n);$$
$$q_n \overset{d}{=} A_1B_1 \vee..\vee A_nB_n \vee (A_1'B_1\cdot..\cdot A_n'B_n); \tag{6.75}$$

$$(A_1|B_1) +..+ (A_n|B_n) = (A_1B_1 +..+ A_nB_n|s_n);\quad s_n \overset{d}{=} B_1\cdot..\cdot B_n. \tag{6.76}$$

(iii) Extend the natural (partial, indeed, lattice) order $\leq$ over R to $(R|R)$ by defining analogous to the case for R,

$$(A|B) \leq (C|D) \text{ iff } (A|B) = (A|B)\cdot(C|D). \tag{6.77}$$

Then, it can be shown

$$(A|B) \leq (C|D) \text{ iff } (C|D) = (A|B) \vee (C|D) \text{ iff } AB \leq CD \ \&\ C'D \leq A'B$$
$$\text{iff } AB \leq CD \ \&\ B \Rightarrow A \leq D \Rightarrow C. \tag{6.78}$$

(iv) Some miscellaneous properties:

Chaining: $(A|B)\cdot B = AB$; $(A|BC)\cdot(C|B) = (AC|B)$; (6.79)

Bayes' Theorem: If $A_1 \vee..\vee A_n \geq B$, then $(A_j|B)=((B|A_j)\cdot A_j|\bigvee_{j=1}^{n}((B|A_j)\cdot A_j))$; (6.80)

$$C \vee (A|B) = (C \vee A|C \vee B)\ ;\quad C\cdot(A|B) = (CA|C \Rightarrow A)\ ;$$
$$(A|B) = (AB \vee B'\cdot(0|0))\ ;\quad (R|R) = R \vee (R\cdot(0|0))\ ; \tag{6.81}$$
$$(B|B) = B \vee (0|0)\ ;\quad (0|B) = B'\cdot(0|0)\ ;$$
$$\mathcal{U} = (R \dashv \{0\}) \vee (0|0)\ ;\quad \mathcal{Z} = (R \dashv \{1\})\cdot(0|0)\ . \tag{6.82}$$

Equal antecedent/reduction to coset operations:

$$(A_1|B) *..* (A_n|B) = (A_1 *..* A_n|B),\ * = \cdot, \vee, +. \tag{6.83}$$

Remarks.

(i) Theorem 6.4 shows that any n-ary boolean function over $(R|R)$ is not only closed but is feasible to compute in terms of the antecedent and consequent consisting of ordinary unconditional boolean operations. Thus, one evaluates any arbitrary combination of conditional or unconditional events (remembering unconditional events are conditional ones with 1 in the antecedent) for a given probability measure $p : R \to u$ as

$$\begin{aligned} &p(\mathrm{comb}((A_1|B_1),...,(A_n|B_n))) \\ &= p((\mathrm{comb}_1(A_1B_1, B_1,..,A_nB_n, B_n)|\mathrm{comb}_2(A_1B_1, B_1,..,A_nB_n, B_n))), \text{ by Thm. 6.4} \\ &= p(\mathrm{comb}_1(A_1B_1, B_1,..,A_nB_n, B_n)|\mathrm{comb}_2(A_1B_1, B_1, ..,A_nB_n, B_n)), \text{ by (6.51')} \end{aligned} \tag{6.84}$$

finally obtained by the usual rules for conditional probability and boolean algebra expansions.

Thus, the original example addressed by material implication in (6.39) becomes

$$p((\text{if } B \text{ then } A) \text{ or } (\text{if } D \text{ then } C)) = p((A|B) \vee (C|D))$$
$$= p((AB \vee /cd|AB \vee CD \vee A'BC'D))$$
$$= p(AB \vee CD|AB \vee CD \vee AA'BC'D)$$
$$= p(AB \vee CD)/(p(AB \vee CD) + p(A'BC'D)), \text{ etc.} \quad (6.85)$$

(ii) Returning to Theorem 6.3 (i), it follows immediately that Theorem 6.4 (iii) (eq. (6.78)) shows the basic compatibility of partial order $\le$ over $(R|R)$ relative to monotonicity of probability and partial ordering of conditional event indicator functions: For any $(A|B), (C|D) \in (R|R)$ not indeterminate with $(A|B)$ not zero-type and $(C|D)$ not unity type, the following statements are equivalent for R assumed atomic:

(I) $1_{(A|B)} \le 1_{(C|D)}$ point-wise over X.

(II) $(A|B) \le (C|D)$.

(III) $p(A|B) \le p(C|D)$, all prob. $p : R \to u$, with $p(B), p(D) > 0$.

(iii) Theorem 6.4 can also be used to show that the algebraic entity $((R|R); \cdot, \vee, (\,)'; 0, 1, (0|0); \le)$ is such that $\cdot, \vee$ are associative, idempotent, commutative operations compatible with $\le$ being a legitimate meet-join lattice ordering over $(R|R)$, bounded below by the zero element wrt $\cdot, \vee$: 0, are bounded above by the unit element wrt $\cdot, \vee$: 1. In addition, $(R|R)$ with this structure has $\cdot$ and $\vee$ being mutually distributive and absorbing, as well as involutive operation $(\,)'$ (though, not in general orthocomplemented, thereby eliminating $(R|R)$ here from being a boolean algebra as R is) such that $(\cdot, \vee, (\,)')$ is a DeMorgan triple.

(iv) Furthermore, it can be shown directly that $(R|R)$ is always relatively pseudocomplemented and hence pseudocomplemented. Specifically, denoting the relative pseudocomplement of $(C|D)$ wrt $(A|B)$ as $(C|D) \triangleright (A|B)$ and the pseudocomplement of $(C|D)$ as $(C|D)^* \overset{d}{=} (C|D) \triangleright 0$, and recalling the well-known results (see Mendelson (1970, p. 182 et passim)) that relative to R, $B \triangleright A = B \Rightarrow A$ and $B = B'$,

$$(C|D) \triangleright (A|B) = \lambda \vee (A|B) = (\lambda \vee A|\lambda \vee B);\ \lambda \overset{d}{=} B'D' \vee C'D;\ (C|D)^* = C'D, \quad (6.86)$$

reducing to the corresponding unconditional situation for R, when $D = B = 1$. The pseudocomplement mapping $(\,)^* : (R|R) \to R$ satisfies the Stone identity

$$(A|B)^* \vee (A|B)^{**} = 1, \text{ all } (A|B) \in (R|R), \quad (6.87)$$

showing $((R|R); \cdot, \vee, 0, 1; \le; (\,)^*)$ is a Stone algebra. Referring, e.g., to Grätzer

(1978), the *skeletal* and *dense sets of* $(R|R)$ are, respectively,

$$(R|R)^* \overset{d}{=} \{(A|B)^* : (A|B) \in (R|\} = R;\ D(R|R) \overset{d}{=} (\ )^{*-1}(0) = \mathscr{U} \cup \{(0|0)\}, \tag{6.88}$$

yielding readily the relations (see also (6.82))

$$D(R|R) = (R|R)^* \vee (0|0);\ (A|B)^{*\prime} = (A|B)^{**},\ \text{all } (A|B) \in (R|R);\ (0|0)^{\prime *} = 0. \tag{6.89}$$

(v) Converse to (iii) and (iv) above, if $(R|R)$ is replaced by an abstract space S and similarly for operations $\cdot$, $\vee$, $(\ )'$, special elements 0, 1, $(0|0)$, partial (lattice) order $\leq$, and pseudocomplement operation $(\ )^*$, so that $(S; \cdot, \vee, (\ )'; 0, 1, (0|0); \leq; (\ )^*)$ is any abstract Stone algebra with involutive operation $(\ )'$ making $(\cdot, \vee, (\ )')$ a DeMorgan triple, such that the formal relations hold in (6.89), then it follows that S with the above structure is isomorphic to $(R|R)$, with the same algebraic operations and relations, where now $R = S^*$ (guaranteed to be a boolean algebra). Independent of the above result initially, it can be shown that if $m : R \to \mathscr{P}(\Omega)$ is the standard injective Stone isomorphism, where Ω is some set dependent upon R, for any given boolean algebra, then $(m|m) : (R|R) \to \mathscr{P}(\Omega)|\mathscr{P}(\Omega))$ is also an isomorphism, extending m, relative to the conditional event algebra structure obtained via functional image extensions of the boolean operations for R and $\mathscr{P}(\Omega)$, where

$$(m|m)(A|B) \overset{d}{=} (m(A)|m(B)),\ \text{all } (A|B) \in (R|R). \tag{6.90}$$

Finally, if the above isomorphic representation of S by $(S^*|S^*)$ is written $h : S \to (S^*|S^*)$, then it follows that the composition $(m|m) \circ h : S \to (\mathscr{P}(\Omega)|\mathscr{P}(\Omega))$ is an injective isomorphism (Ω dependent on S^*), showing a full extension of the Stone Representation Theorem for all such *abstract conditional event algebras.*

(vi) *Higher order conditional events*, i.e., formal quantities $((A|B)|(C|D))$ can be given meaning and reduced, in effect, to single conditional events by use of the relative pseudoinverse operation, where $A, B, C, D \in R$ are arbitrary. This is based upon the following observation resulting from eq. (6.45) applied to the definition of conditional events:

$$(A|B) = \{x : x \in R \ \&\ xB = AB\} \tag{6.91}$$

is the solution set of the conjunctive equation $xB = AB$, which has great intuitive appeal. Thus, it is perfectly reasonable to define the higher order conditional event

$$((A|B)|(C|D)) \overset{d}{=} \{(x|y) : (x|y) \in (R|R) \ \&\ (x|y)\cdot(C|D) = (A|B)\cdot(C|D)\}. \tag{6.92}$$

But it follows from the theory of linear equations in relatively pseudocomplemented lattices (which $(R|R)$ is) (see Grätzer (1978) or Goodman, Nguyen, Walker (1991)), (6.92) becomes

$$((A|B)|(C|D)) = (R|R)\cdot((C|D) \triangleright ((A|B)\cdot(C|D)) \vee ((A|B)\cdot(C|D)). \quad (6.93)$$

Noting that the class union operation $U : \mathcal{P}(\mathcal{P}(R)) \to \mathcal{P}(R)$ is a homomorphism wrt all functionally-imaged extended operations over $\mathcal{P}(R)$ to those over $\mathcal{P}(\mathcal{P}(R))$, it follows that it is natural to inquire: What is the effect applying U to (6.93)? First, note that (6.86) with $(A|B)$ replaced by $(A|B)\cdot(C|D)$ can be shown to have the invariancy

$$(C|D) \triangleright ((A|B)|(C|D)) = \lambda_0 \vee ((A|B)\cdot(C|D)) = \lambda \vee (A|B) = (C|D) \triangleright (A|B),$$

(6.94)

but where now

$$\lambda_0 \overset{d}{=} (B \Rightarrow A)\cdot D' \vee C'D. \quad (6.95)$$

Thus, (6.93) becomes

$$\begin{aligned}((A|B)|(C|D)) &= (R|R)\cdot(\lambda_0 \vee ((A|B)\cdot(C|D))) \vee ((A|B)\cdot(C|D)) \\ &= (R|R)\cdot\lambda_0 \vee ((A|B)\cdot(C|D)), \quad (6.96)\end{aligned}$$

by distributivity and absorption properties of the operations.

Hence, applying U to (6.96), using its homomorphism properties and the calculus of operations from (6.58), (6.68), (6.96),

$$\begin{aligned}U((A|B)|(C|D)) &= U(R|R)\cdot\lambda_0 \vee (ABCD|r_2) = R\cdot\lambda_0 \vee (ABCD|r_2) \\ &= (0|\lambda_0') \vee (ABCD|r_2) = (ABCD|B\cdot(A'D' \vee CD)). \quad (6.97)\end{aligned}$$

Despite the nice algebraic properties of the above reduction, one drawback is that we do not have compatibility with probability in the sense

$$\begin{aligned}p((A|B)|(C|D)) &\overset{d}{=} p((A|B)\cdot(C|D))/p((C|D)) \\ &= p(ABCD|A'B \vee C'D \vee BD)/p(C|D) \\ &\neq p(U((A|B)|(C|D))), \text{ in general}, \quad (6.98)\end{aligned}$$

unlike the single conditional event case where no U is required. More work must be done in this area; forcing closure for higher order conditionals may lead to contradictions, analogous to Lewis' results (1976).

(vii) $(R|R)$ with the fundamental image extensions of operations on R can also be shown to be a modified version of Koopman's comparative conditional qualitative probability structure as discussed in Fine (1973, pp. 183-186).

(viii) Often, it is more appropriate to consider cartesian products or jointness of conditional events in place of direct conjunction, and similarly cartesian sums in place of disjunction. This is especially relevant when e.g. conditional events $(A_j|B_j)$, $j = 1,..,n$ are such that the B_j are all disjoint -- such as in flow chart instructions -- yet eqs. (6.74) and (6.75) show that the conjunction always lead to a trivial zero-type event, and hence zero probability evaluation, while disjunction always dually leads to the equally trivial unity case and a unit probability evaluation! Specifically, using the functional image extension approach as before, it can be shown that for any $(A_j|B_j) \in (R|R)$, $j = 1,..,n$,

$$(A_1|B_1) \times .. \times (A_n|B_n) = (A_1 \times .. \times A_n | B_1 \times .. \times B_n) = (A_1B_1 \times .. \times A_nB_n | B_1 \times .. \times B_n), \tag{6.99}$$

$$(A_1|B_1) \dagger .. \dagger (A_n|B_n) = ((A_1|B_1)' \times .. \times (A_n|B_n)')' = ((A_1' \times .. \times A_n')' | B_1 \times .. \times B_n)$$
$$= (A_1 \dagger .. \dagger A_n | B_1 \times .. \times B_n). \tag{6.100}$$

Of course, with the use of cartesian products and sums, probability evaluations become more complex with joint probability specifications now required. Finally, note that no closure problems arise here, since all cartesian products -- and hence sums -- of boolean algebras are still boolean algebras.

(ix) The calculus of operations and relations obtained by functional image extensions of the boolean ones over R to $(R|R)$ also lead to a sound and complete *conditional probability logic of propositions* with the tautology class being $\mathcal{U}$ and the contradiction class being $\mathcal{Z}$. In connection with this, it can be shown that the only possible *boolean-like* function $f : (R|R)^2 \to (R|R)$, i.e.,

$$f((A|B), (C|D)) = (f_1(AB, B, CD, D) | f_2(AB, B, CD, D)), \text{ all } A, B, C, D \in R, \tag{6.101}$$

for some boolean functions $f_1, f_2 : R^4 \to R$ such that, in the spirit of (ii),

$$f((A|B), (C|D)) \in \mathcal{U} \text{ iff } (A|B) \leq (C|D); \text{ all } A, B, C, D \in R, \tag{6.102}$$

are $f = f^{(1)}$ and $f = f^{(2)}$, where for all $A, B, C, D \in R$,

$$f^{(1)}((A|B), (C|D)) \overset{d}{=} C'D \vee AB \vee B'D'; \quad f^{(2)}((A|B), (C|D)) \overset{d}{=} (C'D \vee AB | B \vee D). \tag{6.103}$$

f(1) is actually the consequent of the *natural isomorphic image* of Lukasiewicz three-valued logical implication, while $f^{(2)}$ is the natural isomorphic image of Sobocinski's three-valued logical material implication. (See Rescher (1969) for expositions on $Ł_3$ and Sob_3. The natural isomorphism connecting any three-valued logic and some choice of conditional event algebra is given below.)

(x) Other topics concerning conditional event algebras have begun to be developed, including: extension of random variables and relations with conditional random variables; problems of assignment of probability to conditional events relative to the functional image assignment of many values in light of the coset representation of conditional events as *sets* of events -- not the traditional single values (see also the latter part of sect. 7 here); extension of the idea of independence to conditional events (see also the Nguyen & Rogers paper in this monograph); and Fréchet-like bounds and probability expansions for various combinations of conditional events (in the same spirit as e.g. Hailperin (1984)).

As a final topic in this review, consider the natural isomorphism between any choice of conditional event algebra -- such as proposed here by functional image extensions, or that proposed commonly (but independently) by Schay, Adams, and Calabrese, or an alternative system also proposed by Schay, to be discussed briefly below -- and any corresponding choice of 3-valued (truth-functional) logic. [We will employ the abbreviation "ce-alg" for "conditional event algebra."]

Recall the operation construction technique of section 3, whereby a given bijection between two spaces X and Y with X having a given algebraic structure induces an isomorphism for Y now having the constructed algebraic structure. Of course, in general, one cannot guarantee that the constructed isomorphic operations over Y will be "recognizable" in some sense. Apropos to this, a basic connection was established between 3-valued indicator functions and conditional events as given in (6.62) -- basic bijection between $Mem_3(X)$ and $(R|R)$ -- and Theorem 6.3 (see also Remark (ii) following Theorem 6.4) -- characterization of ordering. However, no algebraic structure was imposed upon $Mem_3(X)$. Of course, since $Mem_3(X) \subseteq Mem(X)$ (up to the identification of (6.36)), the Zadeh-like operations and relations over the latter cna be used over the smaller class. (More on this later.) In response to the above remarks, the following theorem holds (Goodman (1990)) (see also Goodman et al,1991)):

Theorem 6.5: The three-valued indicator mapping as the natural isomorphism connecting all possible choices of conditional event algebras and all truth-functional three-valued logics.

First, denote the class of all n-ary boolean-like functions $f : (R|R)^n \to (R|R)$, analogous to the binary case given in (6.101), as $bool_n(R|R)$. Recall that the unit interval u is also used in effect as a single value between 0 and 1 and define

$$Q_o \overset{d}{=} \{0, u, 1\} \qquad (6.104)$$

as the common truth set of all three-valued logics to be considered. Any such logic is specified by some set of operations $\not{f} : Q_o^n \to Q_o \in Q_o^{Q_o^n}$. Then, there is a bijection $\theta : bool_n(R|R) \to Q_o^{Q_o^n}$ such that $1_. : ((R|R); bool_n(R|R)) \to (Q_o; Q_o^{Q_o^n})$ is an isomorphism: for all $(\underline{A}|\underline{B}) \overset{d}{=} ((A_1|B_1),..,(A_n|B_n)) \in (R|R)^n$,

$$1_{(\underline{A}|\underline{B})}(x) \overset{d}{=} (1_{(a_1|B_1)}(x),...,1_{(A_n|B_n)}(x)),$$

for all $x \in X$, assuming $R \subseteq \mathcal{P}(X)$, and for all $f \in \text{bool}_n(R|R)$,

$$1_{f(\underline{A}|\underline{B})}(x) = \theta f(1_{(A|B)}(x)). \tag{6.105}$$

Proof: The proof is completely constructive, enabling one to go from any three-valued logical operator to a corresponding conditional event one and vice-versa. (Again, see the cited references.) ∎

In connection with, and as an application of, the above theorem, consider briefly some of the approaches to defining conditional event operations extending the usual unconditional boolean ones, other than the functional image extension approach used so far -- and denoted from now on for convenience as the GN system. As mentioned before, independently Schay (1968), Adams (1975) and Calabrese (1987), denoted commonly as SAC, proposed identical ce-alg's. Actually, Schay also proposed an alternative ce-alg (same reference), which will be denoted simply as S. The complement, conjunction, and disjunction for these ce-alg's are, with the appropriate subscripting, for all $(A|B), (C|D) \in (R|R)$,

$$(A|B)'^{SAC} \overset{d}{=} (A|B)'^{S} \overset{d}{=} (A|B)'^{GN} = (A'|B). \tag{6.106}$$

$$(A|B) \vee_{SAC} (C|D) \overset{d}{=} (AB \vee CD|B \vee D);\ (A|B)\cdot_{SAC} (C|D) \overset{d}{=} ((A|B)' \vee_{SAC} (C|D)')', \tag{6.107}$$

a DeMorgan assumption, whence

$$(A|B)\cdot_{SAC}(C|D) = ((B \Rightarrow A)\cdot(D \Rightarrow C)|B \vee D) = (ABD' \vee B'CD \vee ABCD|B \vee D). \tag{6.108}$$

$$(A|B) \vee_S (C|D) = (AB \vee CD|BD);$$

$$(A|B)\cdot_S(C|D) = (A|B)' \vee_S (C|D)')' = (ABCD|BD). \tag{6.109}$$

Corollary 6.1. 3-valued logic characterizations of SAC, S, GN systems.

Under the mapping $1_{.}$, as in (6.105), the following isomorphisms hold between all operations defined for SAC, S, GN, and corresponding ones to be found in 3-valued logic:

$$\text{SAC} \mapsto \text{Sob}_3;\ \text{S} \mapsto \text{B}_3;\ \text{GN} \mapsto \text{Ł}_3, \tag{6.110}$$

where Sob_3 is Sobocinski's 3-valued logic (see Rescher (1969, pp. 70, 342)), B_3 is Bochvar's 3-valued internal logic (Rescher (1969, pp. 29-34, 339)), and $Ł_3$ is Lukasiewicz' 3-valued logic (Rescher (1969, pp. 22-28, 335)).

Proof: Consequence of Theorem 6.5. ∎

Independently, Dubois & Prade (1989, 1990) have expressed interest in the development of conditional event algebra and, by informal means, pointed out the same correspondences as in Corollary 6.1, without recognizing the more general impact of Theorem 6.5. Recently (Goodman (1989)) a minisymposium was organized on conditional event algebras, as evidence also of the growing interest in the field.

Corollary 6.2. A characterization of GN.

Call any $f, g : (R|R)^2 \to (R|R)$ with f extending ordinary conjunction $\cdot$ over R and g extending ordinary disjunction $\vee$ over R, *monotone preserving* iff

$$1_{f((A|B),(C|D))} \le 1_{(A|B)}, 1_{(C|D)};\ 1_{g((A|B),(C|D))} \ge 1_{(A|B)}, 1_{(C|D)} \tag{6.111}$$

pointwise over X (still assuming throughout here that $R \subseteq \mathscr{P}(X)$).

Also, for any operations $f, g : (R|R)^2 \to (R|R)$ extending $\cdot, \vee$ over R and $h : (R|R) \to (R|R)$ extending negation over R, call the system (f, g, h) a *common antecedent homomorphism* (or *coset compatible*) ce-alg iff for all $A, B, C \in R$,

$$h((A|B)) = (h(AB)|B);\ f((A|B),(C|B)) = (f(AB, CB)|B);$$

$$g((A|B),(C|B)) = (G(AB, CB)|B) \tag{6.112}$$

noting that necessarily $$h(AB) = A'B,$$

whence $$h((A|B)) = (A'|B)\ (=(A'B|B)). \tag{6.113}$$

Then:

(i) of the 81 possible binary boolean-like ce-alg's (f, g, h) extending ordinary conjunction, disjunction, negation, respectively, over R to $(R|R)$, which are DeMorgan for h such that

$$h((A|B)) = (A'|B),\ \text{all } A, B \in R, \tag{6.114}$$

there are 4 which are also commutative and monotone preserving. Letting $f = \cdot_j$, $j = 1, 2, 3, 4$, for all $A, B, C, D \in R$,

$$(A|B)\cdot_1(C|D) = ABCD;\ (A|B)\cdot_2(C|D) = (ABCD|r_2 \vee B'D');$$

$$(A|B)\cdot_3(C|D) = (ABCD|B \vee D); \tag{6.115}$$

$$(A|B)\cdot_4(C|D) = (ABCD|r_2), \tag{6.116}$$

where r_2 is given in (6.73), noting that the SAC and S ce-alg's are not among this group, but GN is (determined through $\cdot_4$).

(ii) The unique boolean-like ce-alg extending ordinary conjunction, disjunction, and negation which is DeMorgan for extended negation h satisfying (6.114) and which is monotone preserving, possesses the common antecedent homomorphism property, and for which its conjunction and disjunction extending operations are mutually distributive

and idempotent is GN.

Proof: Consequence of Theorem 6.5. (Again, see the Goodman and Goodman, Nguyen, Walker references.) ■

Remark. Since Lukasiewicz-$\aleph_1$ (min, max, 1 - ( )) logic is the core of Zadeh's fuzzy set operations relative to the space Mem(X), then Corollary 6.1 shows that the specialization of fuzzy sets and their Zadeh operations to $Ł_3$ for $M_3(X)$ is isomorphic to the GN conditional event algebra over (R|R).

Flou and partitioning sets corresponding to conditional event indicator functions.

With the basic properties of conditional events and their operations and relations established and tied-in with conditional event indicator functions, it is of some interest to reinterpret eqs. (6.27)-(6.31), using the identifications of (6.36)-(6.38): For any A, B ∈ R (⊆ P(X)), the corresponding flou set to $1_{(A|B)}$ is

$$\phi^{-1}(1_{(A|B)}) = \{\phi^{-1}(1_{(A|B)_t}) : t \in u\}; \ \phi^{-1}(1_{(A|B)_t}) = ((\phi^{-1}(1_{(A|B)_t}))_s)_{s\in u}; \quad (6.117)$$

$$\text{for all } s \in u, \ (\phi^{-1}(1_{(A|B)_t}))_s = \begin{cases} X, & \text{if } s = 0, \\ B \Rightarrow A, & \text{if } 0 < s \le t, \\ A \cap B, & \text{if } t < s \le 1, \end{cases} \quad (6.118)$$

and the corresponding partitioning set is

$$(\phi\circ\psi)^{-1}(1_{(A|B)}) = \{(\phi\circ\psi)^{-1}(1_{(A|B)_t}) : t \in u\}, \quad (6.119)$$

with index set

$$J_{(\phi\circ\psi)^{-1}(1_{(A|B)_t})} = \{0, t, 1\}, \quad (6.120)$$

and for any s ∈ {0, u, 1},

$$((\phi\circ\psi)^{-1}(1_{(A|B)_t}))_s = \begin{cases} B \dashv A, & \text{if } s = 0, \\ B', & \text{if } s = t, \\ A \cap B, & \text{if } s = 1. \end{cases} \quad (6.121)$$

Analogous to (6.38) for $Mem_3(X)$, obtain through the identifications of (6.36)-(6.38),

$$Flou_3(X) = \{\phi^{-1}(1_{(A|B)}) : (A|B) \in (R|R)\}, \quad (6.122)$$

$$Part_3(X) = \{(\phi\circ\psi)^{-1}(1_{(A|B)}) : (A|B) \in (R|R)\}, \quad (6.123)$$

and clearly $Mem_3(X)$, $Flou_3(X)$, $Part_3(X)$ are all bijective under the restrictions of ϕ, ψ, $\phi\circ\psi$ (analogous to the bijection part of Theorem 6.1 (ii)).

Again, from the remark following Corollary 6.2, the Zadeh fuzzy set operations for conjunction, disjunction, and negation, i.e., min, max, 1 - ( ), respectively, applied to

$Mem_3(X)$ component-wise yield an isomorphism with GN ce-alg: For $* = \min, \max$, for all $s, t \in u$,

$$(1_{(|B)_t} * 1_{(C|D)_t})_s = (1_{((A|B)\theta^{-1}(*)(C|D))_t})_s \; ; \; 1 - (1_{(A|B)_t})_s = (1_{(A|B)'_t})_s, \quad (6.124)$$

i.e., component-wise over X

$$\min(1_{(A|B)}, 1_{(C|D)}) = 1_{(A|B)\cdot(C|D)}; \; \max(1_{(A|B)}, 1_{(C|D)}) = 1_{(A|B)\vee(C|D)}; \quad (6.125)$$

$$1 - 1_{(A|B)} = 1_{(A|B)'} \quad (6.126)$$

with $(A|B)\cdot(C|D)$, $(A|B) \vee (C|D)$, and $(A|B)'$ all obtainable from GN as in equations (6.68) and (6.69).

Hence, the construction technique of section 3 yields the compatible results for the corresponding flou and partitioning sets, using (6.117)-(6.121) (first, flou):

$$\phi^{-1}(1_{(A|B)}) * \phi^{-1}(1_{(C|D)}) = \phi^{-1}(1_{(A|B)\theta^{-1}(*)(C|D)}), \quad (6.127)$$

i.e., for all $s, t \in u$, $* = \min, \max$, and noting (see sect. 4) $* = \cap_{\min}, \cup_{\max}$, respectively,

$$(\phi^{-1}(1_{(A|B)_t}))_s * (\phi^{-1}(1_{(C|D)_t}))_s = (\phi^{-1}(1_{((A|B)\theta^{-1}(*)(C|D))_t}))_s$$

$$= \begin{cases} X, & \text{if } s = 0 \\ r_2 \Rightarrow (A\cap B\cap C\cap D) = (A\cap B\cap D') \cup (B'\cap C\cap D) \cup (B'\cap D') \cup & \\ \quad \text{if } 0 < s \le t, & \\ (A\cap B\cap C\cap D)\cap r_2 = A\cap B\cap C\cap D, & \\ \quad \text{if } t < s \le 1, & \end{cases} \quad (6.128)$$

for $*$ - min and $\varphi^{-1}(*) = \cdot$.;

$$= \begin{cases} X, & \text{if } s = 0 \\ q_2 \Rightarrow ((A\cap B) \cup (C\cap D)) = (A'\cap B\cap D') \cup (B'\cap C'\cap D) \cup (B'\cap D') & \\ \qquad \cup (A\cap B) \cup (C\cap D) & \\ \quad \text{if } 0 < s \le t, & \\ ((A\cap B) \cup (C\cap D)) \cap q_2 = (A\cap B) \cup (C\cap D) & \\ \quad \text{if } t < s \le 1, & \end{cases} \quad (6.129)$$

for $* = \max$ and $\varphi^{-1}(*) = \vee$;

$$(\phi^{-1}(1_{(A|B)}))' = \phi^{-1}(1_{(A|B)'}), \quad (6.130)$$

i.e., for all $s, t \in u$,

$$(\phi^{-1}(1_{(A|B)'_t}))_s = \begin{cases} X, & \text{if } s = 0 \\ B \Rightarrow A', & \text{if } 0 < s \le t, \\ B \dashv A, & \text{if } t < s \le 1. \end{cases} \tag{6.131}$$

Furthermore, by use of the basic identities

$$(B \Rightarrow A) \cap (D \Rightarrow C) = (r_2 \Rightarrow (A \cap B \cap C \cap D)); \; ((B \Rightarrow A) \cup (D \Rightarrow C) = (q_2 \Rightarrow ((A \cap B) \cup (C \cap D)), \tag{6.132}$$

which, in their own right, are exact material implication parallels of the corresponding conditional event identities in (6.68) and (6.69), it follows by inspection of (6.118), that $*$ in (6.127)-(6.129), for $* = \min$, max, and correspondingly, for $\phi^{-1}(*) = \cdot$, $\vee$, relative to each of the three possible set values component-wise are isomorphic, i.e., symbolically,

$$\begin{pmatrix} X \\ B \Rightarrow A \\ A \cap B \end{pmatrix} * \begin{pmatrix} X \\ D \Rightarrow C \\ C \cap D \end{pmatrix} = \begin{pmatrix} X\,\theta^{-1}(*)X \\ (B \Rightarrow A)\ \theta^{-1}(*)\,(D \Rightarrow C) \\ (A \cap B)\ \theta^{-1}(*)\,(C \cap D) \end{pmatrix}. \tag{6.133}$$

Similarly, for the partitioning sets,

$$(\phi\circ\psi)^{-1}(1_{(A|B)}) * (\phi\circ\psi)^{-1}(1_{(C|D)}) = (\phi\circ\psi)^{-1}(1_{(A|B)\theta^{-1}(*)(C|D)}), \tag{6.134}$$

i.e., for all $t \in u$ and $s \in J_{(\phi\circ\psi)^{-1}(1_{((A|B)\theta^{-1}(*)(C|D))_t})} = \{0, t, 1\}$,

$$((\phi\circ\psi)^{-1}(1_{(A|B)_t}))_s * ((\phi\circ\psi)^{-1}(1_{)C|D)_t}))_s = ((\phi\circ\psi)^{-1}(1_{((A|B)\theta^{-1}(*)(C|D))_t}))_s$$

$$= \begin{cases} r_2 \dashv (A \cap B \cap C \cap D) = (A' \cap B) \cup (C' \cap D), & \text{if } s = 0, \\ r_2' = (A \cap B \cap D') \cup (B' \cap C \cap D) \cup (B' \cap D'), & \text{if } s = t, \\ (A \cap B \cap C \cap D) \cap r_2 = A \cap B \cap C \cap D, & \text{if } s = 1 \end{cases} \tag{6.135}$$

for $* = \min$ and $\phi^{-1}(*) = \cdot$;

$$= \begin{cases} q_2 \dashv ((A \cap B) \cup (C \cap D)) = A' \cap B \cap C' \cap D, & \text{if } s = 0, \\ q_2' = (A' \cap B \cap D') \cup (B' \cap C' \cap D) \cup (B' \cap D'), & \text{if } s = t, \\ ((A \cap B) \cup (C \cap D)) \cap (A \cap B) \cup (C \cap D), & \text{if } s = 1, \end{cases} \tag{6.136}$$

for $* = \max$ and $\phi^{-1}(**) = \vee$;

$$((\phi\circ\psi)^{-1}(1_{(A|B)}))' = (\phi\circ\psi)^{-1}(1_{(A|B)'}) \tag{6.137}$$

i.e., for all $t \in u$ and $s \in \{0, t, 1\}$

$$((\phi\circ\psi)^{-1}(1_{(A|B)'_t})) = \begin{cases} B \dashv A' = A \cap B, & \text{if } s = 0, \\ B' & \text{, if } s = t, \\ A' \cap B = B \dashv A, & \text{if } s = 1. \end{cases} \tag{6.138}$$

In summary:

Theorem 6.6. Apropos to eqs. (6.117)-(6.138), the following diagram holds, superseding Fig. 5.1 for the restriction to three values:

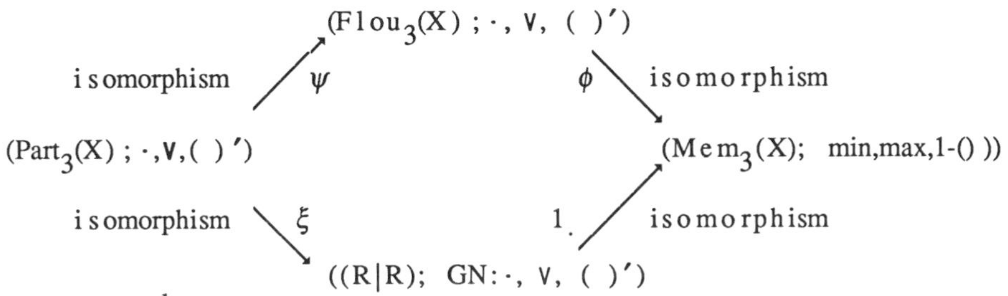

$\xi \overset{d}{=} 1_{\cdot}^{-1}\circ\phi\circ\psi$; $R \subseteq \mathcal{P}(X)$ boolean algebra; $(\cdot, \vee) = (\cap_{min}, \cup_{max})$

Figure 6.1. Summary of isomorphisms among ((R|R); GN), Mem$_3$(X), Flou$_3$(X), Part$_3$(X).

Proof: Combine the results of eqs. (6.117)-(6.138) with the compatible results of Theorem 6.1 (ii). ∎

7. Models and External Probabilities of Fuzzy Sets and Relations with Conditional Event Indicator Functions

The primary purpose of this section is to relate on a firm foundation the concept of a model as a consistent numerical evaluation relative to: fuzzy sets in general, and conditional events, in particular; and an appropriate fixed point relative to all membership functions at that point. In turn, this allows for a rationale to define probabilities for fuzzy sets, in general, and conditional events, in particular. To this end, assume throughout that boolean algebra $R \subseteq \mathcal{P}(X)$. Also, recall (Mendelson (1970)) the concepts of *filters* and *ultrafilters for* R. Call R *atomic*$_0$, if all finite subsets of R -- and hence all subsets of R whose complements are finite -- are in R, which immediately implies R is atomic. For such R, then essentially any ultrafilter $\mathcal{F}$ of R is in the principal ultrafilter form

$$\mathcal{F} = \mathcal{F}_x \overset{d}{=} \{A : x \in A \in R\} \subseteq R, \; x \in X. \tag{7.1}$$

In any case, denote the class of all ultrafilters of R as $\Omega(R)$. Also, define the mapping $\xi : \Omega(R) \times \mathrm{Flou}(X) \to u$, reminescent of the fundamental membership mapping ϕ (see (2.6)), where

$$\xi(\mathcal{F}, a) \overset{d}{=} \sup\{t : t \in u \;\&\; a_t \in \mathcal{F}\}, \text{ all } \mathcal{F} \in \Omega(R), \; a \in \mathrm{Flou}(X). \tag{7.2}$$

Next, define formally a *model of* Flou(X) as any function h: Flou(X) $\to$ u which is a homomorphism relative to $(\cap_{min}, \cup_{max}, (\;)')$ over Flou(X) and (min, max, 1 - ( )) over u, and hence over Mem(X). If, also h is an infinite homomorphism relative to $(\cup_{max}, \max)$ and a homomorphism relative to $(\cap_{prod}, \mathrm{prod})$ for the spaces $\mathrm{Flou}_1(X)$ and $\mathrm{Mem}_1(X)$, then call h a *strong model of* Flou(X). Finally, define

$$\mathrm{Mod}_0(X) \overset{d}{=} \{\xi(\mathcal{F}, \cdot) : \mathcal{F} \in \Omega(R)\} \tag{7.3}$$

and denote the class of all strong models of Flou(X) as $\widetilde{\mathrm{Mod}}(X)$. Before giving the main theorem, the following lemma should be pointed out:

Lemma 7.1. If $R \subseteq \mathcal{P}(X)$ is atomic_0, then for any $\mathcal{F} \in \Omega(R)$, there is a unique corresponding $x \in X$ such that

$$\mathcal{F} = \mathcal{F}_x \;\&\; \zeta(\mathcal{F}_x, a) = \phi(a)(x), \text{ all } a \in \mathrm{Flou}(X). \tag{7.4}$$

Proof: Use the definition of ϕ in (2.6), noting from (7.1), for $a = (a_t)_{t \in u}$,

$$a_t \in \mathcal{F}_x \text{ iff } x \in a_t, \text{ all } x \in X, \; t \in u. \tag{7.5}$$

■

Theorem 7.1. Basic characterization of strong models of Flou(X).

The equation

$$\widetilde{\mathrm{Mod}}(X) = \mathrm{Mod}_0(X) \tag{7.6}$$

is true. More specifically, the following holds:

(i) For each $\mathcal{F} \in \Omega(R)$, $\xi(\mathcal{F}, \cdot)$: Flou(X) $\to$ u is a strong model of Flou(X). In particular, note the case when R is atomic_0: by Lemma 7.1, (7.4) holds.

(ii) For each $h \in \widetilde{\mathrm{Mod}}(X)$,

$$\mathcal{F}_{(h)} \overset{d}{=} \{a : a \in R \;\&\; h(a) = 1\} = h^{-1}(1) \in \Omega(R) \tag{7.7}$$

and

$$\mathscr{h} = \xi(\mathscr{F}_{(h)}, \cdot) \in \mathrm{Mod}_0(X). \tag{7.8}$$

(iii) For each $\mathscr{h} \in \tilde{\mathrm{Mod}}(X)$, there is a unique $x_{\mathscr{h}} \in X$ such that

$$\mathscr{h}(a) = \phi(a)(x_{\mathscr{h}}), \text{ all } a \in \mathrm{Flou}(X). \tag{7.9}$$

If R is also atomic$_0$, then (7.8) and (7.9) combine to become

$$\mathscr{F}_{(\mathscr{h})} = \mathscr{h}^{-1}(1) = \mathscr{F}_{(\mathscr{h})_{x_{\mathscr{h}}}} = (\phi(\cdot)(x_{\mathscr{h}}))^{-1}(1);\ \mathscr{h}(a) = \xi(\mathscr{F}_{(\mathscr{h})_{x_{\mathscr{h}}}}, a) = \phi(a)(x_{\mathscr{h}}), \tag{7.10}$$

all $a \in \mathrm{Flou}(X)$.

(iv)
$$\mathscr{h}(\phi^{-1}(c)) = c, \text{ all } c : X \to u \in \mathrm{Flou}_1(X). \tag{7.11}$$

Proof (i): Let $J \subseteq u$, $a^{(s)} \in \mathrm{Flou}(X)$, $f_s \overset{d}{=} \phi(a^{(s)})$, $s \in J$, and $\mathscr{F} \in \Omega(R)$, all arb. Define $\alpha \overset{d}{=} \xi(\mathscr{F}, \cup_{\min}(a^{(s)}))$ and $\beta \overset{d}{=} \sup_{s \in J}(\xi(\mathscr{F}, a^{(s)}))$. Since $(\max_{s \in J}(f_s))^{-1}[t, 1] \geq f_s^{-1}[t, 1]$, all $s \in J$, then by the definition in (7.2), $\alpha \geq \beta$. Consider the converse: First, as a supremum, for all $\delta > 0$, there exists $s_\delta \in J$ with $f_{s_\delta}(x) \leq \sup_{s \in J}(f_s(x)) < f_{s_\delta}(x) + \delta$.

Since $\mathscr{F}$ is a filter, if $A \overset{d}{=} \{x : x \in X \ \&\ \sup_{s \in J}(f_s(x)) \geq t\} \in \mathscr{F}$, then $B \overset{d}{=} \{x : x \in X \ \&\ f_{s_\delta}(x) \geq t - \delta\} \in \mathscr{F}$, since the above equation implies $A \subseteq B$. Then, for all $\delta > 0$,

using (7.2), letting $C_{s,t} \overset{d}{=} \{x : x \in X * f_s(x) \geq t\}$,

$$\alpha \leq \sup\{t : t \in u \ \&\ B \in \mathscr{F}\}) = \sup_{s \in J}\{\delta + \sup\{t - \delta \varepsilon[-\delta, 1 - \delta] \ \&\ C_{s,t-\delta} \in \mathscr{F}\}$$

$$= \delta + \sup_{s \in J}\{\sup\{t : t \in [0, 1 - \delta] \ \&\ C_{s,t} \in \mathscr{F}\}$$

$$= \delta + \sup_{s \in J}\{\sup\{t : t \in u \ \&\ C_{s,t} \in \mathscr{F}\} = \delta + \beta,$$

implying that $\alpha \leq \beta$. Hence, $\alpha = \beta$ and thus $\xi(\mathscr{F}, \cdot)$ is an infinite homomorph. wrt $(\cup_{\max}, \max)$ for spaces Flou(X) and Mem(X).

Next, for any $a^{(j)} \in \mathrm{Flou}(X)$ and $f_j \overset{d}{=} \phi(a^{(j)})$, $j = 1, 2$, arb., $\xi(\mathscr{F}, \min(f_1, f_2)) \geq \min(\xi(\mathscr{F}, f_1), \xi(\mathscr{F}, f_2))$, slightly abusing notation and using fact that $\mathscr{F}$ is a filter. Conversely, since $f_1^{-1}[t, 1] \cap f_2^{-1}[t, 1] \in \mathscr{F}$ implies $f_j^{-1}[t, 1] \in \mathscr{F}$, by ultrafilter property, the above inequality reverses, showing finally $\xi(\mathscr{F}, \cdot)$ is a homomorphism wrt $(\cap_{\min}, \min)$.

Next, letting $f \overset{d}{=} \phi(a)$, $t_0 \overset{d}{=} \xi(\mathscr{F}, a') = \sup\{t : t \in u \ \&\ D_t \in \mathscr{F}\}$,

$D_t \overset{d}{=} \{x \in X : f'(x) \ge t\}$, $t_1 \overset{d}{=} \xi(\mathcal{F}, a)' = \inf\{t : t \in u \ \& \ E_t \in \mathcal{F}\}$, $E_t \overset{d}{=} \{x \in X : f'(x) \le t\}$. By the definitions of sup and inf, for all $\delta > 0$, there are $t_{0\delta} \le t_0 \le t_{0\delta} + \delta$, $t_{1\delta} - \delta \le t_1 \le t_{1\delta}$ with $D_{t_{0\delta}} \in \mathcal{F}$, $D_{t_0+\delta} \notin \mathcal{F}$, $E_{t_1\delta} \in \mathcal{F}$, $E_{t_1-\delta} \notin \mathcal{F}$. This yields the intersection $\{x : x \in X \ \& \ t_{0\delta} \le f'(x) \le t_{1,\delta}\} \in \mathcal{F}$, from the filter property of $\mathcal{F}$; $t_{0\delta} \le t_{1\delta}$. If $t_{1\delta} - t_{0\delta} > 2\delta$, one could pick midpoint $t_{2\delta}$, $t_{0\delta} < t_{2\delta} < t_{1\delta}$, with $t_{2\delta} - t_{0\delta} > \delta$ and $t_{1\delta} - t_{2\delta} > \delta$. Since $t_{2\delta} > t_{0\delta} + \delta > t_0$, $D_{t_{2\delta}} \notin \mathcal{F}$, by sup property of t_0. Since $\mathcal{F}$ is a filter, $D'_{t_{2\delta}} = \{x \in X : f'(x) < t_{2\delta}\} \subseteq E_{t_{2\delta}} \in \mathcal{F}$. Since $t_{2\delta} < t_{1\delta} - \delta < t_1$, then $E_{2\delta} \notin \mathcal{F}$, by inf property of t_1, a contradiction. Thus, $0 \le t_{1\delta} - t_{0\delta} \le 2\delta$, for all $\delta > 0$ arbitrary.
In turn, the above inequality implies, by the triangle inequality that

$$0 \le t_1 - t_0 \le t_1 - t_{1\delta} + t_{1\delta} - t_{0\delta} + t_{0\delta} - t_0 \le \delta + 2\delta + \delta = 4\delta,$$

which by the arbitrariness of δ, finally implies that $t_1 = t_0$. Hence, $\xi(\mathcal{F}, \cdot)$ is a homomorphism wrt $((\ )', 1 - (\ ))$ for spaces Flou(X) and Mem(X). Finally, by the very definition of $\xi(\mathcal{F}, \cdot)$ applied to $\phi^{-1}(c)$, for any $c \in \mathrm{Mem}_1(X)$, $\xi(\mathcal{F}, \phi^{-1}(c)) = c$, completing the proof of (i).

Proof (ii): Eq. (7.7) follows from the basic properties of filters and ultrafilters. Next, consider the basic identity for any $f = \phi(a) \in \mathrm{Mem}(X)$:

$$f = \sup_{t \in u} \min(1_{f^{-1}[t,1]}, t) \ \ (\text{over } X). \tag{7.12}$$

By properties of inverse functions,

$$a = \phi^{-1}(f) = \sup_{t \in u} \phi^{-1}(\min(1_{f^{-1}[t,1]}, t)),$$

whence for strong model h,

$$h(a) = \sup_{t \in u} h(\phi^{-1}(\min(1_{f^{-1}[t,1]}, t))) = \xi(\mathcal{F}_{(h)}, a).$$

Proof (iii): Consider the identity

$$f = \sup_{x \in X}(f(x) \cdot \delta_x) \ \ (\text{over } X), \tag{7.13}$$

where δ_x is the Krönecker delta function

$$\delta_x(y) = \begin{cases} 0, & \text{if } \ y = x, \ \ y \in X, \\ 1, & \text{if } \ y = x, \ \ y \in X. \end{cases} \tag{7.14}$$

Then, for $f \overset{d}{=} \phi(a)$, $a \in \mathrm{Flou}(X)$,

$$a = \phi^{-1}(f) = \sup_{x \in X} \phi^{-1}(f(x)) \cap_{min} \phi^{-1}(\delta_x),$$

whence for strong model h,

$$h(a) = \sup_{x \in X} \min(h(\phi^{-1}(f(x))), h(\phi^{-1}(\delta_x)))) = \sup_{x \in X} \min(f(x), h(\phi^{-1}(\delta_x))). \tag{7.15}$$

The only remaining thing is to consider what values $h(\phi^{-1}(\delta_x))$ can take:

Case 1. $h(\phi^{-1}(\delta_x)) = 0$, all $x \in X$. But, this case implies by (7.15) that $h(a) = 0$, for all $a \in \text{Flou}(X)$, contradicting the fact that for all $c \in u$, (7.11) holds.

Case 2. $h(\phi^{-1}(\delta_x)) > 0$ for at least two distinct $x_j \in X$, $j = 1, 2$. But, since h is a homomorphism, wrt $\cap_{min}$,

$$0 = h(\phi^{-1}(0)) = h(\phi^{-1}(\delta_{x_1} \cdot \delta_{x_2})) = \min(h(\phi^{-1}(\delta_{x_1})), h(\phi^{-1}(\delta_{x_2}))) > 0,$$

a contradiction!

Case 3. This is the only case left: there is a unique $x_h \in X$ such that $h(\phi^{-1}(\delta_{x_h})) > 0$. Furthermore, since $\min(\delta_{x_h}, \delta'_{x_h}) = 0$, by homomorphism,

$$0 = h(\phi^{-1}(0)) = \min(h(\phi^{-1}(\delta_x)), h(\phi^{-1}(\delta'_x))), \text{ implying } h(\phi^{-1}(\delta'_{x_h})) = 0,$$

whence, by the homomorphism property of h again,

$$h(\phi^{-1}(\delta_{x_h})) = 1. \tag{7.16}$$

Finally, substituting (7.16) into (7.15) yields (7.9), provided that (7.11) is valid. The latter is simply so due to a variation of the standard Cauchy theorem (Aczél (1966, sect. 2.1 et passim)). ■

Corollary 7.1. Characterization of strong models when R is atomic$_o$.

Suppose that boolean algebra R ($\subseteq \mathcal{P}(X)$) is atomic$_o$. Then

$$\tilde{\text{Mod}}(X) = \{\phi(\cdot)(x) : x \in X\}, \tag{7.17}$$

i.e., the strong models of Flou(X) coincide with the fundamental membership evaluations at each fixed point.

Proof: This is a restatement of the right side of (7.10) of Theorem 7.1.

■

The next results, specified to $M_2(X)$ and $M_3(X)$, can be developed without full use of the strong model assumption of Theorem 7.1. Throughout, suppose: boolean algebra $R \subseteq \mathcal{P}(X)$ is atomic$_o$; $\{0, 1\}$ is endowed with the usual classical logic (C_2) operations

$\cdot$, $\vee$, $(\ )' = 1 - (\ )$; $Q_o = \{0, u, 1\}$ has the ordering $0 \le u \le 1$ and is given the $Ł_3$ or, equivalently, Zadeh) structure min, max, $(\ )' = 1 - (\ )$, where now

$$0' = 1,\ 1' = 0,\ u' = \{t' : t \in u\} = u. \tag{7.18}$$

Also, recall the equivalence of $\text{Flou}_2(X)$, $\text{Mem}_2(X)$, and $\mathcal{P}X)$ by Theorem 6.1 (ii) (eqs. (6.17), (6.18)); one can restrict $\text{Flou}_2(X)$ and $\text{Mem}_2(X)$ suitably so that $\mathcal{P}X)$ can be replaced in effect by R. Recall, also with R replacing $\mathcal{P}X)$, the equivalence of $\text{Flou}_3(X)$, $\text{Mem}_3(X)$, and ((R|R); GN) (Theorem 6.6). Thus, the definition of a model remains well-defined when any of the equivalent spaces are interchangeably used. Note also the natural identification for any model $\hbar$

$$\hbar(\{x\}) = \hbar(\delta_x) = \hbar(x), \text{ for all } x \in X. \tag{7.19}$$

Let $\text{Mod}_2(X)$ denote the class of all models of R (i.e., $\text{Flou}_2(X)$), *excluding those models identically zero over all singletons of X -- and hence identically zero over all finite subsets of X, all in R.* Similarly, denote $\text{Mod}_3(X)$ as the class of all models of $\text{mem}_3(X)$ (i.e., ((R|R); GN), etc.) with the same type of exclusion as for $\text{Mod}_2(X)$.

Theorem 7.2. Suppose all of the above hold. Then:

(i) $$\text{Mod}_2(X) = \{1_{\cdot}(x) : 1_{\cdot} \text{ restricted to } R, x \in X\}. \tag{7.20}$$

Hence, for any $\hbar: R \to \{0, 1\}$ model of R, there is a unique $x_\hbar \in X$, such that

$$\hbar(A) = 1_A(x_\hbar), \text{ all } A \in R. \tag{7.21}$$

(ii) $$\text{Mod}_3(X) = \{1_{\cdot}(x) : 1_{\cdot} \text{ restricted to } (R|R), x \in X\}. \tag{7.22}$$

Hence, for any $\hbar: (R|R) \to Q_o$ a model of ((R|R); GN), there is a unique $x_\hbar \in X$ such that

$$\hbar((A|B)) = 1_{(A|B)}(x_\hbar), \quad \text{all } (A|B) \in (R|R). \tag{7.23}$$

Proof (i): If there exists $x_1, x_2 \in X$ with $x_1 \ne x_2$ and $\hbar(x_1), \hbar(x_2) > 0$, then necessarily $\hbar(x_1) = \hbar(x_2) = 1$, implying $0 = \hbar(\emptyset) = \hbar(\{x_1\}) \cap \{x_2\}) = \min(\hbar(x_1), \hbar(x_2))$, implying $\hbar(x_1) = 0$ or $\hbar(x_2) = 0$, a contradiction. Thus, there is a unique $x_\hbar$ with $\hbar(x_\hbar) > 0$, i.e., $\hbar(x_\hbar) = 1$. Next, let $A \in R$ arbitrary. If $x_\hbar \in A$, then

$$\hbar(A) = \hbar(\{x_\hbar\} \cup A - \{x_\hbar\}) = \max(\hbar(x_\hbar), \hbar(A - \{x_\hbar\})) = \max(1, \hbar(A - \{x_\hbar\})) = 1. \tag{7.24}$$

If $x_\hbar \notin A$, then $x_\hbar \in A'$, whence by replacing A by A′ in (7.24), one obtains

$$1 - \hbar(A') = 1 - \hbar(A), \text{ implying } \hbar(A) = 0. \tag{7.25}$$

Thus, (7.24) and (7.25) show (7.21).

Conversely, for any $x \in X$, it follows from standard properties that, in fact, $1_{\cdot}(x) : (R; \cdot, \vee, (\ )') \to (\{0, 1\}; C_2)$ is a homomorphism.

Proof (ii): First note from eq. (6.81) the identity here

$$(A|B) = (A \cap B) \cup (B' \cdot (\emptyset|\emptyset)), \text{ all } A, B \in R, \tag{7.26}$$

with corresponding indicator function form (see also (6.34)

$$1_{(A|B)}(x) = \max(1_{A\cap B}(X), \min(1_{B'}(x), u)), \text{ all } x \in X. \tag{7.27}$$

Now, it follows readily that the restriction of any model $\hbar$ of $((R|R); GN)$ to R is a model of R and hence part (i) above is valid. Thus there exists unique $x_{\hbar} \in X$ such that (7.21) holds. In addition, note that since $(\emptyset|\emptyset)$ has the (unique) property that $(\emptyset|\emptyset)' = (\emptyset|\emptyset)$, then applying $\hbar$,

$$\hbar((\emptyset|\emptyset)') = 1 - \hbar((\emptyset|\emptyset)) = \hbar((\emptyset|\emptyset)) \in Q_o, \tag{7.28}$$

implying by (7.18) that the only possible value of $\hbar((\emptyset|\emptyset))$ satisfying (7.28) is

$$\hbar((\emptyset|\emptyset)) = u. \tag{7.29}$$

Substituting, from the above reasoning, (7./21) and (7.29) into the evaluation of any $(A|B)$ by $\hbar$, using (7.26) and (7.27) yields

$$\hbar((A|B)) = \max(\hbar(A \cap B), \min(\hbar(B'), \hbar((\emptyset|\emptyset))))$$

$$= \max(1_{A\cap B}(x_{\hbar}), \min(1_{B'}(x_{\hbar}), u)) = 1_{(A|B)}(x_{\hbar}). \tag{7.30}$$

Eq. (7.30) shows (7.23) holding.

Conversely, Theorem 6.6 shows (or it can be shown directly) that for any $x \in X$, $1_{\cdot}(x) : ((R|R); GN) \to (Q_o; \min, \max, (\ )')$ is a homomorphism, i.e., for all $A, B, C, D \in R$,

$$1_{(A|B)\cdot(C|D)}(x) = \min(1_{(A|B)}(x), 1_{(C|D)}(x)); \ 1_{(A|B)'}(x) = 1 - 1_{(A|B)}(x);$$
$$1_{(A|B)\vee(C|D)}(x) = \max(1_{(A|B)}(x), 1_{(C|D)}(x)). \tag{7.31}$$

■

External probabilities of fuzzy sets in general, and conditional events and their indicator functions, in particular.

Remarks. With the stage set by the above results, we can now give a natural interpretation to the definition of the *external probability of a fuzzy set* (callled in the fuzzy set literature simply the probability of a fuzzy event -- see e.g., Dubois & Prade (1980, pp. 141 et passim)):

Let $(\Lambda, \mathcal{A}, p)$ be a probability space, (X, R) a measurable space, and $W : \Lambda \to X$ some corresponding random variable. Then, W is not only induces the ordinary probability space $(X, R, p{\circ}W^{-1})$, but more generally the space $(X, \text{Flou}(X), p{\circ}W^{-1})$, where for any $a \in \text{Flou}(X)$,

$$(p_\circ W^{-1})(a) \overset{d}{=} E_W(\phi(a)(W)) = \int_{\omega\in\Lambda} \phi(a)(W(\omega))dP(\omega) = \int_{x\in X} \phi(a)(x)dP(W^{-1}(x)), \tag{7.32}$$

can now be interpreted as the $p_\circ W^{-1}$ -- *averaged model value of flou set* a (or equivalently, of fuzzy set membership function $\phi(a)$). Similarly, the "mean" of a,

$$\text{"E"}(a) \overset{d}{=} E_W(W\cdot\phi(a)(W)), \tag{7.33}$$

when $X \subseteq \mathbb{R}^n$ can be interpreted as the $p_\circ W^{-1}$ -- *averaged model-moment value of flou set* a, etc.

Finally, particularizing the above to conditional event indicator functions in view of the previous results connecting them to fuzzy set membership functions and flou sets, for any choice of $A, B \in R \subseteq \mathcal{P}(X)$, eq. (7.32) yields

$$\begin{aligned}(p_\circ W^{-1})(1_{(A|B)}) &= E_W(1_{(A|B)}(W)) = 1\cdot p(W^{-1}(A\cap B)) + 0\cdot p(W^{-1}(B - A)) \\ &\quad + u\cdot p(W^{-1}(B')) \\ &= p(W^{-1}(A\cap B)) + u\cdot p(W^{-1}(B')).\end{aligned} \tag{7.34}$$

Interpreting u literally as the unit interval, makes (7.34) represent not just a single value but a range of values, so that denoting this further interpretation here by a hat, one obtains easily the closed interval

$$(p\hat{_\circ} W^{-1})(1_{(A|B)}) = [p(W^{-1}(A\cap B)), p(W^{-1}(A\cap B)), p(W^{-1}(B \Rightarrow A))], \tag{7.35}$$

using properties of inverse functions so that

$$p(W^{-1}(B \Rightarrow A)) = 1 - p(W^{-1}(B)) + p(W^{-1}(A\cap B)). \tag{7.36}$$

However, this leaves the basic problem of how to evaluate or replace this interval of values by a single one, which by inspection of the unconditional case should be $p(A|B)$. If formally, u were assigned the value $p(A|B)$ itself, it follows that substituting this ino (7.34) yields back $p(A|B)$! However, this formalism, as intuitively appealing it is, is still onbly a formal mechanism. A more satisfactory approach to this issue can be developed as follows (see also Goodman, Nguyen, Walker (1991) for a brief exposition):

A simple and natural way to assign a single figure-of-merit to a closed interval of real numbers is the computation of a weighted average of the upper and lower boundary points of the interval. Depending on the criterion chosen, the "optimal" choice of weights will vary. In general, the equally weighted mean need not be the choice -- unless a criterion such as the minimization with respect to that point in the interval of the sum of squared distances to every element of the interval is chosen. In line with developing an alternative criterion, consider first the following:

Theorem 7.3. In the following, let $\mathbb{R}$ denote the ordinary real line and let $s_o < t_o \in \mathbb{R}$ be arbitrary fixed and consider the closed interval $[s_o, t_o]$. Let I denote the class of all intervals $[s, t] \subseteq [s_o, t_o]$, with $s < t$. Define mapping $h_1 : \mathbb{R} \times I \to \mathbb{R}$, where

$$h_1(\lambda, [s, t]) \overset{d}{=} \lambda \cdot t + (1 - \lambda) \cdot s; \text{ all } \lambda \in \mathbb{R}, [s, t] \in I, \tag{7.37}$$

the *boundary-weighting function*, and for each positive integer $n \geq 2$, define recursively, the nth *iterate of the boundary weighting function*

$$h_n(\lambda, [s, t]) \overset{d}{=} h_1(h_{n-1}(\lambda, [s, t]), [s, t]); \text{ all } \lambda \in \mathbb{R}, [s, t] \in I. \tag{7.38}$$

Also, define the special subclass of I,

$$I_o \overset{d}{=} \{[s, t] : [s, t] \in I \ \& \ t - s = 1\}. \tag{7.39}$$

Finally, consider for any $[s, t] \in I$, the *boundary-weighting invariance class*

$$H([s, t]) \overset{d}{=} \{\lambda : \lambda \in \mathbb{R} \ \& \text{ eq. (7.41) holds for all } n\} \tag{7.40}$$

$$h_n(\lambda, [s, t]) = h_1(\lambda,. [s, t]); \ n = 1, 2, 3, . \tag{7.41}$$

With the above definitions established, it follows that:

(i) $$H([s, t]) = \emptyset, \text{ for all } [s, t] \in I_o \dashv \{u\}. \tag{7.42}$$

(ii) $$H([s, t]) = \mathbb{R}, \text{ for } [s, t] = u \tag{7.43}$$

(iii) $$H([s, t]) = \{\lambda_{s,t}\}, \text{ for all } [s, t] \in I \dashv I_o, \tag{7.44}$$

where

$$\lambda_{s,t} \overset{d}{=} s/(1 - t + s), \text{ for all } s, t \in \mathbb{R}, t - s \neq 0. \tag{7.45}$$

(iv) In cases (ii) and (iii), the fixed point property also holds

$$h_n(\lambda, [s, t]) = \lambda; \ n = 1, 2, 3, \ldots, \tag{7.46}$$

with λ arbitrary $\in \mathbb{R}$, for (ii) and $\lambda = \lambda_{s,t}$ (uniquely), for (iii).

(v) For all $[s, t] \in I - I_0$,

$$s \leq \lambda_{s,t} \leq t \text{ iff } [s, t] \subset u \ \text{(proper inclus.)} \tag{7.47}$$

Proof: if $\lambda \in H(s, t)$, then, necessarily, choosing in (7.38) $n = 2$ and using (7.41) with $\lambda_1 \overset{d}{=} h_1(\lambda, [s, t])$,

$$\lambda_1 = h_1(\lambda_1, [s, t]) = \lambda_1 \cdot t + (1 - \lambda_1) \cdot s. \tag{7.48}$$

Solving (7.48) for λ_1 immediately leads to the unique solution

$$\S_1 = \lambda_{s,t}, \text{ if } t - s \neq 1. \tag{7.49}$$

In turn, (7.49) through λ is

$$\lambda \cdot t + (1 - \lambda) \cdot s = \lambda_{s,t}, \tag{7.50}$$

which also yields the solution $\lambda = \lambda_{s,t}$, provided $t - s \neq 1$, showing (iii).

Returning back to (7.48), when $t - s = 1$, it becomes

$$\lambda_1 = \lambda_1 + s, \tag{7.51}$$

which, unless $s = 0$ -- whence $t = 1$ in this case and λ_1 can be arbitrary in $\mathbb{R}$, has no solution for λ_1. This shows (i) and (ii). (iv) follows for (iii) from (7.50), while for the case of (ii), it is obvious by inspection that (7.46) always holds. Finally, (v) is shown by consideration of the combination of possibilities $1 - t + s \gtreqless 0$ with $t \gtreqless 1$.

■

Note that Theorem 7.3 (iii) can be generalized in the following sense:

Theorem 7.4. Let $[s, t] \subseteq u$ with $s < t$ and $\lambda \in u$ arbitrary fixed, not necessarily in $H([s, t])$. Then,

$$h_\infty(\lambda, [s, t]) \overset{d}{=} \lim_{n \to \infty} h_n(\lambda, [s, t]) = \lambda_{s,t}, \tag{7.52}$$

with the sequence $(h_n(\lambda, [s, t]))_{n=1,2,\ldots}$ decreasing to, fixed at, increasing to $\lambda_{s,t}$, depending on whether $\lambda \geq \lambda_{s,t}$, $\lambda = \lambda_{s,t}$, $\lambda \leq \lambda_{s,t}$, respectively.

Proof: First, note that if $h_\infty(\lambda, [s, t])$ exists, then, taking limits as $n \to \infty$ in (7.38) yields

$$h_\infty = \lim_{n \to \infty} h_n = h_1(\lim_{n \to \infty} h_{n-1}, [s, t]) = h_1(h_\infty, [s, t]),$$

the same formally as in (7.48) with λ_1 replaced by h_∞. In summary,

$$h_\infty(\lambda, [s, t]) \text{ exists implies } h_\infty(\lambda, [s, t]) = \lambda_s \tag{7.53}$$

Next, analogous to (7.48) with equality replaced by inequality,

$$h_1(\lambda, [s, t]) \leq \lambda \text{ iff } \lambda_{s,t} \leq \lambda. \tag{7.54}$$

In turn, (7.54) shows

$$h_2(\lambda, [s, t]) = h_1(h_1(\lambda, [s, t]), [s, t]) \leq h_1(\lambda, [s, t])$$

iff $\lambda_{s,t} \leq h_1(\lambda, [s, t])$ if $\lambda_{s,t} \leq \lambda$, solving for λ.

Continuing the above process shows the decreasing sequence

$$0 \le \ldots \le h_3(\lambda, [s, t]) \le h_2(\lambda, [s, t]) \le h_1(\lambda, [s, t]) \le \lambda \text{ iff } \lambda_{s,t} \le \lambda \tag{7.55}$$

(7.55) shows that $h_\infty(\lambda, [s, t])$ exists, if $\lambda_{s,t} \le \lambda$. The inequalities in (7.55) reverse, showing finally

$$h_\infty(\lambda, [s, t]) \text{ exists, for all } \lambda \in u. \tag{7.56}$$

Combining (7.53) and (7.56) shows (7.52). ∎

As a consequence of Theorems 7.3 and 7.4, call the assignment

$$h_o([s, t]) \overset{d}{=} h_1(\lambda_{s,t}, [s, t]) = \lambda_{s,t}, \text{ for } [s, t] \subset u, \tag{7.57}$$

the *stable*, or *fixed point, boundary-weighting average of* [s, t]. Extending this idea further, if $\mathscr{A} \subset u$ is arbitrary, the *stable boundary average of* $\mathscr{A}$ is defined through the tightest closed interval around $\mathscr{A}$, $[\inf(\mathscr{A}), \sup(\mathscr{A})]$, provided that $\inf(\mathscr{A}) < \sup(\mathscr{A})$ and $[\inf(\mathscr{A}), \sup(\mathscr{A})] \subset u$:

$$h_o(\mathscr{A}) \overset{d}{=} h_o([\inf(\mathscr{A}), \sup(\mathscr{A})]). \tag{7.58}$$

As a basic application of the above, functionally extend a give prob. $p : R \to u$ ot $\hat{p} : \mathscr{P}(R) \to \mathscr{P}(u)$, analogous to the way ordinary boolean operations were extended from R to $\mathscr{P}(R)$ and then were restricted to the subclass $(R|R)$: (See again the discussion prior to Theorem 6.4)

$$\hat{p}(B) \overset{d}{=} \{p(A) : A \in B\}, \text{ for all } B \in \mathscr{P}(R). \tag{7.59}$$

Hence, (7.59) specializes to the following when $B = (A|B)$, for any $A, B \in R$, noting (6.45) and (6.51) show

$$(A|B) = \{y : y \in R \ \& \ A \cdot B \le y \le B \Rightarrow A\}, \tag{7.60}$$

whereby, using the monotonicity of unconditional probabilities,

$$\hat{p}((A|B)) = \{p(y) : y \in (A|B)\} \subseteq [p(A \cdot B), p(B \Rightarrow A)] \tag{7.61}$$

where

$$\inf(\hat{p}((A|B))) = p(A \cdot B) \ \& \ \sup(\hat{p}((A|B))) = p(B \Rightarrow A) = 1 - p(B) + p(A \cdot B). \tag{7.62}$$

All of this leads to

Theorem 7.5. Justification for assigning conditional probabilities to conditional events:
$p((a|b)) = p(a|b)$.

Let $p : R \to u$ be a given probability measure (R either a boolean algebra, or more strongly, a σ-algebra). Then, for all $A, B \in R$ such that $p(B) > 0$, the stable boundary average of $\hat{p}((A|B))$ coincides with $p(A|B)$.

Proof: In eqs. (7.57) and (7.58) let $\mathcal{A} = \hat{p}((A|B))$, $s = p(AB)$, $t = p(B \Rightarrow A)$, using (7.61) and (7.62), yielding

$$h_o(\hat{p}((A|B))) = h_o([s, t]) = \lambda_{s,t}$$
$$= p(AB)/(1 - p(B \Rightarrow A) + p(AB))$$
$$= p(AB)/p(B) = p(A|B),$$

noting here that Theorem 7.3 (iii) is applicable, since $1 - p(B \Rightarrow A) + p(AB) = 0$ iff $p(B) = 0$, which does not hold here. ■

Of course, other justifications for why $p(A|B)$ is interpreted as the ratio of antecedent to consequent probabilities, *from the standard viewpoint of conditional probabilities, not via conditional events*, are readily available such as the functional equation approach of Azcél (1966, pp. 319-324). See also the game-theoretic admissibility approach using conditional events, Lindley (1982), Goodman et al (1991).

Returning to the computation of probabilities of conditional event indicator functions as part of the more general evaluation of probabilities of fuzzy sets, the basic quandary in eqs. (7.34) and (7.35) can now be solved reasonably. The difficulty with obtaining $(p_\circ W^{-1})(1_{(A|B)})$ is the presence of symbol or "third value" u, which if literally interpreted, yields the equally appearing difficult interval form $(p\hat{_\circ}W^{-1})(1_{(A|B)})$ in eq. (7.35). However, with the use of the stable boundary average of an interval, one now obtains easily

$$h_o((p\hat{_\circ}W^{-1})(1_{(A|B)})) = h_o([p(W^{-1}(A \cap B)), p(W^{-1}(B \Rightarrow A))])$$
$$= p(W^{-1}(A \cap B))/(1 - p(W^{-1}(B \Rightarrow A)) + p(W^{-1}(A \cap B)))$$
$$= p(W^{-1}(A \cap B))/p(W^{-1}(B))$$
$$= (p_\circ W^{-1})(A|B), \tag{7.63}$$

using (7.36), a result that is naturally compatible with, and extends, the classical unconditional case

$$(p_\circ W^{-1})(1_A) = E_W(1_A W)) = p(W^{-1}(A))$$
$$= (p_\circ W^{-1})(A); \text{ all } A \in R. \tag{7.64}$$

8. Summary of Random Set Representation of Fuzzy Sets.

The following development is a summary of results to be found in Goodman & Nguyen (1985, chpts. 5, 6). It is presented here only for purpose of ease of reference and as a background for the concept of conditional fuzzy sets given in the next section.

First, let $(\Lambda, \mathcal{A}, p)$ be a fixed probability space such that $\mathcal{U}: \Lambda \to u$ is a uniformly distributed random variable. Let $(X, \mathcal{B})$ be a fixed measurable space -- $\mathcal{B} \subseteq \mathcal{P}(X)$ is a σ-algebra, and hence a boolean algebra. For each $x \in X$, let $F_x(\mathcal{B}) \overset{d}{=} \{A : x \in A \in \mathcal{B}\}$ be the *filter class on* x *relative to* $\mathcal{B}$ and let $\tilde{\mathcal{C}} \subseteq \mathcal{P}(\mathcal{B})$ be any σ-algebra with $F_x(\mathcal{B}) \in \tilde{\mathcal{C}}$ for all $x \in X$. Call any mapping $S : \Lambda \to \mathcal{B}$ a *random subset of* X iff S is $(\mathcal{A}, \tilde{\mathcal{C}})$-measurable, in which case S induces the probability space $(\mathcal{B}, \tilde{\mathcal{C}}, p \circ S^{-1})$. Denote the class of all random subsets of X as RS(X), distinguishing random subsets only if they differ in their probability evaluations. Denote the corresponding equivalence relation among random subsets of X as $\overset{dis}{=}$ for "equal in distribution". If $S \in RS(X)$ is such that range(S) $\in$ Flou(X), call S a *nested random subset of* X and denote the class of all such as NRS(X) (up to equivalence $\overset{dis}{=}$). Also, identify Mem(X) with the more restricted class of all functions in it which are actually $(\mathcal{B}, B_u)$-measurable. The following theorem is a conglomeration of results from Goodman & Nguyen (1985), modified for the definitions here:

Theorem 8.1. Summary of basic random set representations involving fuzzy sets:

Part 1.

(i) The *one point coverage function* $\nu : RS(X) \to Mem(X)$ is surjective, where

$$\nu(S)(x) \overset{d}{=} p(x \in S) \overset{d}{=} p(S \in F_x) = (p \circ S^{-1})(F_x), \quad \text{all } x \in X, \; S \in RS(X). \tag{8.1}$$

In particular, for any given $f \in Mem(X)$, one can choose (in general, non-unique)

$$S = f^{-1}[\mathcal{U}, 1] \overset{d}{=} \{x : x \in X \;\&\; f(x) \geq \mathcal{U}, \text{ i.e., for any } \omega \in \Lambda,$$

$$S(\omega) = f^{-1}[\mathcal{U}(\omega), 1] = \{\omega_o : \omega_o \in \Lambda \;\&\; f(\omega_1) \geq \mathcal{U}(\omega)\}. \tag{8.2}$$

(ii) The following statements are equivalent:

(I) $S \in NRS(X)$.

(II) There exists $f \in Mem(X)$ such that $S \overset{dis}{=} f^{-1}[\mathcal{U}, 1]$.

(III) There exists $a = (a_t)_{t \in u} \in \text{Flou}(X)$ such that $S \overset{dis}{=} a_{\mathcal{U}}$, where

$$a_{\mathcal{U}}(\omega) \overset{d}{=} a_{\mathcal{U}(\omega)}, \text{ for all } \omega \in \Lambda. \tag{8.3}$$

(IV) There exists $q = (q_t)_{t \in J_q} \in \text{Part}(X)$ such that

$$S \overset{dis}{=} q_{(\mathcal{U})} \overset{d}{=} \bigcup_{\substack{t \in J_q \\ \mathcal{U} \le t < 1}} q_t. \tag{8.4}$$

(iii) For any choice of $f \in \text{Mem}(X)$,

$$S \overset{d}{=} f^{-1}[\mathcal{U}, 1] = q_{(\mathcal{U})} \in \text{NRS}(X), \tag{8.5}$$

where

$$q \overset{d}{=} (f^{-1}(t))_{t \in \text{range}(f)} \in \text{Part}(X), \tag{8.6}$$

noting that (I) and (II) are related via $f = \phi(a)$ (Theorem 2.1).

■

Motivated by the above results, denote for any $a \in \text{Flou}(X)$ and any $q \in \text{Part}(X)$, $a_{\mathcal{U}}$ as a *uniformly randomized flou set* and $f^{-1}(\mathcal{U})$, where $f \overset{d}{=} \phi(\psi(q))$, as a *uniformly randomized partitioning set*; denote the space of all uniformly randomized partitioning sets of X as $\text{Part}(X; \mathcal{U})$. Also denote the obvious bijections where $a \to a_u$ and $q \to (\phi(\psi(q)))^{-1}(\mathcal{U})$, by the common notation $\text{id}_{\mathcal{U}}: \text{Flou}(X) \to \text{Flou}(X; \mathcal{U})$ and $\text{id}_{\mathcal{U}}: \text{Part}(X) \to \text{Part}(X; \mathcal{U})$.

Theorem 8.2. Summary of basic random set representations involving fuzzy sets: Part 2.

The following diagram of isomorphisms holds, extending the isomorphisms of Figure 5.1 to the randomized spaces by use of $\text{id}_{\mathcal{U}}$:

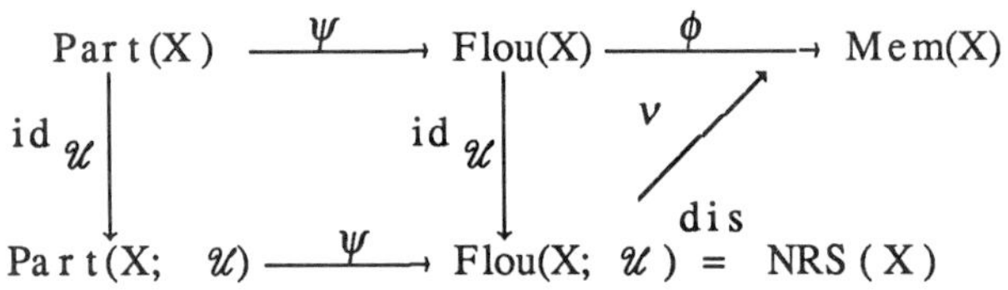

Figure 8.1. Summary of isomorphisms for Part(X), Flou(X),

and their randomizatons and Mem(X). ■

Relative to Fig. 8.1, the following relations hold for all $f \in \mathrm{Mem}(X)$, $a \in \mathrm{Flou}(X)$, $x \in X$:

$$\nu^{-1}(f) = \mathrm{id}_{\mathcal{U}}(\phi^{-1}(f)) = (\phi^{-1}(f))_{\mathcal{U}} = ((f^{-1}[t, 1])_{t \in u})_{\mathcal{U}} = f^{-1}[\mathcal{U}, 1], \tag{8.7}$$

$$a_{\mathcal{U}} = \mathrm{id}_{\mathcal{U}}(a) = \nu^{-1}(\phi(a)) = \phi(a)^{-1}[\mathcal{U}, 1], \tag{8.8}$$

$$f(x) = (\nu(\mathrm{id}_{\mathcal{U}}(\phi^{-1}(f))))(x) = p(x \in (\phi^{-1}(f))_{\mathcal{U}}) = \nu(\nu^{-1}(f))(x) = p(x \in f^{-1}[\mathcal{U}, 1]), \tag{8.9}$$

$$\phi(a)(x) = \nu(\mathrm{id}_{\mathcal{U}}(a))(x) = \nu(a_{\mathcal{U}})(x) = p(x \in a_{\mathcal{U}}) = \nu(\nu^{-1}(\phi(a)))(x) = p(x \in f^{-1}[\mathcal{U}, 1]). \tag{8.10}$$

Also, directly from sect. 4 replacing index variable t by r.v. $\mathcal{U}$, i.e., applying $\mathrm{id}_{\mathcal{U}}$ (see eqs. (4.1), (4.5), (4.10))

$$a_{\mathcal{U}} \cap_{\mathrm{cop}} b_{\mathcal{U}} = (\phi^{-1}(\mathrm{cop}_\circ(\phi(a), \phi(b))))_{\mathcal{U}} = (a \cap_{\mathrm{cop}} b)_{\mathcal{U}};\ a_{\mathcal{U}} \cup_{\mathrm{cocop}} b_{\mathcal{U}} = (a \cup_{\mathrm{cocop}} b)_{\mathcal{U}}, \tag{8.11}$$

similarly;

$$\nu(a_{\mathcal{U}} \cap_{\mathrm{cop}} b_{\mathcal{U}}) = \phi(\mathrm{id}_{\mathcal{U}}^{-1}(a_{\mathcal{U}} \cap_{\mathrm{cop}} b_{\mathcal{U}})) = \phi(a \cap_{\mathrm{cop}} b) = \phi(\phi^{-1}(\mathrm{cop}_\circ(\phi(a), \phi(b)))$$
$$= \mathrm{cop}_\circ(\phi(a), \phi(b)) = \mathrm{cop}_\circ(\nu(a_{\mathcal{U}}), \nu(b_{\mathcal{U}})), \tag{8.12}$$

and

$$\nu(a_{\mathcal{U}} \cap_{\mathrm{cop}} b_{\mathcal{U}})(x) = p(x \in (a_{\mathcal{U}} \cap_{\mathrm{cop}} b_{\mathcal{U}}) = \mathrm{cop}(p(x \in a_{\mathcal{U}}), p(x \in b_{\mathcal{U}})) = \mathrm{cop}(\phi(a)(x), \phi(b)(x)), \tag{8.13}$$

$$\nu(a_{\mathcal{U}} \cup_{\mathrm{cocop}} b_{\mathcal{U}})(x) = p(x \in (a_{\mathcal{U}} \cup_{\mathrm{cocop}} b_{\mathcal{U}})) = \mathrm{cocop}(p(x \in a_{\mathcal{U}}), p(x \in b_{\mathcal{U}}))$$
$$= \mathrm{cocop}(\phi(a)(x), \phi(b)(x)); \tag{8.14}$$

$$a'_{\mathcal{U}} = (\phi^{-1}(1 - \phi(a)))_{\mathcal{U}} = (a')_{\mathcal{U}}, \tag{8.15}$$

$$\nu(a'_{\mathcal{U}}) = \phi(\mathrm{id}_{\mathcal{U}}^{-1}(a'_{\mathcal{U}})) = \phi((\mathrm{id}_{\mathcal{U}}^{-1}(a')_{\mathcal{U}})) = \phi(a') = \phi(a)' = \nu(a_{\mathcal{U}})', \tag{8.16}$$

$$\nu(a'_{\mathcal{U}})(x) = p(x \in a'_{\mathcal{U}}) = 1 - p(x \in a_{\mathcal{U}}) = p(x \in a'_{\mathcal{U}}), \tag{8.16'}$$

noting

$$p(x \in a_{\mathcal{U}}) = p(x \in \phi(a)^{-1}[\mathcal{U}, 1]) = p(\mathcal{U} \le \phi(a)(x)) = \phi(a)(x), \tag{8.17}$$

$$p(x \in b_{\mathcal{U}}) = p(x \in \phi(b)^{-1}[\mathcal{U}, 1]) = p(\mathcal{U} \le \phi(b)(x)) = \phi(b)(x).$$

When cop = min and cocop = max, all of the above can be strengthened as a direct uniformly randomized version of the Negoita-Ralescu representation (1975), extended here in Theorem 4.1. For example,

$$a_{\mathcal{U}} \cap_{\min} b_{\mathcal{U}} = (a \cap_{\min} b)_{\mathcal{U}} = a_{\mathcal{U}} \cap b_{\mathcal{U}} = \phi(a)^{-1}[\mathcal{U}, 1] \cap \phi(b)^{-1}[\mathcal{U}, 1]$$
$$= (\min(\phi(a)(\cdot), \phi(b)\phi(\cdot)))^{-1}[\mathcal{U}, 1]$$
$$= (\phi(a \cap_{\min} b))^{-1}[\mathcal{U}, 1], \qquad (8.18)$$

etc.

In the next development, the single space X is replaced by the family of spaces X_j, $j \in J$ and the single uniform random variable $\mathcal{U}$ is replaced by the stochastic process $\tilde{\mathcal{U}} \overset{d}{=} (\mathcal{U}_j)_{j \in J}$, for some finite or infinite index set J, where $\tilde{\mathcal{U}}$ is determined in distribution by some J-copula cop (with corresponding DeMorgan cocopula cocop), where each $\mathcal{U}_j : \Lambda \to u$ is uniformly distributed. Use the abbreviation

$\text{comb}(\times_{\text{cop}}, \dagger_{\text{cocop}}; \underline{a})$ to denote any typical logical combination of $\underline{a} \overset{d}{=} (a^{(j)})_{j \in k}$, applying operations $\times_{\text{cop}}, \dagger_{\text{cocop}}$ in a well-defined way to $a^{(j)} \in \text{Flou}(X_j)$, $j \in K \subseteq J$, finite. Use also the multivariable notation $\underline{x} \overset{d}{=} (x_j)_{j \in K}$, $\phi(\underline{a}) \overset{d}{=} (\phi(a^{(j)})_{j \in K}$, $\underline{\mathcal{U}} \overset{d}{=} (\mathcal{U}_j)_{j \in K}$, and e.g., the expressions

$$\underline{X} \overset{d}{=} (X_j)_{j \in K}; \ (\underline{x} \in \phi(\underline{a})^{-1}[\underline{\mathcal{U}}, 1]) \overset{d}{=} ((x_j \in \phi(a^{(j)})^{-1}[\mathcal{U}_j, 1]))_{j \in K},$$

etc.

Theorem 8.3. Isomorphic-like evaluations of arbitrary logical combinations of flou sets through membership functions.

With the above assumptions it follows that if the combination is purely a repetitive $\times_{\text{cop}}$ or $\dagger_{\text{cocop}}$, then the results below are valid with this restriction. However, for the general case, the following holds:

(i) For (cop, cocop) $\in$ {(min, max), (pord, probsum)}, then for all $\underline{a} \in \text{Flou}(\underline{X})$ and all $\underline{x} \in \underline{X}$,

$$(\phi(\text{comb}(\times_{\text{cop}}, \dagger_{\text{cocop}}; \underline{a})))(\underline{x}) = p(\text{comb}(\&, \text{or}; (\underline{x} \in \phi(\underline{a})^{-1}[\underline{\mathcal{U}}, 1])))$$
$$= p(\text{comb}(\&, \text{or}; (\underline{\mathcal{U}} \le \phi(\underline{a})(\underline{x}))))$$

$$=p(\operatorname*{or}_{j\in I_o} \operatorname*{\&}_{i\in I_j} (\mathcal{U}_i \le \phi(a^{(i)})(x_i)))$$

$$= \sum_{\emptyset\neq G\subseteq I_o} (-1)^{\mathrm{cart}(G)+1} \cdot \mathrm{cop}((\mathcal{U}_i \le \phi(a^{(i)})(x_i))_{(i\in I_j,\, j\in G)}, \tag{8.19}$$

for some index sets I_j, $j \in I_o$ determined by the combination.

(ii) For (cop, cocop) = (min, max), not only does (i) above hold, but in addition,

$$(\phi(\mathrm{comb}(\times_{\mathrm{cop}}, \dagger_{\mathrm{cocop}}; \underline{a})))(\underline{x}) = \mathrm{comb}(\mathrm{cop}, \mathrm{cocop})(\phi(\underline{a})(\underline{x})). \tag{8.20}$$

■

Note for logical combinations involving negations of compounds of flou sets, reduce by DeMorgan properties the negations to equivalent combinations of $\times$ and $\dagger$ of the flou sets so that essentially one has the original $\mathrm{comb}(\times, \dagger, (\,)'; \underline{a})$ replaced by the equivalent $\mathrm{comb}_0(\times, \dagger; \underline{b})$, where some of the $b^{(j)} = a^{(j)\prime}$ and the remaining $b^{(j)} = a^{(j)}$, $j \in K$.

9. Conditional Fuzzy Sets.

In the past, a number of individuals have attempted to define conditional fuzzy sets. Zadeh (1978, pp. 14-20), based on an analogy "though not completely" with conditional probability, simply defined conditioning as a kind of specification, not at all reducing to conditional probabilities. In particular, if $f : X \times Y \to u$ and f_2 is the Y-marginal of f, i.e.,

$$f_2(y) = \max_{x\in X} f(x, y), \quad \text{all } y \in Y, \tag{9.1}$$

then Zadeh's conditional fuzzy set (or possibility) function of f given f_2 at y is $f(\cdot, y) : X \to u$, i.e., formally the same as f itself with y fixed. Nguyen (1978) also proposed a conditional fuzzy set form not analogous to conditional probability. Nguyen made an assumption that the conditional form should be the ratio of the joint membership function to a function -- to be specified by a suitable criterion which he developed -- of *both* X- and Y-marginals, again, unlike conditional probabilities. This resulted in the form

$$f(y\,|\,x) = f(x, y) \cdot \max(1, f_1(x)/f_2(y))), \quad x \in X, \quad y \in Y. \tag{9.2}$$

Kosko (1986) reconsidering fuzzy entropy, also proposed that fuzzy conditioning could be identified as a "relative subsethood", which for discrete X = y is a single number, not a function of arguments:

$$(f_1 | f_2) \overset{d}{=} 1 - ((\sum_{x \in X} (\max(0, f_1(x)) - f_2(x)))/ \sum_{x \in X} f_1(x))$$

$$= (\sum_{x \in X} \min(f_1(x), f_2(x)))/ \sum_{x \in X} f_2(x). \tag{9.3}$$

Hisdal (1978) proposed the definition, for $f : X \times Y \to u$, f_1 X-marginal,

$$f(y|x) \overset{d}{=} \begin{cases} f(x, y), & \text{if } f_1(x) > f(x, y), \\ [f(x, y), 1], & \text{if } f_1(x) = f(x, y), \end{cases} \tag{9.4}$$

for all $x \in X$, $y \in Y$.

Ramer (1989), on the other hand acknowledging the work of Hisdal and Nguyen, decided that for any $A \subseteq X$ finite and $f : X \to u$, letting

$A = \{x_1,..,x_m\}$, $X = \{x_1,..,x_m, x_{m+1},.., x_n\}$; $0 \leq f(x_1) \leq f(x_2) \leq .. \leq f(x_m) \leq .. \leq f(x_n) \leq 1$,

$$f(x_i | A) \overset{d}{=} \begin{cases} f(x_i), & i = 1, .., m-1 \\ 1 & , i = m. \end{cases} \tag{9.5}$$

From this, Ramer obtains some natural relations satisfied by Hisdal's proposed definition. In addition, he discusses the limiting continuous case and justifies the approach through a minimal cross entropy criterion relative to all possible functions on A. Bouchon (1987) proposed for any two functions $f : X \to u$ and $g : Y \to u$ the two types of conditional forms at any $x \in X$, $y \in Y$

(i) $(f(x) | g(y))_t \overset{d}{=} \sup\{t : t \in u \;\&\; \not{t}(g(y), t) \leq f(x)\}$; $\not{t} : u^2 \to u$ cont. t-norm, (9.6)

with special cases

$$(f(x) | g(y))_{min} = \begin{cases} 1 & , \text{if } f(x) \geq g(y) \\ f(x), & \text{if } f(x) < g(y) \end{cases}; \quad (f(x) | g(y))_{prod} = \min((f(x)/g(y)), 1) \tag{9.7}$$

the left hand side of (9.7) being the well-known intuitionistic implication (Rescher (1969, pp. 44, 45 et passim)).

(ii) $(f(x) | g(y))_{N_h} \overset{d}{=} \max(N_h(g(y)), f(x))$; $N_h(t) \overset{d}{=} h^{-1}(h(0) - h(t))$ a negation, (9.8)

where $h : u \to \mathbb{R}^+$ is nonincreasing continuous with $h(0) \leq +\infty$ and $h(1) = 0$.

Approach (ii) is clearly a generalization of the use of material implication when

$h = 1 - (\ )$. Bouchon, among other properties discussed, points out

$$\mathscr{t}((f(x)\,|\,g\ (y))_{\mathscr{t}}\, g(y)) = \min(f(x), g(y));\ \ \mathscr{t}((f(x)\,|\,g(y))_{N_h}, g(y)) = \mathscr{t}(f(x), g(y)), \tag{9.9}$$

analogous to the usual condition satisfied by conditional probabilities.

Yager (1983) also discussed various approaches to extending or modifying classical material implication for fuzzy sets. (See also Sembi and Mamdani (1979) for a survey and analysis relative to fuzzy decision-making.)

In all of the above approaches, no appeal was made to probability theory, except for the obvious formal similarities. In fact, Mattila (1986) has concluded that fuzzy material implication is not the appropriate counterpart of conditional probability, in keeping with the distinction emphasized in this paper and others relative to the development of conditional event algebra. (Again, see section 6, following eq. (6.38).) Goodman & Stein (1989) attempted a definition for fuzzy conditioning, based upon the fuzzy set analogue of the basic characterization of conditional events as the solution set of a boolean linear equation -- see eq. (6.91). That is, if $\mathscr{S}$ is a generalization of Zadeh's classical $(\min, \max, 1 - (\ ))$ system over Mem(X) (called there a semi-boolean algebra, being a complete bounded distributive DeMorgan lattice) with conjunction $*$ and order $\leq$, for any $f, g \in \mathscr{S}$, the conditional form $(f\,|\,g)$ is given by

$$(f\,|\,g) \overset{d}{=} \{h : h \in \mathscr{S}\ \&\ h*g = f*g\}. \tag{9.10}$$

This led to the form, for any $f, g \in \mathrm{Mem}(X)$, using Zadeh's operations $(\min, \max, 1 - (\ ))$, for $x \in X$,

$$(f\,|\,g)(x) = \begin{cases} f(x) & , \text{ if } f(x) < g(x), \\ [g(x), 1], & \text{if } f(x) \geq g(x), \end{cases} \tag{9.11}$$

reminiscent of Hisdal's earlier independent proposal (see (9.4)). Operations among such conditional entities were defined by use of the functional image technique, as shown earlier here for boolean operations extended to conditional event form (see remarks prior to Theorem 6.4). Unfortunately, unlike the boolean counterpart, closure of operations did not hold, i.e., the functionally extended form for min over conditional forms as in (9.10) did not lead back to the same conditional structure in (9.10).

It will be seen, however, that the approach taken here to defining conditional fuzzy sets comes closest to Bouchon's approach (i) for min = prod (see r.h.s. (9.7)), among all the proposed definitions. However, even in this case there is difference, as will be seen below.

With all of the above background established and *keeping in mind the random set representations of fuzzy sets as summarized in section 8*, the following new approach to fuzzy conditioning is proposed:

Suppose the same setting as in section 8 holds with $(\Lambda, \mathcal{B}, p)$ a fixed probability space, $\tilde{\mathcal{U}} = (\mathcal{U}_j)_{j\in J}$ a stochastic process of uniformly distributed random variables $\mathcal{U}_j : \Lambda \to u$ governed by copula cop, a collection of corresponding spaces $(X_j)_{j\in J}$ with flou spaces $\mathrm{Flou}(X_j)$ and membership function spaces $\mathrm{Mem}(X_j)$, $j \in J$, etc. Consider then w.l.o.g. any $a^{(j)} \in \mathrm{Flou}(X_j)$ and r.v. $\mathcal{U}_j$, $j = 1, 2$. Thus, as in section 8, there are the natural correspondences

$$a^{(j)} \mapsto \phi(a^{(j)})^{-1}[\mathcal{U}_j, 1] \mapsto (\mathcal{U}_j \le \phi(a^{(j)})) \mapsto \mathcal{U}_j^{-1}[0, \phi(a^{(j)})] \in \mathcal{B}^{X_j}$$

$$\begin{aligned}(a^{(1)} \times_{cop} a^{(2)}) &\mapsto \phi^{-1}(\phi(a^{(1)})(\cdot) \times_{cop} \phi(a^{(2)})(\cdot\cdot)) \mapsto (\mathcal{U}_1 \le \phi(a^{(1)}) \,\&\, (\mathcal{U}_2 \le \phi(a^{(2)})\\ &\mapsto ((\mathcal{U}_1, \mathcal{U}_2) \le (\phi(a^{(1)}), \phi(a^{(2)})))\\ &\mapsto (\mathcal{U}_1^{-1}[0, \phi(a^{(1)})]) \cap (\mathcal{U}_2^{-1}[0, \phi(a^{(2)})]) \in \mathcal{B}^{X_1 \times X_2},\end{aligned} \tag{9.12}$$

where the exponentiation of $\mathcal{B}$ refers to the actual relations

$$\mathcal{U}_j^{-1}[0, \phi(a^{(j)})] = (\mathcal{U}_j^{-1}[0, \phi(a^{(j)})(x_j)])_{x_j \in X_j}, \quad j = 1, 2, \tag{9.13}$$

$$\begin{aligned}&\mathcal{U}_1^{-1}[0, \phi(a^{(1)})] \cap \mathcal{U}_2^{-1}[0, \phi(a^{(2)})]\\ &= (\mathcal{U}_1^{-1}[0, \phi(a^{(1)})(x_1)] \cap (\mathcal{U}_2^{-1}[0, \phi(a^{(2)})(x_2)]))_{x_j \in X_j}, \quad j = 1, 2\end{aligned} \tag{9.14}$$

Thus, the marginal flou sets, or equivalently, marginal membership functions correspond via marginal r.v. $\mathcal{U}_j$ to elements in $\mathcal{B}^{X_j}$ and the joint flou sets, correspond via joint r.v. $(\mathcal{U}_1, \mathcal{U}_2)$ to elements in $\mathcal{B}^{X_1 \times X_2}$. Since everything actually depends only on the range of values $\mathcal{B}$ for any choice of x_j, for the most part, we omit the x_1, x_2 arguments, but it will be always understood that these values are present consistently, i.e., for any choice of $(x_1, x_2) \in X_1 \times X_2$, for consequent and same x_2 for antecedent: We have already developed successfully an approach which converts unconditional events in a boolean algebra to conditional ones and allows for feasible computations for naturally extended boolean operations and relations to these conditional forms: namely conditional event algebra, as detailed in sections 6 and 7. Hence, it is proposed that the *conditional flou set* $(a^{(1)} | a^{(2)})_{cop}$, where $f_j = \phi(a^{(j)})$, j = 1, 2, as usual, are identified with the ordinary conditional set,

$$(\alpha|\beta) \overset{d}{=} ((\mathcal{U}_1^{-1}[0, \phi(a^{(1)})]) \cap (\mathcal{U}_2^{-1}[0, \phi(a^{(2)})])| \mathcal{U}_2^{-1}[0, \phi(a^{(2)})]) \in (\mathcal{A} | \mathcal{A}), \tag{9.15}$$

where $(\mathcal{A}|\mathcal{A})$ is the conditional event algebra (with choice of operations such as GN or SAC, etc.) formed from σ-algebra $\mathcal{A}$, in precisely the same way (R|R) was formed from R. Note also that $(\alpha|\beta)$ has a well-defined indicator function $1_{(\alpha|\beta)} : \Lambda \to Q_0 \overset{d}{=} \{0, u, 1\}$, where, as in (6.33),

$$1_{(\alpha|\beta)}(\omega) = \begin{cases} 1, \text{ if } \omega \in \mathcal{U}_j^{-1}[0, \ \phi(a^{(2)})] \cap \mathcal{U}_2^{-1}[0, \phi(a^{(2)})] \\ 0, \text{ if } \omega \in \mathcal{U}_2^{-1}[0, \ \phi(a^{(2)})] \dashv \mathcal{U}_1^{-1}[0, \phi(a^{(1)})] \\ u, \text{ if } \omega \in \Lambda \dashv \mathcal{U}_2^{-1}[0, \phi(a^{(2)})] \ . \end{cases} \tag{9.16}$$

Next, consider the probability evaluation of $(\alpha|\beta)$ by p, based on the usual procedure (see the discussion in section 7 following eq. (7.31) and basic equation (6.51′))

$$p((\alpha|\beta) = p(\alpha|\beta) = p(\alpha \cap \beta)/p(\beta), \ p(\beta) > 0, \tag{9.17}$$

where

$$p(\beta) = p(\mathcal{U}_2^{-1}[0, \phi(a^{(2)})]) = \phi(a^{(2)}), \tag{9.18}$$

since $\mathcal{U}_2$ is uniformly distributed over u, and

$$\begin{aligned} p(\alpha \cap \beta) &= p(\mathcal{U}_1^{-1}[0, \phi(a^{(1)})] \cap \mathcal{U}_2^{-1}[0, \phi(a^{(2)})]) \\ &= \mathrm{cop}_o(\phi(a^{-1})(\cdot), \ \phi(a^{(2)})(\cdot\cdot)), \end{aligned} \tag{9.19}$$

by the very definition of cop. Hence, when $p(\beta) > 0$,

$$(\alpha|\beta) = \mathrm{cop}_o(\phi(a^{(1)})(\cdot), \phi(a^{(2)})(\cdot\cdot))/\phi(a^{(2)})(\cdot\cdot). \tag{9.20}$$

But, since, $\phi(a^{(j)}) = f_j$ is the usual membership function corresponding to flous et $a^{(j)}$, it is clear that (9.20) can be naturally interpreted as the conditional membership function of $\phi(a^{(1)})$ given $\phi(a^{(2)})$, when the latter is not zero. Finally, define for cop fixed:

For any $f_j \in X_j$, j = 1, 2, the conditional membership function

$(f_1|f_2)_{cop} : X_1 \times X_2 \to u$, where

$$(f_1|f_2)_{cop}(x_1, x_2) \overset{d}{=} \mathrm{cop}(f_1(x_1), f(x_2))/f(x_2), \quad x_j \in X_j, \tag{9.21}$$

j = 1, 2, provide at x_2, $f(x_2) > 0$. In order to make this compatible with the three-valued ordinary conditional event indicator function, define

$$(f_1|f_2)_{cop}(x_1, x_2) \overset{d}{=} u, \quad \text{when } f_2(x_2) = 0. \tag{9.22}$$

Combining (9.21) and (9.22) yields the compact form for all $x_j \in X_j$,

$$(f_1|f_2)_{cop} = (cop(f_1(x_1), f(x_2))/f(x_2)) \cdot \delta_{(f_2(x_2)>0)}$$
$$+ \delta_{(f_2(x_2)=0)} \cdot u, \tag{9.23}$$

where, analogous to (6.36), one makes the natural identification

$$(f_1|f_2)_{cop} = \{(f_1|f_2)_{cop,t} : t \in u\}, \tag{9.24}$$

where analogous to (6.33), $(f_1|f_2)_{cop,t}$ is formally the same as $(f_1|f_2)_{cop}$ with u replaced by t, for each $t \in u$.

Similarly, if one starts out with flou sets instead of membership functions, one can define

$$\phi((a^{(1)}|a^{(2)})_{cop}) \overset{d}{=} (\phi(a^{(1)})|\phi(a^{(2)})) \tag{9.25}$$

and procede with $f_j \overset{d}{=} \phi(a^{(j)})$, j = 1, 2, as in (9.21) and on.

Note also the special case where $f_1 = 1_A$, $A \subseteq X_1$, $f_2 = 1_B$, $B \subseteq X_2$,

$$(1_A|1_B)_{cop} = \max(1_{A\times B}, 1_{B'} \cdot u) = 1_{(A\times B|X_1\times B)} = 1_{(A\times X_2|X_1\times B)} \overset{d}{=} 1_{(A|B)}, \tag{9.26}$$

the r.h.s. of (9.25) being for two arguments, one in X_1 and the other in X_2. IF $X_1 = X_2 = X$ and $A, B \subseteq X$ and the arguments are restricted to be the same. $x_1 = x_2 = x$, then (9.25) becomes as in (6.34)

$$(1_A|1_B)_{cop} = 1_{(A|B)} \quad \text{(single argument form)}, \tag{9.27}$$

showing, so far, compatibility of form of fuzzy conditional membership functions with the specialized conditional event indicator functions.

Next, returning to the motivating definition in (9.15), for conditional membershi functions identified as conditional events $(\alpha|\beta)$ in $(\mathcal{A}|\mathcal{A})$, it follows that the natural definition of any operation among membership functions is given through the counterpart over $(\mathcal{A}|\mathcal{A})$:

Analogous to the setting leading to Theorem 8.3, assume (cop, cocop) = (min, max) and that now $\tilde{\mathcal{U}} \overset{d}{=} (\mathcal{U}_{j,i})_{j\in J, i=1,2}$ is a uniformly distributed stochastic process over u, with probability space $(\Lambda, \mathcal{A}, p)$ fixed as before, $\mathcal{U}_{j,i} : \Lambda \to u$ uniformly distributed over u with $\tilde{\mathcal{U}}$ jointly governed by min. Also, assume $(X_{j,i})_{j\in J, i=1,2}$ given spaces with each $X_{j,i}$ corresponding to $\mathcal{U}_{j,i}$ and that $a^{(j)} \in \text{Flou}(X_{j,1})$, $b^{(j)} \in \text{Flou}(X_{j,2})$ arb., $j \in K$.

Select an arbitrary index set $K \subseteq J$ and consider any well-defined logical combination of $(a^{(j)}|b^{(j)})_{min}$ through $\times_{min}$ and $\dagger_{max}$. Expressing this in multivariable notation where e.g., $(\underline{a}|\underline{b}) \overset{d}{=} ((a^{(j)}|b^{(j)})_{min})_{j\in K}$;

$\underline{\mathcal{U}}_i \overset{d}{=} (S\mathcal{C}_{j,i})_{j\in K}$; $\phi(\underline{a}|\underline{b})_{min} = (\phi(a)|\phi(b))_{min} = ((\phi(a^{(j)})|\phi(b^{(j)}))_{min})_{j\in K}$;

$\underline{x}_i \overset{d}{=} (x_{j,i})_{j\in K}$, $x_{j,i} \in X_{j,i}$, $j \in J$, $i = 1, 2$, etc.,

$$\begin{aligned}\phi(\text{comb}(\times_{min}, \dagger_{max}; (\underline{a}|\underline{b})_{min}))(\underline{x}) &\overset{d}{=} \text{comb}(\times_{min}, \dagger_{max}; (\phi(\underline{a})|\phi(\underline{b}))_{min}(\underline{x}))\\ &\overset{d}{=} p(\text{comb}(\cdot, \vee; (\underline{\mathcal{U}}_1^{-1}[\underline{0}, \phi(\underline{a})(\underline{x}_1)]|\, \mathcal{U}_2^{-1}[\underline{0}, \phi(\underline{b})(\underline{x}_2)])))\\ &= p(\text{comb}(\&, \text{or},; ((\underline{\mathcal{U}}_1 \le \phi(\underline{a})(\underline{x}_1))|(\underline{\mathcal{U}}_2 \le \phi(\underline{b})(\underline{x}_2))))),\\ &= p(\alpha_0|\beta_0) = (p(\alpha_0 \cap \beta_0)|p(\beta_0))_{min},\end{aligned} \tag{9.28}$$

with the right hand side of (9.28) interpreted in functional form dependent upon argument $\underline{x}$ and where conditional event $(\alpha_0|\beta_0) \in (\mathcal{A}|\mathcal{A})$ is obtained via the calculus developed out of Theorem 6.4 and evaluated via (6.51′). In particular, consider the single argument case where $K = \{1, 2\}$, $X_{j,i} = X$, $j = 1, 2$, $i = 1, 2$, and for convenience, let $a = a_1$, $b = b_1$, $c = a_2$, $d = b_2$. Then for $*_0 = \cdot\min$, $\vee \max$, $x \in X$, and letting

$$\alpha \overset{d}{=} \mathcal{U}_{1,1}^{-1}[0, \phi(a)(x)] \leftrightarrow (\mathcal{U}_{1,1} \le \phi(a)(x));\ \beta \overset{d}{=} \mathcal{U}_{1,2}^{-1}[0, \phi(b)(x)] \leftrightarrow (\mathcal{U}_{1,2} \le \phi(b)(x)),$$
$$\gamma \overset{d}{=} \mathcal{U}_{2,1}^{-1}[0\cdot\phi(c)(x)] \leftrightarrow (\mathcal{U}_{2,1} \le \phi(c)(x)),\ \delta \overset{d}{=} \mathcal{U}_{2,2}^{-1}[0, \phi(d)(x)] \leftrightarrow (\mathcal{U}_{2,2} \le \phi(d)(x)), \tag{9.29}$$

$$\begin{aligned}\phi((a|b)_{min} *_o (c|d)_{min}) &= (\phi(a)|\phi(b))_{min} *_o (\phi(c)|\phi(d))_{min}\\ &= p((\alpha|\beta)*(\gamma|\delta)) \quad (\phi = \cdot, \vee)\\ &= \begin{cases} p(\alpha\beta\gamma\delta|r_2) = p(\alpha\beta\gamma\delta)/p(r_2), & \text{if } *_o = \cdot_{min} \quad (* = \cdot)\\ p(\alpha\beta \vee \gamma\delta|q_2) = p(\alpha\beta \vee \gamma\delta|q_2), & \text{if } *_o = \vee_{max} \quad (* = \vee)\end{cases}\end{aligned} \tag{9.30}$$

where

$$r_2 \overset{d}{=} \alpha'\beta \vee \gamma'\delta \vee \alpha\beta\gamma\delta;\quad q_2 \overset{d}{=} \alpha\beta \vee \gamma\delta \vee \alpha'\beta\gamma'\delta, \tag{9.31}$$

using (6.68), (6.69), (6.73), and evaluation (6.51′).

Simplifying (9.30) and (9.31) using elementary probability properties,

$$p(\alpha\beta\gamma\delta) = \min(\phi(a)(x), \phi(b)(x), \phi(c)(x), \phi(d)(x)) \quad (9.31)$$

$$p(\alpha\beta \vee \gamma\delta) = \min(\phi(a)(x), \phi(b)(x)) + \min(\phi(c)(x), \phi(d)(x)) - p(\alpha\beta\gamma\delta), \tag{9.32}$$

with $p(\alpha\beta\gamma\delta)$ given in terms of cop and membership functions as in (9.31).

$$p(r_2) = p(\alpha'\beta \vee \gamma'\delta) + p(\alpha\beta\gamma\delta); \; p(q_2) = p(\alpha\beta \vee \gamma\delta) + p(\alpha'\beta\gamma'\delta), \tag{9.33}$$

$$p(\alpha'\beta \vee \gamma'\delta) = p(\alpha'\beta) + p(\gamma'\delta) - p(\alpha'\beta\gamma'\delta), \tag{9.34}$$

$$p(\alpha'\beta) = \phi(b)(x) - \min(\phi(a)(x), \phi(b)(x)); \; p(\gamma'\delta) = \phi(d)(x) - \min(\phi(c)(x), \phi(d)(x)), \tag{9.35}$$

$$\begin{aligned} p(\alpha'\beta\gamma'\delta) &= p(\beta\delta) - p(\beta\gamma\delta) - p(\alpha\beta\delta) + p(\alpha\beta\gamma\delta) \\ &= \min(\phi(b)(x), \phi(d)(x)) - \min(\phi(b)(x), \phi(c)(x), \phi(d)(x)) \\ &\quad - \min(\phi(a)(x), \phi(b)(x), \phi(d)(x)) + p(\alpha\beta\gamma\delta). \end{aligned} \tag{9.36}$$

Even simpler is the negation evaluation:

$$\begin{aligned} \phi((a|b)_{min}{}')(x) &= (\phi(a)|\phi(b))(x)' = p((\alpha|\beta)') = p(\alpha'|\beta) = 1 - p(\alpha|\beta) \\ &= 1 - (\phi(a)|\phi(b))(x), \end{aligned} \tag{9.37}$$

where

$$p(\alpha|\beta) = p(\alpha\beta)/p(\beta) = (\phi(a)(x), \phi(b)(x))/\phi(b)(x) \tag{9.38}$$

if $\phi(b)(x) > 0$.

Thus, (9.30)-(9.38) show that all extended boolean operations over conditional membership functions are closed -- due to the conditional event algebra evaluations -- and feasible to compute: being only simple arithmetic functions of the copula at certain subsets of $\{\phi(a)(x), \phi(b)(x), \phi(c)(x), \phi(d)(x)\}$.

Also, as a check, when $\phi(a) = 1_A$, $\phi(b) = 1_B$, $\phi(c) = 1_C$, $\phi(d) = 1_D$, for any choice of $A, B, C, D \subseteq X$, it is easy to prove, via (9.30), (9.31), and (9.37), that (9.27) shows

$$(1_A|1_B)_{cop} = 1_{(A|B)}, \; (1_C|1_D)_{cop} = 1_{(C|D)} \tag{9.39}$$

and for $*_o = \cdot_{min}, \vee_{max}$, corresponding to $* = \cdot, \vee$,

$$\begin{aligned} (1_A|1_B)_{min} *_o (1_C|1_D)_{min} &= 1_{(A|B)} *_o 1_{(C|D)} = 1_{(A|B)*(C|D)} \\ (1_A|1_B)_{min}{}' &= 1_{(A|B)}{}' = 1_{(A|B)'}, \end{aligned} \tag{9.40}$$

where the R.H.S. of (9.40) are the usual (GN) conditional event operations from Theorem 6.4, given in the indicator function form.

Note that from its very definition, conditional membership functions always satisfy the relations

$$(f|1)_{cop} = f; \text{ if cop is assoc., } (f|g)_{cop} = (cop_{\circ}(f, g)|g)_{cop}; \; (f|g)_{cop} \cdot g = cop_{\circ}(f, g), \tag{9.41}$$

for all $f \in \text{Mem}(X)$, $g \in \text{Mem}(Y)$, and copula cop arbitrary; the dot in the right hand side of (9.41) being ordinary arithmetic product. Finally, it can also be verified directly, using the definition in (9.23) that for f and g as above, together with the assumption now that cop is associative and commutative (such as is the case for cop = min or prod) and Z is any third space and $h \in \text{Mem}(Z)$ is arbitrary such that

$$\sup\{h(z) : z \in Z\} = 1 : \tag{9.42}$$

$$(f|g)_{cop} = \sup\{(f|cop_\circ(g, h(z))_{cop} \cdot (h(z)|g)_{cop} : z \in Z\} . \tag{9.43}$$

The result in (9.43) can be useful as an alternative to Bayes' theorem, where a parameter of interest is described by f, observed data corresponding to g, and auxiliary information in the form of attributes described by h, so that $(f|cop_\circ(g, h(z))_{cop}$ can be interpreted as an inference rule, while $(h(z)|g)_{cop}$ can be thought of as a conditional error form. In practice, both the inference rule and error form may have to be obtained directly, rather than be built up from the antecedent- consequent form, since these individual functions may not be known. The identity in (9.43) corresponds to the well-known expansion

$$p(x|y) = \int_{z \in Z} p(x|y, z) \cdot p(z|y)dz. \tag{9.44}$$

Applications of earlier versions of (9.43) to problems of data fusion (and track association, in particular) can be found in Goodman (1986). Further analysis and discussion of the above results may also be found in Goodman, Nguyen, & Walker (1991, chpt. 8).

Finally, it is of some interest to be able to determine the probability of a conditional fuzzy set. This should extend the unconditional case given in (7.32), as well as the modified conditional event indicator situation as presented in (7.32)-(7.36). There the ambiguity caused by the presence of the u term leads to an interval of probabilities, which was resolved by use of the stable boundary weighting average technique ((7.57), (7.45)), and justified by Theorems 7.3, 7.4). Motivated by the above, suppose that $(\Lambda, \mathcal{A}, p)$ is a fixed probability space, X, Y are given spaces, $(X \times Y, R)$ a measurable space, $W : \Lambda \to X \times Y$ a random variable, and $f \in \text{Mem}(X)$, $g \in \text{Mem}(Y)$ arbitrary, with copula cop fixed. Then,

$$(p_\circ W^{-1})((f|g)_{cop} \overset{d}{=} E_W((f|g)_{cop}(W)) = c_1 \cdot e_1 + c_2 \cdot e_2, \tag{9.45}$$

by standard probability expansion, where also using (9.23),

$$c_1 \overset{d}{=} E_W((f|g)_{cop}(W)|g(W) > 0) = E_W(cop(f(W), g(W))|f(W) > 0), \tag{9.46}$$

$$c_2 \overset{d}{=} E_W((f|g)_{cop}(W)\,|\,g(W) = 0) = u; \quad e_1 \overset{d}{=} p(g(W) > 0); \quad e_2 \overset{d}{=} p(g(W) = 0). \tag{9.47}$$

Hence, analogous to (7.35), substituting (9.47) into (9.45),

$$(p{\circ}W^{-1})((f|g)_{cop}) = c_1 \cdot e_1 + e_2 \cdot u = [c_1 \cdot e_1, c_1 \cdot e_1 + e_2], \tag{9.48}$$

whence the stable boundary average yields

$$h_o((p{\circ}W^{-1})((f|g)_{cop})) = (c_1e_1)/(1 - (c_1e_1 + e_2) + c_1e_1) = c_1e_1/(1 - e_2) = c_1, \tag{9.49}$$

which checks with all special cases (including c.e. indicators, etc.).

Acknowledgements.

The author wishes to express his gratitude for the joint support of this work by: Code 1133 (under Dr. R. Wachter), Office of Naval Research; the Naval Ocean Systems Center Program for Research and Technology (under Dr. J. Silva, Code 014, and with Deputy Director for Research, Dr. A. Gordon, Code 0141, and Deputy Director for Exploratory Development, Dr. K.J. Campbell). Acknowledgements are also given here to the ongoing support of the line management at the Naval Ocean Systems Center (Code 42, Head, J. A. Salzmann, Jr. and Code 421, Head, M.M. Mudurian). Finally, the author wishes to thank: his colleague, Prof. H.T. Nguyen, Mathematics Dept., New Mexico State University at Las Cruces, for many valuable discussions, suggestions, and criticisms, especially during his summer 1990 stay at NOSC as an ASEE Summer Faculty Visitor; his new research associate at NOSC, Dr. P.G. Calabrese (NRC Senior Research Associate), for many comments and penetrating questions.

References.

1. Aczél, J. (1966), *Lectures on Functional Equations and Their Applications*, Academic Press, New York.
2. Adams, E. (1975), *The Logic of Conditionals*, D. Reidel, Dordrecht, Neth.
3. Barr, M. (1989), Fuzzy sets and Toposes, *Proc. 3rd Inter. Fuzzy Sys. Assoc.*, Univ. of Wash., Seattle, (Aug.), 225-228.
4. Belluce, L.P. (1986), Semisimple algebras of infinite valued logic and bold fuzzy set theory, *Canad. J. Math. 38(6)*, 1356-1379.
5. Boole, G. (1854), *An Investigation of the Laws of Thought*, Walton & Maberly, London. Reprinted by Dover Public., New York, 1951. (See especially Chpt. 6 et passim for conditioning concepts.)
6. Bouchon, B. (1987), Fuzzy inferences and conditional possibility distributions, *Fuzzy Sets & Sys. 23*, 23-41.

7. Bruno, G. & Gilio, A. (1985), Confronto fra eventi condizionati di probabililiti nulla nell' inferenza statistica bayesiana (in Italian with English summary), *Rivista di Matemat. per le Scienze Econom. e Soc.* (*Milano*) *8*(2), 141-152.

8. Copeland, A.H. (1950), Implicative boolean algebra, *Math. Zeitschr. 53*(*3*), 285-290.

9. Copeland, A.H. (1956), Probabilities, observations, and predictions, *Proc. 3rd Berkeley Symp. on Math. Stat. & Prob.* (*Vol. II*), 1954-1955 (J. Neyman, ed.), Univ. of CA Press, Los Angeles, 41-47.

10. Calabrese, P.G. (1987), An algebraic synthesis of the foundations of logic and probability, *Info. Sci. 42*, 187-237.

11. DeFinetti, B. (1974), *Theory of Probability*, *Vols. 1* & *2*, John Wiley, New York (Vol. 1: pp. 139, 140; Vol. 2: pp. 266, 267, 322).

12. Dubois, D. & Prade, H. (1980), *Fuzzy Sets & Systems*, Academic Press, New York.

13. Dubois, D. & Prade, H. (1989), Measure-free conditioning, probability, and non-monotonic reasoning, *Proc. 11th Inter. Joint Conf. AI*, Detroit, Mich. (Aug.), 1110-1114.

14. Dubois, D. & Prade, H. (1990), The logical view of conditioning and its application to possibility and evidence theories, *Inter. J. Approx. Reason. 4*, 23-46.

15. Eytan, M. (1981), Fuzzy sets: a topos-logical point of view, *Fuzzy Sets & Sys. 5*, 47-67.

16. Fine, T. (1973), *Theories of Probability*: *An Examination of Foundations*, Academic Press, New York.

17. Gaines, b. (1978), Fuzzy and probability uncertainty logics, *Info. & Control 38*, 154-169.

18. Gentilhomme, Y. (1968), Les ensembles flous en linguistique, *Cahiers de Ling. Théor. et Appliq. 5*, 47-65.

19. Glas, M de (1984), Representation of Lukasiewicz many-valued algebras. The atomic case, *Fuzzy Sets & Sys. 14*, 175-185.

20. Goguen, J.A. (1974), Concept representation in natural and artificial languages: axioms, extensions and applications for fuzzy sets, *Inter. J. Man-Machine Stud. 6*, 531-561.

21. Goodman, I.R. (1981), Fuzzy sets as random level sets: implications and extensions of basic results, in *Applied Systems & Cybernetics, Vol. VI* (G. Lasker, ed.), Pergamon Press, New York, 2757-2766.

22. Goodman, I.R. (1986), *PACT*: *An Approach to Combining Linguistic-Based and Probabilistic Information for Correlation and Tracking*, NOSC Tech. Doc. 878 (March), Naval Ocean Systems Center, San Diego.

23. Goodman, I.R. (1987), A measure-free approach to conditioning, *Proc. 3rd AAAI Workshop Uncert. in AI*, Univ. of Wash., Seattle (July), 270-277.

24. Goodman, I.R. (1989), Chair of "Conditional event algebras and conditional probability computations", minisymposium presented at SIAM Annual Meeting, San Diego, July 21, 1989. Speakers included I.R. Goodman, P.G. Calabrese, H.T. Nguyen, and D.W. Stein. Abstracts of presentations in *Final Program Book of Abstracts of SIAM Meeting*, pp. 19, 20, 34.

25. Goodman, I.R. (1990), Three valued-logic and conditional event algebras, *First Inter. Symp. Uncert. Model & Analy.*, Univ. of Md., College Park, to appear.

26. Goodman, I.R. (1991), Evaluation of combinations of conditioned information: I, a history, accepted for publication in *Info. Sci.*

27. Goodman, I.R. & Nguyen, H.T. (1985), *Uncertainty Models for Knowledge-Based Systems*, North-Holland Press, Amsterdam.

28. Goodman, I.R. & Nguyen, H.T. (1988), Conditional objects and the modeling of uncertainties, in *Fuzzy Computing* (M.M. Gupta & T. Yamakawa, eds.), North-Holland, New York, 119-138.

29. Goodman, I.R. & Nguyen, H.T. (1991), Foundations for an algebraic theory of conditioning, accepted for publication in *Fuzzy Sets & Sys.*

30. Goodman, I.R., Nguyen, H.T., & Rogers, G.S. (1991), On the scoring approach to admissibility of uncertainty measures in expert systems, accepted for publication in *J. Math. Analy. & Applic.*

31. Goodman, I.R., Nguyen, H.T., & Walker, E.A., *Conditional Inference and Logic for Intelligent Systems: A Theory of Measure-Free Conditioning*, monograph accepted for publication by North-Holland.

32. Goodman, I.R. & Stein, D.W., (1989), Extension of the measure-free approach to conditioning of fuzzy sets and other logics, *Proc. 3rd Int. Fuzzy Sys. Assoc.*, Univ. of Wash., Seattle (Aug.), 361-364.

33. Grätzer, G. (1978), *General Lattice Theory*, Birkhäuser Verlag, Basel.

34. Hailperin, T. (1984), Probability logic, *Notre Dame J. Formal Logic 25(3)*, 198-212.

35. Hailperin, T. (1986), *Boole's Logic and Probability, 2nd Ed.*, North-Holland Press, New York.

36. Hisdal, E. (1978), Conditional possibilities, independence, and non-interaction, *Fuzzy Sets & Sys. 1*, 283-297.

37. Höhle, U. (1982), A mathematical theory of uncertainty, in *Fuzzy Set and Possibility Theory: Recent Developments* (R.R. Yager, ed.), Pergamon Press, New York, 344-355.

38. Kosko, B. (1986), Fuzzy entropy and conditioning, *Info. Sci. 40*, 165-174.

39. Lewis, D. (1976), Probabilities of conditionals and conditional probabilities, *The Philos. Rev. 85(3)*, 297-315.

40. Lindley, D.V. (1982), Scoring rules and the inevitability of probability, *Inter. Statis. Rev. 50*, 1-26.

41. Mattila, J.K. (1986), On some logical points of fuzzy conditional decision making, *Fuzzy Sets & Sys. 20*, 137-145.

42. Mazurkiewicz, S. (1956), *Podstawy Rachunku Prawdopodoiénstwa* (in Polish -- Foundations of the Calculus of Probability), Akademia Nauk, Warsaw, Tom 32 (J. Łos, ed.).

43. Mendelson, E. (1970), *Boolean Algebra and Switching Circuits*, Schaum's Outline Series, McGraw-Hill, New York.

44. Negoita, C.V. & Ralescu, D.A. (1975), Representation theorems for fuzzy concepts, *Kybernetes (G. Br.)1*, 169-174.

45. Nguyen, H.T. (1978), On conditional possibility distributions, *Fuzzy Sets & Sys. 1*, 299-309.

46. Nguyen, H.T. & Rogers, G.S. (1991), Conditional operators in a logic of conditionals, in this monograph.

47. Pitts, A.M. (1982), Fuzzy sets do not form a topos, *Fuzzy Sets & Sys. 8*, 101-104.

48. Radecki, T. (1977), Level fuzzy sets, *J. Cybern. 7*, 189-198.

49. Ralescu, D.A. (1979), A survey of the representation of fuzzy concepts and its applications, in *Advances in Fuzzy Set Theory & Applications* (M.M. Gupta, R.K. Ragade, & R.R. Yager, eds.) North-Holland, New York, 77-91.

50. Ramer, A. (1989), Conditional possibility measures, *Cybern. & Sys. 20*, 233-247.

51. Rényi, A. (1970), *Foundations of Probability*, Holden-Day, San Francisco.

52. Rescher, N. (1969), *Many-Valued Logic*, McGraw-Hill Co., New York.

53. Schay, G. (1968), An algebra of conditional events, *J. Math. Analy. & Applic. 24(2)* (Nov.), 334-344.

54. Schweizer, B. & Sklar, A. (1983), *Probabilistic Metric Spaces*, North-Holland Press, New York.

55. Sembi, B.S. & Mamdani, E.H. (1979), On the nature of implication in fuzzy logic, *Proc.* 9th *Inter. Symp. Multi. Logic*, Bath, G. Br., 143-149.

56. Stout, L.N. (1984), Topoi and categories of fuzzy sets, *Fuzzy Sets & Sys. 12*, 169-184.

57. Yager, R.R. (1983), On the implicative operator in fuzzy logic, *Info. Sci. 31*, 141-164.

58. Zadeh, L.A., (1965), Fuzzy sets, *Info. & Control 8*, 338-353.

59. Zadeh, L.A., (1978), Fuzzy sets as a basis for a theory of possibility, *Fuzzy Sets & Sys. 1*, 3-28.

Conditional Logic in Expert Systems
I.R. Goodman, M.M. Gupta, H.T. Nguyen and G.S. Rogers (editors)

DEDUCTION AND INFERENCE USING CONDITIONAL LOGIC AND PROBABILITY

Philip G. Calabrese

National Research Council Senior Research Associate
Naval Ocean System Center, Code 421
San Diego, California 92152

Abstract: *In contrast to the author's 1987 paper, which presented an algebraic synthesis of conditional logic and conditional probability starting with an initial Boolean algebra of propositions, this paper starts with an initial probability space of events and generates the associated propositions as measurable indicator functions (à la the approach of B. De Finetti). Conditional propositions are generated as measurable indicator functions restricted to subsets of positive probability measure. The operations of "and", "or", "not" and "given" are defined for arbitrary conditional propositions. The representation of the resulting conditional event algebra as a 3-valued logic (always possible according to a new theorem due to I. R. Goodman) is given in terms of 3-valued truth tables. Formulas for the conditional probability of complex conditional propositions such as $(q|p) \vee (s|r)$ are proved. A second major theme of the paper concerns deduction in the realm of conditional propositions. It turns out that their are varieties of logical deduction for conditional propositions depending on the particular entailment relation ($\leq$) chosen. These relations are explored including their lattice properties and properties of non-monotonicity. Computational aspects for Artificial Intelligence are also discussed.*

Keywords: Conditional propositions, conditional events, logic, reasoning with uncertainty, 3-valued logic, conditional probability, deduction, inference

1. Introduction

Deep within the foundations of logic and probability, the architects and builders have left a missing stone. Roughly, this foundation stone is to logical propositions what fractions are to integers. Now, with the advent of the computer age, attempts to incorporate more of human intelligence into machines (so-called artificial intelligence) have exposed this lack of foundation and led computer scientists to resort to sub-optimal methods to compute actions from information via some "reasonable" data fusion algorithm. Hence there is no standard theory for combining information in the context of uncertainty. Among the partially overlapping techniques there are:

a. The *fuzzy sets* and other fuzzy language modifiers and methods of L. Zadeh [5],
b. The *belief functions* of Dempster-Shafer [7], and
c. The *probability logic* approach of P. Calabrese [2] and [3].

The author will leave it to the many enthusiasts of fuzziness to crystallize the imprecise and generally wasteful information combining techniques commonly employed by the common man as he commonly goes bumbling through life. This is not to say that we do not need approximate methods by which to combine information in the face of the default of logic and probability to provide more precise methods. Even though fuzzy methods tend to distort information at least these methods come up with solutions, and often an exact solution is not necessary. Nevertheless, science should continually seek to purge all unnecessary natural language ambiguities from its formal mathematical descriptions, not meekly incorporate them! A new theory should also, if possible, merge with the older theory where the older is tested and applicable. *That* the fuzzy approach does not do. Before one adopts a distorting technique, no matter how computationally tractable it may be, one should first extend the classical theories of logic and probability as far as possible, and secondly, merge with them on the boundary of their domain of application. However, except for a few authors (for example, J. Pearl [6] and his important work in conditional independence) this has not been attempted by the new generation of uncertainty workers in so-called artificial intelligence. Instead, many researchers have publicly discounted the practicality of probability theory as a method for reasoning with uncertainty - a notion that has prompted P. Cheeseman [4] to make a "defense of probability theory".

Another technique for reasoning with uncertainty is the belief function approach of Dempster-Shafer [7] which, while striving to be consistent with probability theory, addresses the problem of determining the support for propositions arising from even mutually inconsistent evidence.

The third approach to dealing with uncertainty is actually the oldest. G. Boole himself, the father of the algebra of logic, was developing an algebra of logic *and* probability (see T. Hailperin's cogent account [8]) but he died before completing the work. His unfinished algebraic development was then abbreviated by his successors, who attached his name to the resulting algebra.

In 1932, 1934 and later in 1956, S. Mazurkiewicz [9], [10] and [11] used A. Tarski's [12], [13] new theory of algebraic logic to approach the problem of conditioning in an algebraic setting, but he did not get very far before his death. At the same time N. Kolmogorov [28] was laying down his successful axiomatization of probability theory and he realized that he could not follow logic in equating "if p then q" to "q or not p".

Already, in 1913, B. Russell and A. N. Whitehead [1] had made truth tables and so-called material implication the standard form of implication in logic, and this worked fairly well for 2-valued logic, but Kolmogorov found it to be inappropriate for probability theory. It has also been known at least since 1975, [2] and [3], that the probability $P(q \vee p')$ of the material conditional is, in general, greater than the conditional probability $P(q|p)$ of q given p, unless either $P(p) = 1$ or $P(q|p) = 1$. Furthermore, if $p = 0$ then $q \vee p'$ is certain (=1) but $P(q|p)$ is undefined. This telltale inadequacy of material implication for representing "if - then - " has been noticed by generations of introductory logic students who have questioned why "if p then q" should be true or "valid" in case p is false. This question by pre-indoctrinated logic students has all too often been squelched by their instructors, who blithely appealed to the assignment of exactly *two* truth values to show that "if p then q" must be equivalent to "q or not p". Consequently if p is false then "not p" is true, and so too is $(q \vee p')$, whatever the truth value of q! Thus (the argument goes) "if p then q" is true (valid) when p is false.

Nevertheless, a good scientist does not include cases in his sample for which the premise of his hypothesis is false; he does not count such cases as positive evidence of his hypothesis irrespective of the truth of his conclusion. Nor does a scientist report the probability that either the conclusion of his hypothesis is true or its premise false; rather, he reports the conditional probability of the conclusion of his hypothesis given that its premise is true; and so too must those who would consistently quantify the truth content of partially true statements.

Besides this divergence between the treatments of "if - then -" in the domains of logic versus probability, there also tends to be an inadequate distinction made in logic between propositions that are partially true and propositions that are wholly true. Generally, in a Boolean algebra a proposition need not be either true in all models (interpretations, worlds) or false in all models; a proposition can be true in some and false in others, thus allowing it to have a non-trivial probability. Nevertheless, the lack of a commonly accepted algebraic context for both logic and probability has made the very meaning of the "probability of a proposition" controversial. This is true in spite of the fact that G. Boole [29], R. Carnap and R. C. Jeffrey [30] & [31], H. Gaifman [32], D. Scott and P. Kraus [33], E. W. Adams [19], and T. Hailperin [8] have all defined the probability of a proposition as the probability of its extension set of models, i.e., the probability of the set of models (interpretations, worlds) in which the proposition is true.

Others who have contributed to the expansion of probability logic that should be mentioned include B. De Finetti [14], who first treated propositions as indicator functions from a sample space to {0,1}; P. Rosenbloom [15], whose treatment of algebraic logic was very influential to the author; G. Schay [16], who was probably the first person to define a system of conditional propositions that included operations for combining propositions with different premises; N. Rescher [17], whose monumental 1969 book *Many Valued Logics* (still the standard in the field) included the 3-valued logic of B. Sobocinski [18], which turns out to be equivalent to the author's system less conditional conditionals; E. W. Adams [19], whose operations are equivalent to those of Sobocinski; D. Dubois and H. Prade [20], who have carefully reviewed the recent literature and contrasted the author's conditional logic from that of I. R. Goodman & H. T. Nguyen; and finally I. R. Goodman & H. T. Nguyen, who upon reading an early (1986) manuscript of the author's 1987 paper, immediately realized the crucial importance of conditional events, conducted a comprehensive historical review concerning the problem of conditioning [21], and later contributed to the algebraic foundations of conditionals, initiated new directions for research and discovered significant new results [22]. (I would like to thank these colleagues for discovering the work of G. Schay and B. Sobocinski, and for pointing out similarities between the author's system and those of Schay, Sobocinski and Adams.)

The next section begins with a probability space and defines propositions (à la B. De Finetti [14]) as indicator functions defined on the elementary set of occurrences of a probability space. The meaning of a proposition being partially true or wholly true is defined in the context of the algebraic logic of propositions (see, for instance, Chang and Keisler [26].) The probability of each proposition is then defined in terms of a probability measure on the extensionally associated models (interpretations) that satisfy those propositions.

Conditional propositions (q|p), "q given p", are next defined as domain-restricted P-measurable indicator functions which can be combined by "and", "or", "not" and "given" resulting in another such conditional proposition. The resulting system of conditionals can be represented as a 3-valued logic, as predicted by a recent theorem of I. R. Goodman [22, and this book]. The third value does not represent uncertainty but rather *inapplicability* - falseness of the premise of the conditional proposition. (Uncertainty is automatically represented by non-atomic propositions, that thereby leave various possible facts unspecified.) A new formula is given for the probability of the disjunction, $(q|p) \vee (s|r)$, of two conditional expressions, thereby generalizing the well-known formula $P(q \vee p) =$

$P(q) + P(p) - P(q \wedge p)$. A non-trivial formula for the conjunction of two conditionals is also proved.

In the subsequent section on deduction, two types of deduction in a Boolean algebra are distinguished. One of these types splits into four non-equivalent types of deduction in the realm of conditionals resulting in at least five different kinds of deduction. These types of deduction are characterized in terms of relationships between the original unconditioned propositions.

2. Formal Development

Propositions, Probability Spaces and Indicator Functions: If $\mathcal{P} = (\Omega, \mathcal{B}, P)$ is a probability space then the characteristic function of each P-measurable subset B, $B \in \mathcal{B}$, defines a unique P-measurable indicator function $q: \Omega \rightarrow \{0,1\}$ from Ω to the 2-element Boolean Algebra $\{0,1\}$ as follows:

$$q(\omega) = \begin{cases} 1, \text{ if } \omega \in B, \\ 0, \text{ if } \omega \in B' \end{cases} \tag{1}$$

q is a "proposition" in the sense that for each $\omega \in \Omega$, either q is true for ω (i.e. $q(\omega) = 1$) or q is false for ω (i.e. $q(\omega) = 0$). Let L denote the set of all propositions of $\mathcal{P}$.

Conversely, each P-measurable indicator function q defines a unique P-measurable subset B, $B \in \mathcal{B}$ by

$$B = q^{-1}(1) = \{\omega \in \Omega: q(\omega) = 1\}. \tag{2}$$

B is the P-measurable subset on which q is true, and P(B) is the probability measure of the partial truth of q, and so $P(q) = P(q^{-1}(1))$.

In this correspondence between measurable subsets (probabilistic events) and measurable indicator functions (propositions) the whole set Ω corresponds to the unity indicator function, to those propositions that are true in all ω --- necessary & provable. The empty set Φ corresponds to the zero indicator function, to those propositions that are false in all ω --- impossible and contradictory.

Definition 1: Two propositions (indicator functions) p and q are equivalent if and only if they are equal as functions. That is, p = q if and only if both p and q take the value 1 (or 0) on the same subset of Ω. Thus p = q if and only if $p^{-1}(1) = q^{-1}(1)$ if and only if $p^{-1}(0) = q^{-1}(0)$.

Axioms of Boolean Algebra: A Boolean algebra, as formulated by T. Hailperin [8], is a set of propositions L (including two constants 0 and 1) that is closed under the three operations "and" (juxtaposition or $\wedge$), "or" ($\vee$) and "not" (') and that satisfies these axioms:

$$
\begin{aligned}
pq &= qp, & p \vee q &= q \vee p, \\
(pq)r &= p(qr), & (p \vee q) \vee r &= p \vee (q \vee r), \\
(1)(p) &= p, & 0 \vee p &= p, \\
(p)(p') &= 0, & p \vee p' &= 1, \\
p(q \vee r) &= pq \vee pr, & p \vee (qr) &= (p \vee q)(p \vee r), \\
pp &= p, & p \vee p &= p.
\end{aligned} \tag{3}
$$

Conditional Propositions: In order to incorporate conditions, consider next that each ordered pair, (B|A) of P-measurable subsets B, A in $\mathfrak{B}$ with corresponding pairs (q|p) of indicator functions q, p, defines a unique domain-restrcted P-measurable indicator function (q|p): A $\rightarrow$ {0,1} from A to the 2-element Boolean algebra as follows:

Definition 2:

$$
(q|p)(\omega) = \begin{cases} 1, \text{ if } \omega \in (A \cap B), \\ 0, \text{ if } \omega \in (A \cap B'), \\ \text{undefined, if } \omega \in A' \end{cases} \tag{4}
$$

In terms of the unconditioned propositions p and q this is

$$
(q|p)(\omega) = \begin{cases} q(\omega), \text{ if } p(\omega) = 1, \\ \text{undefined, if } p(\omega) = 0. \end{cases} \tag{5}
$$

(q|p) is a "conditional proposition" in the sense that if p is true on ω then (q|p) is either true on ω or false on ω depending on the truth value of q. If p is false on ω, we say that (q|p) does not apply (i.e., is undefined) for ω. (q|p) is q, restricted to $p^{-1}(1)$, the subset on which p is true. The set of all conditional propositions of $\mathfrak{P}$ will be denoted L/L.

Conversely, each such ordered pair of P-measurable indicator functions (q|p) defines a unique ordered pair, (B|A), of P-measurable subsets where $A = p^{-1}(1)$ and $B = q^{-1}(1)$. A is the measurable subset on which p is true and B is the measurable subset on which q is true. $B \cap A$ is the measurable subset of A on which q is also true, and for non-zero P(A), $P(B \cap A) / P(A)$ is the conditional probability of q given p, denoted P(q|p).

Boolean Operations: The operations "or" ($\vee$), "and" (juxtaposition or $\wedge$) and "not" ('), defined on the Boolean algebra (or sigma-algebra) $\mathfrak{B}$ of events of $\mathfrak{P}$ naturally generate operations on the indicator functions via disjunction, conjunction and negation in the 2-element Boolean algebra {0,1} as follows:

$$\begin{aligned} (p \vee q)(\omega) &= p(\omega) \vee q(\omega), \\ (pq)(\omega) &= p(\omega)q(\omega), \\ p'(\omega) &= (p(\omega))'. \end{aligned} \tag{6}$$

Here, the operations on the right hand side are in the 2-element Boolean algebra.

Note further that the first two operations can be expressed in terms of the minimum and maximum functions on {0,1}:

$$\begin{aligned} p \vee q &= \max\{p, q\} \\ pq &= \min\{p, q\} \end{aligned} \tag{7}$$

Together with the Boolean axioms and truth assignments the set of propositions L forms a Boolean logic, which will formally be denoted $\mathfrak{L}$.

In this framework each probabilistic outcome $\omega \in \Omega$ is a *model* [26, pp. 1-2] of the Boolean logic $\mathfrak{L}$ because firstly, the axioms of the Boolean logic $\mathfrak{L}$ are true in ω and secondly, ω assigns each proposition of $\mathfrak{L}$ an unambiguous truth value of true or false.

The above approach to probability logic starts with a probability space $\mathfrak{P} = (\Omega, \mathfrak{B}, P)$ and generates a Boolean algebra $\mathfrak{L}$ of propositions, each proposition of which has a probability. Another possible approach is to assume a probability measure on a given Boolean algebra of propositions and thereby induce a probability measure on the models of that Boolean algebra. Still another way is to assume a probability measure on the models of a given Boolean algebra and induce a measure on the associated propositions. For the latter approach see P. Calabrese [3].

Now it is known that not every Boolean algebra admits a probability measure P. Nor does every σ-algebra $\mathfrak{B}$ admit a probability measure P. These pathological cases will not be discussed here. Suffice it to say that if a Boolean algebra is finite or at least atomic then there is no problem establishing a probability measure on it.

Equivalence of Conditional Propositions: Having defined conditional propositions as indicator functions, the equivalence of two conditional propositions is easy to define:

Definition 3: Two conditional propositions $(q|p)$ and $(s|r)$ are equivalent, i.e. $(q|p) = (s|r)$, if and only if they are equal as indicator functions, that is, if and only if they have the same domain and are equal on this common domain.

Theorem 1: Two conditionals $(q|p)$ and $(s|r)$ are equivalent if and only if they have equivalent premises and their conclusions are equivalent in conjunction with that premise. That is, $(q|p) = (s|r)$ if and only if $p = r$ and $qp = sr$.

Proof of Theorem 1: By definition $(q|p) = (s|r)$ if and only if they are functionally equal. The common domain of the indicator functions $(q|p)$ and $(s|r)$ is $p^{-1}(1)$ and $r^{-1}(1)$. So $p = r$. The subset of $p^{-1}(1)$ on which $(q|p)$ equals 1 is $[q^{-1}(1)]\ [p^{-1}(1)] = \{\omega \in \Omega$: $q(\omega) = 1$ and $p(\omega) = 1\} = \{\omega \in \Omega: (qp)(\omega) = 1\} = (qp)^{-1}(1)$. Similarly, the subset of $r^{-1}(1)$ on which $(s|r)$ is 1 is $(sr)^{-1}(1)$. Since these subsets are equal, $qp = sr$. Conversely, if $p = q$ and $qp = sr$ then $(q|p)$ and $(s|r)$ have the common domain $p^{-1}(1)$. Furthermore, on $p^{-1}(1)$, which is also $r^{-1}(1)$, $(q|p)(\omega) = q(\omega) = q(\omega)\ p(\omega) = (qp)(\omega)$. Similarly, on $r^{-1}(1)$, $(s|r)(\omega) = (sr)(\omega)$. But $qp = sr$. So $(q|p) = (s|r)$.

The equivalence class of conditional propositions containing the conditional proposition $(q|p)$ is $\{(s|r) \in L/L: (s|r) = (q|p)\} = \{(s|r): r = p \text{ and } sr = qp\} = \{(s|p): sp = qp\}$. and may be denoted $<q|p>$, or when there is no ambiguity simply as $(q|p)$. This class or coset of propositions is the set of all domain-restricted indicator functions which agree with q on the subset $p^{-1}(1)$, where p is has the value 1. The coset $<p|p>$ containing $(p|p)$ is just $\{(s|r) \in L/L: (s|r) = (p|p)\} = \{(s|p): sp = p\}$.

Note that the conditionals $\{(q|0): q \in L\}$ form an equivalence class of wholly undefined conditionals --- conditionals that have impossible premises. Note also that for every conditional proposition $(q|p)$, $(q|p) = (qp|p)$.

Definition 4: A conditional proposition $(q|p)$ is said to be in reduced form if $qp = p$.

Note that if $(q|p)$ is in reduced form, then $P(q|p) = P(q)/P(p)$.

It is instructive to note that in general 2 events A, B (or propositions p, q) generate $2^2 = 4$ nonempty atomic events {AB, AB', A'B, A'B'} and $2^4 = 16$ non-equivalent subsets of these atomic events, and $3^4 = 81$ non-equivalent conditional events (conditional propositions) --- all from just two initial binary variables! (For a proof that the number of non-equivalent conditionals is 3^N, where N is the number of atomic events, see [3], p. 225.) Starting with 4 propositions, $2^{16} = 65{,}536$ non-equivalent propositions and $3^{16} = 43{,}046{,}721$ non-equivalent conditional propositions may be generated!

Operating with Undefined Conditionals: The Boolean operations can be extended in various ways to the domain-restricted indicator functions (i.e. to the conditional propositions) depending upon how one regards the effect of undefined conditionals in combination with defined conditionals.

In this paper a conditional that is undefined for a particular ω will (for that ω) have no effect upon any other conditional with which it may be disjoined or conjoined or which it may condition. That is, if $(s|r)(\omega)$ is undefined then $(s|r)(\omega)$ acts like an operational identity with respect to disjunction, conjunction and when acting as a premise. Furthermore, when acting as a conclusion, such a conditional results in an undefined conditional no matter what the premise. This corresponds to the usual way people handle inapplicable conditionals in practice. These assumptions can be expressed succinctly as follows:

Axioms of Conditional Probability Logic: Let c be an arbitrary conditional proposition and let d be a conditional proposition that is undefined on ω, i.e., $d = (s|r)$ where $r(\omega) = 0$:

$$\begin{aligned} (d(\omega))' &= d(\omega) \\ c(\omega) \vee d(\omega) &= c(\omega) \\ c(\omega)\, d(\omega) &= c(\omega) \\ c(\omega) \mid d(\omega) &= c(\omega) \\ d(\omega) \mid c(\omega) &= d(\omega) \end{aligned} \tag{8}$$

With this understanding, (also see Dubois & Prade [20]), the extensions of the three operations to conditionals takes the following natural functional form:

Definition 5: For arbitrary conditionals $(q|p)$ and $(s|r)$,

$$\begin{aligned} [(q|p) \vee (s|r)](\omega) &= (q|p)(\omega) \vee (s|r)(\omega) \\ [(q|p) \wedge (s|r)](\omega) &= [(q|p)(\omega)] \wedge [(s|r)(\omega)] \\ [(q|p)'](\omega) &= ((q|p)(\omega))' \end{aligned} \tag{9}$$

Theorem 2: In terms of a single conditional of the original propositions q, p, s, and r, these three operations become:

$$\begin{aligned} (q|p) \vee (s|r) &= (qp \vee sr) \mid (p \vee r) \\ (q|p)(s|r) &= [(q \vee p')(s \vee r')] \mid (p \vee r) \\ (q|p)' &= (q'|p) \end{aligned} \tag{10}$$

Proof of Theorem 2: The result follows by using the equations 4, 5 and 9 to express $(q|p)(\omega)$ and $(s|r)(\omega)$ in terms of the original unconditioned propositions q, p, s, & r, and then collecting cases. For instance, the formula for disjunction goes as follows:

$$[(q|p) \vee (s|r)](\omega) = (q|p)(\omega) \vee (s|r)(\omega) \tag{11}$$

$$= \begin{cases} (q|p)(\omega) \vee (s|r)(\omega), & \text{if } (q|p)(\omega) \text{ and } (s|r)(\omega) \text{ are defined,} \\ (q|p)(\omega), & \text{if } (s|r)(\omega) \text{ is undefined,} \\ (s|r)(\omega), & \text{if } (q|p)(\omega) \text{ is undefined} \end{cases} \tag{12}$$

$$= \begin{cases} q(\omega) \vee s(\omega), & \text{if } p(\omega) = 1 \text{ and } r(\omega) = 1, \\ q(\omega), & \text{if } p(\omega) = 1 \text{ and } r(\omega) = 0, \\ s(\omega), & \text{if } p(\omega) = 0 \text{ and } r(\omega) = 1, \\ \text{undefined}, & \text{if } p(\omega) = 0 \text{ and } r(\omega) = 0 \end{cases} \tag{13}$$

$$= \begin{cases} (qp)(\omega) \vee (sr)(\omega), & \text{if } p(\omega) = 1 \text{ or } r(\omega) = 1, \\ \text{undefined}, & \text{if } p(\omega) = 0 \text{ and } r(\omega) = 0 \end{cases} \tag{14}$$

$$= \begin{cases} (qp \vee sr)(\omega), & \text{if } (p \vee r)(\omega) = 1, \\ \text{undefined}, & \text{if } (p \vee r)(\omega) = 0 \end{cases} \tag{15}$$

$$= [(qp \vee sr) \mid (p \vee r)](\omega). \tag{16}$$

Note, for instance, that if $(s|r)(\omega)$ is undefined, i.e. when $r(\omega) = 0$, then $(q|p)(\omega) \vee (s|r)(\omega) = (q|p)(\omega)$.

With the operations of "and" (juxtaposition or $\wedge$), "or" ($\vee$) and "not" (') the set L/L of ordered pairs $(q|p)$ of propositions includes an isomorphic copy of the original Boolean algebra of propositions according to the identification

$$(p|1) \rightarrow p, \tag{17}$$

and for any fixed non-zero proposition p, the conditionals $\{(q|p)\text{: all } q \in L\}$ form a Boolean algebra, which will be denoted $\mathcal{L}/p$. But it is not true that as a whole L/L together with these three operations forms a Boolean algebra. More on this later.

While the above formula for the disjunction ($\vee$) of two conditionals is given in reduced form, the formulas for the other two operations are not. In reduced form these other two become

$$\begin{aligned} (q|p)(s|r) &= (qpr' \vee p'sr \vee qpsr) \mid (p \vee r) \\ (q|p)' &= (q'p \mid p) \end{aligned} \tag{18}$$

De Morgan's Laws for Conditionals: It is interesting to note that De Morgan's formulas have a counterpart here:

Theorem 3:

$$\begin{aligned} [(q|p) \vee (s|r)]' &= (q|p)' \wedge (s|r)' \\ [(q|p) \wedge (s|r)]' &= (q|p)' \vee (s|r)' \end{aligned} \tag{19}$$

Proof of Theorem 3: $[(q|p) \vee (s|r)]' = [(qp \vee sr) \mid (p \vee r)]' = (qp \vee sr)' \mid (p \vee r) = (qp)'(sr)' \mid (p \vee r) = (q' \vee p')(s' \vee r') \mid (p \vee r) = (q'|p) \wedge (s'|r) = (q|p)' \wedge (s|r)'$ using that $(p')' = p$. That proves the first formula. Using the first formula the dual formula follows: $[(q|p) \wedge (s|r)]' = [(q'|p)' \wedge (s'|r)']' = [[(q'|p) \vee (s'|r)]']' = (q'|p) \vee (s'|r) = (q|p)' \vee (s|r)'$.

With respect to priority of operations, when parentheses are omitted, negation (') takes precedence and then conjunction (juxtaposition or $\wedge$) and then disjunction ($\vee$) and then conditioning (|). Thus $(sr \mid q \vee p')$ means $(sr) \mid (q \vee (p'))$.

The Conditional Closure: To obtain closure of operations in L/L, the conditioning process must be extended to the ordered pairs themselves --- to conditional conditionals. These are of the form $(q|p) \mid (s|r)$. [Those of the mixed forms, $((q|p) \mid s)$ and $(q \mid (s|r))$ for propositions q, p, s, and r, can be expressed as $(q|p) \mid (s|1)$ and $(q|1) \mid (s|r)$ respectively.]

Definition 6: For arbitrary conditionals $(q|p)$ and $(s|r)$, define

$$[(q|p) \mid (s|r)](\omega) = (q|p)(\omega) \mid (s|r)(\omega) \tag{20}$$

The following result reduces a conditional conditional to a single conditional of the original propositions.

Theorem 4: For arbitrary conditionals $(q|p)$ and $(s|r)$

$$(q|p) \mid (s|r) = q \mid (p(s \vee r')). \tag{21}$$

Proof of Theorem 4: As with the proof of the other operations above, the result follows by using the definition of $(q|p)(\omega)$ to express $(q|p)(\omega)$ and $(s|r)(\omega)$ in terms of the original unconditioned propositions q, p, s, & r, and then collecting and rephrasing the cases:

$$[(q|p) \mid (s|r)](\omega) = \begin{cases} (q|p)(\omega), & \text{if } (s|r)(\omega) \neq 0, \\ \text{undefined}, & \text{if } (s|r)(\omega) = 0 \end{cases} \tag{22}$$

$$= \begin{cases} (q|p)(\omega), & \text{if } (s|r)(\omega) = 1, \\ (q|p)(\omega), & \text{if } (s|r)(\omega) \text{ is undefined}, \\ \text{undefined}, & \text{if } (s|r)(\omega) = 0 \end{cases} \tag{23}$$

$$= \begin{cases} (q|p)(\omega), & \text{if } s(\omega) = 1 \text{ and } r(\omega) = 1, \\ (q|p)(\omega), & \text{if } r(\omega) = 0, \\ \text{undefined}, & \text{if } s(\omega) = 0 \text{ and } r(\omega) = 1 \end{cases} \tag{24}$$

$$= \begin{cases} (q|p)(\omega), & \text{if } s(\omega) \vee r'(\omega) = 1, \\ \text{undefined}, & \text{if } s(\omega) \vee r'(\omega) = 0 \end{cases} \tag{25}$$

$$= \begin{cases} (q|p)(\omega), & \text{if } (s \vee r')(\omega) = 1, \\ \text{undefined}, & \text{if } (s \vee r')(\omega) = 0 \end{cases} \tag{26}$$

$$= \begin{cases} q(\omega), & \text{if } [p(s \vee r')](\omega) = 1, \\ \text{undefined}, & \text{if } [p(s \vee r')](\omega) = 0 \end{cases} \tag{27}$$

$$= [q \mid p(s \vee r')](\omega). \tag{28}$$

Note that when the premise conditional (s|r) is undefined (i.e. r = 0) it has no effect on the conclusion conditional (q|p).

Corollary to Theorem 4: Applying the above theorem to the mixed form cases mentioned above yields:

$$((q|p) \mid s) = (q \mid ps) \tag{29}$$
$$(q \mid (s|r)) = (q \mid (s \vee r'))$$

Note that as a condition (s|r) is equivalent to (q $\vee$ p').

The collection L/L of all conditional propositions under the four operations "and" (juxtaposition or $\wedge$), "or" ($\vee$), "not" (') and "given" (|) forms a closed system that the author has called the conditional closure of the Boolean logic $\mathfrak{L}$. The conditional closure will formally be denoted $\mathfrak{L}/\mathfrak{L}$.

Since $\mathfrak{L}/\mathfrak{L}$ is closed, compound conditional expressions can be reduced to simple conditionals of Boolean functions, which have well-defined conditional probabilities.

Truth Value Representation: The above development can be expressed in terms of 3-valued truth tables for conditional propositions (or restricted indicator functions). That is, for any fixed $\omega \in \Omega$, a conditional proposition is either true (1), or false (0) or undefined (U). This contrasts from the 2-valued propositions that arise from the characteristic functions of the various events in $\mathfrak{B}$. These 2-valued propositions are either true in ω or false in ω and always defined in ω.

Note that a particular conditional proposition may be true in some ω, false in other ω and undefined in still other ω. It is not accurate (except in a categorical Boolean algebra) to say without regard to a particular ω that each conditional proposition (q|p) is either true, false or undefined.

Note also that the third truth value is designated U for "undefined" not U for "uncertain". Perhaps this value is best expressed as "inapplicable". It is not a value between 0 and 1; it is a completely separate value.

The truth tables for the operations on conditional propositions (q|p) and (s|r) easily follow by considering all possible assignments of T, F, and U (1, 0 and Undefined) to the initial propositions and then applying the operations on conditionals:

	AND	(s|r)(ω) T	F	U
(q|p)(ω)	T	T	F	T
	F	F	F	F
	U	T	F	U

	OR	(s|r)(ω) T	F	U
(q|p)(ω)	T	T	T	T
	F	T	F	F
	U	T	F	U

NOT	T	F	U
	F	T	U

	GIVEN	(s|r)(ω) T	F	U
(q|p)(ω)	T	T	U	T
	F	F	U	F
	U	U	U	U

It can be seen that with an appropriate extension of the functions max and min to include the additional domain value U, "or" corresponds to max, and "and" corresponds to min.

Algebraic Properties of $\mathcal{L}/\mathcal{L}$: While $\mathcal{L}/\mathcal{L}$ contains many Boolean algebras, it is not itself a Boolean algebra. In particular, $\mathcal{L}/\mathcal{L}$ is not wholly distributive. Nor does it in general have absolute complements. Furthermore there are no absolute units except the wholly undefined conditional (1|0). For instance, $(q|p) \wedge 1 = q \vee p' \neq (q|p)$ unless $p = 1$. For an elaboration on these matters see [3], p. 226-7.

Another interesting algebraic consequence of the conditional closure operations in $\mathcal{L}/\mathcal{L}$ is "non-monotonicity" [34]. Unlike the situation in a Boolean algebra, it is not true that the disjunction of two statements is necessarily entailed by each of the two component statements. If this seems strange consider the following example of a compound conditional: "If the store has Pepsi then buy Pepsi or if the store doesn't have Pepsi then buy Coke" The intent of the compound statement is to impose a double constraint. That is, if the store has Pepsi then I need only buy Pepsi for the compound conditional to be true. But if the store doesn't have Pepsi and does have Coke then the Coke must be bought to satisfy the compound conditional. Without the conditional about Coke I would only need to purchase Pepsi if the store has it for the statement to be true, nothing being said in case of no Pepsi at the store. Thus the disjunction of two conditionals (with mutually inconsistent premises) is false when I fail to satisfy each separate conditional when it applies.

It turns out that when the premises of two conditionals are disjoint it doesn't matter whether the conditionals are disjoined or conjoined! The result is the same in English and in the conditional closure algebra. More on this later.

Probability in $\mathcal{L}/\mathcal{L}$: Since complex conditional expressions can be reduced in $\mathcal{L}/\mathcal{L}$ to a single conditional of Boolean expressions, they all have an implied conditional probability. For the disjunction of any two conditional propositions $(q|p)$ and $(s|r)$, the probability can be determined according to the following formula:

Theorem 5: For any conditional propositions $(q|p)$ and $(s|r)$, $P(p) \neq 0 \neq P(r)$,

$$P((q|p) \vee (s|r)) = P(p \mid p \vee r)\, P(q|p) + P(r \mid p \vee r)\, P(s|r) - P(qpsr \mid p \vee r)$$

Note that for $p = r$, this reduces to the ordinary probability of a disjunction.

Proof of Theorem 5: $P((q|p) \vee (s|r)) = P(qp \vee sr \mid p \vee r)$

$$\begin{aligned}
&= P(qp \mid p \vee r) + P(sr \mid p \vee r) - P(qpsr \mid p \vee r)\\
&= P((q|p) \mid p \vee r)\, P(p \mid p \vee r) + P((s|r) \mid p \vee r)\, P(r \mid p \vee r) - P(qpsr \mid p \vee r)\\
&= P(q \mid p(p \vee r))\, P(p \mid p \vee r) + P(s \mid r(p \vee r))\, P(r \mid p \vee r) - P(qpsr \mid p \vee r)\\
&= P(q|p)\, P(p \mid p \vee r) + P(s|r)\, P(r| p \vee r) - P(qpsr \mid p \vee r).
\end{aligned}$$

There is also a non-trivial formula for $P((q|p) \wedge (s|r))$:

Theorem 6: Under the hypothesis of the preceding theorem,

$$P((q|p) \wedge (s|r)) = P(p \mid p \vee r)\, P(q'r'|p) + P(r \mid p \vee r)\, P(sp'|r) + P(qpsr \mid p \vee r).$$

Proof of Theorem 6: $P((q|p) \wedge (s|r)) = P(qpr' \vee srp' \vee qpsr \mid p \vee r)$

$$\begin{aligned}
&= P(qpr' \mid p \vee r) + P(srp' \mid p \vee r) + P(qpsr \mid p \vee r)\\
&= P(p \mid p \vee r)\, P((qr'|p)|(p \vee r)) + P(r \mid p \vee r)\, P((sp'|r)|(p \vee r)) + P(qpsr \mid p \vee r)\\
&= P(p \mid p \vee r)\, P(qr'| p(p \vee r)) + P(r \mid p \vee r) P(sp'| r(p \vee r)) + P(qpsr| p \vee r)\\
&= P(p \mid p \vee r)\, P(qr'|p) + P(r \mid p \vee r)\, P(sp'|r) + P(qpsr \mid p \vee r).
\end{aligned}$$

Note that the last term of the formulas of the last two theorems, namely $P(qpsr \mid p \vee r)$, can be expressed as $P(pr \mid p \vee r)\, P(qs \mid pr)$.

In view of the very large sample spaces associated with even a small number of variables, it is not practical to attempt to enumerate possibilities and calculate probabilities and conditional probabilities from scratch. Formulas like those of Theorems 5 and 6 allowing local calculation of conditional probabilities via partitions are essential for practical determination of conditional probabilities in artificial intelligence applications.

3. Varieties of Deduction

Deduction in $\mathcal{L}$. In a Boolean algebra $\mathcal{L}$, one proposition may (necessarily) imply a second proposition. In the simplest case the truth of a proposition such as $(p \vee 1)$ is implied by the Boolean algebra axioms, which of course, are true in all models ω of $\mathcal{L}$. For instance the truth of $(p \vee 1)$ follows from the laws of complements, associativity and idempotency: $p \vee 1 = p \vee (p \vee p') = (p \vee p) \vee p' = p \vee p' = 1$. In terms of indicator functions, $(p \vee 1)(\omega) = 1$ for all $\omega \in \Omega$. That is, $(p \vee 1)$ is the unity function on Ω. The truth of $(p \vee 1)$ can also be expressed using the following familiar partial ordering on $\mathcal{L}$.

Definition 7: $p \le q$ if and only if $pq = p$.

With this definition it is easy to show the following equivalent form:

$$p \le q \text{ if and only if } p \vee q = q. \tag{30}$$

If $p \le q$ holds, we say p entails (necessarily implies) q. In terms of $\le$ the fact that $(p \vee 1)$ is always true (= 1) can be expressed as $1 \le (p \vee 1)$ and $(p \vee 1) \le 1$. In this way axioms and theorems of the form $p = q$ can all be expressed in terms of $\le$:

$$p = q \text{ if and only if } p \le q \text{ and } q \le p. \tag{31}$$

In terms of indicator functions, $(p \le q)$ is just functional inequality in the 2-element Boolean algebra. That is, $(p \le q)$ means $p(\omega) \le q(\omega)$, for all $\omega \in \Omega$, where $0 \le 1$. Note that if $p \le q$ then easily $q' \le p'$ and for any proposition r, $pr \le qr$ and $(p \vee r) \le (q \vee r)$. The converses are also true. In addition $p \le q$ if and only if $pq' = 0$.

Besides the two equivalent forms given above expressing "p entails q", there are at least two other ways to express $p \le q$:

$$p \le q \text{ if and only if } q \vee p = 1 \tag{32}$$

and

$$p \le q \text{ if and only if } (q|p) = (1|p) \tag{33}$$

The first statement follows because if $p \le q$ then $q = p \vee q$. So $q \vee p' = (p \vee q) \vee p' = 1$. Conversely, if $q \vee p' = 1$ then $(q \vee p')p = (1)(p)$. So $qp \vee p'p = p$. Thus $qp = p$. So $p \le q$.

The second statement follows because if $p \le q$ then $pq = p$. So $(q|p) = (qp|p) = (p|p) = (1|p)$. Conversely, if $(q|p) = (1|p)$ then $qp = (p)(1)$. That is, $qp = p$. So $q \le p$.

According to the definition of equivalent conditionals, the proposition q is equivalent to p in the Boolean algebra $\mathcal{L}/p$ if and only if $(q|p) = (p|p)$, that is, if and only if $qp = p$, which is just $p \le q$. Thus, in $\mathcal{L}/p$, q is equivalent to p if and only if q is entailed by p. We say that q is in the equivalence class generated by p. In other terminology, q is said to be in the *filter class* generated by p or in the *sum ideal* generated by p. This is the equivalence class $<p|p> = \{q \in L: p \le q\}$. Thus, still another way to express "p entails q" is to say that q is in the sum ideal generated by p.

Deduction in $\mathcal{L}/\mathcal{L}$: Unlike the situation existing in $\mathcal{L}$ it is not true that the following two potential definitions for entailment are equivalent in $\mathcal{L}/\mathcal{L}$:

Definition 8 (Conjunctive Implication): $(q|p)$ conjunctively implies $(s|r)$, denoted $(q|p) \le_\wedge (s|r)$, if and only if $(q|p) \wedge (s|r) = (q|p)$. That is,

$$(q|p) \le_\wedge (s|r) \quad \text{if and only if} \quad (q|p) \wedge (s|r) = (q|p)$$

Definition 9 (Disjunctive Implication): $(q|p)$ disjunctively implies $(s|r)$, denoted $(q|p) \le_\vee (s|r)$, if and only if $(q|p) \vee (s|r) = (s|r)$. That is,

$$(q|p) \le_\vee (s|r) \quad \text{if and only if} \quad (q|p) \vee (s|r) = (s|r)$$

In fact if the properties of both definitions hold then, as will be shown below, $p = r$ and $qp \le sr$. Thus the situation reduces to the special case of equal premises, i.e., $q \le s$ on the subset on which p (and r) are true.

In this restricted context of *equivalent premises*, p and r, there are various equivalent ways to express "(q|p) entails (s|p)" including: $(q|p) \le (s|p)$, $(q|p) \le_\vee (s|p)$, $(q|p)' \vee (s|p) = (1|p)$, and $(s|p)|(q|p) = 1|(q|p)$. These are all equivalent to the statement $qp \le sp$. Yet another way to express this is $(s|p) \in <q|p>$, that $(s|p)$ is in the filter class (sum ideal) generated by $(q|p)$. Each of these facts follow in a few steps. Yet it turns out that none of the first four relations are equivalent when the premises of the conditionals are not equivalent!

While $\le_\wedge$ and $\le_\vee$ are not equivalent in $\mathcal{L}/\mathcal{L}$, they do both constitute partial orderings:

Theorem 7: Both $\le_\wedge$ and $\le_\vee$ establish partial orderings on $\mathcal{L}/\mathcal{L}$.

Proof of Theorem 7: The proof follows by routine application of the operations to show reflexivity, antisymmetry and transitivity. For example, reflexivity of $\leq_\wedge$ follows from $(q|p) \wedge (q|p) = [(q \vee p')(q \vee p')] \mid (p \vee p) = [(q \vee p') \mid p] = [(qp \vee p'p) \mid p] = [(qp \vee 0) \mid p] = (qp|p) = (q|p)$.

The following two theorems express the inequalities $(q|p) \leq_\wedge (s|r)$ and $(q|p) \leq_\vee (s|r)$ in terms of the partial ordering on the original propositions.

Theorem 8: $(q|p) \leq_\wedge (s|r)$ if and only if $r \leq p$ and $qp \leq sr \vee r'$.

Corollary to Theorem 8: $(q|p) \leq_\wedge (s|r)$ if and only if $r \leq p$ and $qr \leq sr$.

Theorem 9: $(q|p) \leq_\vee (s|r)$ if and only if $p \leq r$ and $qp \leq sr$.

Corollary to Theorem 9: $(q|p) \leq_\vee (s|r)$ if and only if $p \leq r$ and $qp \leq sp$

Proof of Theorem 8: Suppose $(q|p) \leq_\wedge (s|r)$. Therefore $(q|p)(s|r) = (q|p)$. Then $(qpr' \vee p'sr \vee qpsr \mid p \vee r) = (q|p) = (qp|p)$. So $p \vee r = p$ and $qpr' \vee p'sr \vee qpsr = qp$. From $p \vee r = p$ it follows that $r \leq p$. So $rp' = 0$. Combining these results yields $qp = qpr' \vee p'sr \vee qpsr = qpr' \vee 0 \vee qps = qp(r' \vee s) = qp(r' \vee sr)$. Thus $qp \leq (sr \vee r')$. Conversely, if $(r \leq p)$ and $(qp \leq sr \vee r')$, then $qp = qp(r' \vee sr) = qpr' \vee qpsr = qpr' \vee 0 \vee qpsr = qpr' \vee p'sr \vee qpsr$. Therefore $(q|p) = (qp|p) = (qp \mid p \vee r) = (qpr' \vee p'sr \vee qpsr \mid p \vee r) = (q|p)(s|r)$.

To prove the Corollary to Theorem 8, note that if $(r \leq p)$ and $(qp \leq sr \vee r')$, then $qpr \leq (sr \vee r')r$. So $qr \leq sr$. Conversely, if $(r \leq p)$ and $(qr \leq sr)$, then $qrp \leq srp = sr$. So $qp = qpr \vee qpr' \leq sr \vee qpr' \leq sr \vee r'$.

Proof of Theorem 9: Suppose $(q|p) \leq_\vee (s|r)$. That is, $(q|p) \vee (s|r) = (s|r)$. Therefore $(qp \vee sr \mid p \vee r) = (s|r) = (sr|r)$. So, $p \vee r = r$ and $qp \vee sr = sr$. So $p \leq r$ and $qp \leq sr$. Conversely, if $p \leq r$ and $qp \leq sr$, then $p \vee r = r$ and $qp \vee sr = sr$. So $(s|r) = (sr|r) = (qp \vee sr \mid p \vee r) = (q|p) \vee (s|r)$. That is, $(q|p) \leq_\vee (s|r)$.

To prove the corollary to Theorem 9 note that if $p \leq r$ and $qp \leq sr$ then $qpp \leq srp = sp$. So $qp \leq sp$. Conversely, if $qp \leq sp$ and $p \leq r$ then $qp \leq sp \leq sr$.

Note that as a consequence of Theorem 8 it turns out that $(q \vee p') \leq_\wedge (q|p)$ since $p \leq 1$ and $(q \vee p')p \leq qp$.

Non-Monotonicity of Deduction: As appealing as this definition of entailment seems, it nevertheless appears at first to have a serious flaw, namely: If $(q|p) \leq_\wedge (s|r)$ then it does not follow that $P(q|p) \le P(s|r)$. This issue was brought to the attention of the author by H. T. Nguyen and it also appears in Dubois and Prade [20], both suggesting that a deduction relation is inappropriate as an entailment relation in $\mathcal{L}/\mathcal{L}$ unless it is monotonic in the sense that if $(q|p)$ entails $(s|r)$ then $P(q|p)$ should not be greater than $P(s|r)$. But $\le_\wedge$ does not satisfy this relation:

For example, let $p = 1$, $P(q) = 1/2$, $r = q'$ and $s = q$. Then easily $(q|p) \le_\wedge (s|r)$ but $P(q|p) = 1/2$ while $P(s|r) = 0$. In fact, $(q \vee p') \le_\wedge (q|p)$ but it was shown earlier that $P(q|p) \le P(q \vee p')$, not the other way around. Nevertheless, in thinking about conditional logic and probability one must be flexible with one's conclusions. One must be "non-monotonic" in one's thinking! It might at first seem obvious that $(q|p) \le_\wedge (s|r)$ should imply $P(q|p) \le P(s|r)$. The idea comes swiftly to the mind and just as quickly to the tongue, but is it really so reasonable as a general rule?

Upon second thought, it seems to the author to be rather questionable whether one should insist that whenever one conditional (with its own premise and probability of application) entails a second conditional (with its own premise and probability of application) then their conditional probabilities must be so ordered. Rather, in the propagation of conditional probabilities through a network of logically related conditional propositions, one must perhaps allow for increasing *or decreasing* conditional probabilities. A similar observation can be made for $\le_\vee$. For instance let $0 < P(q) < 1$. Then $(q|q) \le_\vee (q|1)$, i.e., $(q|q)$ disjunctively implies $(q|1)$ because $q \le 1$ and $qq \le (q)1$. However $P(q|1) = P(q) < 1 = P(q|q)$.

In its initial formulation *non-monotonicity* [34] arises from the observation in probability theory that $P(q \mid p \wedge r)$ can be less, more or equal to $P(q|p)$ even though $p \wedge r$ entails p. The lack of monotonicity of $\le_\wedge$ is also well exhibited by considering the two forms $(q|p)$ and $(q \vee p')$. As shown earlier $P(q|p) \le P(q \vee p')$, but it is also true that $(q \vee p') \le_\wedge (q|p)$. On the other hand it is also easy to show that $(q|p) \le_\vee (q \vee p')$.

Nevertheless, if $(q|p) \le_\wedge (s|r)$ then it has been shown that $qp \le sr \vee r'$. That is, whenever $(q|p)$ is true then either $(s|r)$ is true or else r is false. It will later be shown that if $(q|p) \le_\wedge (s|r)$ then $(q \vee p') \le (s \vee r')$ and so $P(q|p) \le P(q \vee p') \le P(sr \vee r')$. That is, if $(q|p) \le_\wedge (s|r)$ then $P(q|p) \le P(sr \vee r')$.

On the other hand, it is not even true in general that if $(q|p) \le_\vee (s|r)$ then $P(q|p) \le P(sr \vee r')$. For instance, let $0 \ne q = p \le s \ne 1 = r$. So $(q|p) \le_\vee (s|r)$. However $P(q|p) = 1 > P(sr \vee r') = P(s)$.

In addition to $\leq_{\wedge}$ and $\leq_{\vee}$ there are at least two other candidates for expressing the notion that an arbitrary conditional (q|p) entails a second arbitrary conditional (s|r). The following two definitions formalize these relations:

Definition 10 (Conditional Implication): (q|p) conditionally implies (s|r), denoted $(q|p) \leq_c (s|r)$, if and only if (s|r) is true given (q|p). That is,

$$(q|p) \leq_c (s|r) \quad \text{if and only if} \quad (s|r)|(q|p) = (1|r)|(q|p).$$

Definition 11 (Material Implication): (q|p) materially implies (s|r), denoted $(q|p) \leq_m (s|r)$, if and only if either (s|r) is true or (q|p) is false. That is,

$$(q|p) \leq_m (s|r) \quad \text{if and only if} \quad (s|r) \vee (q|p)' = (1 \mid r \vee p).$$

The following theorems express these equations in terms of the partial ordering $\leq$ on the original propositions.

Theorem 10: (q|p) conditionally implies (s|r), that is, $(s|r)|(q|p) = (1|r)|(q|p)$ if and only if any one of the following hold:

$$r(q \vee p') \leq s,$$
$$(q \vee p') \leq (s \vee r'),$$
$$rs' \leq pq'.$$

This theorem gives three equivalent ways of expressing the equation $(s|r)|(q|p) = (1|r)|(q|p)$, that (q|p) conditionally implies (s|r): $r(q \vee p') \leq s$ means that if the premise r of the conclusion is true and the premise conditional, (q|p), is not false then the conclusion s is true. $q \vee p' \leq s \vee r'$ means if the premise conditional is not false then the conclusion conditional is not false. $rs' \leq pq'$ means that if the conclusion conditional is false then the premise conditional is false.)

Proof of Theorem 10: Suppose $(q|p) \leq_c (s|r)$. Then $(s|r)|(q|p) = [s \mid r(q \vee p')]$ and $(1|r)|(q|p) = [1 \mid r(q \vee p')]$. So $sr(q \vee p') = r(q \vee p')$. Therefore $r(q \vee p') \leq s$. By reversing the steps the converse follows. The 2nd and 3rd relations of Theorem 10 follow since $r(q \vee p') \leq s$ if and only if $r(q \vee p')s' = 0$ if and only if $rs' \leq (q \vee p')' = pq'$. In addition, $r(q \vee p')s' = 0$ if and only if $(q \vee p') \leq (rs')' = (s \vee r')$.

Here again conditional implication ($\leq_c$) is non-monotonic in the sense that $(q|p) \leq_c (s|r)$ does not imply $P(q|p) \leq P(s|r)$. For instance, let p = 1, s = q, and r = q' with $0 < P(q) < 1$. Then $(q|p) \leq_c (s|r)$ since $q \vee p' = q$ and $s \vee r' = q$. But $P(q|p) = P(q) > 0 = P(s|r)$.

For $\leq_c$ it is true that both $(q|p) \leq_c (q \vee p')$ and $(q \vee p') \leq_c (q|p)$ but clearly, $(q|p) \neq (q \vee p')$. Two propositions may conditionally imply each other without being equivalent. Nevertheless, as is so for both $\leq_\wedge$ and $\leq_m$, if $(q|p) \leq_c (s|r)$ then $P(q|p) \leq P(sr \vee r')$. That is, if $(q|p) \leq_c (s|r)$ then the probability that $(q|p)$ is true is less than or equal to the probability that $(s|r)$ is true or undefined.

The following theorem and its corollaries give three equivalent ways to express that $(q|p)$ materially implies $(s|r)$, i.e., that $(q|p) \leq_m (s|r)$.

Theorem 11: $(s|r) \vee (q|p)' = (1 \mid r \vee p)$ if and only if

$$qp \leq sr \text{ and } r(q \vee p') \leq s.$$

Proof of Theorem 11: $(s|r) \vee (q|p)' = (1 \mid r \vee p)$ if and only if $(sr \vee q'p \mid r \vee p) = (1 \mid r \vee p)$ if and only if $sr \vee q'p = r \vee p$. Multiplying the last equation by qp yields $srqp = rqp \vee qp = qp$. So $qp \leq sr$. Furthermore, multiplying the equation $sr \vee q'p = r \vee p$ by $s'r$ yields $0 \vee q'ps'r = s'r \vee ps'r = s'r$. So $s'r \leq q'p$. So $s'r(q'p)' = 0$. So $s'r(q \vee p') = 0$. Therefore $r(q \vee p') \leq s$. That completes one direction of the proof. Conversely, if $qp \leq sr$ and $r(q \vee p') \leq s$, then $s'r(q \vee p') = 0$. That is, $s'r \leq (q \vee p')' = q'p$. So $qp \leq sr$ and $s'r \leq q'p$. therefore, $sr \vee q'p = (sr \vee qp) \vee (q'p \vee s'r) = (qp \vee q'p) \vee (sr \vee s'r) = p \vee r$. So $sr \vee q'p = r \vee p$. This completes the proof of Theorem 11.

As before the second inequality can be expressed in several ways:

Corollary to Theorem 11: $(s|r) \vee (q|p)' = (1 \mid r \vee p)$ if and only if either of the following hold:

$$qp \leq sr \text{ and } (q \vee p') \leq (s \vee r'),$$
$$qp \leq sr \text{ and } rs' \leq pq'.$$

Clearly from the last two theorems, the statement "(s|r) is true given (q|p) is true" (conditional implication) is weaker than the statement that "either (s|r) is true or (q|p) is false" (material implication).

It is important here as before to determine whether $(q|p) \leq_m (s|r)$ implies $P(q|p) \leq P(s|r)$. It was I. R. Goodman [22] who first proved this result as well as its more difficult converse; H. Prade & D Dubois [20] have also made this observation. The following proof is offered without the requirement of atomicity of the Boolean Algebra $\mathcal{L}$.

Theorem 12: Let a, b, c, and d be four propositions of $\mathcal{L}$. If $P(a|b) \leq P(c|d)$ for every probability measure P on $\mathcal{L}$ for which $P(b) \neq 0 \neq P(d)$ then either $(a|b) \leq_m (c|d)$ or (ab = 0) or (d ≤ c). Conversely, if either (a|b) $\leq_m$ (c|d) or (ab = 0) or (d ≤ c) in $\mathcal{L}/\mathcal{L}$ then P(a|b) ≤ P(c|d).

Proof of Theorem 12: Prove the converse first: If (ab = 0) or (d ≤ c) then easily P(a|b) ≤ P(c|d) since either P(a|b) = 0 or P(c|d) = 1. Otherwise, ab ≤ cd and c'd ≤ a'b. Then P(a|b) = P(ab)/P(b) = P(ab)/[P(ab) + P(a'b)] = 1/[1 + P(a'b)/P(ab)] ≤ 1/[1 + P(c'd)/P(cd)] = P(cd)/[P(cd) + P(c'd)] = P(c|d), which proves the converse. Now suppose that neither (ab = 0) nor (d ≤ c) is true. So ab ≠ 0 and c'd ≠ 0. Now in any case

$$ab = abcd \vee abc'd \vee abcd' \vee abc'd' \tag{34}$$

and

$$c'd = abc'd \vee a'bc'd \vee ab'c'd \vee a'b'c'd \tag{35}$$

Note that in these expansions, only (abc'd) is common to both. The conjunction of any other pair of propositions is 0. Thus any assignment of non-negative probabilities to these seven propositions whose sum is 1 determines a probability measure P on the subalgebra generated by a,b,c and d for which P(b) ≠ 0 ≠ P(d). It will be shown that all but abcd and a'bc'd must be 0 and that the latter must not be 0. Suppose first that the common proposition abc'd ≠ 0. Then assign it probability weight 1. In this case P(b) ≥ P(ab) ≥ P(abc'd) = 1 but P(cd) = P(d) - P(c'd) = 1 - 1 = 0. So P(a|b) = 1 but P(c|d) = 0, which is a contradiction. Next suppose either abcd' or abc'd' is not 0. In this case assign it probability weight 1/2 and assign c'd probability 1/2. Therefore P(ab) ≥ 1/2 but P(cd) = P(d) - P(c'd) = 1/2 - 1/2 = 0. So P(a|b) ≥ 1/2 but P(c|d) = 0, which is again a contradiction. Therefore 0 ≠ ab = abcd. So ab ≤ cd. Next suppose either ab'c'd or a'b'c'd is not 0. In that case assign it probability weight 1/2 and assign abcd probability 1/2. Then P(ab) = 1/2 and P(b) = 1/2 but P(cd) = P(d) - P(c'd) = 1 - 1/2 = 1/2. So P(a|b) = 1 but P(c|d) = 1/2, again a contradiction. Therefore 0 ≠ c'd = a'bc'd. So c'd ≤ a'b. This completes the proof. *(See Editors' Note at the end of this paper.)*

In view of the preceding, since (p)(q|p) ≤ (r)(s|r) is equivalent to pq ≤ sr, having the latter relation together with (q|p) $\leq_c$ (s|r), which is equivalent to s'r ≤ q'p, yields that P(q|p) ≤ P(s|r). If instead of (q|p) $\leq_c$ (s|r), one has (q|p) $\leq_\vee$ (s|r), then again one has (q|p) $\leq_m$ (s|r), and so again P(q|p) ≤ P(s|r) as well as p ≤ r.

The following two theorems and the corollary relate conjunctive and conditional implication:

Theorem 13: If (q|p) $\leq_\wedge$ (s|r) then (q ∨ p') ≤ (s ∨ r'). That is, conjunctive implication implies conditional implication.

Corollary to Theorem 13: If $(q|p) \leq_{\wedge} (s|r)$ then $P(q|p) \leq P(q \vee p') \leq P(s \vee r')$.

Theorem 14: If $(q \vee p') \leq (s \vee r')$ and $r \leq p$ then $(q|p) \leq_{\wedge} (s|r)$. That is, with $(r \leq p)$ conditional implication implies conjunctive implication.

Proofs of Theorems 13 and 14: If conjunctive implication holds then $r \leq p$ and $qr \leq sr$. So $p' \leq r'$. So $q \vee p' = qp \vee p' \leq sr \vee p' \leq sr \vee r' = s \vee r'$. Therefore, $q \vee p' \leq s \vee r'$, which completes the proof of Theorem 13. The corollary is obvious. For Theorem 14, if $(q \vee p') \leq (s \vee r')$ and $r \leq p$ then $qp \leq qp \vee p' = q \vee p' \leq s \vee r' = sr \vee r'$. So $qp \leq sr \vee r'$. Therefore $(q|p) \leq_{\wedge} (s|r)$ by Theorem 8.

While conditional implication is weaker than both conjunctive implication and material implication, conditional implication is not weaker than disjunctive implication. Nor is disjunctive implication weaker than conditional implication. Concerning the relationship between disjunctive and conditional implication there are the following theorems:

Theorem 15: If $(q|p) \leq_{c} (s|r)$ and $p \leq r$ then $(q|p) \leq_{\vee} (s|r)$.

Theorem 16: If $(q|p) \leq_{\vee} (s|r)$ and $p' \leq s \vee r'$ then $(q|p) \leq_{c} (s|r)$.

Proofs of Theorems 15 and 16: For Theorem 15, suppose $(q \vee p') \leq (s \vee r')$ and $p \leq r$. So $(q \vee p')p \leq s \vee r')p$. That is, $qp \leq sp \vee r'p = sp \vee 0 = sp$. So $qp \leq sp$. Therefore $(q|p) \leq_{\vee} (s|r)$. For Theorem 16, suppose $(q|p) \leq_{\vee} (s|r)$ and $p' \leq s \vee r'$. Therefore $q \vee p' = qp \vee p' \leq sp \vee p' \leq s \vee p' = s \vee (s \vee r') = s \vee r'$. That is, $q \vee p' \leq s \vee r'$. So $(q|p) \leq_{c} (s|r)$. This completes the proof of Theorem 16.

Entailment in $\mathcal{L}/\mathcal{L}$: And so it seems that there are different entailments for different situations and most do not impose monotonicity of conditional probability.

From the preceding results it is easy to see the following relationships:

If $(q|p) \leq_{m} (s|r)$ and $r \leq p$ then $(q|p) \leq_{\wedge} (s|r)$ (36)
If $(q|p) \leq_{\wedge} (s|r)$ and $qp \leq sr$ then $(q|p) \leq_{m} (s|r)$ and $r \leq p$

If $(q|p) \leq_{m} (s|r)$ and $p \leq r$ then $(q|p) \leq_{\vee} (s|r)$ (37)
If $(q|p) \leq_{\vee} (s|r)$ and $(q|p) \leq_{c} (s|r)$ then $q|p) \leq_{m} (s|r)$ and $p \leq r$

If $(q|p) \leq_{\wedge} (s|r)$ and $p \leq r$ then $(q|p) \leq_{\vee} (s|r)$ and $p = r$ (38)
If $(q|p) \leq_{\vee} (s|r)$ and $r \leq p$ then $(q|p) \leq_{\wedge} (s|r)$ and $p = r$

If $(q|p) \leq_{m} (s|r)$ then $(q|p) \leq_{c} (s|r)$ (39)
If $(q|p) \leq_{c} (s|r)$ and $qp \leq sr$ then $(q|p) \leq_{m} (s|r)$

It is interesting to note that $\leq_\wedge$, $\leq_\vee$ and $\leq_m$ generate lattices in $\mathcal{L}/\mathcal{L}$ but $\leq_c$ is not a partial ordering because it fails to be antisymmetric.

Nevertheless, $\leq_c$ is a quasi-ordering ([25], p. 4). Of course by equating all conditionals for which $\leq_c$ holds in both directions, a partial ordering arises. However this entails making $(q|p)$ and $(q \vee p')$ equivalent, which is not desirable except when both are certain. The following theorem gives three ways to express the fact that two conditional propositions are equivalent.

Theorem 17: $(q|p) = (s|r)$ if and only if any one of the following are true:

$$(q|p) \leq_\wedge (s|r) \text{ and } (s|r) \leq_\wedge (q|p),$$
$$(q|p) \leq_\vee (s|r) \text{ and } (s|r) \leq_\vee (q|p),$$
$$(q|p) \leq_m (s|r) \text{ and } (s|r) \leq_m (q|p).$$

Proof of Theorem 17: Clearly, if both $(q|p) \leq_\wedge (s|r)$ and $(s|r) \leq_\wedge (q|p)$ then $r \leq p$ and $qr \leq sr$, and $p \leq r$ and $sp \leq qp$. So $p = r$ and $qp \leq sr$, and $sr \leq qp$. So $p = r$ and $qp = sr$. So $(q|p) = (s|r)$. The converse is also easy. Similarly for $\leq_\vee$. Next, if both $(q|p)' \vee (s|r) = (1 \mid p \vee r)$ and $(s|r)' \vee (q|p) = (1 \mid p \vee r)$ then using the Corollary to Theorem 11, $qp \leq sr$, $sr \leq qp$, $s'r \leq q'p$ and $q'p \leq s'r$. So $qp = sr$ and $s'r = q'p$. So $r = sr \vee s'r = qp \vee q'p = p$. Therefore $(q|p) = (s|r)$. Conversely, if $(q|p) = (s|r)$, then $qp = sr$ and $p = r$. So both $qp \leq sr$ and $sr \leq qp$. Therefore, $s'r = s'(q \vee q')r = s'qr \vee s'q'r = s'qp \vee s'q'p = s'(sr) \vee s'q'p = 0 \vee s'q'p \leq q'p$. So $s'r \leq q'p$. By symmetry, $q'p \leq s'r$. So $s'r = q'p$. This completes the proof.

Theorem 18: The conditional closure $\mathcal{L}/\mathcal{L}$ is a lattice under the partial ordering $\leq_\wedge$, where the least upper bound (LUB) and greatest lower bound (GLB) are given by

$$\text{LUB}_\wedge\ (q|p,s|r) = (q \vee s) \mid (pr) = (qp \vee sr) \mid (pr),$$

$$\text{GLB}_\wedge\ (q|p,s|r) = [(q \vee p')(s \vee r')] \mid (p \vee r) = (q|p) \wedge (s|r).$$

Proof of Theorem 18: Firstly, $(q \vee s)|(pr)$ is an upper bound of $(q|p)$ because $pr \leq p$ and $q(pr) \leq (q \vee s)pr$, using the Corollary to Theorem 8. By symmetry $(q \vee s)|(pr)$ is also an upper bound of $(s|r)$. Now if $(t|u)$ is any upper bound of both $(q|p)$ and $(s|r)$ then both $u \leq p$ and $u \leq r$. So $u \leq pr$. By the Corollary, both $qu \leq tu$ and $su \leq tu$. Therefore $(q \vee s)u = qu \vee su \leq tu \vee su \leq tu \vee tu = tu$. Thus $(q \vee s \mid u) \leq_\wedge (t|u)$. But $(q \vee s \mid pr) \leq_\wedge (q \vee s \mid u)$. So by transitivity of $\leq_\wedge$, $(q \vee s \mid pr) \leq_\wedge (t|u)$. Therefore $(q \vee s \mid pr)$ is the LUB of $(q|p)$ and $(s|r)$.

To show that $(q|p) \wedge (s|r) = [(q \vee p')(s \vee r')] \mid (p \vee r)$ is the GLB of $(q|p)$ and $(s|r)$, first note that both $p \leq p \vee r$ and $r \leq p \vee r$. Furthermore, $(q \vee p')(s \vee r')p = (qp \vee 0)(s \vee r') = qp(s \vee r') \leq qp$. Similarly, $(q \vee p')(s \vee r')r = (q \vee p')(sr \vee 0) \leq sr$. Therefore $(q \vee p')(s \vee r') \mid (p \vee r)$ is a lower bound for $(q|p)$ and $(s|r)$. Now if $(t|u)$ is any lower bound of $(q|p)$ and $(s|r)$ then both $p \leq u$ and $r \leq u$, and so $(p \vee r) \leq u$. Furthermore, since both $tp \leq qp$ and $tr \leq sr$, then both $t \leq q \vee p'$ and $t \leq s \vee r'$. This follows from $t = tp \vee tp' \leq qp \vee tp' \leq qp \vee p' = q \vee p'$ and $t = tr \vee tr' \leq sr \vee tr' \leq sr \vee r' = s \vee r'$. Therefore, $t \leq (q \vee p')(s \vee r')$. Thus $(t|u) \leq_{\wedge} (t \mid p \vee r) \leq_{\wedge} (q \vee p')(s \vee r') \mid (p \vee r)$ because $(p \vee r) \leq u$ and $(p \vee r)t \leq (p \vee r)(q \vee p')(s \vee r')$. This completes the proof of Theorem 18.

Theorem 19: $\mathcal{L}/\mathcal{L}$ is a lattice under the partial ordering $\leq_{\vee}$ where the $LUB_{\vee}$ and $GLB_{\vee}$ are given by

$$LUB_{\vee}\ (q|p,s|r) = (q|p) \vee (s|r) = (qp \vee sr)|(p \vee r),$$

$$GLB_{\vee}\ (q|p,s|r) = (qs|pr).$$

Proof of Theorem 19: $(qs|pr)$ is a lower bound of $(q|p)$ and $(s|r)$ because $pr \leq p$ and $pr \leq r$, and because $(qs)(pr) \leq qp$ and $(qs)(pr) \leq sr$. Now if $(t|u)$ is any lower bound of $(q|p)$ and $(s|r)$, then $u \leq p$, $u \leq r$, $tu \leq qp$ and $tu \leq sr$. Therefore $(t|u) \leq_{\vee} (qs|pr)$ because $u \leq pr$ and $tu \leq (qp)(sr)$. This completes the GLB part of the proof. $(qp \vee sr \mid p \vee r)$ is an upper bound of $(q|p)$ and $(s|r)$ because $p \leq p \vee r$ and $r \leq p \vee r$, and because $qp \leq (qp \vee sr)(p \vee r) = qp \vee sr$, and similarly, $sr \leq qp \vee sr$. Now if $(t|u)$ is any upper bound of $(q|p)$ and $(s|r)$, then $p \leq u$, $r \leq u$, $qp \leq tu$ and $sr \leq tu$. Therefore $(qp \vee sr \mid p \vee r) \leq_{\vee} (t|u)$ because $p \vee r \leq u$ and $(qp \vee sr)(p \vee r) = qp \vee sr \leq tu$. This completes the proof.

While disjunctive implication establishes a full lattice in $\mathcal{L}/\mathcal{L}$, it doesn't appear to be universally appropriate for purposes of entailment. For instance consider the two conditionals $(p|p)$ and $(p|1)$ where $p \neq 1$. Then clearly $(p|p) \leq_{\vee} (p|1)$. But $(p|p)$ is certain or undefined whereas $(p|1)$ is just p, and so is uncertain and possibly improbable but it is wholly defined. Nevertheless, $\leq_{\vee}$ is appropriate in some circumstances.

Theorem 20: Material implication $(\leq_m)$ establishes a partial ordering on $\mathcal{L}/\mathcal{L}$.

Proof of Theorem 20: $(q|p) \leq_m (q|p)$ since $(q|p) \vee (q|p)' = (q|p) \vee (q'|p) = (1|p) = (1 \mid p \vee p)$. So $\leq_m$ is reflexive. If $(q|p) \leq_m (s|r)$ and $(s|r) \leq_m (q|p)$ then $qp \leq sr$ and $q \vee p' \leq s \vee r'$, $sr \leq qp$ and $s \vee r' \leq q \vee p'$. So $qp = sr$ and $q \vee p' = s \vee r'$. So $qp = sr$ and $q'p = s'r$. So $q = qp \vee qp' = sr \vee s'r = r$. Therefore $(q|p) = (s|r)$. So $\leq_m$ is antisymmetric. Next for transitivity: If $qp \leq sr$ and $sr \leq tu$, and $q \vee p' \leq s \vee r'$ and $s \vee r' \leq t \vee u'$, then $qp \leq tu$ and $q \vee p' \leq t \vee u'$. So $(q|p) \leq_m (t|u)$. So $\leq_m$ is transitive.

Theorem 21: $\mathcal{L}/\mathcal{L}$ is a lattice under the partial ordering $\leq_m$, where the LUB_m and GLB_m are given by

$$LUB_m\ (q|p,s|r) = (qp \vee sr) \mid (qp \vee sr \vee pr),$$
$$GLB_m\ (q|p,s|r) = (qpsr) \mid (qpsr \vee pq' \vee rs').$$

Proof of Theorem 21: Denoting $(qp \vee sr) \mid (qp \vee sr \vee pr)$ by $(t|u)$, it is clear that $(q|p) \leq_m (t|u)$ and $(s|r) \leq_m (t|u)$ since firstly, $qp \leq qp \vee sr = tu$ and similarly $sr \leq tu$, and furthermore $q \vee p' = qp \vee p' \leq qp \vee sr \vee p' \vee r' = qp \vee sr \vee (pr)' = (qp \vee sr) \vee (qp \vee sr)'(pr)' = (qp \vee sr) \vee [(qp \vee sr) \vee pr]' = t \vee u'$; so $q \vee p' \leq t \vee u'$ and similarly $s \vee r' \leq t \vee u'$. Thus $(t|u)$ is an upper bound of both $(q|p)$ and $(s|r)$. Now if $(x|y)$ is any upper bound of both $(q|p)$ and $(s|r)$ it must be shown that $(x|y)$ is also an upper bound of $(t|u)$. Since $(x|y)$ is an upper bound of $(q|p)$, $qp \leq xy$ and $qp \vee p' \leq xy \vee y'$. Similarly $sr \leq xy$ and $sr \vee r' \leq xy \vee y'$. Therefore $tu = qp \vee sr \leq xy$. Furthermore, $(qp \vee p') \vee (sr \vee r') \leq xy \vee y'$. But the left side of this latter inequality is $(qp \vee sr) \vee p' \vee r' = (qp \vee sr) \vee (pr)' = (qp \vee sr) \vee (qp \vee sr)'(pr)' = (qp \vee sr) \vee (qp \vee sr \vee pr)' = t \vee u'$. So $t \vee u' \leq xy \vee y'$. Therefore $(t|u) \leq_m (x|y)$. Thus $(t|u) = LUB_m\ (q|p,s|r)$.

Next, denoting $(qpsr \mid qpsr \vee pq' \vee rs')$ by $(t|u)$, it is clear that $(t|u)$ is a lower bound of both $(q|p)$ and $(s|r)$ because $tu = qpsr \leq qp$ and similarly $tu \leq sr$, and furthermore because $tu \vee u' = qpsr \vee (qpsr \vee pq' \vee rs')' = qpsr \vee (qpsr)'(pq' \vee rs')' = qpsr \vee (pq' \vee rs')' = qpsr \vee (q \vee p')(s \vee r') \leq q \vee (q \vee p') = q \vee p' = qp \vee p'$; and similarly $tu \vee u' \leq sr \vee r'$. Now if $(x|y)$ is any lower bound of both $(q|p)$ and $(s|r)$, then $xy \leq qp$, $xy \vee y' \leq qp \vee p'$, $xy \leq sr$ and $xy \vee y' \leq sr \vee r'$. So $xy \leq (qp)(sr) = tu$. Furthermore, $xy \vee y' \leq (qp \vee p')(sr \vee r') = (q \vee p')(s \vee r')$ and $tu \vee u' = qpsr \vee (qpsr \vee pq' \vee rs')' = qpsr \vee (qpsr)'(pq' \vee rs')' = qpsr \vee (q \vee p')(s \vee r')$. So $xy \vee y' \leq tu \vee u'$. Therefore $(x|y) \leq_m (t|u)$. Thus $(t|u) = GLB_m\ (q|p,s|r)$. This completes the proof of Theorem 21.

The LUB_m and GLB_m of material implication turn out to be the very operations of disjunction and conjunction derived by I. R. Goodman and H. T. Nguyen [22] by different methods and with somewhat different goals. While these operations have their application, they do not appear to be appropriate for purposes of *general* probability logic. For instance, consider the experiment of rolling a single die once. The compound proposition "if the roll is even then it will be a six or if the roll is odd it will be a five" reduces by the Goodman/Nguyen operations to "if the roll is five or six then it will be five or six", which, of course, is certain and so has conditional probability 1. In contrast, according to the operations of Theorem 2, this compound conditional reduces to "the roll will be five or six" and has probability 2/6 or 1/3, which corresponds nicely with intuition. See also H. Prade and D. Dubois [20] concerning a comparison of these operations.

As mentioned earlier, still another way to express "p entails q" is to say "q is in the equivalence class (sum ideal, filter class) generated by p". In symbols this is $q \in \langle p \rangle$. Now in a Boolean algebra this relation can be expressed in several equivalent ways including $qp = p$, $q \vee p = q$, $q \vee p' = 1$, and $(q|p) = (1|p)$ corresponding to conjunctive, disjunctive, material and conditional implication respectively. However, as has been shown above, these forms are not equivalent in the conditional closure $\mathcal{L}/\mathcal{L}$ of a Boolean algebra $\mathcal{L}$.

The statement "(q|p) entails (s|r)", when extended to conditionals, then becomes "(s|r) is in the equivalence class of conditionals generated by (q|p)". The trouble here is that before an entailment relation is chosen it is not immediately clear what the meaning is of "the equivalence class of conditionals in $\mathcal{L}/\mathcal{L}$ generated by (q|p)". To clarify this matter there is the following:

Definition 12: The equivalence class $\langle q|p \rangle$ of conditional propositions in $\mathcal{L}/\mathcal{L}$ generated by the conditional proposition (q|p) is

$$\langle q|p \rangle = \{(s|r) : (q|p) \leq_c (s|r)\}.$$

Note that this is equivalent to $\langle q|p \rangle = \{(s|r) : q \vee p' \leq s \vee r'\}$. The equivalence class $\langle q|p \rangle$ generated by (q|p) is the set of all conditional propositions (s|r) which are true given (q|p). That is,

$$(s|r) \in \langle q|p \rangle \quad \text{if and only if} \quad [(s|r)|(q|p)] = [(1|r)|(q|p)], \tag{40}$$

where the right hand side is just another way of writing $(q|p) \leq_c (s|r)$.

Note that it follows from Definition 12 that the conditionals (q|p) and (0|pq') and the simple proposition $(q \vee p')$, which is equal to $(q \vee p' \mid 1)$, all generate the same equivalence class in $\mathcal{L}/\mathcal{L}$, namely $\langle q \vee p' \rangle$. If this seems strange recall that these conditionals are equivalent only when they are wholly true, i.e. certain, not when they are merely possible, i.e., having a non-zero probability.

In view of all the foregoing it appears that entailment of conditionals by conditionals is fairly well described in $\mathcal{L}/\mathcal{L}$ by conditional implication ($\leq_c$) even though the lack of anti-symmetry means that conditional implication in both directions is not the same as equivalence of two conditionals. As mentioned previously, $\mathcal{L}/\mathcal{L}$ is quasi-ordered by $\leq_c$ because $\leq_c$ is reflective and transitive.

Since conjunctive implication ($\leq_\wedge$) and material implication ($\leq_m$) individually imply conditional implication, these are stronger forms of entailment than conditional implication. Different circumstances will dictate which kind of implication to use.

To end this section on the recurring issue of non-monotonicity, consider a conditional (q|p) and its contrapositive (p'|q'). As pointed out by the author in [3], pp. 221-2, these two conditionals are equivalent when either is wholly true but otherwise they don't even have the same probability: It is easy to show that if $p \leq q$ then $q' \leq p'$ and conversely. Furthermore a conditional (q|p) conditionally implies its contrapositive (p'|q'):

Theorem 22: $(q|p) \leq_c (p'|q')$

Proof of Theorem 22: $(p'|q') \mid (q|p) = (p' \mid q'(q \vee p')) = (p' \mid q'p') = (1 \mid q'p') = (1 \mid q'(q \vee p')) = (1|q') \mid (q|p)$. So by definition, $(q|p) \leq_c (p'|q')$.

In addition, $P(q|p) = P(p'|q')$ if either is 1. But the conditional probability of a conditional is less than or equal to the conditional probability of its contrapositive if and only if either the corresponding premises or conclusions are so ordered in probability. To make this precise there is the following:

Theorem 23: Suppose $P(p) \neq 0 \neq P(q')$. Then $P(q|p) = 1$ if and only if $P(p'|q') = 1$. Otherwise, $P(q|p) \leq P(p'|q')$ if and only if $P(p) \leq P(q')$ if and only if $P(q) \leq P(p')$.

Proof of Theorem 23: In [3], p.222, it is shown that

$$P(p'|q') = P(q|p) + [1 - P(p)/P(q')]\ [1 - P(q|p)] \tag{41}$$

Clearly, if $P(q|p) = 1$ then so is $P(p'|q') = 1$. By symmetry the converse is also true. Furthermore, $P(q|p) \leq P(p'|q')$ if and only if the product of the brackets is non-negative. Since $[1 - P(q|p)] \geq 0$, this is true if and only if $[1 - P(p)/P(q')] \geq 0$, i.e., if and only if $P(p) \leq P(q')$. So $P(q) \leq P(p')$ using $P(p) = 1 - P(p')$ and $P(q') = 1 - P(q)$.

It is important to realize that in any model in which (q|p) is not false, i.e. not both p true and q false, it is also true that (p'|q') is not false, i.e. not both q' is true and p' is false. However, the fact that these conditionals may be undefined (have truth value U) allows their conditional probabilities to be ordered in either way.

The combining of logic with probability is fraught with the danger of contaminating absolute (certain) information with partially true information, with absolute nonsense being the result. For instance, it is known with certainty (by definition) that "if an animal is a penguin then it is a bird" and it is also known with very high probability that "if an randomly chosen animal is a bird then it will fly". Therefore one might conclude with high probability that "if an animal is a penguin then it will fly." Such examples should give pause to those who would cavalierly fuse data with suboptimal techniques.

References

1. Russell, B. and Whitehead, A. N. (1913) *Principia Mathematica,* Cambridge U. Press.
2. Calabrese, P. G. (Ap 1975) The Probability that p Implies q (preliminary report), *Notices American Mathematical Society* 22(3): A430-A431.
3. Calabrese, P. G. (1987) An Algebraic Synthesis of the Foundations of Logic and Probability, *Information Sciences* **42**, 187-237.
4. Cheeseman, P. (1985) In Defense of Probability, *International Conference on Artificial Intelligence*, Los Angeles, 1002-1009.
5. Zadeh, L. A. (1985) Syllogistic Reasoning in Fuzzy Logic and its Application to Usuality and Reasoning with Dispositions, *IEEE Transactions on Systems, Man, and Cybernetics,* Vol SMC-15, No. 6.
6. Pearl, J. (1988) *Probabilistic Reasoning in Intelligent Systems: Networks of Plausible Inference*, Morgan Kaufman, San Mateo.
7. Shafer, G. (1976) *A Mathematical Theory of Evidence*, Princeton University Press.
8. Hailperin, T. (1976) *Boole's Logic and Probability,* North-Holland.
9. Mazurkiewicz, S. (1932) Zur Axiomatik der Wahrscheinlichkeitslehre, *Comptes rendus des séances de la Société des sciences et des Lettres de Varsovie*, Classe III, Vol 25, pp 1-4.
10. Mazurkiewicz, S. (1934) Über die Grundlagen der Wahrscheinlichkeitsrechnung, Monatshefte für Mathematik und Physik, Vol 41, pp 343-352.
11. Mazurkiewicz, S. (1956) *Podstawy Rachunku Prawdopodobienstwa* (The Foundations of the Calculus of Probability) Monografie Matematyczne, Vol. 32, Panstwowe Wydawnietwo Naukowe, Warszawa.
12. Tarski, A. (1935-36) Wahrscheinlichkeitslehre und Mehrwertige Logik, *Erkenntnis* **5**:174-175.
13. Tarski, A. (1956) *Logic, Semantics, Metamathe-matics --- Papers from 1923 to 1938*, Oxford.
14. De Finetti, B. (1972) *Probability, Induction and Statistics*, Wiley, New York.
15. Rosenbloom, P. (1950) *The Elements of Mathematical Logic,* Dover.
16. Schay, G. (1968) An Algebra of Conditional Events, *Journal of Mathematical Analysis and Applications* **24**, 334-344.

17. Rescher, N. (1969) *Many-Valued Logics*, McGraw-Hill, New York.
18. Sobocinski, B (See Rescher, 1969).
19. Adams, E. W. (1975) *The Logic of Conditionals: An Application of Probability to Deductive Logic*, Reidel, Boston.
20. Dubois, D. and Prade, H. (1990) The Logical View of Conditioning and Its Application to Possibility and Evidence Theories, *International Journal of Approximate Reasoning*, **4**:23-46.
21. Goodman, I. R. (to appear in 1991) Evaluation of Combinations of Conditional Information: I, a History, accepted for publication in *Information Sciences*.
22. Goodman, I. R., Nguyen, H. T. and Walker, E. A., . (to appear in 1991) *Conditional Inference and Logic for Intelligent Systems: A Theory of Measure-Free Conditioning*, accepted for publication by North-Holland.
23. Goodman, I. R., Gupta, M. M., Nguyen, H. T. and Rogers, G. S., eds. (this volume)
24. Lewis, C. I. and Langford, C. H. (1932; 2nd. ed., 1959) *Symbolic Logic*, Century, New York.
25. Birkhoff, G. (1948) *Lattice Theory*, American Mathematical Society Colloquium Publications.
26. Chang, C. C. and Keisler, H. J. (1973; 2nd. ed. 1977) *Model Theory*, North-Holland.
27. Hailperin, T. (1984) Probability Logic, *Notre Dame J. of Formal Logic* 25(3):198-212.
28. Kolmogorov, A. N. (1956; 1st edition 1933: *Grundbegriffe der Wahrscheinlichkeitsrechnung*, Berlin) *Foundations of the Theory of Probability*, Chelsea.
29. Boole, G. (1940; 1st ed., Macmillan, 1854) *An Investigation of the Laws of Thought on which are Founded the Mathematical Theories of Logic and Probabilities*, Open Court.
30. Carnap, R. (1960; 1st ed., 1950) *Logical Foundations of Probability* 2nd. ed., Univ. of Chicago Press.
31. Carnap, R. & Jeffrey, R. C. (1971) *Studies in Inductive Logic and Probability*, Univ. of California Press.
32. Gaifman, H. (1964) Concerning Measures in First Order Calculi, *Israel J. Math.* 2:1-18.
33. Scott, D. and Kraus, P. (1966) Assigning Probabilities to Logical Formulas, in *Aspects of Inductive Logic* , J. Hintikki and P. Suppes, eds., 219-264.
34. Reinfrank, M., de Kleer, J., Ginsberg, M. L. and Sandewell, E., eds. (1988) *Non-monotonic Reasoning*, Proceedings of the 2nd International Workshop, Grassau, FRG, in *Lecture Notes in Artificial Intelligence*, 346, J. Siekmann, ed., Springer-Verlag.

Editors' note: In the proof of Theorem 12 above, the existence of a consistent probability assignment P over *all* $\mathcal{L}$, when $P(\alpha)$ is given for some non-trivial $\alpha \in \mathcal{L}$ was assumed; a proof of this can be found in [22], Chapter 2 .

Conditional Logic in Expert Systems
I.R. Goodman, M.M. Gupta, H.T. Nguyen and G.S. Rogers (editors)

A SIMPLE LOOK AT CONDITIONAL EVENTS

Elbert A. Walker

Department of Mathematical Sciences
New Mexico State University
Las Cruces, NM 88003

Abstract An algebra of "conditional events" is developed, with this algebra playing the role for conditonal events that Boolean algebras play for ordinary events. The primary purpose is to present some of the theory of Goodman, Nguyen, and Walker in [1] in a simpler and more concise fashion, and with a different motivation for the operations defined on the set of conditional events.

Keywords Conditional events, Boolean algebras, probability measures, Stone algebras.

Introduction

The basic item of consideration in this paper is an algebra of "conditional events", with this algebra playing the role for conditional events that Boolean algebras play for ordinary events. If A is a Boolean algebra, for example the algebra of events of some sample space Ω, P is a probability measure on A, and $P(b) \neq 0$, then for any event a, P(a|b), defined to be P(ab)/P(b), is called the "probability of a given b". Now a|b, read "a given b", makes no sense in its own right - it is not an event or any other mathematical entity. But in some applications, such an in AI, there is a need to make sense of a|b and to have logical connectives "and", "or", and "not" for such conditional events, analogous to those for ordinary events. For example, a|b "or" c|d is to be some conditional event e|f, and it would then make sense to ask questions such as "what is the probability of a|b or of c|d"? This question makes no sense in ordinary probability theory. A mathematical model is needed which will legitimize such questions and provide a setting for their answer. This mathematical framework should generalize the theory of Boolean algebras and probability measures on them. Thus the goal is this: provide a mathematical identity for "conditional events" a|b, along with good analogs of union, intersection, and complement for manipulating them, and do it such a way that P(a|b) behaves appropriately with respect to these analogs. Now this, and more, is carried out in [1]. The purpose of this paper is to present some of the theory of that book in a simpler and more concise manner, and particularly with a different motivation for the operations defined on the set of conditional events.

The Space of Conditional Events

The first issue is that of providing a mathematical home for conditional events. What should a conditional event be? One immediate thought is that it should be an event somewhere. In fact, if a and b are events in a probability space and one asks "What is the probability of the event a given the event b?", one may as well take a contained in b, and doing that, there is a new probability space in which a is an event, and in which the answer is "The probability of the event a in that space." To make this precise, let (Ω, A, P) be a probability space. That is, Ω is a set, called the sample space, A is an algebra of subsets of Ω, and P is a probability measure on A. The elements of A are events. Given any b in A for which $P(b) \neq 0$, (b, Ab, P_b) is another probability space. Here $Ab = \{a \cap b : a \in A\}$, and $P_b(a \cap b) = P(a|b)$. Now an event is an element of the Boolean algebra Ab, and it makes sense to define the conditional event a|b to be the event $a \cap b$ *of this latter probability space.* This can be completely specified by the pair ($a \cap b$|b). Summing up, in the setting of the probability space (Ω, A, P), when we ask "What is the probability of a given b?", the answer is "The probability of the event $a \cap b$ in the probability space (b, Ab, P_b)". The conditional event a|b is an event, namely $a \cap b$, but we must keep track of which probability space it is an event of. It should also be understood that we know the master space A of events, from which all our considerations arise.

In [1], a conditional event is defined to be a coset of a principal ideal in a Boolean ring. We prefer to think of a conditional event as just described, that is, as an event in an appropriate probability space. The algebra of conditional events developed in [1] is motivated by the discovery that products, as sets, of cosets of (different) principal ideals of a Boolean ring is again such a coset. (This phenomenon is trivial for the sum of such cosets, but not for the product.) The operations that we will put on conditional events will be motivated by elementary algebraic and probabilistic considerations. The operations between conditional events should satisfy some elementary algebraic properties, and probability should behave properly with respect to these operations. The mathematical models arrived at in the two instances are equivalent - the differences are in points of view. In [1], are extensive discussions and bibliography concerning other efforts along these lines.

More generally, we want to deal just with a Boolean algebra A, not necessarily associated with any sample space, and with no particular probability measure on it. We recall here the various definitions needed.

Definition. A Boolean algebra is a set A with two binary operations $\vee$ and $\wedge$, and a unary operation $'$ which satisfy the following for all a, b, c ε A:

(1) $a \vee a = a$ and $a \wedge a = a$; ($\vee$ and $\wedge$ are idempotent.)

(2) $a \vee b = b \vee a$ and $a \wedge b = b \wedge a$; ($\vee$ and $\wedge$ are commutative.)

(3) $(a \vee b) \vee c = a \vee (b \vee c)$ and $(a \wedge b) \wedge c = a \wedge (b \wedge c)$; ($\vee$ and $\wedge$ are associative.)

(4) $a \vee (b \wedge c) = (a \vee b) \wedge (a \vee c)$ and $a \wedge (b \vee c) = (a \wedge b) \vee (a \wedge c)$; ($\vee$ and $\wedge$ distribute over each other.)

(5) $a \vee (a \wedge b) = a$ and $a \wedge (a \vee b) = a$; (These are the absorption identities.)

(6) There are elements 0 and 1 in A such that $0 \vee a = a$ and $1 \wedge a = a$; ($\vee$ and $\wedge$ have identities.)

(7) For each element a in A, $a \wedge a' = 0$ and $a \vee a' = 1$; (Each element in A has a complement, or A is complemented, or ortho-complemented, or $'$ is a complementation operator on A.)

It can be verified that the identities are unique, and each element a has only one complement a'. For the latter, if b and c are complements of a, that is, if $a \wedge b = 0$ and $a \vee b = 1$, and if $a \wedge c = 0$ and $a \vee c = 1$, then

$$b = b \wedge 1 = b \wedge (a \vee c) =$$
$$(b \wedge a) \vee (b \wedge c) = 0 \vee (b \wedge c) = b \wedge c, \text{ and}$$
$$c = c \wedge 1 = c \wedge (a \vee b) = c \wedge b,$$

whence $c = b$. Also, $'$ satisfies DeMorgan's laws:

(8) $(a \vee b)' = a' \wedge b'$ and $(a \wedge b)' = a' \vee b'$.

For the first equality,

$$(a \vee b) \wedge (a' \wedge b') = (a \wedge (a' \wedge b')) \vee (b \wedge (a' \wedge b')) = 0 \vee 0 = 0.$$

Similarly $(a \vee b) \vee (a' \wedge b') = 1$, whence $a' \wedge b' = (a \vee b)'$. The second equality likewise follows.

There is a partial order relation on A given by $a \leq b$ if $a \wedge b = a$. This makes A into a Boolean lattice, with sup and inf defined by $a \vee b$ and $a \wedge b$, respectively. We forego the details here, referring the reader to [2].

A Boolean algebra can be made into a ring by defining multiplication to be $\wedge$ and defining + by $a + b = (a \wedge b') \vee (a' \wedge b)$. The resulting ring is a called a Boolean ring, and from it the original Boolean algebra is recovered by the equality $a \vee b = a + b + ab$, making the study of Boolean algebras and Boolean rings equivalent. The generic example of a Boolean algebra is the set of all subsets of a given set, with $\wedge$ defined to be intersection, and $\vee$ to be union. Our concern here will be with Boolean algebras in preference to Boolean rings.

The elements of A will be thought of as events, and called so from time to time. The operation $\wedge$ will be called "intersection" or "disjunction" or "multiplication", and in fact $a \wedge b$ will usually be written simply as ab. The operation $\vee$ will be called "union" or "conjunction". Given b in A, Ab = {ab : a in A} is a subalgebra of A, in fact is a Boolean algebra in its own right. For an element a of Ab, we define the conditional event a|b to be simply the pair (a,b). Note that we require that $a \leq b$ in the usual sense of Boolean algebras that ab = a. If a is also in Ad and $b \neq d$, then the conditional events a|b and a|d are not the same. A conditional event is a **pair**, an event a along with its identification b of what space of events it is from.

Definition. Let A be a Boolean algebra. The space $\mathscr{C}(A)$ of conditional events of A is the set $\{(a,b) : a, b \in A, a \leq b\}$.

Note that we have allowed b to be 0 in the definition above. This is for technical reasons having to do with the operations that will be defined subsequently on $\mathscr{C}(A)$.

A calculus of these conditional events, that is, analogs on $\mathscr{C}(A)$ of the Boolean algebra operations of intersection, union, and complement, must extend the operations on ordinary, or unconditional, events. Such events are, of course the conditional events a|1. More generally, the operations on conditional events with the same antecedent should be the ordinary operations in Boolean algebras. For example, the union of a|b and c|b should be $(a \vee c)|b$. The hard question is that of properly defining the operations between conditional events with different antecedents, such as the operation $(a|b) \vee (c|d)$ when $b \neq d$. Our point of view is that the operations should satisfy some elementary algebraic and probabilistic properties demanded by intuition. Probabilistic considerations enter because for any probability measure P on A, we automatically have an extension of P to those conditional events a|b in $\mathscr{C}(A)$ for which $P(b) \neq 0$, namely $P(a|b) = P(ab)/P(b)$. In defining $a|b \vee c|d$, for example, the behavior of P with respect to $\vee$ should have some consideration.

Operations on $\mathscr{C}(A)$

Now we will define operations $\vee$, $\wedge$, and $'$ on $\mathscr{C}(A)$ analogous to the operations $\vee$, $\wedge$, and $'$ on A, and in fact, extending those operations. Note that the conditional events a|1 correspond to the ordinary events of A - they are the "unconditional" events. So a copy of A is in $\mathscr{C}(A)$, and we identify A with that copy. More generally, for each $b \in A$, $b \neq 0$, the conditional events of the form a|b are events of the Boolean algebra Ab, so that $\mathscr{C}(A)$ contains copies of all those Boolean algebras of events. Any extension of $\vee$, $\wedge$, and $'$ to $\mathscr{C}(A)$ should respect those inclusions. This means that $\vee$, $\wedge$, and $'$ on $\mathscr{C}(A)$ must satisfy the following:

(1) For $b \in A$, $a|b \vee c|b = (a \vee c)|b$ and $(a|b) \wedge (c|b) = ac|b$;

(2) $(a|b)' = a'b|b$, where the latter $'$ means complement in A.

Thus there is only one choice for $'$ on $\mathscr{C}(A)$, so there is no further problem there. Our problem is with extensions of $\vee$ and $\wedge$ to $\mathscr{C}(A)$ which satisfy condition (1). Whatever the definition e|f of a|b $\vee$ c|d or of a|b $\wedge$ c|d is, e and f are functions of a, b, c and d. These elements a, b, c, and d are elements of the Boolean algebra A, and the most natural means at our disposal to manipulate them are as elements of A. Thus we require that these functions to be Boolean combinations of them, that is, Boolean polynomials of a, b, c, and d. Further, this is compatible with requirement (1). In any case, we demand the following:

(3) $a|b \vee c|d = \alpha(a,b,c,d)|\beta(a,b,c,d)$, and $a|b \wedge c|d = \gamma(a,b,c,d)|\delta(a,b,c,d)$, where α, β, γ, and δ are Boolean polynomials.

From now on, by extensions of $\vee$ and $\wedge$ to $\mathscr{C}(A)$, we mean those that satisfy condition (1) and condition (3).

A Boolean polynomial of a, b, c, and d may be written in the form of unions of intersections of a,b,c,d and their complements, that is, in its disjunctive normal form. The minimal such polynomials are of the form uvwx, where u is a or its complement, v is b or its complement, and so on. The polynomial is then the union of some of those minimal polynomials. (0 is the union of the empty set of minimal polynomials.) There are 16 of these minimal polynomials, but since we require that $a \leq b$ and $c \leq d$, they reduce to the following 9:

(A) ac	(B) ac′d	(C) a′bc
(D) ad′	(E) a′bc′d	(F) b′c
(G) a′bd′	(H) b′c′d	(I) b′d′

With no requirements on V, this means that there are 2^9 ways to define α and 2^9 ways to define β, and consequently 2^{18} ways to define V. Similarly, there would be 2^{18} ways to define Λ, and consequently 2^{36} ways to define the combination V and Λ. But we have requirement (1) as well as the requirements that α(a,b,c,d) ≤ β(a,b,c,d) and that γ(a,b,c,d) ≤ δ(a,b,c,d). There are some elementary algebraic properties of V and Λ that are in keeping with the intuitive notion that V means "or" and Λ means "and", and we require them:

(4) a|b V c|d = c|d V a|b and a|b Λ c|d = c|d Λ a|b (V and Λ are commutative);

(5) (a|b V c|d) V e|f = a|b V (c|d V e|f) and (a|b Λ c|d) Λ e|f = a|b Λ (c|d Λ e|f) (V and Λ are associative.

We now see what the possibilities are for V and Λ satisfying the requirements laid down so far. First, a|b V c|b = aVc|b, so α(a,b,c,d) must be aVc when b = d. Which polynomials satisfy that? The disjunctive normal form of aVc is ac V a′bc V b′c V ac′d V ad′, and when b = d this reduces to ac V a′bc V ac′d. This means that the possibilities for α(a,b,c,d) are ac V a′bc V ac′d plus any subset of the other minimal polynomials that are contained in ac V a′bc V ac′d when b = d. Those minimal polynomials are ad′, b′c, a′bd′, and b′c′d. However, the commutativity requirement on V dictates that if ad′ were added, then b′c must be added. Similarly for a′bd′ and b′c′d. Being commutative demands that the form does not change when the roles of a and c and of b and d are interchanged. Here are the possibilities for α(a,b,c,d):

α_1(a,b,c,d) = ac V a′bc V ac′d = ad V bc;
α_2(a,b,c,d) = ac V a′bc V ac′d V ad′ V b′c = a V c;
α_3(a,b,c,d) = ac V a′bc V ac′d V a′bd′ V b′c′d = ad V bc V a′bd′ V b′c′d;
α_4(a,b,c,d) = ac V a′bc V ac′d V ad′ V b′c V a′bd′ V b′c′d = a V c V bd′ V b′d.

Now to β(a,b,c,d). When b = d, β(a,b,c,d) must be bd. The disjunctive form of bd is ac V ac′d V a′bc V a′bc′d. Thus β(a,b,c,d) = ac V ac′d V a′bc V a′bc′d plus any subset of the other minimal polynomials that are contained in bd when b = d. Those other minimal polynomials are b′c, ad′, a′bd′, and b′c′d. Using commutativity of V, we wind up with the following possibilities for β(a,b,c,d):

β_1(a,b,c,d) = ac ∨ ac′d ∨ a′bc ∨a′bc′d = bd;
β_2(a,b,c,d) = ac ∨ ac′d ∨ a′bc ∨ a′bc′d ∨ ad′ ∨ b′c = bd ∨ ad′ ∨ b′c
= bd ∨ a ∨ c;
β_3(a,b,c,d) = ac ∨ ac′d ∨ a′bc ∨ a′bc′d ∨ a′bd′ ∨ b′c′d = bd ∨ a′b ∨ c′d;
β_4(a,b,c,d) = ac ∨ ac′d ∨ a′bc ∨ ad′ ∨ bc′ ∨ a′bc′d ∨ a′bd′ ∨ b′c′d = b ∨ d.

To this point, there are 16 possibilities for the definition of ∨, namely the various $\alpha_i|\beta_j$. But $\alpha_2|\beta_1$, $\alpha_2|\beta_3$, $\alpha_3|\beta_1$, $\alpha_3|\beta_2$, $\alpha_4|\beta_1$, $\alpha_4|\beta_2$, and $\alpha_4|\beta_3$ can be ruled out because α_i must be contained in β_j. Further, $\alpha_1|\beta_2$, $\alpha_1|\beta_3$, $\alpha_1|\beta_4$, and $\alpha_3|\beta_3$, $\alpha_3|\beta_4$, can be ruled out because they do not satisfy the associative law. For these cases, 0|b ∨ (c|1 ∨ d|1) ≠ (0|b ∨ c|1) ∨ d|1. Thus we are left with four possibilities for ∨, namely:

a|b ∨ c|d = $\alpha_1|\beta_1$ = (ad ∨ bc)|bd;
a|b ∨ c|d = $\alpha_2|\beta_2$ = (a ∨ c)|(a ∨ c ∨ bd);
a|b ∨ c|d = $\alpha_2|\beta_4$ = (a ∨ c)|(b ∨ d);
a|b ∨ c|d = $\alpha_4|\beta_4$ = (a ∨ c ∨ bd′ ∨ b′d)|(b ∨ d).

These are of course commutative, having been constructed that way, and it is routine to check that they are associative.

Now to the definition of ∧. Let a|b ∧ c|d = γ(a,b,c,d)|δ(a,b,c,d), with γ and δ being polynomials as α and β were above. When b = d, γ(a,b,c,d) = ac and δ(a,b,c,d) = bd = ac ∨ ac′d ∨ a′bc ∨ a′bc′d. Thus we have the same possibilities for δ as we did initially for β, namely β_1, β_2, β_3, β_4 above. The possibilities for γ are these:

γ_1(a,b,c,d) = ac;
γ_2(a,b,c,d) = ac ∨ ad′ ∨ b′c;
γ_3(a,b,c,d) = ac ∨ a′bd′ ∨ b′c′d = ac ∨ bd′ ∨ b′d;
γ_4(a,b,c,d) = ac ∨ ad′ ∨ b′c ∨ a′bd′ ∨ b′c′d = ac ∨ ad′ ∨ b′c ∨ bd′ ∨ b′d.

The combinations $\gamma_2|\beta_1$, $\gamma_3|\beta_1$, $\gamma_4|\beta_1$, $\gamma_2|\beta_3$, $\gamma_3|\beta_2$, $\gamma_4|\beta_2$, and $\gamma_4|\beta_3$ are ruled out because the γ_i is not contained in the β_j for those. The combinations $\gamma_1|\beta_2$, $\gamma_2|\beta_2$, $\gamma_3|\beta_3$, $\gamma_3|\beta_4$, and $\gamma_4|\beta_4$ are ruled out because they do not satisfy the associative law. For these latter combinations, 0|b ∧ (c|1 ∧ d|1) ≠ (0|b ∧ c|1) ∧ d|1. Thus we are left with four possibilities for ∧, namely

$a|b \wedge c|d = \gamma_1|\beta_1 = ac|bd;$
$a|b \wedge c|d = \gamma_1|\beta_3 = ac|(bd \vee a'b \vee c'd);$
$a|b \wedge c|d = \gamma_2|\beta_4 = (ac \vee ad' \vee b'c)|(b \vee d);$
$a|b \wedge c|d = \gamma_1|\beta_4 = ac|(b \vee d).$

Again, these are of course commutative, having been constructed that way, and it is routine to check that they are associative.

At this point, we make the following observation. We could have arrived at the four possibilities for $\wedge$ in a more elegant manner. For each possibility for $\vee$, we could define a corresponding $\wedge$ by the formula

$$a|b \wedge c|d = ((a|b)' \vee (c|d)')'.$$

It is routine to check that such a $\wedge$ satisfies all the requirements. In fact, the four $\wedge$ so constructed are exactly the four above. Further, a $\wedge$ satisfying all the requirement leads to a $\vee$ satisfying all the requirements. The point is that if we find all the possible $\vee$'s, then with the help of $'$, we have all the $\wedge$'s; or if we find all the $\wedge$'s, then with the help of $'$, we have all the $\vee$'s. Further, DeMorgan's laws hold. In our case, of the four possibilities for $\vee$ and the four possibilities for $\wedge$, it is an easy exercise to check that

$(a|b \vee c|d)' = (a|b)' \wedge (c|d)'$, and
$(a|b \wedge c|d)' = (a|b)' \vee (c|d)'$,

where $\vee$ is the i-th of the four $\vee$'s, and $\wedge$ is the i-th of the four $\wedge$'s. Thus for those four pairs, DeMorgan's laws hold. Of course, DeMorgan's law does not hold for any other of these pairs of $\vee$ and $\wedge$. If DeMorgan's law does hold for a pair $\vee$ and $\wedge$, then if one of the operations is commutative and associative, then so will the other be. Thus knowing that the first $\vee$ is associative gets that the first $\wedge$ is associative. Since the first and fourth $\wedge$ are obviously associative, the first and fourth $\vee$ are associative, and since the third $\vee$ is obviously associative, then the third $\wedge$ is associative. Thus the only associative law needing checking is either the second $\vee$ or the second $\wedge$.

At this point, we have the following theorem.

Theorem 1. Let $\mathscr{C}(A) = \{a|b : a, b \in A, a \leq b\}$ be the space of conditional events of the Boolean algebra A, and let $(a|b)' = a'b|b$. Then there are exactly four ways to extend $\vee$

and ∧ to $\mathscr{C}$(A) so that ∨ and ∧ are commutative and associative, and DeMorgan's laws hold. These four ways are

$$a|b \vee c|d = (ad \vee bc)|bd, \text{ and } a|b \wedge c|d = ac|bd;$$
$$a|b \vee c|d = (a \vee c)|(a \vee c \vee bd), \text{ and } a|b \wedge c|d = ac|(a'b \vee c'd \vee bd);$$
$$a|b \vee c|d = (a \vee c)|(b \vee d), \text{ and } a|b \wedge c|d = (ac \vee ad' \vee b'c)|(b \vee d); \text{ and}$$
$$a|b \vee c|d = (a \vee c \vee bd' \vee b'd)|(b \vee d), \text{ and } a|b \wedge c|d = ac|(b \vee d);$$

As indicated, a consideration in defining these operations on $\mathscr{C}$(A) is the behavior of probabilities with respect to them. For a probability measure P on A, we have P defined on $\mathscr{C}$(A) by P(a|b) = P(ab)/P(b) = P(a)/P(b), at least for those b for which P(b) ≠ 0. (We take P(0|0) = 1.) For each such b ε A, P is a probability measure on Ab, and so satisfies the usual properties with respect to ∨, ∧ and ′ on Ab, which is identified with those conditional events of the form a|b. The question is what should be required of P with respect to ∨ and ∧ operating on conditional events with different antecedents? That is, what properties should P(a|b ∨ c|d) and P(a|b ∧ c|d) have? The following requirements seem paramount:

(6) P(a|b ∨ c|d) ≥ P(a|b);
(7) P(a|b ∧ c|d) ≤ P(a|b).

Of course, in view of the commutativity of ∨ and ∧, (6) and (7) require that P(a|b ∨ c|d) ≥ P(c|d) also, and similarly P(a|b ∧ c|d) ≤ P(c|d).

Of the four possibilities

$$a|b \vee c|d = \alpha_1|\beta_1 = (ad \vee bc)|bd,$$
$$a|b \vee c|d = \alpha_2|\beta_2 = (a \vee c)|(a \vee c \vee bd),$$
$$a|b \vee c|d = \alpha_2|\beta_4 = (a \vee c)|(b \vee d), \text{ and}$$
$$a|b \vee c|d = \alpha_4|\beta_4 = (a \vee c \vee bd' \vee b'd)|(b \vee d)$$

for ∨, the third is easily ruled out. Taking c = 0, we get that P(a|b ∨ 0|d) = P(a|(b ∨ d)), which is clearly < P(a|b) in general. Using DeMorgan's laws for the third ∨ and the third ∧, we get that P(a|b ∨ c|d) ≥ P(a|b) for all a|b and d|d if and only if P(a|b ∧ c|d) ≤ P(a|b) for all a|b and c|d. Thus the third ∧ is ruled out by our probabilistic requirements. Similarly, the first possibility for ∧ is ruled out by the probabilistic requirements, and hence the first possibility for ∨ is also ruled out. Of course, one can rule out these various possibilities by looking at specific simple examples. For instance, the first possibility for $\vee$ can be ruled out by taking the discrete sample space $\{x_1, x_2, x_3, x_4\}$, letting $a = \{x_1,x_2\}$, $b = \{x_1, x_2, x_3\}$, $c = \{x_4\}$, and $d = \{x_3, x_4\}$, with $P\{x_i\} = 1/4$. Then $P(a|b) = 2/3$, and $P(a|b \vee c|d) = P((ad \vee bc)|bd) = P(0|\{x_3\}) = 0$.

We are left with two possibilities for $\vee$ and two possibilities for $\wedge$. Using $\cup$ for the case $\alpha_4|\beta_4$ and $\cap$ for the case $\gamma_1|\beta_4$, they are

$$a|b \vee c|d = \alpha_2|\beta_2 = (a \vee c)|(a \vee c \vee bd), \text{ and}$$
$$a|b \cup c|d = \alpha_4|\beta_4 = (a \vee c \vee bd' \vee b'd)|(b \vee d)$$

for "union" and

$$a|b \wedge c|d = \gamma_1|\beta_3 = ac|(bd \vee a'b \vee c'd) \text{ and}$$
$$a|b \cap c|d = \gamma_1|\beta_4 = ac|(b \vee d).$$

for "intersection". We need to check that these four remaining cases do indeed meet the probability requirements. That $P(a|b \cap c|d) = P(ac|(b \vee d)) \leq P(a|b)$ is obvious, and then DeMorgan's law gets that that $P(a|b \cup c|d) = P((a \vee c \vee bd' \vee b'd)|(b \vee d)) \geq P(a|b)$. We prove that $P(a|b \vee c|d) = P((a \vee c)|(a \vee c \vee bd)) \geq P(a|b)$, illustrating a general method. The remaining case then follows from DeMorgan's law. The general idea is to write a, b, $a \vee c$, and $a \vee c \vee bd$, in their disjunctive normal forms, on which then P is additive, and simply verify the inequality desired. Those forms are

$$a = ac \vee ac'd \vee ad',$$
$$b = ac \vee ac'd \vee ad' \vee a'bc \vee a'bc'd \vee a'bd',$$
$$a \vee c = ac \vee ac'd \vee ad' \vee a'bc \vee b'c, \text{ and}$$
$$a \vee c \vee bd = ac \vee ac'd \vee ad' \vee a'bc \vee b'c \vee a'bc'd.$$

We need that $P(a|b \vee c|d) \geq P(a|b)$, which in our case is that

$$P(ac \vee ac'd \vee ad' \vee a'bc \vee b'c)/P(ac \vee ac'd \vee ad' \vee a'bc \vee b'c \vee a'bc'd)$$
$$\geq P(ac \vee ac'd \vee ad')/P(ac \vee ac'd \vee ad' \vee a'bc \vee a'bc'd \vee a'bd').$$

Since all four of the terms a, b, $a \vee c$, and $a \vee c \vee bd$ contain a, we can simplify a bit and keep distinct terms in the expansions disjoint. Just replace the disjunctive form ac ∨ ac′d ∨ ad for a by a itself. Thus we need

$$P(a \vee a'bc \vee b'c)/P(a \vee a'bc \vee b'c \vee a'bc'd) \geq$$
$$P(a)/P(a \vee a'bc \vee a'bc'd \vee a'bd'),$$

or that

$$P(a \vee a'bc \vee b'c)P(a \vee a'bc \vee a'bc'd \vee a'bd') \geq$$
$$P(a)P(a \vee a'bc \vee b'c \vee a'bc'd),$$

or

$$[P(a) + P(a'bc) + P(b'c)][P(a) + P(a'bc) + P(a'bc'd) + P(a'bd')] \geq$$
$$P(a)[P(a) + P(a'bc) + P(b'c) + P(a'bc'd)],$$

which clearly holds.

We now have the following theorem.

Theorem 2. Let $\mathscr{C}(A) = \{a|b : a, b \in A, a \leq b\}$ be the space of conditional events of the Boolean algebra A, and let $(a|b)' = a'b|b$. Then there are exactly two ways to extend ∨ and ∧ to $\mathscr{C}(A)$ so that ∨ and ∧ are commutative and associative, DeMorgan's laws hold, and which satisfy

$$P(a|b \vee c|d) \geq P(a|b), \text{ and}$$
$$P(a|b \wedge c|d) \leq P(a|b).$$

These two ways are the pair

$$a|b \vee c|d = \alpha_2|\beta_2 = (a \vee c)|(a \vee c \vee bd) \text{ and}$$
$$a|b \wedge c|d = \gamma_1|\beta_3 = ac|(bd \vee a'b \vee c'd),$$

and the pair

$$a|b \cup c|d = \alpha_4|\beta_4 = (a \vee c \vee bd' \vee b'd)|(b \vee d) \text{ and}$$
$$a|b \cap c|d = \gamma_1|\beta_4 = ac|(b \vee d).$$

To settle on a single combination of ∨ and ∧ requires other considerations. On an intuitive level, one would like $a|b \wedge b|1 = a|1$. That is, "given b and a|b, then a". Both ∧ and ∩

have this property. In fact, this requirement rules out precisely the possibilities ruled out by our probabilistic requirements, as can be easily checked. However, there are all kinds of things wrong with $\cup$ and $\cap$, even though they are commutative, associative, satisfy DeMorgan's laws, and meet the probabilistic requirements. Here are some shortcomings of these two operations:

(a) $\cap$ is not distributive over $\cup$;
(b) $\cup$ is not distributive over $\cap$;
(c) neither of the absorption laws

$$a|b \cup (a|b \cap c|d) = a|b \text{ nor}$$
$$a|b \cap (a|b \cup c|d) = a|b$$

holds;

(d) there is no identity for $\cup$, nor one for $\cap$.

Examples of the above are easy to come by. For example, $1|1 \cap (0|b \cup 0|d) = 1|1 \cap (bd' \vee b'd)|(b \vee d) = (bd' \cup b'd)|1$, and $(1|1 \cap 0|b) \cup (1|1 \cap 0|d) = 0|1 \cup 0|1 = 0|1$, so $\cap$ does not distribute over $\cup$. Were $x|y$ an identity for $\cup$, then $x|y \cup a|b = a|b = (x \vee a \vee yb' \vee y'b)|(y \vee b)$, and $y \leq b$. So there is no identity for $\cup$.

The other pair $\vee$ and $\wedge$ satisfy all the properties above lacking for $\cup$ and $\cap$. For example, $0|1$ is the identity for $\vee$, and $1|1$ is the identity for $\wedge$. Thus, there are many ways to state requirements that lead to the single pair $\vee$ and $\wedge$. One way is the following:

Theorem 3. Let $\mathscr{C}(A) = \{a|b : a, b \in A, a \leq b\}$ be the space of conditional events of the Boolean algebra A, and let $(a|b)' = a'b|b$. Then there is exactly one way to extend $\vee$ and $\wedge$ to $\mathscr{C}(A)$ so that $\vee$ and $\wedge$ are commutative and associative, have identities, DeMorgan's laws hold, and which satisfy

$$P(a|b \vee c|d) \geq P(a|b), \text{ and } P(a|b \wedge c|d) \leq P(a|b).$$

This extension is given by

$$a|b \vee c|d = (a \vee c)|(a \vee c \vee bd) \text{ and } a|b \wedge c|d = ac|(bd \vee a'b \vee c'd).$$

Now $\mathscr{C}(A)$ with the operations $\vee$ and $\wedge$ has many nice properties. First, $\mathscr{C}(A)$ is a lattice if $a|b \leq c|d$ is defined to mean that $a|b \wedge c|d = a|b$. This lattice has a 0 and 1, namely $0|1$ and $1|1$, respectively (so is bounded), and we have noted that $\mathscr{C}(A)$ is distributive. A further important property of $\mathscr{C}(A)$ is that it has a "pseudocomplement". This means that there is an operator * on $\mathscr{C}(A)$ such that for each $x \in \mathscr{C}(A)$, $x \wedge x^* = 0$, and if $x \wedge y = 0$, then $y \leq x^*$. In $\mathscr{C}(A)$, this operator is $(a|b)^* = (a'b)|1$. In $\mathscr{C}(A)$, it also satisfies $x^* \vee x^{**} = 1$, and this is all expressed by saying that ***$\mathscr{C}$(A) is a Stone Algebra.*** The simplest Stone algebra not a Boolean algebra is $\mathscr{C}(A)$, where A is the Boolean algebra {0,1}. In this case, $\mathscr{C}(A)$ is the three element Stone algebra {0|0, 0|1, 1|1}. A thorough discussion of $\mathscr{C}(A)$ as a Stone algebra may be found in [1].

We close with some comments about $\mathscr{C}(A)$ and its properties. First, we have chosen to define it as the set of all pairs (a,b) = a|b, with $a \leq b$, where a and b come from a Boolean algebra A. In this vein, equivalent definitions are these:

(1) equivalence classes of pairs (a,b) of elements of A, with the equivalence relation given by $(a,b) \approx (c,d)$ if b = d and ab = cd;

(2) all pairs (a,b) of elements of A with $a \geq b'$;

(3) all pairs (a,b) of elements of A with ab = 0.

We chose the set of all pairs (a,b) with $a \leq b$ since that is the way one usually thinks of a "conditional event". That is, condition on b, and then the possible events are those contained in b. If one takes (1) as the definition, then our definition is just choosing a canonical representative of each equivalence class, namely the one with the smallest a. Similarly, definition (2) is choosing the representative with the largest a. Definition (3) is clearly equivalent: $(a,b) \to (a,a'b)$ is a bijection between pairs from our original definition and those of (3). From the point of view of connections with logic, (3) is probably the most appropriate definition. Also, the operations $\vee$ and $\wedge$ assume a particulary simple and suggestive form when (3) is used, becoming $(a,b) \vee (c,d) = (a \vee c, bd)$, and $(a,b) \wedge (c,d) = (ac, b \vee d)$. Furthermore, $(a,b)' = (b,a)$. Since $\vee$ and $\wedge$ are componentwise, it is clear that they are associative, commutative, and so on, just from the fact that the operations on A have these properties. In any case, the system $\mathscr{C}(A)$ may be interpreted as all pairs (a,b) with ab = 0, along with the operations just described.

Finally, we illustrate with an example some of the properties of conditional events and their probabilities with respect to the operations. Consider the simple experiment of rolling a die. Our sample space is {1,2,3,4,5,6}, and A is the set of all subsets of it. Let a = {1,2,}, b = {1,2,3,}, c = {4,5}, and d = {4,5,6}. Then

$$P(a|b \vee c|d) = P((a \vee c)|(a \vee c \vee bd)) = P(a \vee c|a \vee c) = 1.$$

More generally, whenever $bd = 0$, or equivalently whenever $b' \vee d' = 1$, then $P(a|b \vee c|d) = 1$. Does it makes sense for the probability of $\{1,2\}|\{1,2,3\}$ "or" $\{4,5\}|\{4,5,6\}$ to be 1? This seems strange. However, if we take the equivalent definition (3), then a is replaced by $\{1,2,4,5,6\}$ and c by $\{1,2,3,4,5\}$, and $a|b \vee c|d$ becomes $(a \vee c)|(ab \vee ac \vee bd) = \{1,2,3,4,5,6\}|\{1,2,4,5\}$, and it may not seem so strange for the probability of $\{1,2,4,5,6\}|\{1,2,3\}$ "or" $\{1,2,3,4,5\}|\{4,5,6\}$ to be one. A more satisfying rationale for $P(a|b \vee c|d)$ being 1 is this. Thinking in terms of outcomes of experiments, call $a|b$ "true" if the outcome is in a, "false" if the outcome is in $a'b$, and "undecided" if the outcome is in b'. Then $P(a|b)$ should not be thought of as the probability that $a|b$ is "true" but rather as the proportion of time the outcome is "true" of the times it is "true" or "false"; that is $P(a)/P(b)$. An conditional event of the form $x|x$ is either "true" or "undecided". In our example, $a|b \vee c|d = a \vee c|a \vee c$ is of this form, thus is "true" or "undecided", so that the proportion of times it is "true" of the times it is "true" or "false" is simply 1. $P(a|b \wedge c|d) = 0$, as intuition demands.

Of course, P is not really a probability measure on $\mathscr{C}(A)$; in fact $\mathscr{C}(A)$ is not even a Boolean algebra with respect to $\vee$ and $\wedge$, and we should not expect it to behave as one. But for each $b \in A$, it is a probability measure on the subalgebra $\{a|b : a \leq b\}$ of $\mathscr{C}(A)$, and the interplay between P and the operations $\vee$ and $\wedge$ on elements of these distinct subalgebras should be further investigated and clarified. In [1], the space $\mathscr{C}(A)$ of conditional events is investigated rather thoroughly as an algebraic system, and it has a rather rich and interesting structure. Can $\mathscr{C}(A)$, with the function P on it arising from a probability P on A, serve effectively to model important physical situations? Specific non-trivial and convincing examples are needed.

References

1. Goodman, I. R., Nguyen, H. T., and Walker, E. A. (1991) *Conditional Inference and Logic for Intelligent Systems: A Theory of Measure-Free Conditioning*, North Holland, Amsterdam.

2. Gratzer, G. (1978) *General Lattice Theory*, Birkhauser, Basel.

Conditional Logic in Expert Systems
I.R. Goodman, M.M. Gupta, H.T. Nguyen and G.S. Rogers (editors)

CONDITIONING, NON-MONOTONIC LOGIC AND NON-STANDARD UNCERTAINTY MODELS

Didier Dubois Henri Prade

Institut de Recherche en Informatique de Toulouse
Université Paul Sabatier, 118 route de Narbonne
31062 Toulouse Cedex - France

Abstract Conditioning is very often considered in connection with probability; they look strongly entwined in the usual notion of conditional probability. This connection has created a gap between probability theory and logic: while the former seems to ignore material implication when representing conditional knowledge, the latter has no genuine tool to account for conditioning. This unresolved state of affairs on the essence of conditioning has created difficulties with the emergence of alternative numerical models of uncertainty where there is no consensus yet about what is the proper counterpart of conditional probability. This paper intends to bring together various independent works that have shared the concern of modelling conditional knowledge, viewing the concept of conditioning as an entity distinct from probability. It draws from several fields such as logic, philosophy of science, artificial intelligence, statistics, generalized measure theory, and measurement theory. In each of these fields there have been attempts to come to grips with the meaning of conditioning and its possible representations.

Keywords Conditional events, non-monotonic logic, probability theory, possibility theory, belief functions, upper and lower probabilities.

1. Introduction

There are basically two ways of modeling "if... then" rules in Artificial Intelligence : i) material implication in theorem-proving and logic programming ; ii) production rules in expert system shells. However, perhaps due to the fact that, in logic programming, only Horn clauses are used, and disjunctive information is usually not directly processed as such, the two modes of representation are often thought of as equivalent, as it is the case in PROLOG programs for instance. However it is well-known that material implication is a debatable tool for translating if-then statements. Namely $\mathbf{b} \rightarrow \mathbf{a} \triangleq \neg \mathbf{b} \vee \mathbf{a}$ is considered as true when **b** is false, while a production rule "if **b** then **a**" is not applicable in that case. Paradoxes of material implication have motivated the search for non-standard logics.

Another problem occurs, when rules are pervaded with uncertainty, and are assigned numbers such as probability values. It is then interesting to notice that logicians and statisticians split into two groups : logicians interpret these numbers as the probability of the material implication (e.g. Nilsson, 1986). Statisticians use conditional probabilities. The fact that a conditional probability

$$P(\mathbf{a} \mid \mathbf{b}) \triangleq \frac{P(\mathbf{a} \wedge \mathbf{b})}{P(\mathbf{b})}$$

is generally different from $P(\neg\mathbf{b} \vee \mathbf{a})$ has been noticed for a long time. Indeed we have

$$P(\mathbf{a} \mid \mathbf{b}) = \frac{P(\mathbf{b} \rightarrow \mathbf{a}) - P(\neg\mathbf{b})}{1 - P(\neg\mathbf{b})} \qquad (1)$$

In fact $P(\mathbf{a} \mid \mathbf{b})$ and $P(\neg\mathbf{b} \vee \mathbf{a})$ coincide if and only if $P(\mathbf{b}) = 1$, or $P(\neg\mathbf{b} \vee \mathbf{a}) = 1$ with $P(\mathbf{b}) > 0$. Indeed when $P(\mathbf{b}) = 0$, $P(\mathbf{a} \mid \mathbf{b})$ is undefined. The following relationships between $P(\mathbf{a} \mid \mathbf{b})$ and $P(\neg\mathbf{b} \vee \mathbf{a})$ when they take the values 0 or 1, are readily checked, noticing that $P(\neg\mathbf{b} \vee \mathbf{a}) = P(\mathbf{a} \wedge \mathbf{b}) + P(\neg\mathbf{b})$:

if $P(\mathbf{a} \mid \mathbf{b}) = 1$ then $P(\neg\mathbf{b} \vee \mathbf{a}) = 1$; the converse is true only if $P(\mathbf{b}) \neq 0$;
if $P(\neg\mathbf{b} \vee \mathbf{a}) = 0$ then $P(\mathbf{a} \mid \mathbf{b}) = 0$ but $P(\mathbf{a} \mid \mathbf{b}) = 0$ only implies $P(\neg\mathbf{b} \vee \mathbf{a}) < 1$.

These results emphasize the fact that $P(\mathbf{a} \mid \mathbf{b})$ and $P(\neg\mathbf{b} \vee \mathbf{a})$ do not even necessarily coincide when they take the values 0 or 1. Although $P(\mathbf{a} \mid \mathbf{b})$ and $P(\neg\mathbf{b} \vee \mathbf{a})$ are different, the inequality $P(\mathbf{a} \mid \mathbf{b}) \leq P(\neg\mathbf{b} \vee \mathbf{a})$ holds whenever $P(\mathbf{a} \mid \mathbf{b})$ makes sense, i.e. if $P(\mathbf{b}) \neq 0$. Moreover we have $P(\mathbf{b} \rightarrow \mathbf{a}) = P(\neg\mathbf{a} \rightarrow \neg\mathbf{b})$, while $P(\mathbf{a} \mid \mathbf{b}) \neq P(\neg\mathbf{b} \mid \neg\mathbf{a})$ generally. As a consequence, reasoning theories based on conditional probabilities are not easily related to classical logic.

As noticed by Schay (1968), $P(\mathbf{a} \mid \mathbf{b})$ is usually interpreted as "(probability of **a**) given **b**" rather than "probability of (**a** given **b**)" since "**a** given **b**" is not defined in logic. "**a** given **b**" is to be understood as "**a** knowing **b**, and knowing **b** *only*". There has been some work in the past to define the measure-free symbol **a** | **b** in the framework of modal logic (especially Stalnaker, 1968). However the attempts to properly relate **a** | **b** and $P(\mathbf{a} \mid \mathbf{b})$ have been unsuccessful with this approach (e.g. Lewis, 1976 ; Harper et al., 1981). More recently Bruno and Gilio (1985), Calabrese (1987), Nguyen (1987), Goodman (1987), Goodman and Nguyen (1988, 1990), Goodman et al. (1990), and the authors (Dubois and Prade, 1987b, 1988e, 1989, 1990a) have started, independently at the beginning, to investigate the definition of a conditioning relation "**a** | **b**" outside any modal framework, admitting that it cannot be a logical proposition in the usual sense. The aim of Calabrese (1987) is really to be able to define $P(\mathbf{a} \mid \mathbf{b})$ as the probability of something noted "**a** | **b**". In fact these works have rediscovered and developed preliminary findings that already appear in an older, pioneering work by Schay (1968), and can be traced back to De Finetti (1937).

These attempts to introduce measure-free conditioning must be related to Cox's old (1946) axiomatic system that intends to characterize the usual definition of conditional probability on purely non-frequentist grounds. This axiomatic system has been recently proposed as the formal proof of the inevitability of probability theory for uncertainty modeling by Artificial Intelligence researchers (Cheeseman, 1985, 1988 ; Horvitz et al., 1986). See Dubois and Prade (1989, 1990a) for a discussion.

This paper proposes an enquiry into various works that have linked to some extent the issue of conditioning with logic and/or the modeling of uncertainty in the representation of states of knowledge. Indeed, several independent works that were carried out sometimes a long time ago, turn out to be related, for example, Cox's axiomatic framework for conditional probability and Schay's early attempt to define measure-free conditionals. In the measurement literature, Koopman (1940), Luce (1968) and Fine (1973) have considered comparative conditional probabilities and proposed axioms so as to recover numerical models of conditional probabilities. In the more recent field of non-monotonic logic, connexions between postulates of non-monotonic deduction and properties of conditional probabilities have been laid bare by Pearl (1988) and Dubois and Prade (1989). Simultaneously there has been an outburst of non-probabilistic representations of uncertainty, that has been prompted by research in Artificial Intelligence ; see e.g. Dubois and Prade (1988d) for a survey of these models. While the links between the various set-functions that have emerged become more and more mastered, the questions of capturing notions of conditioning, independence, belief revision, data fusion in these new frameworks are pending, and the answers that have been provided so far, are still contradictory and unconclusive. The recent results on measure-free conditioning seem to bring about new justifications for some forms of non-probabilistic conditioning.

The paper is organized as follows. Section 2 deals with measure-free conditioning at large. First, attempts at modeling "if... then" statements by Stalnaker and Lewis in the framework of modal logic are reviewed. Lewis (1976) trivialization results seem to have greatly affected the course of development of this type of view. Then the more recent approach considered by Calabrese (1987), and the authors, is described in detail in the framework of logic, contrasting with the algebraic setting of Goodman and Nguyen (1988). The connection with non-monotonic logic and Adams (1975)'s ε-semantics of conditional logic is then pointed out. Especially, we indicate that conditional objects give rise to a logic that share all the properties of any well-behaved non-monotonic logic whose principles and inference rules have been studied by Kraus, Lehmann and Magidor (1990) .

Section 3 puts together measure-free conditionals and Cox's axiomatic framework for conditional probability. It is shown that notions of conditioning in possibility and evidence theories can be justified on the basis of a variant of Cox's construct. Other types of conditioning in non-additive probabilities are described and discussed.

This paper is only meant as an introduction to a field of research that is currently opening and which the authors think it fruitful to investigate. We use results of two previous papers (Dubois and Prade, 1989, 1990a), augmented by additional background material and new results both in the links between conditional events and non-monotonic logic and in the axiomatic justification of various uncertainty models.

2. Measure-free conditionals

This section reviews various attempts at formalizing "if... then..." statements without referring to any numerical quantification. There are basically three schools of thought : one that tries to capture the idea of subjunctive conditionals (or counterfactuals) in the framework of modal logic ; another tries to build conditional objects that correspond to indicative conditionals in such a way as to remain consistent with probability (something which the first approach cannot handle) ; the third school, only briefly discussed in the conclusion of the paper, tries to supply postulates for comparative conditional probabilities in the spirit of measurement theory. Finally, it is shown that the behavior of conditional objects is consistent with postulates of non-monotonic deduction, that have been put forward recently.

2.1. Conditionals, counterfactuals and modal logics

It is well-known that the sentence "if **b** then **a**" is not satisfactorily translated by the material conditional $\neg\mathbf{b} \vee \mathbf{a}$; the lack of equality between $P(\mathbf{a} \mid \mathbf{b})$ and $P(\neg\mathbf{b} \vee \mathbf{a})$ is only one hint of this disagreement. Basically when **b** is false $\neg\mathbf{b} \vee \mathbf{a}$ is true but it is unpleasant to regard the sentence "if **b** then **a**" as true. In fact, as pointed out by Stalnaker (1968), when the truth of **b** and that of **a** are known, it is not obvious whether "if **b** then **a**" is true or false.

Stalnaker has suggested a procedure to decide whether a conditional sentence "if **b** then **a**" is true or false, based on the so-called Ramsey test : add **b** to your stock of knowledge, and check whether **a** is true. However this procedure only makes sense if **b** is at least considered as possible. But subjunctive conditionals of the form "if it were that **b** then it would be that **a**" make sense even (and especially) if **b** is acknowledged as false. Stalnaker has modified the Ramsey test accordingly so as to encompass the case when **b** is false, using a modal logic formulation and possible world semantics. Informally, checking the truth of the sentence "if **b** then **a**" comes down, when **b** is false, to placing oneself in the situation that is most similar to the actual one where **b** is true, and then checking for the truth of **a**.

Formally, given a Boolean algebra $\mathfrak{B}$ of propositions and a set of possible worlds Ω, Stalnaker considers a selection function f that for any possible world $\omega \in \Omega$, and any sentence $\mathbf{b} \in \mathfrak{B}$ returns another possible world ω' were **b** is true, supposedly the "closest" world to ω where **b** is true. The truth value of a conditional statement if **b** then **a** represented by the conditional connective $\rightarrow$ as $\mathbf{b} \rightarrow \mathbf{a}$ is then assigned as follows :

$\mathbf{b} \rightarrow \mathbf{a}$ is true at ω if **a** is true in f(ω,**b**)
is false at ω if **a** is false in f(ω,**b**)
is true if **b** is ever false

by convention, if **b** is true in ω then f(ω,**b**) = ω, while if **b** is a contradiction then f(ω,**b**) is the absurd world (where everything is true).

Lewis (1973) has questioned this definition on the basis that f(ω,**b**) may contain more than one possible world, and has on such grounds introduced two kinds of subjunctive conditionals $\mathbf{b} \Box\!\!\rightarrow \mathbf{a}$ and $\mathbf{b} \Diamond\!\!\rightarrow \mathbf{a}$ corresponding to the sentences "if it were that **b** then it would be that **a** ("would" conditionals) and "if it were that **b** then it might be that **a**" ("might" conditionals). The formal definition of the "would" conditional is

$\mathbf{b} \Box\!\!\rightarrow \mathbf{a}$ is true at ω if there is a world ω' where $\mathbf{b} \wedge \mathbf{a}$ is true
closer to ω than any world where $\mathbf{b} \wedge \neg\mathbf{a}$ is true

and the "might" conditional is defined by duality

$$\mathbf{b} \Diamond\!\!\rightarrow \mathbf{a} = \neg(\mathbf{b} \Box\!\!\rightarrow \neg\mathbf{a})$$

Basically $\mathbf{b} \Box\!\!\rightarrow \mathbf{a}$ is true in ω if **a** is true in *every* closest world where **b** is true. Lewis' construct also questions the so-called "conditional excluded midde law", that holds in Stalnaker's system, i.e. $(\mathbf{b} \rightarrow \mathbf{a}) \vee (\mathbf{b} \rightarrow \neg\mathbf{a})$. Clearly this axiom is related to the assumption that f(ω,**b**) contains only a single world so that in world f(ω,**b**) either **a** is true or it is false. When f(ω,**b**) corresponds to more worlds, this dichotomy vanishes.

Relating conditionals and probability is tempting, and Stalnaker (1970) tried it assuming the identity between $P(\mathbf{b} \rightarrow \mathbf{a})$ and $P(\mathbf{a} \mid \mathbf{b})$, i.e. following Ramsey, the degree of belief in the conditional $\mathbf{b} \rightarrow \mathbf{a}$ should be equated to the degree of belief in **b**, given that **a** is true. Then the negation law $P(\neg\mathbf{a} \mid \mathbf{b}) = 1 - P(\mathbf{a} \mid \mathbf{b})$ is the numerical version of the conditional excluded middle. In order to include the case when $P(\mathbf{b}) = 0$ (i.e. for counterfactuals), Stalnaker resorts to the extension of conditional probabilities called Popper functions (Popper, 1959).

This attractive proposal received a serious criticism from Lewis (1976) who proved that the assumption $P(\mathbf{b} \rightarrow \mathbf{a}) = P(\mathbf{a} \mid \mathbf{b})$ when $P(\mathbf{b}) > 0$ was untenable but in trivial cases. If the connective $\rightarrow$ does not depend on the chosen probability, a consequence of this identity is that

$$P(\mathbf{b} \rightarrow \mathbf{a} \mid \mathbf{c}) = P(\mathbf{a} \mid \mathbf{c} \wedge \mathbf{b}) \quad \text{when} \quad P(\mathbf{c} \wedge \mathbf{b}) > 0$$

Now let us calculate $P(\mathbf{d}) = P(\mathbf{d} \mid \mathbf{c})P(\mathbf{c}) + P(\mathbf{d} \mid \neg\mathbf{c})P(\neg\mathbf{c})$, where $\mathbf{d} = \mathbf{a} \rightarrow \mathbf{c}$. Assuming $P(\mathbf{a} \wedge \mathbf{c}) > 0$ and $P(\mathbf{a} \wedge \neg\mathbf{c}) > 0$ it comes

$$\begin{aligned} P(\mathbf{a} \rightarrow \mathbf{c}) &= P(\mathbf{a} \rightarrow \mathbf{c} \mid \mathbf{c})P(\mathbf{c}) + P(\mathbf{a} \rightarrow \mathbf{c} \mid \neg\mathbf{c})P(\neg\mathbf{c}) \\ &= 1 \cdot P(\mathbf{c}) + 0 \cdot P(\neg\mathbf{c}) \end{aligned}$$
since $P(\mathbf{a} \rightarrow \mathbf{c} \mid \mathbf{c}) = P(\mathbf{c} \mid \mathbf{a} \wedge \mathbf{c})$ and $P(\mathbf{a} \rightarrow \mathbf{c} \mid \neg\mathbf{c}) = P(\mathbf{c} \mid \mathbf{a} \wedge \neg\mathbf{c})$

and we get $P(\mathbf{c} \mid \mathbf{a}) = P(\mathbf{c})$. This means that $\mathbf{c}$ and $\mathbf{a}$ are stochastically independent whenever $P(\mathbf{c} \wedge \mathbf{a}) > 0$ and $P(\mathbf{a} \wedge \neg\mathbf{c}) > 0$. Particularly any set Ω of alternatives ω_1, ω_2, ω_3 with respective probabilities p_1, p_2, $p_3 = 1 - p_1 - p_2$ being positive will lead to an obvious contradiction to this requirement since if $\mathbf{a}$ corresponds to $\{\omega_1,\omega_2\}$, $\mathbf{c}$ to $\{\omega_2,\omega_3\}$, $P(\mathbf{a} \wedge \mathbf{c}) = p_2$, $P(\mathbf{a} \wedge \neg\mathbf{c}) = p_1$, then $P(\mathbf{c} \mid \mathbf{a}) = p_2 / (p_1 + p_2) \neq P(\mathbf{c}) = 1 - p_1$. So, if $P(\mathbf{a} \mid \mathbf{b}) = P(\mathbf{b} \rightarrow \mathbf{a})$ for some connective $\rightarrow$, no positive probability can be assigned to more than two alternatives. After proving this result Lewis (1976) notices that other ways of updating a probability measure, different from conditioning exist, and introduces the concept of image of a probability measure on a set, that can be defined through the selection function $f(\omega,\mathbf{b})$ of Stalnaker. Namely

$$\forall\, \omega' \in \Omega,\ P_{\mathbf{b}}(\omega') = \Sigma\ \{p(\omega) \mid \omega' = f(\omega,\mathbf{b})\}$$

where $p(\omega)$ is the probability weight of ω, and $f(\omega,\mathbf{b})$ maps ω on the closest world to ω where $\mathbf{b}$ is true. Then it is easy to check that $P(\mathbf{b} \rightarrow \mathbf{a}) = P_{\mathbf{b}}(\mathbf{a})$ built by imaging. Conditioning differs from imaging since in the first case, $P(\neg\mathbf{b})$ is fairly shared among the worlds ω at which $\mathbf{b}$ is true while in imaging, only worlds that are close to worlds where $\mathbf{b}$ is false receive anything.

Lewis concludes that the search for a symbolic counterpart of conditional probability looks hopeless. It is so as long as the formula $\mathbf{b} \rightarrow \mathbf{a}$ cannot be but true or false. However it turns out that relaxing this duality assumption does lead to a connective, called "tri-event" by De Finetti (1937) and denoted hereafter $\mathbf{a} \mid \mathbf{b}$, such that $P(\mathbf{a} \mid \mathbf{b})$ can be the probability of $\mathbf{a} \mid \mathbf{b}$.

2.2. Basic definitions of measure-free conditioning and its truth table interpretation

In the following, the symbol **a** | **b** is informally interpreted as representing a production rule "if **b** then **a**", which means "when **b** is true then **a** can be added to the set of facts (i.e. **b** "produces" **a**), otherwise the rule is not applicable". Viewing **a** | **b** as linking two propositions **a** and **b** of propositional logic, semantics can be given to it under the form of an incomplete truth table, namely denoting t the truth- assignment function, t(**a** | **b**) = 1 when **a** and **b** are both true, t(**a** | **b**) = 0 when **a** is false and **b** is true. When **b** is false, **a** | **b** is considered as inapplicable, which is denoted as t(**a** | **b**) = ?. This symbol means that any truth value in {0,1} can be assigned to **a** | **b**. Such semantics are in accordance with the usual meaning of production rules ; this proposal, made independently by the authors (Dubois and Prade, 1987b), turns out to be exactly equivalent to the definition by Schay (1968). Moreover, it explicitly appears in De Finetti (1937)'s paper on subjective probability and more recently in a paper of Bruno and Gilio (1985). Truth Table 1 exhibits the difference between **b** → **a** and **a** | **b**, while Table 2 is obtained by inversing Table 1 and shows the modus ponens behavior of the conditioning compared to the one of material implication

t(**b**)	t(**a**)	t(**b** → **a**)	t(**a** | **b**)
1	1	1	1
1	0	0	0
0	1	1	?
0	0	1	?

Table 1 : Material implication versus conditioning symbol

t(**b** → **a**)	t(**b**)	t(**a**)		t(**a** | **b**)	t(**b**)	t(**a**)
1	1	1	←(modus ponens)→	1	1	1
1	0	?	←("denial of **a**", but indeterminate truth value)→	1	0	?
0	1	0		0	1	0
0	0	Ø	←(impossible situation) (indeterminate situation)→	0	0	?

Table 2 : Compared modes of inference

In (Dubois and Prade, 1987b) we also notice that t(**a** | **b**) can be implicitly defined by means of the equation :

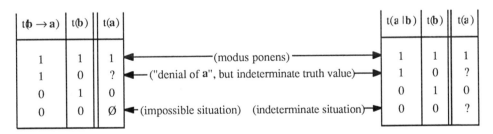

$$t(\mathbf{a} \wedge \mathbf{b}) = t(\mathbf{a} \mid \mathbf{b}) * t(\mathbf{b}) \qquad (2)$$

where $*$ is the conjunction operation on $\{0,1\}$, i.e. $*$ is such that

$$1 * 1 = 1 \text{ and } 1 * 0 = 0 * 1 = 0 * 0 = 0.$$

Indeed if $t(\mathbf{a}) = 1 = t(\mathbf{b})$, (2) entails $t(\mathbf{a} \mid \mathbf{b}) = 1$; if $t(\mathbf{a}) = 0$ and $t(\mathbf{b}) = 1$, (2) entails $t(\mathbf{a} \mid \mathbf{b}) = 0$, while when $t(\mathbf{b}) = 0$, $t(\mathbf{a} \mid \mathbf{b}) = 1$ as well as $t(\mathbf{a} \mid \mathbf{b}) = 0$ are compatible with (2). Min $(t(\mathbf{a} \mid \mathbf{b}), t(\mathbf{b}))$ or their product are examples of possible choices for expressing the operation $*$.

Any proposition $\mathbf{x}$ such that $t(\mathbf{a} \wedge \mathbf{b}) = t(\mathbf{x}) * t(\mathbf{b})$ can stand for $\mathbf{a} \mid \mathbf{b}$. Note that filling the incomplete truth-table can only be done in four ways, equating $\mathbf{a} \mid \mathbf{b}$ to one of the following propositions : $\mathbf{a} \wedge \mathbf{b}$, $\mathbf{a}$, $\mathbf{a} \leftrightarrow \mathbf{b}$, $\mathbf{b} \rightarrow \mathbf{a}$ in a language containing only $\mathbf{a}$ and $\mathbf{b}$ as proposition symbols, and assuming that $t(\mathbf{a})$ and $t(\mathbf{b})$ can be independently valued ($\leftrightarrow$ is the equivalence symbol). The set $\{\mathbf{a} \wedge \mathbf{b}, \mathbf{a}, \mathbf{a} \leftrightarrow \mathbf{b}, \mathbf{b} \rightarrow \mathbf{a}\}$ forms a partially ordered set under the entailment relation, with $\mathbf{a} \wedge \mathbf{b}$ and $\mathbf{b} \rightarrow \mathbf{a}$ being respectively the smallest and the greatest elements (while $\mathbf{a}$ and $\mathbf{a} \leftrightarrow \mathbf{b}$ are not comparable). Thus $\mathbf{a} \mid \mathbf{b}$ can be identified to a set of propositions, for instance $\{\mathbf{a} \wedge \mathbf{b}, \mathbf{a}, \mathbf{a} \leftrightarrow \mathbf{b}, \mathbf{b} \rightarrow \mathbf{a}\}$ here, and "|" does not define a connective in the usual sense.

At this point, it is interesting to give the two following definitions, where $\mathbf{a}$, $\mathbf{b}$, $\mathbf{x}$ denote elements of a *finite* Boolean algebra $\mathcal{B}$

Definition 1 (Goodman and Nguyen, 1988) : $\forall\, \mathbf{a}, \mathbf{b} \in \mathcal{B}$, $\mathbf{a} \mid_G \mathbf{b} = \{\mathbf{x}, \mathbf{x} \wedge \mathbf{b} = \mathbf{a} \wedge \mathbf{b}\}$.

Definition 2 (Calabrese, 1987) : $\forall \mathbf{a}, \mathbf{b} \in \mathcal{B}$, $\mathbf{a} \mid_C \mathbf{b} = \{\mathbf{x}, \exists\, \mathbf{r} \in \partial(\mathbf{b}), \mathbf{x} \wedge \mathbf{r} = \mathbf{a} \wedge \mathbf{r}\}$ where $\partial(\mathbf{b}) = \{\mathbf{b} \vee \mathbf{s}, \mathbf{s} \in \mathcal{B}\}$.

These two definitions are inspired by algebraic considerations. Especially, Goodman and Nguyen (1988) start with the ring properties of $\mathcal{B}$ equipped with conjunction and symmetric difference. It is easy to verify that (2) corresponds to the semantics of definition 1. Moreover, it can be established that definitions 1 and 2 are equivalent. Indeed, taking $\mathbf{r} = \mathbf{b}$ shows that $\mathbf{a} \mid_G \mathbf{b} \subseteq \mathbf{a} \mid_C \mathbf{b}$. Conversely, noticing that $\mathbf{e} \wedge \mathbf{x} = \mathbf{f}$ entails $\exists \mathbf{t}$, $\mathbf{x} = \mathbf{f} \vee \mathbf{t}$ and $\mathbf{e} \wedge \mathbf{t} = \mathbb{O}$ (where $\mathbb{O}$ denotes the smallest element in $\mathcal{B}$), we conclude that if $\mathbf{x} \in \mathbf{a} \mid_C \mathbf{b}$, then $\mathbf{x} = (\mathbf{a} \wedge (\mathbf{b} \vee \mathbf{s})) \vee \mathbf{t}$, with $(\mathbf{b} \vee \mathbf{s}) \wedge \mathbf{t} = \mathbb{O}$, i.e. $\mathbf{b} \wedge \mathbf{t} = \mathbb{O}$ and $\mathbf{s} \wedge \mathbf{t} = \mathbb{O}$. Finally we get, $\mathbf{x} \wedge \mathbf{b} = ((\mathbf{a} \wedge (\mathbf{b} \vee \mathbf{s})) \vee \mathbf{t}) \wedge \mathbf{b} = (\mathbf{a} \wedge (\mathbf{b} \vee \mathbf{s})) \wedge \mathbf{b} = \mathbf{a} \wedge \mathbf{b}$, i.e. $\mathbf{x} \in \mathbf{a} \mid_G \mathbf{b}$.

Note that $\mathbf{a} \mid_G \mathbf{b} = \{\mathbf{a} \wedge \mathbf{b}, \mathbf{a}, \mathbf{a} \leftrightarrow \mathbf{b}, \mathbf{b} \rightarrow \mathbf{a}\}$ as soon as it is required that $\mathbf{x}$ be a Boolean function of independent propositions $\mathbf{a}$ and $\mathbf{b}$ in definition 1. By independent propositions, we mean that $\forall$ **x** $\in$ {**a** $\wedge$ **b**, $\neg$**a** $\wedge$ **b**, **a** $\wedge \neg$**b**, $\neg$**a** $\wedge \neg$**b**}, **x** $\neq \mathbb{O}$. However in any case, **a** $\wedge$ **b** and **b** $\rightarrow$ **a** are the least and greatest elements of **a** $|_G$ **b**, respectively. Let $\leq$ denote the usual partial ordering in the Boolean algebra, expressing entailment, so **b** $\leq$ **a** if and only if $\neg$**b** $\vee$ **a** = $\mathbb{1}$, where $\mathbb{1}$ denotes the greatest element in $\mathcal{B}$; this ordering can also be expressed as : **b** $\leq$ **a** if and only **a** $\wedge$ **b** = **b**. Then **a** $|_G$ **b** = {**a** $\wedge$ **b** $\leq$ **x** $\leq \neg$**b** $\vee$ **a**} (= [**a** $\wedge$**b**,$\neg$**b** $\vee$ **a**] in interval notations).

In the following, we use the notation **a** | **b** to denote the solutions of (2), and we call it a "production rule" which expresses that when **b** is observed or known to be true, **a** can be produced. This is in agreement with the understanding of production rules used in expert systems (Waterman and Hayes-Roth, 1978). Considering a Boolean algebra $\mathcal{B}$ of propositions with tautology $\mathbb{1}$ and contradiction $\mathbb{O}$, we can define the set $\mathcal{B}|\mathcal{B}$ = {**a** | **b**, (**a**,**b**) $\in$ $\mathcal{B}^2$}. $\mathcal{B}$ can be identified as the subset {**a** | $\mathbb{1}$, **a** $\in$ $\mathcal{B}$}. Indeed t(**a** | $\mathbb{1}$) = t(**a**) from (2) (or from Table 1). Note that in the language of expert systems a subset $\mathcal{K}$ of $\mathcal{B}|\mathcal{B}$ is a knowledge base ; $\mathcal{E}$ = $\mathcal{K} \cap \mathcal{B}$ may be viewed as a factual base containing evidence, and $\mathcal{R}$ = $\mathcal{K} \cap (\mathcal{B}|\mathcal{B} - \mathcal{B})$ as a rule base. Rules of the form **a** | $\mathbb{O}$ are not very interesting since they are never applicable (t(**a** | $\mathbb{O}$) = ?, $\forall$**a**) as it can be checked on Table 1. Besides, **a** | **a** = ∂(**a**) = {**x**, **a** $\leq$ **x**} which contains **a** and $\mathbb{1}$; thus **a** | **a** cannot be identified with $\mathbb{1}$. This is natural since the rule **a** | **a** is applicable only if **a** is known to be true, so that t(**a** | **a**) $\in$ {1,?}. More generally, if **b** $\rightarrow$ **a** = $\mathbb{1}$ then t(**a** | **b**) $\neq$ 0 only.

2.3 - Equality and partial ordering on $\mathcal{B}|\mathcal{B}$

It can be shown that (Calabrese, 1987)

$$\mathbf{a} \mid \mathbf{b} = \mathbf{c} \mid \mathbf{d} \text{ if and only if } \mathbf{a} \wedge \mathbf{b} = \mathbf{c} \wedge \mathbf{d} \text{ and } \mathbf{b} = \mathbf{d} \qquad (3)$$

Indeed, {**x**, **x** $\wedge$ **b** = **a** $\wedge$ **b**} = {(**a** $\wedge$ **b**) $\vee$ **s**, with **s** $\wedge$ **b** = $\mathbb{O}$}. When **a** $\wedge$ **b** $\neq$ **c** $\wedge$ **d**, it is clear that **a** $\wedge$ **b** $\notin$ **c** | **d** or **c** $\wedge$ **d** $\notin$ **a** | **b** while **a** $\wedge$ **b** $\in$ **a** | **b** and **c** $\wedge$ **d** $\in$ **c** | **d**. Let us assume that **a** $\wedge$ **b** = **c** $\wedge$ **d**. Then, if **b** $\neq$ **d**, $\exists$**s**, **s** $\wedge$ **b** = $\mathbb{O}$ and **s** $\wedge$ **d** $\neq \mathbb{O}$; it follows that **a** | **b** $\neq$ **c** | **d**. Thus two rules **a** | **b** and **c** | **d** are equal if and only if they have the same applicability condition (i.e. **b** = **d**) and their conclusion parts are identical *when* the condition is satisfied (i.e. **a** $\wedge$ **b** = **c** $\wedge$ **b**). This can be also readily checked using a truth-table and is intuitively satisfactory. (3) was noticed by De Finetti (1937).

The following equalities are worth-noticing and easy to check

$$\mathbf{a} \mid \mathbf{b} = (\mathbf{a} \wedge \mathbf{b}) \mid \mathbf{b} = (\mathbf{a} \leftrightarrow \mathbf{b}) \mid \mathbf{b} = (\mathbf{b} \rightarrow \mathbf{a}) \mid \mathbf{b} \qquad (4)$$

They are in agreement with our interpretation of **a** | **b** in terms of a production rule. Here we have four ways of describing the same rule. However, note that $\mathbf{a} \wedge \mathbf{b}$, $\mathbf{a} \leftrightarrow \mathbf{b}$ or $\mathbf{b} \rightarrow \mathbf{a}$ are not independent of $\mathbf{b}$; then we cannot use (for computing $(\mathbf{a} \wedge \mathbf{b}) \mid \mathbf{b}$ for instance) the equality $\mathbf{a} \mid \mathbf{b} = \{\mathbf{a} \wedge \mathbf{b},\ \mathbf{a},\ \mathbf{a} \leftrightarrow \mathbf{b},\ \mathbf{b} \rightarrow \mathbf{a}\}$ when restricting ourselves to Boolean functions, since it requires the independence of $\mathbf{a}$ and $\mathbf{b}$. For instance, $(\mathbf{a} \wedge \mathbf{b}) \mid \mathbf{b} \neq \{(\mathbf{a} \wedge \mathbf{b}) \wedge \mathbf{b},\ \mathbf{a} \wedge \mathbf{b},\ (\mathbf{a} \wedge \mathbf{b}) \leftrightarrow \mathbf{b},\ \mathbf{b} \rightarrow (\mathbf{a} \wedge \mathbf{b})\} = \{\mathbf{a} \wedge \mathbf{b},\ \mathbf{b} \rightarrow \mathbf{a}\}$, because $(\mathbf{a} \wedge \mathbf{b}) \mid \mathbf{b}$ also contains $\mathbf{a}$ and $\mathbf{a} \leftrightarrow \mathbf{b}$. However, definition $\mathbf{a} \mid \mathbf{b} = [\mathbf{a} \wedge \mathbf{b}, \neg \mathbf{b} \vee \mathbf{a}\ ]$ always makes sense.

Since $\mathbf{a} \mid \mathbf{b} = \{\mathbf{x},\ \mathbf{a} \wedge \mathbf{b} \le \mathbf{x} \le \neg \mathbf{b} \vee \mathbf{a}\}$ and $\mathbf{c} \mid \mathbf{d} = \{\mathbf{y},\ \mathbf{c} \wedge \mathbf{d} \le \mathbf{y} \le \neg \mathbf{d} \vee \mathbf{c}\}$ the following natural partial ordering can be defined on $\mathfrak{B} \mid \mathfrak{B}$ and will be also denoted by '$\le$'

$$\mathbf{a} \mid \mathbf{b} \le \mathbf{c} \mid \mathbf{d} \Leftrightarrow \mathbf{a} \wedge \mathbf{b} \le \mathbf{c} \wedge \mathbf{d} \ \text{ and } \ \neg \mathbf{b} \vee \mathbf{a} \le \neg \mathbf{d} \vee \mathbf{c} \qquad (5)$$

It means that the upper bound of $\mathbf{a} \mid \mathbf{b}$ (resp. : the lower bound) is smaller than the upper bound of $\mathbf{c} \mid \mathbf{d}$ (resp. : the lower bound). It is the natural extension of the ordering on $\mathfrak{B}$ to intervals on $\mathfrak{B}$, since $\mathbf{a} \mid \mathbf{b} \le \mathbf{c} \mid \mathbf{d}$ if and only if for any $\mathbf{x} \in \mathbf{a} \mid \mathbf{b}$ there exists $\mathbf{y} \in \mathbf{c} \mid \mathbf{d}$ such that $\mathbf{x} \le \mathbf{y}$. It also appears that this definition extends the partial ordering in $\mathfrak{B}$ which is recovered by letting $\mathbf{b} = \mathbf{d} = \mathbb{1}$. This definition was already used by Goodman and Nguyen (1988). The relation $\le$ defined by (5) is reflexive and transitive. In the rule interpretation this ordering relation corresponds to an entailment relation. Indeed, $\mathbf{a} \wedge \mathbf{b} \le \mathbf{c} \wedge \mathbf{d}$ means that each time $\mathbf{a} \mid \mathbf{b}$ is true $\mathbf{c} \mid \mathbf{d}$ is true also, and $\neg \mathbf{b} \vee \mathbf{a} \le \neg \mathbf{d} \vee \mathbf{c} \Leftrightarrow \mathbf{b} \wedge \neg \mathbf{a} \ge \mathbf{d} \wedge \neg \mathbf{c}$ means that each time $\mathbf{c} \mid \mathbf{d}$ is false, $\mathbf{a} \mid \mathbf{b}$ is false too. In other words, any example of the rule $\mathbf{a} \mid \mathbf{b}$ is also an example of the rule $\mathbf{c} \mid \mathbf{d}$, and any exception to $\mathbf{c} \mid \mathbf{d}$ is an exception to $\mathbf{a} \mid \mathbf{b}$. For instance "Generally, birds are small flying animals" entails that "Generally, small birds fly", with $\mathbf{a}$ = "small and fly", $\mathbf{b}$ = "bird", $\mathbf{c}$ = "fly", $\mathbf{d}$ = "small bird". Clearly, rule $\mathbf{c} \mid \mathbf{d}$ has more examples and less exceptions than $\mathbf{a} \mid \mathbf{b}$. We can say that the rule $\mathbf{a} \mid \mathbf{b}$ entails the rule $\mathbf{c} \mid \mathbf{d}$.

It can be checked that the equalities $\mathbf{a} \wedge \mathbf{b} = \mathbf{c} \wedge \mathbf{d}$ and $\neg \mathbf{b} \vee \mathbf{a} = \neg \mathbf{d} \vee \mathbf{c}$ entail $\mathbf{b} = \mathbf{d}$ and then we have

$$(\mathbf{a} \mid \mathbf{b} \le \mathbf{c} \mid \mathbf{d} \ \text{ and } \ \mathbf{a} \mid \mathbf{b} \ge \mathbf{c} \mid \mathbf{d}) \Leftrightarrow \mathbf{a} \mid \mathbf{b} = \mathbf{c} \mid \mathbf{d}$$

Besides, in terms of truth-tables, the relation $\le$ defined by (5) corresponds to the ordering $0 \le ? \le 1$, still using the same symbol "$\le$" between values of the truth function. It can be checked that $\mathbf{a} \mid \mathbf{b} \le \mathbf{c} \mid \mathbf{d}$ if and only if $t(\mathbf{a} \mid \mathbf{d}) \le t(\mathbf{c} \mid \mathbf{d})$ in all possible situations. In terms of rules this partial ordering corresponds, as already said, to an entailment relation : if we have the rule $\mathbf{a} \mid \mathbf{b}$ we also have the rule $\mathbf{c} \mid \mathbf{d}$ and it extends the fact that in classical logic if $\mathbf{a} \wedge \mathbf{b}$ (resp.$\mathbf{b} \rightarrow \mathbf{a}$) is true then $\mathbf{c} \wedge \mathbf{d}$ (resp. $\mathbf{d} \rightarrow \mathbf{c}$) is true provided that $\mathbf{a} \wedge \mathbf{b} \le \mathbf{c} \wedge \mathbf{d}$ (resp. : $\mathbf{b} \rightarrow \mathbf{a} \le \mathbf{d} \rightarrow \mathbf{c}$). In particular, we have

$$\forall \mathbf{c},\ \mathbf{a} \mid \mathbf{b} \le (\mathbf{a} \vee \mathbf{c}) \mid \mathbf{b} \qquad (6)$$

which means that if the rule $\mathbf{a} \mid \mathbf{b}$ holds, any more imprecise conclusion $\mathbf{a} \vee \mathbf{c}$ can be also produced. This is already the case with the material implication since $\mathbf{b} \rightarrow (\mathbf{a} \vee \mathbf{c})$ is true as soon as $\mathbf{b} \rightarrow \mathbf{a}$ is. But,

there is no universal ordering between $\mathbf{a} \mid (\mathbf{b} \wedge \mathbf{c})$ *and* $\mathbf{a} \mid \mathbf{b}$ (7)

Indeed $\mathbf{a} \wedge \mathbf{b} \wedge \mathbf{c} \leq \mathbf{a} \wedge \mathbf{b}$ but $\neg\mathbf{b} \vee \neg\mathbf{c} \vee \mathbf{a} \geq \neg\mathbf{b} \vee \mathbf{a}$. In other words, the rule $\mathbf{a} \mid \mathbf{b}$ may be true as well as false while the rule $\mathbf{a} \mid (\mathbf{b} \wedge \mathbf{c})$ is not applicable. This contrasts with the material implication for which $\mathbf{b} \rightarrow \mathbf{a}$ true entails that $(\mathbf{b} \wedge \mathbf{c}) \rightarrow \mathbf{a}$ is true. It also contrasts with the entailment relation ($\leq$) in $\mathfrak{B}$ for which $\mathbf{b} \leq \mathbf{a}$ implies $\mathbf{b} \wedge \mathbf{c} \leq \mathbf{a}$. We have $\mathbf{b} \leq \mathbf{a} \Leftrightarrow t(\mathbf{a} \mid \mathbf{b}) \in \{?,1\}$, as it can be easily checked on truth-tables. But this does not cover the case where $\mathbf{a}$ is false when $\mathbf{b}$ is true. The statement of fact (7) corresponds to a form of non-monotonicity. But, it can be seen on truth-tables that we cannot have the rules $\mathbf{a} \mid \mathbf{b}$ and $\neg\mathbf{a} \mid (\mathbf{b} \wedge \mathbf{c})$ simultaneously true. This is not very surprizing since, for instance, being both a flying bird and a non-flying ostrich is not possible (with $\mathbf{b}$ = bird, $\mathbf{a}$ = flying, $\mathbf{c}$ = ostrich). Note also that $P(\mathbf{a} \mid \mathbf{b}) = 1$ and $P(\neg\mathbf{a} \mid \mathbf{b} \wedge \mathbf{c}) = 1$ are incompatible since the former entails $P(\neg\mathbf{a} \wedge \mathbf{b}) = 0$ and thus $P(\neg\mathbf{a} \wedge \mathbf{b} \wedge \mathbf{c}) = 0$, while the latter entails $P(\mathbf{a} \wedge \mathbf{b} \wedge \mathbf{c}) = 0$, which leads to $P(\mathbf{b} \wedge \mathbf{c}) = 0$ making $P(\neg\mathbf{a} \mid \mathbf{b} \wedge \mathbf{c})$ undefined. But, a numerical uncertainty measure g compatible with the partial ordering in $\mathfrak{B}|\mathfrak{B}$, will remain free, due to (7), to be such $g(\mathbf{a} \mid \mathbf{b} \wedge \mathbf{c}) < g(\mathbf{a} \mid \mathbf{b})$; see section 3. Thus we shall be able to capture a form of non-monotonicity in this framework, which is in agreement with the rule interpretation, in commonsense knowledge (e.g. generally birds fly but special kinds of birds don't).

Besides, we have the following ordering which is easy to check

$$(\mathbf{a} \wedge \mathbf{b}) \mid \mathbb{1} \leq \mathbf{a} \mid \mathbf{b} \leq (\neg\mathbf{b} \vee \mathbf{a}) \mid \mathbb{1} \qquad (8)$$

and enables us to compare $\mathbf{a} \mid \mathbf{b}$ with $\mathbf{a} \wedge \mathbf{b}$ and with $\neg\mathbf{b} \vee \mathbf{a}$ in $\mathfrak{B}|\mathfrak{B}$ in a way that is in agreement with our intuition.

Lastly, the following property, which is easy to check, expresses the compatibility of the entailment relation $\leq$ with the union operation performed on the left side of the conditioning symbol "|".

$$\left\{ \begin{array}{l} \mathbf{a} \mid \mathbf{e} \leq \mathbf{c} \mid \mathbf{f} \\ \mathbf{b} \mid \mathbf{e} \leq \mathbf{d} \mid \mathbf{f} \end{array} \right. \Rightarrow (\mathbf{a} \vee \mathbf{b}) \mid \mathbf{e} \leq (\mathbf{c} \vee \mathbf{d}) \mid \mathbf{f} \qquad (9)$$

Statement (9) reduces to (6) for $\mathbf{b} = \mathbb{O}$, $\mathbf{c} = \mathbf{a}$, $\mathbf{d} = \mathbf{c}$, $\mathbf{e} = \mathbf{b}$, $\mathbf{f} = \mathbf{b}$.

Bruno and Gilio (1985) use another definition of entailment between conditional objects namely :

$$\mathbf{a} \mid \mathbf{b} \subseteq \mathbf{c} \mid \mathbf{d} \text{ if and only if } \mathbf{a} \le \mathbf{c} \text{ and } \mathbf{b} \le \mathbf{d}$$

This definition is however unrelated to $\le$ on $\mathfrak{B} \mid \mathfrak{B}$, although both definitions coincide on $\mathfrak{B}$.

2.4. Connectives for conditionals

The problem of extending operations such as negation, intersection and union to $\mathfrak{B} \mid \mathfrak{B}$ has been addressed by Schay (1968), Bruno and Gilio (1985), Calabrese (1987) and Goodman and Nguyen (1988). There is a consensus about negation, i.e.

$$\neg(\mathbf{a} \mid \mathbf{b}) = (\neg\mathbf{a} \mid \mathbf{b}) \qquad (10)$$

In terms of a truth-table, it corresponds to extending the negation operation by postulating that $t(\neg\mathbf{a}) = ?$ if $t(\mathbf{a}) = ?$. That is to say, $\neg(\mathbf{a} \mid \mathbf{b})$ corresponds to the converse rule "if **b** then not **a**". This is quite different from what happens with the material implication where $\neg(\mathbf{b} \to \mathbf{a}) = \mathbf{b} \wedge \neg\mathbf{a} \ne \mathbf{b} \to \neg\mathbf{a}$! Here, the negation of a rule is another rule with the same condition of application and the opposite conclusion. It contrasts with the logic programming point of view where a conditional is expressed under the form of a clause $\neg\mathbf{b} \vee \mathbf{a}$ (whose negation is no longer a clause). Besides, this difference seems similar to the one between $\mathbf{b} \vdash \mathbf{a}$ (which is a bit like $\mathbf{a} \mid \mathbf{b}$) and $\vdash \mathbf{b} \to \mathbf{a}$, which are equivalent in classical logic, but no longer in many non-standard systems. Lastly, note that (10) is in accordance with Stalnaker's conditionals introduced in Section 2.1.

There exist three different proposals for defining the conjunction of $(\mathbf{a} \mid \mathbf{b})$ and $(\mathbf{c} \mid \mathbf{d})$, which may appear under various equivalent forms, since due to (4) there are at least four ways of describing the same rule (the forms used below are not necessarily the ones used by the author(s) who introduced the definitions)

$$(\mathbf{a} \mid \mathbf{b}) \mathbin{\pmb{\wedge}} (\mathbf{c} \mid \mathbf{d}) = ((\mathbf{b} \to \mathbf{a}) \wedge (\mathbf{d} \to \mathbf{c})) \mid (\mathbf{b} \vee \mathbf{d}) \qquad (11) \text{ (Schay, Calabrese)}$$
$$(\mathbf{a} \mid \mathbf{b}) \cdot (\mathbf{c} \mid \mathbf{d}) = (\mathbf{a} \wedge \mathbf{c}) \mid ((\neg\mathbf{a} \wedge \mathbf{b}) \vee (\neg\mathbf{c} \wedge \mathbf{d}) \vee (\mathbf{b} \wedge \mathbf{d})) \qquad (12) \text{ (Goodman and Nguyen)}$$
$$(\mathbf{a} \mid \mathbf{b}) \cap (\mathbf{c} \mid \mathbf{d}) = (\mathbf{a} \wedge \mathbf{c}) \mid (\mathbf{b} \wedge \mathbf{d}) \qquad (13) \text{ (Schay, Bruno and Gilio)}$$

In terms of truth tables, it can be checked that these three definitions correspond to three possible extensions of the binary conjunction operation which preserve the symmetry and which take into account the symbol ? introduced in Table 1. This point is not really made clear by the authors who introduce the definitions. Namely, using the same notations for combining propositions or their truth values,

- (11) can be obtained by postulating $1 \wedge ? = 1$; $0 \wedge ? = 0$; $? \wedge ? = ?$
- (12) can be obtained by postulating $1 \cdot ? = ?$; $0 \cdot ? = 0$; $? \cdot ? = ?$
- (13) can be obtained by postulating $1 \cap ? = ?$; $0 \cap ? = ?$; $? \cap ? = ?$

The first conjunction is such that the combination of something true (resp. false) with something inapplicable is true (resp. false). The second conjunction is defined in agreement with the ordering $0 \le ? \le 1$ i.e. the natural interval ordering between 0,{0,1}, and 1. Note that these conjunction operations were first considered in the framework of trivalent logics, by Sobocinski, Lukasiewicz and Bochvar respectively ; see Rescher (1969).

The main practical difference between definitions (11), (12) and (13) lies in the domain where the resulting rule is applicable, $\cap$ being the the most restrictive (it requires $\mathbf{b} \wedge \mathbf{d}$ true) and $\wedge$ being the least restrictive, while ' $\cdot$ ' is intermediary. From the point of view of rule-based systems, $\wedge$ means that the two rules $\mathbf{a} \mid \mathbf{b}$ and $\mathbf{c} \mid \mathbf{d}$ are available and form a rule base. It is natural to define the applicability of a rule base $\{\mathbf{a}_i \mid \mathbf{b}_i, i = 1,n\}$ to a factual base $\mathcal{F}$ whenever at least one rule i is applicable to $\mathcal{F}$, i.e. $\vee_{i=1,n} \mathbf{b}_i$ is true. This remark emphasizes the natural appeal of operation $\wedge$ in the scope of rule-based systems.

Note that $\cap$ would mean in this interpretation that a rule base is applicable whenever *all* rules are applicable, which is not satisfactory. However the operation $\cap$ corresponds to the building from two rules, of a rule with a more specific condition and a more specific conclusion. It means that if **a** (resp. **c**) is produced when **b** (resp. **d**) is known to be true, then the conjunction $\mathbf{a} \wedge \mathbf{c}$ can be produced when both **b** and **d** are known to be true. It is similar to the fact that in logic $\mathbf{b} \rightarrow \mathbf{a}$ and $\mathbf{d} \rightarrow \mathbf{c}$ entails $(\mathbf{b} \wedge \mathbf{d}) \rightarrow (\mathbf{a} \wedge \mathbf{c})$. However, due to (7), the rule $(\mathbf{a} \wedge \mathbf{c}) \mid (\mathbf{b} \wedge \mathbf{d})$ may be rejected, when $\mathbf{a} \mid \mathbf{b}$ and $\mathbf{c} \mid \mathbf{d}$ are correct.

As already said the conditions of applicability of $(\mathbf{a} \mid \mathbf{b}) \cdot (\mathbf{c} \mid \mathbf{d})$ are intermediary ; indeed it requires only, either that both rules are applicable or if only one of them is applicable, that its conclusion is false, as it can be seen on (12). Goodman and Nguyen (1988) advocate this definition as being the natural extension of conjunctions from elements of $\mathcal{B}$ to conditional objects viewed as intervals, that is

$$(\mathbf{a} \mid \mathbf{b}) \cdot (\mathbf{c} \mid \mathbf{d}) = \{\mathbf{x} \wedge \mathbf{y}, \text{ for any } \mathbf{x} \in \mathbf{a} \mid \mathbf{b} \text{ and for any } \mathbf{y} \in \mathbf{c} \mid \mathbf{d}\}.$$

This definition (12) of the conjunction of two rules also parallels the following identity which holds in classical logic

$$(\mathbf{b} \rightarrow \mathbf{a}) \wedge (\mathbf{d} \rightarrow \mathbf{c}) = ((\neg \mathbf{a} \wedge \mathbf{b}) \vee (\neg \mathbf{c} \wedge \mathbf{d}) \vee (\mathbf{b} \wedge \mathbf{d})) \rightarrow (\mathbf{a} \wedge \mathbf{c}) \qquad (14)$$

However the right part of (14) does not appear as a very natural expression of the conjunction of the two implications $\mathbf{b} \to \mathbf{a}$ and $\mathbf{d} \to \mathbf{c}$, although it expresses that the conjunction of the two conclusions can be deduced from **b** and **d** if the two implications are true and cannot be deduced if one of them is false. Similarly, the definition (12) is not intuitively appealing, at least using the rule interpretation. Indeed if $t(\mathbf{a} \mid \mathbf{b}) = 0$ or $t(\mathbf{c} \mid \mathbf{d}) = 0$, the condition part of the resulting rule is satisfied, so that this rule turns out to be false since then $t((\mathbf{a} \mid \mathbf{b}) \cdot (\mathbf{c} \mid \mathbf{d})) = 0$. It is more natural to require that when one of two rules is false their conjunction is either false or not applicable, i.e definition (11). And indeed, the conjunction of the two implications above can also be written equivalently

$$(\mathbf{b} \to \mathbf{a}) \wedge (\mathbf{d} \to \mathbf{c}) = (\mathbf{b} \vee \mathbf{d}) \to ((\mathbf{a} \wedge \mathbf{c}) \vee (\mathbf{a} \wedge \neg\mathbf{d}) \vee (\mathbf{c} \wedge \neg\mathbf{b})) \qquad (15)$$

This latter writing seems more satisfactory from an intuitive point of view. It can be checked that

$$((\mathbf{a} \wedge \mathbf{c}) \vee (\mathbf{a} \wedge \neg\mathbf{d}) \vee (\mathbf{c} \wedge \neg\mathbf{b})) \mid (\mathbf{b} \vee \mathbf{d}) \;=\; ((\mathbf{b} \to \mathbf{a}) \wedge (\mathbf{d} \to \mathbf{c})) \mid (\mathbf{b} \vee \mathbf{d})$$

using $(\neg B \vee A) \wedge B = A \wedge B$ with $B = \mathbf{b} \vee \mathbf{d}$ and $\neg B \vee A = (\mathbf{b} \to \mathbf{a}) \wedge (\mathbf{d} \to \mathbf{c})$. Then the definition (11) has an equivalent form whose condition and conclusion parts respectively coincide with the condition and conclusion parts of the right part of (15). This confirms the intuitive appeal of definition (11). Of course when $\mathbf{b} = \mathbf{d}$, (11), (12) and (13) coincide.

The following identities or relations are worth noticing :

$$\mathbf{a} \mid \mathbf{b} \le \mathbf{c} \mid \mathbf{d} \Leftrightarrow (\mathbf{a} \mid \mathbf{b}) \cdot (\mathbf{c} \mid \mathbf{d}) = (\mathbf{a} \mid \mathbf{b}) \qquad (16)$$

$$(\mathbf{a} \mid \mathbf{b}) \cdot (\mathbf{c} \mid \mathbf{d}) \le (\mathbf{a} \mid \mathbf{b}) \,\boldsymbol{\wedge}\, (\mathbf{c} \mid \mathbf{d}) \;;\; (\mathbf{a} \mid \mathbf{b}) \cdot (\mathbf{c} \mid \mathbf{d}) \le (\mathbf{a} \mid \mathbf{b}) \cap (\mathbf{c} \mid \mathbf{d}) \qquad (17)$$

$$(\mathbf{a} \wedge \mathbf{b}) \mid \mathbb{1} = (\mathbf{a} \mid \mathbf{b}) \,\boldsymbol{\wedge}\, (\mathbf{b} \mid \mathbb{1}) = (\mathbf{a} \mid \mathbf{b}) \cdot (\mathbf{b} \mid \mathbb{1}) \qquad (18)$$

$$(\mathbf{b} \wedge \mathbf{c}) \mid \mathbf{a} = (\mathbf{b} \mid \mathbf{a}) \,\boldsymbol{\wedge}\, (\mathbf{c} \mid (\mathbf{a} \wedge \mathbf{b})) = (\mathbf{b} \mid \mathbf{a}) \cdot (\mathbf{c} \mid (\mathbf{a} \wedge \mathbf{b})) \qquad (19)$$

$$(\mathbf{c} \mid (\mathbf{a} \wedge \mathbf{b})) \,\boldsymbol{\wedge}\, (\mathbf{c} \mid (\mathbf{a} \wedge \neg\mathbf{b})) = \mathbf{c} \mid \mathbf{a} \qquad (20)$$

The equivalence (16) is used by Goodman and Nguyen (1988) as defining the partial ordering ; it can be easily checked, as well as (17) and (18) on truth-tables. (19) is easy to prove. Indeed

$$\begin{aligned}(\mathbf{b} \mid \mathbf{a}) \,\boldsymbol{\wedge}\, (\mathbf{c} \mid (\mathbf{a} \wedge \mathbf{b})) &= ((\mathbf{a} \to \mathbf{b}) \wedge ((\mathbf{a} \wedge \mathbf{b}) \to \mathbf{c})) \mid \mathbf{a} \\ &= (\neg\mathbf{a} \vee (\mathbf{b} \wedge (\neg\mathbf{b} \vee \mathbf{c}))) \mid \mathbf{a} = (\neg\mathbf{a} \vee (\mathbf{b} \wedge \mathbf{c})) \mid \mathbf{a} \\ &= (\mathbf{a} \to (\mathbf{b} \wedge \mathbf{c})) \mid \mathbf{a} = (\mathbf{b} \wedge \mathbf{c}) \mid \mathbf{a} \text{ due to (4).}\end{aligned}$$

Similarly, $(\mathbf{b} \mid \mathbf{a}) \,\boldsymbol{\wedge}\, (\mathbf{c} \mid (\mathbf{a} \wedge \mathbf{b})) = (\mathbf{b} \wedge \mathbf{c}) \mid ((\mathbf{a} \wedge \neg\mathbf{b}) \vee (\neg\mathbf{c} \wedge \mathbf{a} \wedge \mathbf{b}) \vee (\mathbf{a} \wedge \mathbf{b})) = (\mathbf{b} \wedge \mathbf{c}) \mid \mathbf{a}$. But (19) does not hold for the third conjuction. Obviously (18) is a particular case of (19) (with $\mathbf{a} = \mathbb{1}$ and $\mathbf{c} = \mathbf{a}$). The identity (19) is the symbolic counterpart of a well-known (basic)

relation between conditional probabilities, namely

$$\mathrm{Prob}(\mathbf{b} \wedge \mathbf{c} \mid \mathbf{a}) = \mathrm{Prob}(\mathbf{b} \mid \mathbf{a}) \cdot \mathrm{Prob}(\mathbf{c} \mid \mathbf{a} \wedge \mathbf{b}).$$

Note that there is no ordering between $(\mathbf{a} \mid \mathbf{b}) \curlywedge (\mathbf{c} \mid \mathbf{d})$ and $(\mathbf{a} \mid \mathbf{b}) \cap (\mathbf{c} \mid \mathbf{d})$. This is natural, since in the particular case where $\mathbf{a} = \mathbf{c}$, these two expressions reduce to $\mathbf{a} \mid (\mathbf{b} \vee \mathbf{d})$ and to $\mathbf{a} \mid (\mathbf{b} \wedge \mathbf{d})$ respectively and due to (7) there is no universal ordering between them. The equality (20) is easy to prove ; indeed the left side of (20) is equal to

$$(((\mathbf{a} \wedge \mathbf{b}) \rightarrow \mathbf{c}) \curlywedge ((\mathbf{a} \wedge \neg\mathbf{b}) \rightarrow \mathbf{c})) \mid \mathbf{a} = (\mathbf{a} \rightarrow \mathbf{c}) \mid \mathbf{a} = \mathbf{c} \mid \mathbf{a} \text{ using (4).}$$

Note that (20) has no perfect counterpart in probability theory. The following entailment relation is also worth noticing

$$\mathbf{a} \mid \mathbf{b} \curlywedge \neg\mathbf{a} \mid (\mathbf{b} \wedge \mathbf{c}) \leq \neg\mathbf{c} \mid (\mathbf{a} \wedge \mathbf{b})$$

It is easy to check ; indeed $((\mathbf{b} \rightarrow \mathbf{a}) \wedge ((\mathbf{b} \wedge \mathbf{c}) \rightarrow \neg\mathbf{a})) \mid \mathbf{b} \leq \neg\mathbf{c} \mid (\mathbf{a} \wedge \mathbf{b})$
since $(\neg\mathbf{b} \vee \mathbf{a}) \wedge (\neg\mathbf{b} \vee \neg\mathbf{c} \vee \neg\mathbf{a}) \wedge \mathbf{b} = \mathbf{a} \wedge \mathbf{b} \wedge \neg\mathbf{c}$
and $\neg\mathbf{b} \vee ((\neg\mathbf{b} \vee \mathbf{a}) \wedge (\neg\mathbf{b} \vee \neg\mathbf{c} \vee \neg\mathbf{a})) = \neg\mathbf{b} \vee (\mathbf{a} \wedge \neg\mathbf{c}) \leq \neg\mathbf{a} \vee \neg\mathbf{b} \vee \neg\mathbf{c}$.
This completes the discussion of statement (7) above by showing not only that there is no entailment relation between $\mathbf{a} \mid \mathbf{b}$ and $\mathbf{a} \mid (\mathbf{b} \wedge \mathbf{c})$, but also that a conjunction of $\mathbf{a} \mid \mathbf{b}$ and $\neg(\mathbf{a} \mid (\mathbf{b} \wedge \mathbf{c}))$ entails something in agreement with our intuition. It is also in agreement with probability calculus since it can be shown that

$$P(\neg\mathbf{c} \mid \mathbf{a} \wedge \mathbf{b}) \geq 1 - \frac{1 - P(\neg\mathbf{a} \mid \mathbf{b} \wedge \mathbf{c})}{P(\mathbf{a} \mid \mathbf{b})}$$

which expresses that if $P(\mathbf{a} \mid \mathbf{b})$ and $P(\neg\mathbf{a} \mid \mathbf{b} \wedge \mathbf{c})$ are both close to 1, $P(\neg\mathbf{c} \mid \mathbf{a} \wedge \mathbf{b})$ is also close to 1 (however remember that $P(\mathbf{a} \mid \mathbf{b}) = 1$ and $P(\neg\mathbf{a} \mid \mathbf{b} \wedge \mathbf{c}) = 1$ are incompatible as already said).

Disjunction operations can be derived using De Morgan laws and the definition of the negation of conditionals. For instance, the dual of $\curlywedge$ is (Calabrese, 1987)

$$(\mathbf{a} \mid \mathbf{b}) \curlyvee (\mathbf{c} \mid \mathbf{d}) = ((\mathbf{a} \wedge \mathbf{b}) \vee (\mathbf{c} \wedge \mathbf{d})) \mid (\mathbf{b} \vee \mathbf{d}) \qquad (21)$$

It has been proposed by Bruno and Gilio (1985), and also by Schay (1968) under a different appearance. This disjunction produces a rule which can be triggered by disjunctive information, weaker than that which triggers $\mathbf{a} \mid \mathbf{b}$ or $\mathbf{c} \mid \mathbf{d}$. Using (6), we deduce the ordering relation

$$(\mathbf{a} \mid \mathbf{b}) \curlyvee (\mathbf{c} \mid \mathbf{d}) \leq (\mathbf{a} \vee \mathbf{c}) \mid (\mathbf{b} \vee \mathbf{d}) \qquad (22)$$

since $(\mathbf{a} \wedge \mathbf{b}) \vee (\mathbf{c} \wedge \mathbf{d}) \leq \mathbf{a} \vee \mathbf{c}$. Thus the disjunction of two rules (in the sense of $\curlyvee$) entails that if one the conditions is satisfied then at least one of **a** and **c** must be true, which is in agreement with the intuition. Moreover it can checked that we have the ordering relation

$$(\mathbf{a} \mid \mathbf{b}) \curlywedge (\mathbf{c} \mid \mathbf{d}) \leq (\mathbf{a} \mid \mathbf{b}) \curlyvee (\mathbf{c} \mid \mathbf{d}) \qquad (23)$$

But no such relation exists between **a** | **b** and its disjunction or conjunction with another rule **c** | **d**. This is due to the fact that **a** | **b** may be not applicable while **c** | **d** is ; however in this case we have the relations $(\mathbf{a} \mid \mathbf{b}) \curlywedge (\mathbf{c} \mid \mathbf{d}) \leq \mathbf{c} \mid \mathbf{d} \leq (\mathbf{a} \mid \mathbf{b}) \curlyvee (\mathbf{c} \mid \mathbf{d})$ for the other rule.

It is interesting to check Stalnaker(1968)'s conditional law of excluded middle in this setting. The disjunction of **a** | **b** and ¬**a** | **b** is, whatever the considered disjunction, $\mathbb{1} \mid \mathbf{b}$. The law holds when **b** is true and is not applicable otherwise.

The disjunction operations $\curlyvee$, $\perp$, $\cup$ can be expressed in terms of truth-values by duality with respect to conjunctions $\curlywedge$, $\cdot$, $\cap$. Namely, $\forall x \in \{0, ?, 1\}$

> $x \curlywedge ? = x = ? \curlywedge x$ yields $x \curlyvee ? = x = ? \curlyvee x$
> $x \,.\, ? = \min(x, [0,1]) = ? \,.\, x$ yields $x \perp ? = \max(x, [0,1]) = ? \perp x$ where $[0,1]$ is identified with ?
> $x \cap ? = ? = ? \cap x$ yields $x \cup ? = ? = ? \cup x$.

Note that ?, with respect to both $\curlywedge$ and $\curlyvee$, plays the rôle of a neutral element (it has been called a "nought element" by Sanchez (1989) who considered it for discussing a problem of importance weighting in information retrieval), while ? is an universally absorbing element with respect to both $\cap$ and $\cup$. Again, the pairs $(\curlywedge,\curlyvee)$, $(.,\perp)$, $(\cap,\cup)$ were first considered in the framework of trivalent logics, as conjunction and disjunction operations, by Sobocinski, Lukasiewicz and Bochvar respectively ; see Rescher (1969).

Schay (1968) indicates that $\curlyvee$ and $\curlywedge$ are not distributive with respect to each other so that *$\mathcal{B}/\mathcal{B}$ is no longer a Boolean algebra*. See also Calabrese (1987). Moreover the algebraic structure of $(\mathcal{B}|\mathcal{B}, \curlywedge, \curlyvee, \cdot, \perp, \cap, \cup, \neg)$ is still to investigate. Let us mention the distributivity of $\curlywedge$ with respect to $\perp$, i.e.

$$\mathbf{a} \mid \mathbf{b} \curlywedge (\mathbf{c} \mid \mathbf{d} \perp \mathbf{e} \mid \mathbf{f}) = (\mathbf{a} \mid \mathbf{b} \curlywedge \mathbf{c} \mid \mathbf{d}) \perp (\mathbf{a} \mid \mathbf{b} \curlywedge \mathbf{e} \mid \mathbf{f})$$

as well as the distributivity of $\cap$ with respect to $\curlyvee$ (Bruno and Gilio (1985)) ; this is no longer true for $\cap$ with respect to $\perp$. However, all the binary connectives are associative, commutative, and idempotent.

The following monotonicity property holds with respect to the relation ≤ :

$$\text{if } \mathbf{a}_1 \mid \mathbf{b}_1 \leq \mathbf{a}_2 \mid \mathbf{b}_2 \text{ and } \mathbf{c}_1 \mid \mathbf{d}_1 \leq \mathbf{c}_2 \mid \mathbf{d}_2 \text{ then } \mathbf{a}_1 \mid \mathbf{b}_1 \wedge \mathbf{c}_1 \mid \mathbf{d}_1 \leq \mathbf{a}_2 \mid \mathbf{b}_2 \wedge \mathbf{c}_2 \mid \mathbf{d}_2$$

This property holds too for connectives $\cup$, $\cdot$, $\perp$ but not for $\cap$, $\vee$.

Lastly it is interesting to iterate the conditioning process in such a way that $\mathfrak{B}|\mathfrak{B}$ remains closed under this process. The following definition is natural (Calabrese, 1987)

$$(\mathbf{a} \mid \mathbf{b}) \mid \mathbf{c} = \mathbf{a} \mid (\mathbf{b} \wedge \mathbf{c}) \qquad (24)$$

Indeed "If **c** is true then (if **b** is true then **a** is produced)" means that **b** and **c** are the conditions required to produce **a**. In terms of truth-table, (24) is obtained with the convention $? \mid 0 = ? = ? \mid 1$ (using the same symbol '|' for propositions and for values of the truth function). However the companion expression $\mathbf{a} \mid (\mathbf{b} \mid \mathbf{c})$ is less easy to interpret. Two meanings can be envisaged

1) if $\mathbf{b} \mid \mathbf{c}$ is true then **a** is produced. That is to say : if **c** is true, **b** is held for true then **a** is produced. This is equivalent to let | be associative and $\mathbf{a} \mid (\mathbf{b} \mid \mathbf{c}) = \mathbf{a} \mid (\mathbf{b} \wedge \mathbf{c})$. It corresponds to the convention $1 \mid ? = ? = 0 \mid ?$.

2) if $\mathbf{b} \mid \mathbf{c}$ is not false then **a** is produced. Note that it means that **a** is produced as long as $\mathbf{b} \mid \mathbf{c}$ is acceptable as a rule (even a non-applicable one), i.e. it sounds like a meta-rule (a rule depending upon rules). That is to say : if $\neg(\mathbf{c} \wedge \neg\mathbf{b})$ is true then **a** is produced. In that case | is not associative and $\mathbf{a} \mid (\mathbf{b} \mid \mathbf{c}) = \mathbf{a} \mid (\mathbf{c} \rightarrow \mathbf{b})$. This is Calabrese's definition. It corresponds to set $1 \mid ? = 1$ and $0 \mid ? = 0$.

This problem leads to alternative definitions for the conditioning between rules :

$$(\mathbf{a} \mid \mathbf{b}) \mid (\mathbf{c} \mid \mathbf{d}) = \mathbf{a} \mid (\mathbf{b} \wedge \mathbf{c} \wedge \mathbf{d}) \qquad \text{(associative definition)}$$

$$\text{or} \quad \mathbf{a} \mid (\mathbf{b} \wedge (\mathbf{d} \rightarrow \mathbf{c})) \qquad \text{(second point of view).}$$

Goodman and Nguyen (1988) propose to define $(\mathbf{a} \mid \mathbf{b}) \mid (\mathbf{c} \mid \mathbf{d})$ by applying again definition 1. Then, we do not get an element of $\mathfrak{B}|\mathfrak{B}$ but an interval therein. This proposal, if formally sound, leads to an infinite expansion process where intuition may be lost. See, however, Goodman et al. (1990), chapter 8. Weber (1988b) has recently extended the notion of conditional objects to weaker structures than Boolean algebras, namely residuated lattice-ordered semi-groups. This way, the extension of conditional objects to fuzzy events can be contemplated. See also Goodman et al. (1990), chapter 7.

2.5 - Measure-free conditionals as default rules

Several authors, including Zadeh (1985), Pearl (1988), and Dubois and Prade (1988a), have suggested that a default rule such as "Generally, **b**'s are **a**'s" could be interpreted as Probability($\mathbf{a} \mid \mathbf{b}$) = HIGH. Interpretations of HIGH vary from a probability infinitesimally close to 1 (following Adams, 1975) to fuzzy quantifiers. It may be tempting to consider the measure-free conditional $\mathbf{a} \mid \mathbf{b}$ as a model of normal default, in the spirit of Reiter's logic (1980). That is, if **a** is true then, unless **b** can be proved false, **b** is true without referring to any statistical interpretation, considering that the statistical component is carried by the probability attached to the conditional, and not by the conditional itself.

There are two conditions under which $\mathbf{a} \mid \mathbf{b}$ could represent a default :

1) there exists at least one interpretation for which $t(\mathbf{a} \mid \mathbf{b}) = 1$ (otherwise $\mathbf{a} \wedge \mathbf{b} = \mathbb{O}$ and it makes no sense to assert $\mathbf{a} \mid \mathbf{b}$)

2) there may exist exceptions to the rule, i.e. interpretations for which $t(\mathbf{a} \mid \mathbf{b}) = 0$ (otherwise $\mathbf{a} \leq \mathbf{b}$ holds and $\mathbf{a} \mid \mathbf{b}$ is nothing but a standard monotonic inference rule ; particularly, for any probability measure P, $P(\mathbf{a} \mid \mathbf{b}) = 1$, while here we wish to allow for $P(\mathbf{a} \mid \mathbf{b}) \in (0,1)$).

Asserting "$\mathbf{a} \mid \mathbf{b}$" should thus be interpreted as : $\mathbf{b} \neq \mathbb{O}$ and $(\mathbf{a} \mid \mathbf{b}) \neq (\mathbb{O} \mid \mathbf{b})$; these two conditions hold if and only if $\mathbf{a} \wedge \mathbf{b} \neq \mathbb{O}$, so that $\mathbf{a} \mid \mathbf{b}$ means "there are examples of **b**'s that are **a**'s", i.e. the weakest kind of default rule one may apparently think of. The condition $\mathbf{b} \neq \mathbb{O}$ can be relaxed since conditionals of the form $\mathbf{a} \mid \mathbb{O}$ correspond to never applicable rules. Hence we define the acceptance of asserting $\mathbf{a} \mid \mathbf{b}$ as the fact of assuming $\mathbf{a} \mid \mathbf{b} \neq \mathbb{O} \mid \mathbf{b}$. Note that despite the isomorphism between $\mathfrak{B}$ and $\{\mathbf{a} \mid \mathbb{1}, \mathbf{a} \in \mathfrak{B}\}$, asserting a proposition **a** (also denoted $\vdash \mathbf{a}$) is different from (and much stronger than) asserting $\mathbf{a} \mid \mathbb{1}$ since the latter comes down to only assuming $\mathbf{a} \neq \mathbb{O}$. Similarly, $\mathbf{b} \vdash \mathbf{a}$ (or equivalently, $\vdash \neg\mathbf{b} \vee \mathbf{a}$, or still, $\neg\mathbf{b} \vee \mathbf{a} = \mathbb{1}$) is stronger than asserting $\mathbf{a} \mid \mathbf{b}$ since it admits of no exception. The property "$\mathbf{b} \vdash \mathbf{a}$ implies $\mathbf{a} \mid \mathbf{b}$" is easy to check and corresponds to the property of "supraclassicality" in non-monotonic logic.

As a next step, it seems possible to use the ordering relation $\leq$ between defaults and the conjunction $\curlywedge$ for the definition of a consequence relation. A default $\mathbf{e} \mid \mathbf{f}$ can be deduced from $\{\mathbf{a} \mid \mathbf{b}, \mathbf{c} \mid \mathbf{d}\}$ if and only if

$$(\mathbf{a} \mid \mathbf{b}) \curlywedge (\mathbf{c} \mid \mathbf{d}) \leq (\mathbf{e} \mid \mathbf{f}) \qquad (25)$$

(25) means the following : any example of one of the rules $\mathbf{a} \mid \mathbf{b}$ or $\mathbf{c} \mid \mathbf{d}$, that is not an

exception to the other rule is an example of $\mathbf{e} \mid \mathbf{f}$; and any exception to $\mathbf{e} \mid \mathbf{f}$ is an exception to one of the rules $\mathbf{a} \mid \mathbf{b}$, or $\mathbf{c} \mid \mathbf{d}$. Particularly $(\mathbf{a} \mid \mathbf{b}) \boldsymbol{\wedge} (\mathbf{c} \mid \mathbf{d}) \leq (\mathbf{a} \mid \mathbf{b})$ does not hold because an example of $\mathbf{c} \mid \mathbf{d}$ can be simply irrelevant for $\mathbf{a} \mid \mathbf{b}$ (i.e. $t(\mathbf{c} \wedge \mathbf{d}) = 1$ and $t(\mathbf{b}) = 0$ so that $t((\mathbf{a} \mid \mathbf{b}) \boldsymbol{\wedge} (\mathbf{c} \mid \mathbf{d})) = 1$ while $t(\mathbf{a} \mid \mathbf{b}) = ?$). On the contrary a rule $\mathbf{e} \mid \mathbf{f}$ that satisfies (25) takes into account *both* rules since its examples are at least all those of each rule when the two rules do not contradict each other. This remark suggests that (25) defines $\mathbf{e} \mid \mathbf{f}$ as a weak substitute to the set of defaults $\{\mathbf{a} \mid \mathbf{b}, \mathbf{c} \mid \mathbf{d}\}$ in which both rules are still acting. By contrast $(\mathbf{a} \mid \mathbf{b}) \cdot (\mathbf{c} \mid \mathbf{d}) \leq (\mathbf{a} \mid \mathbf{b})$ is always true with the conjunction defined by (12). Hence using this conjunction in a consequence relation on an algebra of conditional objects does not look natural when the conditional objects are viewed as production rules.

The following properties of the consequence relation $\leq$ are noticeable, and easily checked using truth-tables, or equivalently, using the definition (5) of $\leq$ and the conjunctions (11) and (12) (hereafter written using $\boldsymbol{\wedge}$) :

$$(\mathbf{a} \mid \mathbf{b}) \boldsymbol{\wedge} (\mathbf{c} \mid \mathbf{b}) \leq \mathbf{c} \mid (\mathbf{a} \wedge \mathbf{b}) \tag{26}$$

$$(\mathbf{a} \mid \mathbf{b}) \boldsymbol{\wedge} (\mathbf{c} \mid (\mathbf{a} \wedge \mathbf{b})) \leq \mathbf{c} \mid \mathbf{b} \tag{27}$$

$$(\mathbf{a} \mid \mathbf{b}) \boldsymbol{\wedge} (\mathbf{c} \mid \mathbf{b}) \leq (\mathbf{a} \wedge \mathbf{c}) \mid \mathbf{b} \tag{28}$$

$$(\mathbf{a} \mid \mathbf{b}) \boldsymbol{\wedge} (\mathbf{b} \mid \mathbf{a}) \boldsymbol{\wedge} (\mathbf{c} \mid \mathbf{a}) \leq \mathbf{c} \mid \mathbf{b} \tag{29}$$

$$\mathbf{c} \mid (\mathbf{a} \wedge \mathbf{b}) \leq (\neg \mathbf{b} \vee \mathbf{c}) \mid \mathbf{a} \tag{30}$$

$$(\mathbf{c} \mid \mathbf{a}) \boldsymbol{\wedge} (\mathbf{c} \mid \mathbf{b}) \leq \mathbf{c} \mid (\mathbf{a} \vee \mathbf{b}) \tag{31}$$

<u>Proof</u> : (26) holds for all three conditional conjunctions since

$$(\mathbf{a} \mid \mathbf{b}) \boldsymbol{\wedge} (\mathbf{c} \mid \mathbf{b}) = (\mathbf{a} \mid \mathbf{b}) \cdot (\mathbf{c} \mid \mathbf{b}) = (\mathbf{a} \mid \mathbf{b}) \cap (\mathbf{c} \mid \mathbf{b}) = (\mathbf{a} \wedge \mathbf{c}) \mid \mathbf{b} \leq \mathbf{c} \mid (\mathbf{a} \wedge \mathbf{b})\,;$$

(27) is a weak version of (19), and also holds for conjunction $\cdot$. (28) holds with equality for all conjunctions. (29) is easily proved as follows :

$$\begin{aligned}(\mathbf{a} \mid \mathbf{b}) \boldsymbol{\wedge} (\mathbf{b} \mid \mathbf{a}) \boldsymbol{\wedge} (\mathbf{c} \mid \mathbf{a}) &= (\mathbf{a} \mid \mathbf{b}) \boldsymbol{\wedge} (\mathbf{b} \wedge \mathbf{c} \mid \mathbf{a}) \\ &= ((\neg \mathbf{b} \vee \mathbf{a}) \wedge (\neg \mathbf{a} \vee (\mathbf{b} \wedge \mathbf{c}))) \mid (\mathbf{a} \vee \mathbf{b})\end{aligned}$$

now, $$\begin{aligned}(\neg \mathbf{b} \vee \mathbf{a}) \wedge (\neg \mathbf{a} \vee (\mathbf{b} \wedge \mathbf{c})) \wedge (\mathbf{a} \vee \mathbf{b}) &= \mathbf{a} \wedge (\neg \mathbf{a} \vee (\mathbf{b} \wedge \mathbf{c})) \\ &= \mathbf{a} \wedge \mathbf{b} \wedge \mathbf{c} \leq \mathbf{c} \wedge \mathbf{b}\end{aligned}$$

moreover, $$\begin{aligned}(\neg \mathbf{a} \wedge \neg \mathbf{b}) \vee ((\neg \mathbf{b} \vee \mathbf{a}) \wedge (\neg \mathbf{a} \vee (\mathbf{b} \wedge \mathbf{c}))) &= (\neg \mathbf{b} \vee \mathbf{a}) \wedge (\neg \mathbf{a} \vee (\mathbf{b} \wedge \mathbf{c})) \\ &= (\neg \mathbf{b} \wedge \neg \mathbf{a}) \vee (\mathbf{a} \wedge \mathbf{b} \wedge \mathbf{c}) \leq \neg \mathbf{b} \vee \mathbf{c}\end{aligned}$$

(29) does not hold for conjunction $\cap$, however ; but it holds with conjunction $\cdot$. (30) is proved similarly due to $\mathbf{a} \wedge \mathbf{b} \wedge \mathbf{c} \leq \mathbf{a} \wedge (\neg \mathbf{b} \vee \mathbf{c})$ and $\neg(\mathbf{a} \wedge \mathbf{b}) \vee \mathbf{c} = \neg \mathbf{a} \vee \neg \mathbf{b} \vee \mathbf{c}$. (31)

holds, with equality ; indeed noticing that $(\mathbf{c} \mid \mathbf{a}) \wedge (\mathbf{c} \mid \mathbf{b}) = (\neg\mathbf{a} \vee \mathbf{c}) \wedge (\neg\mathbf{b} \vee \mathbf{c}) \mid (\mathbf{a} \vee \mathbf{b})$, the condition of equality (3) is easily checked, i.e. $(\mathbf{a} \vee \mathbf{b}) \wedge (\neg\mathbf{a} \vee \mathbf{c}) \wedge (\neg\mathbf{b} \vee \mathbf{c}) = (\mathbf{a} \vee \mathbf{b}) \wedge \mathbf{c}$. (31) also holds (but not with equality) for conjunction $\cdot$ and does not hold for conjunction $\cap$.

Q.E.D.

(26-27) and (29-31) have the following probabilistic counterparts :

$$P(\mathbf{c} \mid \mathbf{a} \wedge \mathbf{b}) \geq P(\mathbf{a} \wedge \mathbf{c} \mid \mathbf{b})$$
$$P(\mathbf{c} \mid \mathbf{b}) \geq P(\mathbf{a} \mid \mathbf{b}) \cdot P(\mathbf{c} \mid \mathbf{a} \wedge \mathbf{b})$$
$$P(\mathbf{c} \mid \mathbf{b}) \geq P(\mathbf{a} \mid \mathbf{b}) \cdot P(\mathbf{b} \wedge \mathbf{c} \mid \mathbf{a})$$
$$P(\neg\mathbf{b} \vee \mathbf{c} \mid \mathbf{a}) \geq P(\mathbf{c} \mid \mathbf{a} \wedge \mathbf{b})$$
$$P(\mathbf{c} \mid \mathbf{a}) > \varepsilon,\ P(\mathbf{c} \mid \mathbf{b}) > \varepsilon' \;\Rightarrow\; P(\mathbf{c} \mid \mathbf{a} \vee \mathbf{b}) > \varepsilon''.$$

In conditional logic of the Adams (1975), $\mathbf{a} \mid \mathbf{b}$ is interpreted as $P(\mathbf{a} \mid \mathbf{b}) \geq 1 - \varepsilon$ where ε is arbitrarily close to 0 and denoted as $\mathbf{b} \to \mathbf{a}$. This interpretation is much more demanding than ours, which corresponds only to $P(\mathbf{a} \mid \mathbf{b}) > 0$. However Adams (1975) found inference rules that are exact counterparts of (26, 27) and(31), namely :

triangularity :	$\mathbf{b} \to \mathbf{a},\ \mathbf{b} \to \mathbf{c} \;\Rightarrow\; (\mathbf{b} \wedge \mathbf{a}) \to \mathbf{c}$
Bayes rule :	$\mathbf{b} \to \mathbf{a},\ (\mathbf{a} \wedge \mathbf{b}) \to \mathbf{c} \;\Rightarrow\; \mathbf{b} \to \mathbf{c}$
disjunction :	$\mathbf{a} \to \mathbf{c},\ \mathbf{b} \to \mathbf{c} \;\Rightarrow\; (\mathbf{a} \vee \mathbf{b}) \to \mathbf{c}$

These rules are used by Pearl (1988) to build a probabilistic-like default logic.

By contrast, starting from purely logical assignments, Gabbay (1985) proposed several axioms that a non-monotonic deduction operation $\mathrel{|\!\sim}$ should satisfy, and especially :

$$\frac{\mathbf{b} \mathrel{|\!\sim} \mathbf{a}\ ;\ \mathbf{b} \mathrel{|\!\sim} \mathbf{c}}{\mathbf{b}, \mathbf{a} \mathrel{|\!\sim} \mathbf{c}} \quad \text{and} \quad \frac{\mathbf{b} \mathrel{|\!\sim} \mathbf{a}\ ;\ \mathbf{a}, \mathbf{b} \mathrel{|\!\sim} \mathbf{c}}{\mathbf{b} \mathrel{|\!\sim} \mathbf{c}}$$

(restricted monotonicity) (cut)

Clearly, restricted monotonicity becomes triangularity in the probabilistic setting and correspond to (26), while (27), related to Bayes rule, is simply a weak form of transitivity (often called "cut") that non-monotonic deduction must satisfy. Note that in the above patterns of inference, the terms $\mathbf{a}, \mathbf{b} \mathrel{|\!\sim} \mathbf{c}$ and $\mathbf{b} \mathrel{|\!\sim} \mathbf{c}$ are exchanged, as pointed out by Mackinson (1989). It is then possible to put these two patterns together and claim that given $\mathbf{b} \mathrel{|\!\sim} \mathbf{a}$, the non-monotonic deductions $\mathbf{a}, \mathbf{b} \mathrel{|\!\sim} \mathbf{c}$ and $\mathbf{b} \mathrel{|\!\sim} \mathbf{c}$ are equivalent. This is what Mackinson (1989) calls the cumulativity condition. For conditional objects it holds under the form : if $t(\mathbf{a} \mid \mathbf{b}) \neq 0$ then $\mathbf{c} \mid (\mathbf{a} \wedge \mathbf{b}) = \mathbf{c} \mid \mathbf{b}$.

The reflexivity property, i.e. $\mathbf{a} \mathrel{|\!\sim} \mathbf{a}$, also holds for conditional objects since, generally, $\mathbf{a} \mid \mathbf{a} \neq \mathbb{O}$ (even if $\mathbf{a} = \mathbb{O}$). Other noticeable properties of conditional objects that make them look like non-monotonic consequence operators are the following :

- if $\mathbf{a} = \mathbf{b}$ then $\mathbf{c} \mid \mathbf{a} = \mathbf{c} \mid \mathbf{b}$, which corresponds to the "left logical equivalence" property of Kraus et al. (1990) :

$$\frac{\vdash \mathbf{a} \leftrightarrow \mathbf{b} \ ; \ \mathbf{a} \mathrel{|\!\sim} \mathbf{c}}{\mathbf{b} \mathrel{|\!\sim} \mathbf{c}}$$

- if $\mathbf{a} \leq \mathbf{b}$ then $\mathbf{a} \mid \mathbf{c} \leq \mathbf{b} \mid \mathbf{c}$ which corresponds to the property of "right weakening" by Kraus et al. (1990) :

$$\frac{\vdash \mathbf{a} \rightarrow \mathbf{b} \ ; \ \mathbf{c} \mathrel{|\!\sim} \mathbf{a}}{\mathbf{c} \mathrel{|\!\sim} \mathbf{b}}$$

These properties, along with reflexivity, restricted monotonicity (26) and cut (27), characterize the so-called system C of Kraus et al. (1990). They indicate that counterparts of (28) and (29) are consequences of these properties namely

$$\frac{\mathbf{a} \mathrel{|\!\sim} \mathbf{b} \ ; \ \mathbf{a} \mathrel{|\!\sim} \mathbf{c}}{\mathbf{a} \mathrel{|\!\sim} \mathbf{b} \wedge \mathbf{c}} \qquad \text{("right and")}$$

$$\frac{\mathbf{a} \mathrel{|\!\sim} \mathbf{b} \ ; \ \mathbf{b} \mathrel{|\!\sim} \mathbf{a} \ ; \ \mathbf{a} \mathrel{|\!\sim} \mathbf{c}}{\mathbf{b} \mathrel{|\!\sim} \mathbf{c}} \qquad \text{("reciprocity")}$$

The name "reciprocity" can be found in Mackinson (1989). Moreover, (30) corresponds to one of two halves of the deduction theorem, i.e. following again Kraus et al. (1990) :

$$\frac{\mathbf{a} \wedge \mathbf{b} \mathrel{|\!\sim} \mathbf{c}}{\mathbf{a} \mathrel{|\!\sim} \neg\mathbf{b} \vee \mathbf{c}} \qquad \text{(HD1)}$$

These authors indicate that the converse inference (that does not hold for conditional objects) leads to the collapse of the C system onto classical logic. Lastly, (31) is called a distribution property by Gärdenfors and Mackinson (1990), and is a consequence of the (HD1) property added to the C-like axioms. It can be written in the style of non-monotonic consequence axioms as :

$$\frac{\mathbf{a} \mathrel{|\!\sim} \mathbf{c} \ ; \ \mathbf{b} \mathrel{|\!\sim} \mathbf{c}}{\mathbf{a} \vee \mathbf{b} \mathrel{|\!\sim} \mathbf{c}} \qquad \text{(distribution)}$$

Let us proceed to a formal derivation, in the setting of conditional objects, of (28) and (29) from (27), (26), the reflexivity property, the left logical equivalence and the right weakening. We also need the fact that the operation denoted ";" in the non-monotonic patterns, is associative and idempotent. Fortunately, the conjunction $\wedge$ is indeed associative and idempotent, (as well as the other conditional conjunctions). Moreover, in the patterns of non-monotonic inference, reflexivity means that terms of the form $\mathbf{a} \mid\!\sim \mathbf{a}$ can always be added to a set of non-monotonic deductions $\mathbf{a}_i \mid\!\sim \mathbf{b}_i$, and by the right weakening axiom, any term of the form $\mathbf{a} \mid\!\sim \mathbf{a} \vee \mathbf{b}$ can also be added. With conditionals objects it comes down to verifying that $(\mathbf{a} \mid \mathbf{b}) \wedge (\mathbf{c} \mid \mathbf{c}) = \mathbf{a} \mid \mathbf{b}$, but this only holds if $\mathbf{c} \vdash \mathbf{b}$; $(\mathbf{a} \mid \mathbf{b}) \wedge (\mathbf{d} \vee \mathbf{c} \mid \mathbf{c}) = \mathbf{a} \mid \mathbf{b}$ also holds when $\mathbf{c} \vdash \mathbf{b}$. But it will be enough for the derivations. Lastly the ";" symbol and the horizontal line indicating higher-order entailment in the C patterns are such that it is possible to simulaneously add a term $\mathbf{a} \mid\!\sim \mathbf{b}$ above the horizontal line and below it. This is consistent with the fact that operation $\wedge$ is monotonic with respect to $\geq$. Now we are in a position to prove (28) and (29) from (27), (26), the reflexivity property, the left logical equivalence and the right weakening.

<u>Proof of (28)</u> :

$$
\begin{aligned}
(\mathbf{a} \mid \mathbf{b}) \wedge (\mathbf{c} \mid \mathbf{b}) &= ((\mathbf{a} \mid \mathbf{b}) \wedge (\mathbf{c} \mid \mathbf{b})) \wedge (\mathbf{a} \wedge \mathbf{c} \mid (\mathbf{b} \wedge \mathbf{c}) \wedge \mathbf{a}) \wedge (\mathbf{a} \mid \mathbf{b}) \\
&\leq ((\mathbf{c} \mid \mathbf{a} \wedge \mathbf{b}) \wedge (\mathbf{a} \wedge \mathbf{c} \mid (\mathbf{b} \wedge \mathbf{c}) \wedge \mathbf{a})) \wedge (\mathbf{a} \mid \mathbf{b}) && \text{(by (26))} \\
&\leq (\mathbf{a} \wedge \mathbf{c} \mid \mathbf{a} \wedge \mathbf{b}) \wedge (\mathbf{a} \mid \mathbf{b}) && \text{(by (27) : cut on } \mathbf{b}) \\
&\leq (\mathbf{a} \wedge \mathbf{c} \mid \mathbf{b}) && \text{(by (27) again cut on } \mathbf{c})
\end{aligned}
$$

<u>Proof of (29)</u> :

$$
\begin{aligned}
&(\mathbf{a} \mid \mathbf{b}) \wedge (\mathbf{b} \mid \mathbf{a}) \wedge (\mathbf{c} \mid \mathbf{a}) = \\
&\quad = (\mathbf{a} \mid \mathbf{b}) \wedge (\mathbf{a} \mid \mathbf{b}) \wedge (\mathbf{b} \mid \mathbf{a}) \wedge (\mathbf{c} \mid \mathbf{a}) \leq ((\mathbf{a} \mid \mathbf{b}) \wedge (\mathbf{b} \wedge \mathbf{c} \mid \mathbf{a})) \wedge (\mathbf{a} \mid \mathbf{b}) \\
&\quad\quad \text{(using the just proved result)} \\
&\quad \leq ((\mathbf{b} \wedge \mathbf{c}) \mid (\mathbf{a} \wedge \mathbf{b})) \wedge (\mathbf{a} \mid \mathbf{b}) && \text{(using (26))} \\
&\quad \leq (\mathbf{b} \wedge \mathbf{c}) \mid \mathbf{b} && \text{(using (27), cut on } \mathbf{a}) \\
&\quad \leq \mathbf{c} \mid \mathbf{b} \quad \text{from (4)}
\end{aligned}
$$

Similarly, accepting (30) on top, we can prove (31) as follows

$$
\begin{aligned}
(\mathbf{c} \mid \mathbf{b}) \wedge (\mathbf{c} \mid \mathbf{a}) &\leq (\mathbf{c} \mid (\mathbf{a} \vee \mathbf{b}) \wedge \mathbf{b}) \wedge (\mathbf{c} \mid (\mathbf{a} \vee \mathbf{b}) \wedge \mathbf{a}) && \text{(by "left equivalence")} \\
&\leq (\neg\mathbf{b} \vee \mathbf{c} \mid \mathbf{a} \vee \mathbf{b}) \wedge (\neg\mathbf{a} \vee \mathbf{c} \mid \mathbf{a} \vee \mathbf{b}) && \text{(by (30) twice, and monotonicity of } \wedge \text{ with respect to } \leq) \\
&\leq ((\neg\mathbf{b} \vee \mathbf{c}) \wedge (\neg\mathbf{a} \vee \mathbf{c}) \mid \mathbf{a} \vee \mathbf{b}) && \text{(by (28))} \\
&= (\neg(\mathbf{a} \vee \mathbf{b}) \vee \mathbf{c} \mid \mathbf{a} \vee \mathbf{b}) \wedge (\mathbf{a} \vee \mathbf{b} \mid \mathbf{a} \vee \mathbf{b})
\end{aligned}
$$

$\leq (\mathbf{c} \mid \mathbf{a} \vee \mathbf{b})$ (by (28) and (6)) Q.E.D.

The entailment relation mentioned above

$$\mathbf{a} \mid \mathbf{b} \curlywedge \neg\mathbf{a} \mid (\mathbf{b} \wedge \mathbf{c}) \leq \neg\mathbf{c} \mid \mathbf{a} \wedge \mathbf{b}$$

can also be derived using (26) and (30). Namely

$$\mathbf{a} \mid \mathbf{b} \curlywedge \neg\mathbf{a} \mid (\mathbf{b} \wedge \mathbf{c}) \leq \mathbf{a} \mid \mathbf{b} \curlywedge (\neg\mathbf{a} \vee \neg\mathbf{c}) \mid \mathbf{b} \qquad \text{(by (30))}$$
$$\leq (\neg\mathbf{a} \vee \neg\mathbf{c}) \mid (\mathbf{a} \wedge \mathbf{b}) = \neg\mathbf{c} \mid (\mathbf{a} \wedge \mathbf{b}) \qquad \text{(by (26))}.$$

Note that monotonicity of $\curlywedge$ with respect to $\leq$ is useful throughout. These results could be derived similarly with the conditional conjunction " $\cdot$ " instead of $\curlywedge$, but not all of them with $\cap$ (since the latter is not monotonic with respect to $\leq$). Gärdenfors and Mackinson (1990) prove similar derivations with operations of revision on sets of formulas instead of non-monotonic deduction operations.

There is more than an analogy between conditional objects and non-monotonic deduction operations. Namely we can think of building a high-level inference system for conditional objects having all the inference rules of a well-behaved non-monotonic logic, where inference patterns of the form

$$\frac{\mathbf{a} \mid\!\sim \mathbf{b} \ ; \ \mathbf{c} \mid\!\sim \mathbf{d}}{\mathbf{e} \mid\!\sim \mathbf{f}}$$

are replaced either by

$$(\mathbf{b} \mid \mathbf{a}) \curlywedge (\mathbf{d} \mid \mathbf{c}) \leq \mathbf{f} \mid \mathbf{e}$$

or by

$$(\mathbf{b} \mid \mathbf{a}) \cdot (\mathbf{d} \mid \mathbf{c}) \leq \mathbf{f} \mid \mathbf{e}.$$

From a computational point of view, the two forms of inference rules are not equivalent. Indeed, we may wonder about the properties of the pairs ($\curlywedge$,$\geq$) and ($\cdot$,$\geq$) viewed as the basis for an inference mechanism. In a non-monotonic logic, the deduction operation $\mid\!\sim$ is non-monotonic, but the higher level deduction operation using (;,—) has all the properties of a well-behaved classical deduction operation, i.e. letting $\mathbb{A}$ be a set of non-monotonic deduction rules $\mathbf{a}_i \mid\!\sim \mathbf{b}_i$, we can check that

$$\frac{\mathbb{A}}{\mathbb{A}} \text{ (reflexivity) ; } \frac{\mathbb{A}}{\mathbb{B}} \text{ and } \frac{\mathbb{B}}{\mathbb{C}} \text{ imply } \frac{\mathbb{A}}{\mathbb{C}} \qquad \text{(transitivity)}$$

and $\frac{\mathbb{A}}{\mathbb{B}}$ imply $\frac{\mathbb{A} \cup \mathbb{C}}{\mathbb{B}}$ (monotonicity)

It is clear that ≤ does satisfy transitivity and reflexivity properties for conjunctions of conditional objects (since these reduce to conditional objects, and ≤ is a reflexive and transitive relation). However, while · and $\wedge$ are both monotonic with respect to ≥, ≥ is monotonic with respect to · but not with respect to $\wedge$, i.e.

$$\mathbf{a} \mid \mathbf{b} \le \mathbf{c} \mid \mathbf{d} \text{ implies } \mathbf{a} \mid \mathbf{b} \cdot \mathbf{e} \mid \mathbf{f} \le \mathbf{c} \mid \mathbf{d}$$

but $$\mathbf{a} \mid \mathbf{b} \le \mathbf{c} \mid \mathbf{d} \text{ does not imply } \mathbf{a} \mid \mathbf{b} \wedge \mathbf{e} \mid \mathbf{f} \le \mathbf{c} \mid \mathbf{d}$$

A counter-example to the monotonicity of ($\wedge$,≥) was given above when $\mathbf{c} \mid \mathbf{d} = \mathbf{a} \mid \mathbf{b}$.

What this means is that an inference system based on ($\wedge$,≥) will be very difficult to implement, since it makes no sense to saturate a knowledge base of conditionals through local forward deduction when the inference is non-monotonic. It means that a logic of non-monotonic production rules may be hopeless, since the preference for conjunction $\wedge$ is linked to a production-rule interpretation of conditional operations.

On the other hand, inference systems based on (· ,≥) will be monotonic, and are in accordance with the handling of conditional probabilities, as pointed out by Goodman et al. (1990). Hence we can envisage an inference system similar to Adams' conditional logic, but where the semantics differs (here it is a three-valued logic of conditionals). In such a system, we can think of proceeding as follows ; given a set $\mathcal{R}$ of conditional objects, a set $\mathcal{E}$ of propositions taken as evidence and a proposition $\mathbf{p}$ to be established, the problem is to derive from $\mathcal{R}$ a conditional object of the form $\mathbf{p} \mid (\mathbf{a}_1 \wedge \mathbf{a}_2 \wedge \ldots \wedge \mathbf{a}_n)$ where $\mathcal{E} = \{\mathbf{a}_1, \ldots, \mathbf{a}_n\}$, using the inference rules of the logic C, to which (HD1) is added.

Let c($\mathcal{R}$) be the set of conditionals obtained by these inference rules. c($\mathcal{R}$) is unique since deduction is monotonic but is generally infinite so that it is not to be computed in practice. Note that such an inference system does embed non-monotonicity, and can handle exceptions since if we add a new piece of evidence to $\mathcal{E}$, say $\mathbf{a}_{n+1}$, the set

$$\{\mathbf{b} \text{ such that } \mathbf{b} \mid (\mathbf{a}_1 \wedge \mathbf{a}_2 \wedge \ldots \wedge \mathbf{a}_n) \in c(\mathcal{R})\}$$

may not be included in the set $\{\mathbf{b} \text{ such that } \mathbf{b} \mid (\mathbf{a}_1 \wedge \mathbf{a}_2 \wedge \ldots \wedge \mathbf{a}_{n+1}) \in c(\mathcal{R})\}$. However the inference system itself will be monotonic.

The above proposal is only tentative, and several open problems remain, namely

- are the inference rules between conditional objects described above sufficient ? This entails a study into the semantics of conditional objects, in order to prove that the chosen set of inference rules is sound and complete with respect to the 3-valued semantics of conditional objects.
- what are the precise links between non-monotonic logic and our conditional objects, on the one hand, and how does it relate to probability theory ? This means going beyond Adams' ε-semantics as studied by Pearl (1988).
- what is the link between revision theory (e.g. Gärdenfors (1988)) and conditional objects ?

If the answer is yes to the first point, it means that conditional objects offer another kind of semantics to non-monotonic logic, different from the ones based on preferential models as studied by Kraus et al. (1990). If the connection with probability theory turns out to be a deep one, the calculus of conditionals may turn out to be the proper qualitative counterpart of some probabilistic logics.

At this point it would be worthwhile to investigate the links between the entailment relation $\leq$ between conditional objects, and comparative conditional probability. This will be done in the future. The remainder of the paper is more concerned with the compatibility between conditional objects and conditional measures of uncertainty.

These remarks suggest that a non-monotonic logic where defaults are modelled by measure-free conditionals is likely to have all the properties that a well-behaved non-monotonic logic should satisfy, especially the possibility to infer new defaults, and the reasoning by cases (due to (18)).

3. Conditional measures of uncertainty

A measure of uncertainty on a Boolean algebra $\mathfrak{B}$ is a function $g : \mathfrak{B} \to [0,1]$ which assigns to each proposition $\mathbf{a} \in \mathfrak{B}$ a degree $g(\mathbf{a})$ such that $g(\mathbb{1}) = 1$, $g(\emptyset) = 0$ and $g(\mathbf{a}) \geq g(\mathbf{b})$ whenever $\mathbf{a}$ is entailed by $\mathbf{b}$ (i.e. $\mathbf{b} \leq \mathbf{a}$). The fact that $\mathfrak{B}$ is a Boolean algebra forbids the compositionality of g over $\mathfrak{B}$ as soon as g takes values other than 0 and 1, i.e. there is no isomorphism Φ between $\mathfrak{B}$ and [0,1] such that

$$\forall \mathbf{a}, \quad g(\neg \mathbf{a}) = \Phi_{\neg}(g(\mathbf{a})) \tag{32}$$

$$\forall \mathbf{a}, \forall \mathbf{b}, \quad g(\mathbf{a} \wedge \mathbf{b}) = \Phi_{\wedge}(g(\mathbf{a}), g(\mathbf{b})) \tag{33}$$

$$\forall \mathbf{a}, \forall \mathbf{b}, \quad g(\mathbf{a} \vee \mathbf{b}) = \Phi_{\vee}(g(\mathbf{a}), g(\mathbf{b})) \tag{34}$$

See Dubois and Prade (1988b) for a detailed discussion. For instance if g is a probability measure $g(\mathbf{a} \wedge \mathbf{b}) = g(\mathbf{a}) \cdot g(\mathbf{b})$ assumes stochastic independence and does not hold in general (e.g. if $\mathbf{b} = \neg\mathbf{a}$) ; moreover $g(\mathbf{a} \vee \mathbf{b}) = g(\mathbf{a}) + g(\mathbf{b})$ requires $g(\mathbf{a} \wedge \mathbf{b}) = 0$.

The fact that $\mathcal{B}|\mathcal{B}$ is no longer a Boolean algebra allows compositionality of measures of uncertainty acting on conjunctions of the form $\mathbf{a} \wedge \mathbf{b}$, when decomposed as $(\mathbf{a} \mid \mathbf{b}) \wedge \mathbf{b}$, in the sense of (18). Indeed, what creates problems on $\mathcal{B}$ for an identity like $g(\mathbf{a} \wedge \mathbf{b}) = g(\mathbf{a}) * g(\mathbf{b})$ is that when $\mathbf{a} = \mathbf{b}$ we get $g(\mathbf{a}) = g(\mathbf{a}) * g(\mathbf{a})$ which forces $g(\mathbf{a}) = 1$ as soon as $* \neq \min$. And a probability measure that satisfies $\min(g(\mathbf{a}), g(\mathbf{b})) = g(\mathbf{a} \wedge \mathbf{b})$, $\forall \mathbf{a}, \mathbf{b}$, is a Dirac measure (since $\min(g(\mathbf{a}), g(\neg\mathbf{a})) = 0$, $\forall \mathbf{a}$). On the contrary the idempotence of $\wedge$ no longer creates problem when $\mathbf{a} \mid \mathbf{b}$ and $\mathbf{b}$ are combined, since $\forall \mathbf{b}$, $(\mathbf{b} \mid \mathbf{b}) \neq \mathbf{b}$, if $\mathbf{b} \neq \mathbb{1}$. Then it is consistent to state a decomposability axiom of the form

$$\text{A1} \quad g(\mathbf{a} \wedge \mathbf{b}) = g(\mathbf{a} \mid \mathbf{b}) * g(\mathbf{b})$$

identifying $\mathbf{a} \wedge \mathbf{b} \mid \mathbb{1}$ with $\mathbf{a} \wedge \mathbf{b}$ and $\mathbf{b} \mid \mathbb{1}$ with $\mathbf{b}$. By convention $g(\mathbf{a} \mid \mathbf{b})$ is defined only when $t(\mathbf{a} \mid \mathbf{b}) \neq ?$; moreover $g(\mathbf{a} \mid \mathbf{b}) = 0$ when $t(\mathbf{a} \mid \mathbf{b}) = 0$. Then, $g(\cdot \mid \mathbf{b})$ defines a monotonic function $(\mathbf{a} \leq \mathbf{c}) \Rightarrow g(\mathbf{a} \mid \mathbf{b}) \leq g(\mathbf{c} \mid \mathbf{b}))$ with $g(\mathbf{b} \mid \mathbf{b}) = 1$.

Besides, it would be desirable to have the following monotonicity property satisfied

$$\text{A0} \quad \mathbf{a} \mid \mathbf{b} \leq \mathbf{c} \mid \mathbf{d} \Rightarrow g(\mathbf{a} \mid \mathbf{b}) \leq g(\mathbf{c} \mid \mathbf{d})$$

due to the understanding of the partial ordering "≤" in terms of entailment in the rule interpretation. Note that A0 implies the following noticeable inequalities, when $g(\mathbf{a} \mid \mathbf{b})$ is defined

$$g(\mathbf{a} \wedge \mathbf{b}) \leq g(\mathbf{a} \mid \mathbf{b}) \leq g(\mathbf{b} \to \mathbf{a}) \qquad (35)$$

Axioms A0 and A1 lead to a definition of conditional measures of uncertainty that are in accordance with both probability theory and measure-free conditionals. As will be seen later there is room for other kinds of definitions of conditioning as well.

In the following we shall consider the case of probability measures, belief and plausibility functions (Shafer, 1976), possibility measures (Zadeh, 1978 ; Dubois and Prade, 1988c), upper and lower probabilities (e.g. Chateauneuf and Jaffray, 1989), and decomposable measures(Dubois and Prade, 1982 ; Weber, 1984). See Dubois and Prade (1988d) for an organised presentation of these notions. Here we assume that the reader has some familiarity with these notions.

3.1. The probabilistic case

The axiom A1 has been proposed by Cox (1946), along with the two following ones

A2 $g(\neg \mathbf{a}) = S(g(\mathbf{a}))$

A3 $*$ and S have continuous second-order derivatives

As pointed out by Cox (1946), the compatibility of A1 with the Boolean structure entails that $*$ should be associative. Under the assumptions A1, A2 and A3 this author proves that $*$ is the product, $S(x) = 1 - x$ (up to an isomorphism) and that g is a probability measure. It can be shown that conditional probability satisfies A0, as already said by Goodman and Nguyen(1988).

<u>Proposition 1</u> : When P is a probability measure, $\mathbf{a} \mid \mathbf{b} \leq \mathbf{c} \mid \mathbf{d}$ implies $P(\mathbf{a} \mid \mathbf{b}) \leq P(\mathbf{c} \mid \mathbf{d})$.

<u>Proof</u> : Let g be a monotonic function, i.e. such that $\mathbf{a} \leq \mathbf{b}$ implies $g(\mathbf{a}) \leq g(\mathbf{b})$. Let $\mathbf{a} \mid \mathbf{b} \leq \mathbf{c} \mid \mathbf{d}$; then $g(\mathbf{a} \wedge \mathbf{b}) \leq g(\mathbf{c} \wedge \mathbf{d})$ and $g(\neg\mathbf{b} \vee \mathbf{a}) \leq g(\neg\mathbf{d} \vee \mathbf{c})$ due to the monotonicity of g ; the latter inequality is $g(\mathbf{b} \wedge \neg\mathbf{a}) \geq g(\mathbf{d} \wedge \neg\mathbf{c})$, since $\mathbf{d} \wedge \neg\mathbf{c} \leq \mathbf{b} \wedge \neg\mathbf{a}$. Now assume g is a probability measure. Then $P(\mathbf{a} \mid \mathbf{b}) = f\left(\dfrac{P(\neg\mathbf{a} \wedge \mathbf{b})}{P(\mathbf{a} \wedge \mathbf{b})}\right)$ with $f(x) = 1/(1 + x)$. The above inequalities imply $\dfrac{P(\neg\mathbf{a} \wedge \mathbf{b})}{P(\mathbf{a} \wedge \mathbf{b})} \geq \dfrac{P(\neg\mathbf{c} \wedge \mathbf{d})}{P(\mathbf{c} \wedge \mathbf{d})}$, hence $P(\mathbf{a} \mid \mathbf{b}) \leq P(\mathbf{c} \mid \mathbf{d})$. Q.E.D.

Shafer (1988) has criticized A1 as being natural only for someone who is familiar with the usual definition of conditional probability. For instance conditional probability can also be defined as

$$P(\mathbf{a}|\mathbf{b}) = \frac{P(\mathbf{a} \wedge \mathbf{b})}{P(\mathbf{b})} = \frac{P(\mathbf{a} \wedge \mathbf{b})}{P(\mathbf{a} \wedge \mathbf{b}) + P(\neg\mathbf{a} \wedge \mathbf{b})} = \frac{P(\mathbf{a} \wedge \mathbf{b})}{P(\mathbf{a} \wedge \mathbf{b}) + 1 - P(\neg\mathbf{b} \vee \mathbf{a})}$$

and it may look natural to start with the "natural" requirement that $P(\mathbf{a} \mid \mathbf{b})$ be defined as a function of $P(\mathbf{a} \wedge \mathbf{b})$ and $P(\neg\mathbf{a} \wedge \mathbf{b})$ only, since it reflects the relative strength of **a** and $\neg\mathbf{a}$ in the environment where **b** is true. Besides the above equalities also indicate that $P(\mathbf{a} \mid \mathbf{b})$ is also monotonically increasing function of $P(\mathbf{a} \wedge \mathbf{b})$ and $P(\neg\mathbf{b} \vee \mathbf{a})$ only . This latter form is well in accordance with the fact that a measure free conditional is of the form of an interval $[\mathbf{a} \wedge \mathbf{b}, \neg\mathbf{b} \vee \mathbf{a}]$. It suggests that the value of a conditional measure $g(\mathbf{a} \mid \mathbf{b})$ depends only on the values of g at the end points of the interval. It would lead to an axiom

A´1 : $P(\mathbf{a} \mid \mathbf{b}) = F(P(\mathbf{a} \wedge \mathbf{b}), P(\neg\mathbf{b} \vee \mathbf{a}))$

which explicitly defines $P(\mathbf{a} \mid \mathbf{b})$ while A1 only provides an implicit definition. It is hard to choose between A1 and A´1 as to which is the most natural axiom !

Axiom A2 clearly requires the negation of a measure-free conditional as it appears in (10).

However this axiom also presupposes that the meaning of the extreme values of P(**a** | **b**) (i.e. 0 and 1) is well-understood. This is clearly a matter of convention. Cox's convention is that 1 means certainty (Probability = 1) and 0 means impossibility (Probability = 0). Axiom A2 becomes very natural since it means (along with A3) the more probable **a**, the less probable ¬**a**.

As noticed by Heckerman (1989), A3 can be relaxed into continuity and strict increasingness of $*$ in each place. Then $*$ = product is still the only solution of A1, due to results in functional equations by Aczel (1966). See also Aleliunas (1988) for a slightly different approach to the same question. These arguments have been proposed as a proof of the uniqueness of probability measures as proper measures of uncertainty. This is questionable because axiom A2 implicitly rejects all representations of uncertainty based on two degrees $(\Pi(\mathbf{a}),C(\mathbf{a}))$ distinguishing between ideas of possibility and certainty, for which $\Pi(\mathbf{a}) = S(C(\neg\mathbf{a}))$ replaces A2 and means that certainty of **a** $(C(\mathbf{a}) = 1)$ is equivalent to the impossibility of ¬**a** $(\Pi(\neg\mathbf{a}) = 0)$. This is the case with upper and lower probability models. Besides, the properties of $*$ can be relaxed to be simply increasing in the wide sense, in which case any triangular norm can be a candidate.

A triangular norm is a binary operation $*$ defined in [0,1], such that i) $*$ is associative ; ii) $*$ is commutative ; iii) $x \le y$ and $z \le t \Rightarrow x * z \le y * t$; iv) $0 * 0 = 0$; $x * 1 = x$. There are mainly three kinds of continuous triangular norms whose prototypes are respectively $x * y = \min(x,y)$, $x * y = xy$ and $x * y = \max(0, x + y - 1)$. See Schweizer and Sklar (1983). More specifically we consider here three relaxations of A3

A3′ : $*$ is continuous and strictly monotonic in both places (i.e. a strict-triangular norm isomorphic to product)

A3″ : $*$ is continuous and isotonic i.e. $x > x'$ and $y > y' \Rightarrow x * y > x' * y'$

A3‴ : $*$ is a continuous triangular norm.

As for operation S, we must keep it strictly decreasing in A2, due to the involutive property (i.e. $g(\mathbf{a}) = S \cdot S(g(\mathbf{a}))$, $\forall\mathbf{a}$), and it is known (Trillas 1979) that $S(x) = 1 - x$ up to an isomorphism in [0,1].

We can prove the following results

1. $*$ = minimum is compatible with A1 and A2. But, it leads to a function g which may fail to be decomposable, in the sense that $\nexists\perp$, $\forall\mathbf{a}$, $\forall\mathbf{b}$, $g(\mathbf{a} \vee \mathbf{b}) = g(\mathbf{a}) \perp g(\mathbf{b})$ if $\mathbf{a} \wedge \mathbf{b} = \mathbb{O}$; it contrasts with probability and possibility measures (see Appendix). An example of a function g which satisfies (C) and $\forall\mathbf{a}$, $g(\neg\mathbf{a}) = S(g(\mathbf{a}))$ is the following

$g(\mathbf{a} \wedge \mathbf{b}) = .7$;	$g(\mathbf{b}) = .75$;	$g((\neg\mathbf{a} \wedge \mathbf{b}) \vee (\mathbf{a} \wedge \neg\mathbf{b})) = .3$;	$g(\neg\mathbf{a} \vee \neg\mathbf{b}) = .3$;
$g(\neg\mathbf{a} \wedge \mathbf{b}) = .3$;	$g(\neg\mathbf{b}) = .25$;	$g((\mathbf{a} \wedge \mathbf{b}) \vee (\neg\mathbf{a} \wedge \neg\mathbf{b})) = .7$;	$g(\mathbf{a}\vee\neg\mathbf{b}) = .7$;
$g(\mathbf{a} \wedge \neg\mathbf{b}) = .2$;	$g(\mathbf{a}) = .7$;	$g(\mathbb{0}) = 0$;	$g(\neg\mathbf{a} \vee \mathbf{b}) = .8$;
$g(\neg\mathbf{a} \wedge \neg\mathbf{b}) = .25$;	$g(\neg\mathbf{a}) = .3$;	$g(\mathbf{a} \vee \mathbf{b}) = .75$;	$g(\mathbb{1}) = 1$

g is not decomposable since $g(\mathbf{a} \wedge \mathbf{b}) = g(\mathbf{a}) = .7$; $g(\neg\mathbf{a} \wedge \mathbf{b}) = g(\neg\mathbf{a}) = .3$ but $g(\mathbf{b}) = .75$ while $g(\mathbb{1}) = 1$.

2. Nilpotent triangular norms such as $x * y = \max(0, x + y - 1)$ are not compatible with A1.

Proof : In case of a nilpotent triangular norm such as $x * y = \max(0, x + y - 1)$ (see Schweizer and Sklar, 1983)), A1 can be written under the form

$$f(g(\mathbf{a} \wedge \mathbf{b})) = f(g(\mathbf{a} \mid \mathbf{b})) + f(g(\mathbf{b}))$$

where f is strictly decreasing function such that $f(0) = 1$ and $f(1) = 0$. Letting $\mathbf{b} = \neg\mathbf{a}$, we get

$$f(0) = f(g(\mathbf{a} \mid \neg\mathbf{a})) + f(g(\mathbf{b}))$$

Since it seems natural to require that $\forall\mathbf{a},\ g(\mathbf{a} \mid \neg\mathbf{a}) = 0$ (indeed it corresponds to a rule always false when applicable), we conclude that

$$\forall\mathbf{b} \neq \mathbb{0},\ f(g(\mathbf{b})) = 0, \text{ i.e. } g(\mathbf{b}) = 1.$$

This is the total ignorance function of possibility theory which is not compatible with A2 (since $S(g(\mathbb{0})) = S(0) = 1 = S(g(\mathbb{1}))$. Q.E.D.

These results tend to indicate the reasonableness of the strict monotonicity assumption for operation $*$ in conjunction with A1 *and* A2.

Moreover, it can be established that the only possible candidate for $*$ when g is a probability measure is the product, assuming only the non-decreasingness of $*$ with respect to its first argument. Indeed the summation of the two equalities

$$\text{Prob}(\mathbf{a} \wedge \mathbf{b}) = \text{Prob}(\mathbf{a} \mid \mathbf{b}) * \text{Prob}(\mathbf{b})$$
$$\text{Prob}(\neg\mathbf{a} \wedge \mathbf{b}) = \text{Prob}(\neg\mathbf{a} \mid \mathbf{b}) * \text{Prob}(\mathbf{b})$$

leads to $\text{Prob}(\mathbf{b}) = \text{Prob}(\mathbf{a} \mid \mathbf{b}) * \text{Prob}(\mathbf{b}) + (1 - \text{Prob}(\mathbf{a} \mid \mathbf{b})) * \text{Prob}(\mathbf{b})$

i.e. to the functional equation

$$x = y * x + (1 - y) * x$$

It was proved by Alsina (1985) that the general solution of this equation (which he encountered when discussing connectives for fuzzy sets), is the product provided that $*$ is an associative binary operation on [0,1] which is non-decreasing in its first variable. This result clearly proves, if needed, that solutions to A1, A2 and A3´´ (with $* = \min$) cannot be probability measures.

Weber (1987, 1988a) has recently investigated conditional measures issued from decomposable measures based on Archimedean triangular co-norms $\perp$. A triangular co-norm $\perp$ is obtained from a triangular norm $*$ by letting $x \perp y = 1 - (1 - x) * (1 - y)$; it is Archimedean if we have $x \perp x > x$, for $x \in (0,1)$. Then a decomposable measure g on a Boolean algebra $\mathfrak{B}$ satisfies $g(\mathbf{a} \vee \mathbf{b}) = g(\mathbf{a}) \perp g(\mathbf{b})$ whenever $\mathbf{a} \wedge \mathbf{b} = \mathbb{O}$ (see Dubois and Prade, 1982 ; Weber, 1984). Weber (1987, 1988a) concentrates on decomposable measures based on nilpotent triangular norms, i.e. isomorphic to $\min(1, x + y)$. They are of the form $x \perp y = f^{-1}(\min(1, f(x) + f(y)))$ for a continuous, bijectively increasing mapping from [0,1] to itself. Clearly, in that case $f \circ g$ is a probability measure and Weber proposes to define $g(\mathbf{a} \mid \mathbf{b}) = f^{-1}(f(g(\mathbf{a} \wedge \mathbf{b})) / f(g(\mathbf{b})))$. Clearly, this is in accordance with Cox axiomatics.

3.2. Conditioning in evidence and possibility theories: an axiomatic setting

From now on, we relax the assumption A2, and we define two types of measures of uncertainty, called certainty measure (denoted C) and possibility measure (denoted Π) which obey the following conventions that differ from the ones of probability. For the possibility function, 1 means complete possibility (i.e. consistency with available knowledge) and 0 means impossibility. Under this new convention, A2 does not sound reasonable at all for Π, since it would mean, along with A3 : the more possible **a**, the less possible $\neg$**a**. But in the case of incomplete knowledge, one may find that **a** and $\neg$**a** are equally and totally possible. A more natural substitute to A2 would be : the more impossible $\neg$**a**, the more certain **a**. In other words, when $\Pi(\mathbf{a} \mid \mathbf{b})$ ranges from impossibility (0) to possibility (1), $S(\Pi(\mathbf{a} \mid \mathbf{b}))$ denoted $C(\neg\mathbf{a} \mid \mathbf{b})$ does not qualify $\neg$**a** in the same way : $C(\neg\mathbf{a} \mid \mathbf{b}) = 1$ means that $\neg$**a** is certain while $C(\neg\mathbf{a} \mid \mathbf{b}) = 0$ means that $\neg$**a** is totally *uncertain* (i.e. it corresponds to a state of ignorance). Hence changing the meaning of the end-points of the unit interval may lead to droping axiom A2, and considering two set-functions, one for possibility, say Π, one for certainty say C, that exchange via the duality property

$$\Pi(\mathbf{a} \mid \mathbf{b}) = S(C(\neg\mathbf{a} \mid \mathbf{b})) \qquad (36)$$

and may act as a weak substitute to A2. Moreover, other natural constraints on Π and C are :

$$C(\mathbf{a}) \leq \Pi(\mathbf{a}) \tag{37}$$

$$C(\mathbf{a}) = 1 \Rightarrow C(\neg\mathbf{a}) = 0 \tag{38}$$

The inequality (37) means that certainty demands more than mere possibility. (38) means that if **a** is certain then $\neg$**a** cannot be certain to the least degree. (36) could be strengthenedened into $C(\mathbf{a}) = 1-\Pi(\neg\mathbf{a})$ since S must be involutive and strictly decreasing, i.e. $S(x) = 1 - x$ up to an isomorphism, once again. In the following, (36) is thus turned into

$$\Pi(\mathbf{a}|\mathbf{b}) = 1-C(\neg\mathbf{a}|\mathbf{b}) \tag{39}$$

Clearly (37) and (39) imply (38) and also $C(\mathbf{a}) + C(\neg\mathbf{a}) \leq 1$, $\Pi(\mathbf{a}) + \Pi(\neg\mathbf{a}) \geq 1$. $C(\mathbf{a}) = C(\neg\mathbf{a}) = 0$ (equivalently : $\Pi(\mathbf{a}) = \Pi(\neg\mathbf{a}) = 1$) is permitted and expresses total ignorance about **a** (lack of certainty). On the contrary $\Pi(\mathbf{a}) = 0$ means impossibility of **a**, which by (38) implies and is implied by $C(\neg\mathbf{a}) = 1$, i.e. certainty about $\neg$**a**. Note that (37-39) is weaker than A2 (or (32)). Hence as long as A1 and A2 are consistent with the structure of $\mathcal{B}|\mathcal{B}$, A1 along with (36-38) will be consistent with it too. Examples of functions Π are possibility measures (Zadeh, 1978), plausibility functions (Shafer, 1976), and upper probabilities (e.g. Chateauneuf and Jaffray, 1989), while C can be necessity measures, belief functions or lower probabilities.

Let us give brief definitions of these uncertainty measures. Π (resp. C) is an upper (resp. lower) probability function if there is a family $\mathcal{P}$ of probability measures such that for all **a** in $\mathcal{B}$, $\Pi(\mathbf{a}) = \sup\{P(\mathbf{a}), P \text{ in } \mathcal{P}\}$ (resp. $C(\mathbf{a}) = \inf\{P(\mathbf{a}), P \text{ in } \mathcal{P}\}$). A particular case of upper probability is obtained when Π can be constructed from a so-called basic probability assignment m, i.e. a mapping from $\mathcal{B}$ to [0,1] such that $m(\mathbb{O}) = 0$ and all the $m(\mathbf{a})$ sum to 1. Elements **a** such that $m(\mathbf{a}) > 0$ are called focal elements. Then Π (resp. C) is called a plausibility (resp. belief) function if and only if

$$\Pi(\mathbf{a}) = \Sigma_{\mathbf{b}:\mathbf{a}\wedge\mathbf{b}\neq\mathbb{O}}\ m(\mathbf{b}) \quad (\text{ resp : } C(\mathbf{a}) = \Sigma_{\mathbf{b}:\mathbf{b}\leq\mathbf{a}}\ m(\mathbf{b})\ )$$

When Π is a more general upper probability function, the weights $m(\mathbf{a})$ can still be computed (via Möbius inversion, see Shafer, 1976 ; Chateauneuf and Jaffray, 1989) but some may then be negative. A plausibility (resp. belief) function Π (resp. C) is called a possibility (resp. necessity) measure if and only if for all **a**, **b**, $\Pi(\mathbf{a} \vee \mathbf{b}) = \max(\Pi(\mathbf{a}),\Pi(\mathbf{b}))$ (resp : $C(\mathbf{a} \wedge \mathbf{b}) = \min(C(\mathbf{a}),C(\mathbf{b}))$). In that case and only in that case, the set of focal elements of Π is totally ordered by the entailment relation $\leq$.

A first question regarding these uncertainty measures is whether we apply A1 to *both* C and Π, or to one of them only, and then which one. It is easy to see that if $\Pi(\mathbf{a} \mid \mathbf{b})$ satisfies

$$\Pi(\mathbf{a} \wedge \mathbf{b}) = \Pi(\mathbf{a} \mid \mathbf{b}) * \Pi(\mathbf{b}) \qquad (40)$$

then due to (39) $C(\neg\mathbf{a} \mid \mathbf{b})$ is the solution to the equation

$$1 - C(\neg\mathbf{a} \vee \neg\mathbf{b}) = (1 - C(\neg\mathbf{a} \mid \mathbf{b})) * (1 - C(\neg\mathbf{b})) \qquad (41)$$

Let us consider the two basic possible operations for $*$, namely the product and the minimum. For instance, if $*$ = product, $C(\neg\mathbf{a} \mid \mathbf{b}) = \dfrac{C(\neg\mathbf{a} \vee \neg\mathbf{b}) - C(\neg\mathbf{b})}{1 - C(\neg\mathbf{b})}$. We are back to equation (1) with C instead of probability. (40) corresponds to the Dempster rule of conditioning when Π is a plausibility function. If we further want the counterpart of (40) for C, we should have

$$C(\mathbf{a} \wedge \mathbf{b}) = C(\mathbf{a} \mid \mathbf{b}) * C(\mathbf{b}) \qquad (42)$$

This is the geometric rule of conditioning (Suppes and Zanotti, 1977) when C is a belief function and $*$ is the product. Requiring that (41) and (42) define the same conditional certainty is a strong requirement. Solutions to (41) and (42) will be different in the case when $*$ is the product. Indeed (40) and (42) lead to

$$C(\mathbf{a} \mid \mathbf{b}) = \frac{C(\mathbf{a} \vee \neg\mathbf{b}) - C(\neg\mathbf{b})}{1 - C(\neg\mathbf{b})} = \frac{C(\mathbf{a} \wedge \mathbf{b})}{C(\mathbf{b})}$$

This property is not satisfied by belief functions generally since it is easy to construct examples of **a** and **b** where $C(\mathbf{a} \wedge \mathbf{b}) = 0$, but $C(\neg\mathbf{a} \vee \mathbf{b})$ and $C(\mathbf{b})$ are positive and $C(\neg\mathbf{b}) = 0$; for instance, allocate probability masses $m(\mathbf{a} \vee \neg\mathbf{b}) > 0$, $m(\mathbf{b}) > 0$, $m(\mathbf{c}) = 0$ for all implicants **c** of $\neg\mathbf{b}$ and $\mathbf{a} \wedge \mathbf{b}$. Moreover, in order to maintain the above equality, the two expressions need to be defined in the same situations, namely $C(\mathbf{b}) > 0$ if and only if $1 - C(\neg\mathbf{b}) > 0$ for all events **b**. It is easy to check that only belief functions that are probability measures satisfy this condition. This is because when focal elements (**c** such that $m(\mathbf{c}) > 0$) are not atoms of the Boolean algebra, the equalities $C(\mathbf{b}) = 0$ and $C(\neg\mathbf{b}) < 1$ are compatible at least for one **b**. Hence the conditioning axioms A1 should be independently specified either for Π or for C.

On the contrary, when $*$ = min, (40) and (42) are compatible, as seen in the following

If we choose to define $C(\mathbf{a} \mid \mathbf{b})$ by (42) where $*$ must clearly be a triangular norm, we find that $C(\mathbf{a} \mid \mathbf{b})$ is undefined as soon as $C(\mathbf{b}) = 0$ ($\Rightarrow C(\mathbf{a} \wedge \mathbf{b}) = 0$), i.e. as soon as **b** is completely uncertain ; in contrast, in the set $\mathfrak{B} \mid \mathfrak{B}$, $\mathbf{a} \mid \mathbf{b}$ is inapplicable only when **b** is false. As a consequence (40) seems to be preferable to (42) since $\Pi(\mathbf{a} \mid \mathbf{b})$ (hence $C(\mathbf{a} \mid \mathbf{b})$) is not defined only when **b** is impossible, in accordance with measure-free conditionals. Note that (40) or (42) enable extensions of Bayes theorem to be stated, e.g.

$$C(\mathbf{a} \mid \mathbf{b}) * C(\mathbf{b}) = C(\mathbf{b} \mid \mathbf{a}) * C(\mathbf{a}) \quad (43)$$

$$\Pi(\mathbf{a} \mid \mathbf{b}) * \Pi(\mathbf{b}) = \Pi(\mathbf{b} \mid \mathbf{a}) * \Pi(\mathbf{a}) \quad (44)$$

But as noted by Suppes and Zanotti (1977), (43) forbids any updating of $C(\mathbf{b})$ into $C(\mathbf{b} \mid \mathbf{a})$ when $C(\mathbf{b}) = 0$ i.e. with an initial state of knowledge expressing total ignorance, while (44) permits such an updating. Indeed in that case $\Pi(\mathbf{b}) = 1$ and $\Pi(\mathbf{b} \mid \mathbf{a})$ is obtained by solving equation $\Pi(\mathbf{a} \mid \mathbf{b}) = \Pi(\mathbf{b} \mid \mathbf{a}) * \Pi(\mathbf{a})$. Hence with the adopted conventions as to the meaning of functions Π and C, applying axiom A1 to Π looks more natural.We shall thus consider the axiom system, as being the most adapted to the spirit of possibility and evidence theories :

B1 : $\Pi(\mathbf{a} \wedge \mathbf{b}) = \Pi(\mathbf{a} \mid \mathbf{b}) * \Pi(\mathbf{b})$

B2 : $C(\mathbf{a}) = 1 - \Pi(\neg\mathbf{a})$

B3 : $*$ is an *isotonic* triangular norm (this is motivated by the incompatibility result of section 3.1 for nilpotent triangular norms)

3.3. Some solutions to the axiomatic system

The main solutions for $*$ are product and minimum as recalled above. For $*$ = minimum, we obtain several solutions for the definition of conditional possibility :

- if $\Pi(\mathbf{a} \wedge \mathbf{b}) < \Pi(\mathbf{b})$, then $\Pi(\mathbf{a} \mid \mathbf{b}) = \Pi(\mathbf{a} \wedge \mathbf{b})$;
- if $\Pi(\mathbf{a} \wedge \mathbf{b}) = \Pi(\mathbf{b})$, then $\Pi(\mathbf{a} \mid \mathbf{b})$ is freely choosen in $[\Pi(\mathbf{b}), 1]$.

This definition of conditional possibility was first proposed by Hisdal (1978) and subsequently used by the authors (Dubois and Prade, 1986, 1988c) in the framework of Zadeh's possibility theory. It is convenient to define $\Pi(\mathbf{a} \mid \mathbf{b}) = 1$ in the undeterminate case, by consistency with the probabilistic case, and the principle of minimum specificity (Dubois and Prade, 1987a) which expresses that possibility degrees should remain as large as possible provided they do not violate the existing constraints. Ramer (1989) also studies this kind of conditioning but selects another solution for the sake of preserving robustness when Π is slightly changed.

An advantage of the choice $*$ = minimum is a reconciliation between the material implication and the conditional **a** | **b**. Indeed, we have by duality

$$C(\mathbf{a} \mid \mathbf{b}) = \begin{cases} C(\mathbf{b} \to \mathbf{a}) \text{ if } C(\mathbf{b} \to \mathbf{a}) > C(\neg\mathbf{b}) \\ \text{freely choosen in } [0, C(\neg\mathbf{b})] \text{ if } C(\mathbf{b} \to \mathbf{a}) = C(\neg\mathbf{b}) \end{cases}$$

and the identity (42), $C(\mathbf{a} \wedge \mathbf{b}) = \min(C(\mathbf{a} \mid \mathbf{b}), C(\mathbf{b}))$ is valid. To check it, notice first that the identity $C(\mathbf{a} \wedge \mathbf{b}) = \min(C(\mathbf{b} \rightarrow \mathbf{a}), C(\mathbf{b}))$ always holds. Consider now the case when $C(\mathbf{b} \rightarrow \mathbf{a}) = C(\neg\mathbf{b})$. Clearly it is enough to check (42) when $C(\mathbf{a} \mid \mathbf{b}) = 0$. In possibility theory, the identity $\min(C(\mathbf{b}), C(\neg\mathbf{b})) = 0$ holds. If $C(\mathbf{b}) = 0$, (42) trivially holds. If $C(\neg\mathbf{b}) = 0$, $C(\mathbf{a} \mid \mathbf{b})$ is no longer freely chosen and coincides with $C(\mathbf{b} \rightarrow \mathbf{a})$.

In other words, material implication is a solution to the Coxian axiomatic system {B2,(42),B3}, and the more complete axiom system {B1,(42),B2,B3}is consistent, contrary to the case when * is a product.

It is easy to check that the requirement A0 is satisfied by Π and C, taking $\Pi(\mathbf{a} \mid \mathbf{b}) = \Pi(\mathbf{a} \wedge \mathbf{b})$ and $C(\mathbf{a} \mid \mathbf{b}) = C(\mathbf{b} \rightarrow \mathbf{a})$. Besides, if we take $\Pi(\mathbf{a} \mid \mathbf{b}) = 1$ when $\Pi(\mathbf{a} \wedge \mathbf{b}) = \Pi(\mathbf{b})$ (and dually $C(\mathbf{a} \mid \mathbf{b}) = 0$ if $C(\mathbf{b} \rightarrow \mathbf{a}) = C(\neg\mathbf{b})$), A0 is still satisfied if Π is a possibility measure and C the dual necessity measure.

<u>Proof</u> : Indeed, we have only to make sure that $\Pi(\mathbf{a} \mid \mathbf{b}) = 1$ entails $\Pi(\mathbf{c} \mid \mathbf{d}) = 1$. For any plausibility function Π we have $\Pi(\mathbf{b}) \geq \max(\Pi(\mathbf{a} \wedge \mathbf{b}), \Pi(\neg\mathbf{a} \wedge \mathbf{b}))$. If $\Pi(\mathbf{a} \wedge \mathbf{b}) = \Pi(\mathbf{b})$, it follows that $\Pi(\mathbf{a} \wedge \mathbf{b}) \geq \Pi(\neg\mathbf{a} \wedge \mathbf{b})$. If $\mathbf{a} \mid \mathbf{b} \leq \mathbf{c} \mid \mathbf{d}$, the monotonicity of Π and the transitivity lead to $\Pi(\mathbf{c} \wedge \mathbf{d}) \geq \Pi(\neg\mathbf{c} \wedge \mathbf{d})$ since $\mathbf{a} \wedge \mathbf{b} \leq \mathbf{c} \wedge \mathbf{d}$ and $\neg\mathbf{a} \wedge \mathbf{b} \geq \neg\mathbf{c} \wedge \mathbf{d}$. Then if Π is a possibility measure (Zadeh, 1978), we have

$$\Pi(\mathbf{d}) = \max(\Pi(\mathbf{c} \wedge \mathbf{d}), \Pi(\neg\mathbf{c} \wedge \mathbf{d})) = \Pi(\mathbf{c} \wedge \mathbf{d}), \text{ i.e. } \Pi(\mathbf{c} \mid \mathbf{d}) = 1.$$

Dually, it can be shown that $C(\mathbf{c} \mid \mathbf{d}) = 0$ entails $C(\mathbf{a} \mid \mathbf{b}) = 0$. Q.E.D.

On the whole, when * = min in the setting of Zadeh's possibility theory, conditional possibility and certainty almost coincide (and are allowed to coincide) with the possibility of conjunction and the certainty of material implication, respectively. This is natural since a measure-free conditional can be viewed as the interval of propositions limited by conjunction and material implication, which could be symbolically represented by

$$(C,\Pi)(\mathbf{a} \mid \mathbf{b}) = (C,\Pi)([\mathbf{a} \wedge \mathbf{b}, \mathbf{b} \rightarrow \mathbf{a}]) = (C(\mathbf{b} \rightarrow \mathbf{a}),\Pi(\mathbf{a} \wedge \mathbf{b})).$$

In other words we are back to the Boolean algebra. This result justifies the setting of possibilistic logic (Dubois and Prade, 1990b), that is, propositional logic to which degrees of possibility and certainty are allocated to propositions.

However this approach to the problem of conditioning is somewhat limited because it does not extend beyond possibility theory. Indeed the solution to the Coxian axiomatic system for belief functions must encompass the probabilistic solution. But as shown in 3.1, the set-functions satisfying Cox axioms for $*$ = min are not probability measures. Hence the alternative $*$ = min must be given up for general belief functions as well as for more general upper and lower probability systems. On the other hand, one of the main interests of conditioning in probability is to provide a solution to the problem of learning from successive experiments ; a purpose which can be better reached using $*$ = product, since then $*$ has an inverse operation. Anyway, this question needs further investigation.

For $*$ = product, we obtain Shafer's proposal, i.e. $\Pi(\mathbf{a} \mid \mathbf{b}) = \dfrac{\Pi(\mathbf{a} \wedge \mathbf{b})}{\Pi(\mathbf{b})}$ which is exactly the Dempster rule of conditioning. Axiom A0 holds for belief and plausibility measures in the sense of Shafer as proved in the following :

<u>Proposition 2</u> : $\mathbf{a} \mid \mathbf{b} \leq \mathbf{c} \mid \mathbf{d}$ implies $\Pi(\mathbf{a} \mid \mathbf{b}) \leq \Pi(\mathbf{c} \mid \mathbf{d})$ where Π is a plausibility measure or a possibility measure.

<u>Proof</u> : it is enough to express

$$\Pi(\mathbf{a}|\mathbf{b}) = \frac{\Pi(\mathbf{a} \wedge \mathbf{b})}{\Pi(\mathbf{b})} \quad \text{as} \quad \frac{\Pi(\mathbf{a} \wedge \mathbf{b})}{\Pi(\mathbf{a} \wedge \mathbf{b}) + K(\mathbf{a},\mathbf{b})}$$

where $K(\mathbf{a},\mathbf{b}) = \Sigma\{m(\mathbf{e}) \mid \mathbf{e} \wedge \mathbf{b} \neq \mathbb{O},\ \mathbf{e} \wedge \mathbf{a} \wedge \mathbf{b} = \mathbb{O}\}$, and m denotes the basic probability assignment defining Π. $K(\mathbf{a},\mathbf{b})$ is the weight bearing on exceptions to the rule $\mathbf{a} \mid \mathbf{b}$. If $\mathbf{a} \mid \mathbf{b} \leq \mathbf{c} \mid \mathbf{d}$ then $\Pi(\mathbf{a} \wedge \mathbf{b}) \leq \Pi(\mathbf{c} \wedge \mathbf{d})$, and we further need. $K(\mathbf{a},\mathbf{b}) \geq K(\mathbf{c},\mathbf{d})$. The latter inequality reads

$$\Sigma_{\substack{\mathbf{e}\wedge\mathbf{b}\neq\mathbb{O} \\ \mathbf{e}\wedge\mathbf{a}\wedge\mathbf{b}=\mathbb{O}}} m(\mathbf{e}) \ \geq\ \Sigma_{\substack{\mathbf{f}\wedge\mathbf{d}\neq\mathbb{O} \\ \mathbf{f}\wedge\mathbf{c}\wedge\mathbf{d}=\mathbb{O}}} m(\mathbf{f})$$

It holds since m is non-negative and there are more terms in the left hand sum ; indeed,

$\mathbf{f} \wedge \mathbf{c} \wedge \mathbf{d} = \mathbb{O} \Rightarrow \mathbf{f} \wedge \mathbf{a} \wedge \mathbf{b} = \mathbb{O}$ due to $\mathbf{a} \wedge \mathbf{b} \leq \mathbf{c} \wedge \mathbf{d}$;
the focal elements $\mathbf{f}$ which are taken into account in the right hand part of the above inequality are such that $\mathbf{f} \wedge \neg\mathbf{c} \wedge \mathbf{d} \neq \mathbb{O}$ and then are also such that $\mathbf{f} \wedge \neg\mathbf{a} \wedge \mathbf{b} \neq \mathbb{O}$ (due to $\neg\mathbf{a} \wedge \mathbf{b} \geq \neg\mathbf{c} \wedge \mathbf{d}$), hence $\mathbf{f} \wedge \mathbf{b} \neq \mathbb{O}$.

When Π is a possibility measure, the result also holds since Π is a plausibility measure such that $\Pi(\mathbf{a} \vee \mathbf{b}) = \max(\Pi(\mathbf{a}), \Pi(\mathbf{b}))$, $\forall \mathbf{a}, \mathbf{b}$. A direct proof is to use the one of Proposition 1 changing $f(x) = 1/(1 + x)$ into $f(x) = \min(1, 1/x)$. Q.E.D.

For belief functions the result is easily deduced from (41) and the duality between C and Π. As pointed out by Smets (1988), $C(\mathbf{a} \mid \mathbf{b}) = C(\mathbf{b} \to \mathbf{a})$ is again valid whenever $C(\mathbf{b}) = 0$, i.e. for a wider range of situations than with standard probability measures.

3.4. Upper and lower conditional probabilities

As noticed by Kyburg (1987), if Π is an upper probability function, $\Pi(\cdot \mid \mathbf{b})$ is generally not an upper conditional probability $P^*(\cdot \mid \mathbf{b})$, i.e. $\Pi(\mathbf{a} \mid \mathbf{b}) < P^*(\mathbf{a} \mid \mathbf{b})$ where

$$P^*(\mathbf{a} \mid \mathbf{b}) = \max\{P(\mathbf{a} \mid \mathbf{b}) \mid P(\mathbf{a} \wedge \mathbf{b}) \in [C(\mathbf{a} \wedge \mathbf{b}), \Pi(\mathbf{a} \wedge \mathbf{b})], P(\mathbf{b}) \in [C(\mathbf{b}), \Pi(\mathbf{b})]\}.$$

Letting the lower conditional probability P_* be defined as $P_*(\mathbf{a} \mid \mathbf{b}) = 1 - P^*(\neg\mathbf{a} \mid \mathbf{b})$, the interval $[C(\mathbf{a} \mid \mathbf{b}), \Pi(\mathbf{a} \mid \mathbf{b})]$ is thus narrower than $[P_*(\mathbf{a} \mid \mathbf{b}), P^*(\mathbf{a} \mid \mathbf{b})]$. Although the Dempster rule of conditioning makes sense with belief functions, the other conditioning rule is more natural in the framework of upper and lower probabilities. However it is unlikely that axiom A0 will be satisfied for upper conditional probabilities other than plausibility measures of Shafer since as shown by Chateauneuf and Jaffray (1989), upper and lower probability functions lead to possibly negative masses $m(\mathbf{e})$ through Möbius inversion. Besides upper conditional probabilities violate axiom B1, i.e. the Coxian axiomatics does not fit the upper and lower probability framework.

The proper axiomatic setting for monotonic set functions more general than belief and plausibility functions is rather given by means of the axiom alternative to B1 suggested in 3.1, that is

B'1 : $\Pi(\mathbf{a} \mid \mathbf{b}) = F(\Pi(\mathbf{a} \wedge \mathbf{b}), \Pi(\neg\mathbf{b} \vee \mathbf{a}))$
B2 : $C(\mathbf{a}) = 1 - \Pi(\neg\mathbf{a})$
B'3 : $F(x,y)$ is a strictly monotonic function in both places when $x \neq 0$, $y \neq 1$; for all x, y, $F(0,y) = 0$ and $F(x,1) = 1$

Indeed a solution to these axioms is the following definition of conditional upper probability (De Campos et al., 1990)

$$\Pi'(\mathbf{a} \mid \mathbf{b}) = \frac{\Pi(\mathbf{a} \wedge \mathbf{b})}{\Pi(\mathbf{a} \wedge \mathbf{b}) + C(\neg\mathbf{a} \wedge \mathbf{b})}$$

This is easy to check using B2 ; namely, $F(x,y) = x/(x + 1 - y)$. Note that in the axiom system, $F(x,y)$ is defined only for $x \leq y$, since $\Pi(\mathbf{a} \wedge \mathbf{b}) \leq \Pi(\neg\mathbf{b} \vee \mathbf{a})$ due to the monotonicity of Π. The conditions $F(0,y) = 0$ and $F(x,1) = 1$ are respectively induced by the constraints $\Pi(\mathbf{a} \mid \mathbf{b}) = 0$ if **a** and **b** are contradictory and $\Pi(\mathbf{b} \mid \mathbf{b}) = 1$. Moreover axiom B'1 also holds for the dual set functions $C'(\mathbf{a} \mid \mathbf{b}) = 1 - \Pi'(\neg\mathbf{a} \mid \mathbf{b})$ since

$$\begin{aligned} C'(\mathbf{a} \mid \mathbf{b}) &= 1 - \Pi'(\neg\mathbf{a} \mid \mathbf{b}) \\ &= (C'(\mathbf{a} \wedge \mathbf{b}) + \Pi(\neg\mathbf{a} \wedge \mathbf{b}) - \Pi(\neg\mathbf{a} \wedge \mathbf{b}))/(C(\mathbf{a} \wedge \mathbf{b}) + \Pi(\neg\mathbf{a} \wedge \mathbf{b})) \\ &= C(\mathbf{a} \wedge \mathbf{b})/(C(\mathbf{a} \wedge \mathbf{b}) + \Pi(\neg\mathbf{a} \wedge \mathbf{b})) = F(C(\mathbf{a} \wedge \mathbf{b}), C(\neg\mathbf{b} \vee \mathbf{a})) \end{aligned}$$

It can be shown (De Campos et al., 1990) that this definition of conditional set functions coincides with upper and lower conditional probabilities in the sense of Kyburg, introduced above, as soon as Π is a Choquet capacity of order 2, i.e. $\Pi(\mathbf{a} \wedge \mathbf{b}) + \Pi(\mathbf{a} \vee \mathbf{b}) \leq \Pi(\mathbf{a}) + \Pi(\mathbf{b})$. In that case $\Pi'(\mathbf{a} \mid \mathbf{b}) = P^*(\mathbf{a} \mid \mathbf{b})$.

With the definition of conditioning satisfying axioms B'1, B2, B'3, axiom A0 is trivially satisfied, i.e $\mathbf{a} \mid \mathbf{b} \leq \mathbf{c} \mid \mathbf{d}$ implies $\Pi'(\mathbf{a} \mid \mathbf{b}) \leq \Pi'(\mathbf{c} \mid \mathbf{d})$ and the same for the dual measure C. This result indicates that the usual notion of conditioning for a large class of upper and lower probabilities is consistent with the algebra of measure-free conditionals. On top of that, we are again in the case where B'1, B2, B'3 are satisfied for both Π and C, as in the case of possibility theory with * = min.

4. Conclusion

This paper, as noted in the beginning, expands the contents of two previous ones by relating the theory of measure-free conditionals to non-monotonic logic on the one hand and to the axiom system of Cox for probability theory on the other hand. Along the first line of thought it seems that measure-free conditionals offer a genuine example of a non-monotonic logic that satisfy all the natural postulates thereof. On the side of numerical reasoning, almost all notions of conditioning outside probability theory have been cast in the setting of measure-free conditionals. Only the proposal of Planchet (1989) for belief functions that is,

$$C(\mathbf{a} \mid \mathbf{b}) = \frac{C(\mathbf{a}) - C(\mathbf{a} \wedge \neg\mathbf{b})}{1 - C(\neg\mathbf{b})}$$

still escapes our work. Besides, there are some obvious open problems and areas to investigate :

- find all candidate solutions to the axiomatic system inspired by Cox for the case of measures of uncertainty obeying the duality property of possibility and certainty (axiom B2). Namely are belief functions the only solutions when $*$ = product ?

- prove the unicity of the form of the function F that define conditional monotonic set functions from the knowledge of the values of the set function for the conjunction and the material implication of two propositions. Note that Weber (1988b) has devised axioms of the form B'1 for conditional measures, where the function F is taken to be a residuated implication (e.g Dubois and Prade's book, 1988c chap. 4, and Smets'contribution in this book) or a mean value function.
- the axiomatic setting by Cox, once relaxed to encompass possibility measures and belief functions can serve as a basis for a theory of belief updating that parallels the one developed by Heckerman (1989) in a probabilistic setting. However in the case of upper and lower probabilities it seems that another setting is to be searched for. The one outlined in 3.4 has still to be analyzed.
- it may be interesting to bridge the gap between the logical view of conditioning developed here and past studies on comparative (qualitative) conditional probabilities (Fine, 1973, Chap. 2 ; Kranz et al., 1971, Chap. 5). The latter approaches start with a weak order (expressing "more probable than") among conditional objects $\mathbf{a} \mid \mathbf{b}$ and state axioms this ordering should intuitively satisfy in order to find conditional probabilities as its unique numerical counterpart. The ordering relation introduced in this paper (defined by (5)) is not a weak order because it does not satisfy the connectedness property (i.e. $\mathbf{a} \mid \mathbf{b} \leq \mathbf{c} \mid \mathbf{d}$ or $\mathbf{c} \mid \mathbf{d} \leq \mathbf{a} \mid \mathbf{b}$ for any $\mathbf{a}$, $\mathbf{b}$, $\mathbf{c}$, $\mathbf{d}$). The qualitative probability relations considered in (Fine, 1973 ; Kranz et al., 1971) are indeed consistent with but stronger than the relation $\leq$ considered here.

APPENDIX

Compatibility of * = minimum with A1 and A2

A1 yields

$$g(\mathbf{a} \wedge \mathbf{b}) = \min(g(\mathbf{a} \mid \mathbf{b}), g(\mathbf{b}))$$
$$g(\neg\mathbf{a} \wedge \mathbf{b}) = \min(g(\neg\mathbf{a} \mid \mathbf{b}), g(\mathbf{b}))$$

Then, it has the following consequence

$$\forall \mathbf{a}, \forall \mathbf{b}, g(\mathbf{a} \wedge \mathbf{b}) < g(\mathbf{b}) \text{ and } g(\neg\mathbf{a} \wedge \mathbf{b}) < g(\mathbf{b}) \Rightarrow g(\mathbf{a} \wedge \mathbf{b}) = g(\neg\mathbf{b} \vee \mathbf{a}) = g(\mathbf{a}) \qquad \text{(C)}$$

Indeed, $g(\mathbf{a} \wedge \mathbf{b}) < g(\mathbf{b})$, $g(\neg\mathbf{a} \wedge \mathbf{b}) < g(\mathbf{b})$ and A2 entails

$$g(\mathbf{a} \wedge \mathbf{b}) = g(\mathbf{a} \mid \mathbf{b}) = S(g(\neg\mathbf{a} \mid \mathbf{b})) = S(g(\neg\mathbf{a} \wedge \mathbf{b})) = g(\neg\mathbf{b} \vee \mathbf{a}) = g(\mathbf{a})$$

The last equality is due to the monotonicity of g with respect to the partial ordering in $\mathcal{B}$. Similarly we have, changing **a** into ¬**a**,

$$g(\neg \mathbf{a} \wedge \mathbf{b}) < g(\mathbf{b}) \text{ and } g(\mathbf{a} \wedge \mathbf{b}) < g(\mathbf{b}) \Rightarrow g(\neg \mathbf{a} \wedge \mathbf{b}) = g(\neg \mathbf{a})$$

and

$$g(\mathbf{a} \wedge \neg \mathbf{b}) < g(\neg \mathbf{b}) \text{ and } g(\neg \mathbf{a} \wedge \neg \mathbf{b}) < g(\neg \mathbf{b}) \Rightarrow g(\mathbf{a} \wedge \neg \mathbf{b}) = g(\mathbf{a}) \text{ and } g(\neg \mathbf{a} \wedge \neg \mathbf{b}) = g(\neg \mathbf{a})$$

Letting $g(\mathbf{a}) = \alpha$, $g(\mathbf{b}) = \beta$, these conditions become

$$\alpha < \min(\beta, S(\beta)) \text{ and } S(\alpha) < \min(\beta, S(\beta))$$

which is impossible. Then we should have

$$\begin{aligned} \forall \mathbf{a}, \forall \mathbf{b}, \ & g(\mathbf{b}) = \max(g(\mathbf{a} \wedge \mathbf{b}), g(\neg \mathbf{a} \wedge \mathbf{b})) \\ \underline{\text{or}} \ & g(\neg \mathbf{b}) = \max(g(\mathbf{a} \wedge \neg \mathbf{b}), g(\neg \mathbf{a} \wedge \neg \mathbf{b})) \end{aligned}$$

Note that we cannot have these two equalities simultaneously for *any* **a** or **b**, since then g would be a possibility measure, which is not compatible with A2.

Starting with a function g which satisfies the condition (C), it is always possible to define $g(\mathbf{a} \mid \mathbf{b})$ consistently with A1 and A2. Indeed, due to A1 we should have

$$\begin{aligned} g(\mathbf{a} \mid \mathbf{b}) \ & = g(\mathbf{a} \wedge \mathbf{b}) \quad \text{if } g(\mathbf{b}) < g(\mathbf{a} \wedge \mathbf{b}) \\ & \geq g(\mathbf{a} \wedge \mathbf{b}) \quad \text{if } g(\mathbf{b}) = g(\mathbf{a} \wedge \mathbf{b}) \end{aligned}$$

$$\begin{aligned} g(\neg \mathbf{a} \mid \mathbf{b}) \ & = g(\neg \mathbf{a} \wedge \mathbf{b}) \quad \text{if } g(\mathbf{b}) < g(\neg \mathbf{a} \wedge \mathbf{b}) \\ & \geq g(\neg \mathbf{a} \wedge \mathbf{b}) \quad \text{if } g(\mathbf{b}) = g(\neg \mathbf{a} \wedge \mathbf{b}) \end{aligned}$$

together with A2, i.e. $g(\neg \mathbf{a} \mid \mathbf{b}) = S(g(\mathbf{a} \mid \mathbf{b}))$. Four cases have to be distinguished

- $\begin{cases} g(\mathbf{a} \wedge \mathbf{b}) < g(\mathbf{b}) \\ g(\neg \mathbf{a} \wedge \mathbf{b}) < g(\mathbf{b}) \end{cases} \Rightarrow \begin{cases} g(\mathbf{a} \mid \mathbf{b}) = g(\mathbf{a}) \\ g(\neg \mathbf{a} \mid \mathbf{b}) = g(\neg \mathbf{a}) \end{cases}$ due to (C)

- $\begin{cases} g(\mathbf{a} \wedge \mathbf{b}) < g(\mathbf{b}) \\ g(\neg \mathbf{a} \wedge \mathbf{b}) = g(\mathbf{b}) \end{cases} \Rightarrow \begin{cases} g(\mathbf{a} \mid \mathbf{b}) = g(\mathbf{a} \wedge \mathbf{b}) \\ g(\neg \mathbf{a} \mid \mathbf{b}) = g(\neg \mathbf{a} \vee \neg \mathbf{b}) \geq g(\neg \mathbf{a} \wedge \mathbf{b}) \end{cases}$

- $\begin{cases} g(\mathbf{a} \wedge \mathbf{b}) = g(\mathbf{b}) \\ g(\neg \mathbf{a} \wedge \mathbf{b}) < g(\mathbf{b}) \end{cases} \Rightarrow \begin{cases} g(\neg \mathbf{a} \mid \mathbf{b}) = g(\neg \mathbf{a} \wedge \mathbf{b}) \\ g(\mathbf{a} \mid \mathbf{b}) = g(\mathbf{a} \vee \neg \mathbf{b}) \geq g(\mathbf{a} \wedge \mathbf{b}) \end{cases}$

$$- \begin{cases} g(\mathbf{a} \wedge \mathbf{b}) = g(\mathbf{b}) \\ g(\neg\mathbf{a} \wedge \mathbf{b}) = g(\mathbf{b}) \end{cases} \Rightarrow \begin{cases} g(\mathbf{a} \mid \mathbf{b}) \geq g(\mathbf{a} \wedge \mathbf{b}) = g(\mathbf{b}) \\ g(\neg\mathbf{a} \mid \mathbf{b}) \geq g(\neg\mathbf{a} \wedge \mathbf{b}) = g(\mathbf{b}) \end{cases}$$

$$\Rightarrow \begin{cases} g(\mathbf{a} \wedge \mathbf{b}) = g(\mathbf{b}) \leq g(\mathbf{a} \mid \mathbf{b}) \leq g(\neg\mathbf{b}) = g(\mathbf{a} \vee \neg\mathbf{b}) \\ g(\neg\mathbf{a} \wedge \mathbf{b}) = g(\mathbf{b}) \leq g(\neg\mathbf{a} \mid \mathbf{b}) \leq g(\neg\mathbf{b}) = g(\neg\mathbf{a} \vee \neg\mathbf{b}) \end{cases}$$

Thus it is possible to define $g(\mathbf{a} \mid \mathbf{b})$ consistently with A1 and A2 when (C) holds. An example is given in the text.

References

1. Aczel, J. (1966) *Lectures on Functional Equations and their Applications*, Academic Press, New York.

2. Adams, E.W. (1975) *The Logic of Conditionals*, D. Reidel, Dordrecht.

3. Aleliunas, R. (1988) A new normative theory of probabilistic logic, *Proc. of the 7th Biennial Conference of the Canadian Society for Computational Studies of Intelligence* (R. Goebel, ed.), Edmonton, Alberta, Canada, June, 67-74.

4. Alsina, C. (1985) On a family of connectives for fuzzy sets, *Fuzzy Sets and Systems* (16), 231-235.

5. Bruno, G., Gilio, A. (1985) Confronto fra eventi condizionati di probabilità nulla nell'inferenza statistica bayesiana, *Rivista di Matematica per le Scienze Economiche e Sociali*, Anno 8°, Fascicolo 2°, 141-152.

6. Calabrese, P. (1987) An algebraic synthesis of the foundations of logic and probability, *Information Sciences* (42), 187-237.

7. Chateauneuf, A., Jaffray, J.Y. (1989) Some characterizations of lower probabilities and other monotone capacities through the use of Möbius inversion, *Mathematical Social Sciences* (17), 263-283.

8. Cheeseman, P. (1985) In defense of probability, *Proc. 9th Inter. Joint Conf. on Artificial Intelligence*, Los Angeles, 1002-1009.

9. Cheeseman, P. (1988) An inquiry into computer understanding, (With 23 discussions and a reply), *Computational Intelligence* (4), 58-142.

10. Cox, R.T. (1946) Probability, frequency and reasonable expectation, *Amer. J. Phys.* (14), 1-13.

11. De Campos, L.M., Lamata, M.T., Moral, S. (1990) The concept of conditional fuzzy measure, *Int. J. of Intelligent Systems* (5), 237-246.

12. De Finetti, B. (1937) La prévision, ses lois logiques et ses sources subjectives, *Ann. Inst. H. Poincaré 7, 1937*, translated by H. Kyburg Jr., in : *Studies in Subjective Probability* (H. Kyburg Jr., H. Smokler, eds.), Wiley, New York, 95-158, 1964.

13. Dubois, D., Prade, H. (1982) A class of fuzzy measures based on triangular norms – A general framework for the combination of uncertain information, *Int. J. of General Systems* (8), 43-61.

14. Dubois, D., Prade, H. (1986) Possibilistic inference under matrix form, In : *Fuzzy Logic in Knowledge Engineering* (H. Prade, C.V. Negoita, eds.), Verlag TÜV Rheinland, Köln, 112-126.

15. Dubois, D., Prade, H. (1987a) Properties of measures of information in evidence and possibility theories, *Fuzzy Sets and Systems* (24), 161-18.

16. Dubois, D., Prade, H. (1987b) *Théorie des Possibilités. Applications à la Représentation des Connaissances en Informatique*, Masson, Paris. 2nd edition, 135-138 and 140-143.

17. Dubois, D., Prade, H. (1988a) On fuzzy syllogisms, *Computational Intelligence* (4), 171-179.

18. Dubois, D., Prade, H. (1988b) An introduction to possibilistic and fuzzy logics, In: *Non-Standard Logics for Automated Reasoning* (P. Smets, E.H. Mamdani, D. Dubois, H. Prade, eds.), Academic Press, London & New York, 287-315.

19. Dubois, D. Prade, H. (1988c) *Possibility Theory - An Approach to Computerized Processing of Uncertainty* Plenum Press, New York.

20. Dubois, D., Prade, H. (1988d) Modeling uncertainty and inductive inference, *Acta Psychologica* (68), 53-78.

21. Dubois, D., Prade, H. (1988e) Conditioning in possibility and evidence theories –A logical viewpoint–, In : *Uncertainty and Intelligent Systems* (Proc. of the 2nd Inter. Conf. on Information Processing and Management of Uncertainty in Knowledge-Based Systems (IPMU'88), Urbino, Italy, July, 1988) (B. Bouchon, L. Saitta, R.R. Yager, eds.), Springer Verlag, Berlin, 401-408.

22. Dubois, D., Prade, H. (1989) Measure-free conditioning, probability and non-monotonic reasoning, *Proc. of the 11th Inter. Joint Conf. on Artificial Intelligence*, Detroit, 1110-1114.

23. Dubois, D. Prade, H. (1990a) The logical view of conditioning and its applications to possibility and evidence theories, *Int. J. of Approximate Reasoning* (4), 23-46.

24. Dubois, D., Prade H., H. (1990b) Resolution principles in possibilistic logic, *Int. J. of Approximate Reasoning* (4), 1-21.

25. Fine, T.L. (1973) *Theories of Probability*, Academic Press, New York.

26. Gabbay, D.M. (1985) Theoretical foundations for non- monotonic reasoning in expert systems, In : *Logics and Models of Concurrent Systems* (K.R. Apt, ed.), Springer Verlag, Berlin, 439-457.

27. Gärdenfors, P. (1988) *Knowledge in Flux – Modeling the Dynamics of Epistemic States*, MIT Press, Cambridge, Mass..

28. Gärdenfors, P., Makinson, D. (1990) Relations between the logic of theory change and non-monotonic logic, *Proc. of RP2 Meeting Defeasible Reasoning Uncertainty*

Management Systems Project (ESPRIT-BRA), Albi, (available from IRIT, Univ. P. Sabatier, Toulouse, France), 171-193.

29. Goodman, I.R. (1987) A measure-free approach to conditioning, *Proc. of the 3rd AAAI Workshop on Uncertainty in Artificial Intelligence*, Seattle, July, 270-277.

30. Goodman, I.R., Nguyen, H.T.(1988) Conditional objects and the modeling of uncertainties, In : *Fuzzy Computing - Theory, Hardware and Applications* (M.M. Gupta, T. Yamakawa, eds.), North- Holland, 119-138.

31. Goodman, I.R., Nguyen, H.T. (1990) Foundations for an algebraic theory of conditioning, *Fuzzy Sets and systems*, to appear.

32. Goodman, I.R., Nguyen, H.T., Walker, E.A. (1990) *Conditional Inference and Logic for Intelligent Systems : A Theory of Measure-Free Conditioning*, North-Holland, to appear.

33. Harper, W.L., Stalnaker, R., Pearce, G. (eds.) (1981) *Ifs. Conditionals, Belief, Decision, Chance and Time*, Reidel, Dordrecht.

34. Heckerman, D.E. (1989) An axiomatic framework for belief updates, In : *Uncertainty in Artificial Intelligence 2* (J.F. Lemmer, L.N. Kanal, eds.), North-Holland, 11-22.

35. Hisdal, E. (1978) Conditional possibilities : independence and non-interaction, *Fuzzy Sets and Systems* (1), 283-297.

36. Horvitz, E.J., Heckerman, D.E., Langlotz, C.P. (1986) A framework for comparing alternative formalisms for plausible reasoning, *Proc. Amer. Assoc. for Artificial Intelligence Conference (AAAI-86)*, Philadelphia, 210-214.

37. Koopman, B.O. (1940) The bases of probability, *Bulletin of the American Mathematical Society* (46), 763-774.

38. Krantz, D.H., Luce, R.D., Suppes, P., Tversky, A. (1971) *Foundations of Measurement - Vol. 1 : Additive and Polynomial Representations*, Academic Press, New York.

39. Kraus, K., Lehmann, D., Magidor, M. (1990) Nonmonotonic reasoning, preferential models and cumulative logics, *Artificial Intelligence* (44), 167-207.

40. Kyburg, H. (1987) Bayesian and non-Bayesian evidential updating, *Artificial Intelligence* (31), 271-293.

41. Lewis, D. (1973) Counterfactuals and comparative probability, *J. of Philosophical Logic* (2).

42. Lewis, D. (1976) Probabilities of conditionals and conditional probabilities, *Phil. Rev.* (85), 297-315. Also in Harper et al. (129-150, 1981).

43. Luce, R.D. (1968) On the numerical representation of qualitative conditional probability, *Ann. Math. Statist.* (39), 481-491.

44. Makinson, D. (1989) General theory of cumulative inference, In : *Non-Monotonic Reasoning* (Proc. of the 2nd Inter. Workshop, Grassau, FRG, June 13-15, 1988) (M. Reinfranck, J. De Kleer, M.L. Ginsberg, E. Sandewall, eds.), Springer Verlag, 1-18.

45. Nguyen, H.T. (1987) On representation and combinability of uncertainty, *Preprints of 2nd Inter. Fuzzy Systems Association Congress*, Tokyo, July, 506-509.

46. Nilsson, N. (1986) Probabilistic logic, *Artificial Intelligence* (28), 71-87.

47. Pearl, J. (1988) *Probabilistic Reasoning in Intelligent Systems : Networks of Plausible Inference*, Morgan Kaufmann, San Mateo, Ca..

48. Planchet, B. (1989) Credibility and conditioning, *J. of Theoretical Probability* (2), 289-299.

49. Popper, S.K. (1959) *The Logic of Scientific Discovery*, Harper Torchbooks, Harper & Row, Publ..

50. Ramer, A. (1989) Conditional possibility distributions, *Proc. of the 3rd Inter. Fuzzy Systems Assoc. (IFSA) Congress*, Seattle, 412-415.

51. Reiter, R. (1980) A logic for default reasoning, *Artificial Intelligence* (13), 81-132.

52. Rescher, N. (1969) *Many-Valued Logic*, McGraw- Hill, New York.

53. Sanchez, E. (1989) Importance in knowledge systems, *Information Systems*, 14(6), 455-464.

54. Schay, G. (1968) An algebra of conditional events, *Journal of Mathematical, Analysis and Applications* (24), 334-344.

55. Schweizer, B., Sklar, A. (1963) Associative functions and abstract semigroups, *Publ. Mathe.* (Debrecen.) (10), 69-81.

56. Shafer, G. (1976) *A Mathematical Theory of Evidence*, Princeton University Press, New Jersey.

57. Shafer, G. (1988) Comments on An inquiry into computer understanding by Peter Cheeseman, *Computational Intelligence* (Canada) (4), 121-124.

58. Smets, P. (1988) Belief functions, In : *Non-Standard Logics for Automated Reasoning* (P. Smets, E.H. Mamdani, D. Dubois, H. Prade, eds.), Academic Press, New York, 253-286.

59. Stalnaker, R. (1968) A theory of conditionals, In : *Studies in Logical Theory* (N. Rescher, ed.), Blackwell, Oxford. Also in Harper et al. (41-55, 1981).

60. Stalnaker, R. (1970) Probability and conditionals, *Philosophy of Science* (37), 64-80.

61. Suppes, P., Zanotti, M. (1977) On using random relations to generate upper and lower probabilities, *Synthese* (36), 427-440.

62. Trillas, E. (1979) Sobre funciones de negación en la teoría de conjuntos difusos, *Stochastica* (III, n° 1), 47-59.

63. Waterman, D.A., Hayes-Roth, F. (Eds.) (1978) *Pattern-Directed Inference*

Systems, Academic Press, New York.

64. Weber, S. (1984) ⊥-decomposable measures and integrals for Archimedean t-conorms⊥, *J. of Mathematical, Analysis and Applications* (101).

65. Weber, S. (1987) Conditional measures and their applications to fuzzy sets, *Preprints of the Second Inter. Fuzzy Systems Association Congress*, Tokyo, July, 412-415.

66. Weber, S. (1988a) Conditional measures based on Archimedean semi-groups, *Fuzzy Sets and Systems* (27), 63-72.

67. Weber, S. (1988b) Decomposable measures for conditional objects, *10th Inter. Seminar on Fuzzy Set Theory "Measures and Integrals – Alternative Concepts"*, Linz, Austria, September.

68. Zadeh, L.A. (1978) Fuzzy sets as a basis for a theory of possibility, *Fuzzy Sets and Systems* (1), 3-28.

69. Zadeh, L.A. (1985) Syllogistic reasoning in fuzzy logic and its application to reasoning with dispositions, *IEEE Trans. on Systems, Man and Cybernetics* (15), 754-763.

Conditional Logic in Expert Systems
I.R. Goodman, M.M. Gupta, H.T. Nguyen and G.S. Rogers (editors)

CONDITIONING OPERATORS IN A LOGIC OF CONDITIONALS

Hung T. Nguyen and Gerald S. Rogers

Department of Mathematical Sciences
New Mexico State University
Las Cruces, NM, 88003

Abstract: Following work of Goodman, Nguyen, and Walker (1990), we present a simple view of a "conditional operator" within a mathematical theory of conditional logic where "conditionals" become mathematical entities. We show that in the inference model of Pearl (1988), the associated "logical consequent relation" turns out to be non-monotonic. Then we discuss notions of qualitative conditional independence. Finally, we look at the combination of evidence and at some computational aspects of conditional logic when uncertainty is taken in a specific quantitative form.

Keywords: Conditional events, conditional logic, combination of evidence, qualitative conditional independence

1. Introduction

One of the main tasks in the design of intelligent systems is the modeling of reasoning with uncertain conditional information. In the beginning, a logic of implicative statements, or conditionals, in a natural language is required; one model was given by Adams (1975). However, the basic objects in his work, namely conditionals or conditional events, were taken as primitives in natural language; also, his logical operations among these primitives were proposed on intuitive grounds. Thus the principal component in the logic of reasoning, the "logical consequent relation", came to be defined semantically and applicable only for the "defaults". His ε-semantics was popularized by Pearl (1988) for "plausible reasoning". It is not clear how such semantics can be modified to handle more arbitrary rules of expert systems. At the same time, there is no syntactic counterpart for the logical consequent relation. In this paper, we discuss the foundations of these concepts and related issues.

2. Conditioning operators

As in traditional symbolic logic, the basic objects are elements of an abstract Boolean ring $\mathscr{R}$ (Halmos, 1963). While this is general enough to contain measurable spaces, since the σ-additivity of the probability measures does not enter the analysis herein, it is sufficient to consider finitely additive probability measures on $\mathscr{R}$.

Logical operations on $\mathscr{R}$ are denoted by:

$\vee$ (disjunction or union), $\cdot$ (conjunction or intersection),

$'$ (negation or set complement), $+$ (addition or symmetric difference). Also, 0 is ϕ and 1 is Ω (in the case that $\mathscr{R}$ is a field of subsets of some set Ω). The algebraic system

$$[\mathscr{R}, \vee, \cdot, ', 0, 1]$$

is equivalent to the Boolean ring

$$[\mathscr{R}, +, \cdot, 0, 1] .$$

The order relation on $\mathscr{R}$ is $a \leq b$ iff $ab = a \cdot b = b$. $\mathscr{R}$ is the syntax part of logic.

When dealing with conditional information or implicative propositions, an extended logic, the conditional logic, is needed, in the same spirit as the extension "from probability measures to conditional probability measures" . Although the lack of a definition of conditional events before that of conditional probabilites may not create any difficulties in the ordinary theory of probability and statistics, there is no reason to expect this nicety in logic, especially for the reasoning purposes in automated intelligent systems. Indeed, in his approach to plausible reasoning, Pearl (1988) mentioned the lack of conditioning operators in logic. (See also, Dubois and Prade 1989, 1990). The full impact of the use of conditioning operators in logic is yet to be developed but, as Goodman et al (1990) put it, the mathematical problem is interesting in itself. In this section, we re-examine the axiomatic derivation of conditioning operators which are compatible with probability.

The search is for maps f of $\mathscr{R} \times \mathscr{R}$ with values in some space $\mathscr{S}$ which capture the basic aspects of conditioning and are compatible with conditional probability evaluations. The following is similar to discussions in Goodman, et al (1990).

In view of Lewis' triviality result (see Adams, 1975), we see that the range $\mathscr{S}$ of f should be strictly larger than $\mathscr{R}$ (actually, the containement is under suitable identification). The following simple test case brings out a further property.

Example: $g : \mathcal{R}\times\mathcal{R} \to \mathcal{R}$ has values $g(a,b) = ab$. Then, g has two properties of conditioning:

i) $g(\mathcal{R},1) = \mathcal{R}$, that is, conditional events are generalizations of unconditional events;

ii) $g(a,b) = g(ab,b)$, that is, conditioning a on b is the same as conditioning ab on b.

But g is not compatible with probability:

iii) $P(g(a,b)) = P(ab) \neq P(a|b)$;

iv) since for some a,b,c,d with $P(b)\cdot P(d) > 0$, it is possible that $ab = cd$ while $b \neq d$, it follows that

$g(a,b) = g(c,d)$ does not imply $P(a|b) = P(c|d)$ for all probability measures P on $\mathcal{R}$.

Taking these results into account, we conclude that the range of f(,b), which is $\mathcal{R}b$, is to be viewed as a subset of $\mathcal{R}$ and the range of f is to be the union $\mathcal{S} = \bigcup_{b\in\mathcal{R}} \mathcal{R}b$.

If this union is taken to be "disjoint union", then $\mathcal{S}$ is strictly larger than $\mathcal{R}$. Specifically, elements of $\mathcal{R}b$ are to be distinguished from elements of $\mathcal{R}d$ when $b \neq d$, even though, as elements of $\mathcal{R}$ itself, they may coincide ($\{bd\} = \{db\}$); if $a \leq b$ and $c \leq d$ and $b \neq d$, then we have two distinct elements in $\mathcal{S}$. In order to emphasize this distinction in discourse, we write elements of $\mathcal{R}b$ as (a,b), using b to index the "home" of a ; thus when $b \neq d$, $(a,b) \neq (a,d)$. This formalizes the intuitive notion that conditioning on different antecedents leads to different conditional events.

Example,cont: When this "disjoint union concept" is applied to $\mathcal{S}$ for the g considered above, g becomes "probability compatible". Actually, we modify g to have values

$$g(a,b) = (ab,b)$$

and assign probability $\tilde{P}(ab,b) = P(a|b)$. Then,

$$g(a,b) = g(c,d) \text{ implies } b = d \text{ and } ab = cd$$

whence $P(a|b) = P(ab)/P(b) = P(cd)/P(b) = P(c|d)$.

This suggests the following axioms for conditioning operators.

Definition A conditioning operator f mapping $\mathcal{D} = \mathcal{R}\times\mathcal{R}$ into some set $\mathcal{S}$ has the properties:

I. $f(a,b) = f(ab,b)$ for all $(a,b) \in \mathcal{D}$;

II. $f(a,b) = f(c,d)$ imples $b = d$ or, equivalently, $\mathcal{S}$ is the disjoint union of the $f(\mathcal{R},b)$;

III. f is probability-compatible, that is, $f(a,b) = f(c,d)$ implies $P(a|b) = P(c|d)$ for all probability measures on $\mathcal{R}$ such that $P(b)\cdot P(d) > 0$.

Note that in view of II, III is a "local" compatibility condition equivalent to

"$f(a,b) = f(c,b)$ implies $P(ab) = P(cb)$

for all P such that $P(b) > 0$."

In the example with $g(a,b) = (ab,b)$, the implication is a bit stronger, namely, $g(a,b) = g(c,b)$ implies $ab = cb$. It is shown in Goodman et al (1990), that when $\mathcal{R}$ is atomic, these two implications are also equivalent. Then, III can be modified to

$$\text{IV. } f(a,b) = f(c,b) \text{ implies } ab = cb .$$

In this case, $f(\mathcal{R},1)$ is a true copy of $\mathcal{R}$.

The search for f satisfying I, II, IV proceeds as follows. For each $b \in \mathcal{R}$, consider the map $f(\ ,b) : \mathcal{R} \to f(\mathcal{R},b) = \mathcal{S}_b$. To satisfy I, the restriction of $f(\ ,b)$ to $\mathcal{R}b$ must be onto $\mathcal{S}_b$; then imposing IV makes this restriction be one-to-one. Thus $f(\ ,b)$ induces a natural Boolean ring on $\mathcal{S}_b$ (operations $+_b$, $\cdot_b$, with 0_b, 1_b) making $f(\ ,b) : \mathcal{R} \to \mathcal{S}_b$ a homomorphism. Now let $I(b)$ be the kernel of $f(\ ,b)$, that is, $I(b) = \{x \in \mathcal{R} : f(x,b) = f(0,b) = 0_b\}$. The following is the usual form of an equivalence relation on $\mathcal{R}$: $x \approx_f y$ iff $f(x,b) = f(y,b)$, or, equivalently, $x + y \in I(b)$.

Let $\hat{f}(\ ,b) : \mathcal{R} \to \mathcal{R}/I(b)$ have values $\hat{f}(a,b) = a + I(b)$, the equivalence class containing a. Now I. implies $a \approx_f ab$ for all $a \in \mathcal{R}$ so that $a + ab = ab' \in I(b)$ or $\mathcal{R}b' \subseteq I(b)$. Conversely, let $a \in I(b)$; then $f(a,b) = f(ab,b) = 0_b$. But since the restriction of $f(\ ,b)$ to $\mathcal{R}b$ is an isomorphism, $ab = 0$, that is, $a \in \mathcal{R}b'$ or $I(b) \subseteq \mathcal{R}b'$. This makes

$$\hat{f}(a,b) = a + \mathcal{R}b' \text{ in } \mathcal{R}/\mathcal{R}b' .$$

It is easy to see that $\hat{f}$ satisfies I, II, IV. Since each $\mathcal{S}_b$ is isomorphic to $\mathcal{R}/\mathcal{R}b'$, all f satyisfying I, II, IV are obtained from $\hat{f}$ through bijections; specifically,

$$f : \mathcal{R} \times \mathcal{R}^* \to \mathcal{S} = \cup_{b \in \mathcal{R}} \mathcal{S}_b$$

where the union is "disjoint" and the "marginal" maps $f(\ ,b)$ are for a fixed collection $\{\mathcal{S}_b : b \in \mathcal{R}\}$. (There is also a bijection between $\cup_{b \in \mathcal{R}} \mathcal{R}/\mathcal{R}b'$ and S.) The values $f(a,b)$ are viewed as the measure-free conditional events. To simplify the discussion, the canonical form of $f(a,b)$ is taken to be $(a|b) = a + \mathcal{R}b'$, a coset of a principal ideal; then the space of conditional events, the mathematical conditional extension of logic, is $\mathcal{R}/\mathcal{R} = \cup_{b \in \mathcal{R}} \mathcal{R}/\mathcal{R}b'$, taken as the disjoint union of the quotient rings.

An interpretation of $(a|b)$ in algebraic logic (Halmos, 1962) goes as follows. An $\mathcal{R}$-filter is a set

$$\mathcal{R} \vee b = \{x \vee b : x \in \mathcal{R}\} = \{y \in \mathcal{R} : y \geq b\}$$

where $y \geq b$ means $yb = b$. This filter represents the set of all "consequents of b" (if b is true then $x \vee b$ is true for $x \in \mathcal{R}$). This suggests that $(a|b)$ should represent events y equivalent to a under that filter. Here, y is equivalent to a under $\mathcal{R} \vee b$, written $y \approx_b a$, if there is an $r \in \mathcal{R}$, such that $(r \vee b)y = (r \vee b)a$. Hence we define a conditional event to be an equivalence class:

$$(a|b) = a[\mathcal{R} \vee b] = \{y : y \approx_b a\} .$$

But from $y \in (a|b)$ such that $(r \vee b)y = (r \vee b)a$, we get

$$(1 + (r \vee b)')y = (r \vee b)a$$

whence

$$\begin{aligned} y &= (r \vee b)a + (r \vee b)'y \\ &= ba + r(1 + b)a + r'b'y \\ &= a + (a + ra + r'y')b' \end{aligned}$$

so that $y \in a + \mathcal{R}b'$. Conversely, $x = a + sb'$ implies

$$(r \vee b)x = (r \vee b)a \quad \text{when} \quad r = b .$$

This means that $x \approx_b a$ so that $(a|b) = a + \mathcal{R}b'$.

3. Non-monotonic conditional reasoning

Each reasoning procedure in an intelligent system is based upon a logical consequence (or logical entailment) relation in a given logic. In classical first-order logic, the entailment relation $\Rightarrow$ is the order relation $\leq$ in the Boolean ring $\mathcal{R}$ and is obviously monotonic:

$$\text{if } a \leq b \text{ then } \forall c \in \mathcal{R}, \text{ we have } ac \leq b.$$

More specifically, for $A \subseteq \mathcal{R}$, and $Th(A) = \{x \in \mathcal{R} : A \Rightarrow x\}$, we say that $\Rightarrow$ is monotonic

$$\text{if } A \subseteq B \subseteq \mathcal{R} \text{ implies } Th(A) \subseteq Th(B).$$

The rule $\Rightarrow$ is non-monotonic if it is not monotonic. By some abuse of language, a reasoning procedure is said to be monotonic or non-monotonic according as $\Rightarrow$ is monotonic or not. The terms "inference", "reasoning" and "logic", as in probabilistic inference, probabilistic reasoning, and probabilistic logic, should be used with care! For example, while probability logic is monotonic, probabilistic reasoning claims to capture a non-monotonicity property! It turns out that this all depends on the structure of the syntax of the logic used. To make things precise, by conditional inference (or reasoning), we mean $E \underset{K}{\Rightarrow} a$ (a follows logically from E in the context of K), where $T = <K, E>$ is a theory (Pearl, 1988), K is the knowledge base and E is the evidence. In this framework, $\Rightarrow$ acts like a set-valued function with two arguments (K, E).

The non-monotonicity of $\Rightarrow$ is in general relative to E, i.e. to the addition of facts or evidence. This explains why the conditional probability operator is referred to as being non-monotonic: for fixed $a \in \mathcal{R}$, the set-function $P(a \mid \cdot)$ is not monotonic with respect to $\leq$ on $\mathcal{R}$.

The search for logical operations on $\mathcal{R} | \mathcal{R}$ extending those on $\mathcal{R}$ is based on the following natural observation. (See Goodman, et al, 1990.)

The usual (ring) operations on the Boolean quotient ring $\mathcal{S}_b$, for each fixed b, are coset operations in algebra:

$$(a|b) + (c|b) = (a + c|b) ;$$
$$(a|b) \cdot (c|b) = (ac|b) ;$$
$$(a|b) \vee (c|b) = (a|b) + (c|b) + (a|b)(c|b) ;$$
$$(a|b)' = (a'|b) .$$

But $\mathcal{R} | \mathcal{R}$ is the union of all $\mathcal{S}_b$, $b \in \mathcal{R}$. For different antecedents, i.e. for conditionals from different quotient rings, there are no operations available in the literature of ring theory, perhaps because of a lack of motivation. Now observe that the above coset operations on each S_b can be rewritten as:

$$(a|b) + (c|b) = \{x + y : x \in (a|b), y \in (c|b)\}$$
$$(a|b) \cdot (c|b) = \{xy : x \in (a|b), y \in (c|b)\} .$$

Therefore it is natural to define operations on $\mathcal{R} | \mathcal{R}$ as:

$$(a|b) + (c|d) = \{x + y : x \in (a|b), y \in (c|d)\}$$
$$(a|b) \cdot (c|d) = \{xy : x \in (a|b), y \in (c|d)\} .$$

The striking result is that these operations are closed on $\mathcal{R} | \mathcal{R}$, i.e. they do yield cosets. It can be shown that

$$(a|b) + (c|d) = (a + c|bd)$$
$$(a|b) \cdot (c|d) = (ac|a'b \vee c'd \vee bd)$$
$$(a|b) \vee (c|d) = (a \vee c|ab \vee cd \vee bd) .$$

However, $\mathcal{R} | \mathcal{R}$ with these operations is not quite a ring because of the lack of additive inverses.

For inference purposes, an extension of the order relation to $\mathcal{R}|\mathcal{R}$ is useful. Define

$$(a|b) \le (c|d) \text{ as } (a|b)\cdot(c|d) = (a|b).$$

This happens when $ab \le cd$ and $c'd \le a'b$. Indeed, we need to check when $ab = abcd$ and $b = a'b \vee c'd \vee bd$. Since $ab \le cd$, we have $ab = abcd$. Since $c'd \le a'b$, we have

$$a'b \vee c'd \vee bd = a'b \vee bd = b(a' \vee d).$$

But $b = ab + a'b \le cd \vee a' \le d \vee a'$, and hence $b(a' \vee d) = b$. Conversely, $ab = abcd$ implies that $ab \le cd$; multiplying $b = a'b \vee c'd \vee bd$ by a', we get

$$a'b = a'b \vee a'c'd, \text{ i.e. } a'c'd \le a'b.$$

But from $c'd \le b$ we have $ac'd \le ab \le cd$, meaning that $ac'd = 0$, i.e. $c'd \le a'b$.

Also, it can be shown that if $(a|b) \le (c|d)$, then, for any probability measure P, we have $P(a|b) \le P(c|d)$.

Now the conditioning operator $(\cdot|\cdot)$ is non-monotonic relative to the second argument. Indeed, for $a, b, c \in \mathcal{R}$, we have in general $ab \le abc$ and $a'b \le a'bc$, so that $(a|b)$ and $(a|bc)$ are not comparable. This fact also explains the non-monotonicity of the conditioning probability operator. See also Dubois and Prade (1989, 1990).

4. Measure-free concepts of independence and valuations

In the previous section, conditional events were treated in an environment totally measure-free; now we need to introduce some numerical aspects. We suggest that our approach herein is more self-consistent than that of some other published works. For example, Bundy (1985) began his incidence calculus by taking uncertainty in terms of sets but used probability to assess "a given b". But, it is not clear to us how this would lead to a combination of

"If b then a" with "If c then d".

Moreover, what we have done here is also consistent with the foundations of conditional probability spaces in Renyi (1970). He proposes properties for (our notation) $Q : \mathcal{R} \times \mathcal{B} \to [0,1]$ where the "bunch" $\mathcal{B}$ is a subset of $\mathcal{R}$, not containing ϕ, closed under finite unions with $\cup_{n=1}^{\infty} b_n = \Omega$ for some sequence in $\mathcal{B}$; when $\mathcal{B} = \{\Omega\}$, Q is a probability. He shows that there is a σ-finite measure μ on $\mathcal{R}$ such that for $b \in \mathcal{B}$, $0 < \mu(b) < \infty$ and

$$Q(a,b) = \mu(ab)/\mu(b).$$

Taking $\tilde{P}$ restricted to $\tilde{\mathscr{R}}_{\mathscr{B}} = \cup_{b \in \mathscr{B}} \mathscr{A} \mathscr{A} b'$ to have values $\tilde{P}(a|b) = Q(a,b)$ or, visa-versa, defining Q by the same equation, is a perfectly respectable extension. Moreover, in the ordinary case, a and b are independent given c iff

$$P(ab|c) = P(a|c) \cdot P(b|c) .$$

But now this can be written as $\tilde{P}((ab|c)) = \tilde{P}((a|c)) \cdot \tilde{P}((b|c))$ for $\tilde{P}$ on $\tilde{\mathscr{R}}_{\Omega}$. This suggests that we define $(a|b)$ and $(c|d)$ to be independent with respect to $\tilde{P}$ iff

$$\tilde{P}((a|b) \cdot (c|d)) = \tilde{P}((a|b)) \cdot \tilde{P}((c|d)) .$$

Rényi (1970) also included a discussion of "qualitative independence" and showed that independence in ordinary probability was stronger: if a and b are independent and non-trivial so that $P(a \cap b) = P(a) \cdot P(b) > 0$, then a and b are *qualitatively independent*; that is, ab , a′b , ab′, a′b′ are all non-empty. Coincidentally, these events also have positive probabilities.

Our motivation for considering "independence" comes from knowledge representation in inference networks of expert systems. For example, in some models for medical diagnosis, the variables of interest can be represented as nodes or vertices in a graph; then causal relationships are represented by edges of the graph and the strengths of such relationships are quantified by an uncertainty measure; in others, Dempster-Shafer belief functions (Shafer, 1976) or possibility measures (Zadeh, 1978) are used. Since there is no general agreement on the choice of such measures, the construction of the inference network (also called the influence diagram) should be done without reference to the measure of uncertainty used. As some "independence" assumption generally simplifies the calculations within the representation, it will be helpful to have such a concept a priori.

In the following, we discuss in detail qualitative independence and conditional qualitative independence of variables. Of course, this includes the qualitative independence of events in Rényi (1970).

We proceed now to the formulation of measure-free (that is, qualitative or algebraic) concepts of unconditional and conditional independence of events, and more generally, variables, in the discrete and "continuous" cases. These concepts turn out to be less restrictive than their counterparts in probability theory in the sense that, roughly,

"Stochastic (P) independence implies
qualitative (Q) independence."

First we give a brief historical background.

The concept of qualitiative independence was treated in some detail in Rényi (1970). Let $\mathscr{R}$, +, $\cdot$, 0, 1 be a Boolean (σ-)ring with the logical operations $\forall$ and $'$. For $a, b \,\varepsilon\, \mathscr{R}$, one says that a and b are Q-independent iff

$$ab,\ ab',\ a'b,\ a'b' \text{ are all not } \phi$$

(implying also that a, a', b, b' are all not ϕ). Some justification comes about by treating the elements of $\mathscr{R}$ as realizations or occurrences of events. For example, if $a'b = \phi$, then $b \le a$, $(b \subset a)$ so that when b is realized, a is also realized; then a and b cannot be "independent". Rényi showed that "P-independence implies Q-independence":

$$P(a \cap b) = P(a) \cdot P(b) > 0 \text{ imples } a \cap b \neq \phi$$

and the rest follow by the use of complements.

Q-independence of non-empty a and b can be reformulated as follows. Let $\pi(a) = \{a, a'\}$ and $\pi(b) = \{b, b'\}$ be partitions of $1\ (= \Omega)$. Then a and b are Q-independent iff

$$\text{for all } \alpha \,\varepsilon\, \pi(a) \text{ and all } \beta \,\varepsilon\, \pi(b),\ \alpha\beta \neq \phi .$$

If we fix a and b through their indicator variables 1_a and 1_b, then the following equivalent definition leads into that for other variables. The σ-field generated by 1_a is a sub σ-field of $\mathscr{R}$; say, $\sigma(1_a) = \{0, 1, a, a'\}$; similarly,

$$\sigma(1_b) = \{0, 1, b, b'\}.$$

Then a and b are Q-independent iff for all $\alpha \,\varepsilon\, \sigma(1_a) - \{0\}$ and all $\beta \,\varepsilon\, \sigma(1_b) - \{0\}$, $\alpha\beta \neq \phi$.

Let X, Y be measurable functions on $(\Omega, \mathscr{R})$ with countable ranges in the real line; let the countable partitions (with no empty subsets) generated by X and Y be, correspondingly, $\pi(X) = \{a_n\}$ and $\pi(Y) = \{b_m\}$. Then X, Y are Q-independent iff $\pi(X)$ and $\pi(Y)$ are Q-independent in the sense that

$$\text{for all } a \,\varepsilon\, \pi(X) \text{ and all } b \,\varepsilon\, \pi(Y),\ ab \neq \phi .$$

Now note that $\sigma(X) = \{\cup_{i\varepsilon I}\, a_i : I \subset X(\Omega)\}$ where $a_i = X^{-1}(i)$ for $i \,\varepsilon\, X(\Omega)$ and I could be ϕ. X and Y are Q-independent iff for all $a \,\varepsilon\, \sigma(X) - \{\phi\}$ and all $b \,\varepsilon\, \sigma(Y) - \{\phi\}$, $ab \neq \phi$.

As far as we know, Q-independence of "continuous" variables has not been discussed in the literature; in Rényi (1970), Q-conditional independence was not addressed. Shafer, et al (1987), in inference networks in expert systems, defined Q-conditional independence for finite partitions, that is, variables with finite ranges. They did not consider the concept of Q-conditional independence of events. The rest of this section is a comprehensive discussion of all these notions with the following notation.

Definition: Let $\mathcal{R}$, +, ·, 0, 1, $\forall$, ′ be a Boolean (σ-)ring.

1. Let A and B be two subsets of $\mathcal{R}$ consisting of non-zero (not 0) elements. Then

$$\underset{\mathcal{R}}{\perp} B \text{ iff for all } a \in A \text{ \& all } b \in B,\ a\cdot b \neq 0 .$$

2. Let a and b $\in \mathcal{R}$. Then

$$a \underset{\mathcal{R}}{\perp} b \text{ iff } \pi(a) = \{a, a'\} \underset{\mathcal{R}}{\perp} \pi(b) = \{b, b'\} .$$

3. Let X and Y be discrete variables. Then

$$X \underset{\mathcal{R}}{\perp} Y \text{ iff } \pi(X) \underset{\mathcal{R}}{\perp} \pi(Y) \text{ iff}$$

for all $a \in \sigma(X) - \{0\}$ & all $b \in \sigma(Y) - \{0\}$, $ab \neq 0$.

4. Let a, b and c $\in \mathcal{R}$. Then

$$a \underset{P}{\perp} b \mid c \text{ iff } P(ab|c) = P(a|c)\cdot P(b|c),$$

equivalently, $\tilde{P}((a|c)\otimes(b|c)) = \tilde{P}(a|c)\cdot\tilde{P}(b|c)$.

5. Let a, b and c $\in \mathcal{R}$. Then

$$a \underset{Q}{\perp} b \mid c \text{ iff } (a|c) \underset{\mathcal{R}/\mathcal{R}c'}{\perp} (b|c) \text{ iff}$$

$$\text{or all } (\alpha|c) \in \pi(a|c) = \{(a|c), (a'|c)\} \text{ and}$$
$$\text{all } (\beta|c) \in \pi(b|c) = \{(b|c), (b'|c)\} ,$$
$$(\alpha|c) \otimes (\beta|c) \neq (0|c) .$$

Note here that $(\alpha|c) \otimes (\beta|c) \neq 0$ is equivalent to

$$(\alpha\beta|c) \neq (0|c) \text{ or to } \alpha\beta c \neq 0 .$$

Also, in considering $\pi(a|c)$ it is implicitly assumed that $(a|c)$ and $(a'|c)$ are not $(0|c)$ which is equivalent to $ac \neq 0$ and $a'c \neq 0$. Moreover, we can show that the Q-conditional independence in Definition 5 is *strictly weaker* than that for finite partitions as in Shafer, et al, (1987). First, we write their definition in our notation.

Definition: Let X, Y, Z be discrete variables; let

$$A^{c}_{\pi(X)} = \{(a|c) : a \in \pi(X) \text{ and } ac \neq 0\} .$$

Then, $X \underset{Q}{\perp} Y \mid Z$ iff $\pi(X) \underset{Q}{\perp} \pi(Y) \mid \pi(Z)$ iff

$$A^{c}_{\pi(X)} \underset{\mathcal{R}/\mathcal{R}c'}{\perp} A^{c}_{\pi(Y)} \quad \text{for all } c \in \pi(Z) .$$

We see that if $1_a \underset{Q}{\perp} 1_b \mid 1_c$ according to this last definition, then $a \underset{Q}{\perp} b \mid c$ according to Definition 5 but that the converse does not hold. Unlike the unconditional case, Q-conditional independence of events cannot be defined in terms of variables.

In order to define a Q-independence which will be compatible with stochastic independence for "continuous variables", it is necessary to pay attention to "small sets". In probability theory, these are the P-null sets; here these are abstracted to σ-ideals (Halmos, 1963), a dual of the "bunch" of Rényi (1970). In the discrete case, it is necessary to consider only the zero ideal $\mathcal{M}_o = \{0\}$ which is a trivial σ-ideal.

When P is a probability on $\mathcal{R}$,

$$\mathcal{M}_P = \{a \in \mathcal{R}: P(a) = 0\} \text{ is a } \sigma\text{-ideal.}$$

Now $X \underset{P}{\perp} Y$ iff $\sigma(X) \underset{P}{\perp} \sigma(Y)$ in the sense that for all $a \in \sigma(X)$, $b \in \sigma(Y)$, $P(ab) = P(a) \cdot P(b)$. If $a \in \sigma(X) - \mathcal{M}_P$ and $b \in \sigma(Y) - \mathcal{M}_P$, then $P(ab) > 0$ which implies that $ab \notin \mathcal{M}_P$ so that $ab \neq 0$. If one requires only $a \in \sigma(X)-\{0\}$, it could happen that $P(a) = 0$ or $ab = 0$. Thus we are lead to the following continuation.

Definition: Let X, Y, Z be real measurable functions on $\mathcal{R}$.

6) $X \underset{Q}{\perp} Y$ iff $\sigma(x) - \mathcal{M} \underset{\mathcal{R}}{\perp} \sigma(Y) - \mathcal{M}$ as in Definition 1) iff there is a σ-ideal $\mathcal{M}$ such that

$$\text{for all } a \in \sigma(X) - \mathcal{M} \text{ and all } b \in \sigma(Y) - \mathcal{M},\ ab \neq 0 .$$

7) $X \underset{Q}{\perp} Y \mid Z$ iff there is a σ-ideal $\mathcal{M}$ such that for all $a \in \sigma(X) - \mathcal{M}$ and all $b \in \sigma(Y) - \mathcal{M}$ and all $c \in \sigma(Z) - \mathcal{M}$, $a \underset{Q}{\perp} b \mid c$ as in Definition 4.

5. Combination of evidence

This discussion of combination of evidence in artificial intelligence, in particular, expert systems, has just two goals: i) to give an elementary presentation of the problem in a setting more familiar to statisticians yet one which can lead to other approaches in modeling uncertainty; ii) to point out the possibility of using conditional events and their extensions in this problem.

For example, one (simply stated) problem in the combination of evidence in a probabilistic setting is to say something about $P(a|bc)$ from knowledge of $P(a|b)$ and $P(a|c)$; details of many situations need to be worked out. Here we will examine one computational procedure.

Consider the reasoning frame $T = \langle K,E \rangle$, as in Pearl (1988), where $K \subseteq \mathcal{R}/\mathcal{R}$ and $E \subseteq \mathcal{R}$. Conditionals of interest are of the form $(a|E)$ for $a \in \mathcal{R}$ and, in this mode, E stands for the conjunction of all events in E . When K is given along with conditional probabilities $\alpha_i = P(c_i|d_i)$, $i = 1(1)n$, with $(c_i|d_i) \in K$, the value of $P(a|E)$ represents a degree of logical entailment. The computational procedure is simply a generalization of Hailperin (1984). (See also Nilsson, 1986.)

Recall that $\mathcal{R}$ as a field of subsets of some set Ω. First, observe that

$$P(a|b) = P(ab) + P(a|b)P(b'). \quad (*)$$

Thus, if $\mathcal{P}$ is a finite $\mathcal{R}$-partition of Ω, of size m, say $\mathcal{P} = \{c_1, c_2, ..., c_m\}$, and ab, b′ can be expressed in terms of the c_j's, say, $ab = \sum_{j \in N} c_j$, $b' = \sum_{j \in M} c_j$ with $N, M \subseteq \{1, 2, ..., m\}$, then $P(a|b)$ is related to $P(c_j)$, $j \in N \cup M$, in a linear fashion. Hence the problem of computation of, say,

$$P(a_{n+1}|b_{n+1}), \text{ given } P(a_i|b_i), i = 1, 2, ..., n,$$

can be described as follows.

From the collection of $2(n + 1)$ events

$$\{a_1, b_1; a_2, b_2; \cdots; a_{n+1}, b_{n+1}\},$$

form the canonical partition $\mathcal{P}$ of Ω consisting of all events of the form

$$a_1^{\alpha_1} b_1^{\beta_1} a_2^{\alpha_2} b_2^{\beta_2} \cdots a_{n+1}^{\alpha_{n+1}} b_{n+1}^{\beta_{n+1}},$$

where $\alpha_j, \beta_j \in \{0, 1\}$, with

$$a_j^1 = a_j, \quad b_j^1 = b_j, \quad a_j^0 = a_j', \quad b_j^0 = b_j'.$$

All events $a_j b_j$, b_j' are decomposable in terms of the elements of this canonical partition. Let m be size of $\mathcal{P}$, $m \le 2^{2(n+1)}$, and label these elements as

$c_1, c_2, \cdots, c_m$. In view of (*), a coding or "design" n by m matrix Π is defined as $\Pi = [\Pi_{ij}]$, where

$$\Pi_{ij} = 0\,,\ 1\,,\ \text{or}\ \ P(a_i|b_i)$$

according as $c_j \leq a_i'b_i$, $\leq a_ib_i$, or $\leq b_i'$. Suppose that $\Lambda_j = P(c_j)$, $j = 1, \cdots, m$ are solutions of the system of equations: $\sum_{j=1}^{m} \Lambda_j\Pi_{ij} = P(a_i|b_i)$, $i = 1, \cdots, n$; then

$P(a_{n+1}|b_{n+1}) = \sum_{j=1}^{m} \Lambda_j\Pi_{n+1,j}$, where as before,

$$\Pi_{n+1,j} = 0\,,\ 1\,,\ \text{or}\ \ P(a_{n+1}|b_{n+1})$$

according as $c_j \leq a_{n+1}'b_{n+1}$, $\leq a_{n+1}b_{n+1}$, or $\leq b_{n+1}'$.

Of course, as in the case of unconditional probabilities, the solutions for the Λ_j's is not, in general, unique but bounds for $P(a_{n+1}|b_{n+1})$ can be obtained using linear programming techniques. For practical computational purposes, stochastic optimization might be helpful.

We illustrate the use of the algebraic structure of measure-free conditional events to provide approximations for bounds on $(a|b)$ and numerical Frechet-like bounds on $P(a|bc)$.

For very practical reasons, we consider a finite set Θ representing either a parameter space as in a statistical model or a collection of all possible answers to the question of interest. We reserve the triple $(\Omega, \mathcal{A}, P)$ as the underlying probability space on which all random functions are defined. In the Bayesian spirit, it is assumed that the true parameter θ_o is a random variable from Ω into Θ with a distribution P_o on the power set $\mathcal{R} = \mathcal{P}(\Theta)$.

In the case of *complete prior information* P_o is known, that is, $P_o(a)$ is known for all $a \in \mathcal{R}$. Suppose now that some event b is realized; then the prior information P_o (representing our knowledge about θ_o) can be modified or updated into a conditional probability P_b . In expert systems, the sense of "evidence b" is that the value of θ_o is in b ; for example, in a medical diagnosis, the patient exhibits the symptom(s) in the set b .

In practice, this kind of updating of knowledge is not possible since P_o is not known. Then this is a Bayesian case of *incomplete prior information*; the existence of P_o is postulated but the only known information is b and the value $P_o(b) = \alpha$. A main question, as in Dempster (1967), is, "What can be said about the values $P_o(a)$ for the other $a \varepsilon \mathcal{R}$?"

We affirm that our knowledge at each state is expressed by a probability measure; when new evidence is obtained, this is to be "updated" by some "combining". The concept of evidence is very intuitive yet it is often understood in natural language and semantics. We interpret it as a realized event supplied by some "test" which might be merely the opinion of an expert. This lack of precision in evidence suggests looking at a less precise formulation of randomness than that in random variables. Thus we turn to *random sets*

A random set is simply a measurable (in terms of $\mathcal{A}$ and the power set $\mathcal{P}(\mathcal{R}) = \mathcal{P}(\mathcal{P}(\Theta)))$ function S from Ω to $\mathcal{R}$. Herein we limit the values of S to be not ϕ : $P(S = \phi) = 0$. This restriction is to limit the random sets to those which are direct generalizations of random variables where the empty set is not a possible value. Then combination = conjoining = intersection of evidence leading to S with evidence leading to T is the intersection $S \cap T$. Our contention is that S or its distribution P_S models evidence or knowledge in the most general form.

For example, to address the question posed above, we take the particular function S to have "density"

$$P(S = b_1 = b) = P_o(b) = \alpha \text{ , } P(S = b_2 = b') = 1 - \alpha \text{ .}$$

The "CDF" of S is $F_S : \mathcal{R} \to [0,1]$ with

$$F_S(a) = P(S \leq a)$$

$$= \sum_{b_i \leq a} P_o(b_i) = \begin{cases} 1 & \text{if } b_1 \cup b_2 \subset a \\ \alpha & \text{if only } b_1 \subset a \text{ .} \\ 1 - \alpha & \text{if only } b_2 \subset a \\ 0 & \text{otherwise} \end{cases}$$

Obviously, "$S \leq a$" is the weak sub-set inequality. It is easy to see that for all $a \varepsilon \mathcal{R}$, $F_S(a) \leq P_o(a)$. Replacing a by a$'$ in this inequality, yields

$$F_S(a') \le 1 - P_o(a) \text{ or } P_o(a) \le 1 - F_S(a') .$$

Thus one interval approximation for $P_o(a)$ is

$$[F_S(a) , 1 - F_S(a')] .$$

Then, when b is (evidence) realized,
$P_o(a|b) = P_o(ab)/P_o(b)$ has the interval approximation

$$\left[\frac{F_S(ab)}{\alpha}, \frac{1 - F_S((ab)')}{\alpha}\right] .$$

The symbolism in this example is quite general. Since $\mathcal{R}(\mathcal{R})$ is also finite, the probabilities are completely determined by the density P_S on $\mathcal{R}$, or, equivalently, by the CDF
$F_S : \mathcal{R}(\mathcal{R}) \to [0,1]$. Indeed,

$$\begin{aligned} F_S(a) &= \Pr(S \le a) = \Pr(\{\omega : S(\omega) \subset a\}) \\ &= \Pr(S(\omega) = a_1 \subset a , S(\omega) = a_2 \subset a , \cdots) \\ &= \sum_{a_i \le a} P_S(a_i) \end{aligned}$$

and, conversely, $P_S(\{a\}) = F_S(a) - \sum_{b < a} P_S(b)$ where the last inequality is for proper subsets; of course, the sums are on sets in $\mathcal{R}$. Moreover, if X is a random variable with density m on $\Theta = \{\theta_1, \cdots, \theta_N\}$, then X can also be considered as a random set, say $\underset{\sim}{X}$, with range $\{\theta_1\} , \cdots, \{\theta_N\}$ contained in $\mathcal{R}(\mathcal{R}(\Theta))$ and

$$F_{\underset{\sim}{X}}(a) = \sum_{\{\theta_i\} \, \varepsilon \, a} m(\theta_i) \text{ for all } a \ \varepsilon \ \mathcal{R}(\mathcal{R}) .$$

Indeed, this $F_{\underset{\sim}{X}}$ is actually a probability measure on $\mathcal{R}(\mathcal{R})$.

We now consider other examples beginning with the simplest random set which is like the simplest Dirac (degenerate) random variable.

Example 1. Fix $a \ne \Theta$ in $\mathcal{R}(\Theta)$ .Let $X_a(\omega) = a$ for all $\omega \ \varepsilon \ \Omega$. Then on $\mathcal{R}(\Theta)$, the density

$$\Pr(X_a = b) = P_{X_a}(b) = 1 \text{ if } b = a \text{ and } 0 \text{ otherwise.}$$

But on $\mathcal{R}(\mathcal{R}(\Theta))$, the probability measure is

$$F_{X_a}(b) = 1 \text{ if } a \le b \text{ and } 0 \text{ otherwise.}$$

Example 2. Let X be a measurable function from Ω <u>onto</u> $\Theta = \{2, 3\}$ such that $\Omega_2 = X^{-1}(2)$ and $\Omega_3 = X^{-1}(3)$ are non-empty. Let the density of X on Θ have values

$$P_X(2) = \Pr(X = 2) = p_2 \,, \; P_X(3) = \Pr(X = 3) = p_3 \,.$$

Then the CDF is $F_X(a) = \Pr(X \le a) = \begin{cases} 0 & \text{if } a < 2 \\ p_2 & \text{if } 2 \le a < 3 \,. \\ 1 & \text{if } 3 \le a \end{cases}$

This also generates a probability measure Q_X on the field

$\mathcal{A}(\Theta) = \{\phi, \{2\}, \{3\}, \Theta\}$ with values

$$Q_X(\phi) = 0 \,, \; Q_X(\{2\}) = p_2 \,, \; Q_X(\{3\}) = p_3 \,, \; Q_X(\Theta) = 1 \,.$$

Now we "lift" X to a set function on Ω with values

$$\underset{\sim}{X}(\omega) = \begin{cases} \{2\} & \text{if } \omega \in \Omega_2 \\ \{3\} & \text{if } \omega \in \Omega_3 \end{cases} .$$

Since $\Omega_2 \cup \Omega_3 = \Omega$, $\underset{\sim}{X}$ maps Ω <u>into</u> $\mathcal{R} = \mathcal{A}(\Theta)$. The corresponding density has values

$$P_{\underset{\sim}{X}}(\phi) = P_{\underset{\sim}{X}}(\Theta) = 0 \,, \; P_{\underset{\sim}{X}}(\{2\}) = p_2 \,, \; P_{\underset{\sim}{X}}(\{3\}) = p_3 \,.$$

For $a \in \mathcal{A}(\mathcal{R})$, the CDF $F_{\underset{\sim}{X}}(a) = \sum_{b \le a} P_{\underset{\sim}{X}}(b)$; we table the values:

ϕ	$\{2\}$	$\{3\}$	Θ	$\phi, \{2\}$	$\phi, \{3\}$	ϕ, Θ
0	p_2	p_3	0	p_2	p_2	0

$\{2\}, \{3\}$	$\{2\}, \Theta$	$\{3\}, \Theta$	$\phi, \{2\}, \{3\}$
1	p_2	p_3	1

$\phi, \{2\}, \Theta$	$\phi, \{3\}, \Theta$	$\{2\}, \{3\}, \Theta$	$\phi, \{2\}, \{3\}, \Theta$
p_2	p_3	1	1

Example 3. Let Y be a random variable with positive density $P_o(\theta_i)$ on $\Theta = \{\theta_1, \cdots, \theta_N\}$; let $\underset{\sim}{Y}$ be its corresponding random set. Suppose that $b = \{\theta_{i1}, \cdots, \theta_{ik}\}$ is realized; let X_b be its corresponding random set. Then, $Z = \underset{\sim}{Y} \cap X_b$ has the values $\{\theta_{i1}\}, \cdots, \{\theta_{ik}\}, \phi$

and

$$P(Z = \phi) = \sum_{\theta_i \notin b} P_o(\theta_i) .$$

Since these values are all positive, we can truncate Z to $\underset{\sim}{Z}$ with range $\{\theta_i\} \varepsilon\, b$ and probabilities

$$P(\underset{\sim}{Z} = \{\theta_i\}) = P_o(\theta_i)/P_o(\phi) .$$

Of course, this is the conditional probability distribution of Y given b on $\mathcal{R} = \mathcal{A}(\Theta)$.

Example 4. Let X , Y be random variables with the respective probabilities P_1, P_2 on $\mathcal{A}(\Theta)$; suppose that X and Y are independent with respect to P . The corresponding random sets are denoted by $\underset{\sim}{X}$, $\underset{\sim}{Y}$. Let $Z = \underset{\sim}{X} \cap \underset{\sim}{Y}$ have the range ϕ, $\theta_1, \cdots, \theta_n$. Here $Z(\omega) = \underset{\sim}{X}(\omega) \cap \underset{\sim}{Y}(\omega) = \phi$ if

$$X(\omega) = \theta_1 \neq \theta_2 = Y(\omega) .$$

Again, deleting ϕ , we get

$$P(\underset{\sim}{Z} = \{\theta_i\}) = P_1(\theta_i)\cdot P_2(\theta_i)/\sum_{j=1}^{n} P_1(\theta_j)\cdot P_2(\theta_j) .$$

Example 5. Here we turn to the problem of the (parallel) combining of two pieces of evidence. Suppose that b and c are P_o-independent and $P_o(b) = \alpha$, $P_o(c) = \beta$ are known; what is to be said about $P_o(a|bc)$? First, since

$$P_o(a|bc) = P_o(abc)/P_o(bc) = P_o(abc)/\alpha\beta ,$$

it may be sufficient to approximate $P_o(abc)$. Now note that there are two levels at which to proceed, that of events and that of random sets.

A: Combining the evidence (events) first. With $P_o(bc) = \alpha\beta$, we proceed as above, taking the random set S_1 to have density $P(S_1 = bc) = \alpha\beta$ and $P(S_1 = (bc)') = 1 - \alpha\beta$. For all $a \,\varepsilon\, \mathcal{R}$, $F_{S_1}(a) \le P_o(a) \le 1 - F_{S_1}(a')$.

B: Combining the random sets. Let S_b have range b, b′ with probabilities α, $1\text{-}\alpha$; let S_c have range c, c′ with probabilities β, $1\text{-}\beta$. Let F_{S_b} and F_{S_c} be the corresponding CDFs. Then $S_2 = S_b \cap S_c$ has range

bc, bc′, b′c, b′c′

with density values (via independence)

$$\alpha\beta,\ \alpha(1-\beta),\ (1-\alpha)\beta,\ (1-\alpha)(1-\beta)\ .$$

Then for all $a \in \mathscr{R}$, $F_{S_2}(a) \leq P_o(a) \leq 1 - F_{S_2}(a')$. These bounds are "sharper" than those obtained in A since the partition

$$b_1 = bc,\ b_2 = bc',\ b_3 = b'c,\ b_4 = b'c'$$

is finer than the partition

$$d_1 = bc,\ d_2 = (bc)' = b_2 \cup b_3 \cup b_4\ .$$

More precisely,

$$F_{S_1}(a) = \sum_{d_i \leq a} P_o(d_i) \leq \sum_{b_i \leq a} P_o(b_i) = F_{S_2}(a)$$

and so also $1 - F_{S_2}(a') \leq 1 - F_{S_1}(a')$. Thus an interval approximation can be taken as

$$P_o(a\,|\,bc)\ \varepsilon \left[\frac{F_{S_2}(a)}{\alpha\beta}, \frac{1 - F_{S_2}(a)}{\alpha\beta}\right].$$

Once such "confidence intervals" have been obtained, they can be used in succeeding decision processes. This is to be contrasted with the use of Frechet bounds

$$P_o(abc) \leq \min\{P_o(a), P_o(bc)\}$$

wherein $P_o(a)$ has to be estimated by some other means.

The following example illustrates an application in conditional evidence. This is a typical situation where the use of measure-free conditional events and their algebraic structure is truly necessary.

Example 6. Suppose that P_o is unknown but we are given (by an expert) that a and c are independent given b ,

that $P_o(a\,|\,b) = \alpha$,

and that $P_o(c\,|\,b) = \beta$.

(If b = 1 , this reduces to the first example on interval approximations.) The random set X has range

$$\{(a\,|\,b), (a'\,|\,b)\}\ ;$$

the random set Y has range $\{(c\,|\,b), (c'\,|\,b)\}$, each a subset of $\mathscr{R}/\mathscr{R}b'$. Also,

$$P(X = (a\,|\,b)) = \alpha = 1 - P(X = (a'\,|\,b))\ ,$$

$$P(Y = (c\,|\,b)) = \beta = 1 - P(Y = (c'\,|\,b))\ .$$

Now $Z = X \otimes_b Y$ has range $(ac\,|\,b), (ac'\,|\,b), (a'c\,|\,b), (a'c'\,|\,b)$ with probabilities $\alpha\beta$,

$\alpha(1-\beta)$, $(1-\alpha)\beta$, $(1-\alpha)(1-\beta)$. Then $F_Z : \mathcal{R}/\mathcal{R}b \to [0,1]$ has values

$$F_Z(r|b) = \sum_{(a_ic_i|b) \le (r|b)} P_Z(a_ic_i|b)$$

where a_i is a or a′, and c_i is c or c′ . Here we note that $(a_ic_i|b) \le (r|b)$ iff $(a_ic_i|b)\cdot(r|b) = (a_ic_i|b)$

$$\text{iff } a_ic_ib \le r$$

by taking b = d in the lemma which follows. Then, as in the unconditional case, $F_Z(r|b) \le P_Z(r|b)$; the interval approximation is

$$F_Z(r|b) \le P_Z(r|b) \le 1 - F_Z(r'|b) \text{ for } (r|b) \in \mathcal{R}/\mathcal{R}b' .$$

Lemma. On $\mathcal{R}/\mathcal{R}b'$, $(a|b) \le (c|d)$ implies $\tilde{P}(a|b) \le \tilde{P}(c|d)$.

Proof: By hypothesis and properties of $\vee$,

$$(c|d) = (c|d) \vee (a|b) = (a \vee c|ab \vee cd \vee bd) .$$

By definition of $\tilde{P}$, we get

$$\tilde{P}(c|d) = P(ab \vee cd)/P(ab \vee cd \vee bd) .$$

Since $ab \vee cd \vee bd \le b \vee cd$, $P(ab \vee cd) \le P(b \vee cd)$ and so

$$P(ab \vee cd)/P(ab \vee cd \vee bd) \ge P(ab \vee cd)/P(b \vee cd) .$$

Now $ab \vee cd = ab + (ab)'cd \ge ab + b'cd$ and

$$b \vee cd = b + b'cd ;$$

so that $P(ab \vee cd) \ge P(ab) + P(b'cd)$,

$$P(b \vee cd) = P(b) + P(b'cd) .$$

Putting these together yields

$$\tilde{P}(c|d) \ge \frac{P(ab) + P(b'cd)}{P(b) + P(b'cd)} .$$

It is easy to see that $\dfrac{P(ab) + t}{P(b) + t}$ is decreasing in $t \ge 0$ so that

$$\tilde{P}(c|d) \ge \frac{P(ab)}{P(b)} = \tilde{P}(a|b) .$$

Example 7. Another simply stated problem is to treat the expert knowledge of the material implication $b \to a$ with probability (certainty) α . The following results may aid in looking for Frechet-like bounds.

i) $(a|b) = (b \to a|b)$ since this holds iff

$$(a|b) = (b' \vee a|b) \text{ iff } ab = (b' \vee a)b \text{ which is obvious.}$$

ii) Since $ab = (ab|1) = (ab|1)(a|b) = (ab|(ab)' \vee a'b \vee b)$,

$$ab \leq (a|b) ;$$

iii) Since $(a|b)(b' \forall a) = (a(b' \forall a)|a'b \forall ba' \forall b) = (a|b)$,

$$(a|b) \leq b \rightarrow a .$$

In general, as in our examples, "evidence" does not specify probabilities for all of $\mathcal{R}$ or even all of Θ ; this means that we are in fact limited to approximations such as the intervals above. At the same time, the "CDFs" $F_X, F_Z, \cdots$ from $\mathcal{R}$ to [0,1] are generally not additive. It is also possible that the distribution might be given in a different form as in Henkind and Harrison (1988). But at least such a CDF as F_X is computable from the data/evidence and could be taken as a belief function. By extracting appropriate axioms for F_X , one will be lead to the belief function of Dempster-Shafer. This makes the belief function a CDF for a random set and part of generalized theory of probability (Nguyen, 1978).

The idea of focusing on belief functions is a truly ingenious one as is indicated by its apparent success in "AI" problems. This is due not only to its ability to represent empirical knowledge in a mathematical form but also to the fact that the rule of combination makes the associated logic truth functional. Recall that probability logic is not truth functional (Hailperin, 1984).

It should be noted that the use of random sets also clarifies the concept of independent pieces of evidence; moreover, there is no disagreement with Lindley's argument (Lindley, 1982) about admissibility if one views belief functions as equivalent to probability measures on $\mathcal{P}\mathcal{R}(\Theta))$; see also Goodman, et al (1990). Finally, at the computational (complexity) level, approximations of belief functions can be made by using bounds obtained from inclusions between random sets (Dubois and Prade, 1986; Yager 1986).

REFERENCES

1. E. Adams (1975), *The logic of conditionals*, Dardrecht, North-Holland, D. Reidel.

2. A. Bundy (1985), Incidence calculus: a mechanism for probabilistic reasoning, *J. of Automated Reasoning* 1, 263-283.

3. A.P. Dempster (1976), Upper and lower probabilities induced by a multivalued mapping, *Ann. Math. Statist.* 38, 325-339.

4. D. Dubois and H. Prade (1986), A set theoretic view of belief functions, *Inter. J. of General Systems* 12, 193-226.

5. D. Dubois and H. Prade (1989), Measure-free conditioning, probability, and non-montonic reasoning, *Eleventh Inter. Joint Conf. AI Proceedings*,Detroit, MI, Vol 2, 1110-1114.

6. D. Dubois and H. Prade (1990), The logical view of conditioning and its applications to possibility and evidence theories, *Int. J. Approx. Reasoning* 4(1), 23-46.

7. I.R. Goodman and H.T. Nguyen (1985), *Uncertainty Models for Knowledge Based Systems,* Amsterdam: North-Holland.

8. I.R. Goodman, H.T. Nguyen and E.A. Walker (1990), *Conditional Inference for Intelligent Systems: A Theory of Measure-free Conditioning*, North-Holland, to appear.

9. I.R. Gooodman, H.T. Nguyen and G.S. Rogers (1990), On the scoring approach to admissibility of uncertainty measures in expert systems, To appear in *J. Math. Anal. and Appl.*

10. T. Hailperin (1984), Probability Logic, *Notre Dame J. of Formal Logic,* 25(3), 198-212.

11. P.R. Halmos (1962), *Algebraic Logic,* New York : Chelsea.

12. P.R. Halmos (1963), *Lectures on Boolean Algebras,* New York: Springer-Verlag.

13. S.J. Henkind and M.C. Harrison (1988), . An analysis of four uncertainty calculi, *IEEE Trans. Systems Management and Cybernetics* 18(5), 700-714.

14. D.V. Lindley (1982), Scoring rules and the inevitability of probability, *Inter. Statist. Review* 50, 1-26.

15. N.J. Nilsson (1986), Probability Logic, *Artificial Intelligence,* 28(1), 71-87.

16. H.T. Nguyen (1978), On random sets and belief functions, *J. Math. Anal. and Appl.* (65), 531-542.

17. J. Pearl (1988), *Probabilistic Reasoning in Intelligent Systems,* San Mateo: Morgan Kaufmann.

18. A. Rényi. *Foundations of Probability Theory,* San Franisco: Holden-Day (1970).

19. G. Shafer (1976), *A Mathematical Theory of Evidence,* Princeton: Princeton University Press.

20. G. Shafer, P.P. Shenoy and K. Mellouli (1987), Propagation of belief functions in qualitative Markov trees, *Inter. J. of Approximate Reasoning* 1(4), 349-400.

21. R.R. Yager (1986), The entailment principle for Dempster-Shafer granules, *Inter. J. Intelligent Systems* 1, 247-262.

22. L.A. Zadeh (1978), Fuzzy sets as a basis for a theory of possibility theory, *Fuzzy Sets and Systems,* 1, 3-28.

Conditional Logic in Expert Systems
I.R. Goodman, M.M. Gupta, H.T. Nguyen and G.S. Rogers (editors)

COMBINATION OF EVIDENCE WITH CONDITIONAL OBJECTS AND ITS APPLICATION TO COGNITIVE MODELING

Marcus Spies
Research Institute for Applied Knowledge Processing (F A W)
Helmholtzstr. 16; D - 7900 Ulm
IBM Germany — Scientific Center
Institute for Knowledge-based Systems
Schlosstr. 70; D - 7000 Stuttgart 1

Abstract: In the *introduction*, a paradoxical situation of cognitive science w.r.t. the relationship between human and formal representation of uncertainty is sketched. The use of conditional objects seems essential in overcoming the paradox. In the *second* part, valued conditional objects are introduced. They allow for an easy knowledge representation with conditional objects. In the *third* part, the general significance of conditional objects is stressed. A theorem demonstrates that combining evidence with conditional objects implies a strong qualitative independence property. Moreover, it is shown that inferences with valued conditional objects agree with the likelihood combination rule. In the *fourth* part, the treatment of the paradox in cognitive science is resumed. It is well known from cognitive psychology that human inferences differ from formal uncertainty models. This phenomenon is usually attributed to human misrepresentation. It is shown that at least some of these biases become explainable if a conditional-object model of inferential situations is specified. A *final* part gives an outlook concerning this perspective. It establishes a link between conditional objects and contingency tables. It is demonstrated that incomplete contingency tables do have sound numerical models equivalent to the calculus of valued conditional objects. Some implications of this result are briefly characterized.

Keywords: Dempster/Shafer theory, Combination of Evidence, Conditional Objects, Human Information Processing

1 Introduction

When I first heard about conditional objects in a very short introduction given by Hung T. Nguyen at the IFSA conference in Tokyo, 1987, I was both fascinated and sceptical. The fascination arose from the elegant definition of conditional events that ingeniously answered the question "Where is the event 'B given A'?" This question, or, rather, the lack of an answer to it, had made understanding conditional probability a matter of accepting a definition when I had been a student. The scepticism arose from the fact that the new notion introduced a new degree of complexity, since it passed from points to sets (i.e., from elements to subsets of a σ-algebra). After fuzzy sets and random sets this was the third time I encountered such a situation. Fuzzy sets can be viewed as sets of their level sets (which are crisp) and random sets are set-valued random variables. In each case passing from simple to complex objects necessitated altering one's level of thinking, using a new notation and more complex programming techniques, and so on. Conditional objects promised to be the third case of this kind (of course, intimately related to the two former ones). However, the fascination was greater than the scepticism, and so I started playing through inferences under uncertainty with conditional objects. This was how I saw that there is an intimate relationship of this new kind of complex objects to a highly virulent problem in cognitive psychology (or cognitive science, if you prefer). This is the problem of human biases in judgment and inference under uncertainty.

This problem is the reason why many people in the expert systems area, who once upon a time swore by the importance of data from human experts, by now swear at this seemingly unreliable source of information. Simply stated, humans are bad intuitive statisticians. This is no wonder at all, since humans are no good manometers or thermometers (or ...) either. The reason why people are more disappointed by the failure of humans to judge probability (or other kinds of uncertainty) than by their inability to, say, measure temperature by judgments is that uncertainty valuations very often are genuinely subjective *while being objectively reasonable and reliable.* This seems to be the reason of the astounding success of fuzzy control systems and neural networks. They capture the reliable part of human judgment by approximation or simulation and do not bother with the unreliable part. Thus, the cognitive psychologist is left with the paradoxical situation that something in his/her field of scientific interest gives rise to systems that perform particularly well while according to the model language being used it is just fallacious, unreliable, and biased.

In my view, conditional objects can help resolving this paradoxical situation. They can be used to formulate a mathematical model of cognitive processes in reasoning under uncertainty that promises to make much of the unreliability / fallaciousness / biasedness discussion obsolete. This is because conditional objects allow for looking primarily at sets where psychologists have mainly looked at numbers. Using a good set-theoretic representation of uncertain inferences, at least some of the human biases can be rationally explained. The model makes some assumptions that can be empirically tested (this is still to be done). And it can be plugged into a neural network that learns membership functions for simulation purposes (this, again, is still to be done). Finally, the weakness of the present status of the model is the assumption of finite sets made almost everywhere in this paper (except in theorem 1). However, this assumption will allow to formulate a database-like descriptive model of partial relational knowledge supposed to underly human representation of uncertainty.

2 Valued Conditional Objects

A common property of models for the combination of evidence is that they make use of conditioning. Of course, this is true for probabilistic models (see Lauritzen &Spiegelhalter, 1988; Pearl, 1988). But even more general models cannot dispense with a notion of conditioning in order to justify formalisms for combining evidence.

For instance, Zadeh (1985) extends the likelihood combination rule (see Goodman & Nguyen, 1985; Heckerman, 1986) to fuzzy quantifiers. Now, a fuzzy quantifier describes the fuzzy relative quantity of, say, B's among A's as a fuzzy conditional probability $Q(B|A)$. To give but one more example, in Baldwin's support logic (see Baldwin, 1986), a support pair associated with a rule $p : -q$ asserts degrees of necessary and possible support of p conditional on the assumption that q holds.

In Dempster's and Shafer's theory of evidence (see Shafer, 1976), conditioning is just a special case of combining evidence. However, the problem of knowing only conditional information remains untreated in this framework (see Shafer, 1982; Pearl, 1988).

It is important to observe (see Goodman & Nguyen, 1988) that there is no element X of any σ-algebra $\mathcal{A}$ such that X is obtained as Boolean function of A, B, ..., and that in probability space $(\Omega, \mathcal{A}, P)$ $P(B|A) = P(X)$. for any $A, B \in \mathcal{A}$. Similarly, $p : -q$ is not an element of a boolean algebra of sets. The desire to "locate" conditionals in a set-theoretic sense has led to the definition of conditional objects in Goodman & Nguyen (1988); see also Dubois).

Let $\mathcal{R}(+, \star)$ denote a Boolean ring of sets over a universe U; i.e., a ring with unit element 1 and such that $a \star a = a$, $\forall a \in \mathcal{R}$. This is the idempotency property. It follows that $\mathcal{R}$ is commutative and has the characteristic **2**, i.e., $a + a = 0$, $\forall a \in \mathcal{R}$, where 0 is the zero element of $\mathcal{R}$.

Thus, in the set-theoretic sense, + corresponds to symmetric difference, while $\star$ corresponds to intersection. The usual set union can be written as $a \cup b := a + b + a \star b$ assuming standard operator priorities. Complementation is denoted $a' := 1 + a$. Therefore, a Boolean ring of sets corresponds in a direct way to a Boolean lattice with

$$x \sqcap y = x \star y$$
$$x \sqcup y = x + y + x \star y.$$

In the sequel $x \star y$ will mostly be abbreviated by xy. Similarly, in some formulae $1 + x$ will be abbreviated by x'.

A *conditional object* is defined is defined by Goodman & Nguyen (1988) as a set of subsets which all fulfill a given implication. The conditional object $[b|a]$ is a set of elements x of $\mathcal{R}$ such that the intersection of x with a is the same as the intersection of b with a:

$$[b|a] := \{x \in \mathcal{R} | x \star a = b \star a\}.$$

Equivalently,

$$[b|a] := \{x \in \mathcal{R} | x = a \star b + y \star a', \ \forall y \in \mathcal{R}\}.$$

$\mathcal{R}(+, \star)$ is a lattice. We denote the infimum and supremum of $[b|a]$ by $\sqcap[b|a]$ and $\sqcup[b|a]$, respectively.

In a recent paper, Nguyen & Rogers (1990) have provided a more general view of conditional objects in terms of partitions of a Boolean ring modulo an ideal. The basic point is that the definition of conditional objects can be equivalently written as

$$[b|a] = b + \mathcal{R}a'.$$

Since the term $\mathcal{R}a'$ denotes a (principal) ideal of a Boolean ring, there is a partition of this ring modulo this ideal, written as $\mathcal{R}_{/\mathcal{R}a'}$. Thus, the conditional objects of a given antecedent are cosets (or equivalence classes) of this partition. The conditional object of a particular consequent is the coset containing this consequent. These results will be used in the section on combination of evidence.

If we use only those sets in a conditional object that are Boolean functions of antecedent and consequent, we obtain a more restricted expression. This will be called *term-generated conditional object* in the sequel. For example, abbreviating $a \star b$ by ab, for a simple object like $[b|a]$ we obtain:

$$[b|a] \supseteq \{ab, b, 1 + a + b, 1 + a + ab\}$$

Definition 1 *A term-generated conditional object is the subset of a conditional object that can be obtained by using Boolean functions of antecedent and consequent:*

$$[b|a]^T = \{ab, b, 1 + a + b, 1 + a + ab\}$$

Since $a \star b$ and $y \star a'$ can never intersect, it follows from the second definition formula that

1. $\sqcap[b|a] = a \star b$
2. $\sqcup[b|a] = a \star b + 1 + a = a' \cup b$, i.e. standard implication.

From the monotonicity of probability measures, it follows that

$$p(x) \in [p(a \star b), p(a' \cup b)\}] \; \forall x \in [b|a].$$

Conversely, Goodman & Nguyen (1988) show that, for any probability measure,

$$p(a \star b) \leq p(b|a) \leq p(1 + a + a \star b)$$

We call

- $p(\sqcap[b|a])$ DEGREE OF VERIFICATION,
- $1 - p(\sqcup[b|a]) = p(a + a \star b)$ DEGREE OF FALSIFICATION.

If a probability measure is given on U, the conditional probability $p(b|a)$ can be recovered from $p(\sqcap[b|a])$ and $p(\sqcup[b|a])$ by

$$p(b|a) := \frac{p(\sqcap[b|a])}{1 - (p(\sqcup[b|a]) - p(\sqcap[b|a]))}.$$

This is equivalent to the results on Bayesian Conditioning investigated in Jaffray (1990). This equation implies that

- the conditional probability $p(b \mid a)$ equals one iff there are no falsifying elements, and
- the conditional probability $p(b \mid a)$ equals zero iff there are no verifying elements.

Thus, not all elements need to verify an implication in order to force a conditional probability to unity. This is in accordance with classical definitions. The difference between the complement of the degree of falsification and the degree of verification expresses how much the evidence is scattered between verifying and non-falsifying elements. If there are no verificative elements, the degree of falsification is simply $p(a)$.

The partition induced by a term generated conditional object $[b|a]^T$ (written $\Phi_{[b|a]^T}$) is the finest partition on the universe U such that all its elements are intersections of elements in $[b|a]^T$. Example: The partition induced by $[b|a]^T$ can be written

$$\Phi_{[b|a]^T} = \{ab, b + ab, a + ab, 1 + a + b + ab\}.$$

I mention the following lemma:

Lemma 1 *The partition induced by $[b|a]^T$ is the set of atoms of the $\sigma-$ring generated by $\{a, b, 1\}$. As a consequence,*

$$\Phi_{[b|a]^T} = \Phi_{[\bar{b}|a]^T} = \Phi_{[b|\bar{a}]^T}.$$

PROOF: A $\sigma-$ring is closed under set differences and countable unions, and therefore under countable symmetric differences. Hence, using these operations on $a, b, 1$, one can generate $1+a$, $1+b$, and thus $1+((1+a)\cup(1+b)) = ab$. Applying set difference again one obtains $b+ab$, $a+ab$. Now $1+(ab \cup a+ab \cup b+ab) = 1+a+b+ab$. Because there is no further intersection to be generated that is contained in these partition elements, they are the atoms of the σ-ring. Since a and b play symmetric roles, the generated σ-rings remain the same if antecedent and consequent are interchanged. Negation leaves the generated σ-ring S unchanged because $\{a, b, 1\} \subset S \Leftrightarrow \{1+a, 1+b, 1\} \subset S$. $\diamond$

In the first line, conditional objects are useful for a general understanding of conditioning. However, as I tried to indicate, their definition was already inspired by thinking in terms of probability measures and the set algebra they are defined on. In this paper I wish to explore more deeply (albeit not exhaustively) what happens if we use conditional objects to answer conventional questions, in particular the question of combination of evidence. This question is of paramount importance in expert systems. In order to do this, it is necessary to introduce valuations of conditional objects. I will restrict these valuations to the subsets of conditional objects that correspond to Boolean functions of antecedent and consequent.

Definition 2 *A valued conditional object (VCO) is a pair (C, S), where C is a term-generated conditional object and S is a belief function carried by Φ_C. A belief function on conditional object $[b|a]$ is written as $Bel([b|a])$.*

For the definition of belief functions carried by partitions, see Shafer et al., 1987. The preceding lemma, in this context, shows that the partition generated by a term-generated conditional object is a convenient frame on which to base reasoning on any conditional information between two terms of a propositional algebra.

A belief function on a TG-conditional object can be specified in two ways. Either, we immediately use the partition generated by the object and give a belief function focussed on the field of subsets generated by this partition. Or, we use the conditional object in its primitive formulation to assign belief values or m-numbers. In any case, if belief values are given, the m-numbers for the field of partition elements can be iteratively deduced. The main difference between the two approaches is that only the first allows a direct specification of a degree of falsification. Moreover, it seems that a probability distribution S on Φ_C suffices to simulate inferences like those of humans; therefore they will be used in the sections on cognitive modeling.

A term-generated conditional object can be visualized conveniently as follows. We write down the diagram of the sublattice of its elements:

```
1 + a + ab
  /     \
 /       \
b       1 + a + b
 \       /
  \     /
    ab
```

The smallest element is the set corresponding to the degree of verification, the greatest element is the complement of the set corresponding to the degree of falsification (i.e. it is the set of all non-falsifying instances of the statement "if $x \in a$, then $x \in b$"). The element b corresponds to the base rate, the element $1 + a + b$ is the set containing all examples and all irrelevant instances of the implication statement.

A belief function carried by the partition obtained from the intersections of the four elements of the term-generated conditional object could have any disjunctions of these elements as focal elements. For the purpose of a proof in the next section and for the cognitive interpretation of conditional objects, however, it suffices to consider probability measures on the partition of a term-generated conditional object. For this special case, the following notation will be used in the sequel for the object $[b|a]$:

$$\begin{aligned} m_1 &= m(ab) \\ m_2 &= m(b + ab) \\ m_3 &= m(a + ab) \\ m_4 &= m(1 + a + b + ab) \\ m_1 + m_2 + m_3 + m_4 &= 1 \end{aligned}$$

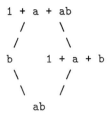

Let us again take the VCO on $[b|a]$ as a valuation of meaning facets of the implication statement "if $x \in a$, then $x \in b$". Then, the four m-numbers have these meanings: m_1 is the probability of examples (or degree of verification), m_2 is the probability of trivial cases, which fulfill the implication because the consequent is true without being examples, m_3 is the probability of exceptions (or degree of falsification), and m_4 is the probability of irrelevant cases. Each of the m-numbers, therefore, has a clear intuitive meaning. It is a matter of practice to see in which application domains which numbers can be estimated from screenings and which have to be asked from experts. I mean that the language of VCOs is much clearer in terms of logic than the language of classical conditional probability. Shafer & Tversky (1985) discuss designs for probability judgment. The VCO language gives rise to an additional design and its relative merits seem worth an encompassing evaluation.

3 Combination of Evidence with Valued Conditional Objects

A very useful property in combining evidence has been established in a series of papers by Shafer, Shenoy, and Mellouli (published in Shafer et al., 1987: see also Kong, 1986). This property is purely qualitative; its validity must be verified prior to any valuations of the objects to be combined. In this, it is similar to the qualitative dependency notions found in Pearl (1988). Here is how this property is defined:

Definition 3 *Let Φ_i, for $i \in I$, be a collection of partitions of a set U. Then, for $j \in J \subseteq I$, the partitions Φ_j are called qualitative independent (short: Q-independent), if $\forall A_j \in \Phi_j$ the following holds:$\bigcap_{j \in J} A_j \neq \emptyset$.*

Q-independence, in general, is much too strong for applications. For example, if you are given a set of poisonous substances, a set of possible emission sources of these substances, and a set of possible damages, you usually won't have Q-independence of the partitions generated by these three sets on their cartesian product. That is, some substances cause specific damages and are only emitted by certain sources. However, concentrating on a single substance, it can be reasonable to assume that the damages it can cause are independent of the source from which it stems (which is reasonable if you do not want to make a model of substance diffusion in the environment). This idea leads to the notion of qualitative *conditional* independence (for the definition of infima and suprema of partitions, see Shafer et al., 1987):

Definition 4 *Let J, K, L be subsets of the index set I of partitions. Let $\Phi_J = \sqcap_{j \in J} \Phi_j$ (similarly, define Φ_K and Φ_L). Then Φ_L and Φ_J are qualitative conditional independent (short QC-independent) given Φ_K, if $\forall A_k \in \Phi_K$, $\forall B_l \in \Phi_L$, $\forall C_j \in \Phi_J$, the following holds: $A_k \cap B_l \neq \emptyset$ and $A_k \cap C_j \neq \emptyset$ implies $A_k \cap B_l \cap C_j \neq \emptyset$.*

This definition needs some comments. First, its use in the framework of Dempster/Shafer theory requires the partitions involved to be defined on a finite universe. Otherwise, the correspondence between a partition and a σ-algebra which holds for finite universes can no longer be assumed (see Shafer et al., 1987, p.354). Finite partitions are, of course, limited if one wants to treat random variables on the basis of QC-independence. A more general approach to QC-independence can be found in Nguyen & Rogers (1989). It should be noted, however, that the definition by itself does not preclude the case of an infinite universe. For instance, the partitions of the ring of integers modulo two arbitrary integers are QC-independent given the partition modulo the *gcd* (greatest common denominator) of these numbers.

Second, the definition does *not* assume that the index sets J, K, L are mutually disjoint. It is even possible to show that arbitrary partitions are QC-independent given the infimum of these partitions:

Lemma 2 *Let $K \supseteq K_1 \cup K_2$. For any A_k in Φ_K ($k \in K$), there are sets P, Q in Φ_{K_1} and Φ_{K_2} such that $A_k = P \cap Q$. Since the infimum condition implies that A_k does not intersect with any other elements from the partitions Φ_{K_1} and Φ_{K_2}, the QC-independence is trivially fulfilled.*

Any set of variables can be viewed as a conditioning set w.r.t to its subsets. On the other hand, it is this property that approaches QC-independence to a very important class of dependencies known from database design theory, namely multivalued dependencies defined in Fagin (1977), Beeri et al. (1977). In a previous paper, Spies (1988), I have proved that the QC-independence and multivalued dependencies are actually equivalent. This allows to use algorithms like the one described in Ozsoyoglu & Yuan (1987) to construct knowledge representations from quite elementary inputs. For a more recent account of the related results, including a discussion of embedded multivalued dependencies, see Spies (1990b).

There is an important relationship between conditional objects and QC - independence which I will state now. COs, as could be seen in the preceding section, are cosets (or equivalence classes) in a ring being partitioned modulo the ideal generated by the negated antecedent of the CO. For antecedent b we have

$$\forall a \in \mathcal{R} : [a|b] \in \mathcal{R}_{/\mathcal{R}b'}.$$

As stated in Nguyen & Rogers (1990), the problem of combining evidence w.r.t. different antecedents amounts to combining cosets from different quotient rings. Thus, the problem of combination of evidence can be stated in the most general form as follows:

$$\textit{Given } [a|b] \textit{ and } [a|c] \text{ , } \textit{what is } [a|b \star c] \text{ ?}$$

This is the well-known antecedent-conjunction problem (ANC). It has been solved by the classical likelihood combination rule derived from the Bayes-formula and reformulated for fuzzy quantifiers by Zadeh (1985), Spies (1989). Henceforth, the *given* conditionals will be referred to as the *premises*, while the conditional being asked for will be called the *conclusion*. Of course, any number of premises can occur. In the light of the definition of COs, the problem of combining evidence is contained in the problem of combining the partitions corresponding to the different antecedents. In this perspective, the quotient ring generated by an antecedent distinguishes between certain consequents and treats others as equal (those being contained in the same coset). Dubois & Prade (1989) have pointed out that the antecedent conjunction object has no general ordering relationship to the premise conditionals.

The main result of the present paper is that antecedent conjunction problems can be solved with conditional objects without having to take care of any qualitative independence assumptions. That is, using conditional objects you move in a much more complex world, and things you have to assume in a simpler world are included in the model governing the more complex world. Using conditional objects you lose simplicity and you gain inferential richness. The consequences of the following developments for the combination of evidence of correlated sources of information are still to be drawn.

In order to prove the theorem on combination of evidence with conditional objects, a few results from the theory of Boolean lattices are needed. I quote them from Erné (1987), chapter 6.

Definition 5 (Erné (1987)) *A congruence relation on a lattice S is an equivalence relation θ such that $x\theta x'$ implies $x \sqcup y \;\theta\; x' \sqcup y$ and $x \sqcap y \;\theta\; x' \sqcap y$.*

Lemma 3 (Erné (1987)) *The congruence relations of a lattice form a closed sublattice of the lattice of equivalence relations. In particular, the supremum of a set of congruence relations is the transitive closure of their union:*

$$\bigsqcup_{i\in I} \theta_i = cl(\bigcup_{i\in I} \theta_i)$$

(where cl denotes transitive closure).

Lemma 4 (Erné (1987)) *In a Boolean lattice there is an isomorphism from the lattice of congruence relations to the lattice of ideals given by $\theta \to \theta\bot$.*

As a consequence, in a Boolean lattice each partition modulo an ideal is equivalent to a congruence relation. In other words, the set of conditional objects from a given antecedent is the set of equivalence classes of a congruence relations over the Boolean lattice being used. Now, combination of evidence with different antecedents leads to examining conditional objects with conjunctions of antecedents. The relationship between them and the quotient rings generated from single antecedents is surprisingly simple. Here, the lemma concerning the existence of suprema of congruence relations is used. Since we are dealing with Boolean rings, this description of suprema of congruence relations extends immediately to ring partitions modulo an ideal. This gives us the notation necessary for the following lemma:

Lemma 5 *The congruence relation corresponding to the set of conditional objects of a conjunction of antecedents is the supremum of the congruence relations corresponding to the sets of conditional objects of the single antecedents:*

$$\mathcal{R}_{/\mathcal{R}(\sqcap X)'} = \bigsqcup_{x \in X} \mathcal{R}_{/\mathcal{R}x'}$$

PROOF: Because of the De Morgan property in Boolean lattices we have $(\sqcap X)' = \bigsqcup_{x \in X} x'$. Therefore, in view of the preceding lemmata, the congruence relation corresponding to the principal ideal of the complement of the conjunction of antecedents is equivalent to the partition of $\mathcal{R}$ modulo the ideal $\mathcal{R} \bigsqcup_{x \in X} x'$. Moreover, in a Boolean lattice there is a trivial isomorphism between the lattice itself and the lattice of the ideals, ordered by usual set inclusion. Therefore,

$$\mathcal{R} \bigsqcup_{x \in X} x' = \bigsqcup_{x \in X} \mathcal{R}x'.$$

Because of the preceding lemma there is an isomorphism between ideals and congruence relations. This isomorphism takes suprema of ideals to suprema of congruence relations. Thus,

$$\mathcal{R}_{/\bigsqcup_{x \in X} \mathcal{R}x'} = \bigsqcup_{x \in X} \mathcal{R}_{/\mathcal{R}x'}$$

and the proof is complete. ◇

Putting together the results collected in the preceding lemmata, it is clear that antecedent conjunction of partitions corresponding to conditional objects can be conveniently described as a supremum formation of congruence relations. Now, if there are only two such relations for forming the supremum, it can be shown that Q-conditional independence must hold. Denoting, as before, the partition generated by the complement of antecedent x, relative to the ring universe $\mathcal{R}$, as $\mathcal{R}_{/\mathcal{R}x'}$, and conditional Q-independence by the operator $\perp_Q$ between conditional independent partitions, and by separating the conditioning partition from these by a $|$, we have:

Theorem 1 *The set of conditional objects corresponding to a conjunction of two antecedents forms a partition that is qualitative conditional independent from the partitions corresponding to the set of conditional objects of each antecedent:*

$$\mathcal{R}_{/\mathcal{R}x'} \perp_Q \mathcal{R}_{/\mathcal{R}y'} | \mathcal{R}_{/\mathcal{R}(xy)'}$$

PROOF: From the preceding lemmata, we know that the right-hand side is the supremum of the congruence relations of the left-hand side. Let $\theta_1, \ldots, \theta_n$ be a set of congruence relations. Then the supremum of them is the transitive closure of their union. Denoting this supremum by θ (without subscript) we find that $x\theta x'$ holds if

$$\exists x_0, \ldots, x_n, \ s.t. \ x_{i-1}\theta_i x_i,$$

where $x_0 = x$ and $x_n = x'$ and $i \in \{1, \ldots, n\}$. Since the θ_i describe equivalence classes it follows that any elements are in a class of θ if they are equivalent w.r.t. any θ_i (because the x_i need not be different, we can use reflexivity to "skip" some of the chain of the θ_i). Thus, any coset in θ is a union of cosets in some θ_i with nonempty intersections. Therefore, if there are only two cosets to be combined, the combined coset will intersect both cosets and will be equal to their union. In this situation, the defining condition of QC-independence holds trivially. $\diamond$

This theorem does not assume a finite universe. The combination of evidence with conditional objects yields a congruence relation given which the congruence relations in the premises are pairwise QC-independent. Combination of evidence with conditional objects *always* satisfies the QC-independence for *pairs of premises*. Of course, theorem 1 can be applied iteratively to account for conjunctions of more than two antecedents. *No qualitative independence assumptions have to be checked.* This is a much weaker requirement than in any formalism for combination of evidence known up to now (see Heckerman, 1986).

In view of lemma 2, one might argue that the result of theorem 1 is simple, if not trivial. It might seem so, because qualitative conditional independence always holds given a superset of variables between its various subsets. However, the analogy to conditional objects is not as easy as this. First, theorem 1 does NOT hold for arbitrary many combined antecedents. Moreover, each conditional object does not always act like a dimension in a multidimensional space. Conditional objects with similar antecedents (similar in the sense that their infimum is not the bottom element of the lattice) are not "independent" in an intuitive sense like orthogonal dimensions in a multivariate model.

In Boolean rings with few elements, the antecedent conjunction can lead to the trivial congruence relation $U \times U$, since the partition of the conclusion is always coarser than the partitions of the premises. Therefore, theorem 1 should not be seen as a proposal for computational simplification of an otherwise untractable problem. It rather establishes a formal property in order to help understanding the broader picture we may have of combination of evidence once conditional objects are used.

As far as I can judge by now, for practical purposes a different approach seems necessary. QC-independence can be shown to hold in a different way for conditional objects if we concentrate on one single consequent at a time. The basic simplification is the use of term-generated subsets of conditional objects. Using these subsets, partitions can easily be described and some inferences can be formulated in the framework of qualitative Markov properties used by Shafer et al. (1987). Basically, term-generated COs are homomorphisms from COs to those elements that can be expressed as Boolean functions of the antecedent and consequent terms only.

A Qualitative Markov Tree (QMT, Shafer et al., 1987) is a tree whose nodes represent partitions and whose edges at each node represent qualitative conditional independence (QCI) of the infima of partitions of each subtree they connect to the node given the partition at the node itself. Now, there is a close relationship between QMTs and term-generated conditional objects.

Theorem 2 *The partitions of premises in an antecedent conjunction problem* $\Phi_{[b|a]^T}$ *and* $\Phi_{[b|c]^T}$ *are QC-independent given the partition of the conclusion* $\Phi_{[b|a\star c]^T}$.

PROOF: The partition produced by $[b|a \star c]^T$ is the infimum of the partitions contributed from the premises. This follows from the fact that each element in $\Phi_{[b|a\star c]^T}$ is an intersection of elements in $\Phi_{[b|a]^T}$ and $\Phi_{[b|c]^T}$ and that all such intersections are taken in building up the partition of the consequent. Note that this only holds for finite partitions. The conditional qualitative Markov property holds then trivially. ◇

Therefore, a belief function for a valued conditional object can be computed quite elegantly using the results from Shafer et al. (1987). Omitting the superscripts "T" we simply have:

$$Bel_{\Phi_{[b|a\star c]}} = Bel([b|a])_{\Phi_{[b|a\star c]}} \oplus Bel([b|c])_{\Phi_{[b|a\star c]}}.$$

The subscripts to *Bel* denote coarsenings of a belief function such that it is carried by the indicated partition. Note that the coarsenings on the right hand side are actually trivial, since

$$\Phi_{[b|a\star c]} = \sqcap\{\Phi_{[b|a]}, \Phi_{[b|c]}\},$$

where the $\sqcap$ denotes the coarsest common refinement of the partitions in the bracket.

In a broader perspective, antecedent conjunction problems can thus be formulated with valued conditional objects in qualitative Markov trees and processed in a comparatively efficient manner. Let us now examine whether these solutions agree with classical solutions from Bayesian updating.

Lemma 6 *The calculations proposed for conditional objects agree with Bayes' rule.*

PROOF: We have

$$p(b \mid a) = \frac{p(a \mid b)p(b)}{p(a)}.$$

With conditional objects, using the notation from section 2 and the rule relating conditional probabilities to probabilities of elements of a VCO, the left hand side reads:

$$\frac{m_1}{1-((1-m_3)-m_1)} = \frac{m_1}{m_1+m_3}$$

For the right side, one obtains

$$\frac{\frac{m_1}{m_1+m_2}(m_1+m_2)}{m_1+m_3} = \frac{m_1}{m_1+m_3},$$

which is the desired equality. $\diamond$

One can view a VCO as a representation of a conditional probability by unconditional prbabilities. What the (I admit, simple) preceding lemma shows is that ANY such representation yields a solution compatible with Bayes' theorem. Moreover, it can be shown that combination of valued conditional objects with Dempster's rule reduces to the likelihood combination rule (analyzed in Heckerman, 1986; Goodman & Nguyen, 1985) if there is Bayesian ignorance, i.e., the base rate of the hypothesis equals 0.5. At first glance, this seems a weak result. However, with conditional objects and Dempster's rule, base rates can be *different between sources*, therefore, the situation can only agree in very special cases with a situation assuming a fixed base rate. I add that the role of the base rate is implicit in the likelihood combination rule. Therefore, the base rate cannot be seen as an additional item of evidence to be combined with the premise informations via Dempster's rule (actually, if one tries to do the calculations, one ends up with the inverse value of the base-rate effect than with the likelihood combination rule; this is funny, but nothing else).

It should be noted that the equivalence of Dempster's rule and the likelihood combination rule is not produced by using VCOs; it is only easier to make it clear if one uses this representation.

Theorem 3 *The antecedent combination of valued conditional objects (VCOs) agrees with the likelihood combination rule under the assumption of base rates equal to 0.5.*

PROOF:

The notation established in section 2 is used. Thus, one source of evidence corresponds to m-numbers m_1 through m_4, and the second source corresponds to m-numbers n_1 through n_4. Then, we have $p(b \mid a) = \frac{m_1}{m_1+m_3}$, $p(b \mid c) = \frac{n_1}{n_1+n_3}$. $p(b)$ could be estimated from each of the conditional objects. Since it contributes the base rate information in the Bayesian approach, no such such estimate is used. The likelihood combination rule (assuming the usual quantitative conditional independence relations described in Heckerman, 1986), written as in Goodman & Nguyen (1985), p. 480, gives

$$p(b \mid ac) = \left[1 + \frac{\left(1-\frac{n_1}{n_1+n_3}\right)\left(1-\frac{m_1}{m_1+m_3}\right)p(b)}{\frac{n_1}{n_1+n_3}\frac{m_1}{m_1+m_3}p(\bar{b})}\right]^{-1}.$$

Rearranging terms, the fraction simplifies to

$$\frac{n_3 m_3}{n_1 m_1}\frac{p(b)}{p(\bar{b})}.$$

This is the inverse of the posterior odds; note that this reduces to a ratio of multiplied degrees of verification and falsification, weighted by a base rate factor! Calculating the posterior probability using this simplified expression we obtain

$$p(b \mid ac) = \frac{n_1 m_1}{n_1 m_1 + n_3 m_3 \frac{p(b)}{p(\bar{b})}},$$

which reduces, by Bayesian ignorance, to

$$\frac{n_1 m_1}{n_1 m_1 + n_3 m_3}.$$

Using Dempster's rule without taking care of the base rate, we obtain

$$k = (m_1 + m_2)n_4 + (n_1 + n_2)m_4 + (m_1 + m_2)n_3 + (n_1 + n_2)n_3$$

which simplifies to

$$k = (m_1 + m_2)(n_3 + n_4) + (m_3 + m_4)(n_1 + n_2).$$

Since, for comparability with the classical approach, we assumed a Bayesian belief function, we have

$$Bel(\sqcap[b|a \star c]) = \frac{m_1 n_1}{1-k},$$

where the numerator is the product of degrees of verification, and

$$Bel(\sqcup[b|a \star c]) = 1 - \frac{m_3 n_3}{1-k},$$

where the numerator is the product of the degrees of falsification. From the formula relating the probability intervals of conditional objects to conditional probability (see section 2), one obtains

$$p(b \mid ac) = \frac{Bel(\sqcap[b|a \star c])}{1 - (Bel(\sqcup[b|a \star c]) - Bel(\sqcap[b|a \star c]))} = \frac{m_1 n_1}{m_3 n_3 + m_1 n_1}.$$

◇

This proof shows that information on trivial and irrelevant cases is discarded when computing a conditional probability from a conditional object. The formula obtained from the VCO-approach before accounting for base rates looks somewhat like the old rule "favorable cases divided by all relevant cases". The reformulation of the likelihood combination rule with VCOs leads to a particularly simple and elegant expression of this rule. Moreover, the combination of valued conditional objects in the antecedent conjunction problem does *not* assume equal base rates in both premises by default. If we view the "premises" as two independent sources of information, this seems a very desirable relaxation of the assumptions underlying older combination paradigmata. The fact that VCO combination does not implicitly correct for base rates follows from this property. Therefore, it should be clear that any "prior" distribution that is different from a uniform distribution has to be explicitly combined via Dempster's rule with further conditional information in order to maintain the equivalence of the present or any Dempster/Shafer-like formalism to Bayes' rule.

Let us turn to an example in order to assess what the combination of evidence using VCOs can do. The example presented here is a re-analysis of an example given by Kohlas (1990). It is not set out to establish a new reasoning mechanism but solely to demonstrate the ability of conditional objects to emulate well-known patterns of inference.

Suppose you have a machine and an alarm system for this machine. The alarm system is supposed to give a sound when the machine is out of order. However, since switching off the machine is expensive and the alarm devie might be faulty, the question to be answered is "how probable is a machine fault, if the alarm system rings?" The interesting fact is that the data that can be obtained do not have an immediate impact on this question. The data consist of two pieces of evidence:

- A set of m-numbers (adding up to one) for the following cases:
    1. The system works correctly (either we have a faulty machine and a signal from the system or the machine works well and the alarm system keeps silent): m_c.
    2. The alarm system is oversensitive (it rings no matter which state the machine is in): m_o.
    3. The alarm system is out of order (it never rings): m_u.
    4. The alarm system is incorrectly wired (either the machine works well and the alarm goes on or there is no alarm despite the machine being out of order): m_w.
- The probabilities of the machine being at fault or not: p_f and p_n, where $p_n = 1 - p_f$.

To simplify the formulae, the following abbreviations will be used:

- s means "there is a signal from the alarm system", $\bar{s}$ means the negation of this statement.
- f means "there is a fault in the machine", $\bar{f}$ means the negation of this statement.

Then, the data can be written as follows:

$$\begin{aligned} m_c &= m(fs \vee \bar{f}\bar{s}) = m(1+s+f) \\ m_o &= m(s) \\ m_u &= m(\bar{s}) = m(1+s) \\ m_w &= m(s\bar{f} \vee \bar{s}f) = m(s+f) \\ p_f &= p(f) = 1 - p(1+f) \end{aligned}$$

Let us take the m-numbers as "prior" information on the conditional object. Since the focal elements do not coincide with those of $[f \mid s]$, we have to project the basic probability assignment in order to write down belief / plausibility intervals for this information. They look as follows:

$$\begin{aligned} Bel(sf) &= 0 & Pl(sf) &= m_c + m_o \\ Bel(f+sf) &= 0 & Pl(f+sf) &= m_u + m_w \\ Bel(1+s+f+sf) &= 0 & Pl(1+s+f+sf) &= m_c + m_u \\ Bel(s+sf) &= 0 & Pl(s+sf) &= m_o + m_w \end{aligned}$$

Note that without conditional objects you could not assess any prior information at this stage, because neither the conditional probability of f given s nor of s given f can be calculated. All one can tell is that the upper bound of , say, $p(f \mid s)$ is somewhere in the interval $[m_c + m_u, 1]$ and that its lower bound is somewhere in $[0, m_c + m_o]$. This situation is very close to what happens in applications: The conditional data are known only up to intervals of verifying or falsifying instances. Take statistics from patients in a clinic: You have verifying and falsifying instances but no base rates available. And this is what VCOs can account for in inferences.

Now, the second piece of evidence (p_f, p_n) corresponds precisely to some base rate information coming in on the antecedent of the conditional object describing our question "how probable is a fault, given an alarm sound?" One can apply Dempster's rule to obtain a posterior information concerning this question. The remarkable fact is that now *all focal elements are in the term-generated partition of* $[f \mid s]$. It is easily seen that this must hold, since the two pieces of evidence can be viewed as restrictions on cell sums of a two-dimensional dichotomous contingency table and the combination according to Dempster's rule yields the intersections corresponding to the cells of the table. These cells, in turn, are just what the partition of a term-generated conditional object for dichotomous variables gives. The general relation of conditional objects to multivariate structures (like those discussed in Kong, 1986, and Kohlas, 1990) is still to be examined.

Finally, as the third piece of evidence, we are told that the alarm rings, i.e. that s is true. We are interested in the m-numbers for the VCO on conditional object $[f|s]$, i.e., on the conditional evidence that there is a fault in the machine, given the previous evidences and the fact that the alarm system rings. The result of combining the belief functions (according to Dempster's rule!) and discarding all elements contained in or equal to $\bar{s}$ leads to the following result:

$$\begin{aligned} m_1 &= \frac{p_f(m_c + m_o)}{1 - m_u} \\ m_2 &= \frac{p_f m_w}{1 - m_u} \\ m_3 &= \frac{p_n(m_o + m_w)}{1 - m_u} \\ m_4 &= \frac{p_n m_c}{1 - m_u} \end{aligned}$$

As a consequence,

$$p(f|s) = \frac{m_1}{m_1 + m_3} = \frac{p_f(m_c + m_o)}{p_f(m_c + m_o) + p_n(m_o + m_w)}$$

This is equal to

$$\frac{p_f Pl(s|f)}{p_f Pl(s|f) + p_n Pl(s|\bar{f})}$$

calculating the Pl from the first item of evidence (e.g.,

$$Pl(s|f) = \frac{Pl(sf)}{1 - (Pl(f + sf) - Pl(sf))}).$$

This again shows Bayes' rule recovered by Dempster's combination rule applied to a representation of conditional information by VCOs. However, the representation is more conservative than a plain application of Bayes' rule, since the result appears only via plausibility values. This reflects the fact that no evidence implying only verifying instance of the rule "IF the alarm fires, THEN the system is at fault" has been observed! Thus, VCOs make some quite important differentiations that vanish if one just combines probabilities.

Other inferences, like the intersection / product or chaining syllogisms can also be formulated with valued conditional objects, see Zadeh (1985); empirical studies are reported in Spies (1989). However, the QC-independence condition is not fulfilled for these problems, which complicates their treatment. For instance, a chaining problem requires "multiplying out" all elements of the contributing conditional objects' partitions. This leads to the exponential algorithmic behaviour of Dempster's rule that is encountered in classical applications, see Shafer et al. (1987). A good software implementing the present approach must incorporate fast algorithms for set algebra in order to keep in pace with with the demands of a real-world expert system.

4 Modelling Human Inferences with Valued Conditional Objects

Results from cognitive psychological experiments have brought to our knowledge many so-called biases in human processing of quantitative evidence (see Kahneman et al. (eds., 1982); Scholz (1987)). Humans process quantitative evidence in a way that often is at variance with probabilistic models. It has been known since the basic work of Wason & Johnson-Laird (1972) that human inference uses implications different from those found in classical and even multivalued or fuzzy logic. In a more recent approach, Klayman & Ha (1987) have demonstrated that psychologically plausible notions of confirmation and disconfirmation in hypothesis testing lead to reasonable behaviour in many real-world situations, i.e. they help reducing verification or falsification effort. Therefore, one might conclude, it seems no longer justified to call psychological behaviour fallacious, as it was implied by concepts like "verification bias" in earlier research. In a similar vain, Scholz (1987) examines strategies of stochastic thinking which lead humans to represent stochasticially equivalent situations differently depending on the context of the problem they are asked to solve.

Humans are bad intuitive statisticians. They tend to ignore base rates, they combine evidence in a rather conservative manner in comparison to Bayes' theorem, they use heuristics like availability to estimate probability, and so forth (for an account of empirical findings concerning these facts, see Kahneman et al. (eds., 1982); Scholz (1987)). If humans are confronted with inference problems in a fuzzy or Dempster/Shafer setting (Spies, 1989), some of these biases disappear and some new ones occur.

The basic problem for the cognitive scientist dealing with these phenomena was that, up to now, no sufficiently general model was available to express *all normatively possible solutions simultaneously.* That is, you could compare human behaviour with Bayes' theorem, or, in a different task setting, with Dempster's combination rule, or with arbitrary rules made up for descriptive purposes only. However, you could not put human behaviour in the framework of *all possibly legitimate* solutions at once.

The principal gain in using conditional objects is precisely that this is now possible, since we have a purely set-theoretical framework in which to express any inference problem under uncertainty. In this paper, I will not show how an empirical test procedure for "locating" human behaviour w.r.t. a conditional object model could be devised. Such a construction is still under study. What I want to do is simply to show how *two of the more prominent human "biases" in inference under uncertainty can be rationally explained if a conditional object model is used as descriptive model of the underlying cognitive process.*

One possible root of the obvious deviances of human processing from probabilistic models is the lack of accounting for uncertainty in the sense of vagueness that is inherent to classical probabilistic modelling. Therefore, one might be inclined to assume that extending probabilistic inference models to models that account for more vagueness and imprecision is sufficient for explaining and simulating so-called human biases. After all, they might turn out not to be biases but mere "shifts of accent" due to an underlying inherent vagueness of the problem representation in the human mind.

A first attempt at accounting for uncertainty leads to using extended versions of probability calculus as candidate models. First, there is Zadeh's (1985) theory of fuzzy quantifiers. Fuzzy quantifiers extend the calculus of conditional probabilities to fuzzy probabilities. In an empirical study (Spies, 1989), I could show that using monotonic fuzzy quantifiers and allowing for medium degrees of entropy/nonspecificity actually did enhance the consensus of human performance with formal inferences. However, some typical "biases" of human inference under uncertainty reappeared in the fuzzy framework almost unmodified. Among them, the most prominent is the *base rate enhancement bias* in combination of evidence (see Spies, 1990a) that has been studied for crisp probabilities already in Edwards (1982). This bias is conventionally called "conservatism". The phenomenon being observed is that humans in general do not allow for several confirming evidences to add up to a stronger confirming evidence, and, conversely, to underestimate the joint effect of several disconfirming evidences on a hypothesis. Thus, the direction of research was correct, but mere fuzzification of quantitative evidence did not turn out to be a sufficient answer to the quest for explanations for human "biases".

Second, there is Baldwin's (1986) model of support logic. In it, we need not process quantities but rather degrees of support in favor of and/or against a rule or a fact. Again, I could show empirically, that allowing for an interval-valued support turned out to increase consensus of human inferences with model inferences if medium-wide and "monotonic" intervals could be used instead of narrow ones (a monotonic support interval is either $[0, a]$ or $[a, 1]$ with $0 \leq a \leq 1$). However, in combination of evidence, an effect analogous to the base rate enhancement bias could be detected. Moreover, clear differences in evaluating implications between humans and models of support logic could be observed, as well as a strikingly different pattern of combining conflicting evidence. While, for support pairs, Dempster's rule leads to an increase of specificity in combining evidence, humans rather tend to relax specificity if there is a sufficiently high amount of conflict between the sources to be combined (proof and details in Spies, 1989). Moreover, the base rate enhancement bias could be observed again in this different framework. As a consequence, the use of interval-valued supports seemed a step in the good direction but it did not really show a way through the apparent labyrinth of human processing of uncertain inferences.

To say it clearly, the purpose of these considerations is *not* to *explain away* human biases. That they exist, and that their consequences can be severe is not to be doubted. Rather, the purpose is to *explain* them, i.e., to give rational reasons that establish under which conditions we may expect them. As a by-product of this effort, some of the biases will appear harder than others.

There are two ways in which to use VCOs to model human inferences. First, one might ask humans to provide us with the input to a full model. Thus, humans would have to be asked to specify degrees of verification and degrees of falsification in addition to a conditional probability. Second, one might *estimate* a belief function on a conditional object given more or less specific information. The basic rationale of estimating would be the optimization of an uncertainty measure, quite in the spirit of the maximum entropy principle in statistical mechanics. Thus, one would formulate a nonlinear optimization problem (NLP) for valued conditional objects. (Recall that valued conditional objects were defined as those elements of an arbitrary CO that are Boolean functions of antecedent and consequent).

In the present text, I wish to elaborate on the second way, since here, with quite simple assumptions, models that seem adequate to human inferences can be built. The first way will be followed in an empirical study that is currently being planned.

The motivation for using an NLP-approach can be summarized as follows:

1. Point-valued conditional probabilities may be all we can get from an expert– degrees of verification / falsification being too difficult to estimate for a human expert.
2. However, the "true" conditional probability in the expert's mind is assumed to be imprecise.
3. Then, a belief function over the partition generated by conditional object $[b|a]$ can be estimated by maximizing belief-entropy, which has been called "degree of confusion" in Dubois & Prade (1987).

In the simplest case *a probability distribution is to be estimated for a partition generated by a TG-conditional object that maximizes belief-entropy.* The notation $m_1, \ldots, m_4$ is used as introduced in section 2.

Then, the simplest NLP, given $p(b|a)$, reads:

$$MAXBelEntropy = - \sum_{x \in \Phi_{[b|a]}} m(x) ln Bel(x)$$

s.t.

$$\sum_{i=1}^{4} m_i = 1, \quad \frac{m_1}{m_1 + m_3} = p(b|a)$$

$$0 \leq m_i \leq 1 \, \forall i \in \{1, ..., 4\}$$

This can be reduced to a convex optimization problem. A rough approximation for $p(b|a) = 0.50$ yields a degree of verification of 0.10, and a degree of falsification of 0.18, with a value of 0.79 for the objective function. Note that in this simple formulation of the problem two of the m_i play symmetric roles; in terms of the solution obtained, this means that $m_{opt}(a + ab) = m_{opt}(b + ab)$. Moreover, the optimal solution has the property that $Bel_{opt}(b) \approx p(b|a)$.

If we use NLPs of this kind to approximate belief functions carried by partitions that are generated by conditional objects, and if we use these approximations in inferences, we get a model of how a human being might infer. *This model is actually rich enough to simulate some or all of the so-called human biases in inferences under uncertainty. Note that this becomes possible by the psychological assumption of an underlying vagueness of the meaning of a conditional probability (or a support given w.r.t. a rule). This vagueness can be modelled by means of a possibility distribution on a conditional object (actually, an L−fuzzy set).*

To substantitate this claim, I would like to refer to the two biases in combination of evidence mentioned before. The base rate enhancement bias can be simulated with the model for inferences using approximated conditional objects. If we use probability distributions on the partitions generated by the premises, the resulting belief function for combined evidence will be compatible with the belief functions being combined. In this *particular case* , we have, for the first premise,

$$Bel([b|a \star c])_{\Phi_{[b|a]}} = Bel([b|a]).$$

Therefore, set inclusion relations between the elements of $[b|a], [b|c]$ and $[b|a \star c]$, respectively, translate into inequality relations of the corresponding Bel-numbers. For instance, we obtain

$$Bel([b|a \star c])(abc) \leq min(Bel([b|a])(ab), Bel([b|c])(bc)).$$

Similarly,

$$Bel([b|a \star c])(1 + ac + abc) \geq max(Bel([b|a])(1 + a + ab), Bel([b|c])(1 + c + bc)).$$

Noting that $abc = \sqcap([b|a \star c])$ and $1 + (a + ab)c = 1 + (c + bc)a = \sqcup([b|a \star c])$ we can say that combining evidence with conditional objects *always* enlarges the scope of the objects being combined. Therefore, we find belief weight assigned to verificative elements of the conditional object that certainly is below the combined conditional probability and below both of the premise-probabilities. Conversely, we always find belief weight assigned to non-falsifying elements of the conditional object that is higher than the combined conditional probability and higher than both of the premise-probabilities. As a consequence, if more subjective weight is put on degrees of verification in combining confirming evidences, a legitimate result of the combination process is a point below the combined probability of the likelihood combination rule. Conversely, if more subjective weight is put on falsification degrees for disconfirming evidences, a legitimate result of combining them is a point above the combined probability of the likelihood combination rule. This also holds true, mutatis mutandis, for fuzzy quantifier problems and support pair combinations. What is needed to verifiy this model is empirical evidence for subjective weights that supports these assumptions.

Similarly, the property of human combination of conflicting evidence by relaxing specificity can easily be reconstructed from the present model, if we use again the above equations.

We may thus state that there is always a possibility distribution on the lattice defined by VCOs such that a human answer with the biases treated here can be simulated. A simple way to obtain this is to take the interval $[b \sqcap [b|a \star c], b \sqcup [b|a \star c]]$. A boxplot of data from Spies (1989) reveals that most subjects move from premises to conclusions in parallel with the boundaries of the VCOs. More sophisticated predictions are still under study. Note that the inherent variability fo the assumed subjective imprecise representation of evidence quantities or supports would render a point-valued prediction quite useless. As it was shown in theorem 3, VCO combination of evidence does not implicitly account for base rates. The relationship of this property to the very common base rate fallacy in human judgment seems to be one more promising application of the present approach (cf. Scholz, 1987).

5 A cognitive model for human Combination of Evidence

The NLP approach to using conditional objects in evaluating expert judgments assumes that, psychologically spoken, the "true" conditional probability in the subject's mind is imprecise. This assumption has a good psychological tradition. For instance, in psychophysiological measurement, category boundaries for stimulus discrimination are modelled as –usually– overlapping probability distributions (see Torgerson (1958), ch. 8 - 10). However, it is difficult to substantiate what an imprecise probability in a subject's mind could be. It is not very plausible to postulate psychological reality of such a thing as a valued conditional object. Moreover, it does not seem to suffice to assume that imprecision comes in by the linguistic representation of probabilities as the traditional approaches in fuzzy set theory do. This is so because linguistic imprecision is not sufficient to describe the peculiarities of *human inferences* under uncertainty (not just representation of terms expressing this or the other kind of uncertainty). Thus, if linguistic modelling of uncertainty does not provide a sufficiently rich model language we have to go back to human representation of events and frequencies in order to establish a model of subjective representation of imprecise probabilities. In this section I try to give an outline of a cognitive model that embodies imprecise probabilities in an obvious and plausible manner.

The key notion for expressing the meaningfulness of conditional objects in describing cognitive structures is that of the *incomplete contingency tables paradigm.* Intuitively, an incomplete table is a relation in the sense of relational database theory with some tuples having null values at arbitrary places. An incomplete table may arise from badly recording data sets from customers, or from lack of precise information. This is only one interpretation of null values, the other being that for a tuple with a null value in an attribute this attribute is not defined. In the present model, the first interpretation is used throughout. An incomplete contingency table (ICT) is an incomplete table with a counting measure defined on it.

Before stressing its impact on cognitive modelling, let me comment on some general properties of the incomplete table paradigm. Statistically spoken, incomplete tables are contingency tables with missing entries. An entry is called missing if at least one of the dimensions of the contingency table is not specified. A simple example is the following record from a jeans shop. It is structured as data of a two-dimensional contingency table. One dimension is the approximate age of the customer, the other dimension is the jeans this customer bought. A example of a missing entry would be an age record of a customer with missing specification of the colour of the jeans he/she bought or a record of a jeans sold with missing information on the age group of the customer. The definition of a missing entry should reasonably exclude the case of a "record" of which no dimension at all is specified. Note that the presence of missing entries implies that the cell counts do not always add up to the marginals as in usual contingency tables.

The dashed lines refer to entries relevant to assessing the probability that people in their thirties buy blue jeans (i.e., $p(\ Jeans = blue |\ Customer = in30ies)$).

COMPLETE | INCOMPLETE

TABLE

CUSTOMER	JEANS		CUSTOMER	JEANS
in 30ies	blue	—	in 30ies	blue
in 40ies	blue		*******	blue
in 20ies	red		*******	red
old	black		*******	black
in 30ies	black	—	*******	black
in 50ies	green		in 50ies	green
in 40ies	white		in 40ies	*******
young	white		young	white
in 20ies	green		in 20ies	*******
in 30ies	green	—	in 30ies	*******
in 50ies	green		in 50ies	*******
in 30ies	blue	—	in 30ies	blue
in 50ies	white		in 50ies	white
old	black		old	black
old	black		*******	black
young	blue		*******	blue
young	blue		young	blue
young	black		young	black

The essential point about incomplete tables is that they render senseless any classical probabilistic evaluation in terms of relative frequencies. That is, if we have a counting measure on the complete table, we have only a belief function on the incomplete table. Therefore, if you wish to assess the conditional probability of, say, a blue jeans sold to a customer in his/her thirties, the classical formula willfail to give you a reasonable answer. (In the table presented here, the classical formula, for the complete version, yields 1/2. For the incomplete table, we obtain 2/3!) This is a noticeable property because of the simplicity of this paradigm. The classical probabilistic evaluation of conditional probabilities leads to absurd estimates. The way out is again surprisingly simple: Use lower and upper probabilities of conditional objects to approximate the true conditional probability in the complete table. *In an ICT, the upper and lower probabilities of a given conditional bound the true conditional probability. A conditional probability calculated on the basis of an incomplete table is, in general, not bounded by upper and lower probabilities of a conditional.* The formal statement and proof of this conjecture needs more notation and space than adequate for this brief outlook on a modeling perspective.

An incomplete version of a given relation is defined to be the relation modified by arbitrary replacements of occurences of attribute values in tuples of the relation by null values. Thus, an incomplete version is neither a projection nor a selection from a given relation. It is a very simple model of partial knowledge of a relation, likely to hold both for a little jeans store without automatic cash register and for human memory.

The incomplete table paradigm provides a very simple framework for establishing the necessity of using conditional objects. Actually, this paradigm is a very simple measure-free uncertainty model.

As such, it tells us how to treat missing data in contingency tables. This might become an important application of conditional objects in the future. Moreover, in the ICT paradigm, calculations with conditional objects are equivalent to Bayesian conditioning treated in Jaffray (1990). This is a subject for further study.

On the other hand, the incomplete table paradigm can be taken as a cognitive model. In his book on mental models, Johnson-Laird (1983) introduced the list paradigm for explaining specific properties of human processing of quantitative inferences. It is tempting to view the ICT paradigm as a generalization of his model to reasoning under uncertainty. As such, it seems to model quite well what happens in an expert's mind when asked to assess the probability of disease A, given symptom B. What he or she has in his/her mind, might very well look like an incomplete table, with a column for diseases and a column for symptoms and one tuple for each patient. For some patients, parts of the information in one or the other column is wiped out, and this is why a conditional event is cognitively more complex than a conditional probability. The expert's evaluation of his/her memory, according to this model, can be captured by upper and lower probabilities of conditional objects.

The psychological purpose behind this generalization is the explanation of the so-called human biases in evaluating probabilistic and more general inferences under uncertainty.

6 Acknowledgement

I wish to thank Prof. Hung T. Nguyen and Prof. Irwin Goodman for thoroughly discussing the approach presented here with me at the third IFSA conference in Seattle (1989). Moreover, I have learned much from discussions with Dr. Roland Scholz, and Prof. Michael Smithson. In preparing the final version, I had very useful advice by Prof. Jean-Yves Jaffray, Prof. Juerg Kohlas, Prof. Franz-Josef Radermacher, and some other participants of the FAW Workshop on Uncertainty Modeling in July 1990.

References

[1] Baldwin, J. F. (1986): Support logic programming. In: A. Jones, A. Kaufmann, H.-J. Zimmermann (eds.): Fuzzy Sets Theory and Applications, NATO ASI Series, Reidel, Dordrecht - Boston, 133- 170.

[2] Beeri, C., Fagin, R., Howard, J. (1977): A complete Axiomatization for functional and Multivalued Dependencies in Database Relations. Int. Conf. Mgmt. of Data, ACM, NY, 47-61.

[3] Bishop, Y., Fienberg, S., Holland, P. (1975): Discrete Multivariate Analysis: Theory and Practice. MIT Press, Cambridge, MA.

[4] Dubois, D., Prade, H. (1987): Properties of measures of information in evidence and possibility theories. Fuzzy Sets and Systems, 24, 2, 161-182.

[5] Dubois, D., Prade, H. (1988): Conditioning in Possibility and Evidence Theories - A logical Viewpoint. In: B. Bouchon, L. Saitta, R. Yager (eds.): Uncertainty and Intelligent Systems (Proc. Second IPMU, Urbino 1988), 401-408.

[6] Dubois, D., Prade, H. (1989): Measure-free Conditioning, Probability, and Non-monotonic Reasoning. Proc. 11th IJCAI, Detroit, 1110 - 1114.

[7] Edwards, W. (1982): Conservatism in human information processing. In: Kahneman, Slovic, Tversky (eds.): Judgment under uncertainty, New York, Cambridge University Press, 359-369.

[8] Erné, M. 1987: Ordnungs- und Verbandstheorie, University of Hagen Press.

[9] Fagin, R. (1977): Multivalued Dependencies and a new Normal Form for relational Databases. ACM Transactions on Database Systems, 2, 262-278.

[10] Goodman, I., Nguyen, H. (1985): Uncertainty Models for Knowledge-based Systems. North Holland, Amsterdam.

[11] Goodman, I., Nguyen, H. (1988): Conditional Objects and the Modelling of Uncertainties. In M. Gupta, T. Yamakawa (eds.): Fuzzy Computing, Elsevier Science, New York, 119 - 138.

[12] Heckerman, D. (1986): Probabilistic interpretations for MYCIN's Certainty Factors. In: L.N. Kanal, J.F. Lemmer (eds.): Uncertainty in Artificial Intelligence (1), North Holland, 167 - 196.

[13] Jaffray, J.-Y. (1990): Bayesian Conditioning and Belief Functions. Working Paper. Université Paris VI, Laboratoire d' Informatique de la décision.

[14] Kohlas, J. (1990): Evidenztheorie: Ein Kalkuel mit Hinweisen. FAW, University of Ulm, Research Report FAW-TR-90002.

[15] Kong, A. (1986): Multivariate Belief Functions and Graphical Models, Diss., Dept. of Statistics, Harvard University.

[16] Johnson-Laird, P.N. (1983): Mental Models, Cambridge University Press, Cambridge.

[17] Kahneman, D., Slovic, P., Tversky, A. (eds., 1982): Judgment under Uncertainty: Heuristics and Biases. New York, Cambridge University Press.

[18] Klayman, J., Ha, Y.-W. (1987): Confirmation, Disconfirmation, and Information in Hypothesis Testing. Psychologial Review, 94, 2, 211 - 228.

[19] Lauritzen, S., Spiegelhalter, D. (1988): Local Computations with Probabilities on Graphical Structures and their Application to Expert Systems. J. R. Statistical Society, 50, 2, 157 - 224.

[20] Nguyen, H.T., Rogers, G. (1990): Conditioning Operators in a Logic of Conditionals. (This volume)

[21] Ozsoyoglu, Z. M., Yuan, L.Y. (1987): A new Normal Form for Nested Relations. ACM Transactions on Database Systems, 12, 1, 111-136.

[22] Pearl, J. (1988): Probabilistic Reasoning in intelligent Systems: Networks of Plausible Inference. Morgan Kaufman, San Mateo, CA.

[23] Shafer, G. (1976): A mathematical Theory of Evidence. Princeton, Princeton University Press.

[24] Shafer, G. (1982): Belief Functions and Parametric Models. J. R. Stat. Society, B, 44 (3), 322 - 352.

[25] Shafer, G., Tversky, A. (1985): Languages and Designs for Probability Judgment, Cognitive Science, 9, 309 - 339.

[26] Shafer, G., Shenoy, P., Mellouli, K. (1987): Propagating Belief Functions in Qualitative Markov Trees. Int. J. Approx. Reasoning, 1 (4), pp. 349-400.

[27] Scholz, R. (1987): Cognitive Strategies in Stochastic Thinking. Reidel, Dordrecht - Boston.

[28] Spies, M. (1988): A Model for the Management of imprecise Queries in relational Databases. in: B. Bouchon, L. Saitta, R. Yager (eds.): Uncertainty and Intelligent Systems. Springer Lecture Notes on Computer Science, vol. 313, Heidelberg; 146-153.

[29] Spies, M (1989): Syllogistic inference under uncertainty–An empirical contribution to uncertainty modelling in knowledge-based systems with fuzzy quantifiers and support logic. Munich, Psychologie Verlags Union.

[30] Spies, M. (1990a): Imprecision in Human Combination of Evidence. In: W. Janko, M. Roubens, H.-J. Zimmermann (eds.): Advances in Fuzzy Systems. Kluwer, Boston, 161 - 175.

[31] Spies, M. (1990b): Application Aspects of Qualitative Conditional Independence. Proc. 3rd IPMU Conference, ENSTA, Paris, 7/2 - 7/6, 1990.

[32] Torgerson, W. (1958): Theory and Methods of Scaling, Wiley, New York.

[33] Wason, J., Johnson-Laird, P.N. (1972): Psychology of Reasoning: Structure and Content, Batsford, London.

[34] Zadeh, L.A. (1985): Syllogistic reasoning in fuzzy logic and its application to usuality and reasoning with dispositions, University of California at Berkeley. Institute of Cognitive Studies, Report 34.

Conditional Logic in Expert Systems
I.R. Goodman, M.M. Gupta, H.T. Nguyen and G.S. Rogers (editors)

CONNECTIVES (AND, OR, NOT) AND T-OPERATORS IN FUZZY REASONING

M.M. Gupta and J. Qi

Intelligent Systems Research Laboratory
College of Engineering
University of Saskatchewan
Saskatoon, Sask.
Canada, S7N OWO

Abstract In this paper, the theory of T-norm and T-conorm is reviewed and the T-norm, T-conorm and negation function are defined as a set of T-operators which can be used to define the connectives AND, OR and NOT for fuzzy reasoning applications. Some typical T-operators and their mathematical properties are presented. Finally, the T-operators are extended to the conventional fuzzy reasoning methods which are based on the MIN and MAX operators. This extended fuzzy reasoning method provides both a general and a flexible algorithm for the design of fuzzy logic controllers and, more generally, for the modelling of any decision-making process and expert systems.

Keywords Connectives AND, OR, and NOT, T-norms, T-conorms, T-operators, Fuzzy Inference, Fuzzy Logic Controller, Expert Systems.

1. Introduction

The triangular norm (T-norm) and the triangular conorm (T-conorm) originated from the studies of probabilistic metric spaces, Menger (1942) and Schweizer et al (1983), in which triangular inequalities were extended using the theory of T-norm and T-conorm. Later, Hohle (1978), Alsina et al (1983), etc. introduced the T-norm and the T-conorm into fuzzy set theory and suggested that the T-norm and the T-conorm be used for the intersection and union of fuzzy sets. Since then, many other researchers have presented various types of T-operators for the same purpose, for example, Yager (1983), Dombi (1982) and Weber (1983), and even proposed some methods to generate the variations of these operators, for example, Kaufmann et al (1988), which are given in the Appendix.

Zadeh's conventional T-operators, MIN and MAX, have been used in almost every design of fuzzy logic controllers and even in the modelling of other decision-making processes and expert systems. However, some theoretical and experimental studies seem to indicate that other types of T-operators may work better in some situations, especially in the context of decision-making processes. For example, the product operator may be preferred to the MIN operator, Dubois et al (1986). On the other hand, when choosing a set of T-operators for a given decision-making process, one has to consider their properties, the accuracy of the model, their simplicity, computer and hardware implementation, etc. For these and other reasons, it is of interest to use other sets of T-operators in the modelling of decision-making processes, so that multiple options are available for selecting T-operators that may be better suited for given problems.

Expert system, in a way, is a process of emulation of human knowledge and inference mechanism in the form of an algorithm which can be implemented on a machine. The knowledge base derived from a human expert appears in the form of 'If...Then' rules with connectives such as 'AND', 'OR', and 'NOT'. Some examples of such rules are:

If A_1 AND B_1 then C_1

If A_2 OR B_2 then C_2

If A_3 OR (B_3 AND B_2) then C_3

If A_4 AND (NOT B_4) then C_4

where A_i, B_i and C_i (i=1,2,3,4) are fuzzy sets over the universes of discourses A, B, and C respectively.

Let the membership functions of these variables A_i, B_i, and C_i be represented by x_i y_i, and z_i respectively, where x_i, y_i, and $z_i \in [0, 1]$. Then the connectives AND, OR and NOT in fuzzy logic can be represented by the T-norm T, T-conorm T* and the negation function N respectively. For example,

A_1 AND B_1 -> $T(x_1, y_1)$

A_2 OR B_2 -> $T^*(x_2, y_2)$

A_3 OR (B_3 AND B_2) -> $T^*(x_3, T(y_3, y_2))$

A_4 AND (NOT B_4) -> $T(x_4, N(y_4))$

Thus, the connectives AND, OR, and NOT in a knowledge base can be expressed in the form of T-norm, T-conorm and negation operation. Also, these operators are very useful in implementing the human-like reasoning functions for the design of expert systems; these reasoning functions are based on implication functions, and the compositional rule of inference.

In this paper we will give a detailed exposition of the theory of T-operators, some methods of their generations, and possible applications in fuzzy reasoning processes.

2. Definitions of T-operators

The T-norm, the T-conorm and the negation function are defined as T-operators and are used to calculate the membership values of intersection, union and complement of fuzzy sets, respectively. The definitions of T-operators have been given by many researchers. In this section, however, an attempt is made to give a complete set of definitions to T-operators.

Definition 1

Let T: $[0, 1] \times [0, 1] \rightarrow [0, 1]$, T is a T-norm, if and only if (iff)

(1.1) $T(x, y) = T(y, x)$ (Commutativity)

(1.2) $T(x, y) \leq T(x, z)$, if $y \leq z$ (Monotonicity)

(1.3) $T(x, T(y, z)) = T(T(x, y), z)$ (Associativity)

(1.4) $T(x, 1) = x$.

For all $x, y, z \in [0, 1]$.

A T-norm is Archimedean, iff

(1.5) $T(x, y)$ is continuous

(1.6) $T(x, x) < x \quad \forall x \in (0, 1)$.

An Archimedean T-norm is strict, iff

(1.7) $T(x', y') < T(x, y)$, if $x' < x$, $y' < y$, $\forall x', y', x, y \in (0, 1)$

Definition 2

Let T^*: $[0, 1] \times [0, 1] \rightarrow [0, 1]$, T^* is a T-conorm, iff

(2.1) $T^*(x, y) = T^*(y, x)$ (Commutativity)

(2.2) $T^*(x, y) \leq T^*(x, z)$, if $y \leq z$ (Monotonicity)

(2.3) $T^*(x, T^*(y, z)) = T^*(T^*(x, y), z)$ (Associativity)

(2.4) $T^*(x, 0) = x$.

For all $x, y, z \in [0, 1]$.

A T-conorm is Archimedean, iff

(2.5) T^* is continuous

(2.6) $T^*(x, x) > x \quad \forall x \in (0, 1)$.

An Archimedean T-conorm is strict, iff

(2.7) $T^*(x', y') < T^*(x, y)$, if $x' < x$, $y' < y$, $\forall x', y', x, y \in (0, 1)$.

Note that for a T-norm T and a T-conorm T^*

$T(0, 0) = 0, \quad T(1, 1) = 1$

$T^*(0, 0) = 0, \quad T^*(1, 1) = 1.$

Definition 3

Let N: $[0, 1] \rightarrow [0, 1]$, N is a negation function, iff

(3.1) $N(0) = 1$, $N(1) = 0$

(3.2) $N(x) \leq N(y)$, if $x \geq y$. (Monotonicity)

A negation function is strict, iff

(3.3) N(x) is continuous

(3.4) $N(x) < N(y)$, for $x > y$ $\forall\, x, y \in [0, 1]$.

A strict negation function is involutive, iff

(3.5) $N(N(x)) = x$, $\forall\, x \in [0, 1]$.

3. Some Typical T-operators

In this section, eleven sets of T-operators are given and some of their relevant properties are studied.

Zadeh's T-operators are the most popular ones in the literature, and are defined as follows:

$$T_1(x, y) = \mathrm{MIN}\,(x, y) \qquad (1.a)$$

$$T_1^*(x, y) = \mathrm{MAX}\,(x, y) \qquad (1.b)$$

$$N_1(x) = 1 - x. \qquad (1.c)$$

Weber (1983), Bandler et al (1980), and others proposed and studied a set of T-operators which are also called probabilistic operators defined as,

$$T_2(x, y) = x \cdot y \qquad (2.a)$$

$$T_2^*(x, y) = x + y - x\,y \qquad (2.b)$$

$$N_2(x) = 1 - x. \qquad (2.c)$$

A set of T - operators such as,

$$T_3(x, y) = \mathrm{MAX}\,(x + y - 1, 0) \qquad (3.a)$$

$$T_3^*(x, y) = \mathrm{MIN}\,(x + y, 1) \qquad (3.b)$$

$$N_3(x) = 1 - x \qquad (3.c)$$

are called Lukasiewicz logics and have been studied by Giles (1976) and others.

Another set of T-operators are defined as,

$$T_4(x, y) = \frac{xy}{x + y - xy} \qquad (4.a)$$

$$T_4^*(x, y) = \frac{x + y - 2xy}{1 - xy} \qquad (4.b)$$

$$N_4(x) = 1 - x. \qquad (4.c)$$

Weber (1983) and others studied a set of T-operators which are given by,

$$T_5(x, y) = \begin{cases} x, & \text{if } y = 1 \\ y, & \text{if } x = 1 \\ 0, & \text{otherwise} \end{cases} \qquad (5.a)$$

$$T_5^*(x, y) = \begin{cases} x, & \text{if } y = 0 \\ y, & \text{if } x = 0 \\ 1, & \text{otherwise} \end{cases} \tag{5.b}$$

$$N_5(x) = 1 - x. \tag{5.c}$$

This set of operators is the only one which is not continuous.

Weber (1983) and others proposed a set of T-operators which are defined as,

$$T_6(x, y) = \frac{\lambda xy}{1 - (1 - \lambda)(x + y - xy)} \tag{6.a}$$

$$T_6^*(x, y) = \frac{\lambda(x + y) + xy(1 - \lambda)}{\lambda + xy(1 - \lambda)} \tag{6.b}$$

$$N_6(x) = 1 - x. \tag{6.c}$$

Note the following limiting case for T_6 and T_6^*:

(i) For $\lambda \to 0$, $T_6 \to T_5$, and $T_6^* \to T_5^*$;

(ii) For $\lambda = 1$, $T_6 = T_2$, and $T_6^* = T_2^*$; and

(iii) For $\lambda \to \infty$, $T_6 = T_4$, and $T_6^* = T_4^*$.

Yager (1983) proposed a set of T-operators which is defined as follows:

$$T_7(x, y) = \text{MAX}\,(1 - ((1 - x)^p + (1 - y)^p)^{1/p},\ 0) \tag{7.a}$$

$$T_7^*(x, y) = \text{MIN}\,((x^p + y^p)^{1/p},\ 1) \tag{7.b}$$

$$N_7(x) = 1 - x. \tag{7.c}$$

Again, note the following:

(i) For $p = 1$, $T_6 = T_3$, and $T_6^* = T_3^*$, and

(ii) For $p \to \infty$, $T_6 \to T_1$, and $T_6^* \to T_1^*$.

Dombi (1982) presented the following set of T-operators:

$$T_8(x, y) = \frac{1}{1 + ((\frac{1}{x} - 1)^{\lambda} + (\frac{1}{y} - 1)^{\lambda})^{1/\lambda}} \tag{8.a}$$

$$T_8^*(x, y) = \frac{1}{1 + ((\frac{1}{x} - 1)^{-\lambda} + (\frac{1}{y} - 1)^{-\lambda})^{-1/\lambda}} \tag{8.b}$$

$$N_8(x) = 1 - x. \tag{8.c}$$

Note the following:

(i) For $\lambda \to 0$, $T_8 \to T_5$, and $T_8^* \to T_5^*$;

(ii) For $\lambda = 1$, $T_8 = T_4$, and $T_8^* = T_4^*$; and

(iii) For $\lambda \to \infty$, $T_8 \to T_1$, and $T_8^* \to T_1^*$.

Dubois et al (1986) also gave a set of T - operators defined as,

$$T_9(x, y) = \frac{xy}{\max(x, y, \lambda)} \tag{9.a}$$

$$T_9^*(x, y) = 1 - \frac{(1 - x)(1 - y)}{\max(1 - x, 1 - y, \lambda)} \tag{9.b}$$

$$N_9(x) = 1 - x. \tag{9.c}$$

Note the following:

(i) For $\lambda = 0$, $T_9 = T_1$, and $T_9^* = T_1^*$, and

(ii) For $\lambda = 1$, $T_9 = T_2$, and $T_9^* = T_2^*$.

Weber (1983) proposed another set of T-operators which are defined as

$$T_{10}(x, y) = \mathrm{MAX}\left(\frac{x + y - 1 + \lambda x y}{1 + \lambda}, 0\right) \tag{10.a}$$

$$T_{10}^*(x, y) = \mathrm{MIN}(x + y + \lambda x y, 1) \tag{10.b}$$

$$N_{10}(x) = \frac{1 - x}{1 + \lambda x}. \tag{10.c}$$

Note the following:

(i) For $\lambda = 0$, $T_{10} = T_3$, and $T_{10}^* = T_3^*$;

(ii) For $\lambda \to -1$, $T_{10} \to T_5$, and $T_{10}^* \to T_2^*$; and

(iii) For $\lambda \to \infty$, $T_{10} \to T_2$, and $T_{10}^* = T_5^*$.

Yu Yandong (1985) studied a set of T-operators which are given by

$$T_{11}(x, y) = \mathrm{MAX}((1 + \lambda)(x + y - 1) - \lambda x y, 0) \tag{11.a}$$

$$T_{11}^*(x, y) = \mathrm{MIN}(x + y + \lambda x y, 1) \tag{11.b}$$

$$N_{11}(x) = 1 - x. \tag{11.c}$$

Note the following:

(i) For $\lambda \to -1$, $T_{11} \to T_2$, and $T_{11}^* \to T_2^*$;

(ii) For $\lambda = 0$, $T_{11} = T_3$, and $T_{11}^* = T_3^*$; and

(iii) For $\lambda \to \infty$, $T_{11} \to T_5$, and $T^*_{11} \to T^*_5$.

4. Some Properties of T-Operators

In the following, some important mathematical properties of T-operators are presented. For simplicity, all proofs are omitted.

According to the definitions, T and T^* possess the following two important properties:

P_1: Commutativity:

$$T(x, y) = T(y, x) \tag{12.a}$$
$$T^*(x, y) = T^*(y, x). \tag{12.b}$$

P_2: Associativity:

$$T(x, T(y, z)) = T(T(x, y), z) \tag{13.a}$$
$$T^*(x, T(y, z)) = T^*(T^*(x, y), z). \tag{13.b}$$

Also, consider the following additional important properties for T-operators.

P_3: Distributivity:

$$T(x, T^*(y, z)) = T^*(T(x, y), T(x, z)) \tag{14.a}$$
$$T^*(x, T(y, z)) = T(T^*(x, y), T^*(x, z)). \tag{14.b}$$

P_4: Absorption:

$$T(T^*(x, y), x) = x \tag{15.a}$$
$$T^*(T(x, y), x) = x. \tag{15.b}$$

P_5: Idempotency:

$$T(x, x) = x \tag{16.a}$$
$$T^*(x, x) = x. \tag{16.b}$$

Theorem 1:

$$\text{Distributivity} \to \text{Absorption} \to \text{Idempotency} \to \begin{matrix} T & = & T_1 \\ T^* & = & T^*_1 \end{matrix}$$

According to this theorem, it is clear that all T-norms and T-conorms do not satisfy the properties: P_3, P_4 and P_5 except for T_1 and T^*_1.

The excluded-middle laws are stated as,

$$P_6:\ T(x, N(x)) = 0 \tag{17.a}$$
$$P_7:\ T^*(x, N(x)) = 1. \tag{17.b}$$

Theorem 2:

If T and T^* satisfy P_6 and P_7, then they do not have P_3, P_4 and P_5.

(T_3, T_3^*, N_3), (T_5, T_5^*, N_5), $(T_{10}, T_{10}^*, N_{10})$ and $(T_{11}, T_{11}^*, N_{11})$ are the only ones in Table 1 which satisfy P_6 and P_7 and, therefore, do not have properties, P_3, P_4 and P_5. Note that $(T_{11}, T_{11}^*, N_{11})$ has P_6 and P_7 only when $\lambda \geq 0$.

The well known De Morgan's laws for T-operators are stated as follows:

$$P_8:\ N(T(x, y) = T^*(N(x), N(y)) \qquad (18.a)$$

$$P_9:\ N(T^*(x, y)) = T(N(x), N(y)). \qquad (18.b)$$

Theorem 3:

If N(x) is involutive, Equations (18.a) and (18.b) are equivalent, and the following equations are also true:

$$P_{10}:\ T(x, y) = N(T^*(N(x), N(y))) \qquad (19.a)$$

$$P_{11}:\ T^*(x, y) = N(T(N(x), N(y))). \qquad (19.b)$$

All eleven sets of T-operators satisfy De Morgan's laws, although $(T_{10}, T_{10}^*, N_{10})$ is needed to satisfy the requirement: $x + y + \lambda\, x\, y \geq 1$ ($\lambda \neq 0$).

There are some other important properties which are described by the following inequalities.

$$P_{12}:\ T_5(x, y) \leq T(x, y) \leq T_1(x, y) \qquad (20.a)$$

$$P_{13}:\ T_1^*(x, y) \leq T^*(x, y) \leq T_5^*(x, y) \qquad (20.b)$$

$$P_{14}:\ T_5(x, y) < T_3(x, y) < T_2(x, y) < T_4(x, y) < T_1(x, y) \qquad (21.a)$$

$$P_{15}:\ T_1^*(x, y) < T_4^*(x, y) < T_2^*(x, y) < T_3^*(x, y) < T_5^*(x, y). \qquad (21.b)$$

These conclusions are also demonstrated in Fig. 1 for triangular fuzzy numbers.

5. Fuzzy Inference Methods Based on T-Operators

In this section, a generalized fuzzy reasoning method is proposed by extending T-operators to conventional fuzzy reasoning algorithms in which MIN and MAX operators are widely being used. Then, by using the Mamdani's implication function, which is simple and easy to implement, a series of examples are given based on the proposed fuzzy reasoning methods.

As discussed before, theoretical and experimental studies have indicated that some T-operators work better in some situations, especially in the context of decision-making processes, than MIN and MAX operators which have been widely used for the same purpose. In fact, the choice of an operator is always a matter of context, and it mostly depends on the real-world problem which is to be modelled. It is appropriate, therefore, to use the general concept of T-operators in the modelling of decision-making process, in addition to the MIN and MAX operators so as to provide more options and flexibility for the selection of T-operators that may be better suited for a given problem.

In decision-making environments, the human brain tends to make inferences in which fuzzy expressions are often involved. These types of inferences cannot be satisfactorily modelled by using classical two-valued logic. A fuzzy inference means deducing new conclusions from the given information in the form of 'IF-THEN' rules in which antecedents and consequents are fuzzy sets. The following are the forms of fuzzy inferences:

Implication: if x is A, then y is B

Premise: x is A'

Conclusion: y is B'

where x and y are linguistic variables, such as position, velocity, pressure and temperature, etc., and A, A', B and B' are fuzzy sets representing linguistic labels over the universes of discourse X, X, Y and Y respectively, such as SMALL, MEDIUM, HIGH and VERY LOW, etc.

This type of inference is called generalized modus ponens which reduces to classical modus ponens for A' = A and B' = B.

The following is an example of the above form of inference which may be used in a temperature control system.

Implication: If temperature is high then fuel input is low

Premise: the temperature is very high

Conclusion: the fuel input is very low

Consider another form of inference,

Implication: if x is A, then y is B

Premise: y is B'

Conclusion: x is A'

Similarly, if A' = $\bar{A}$ and B' = $\bar{B}$, this inference becomes modus tollens. Therefore, it is called the generalized modus tollens.

In the design of fuzzy logic controllers, the fuzzy inference with the form of generalized modus ponens is used as shown in the following:

Implication: If control condition A, then control action B

Premise: control condition A'

Conclusion: Control action B'

Consider a fuzzy logic controller as an example of a fuzzy reasoning process. Suppose that an experienced human operator provides verbal descriptions of his expert knowledge about the process to be controlled in the form of 'IF - THEN' rules as follows:

Rule 1: If x is A_1, then y is B_1

Rule 2: If x is A_2, then y is B_2

... ...

Rule i: If x is A_i, then y is B_i

... ...

Rule N: If x is A_N, then y is B_N

or, this set of control rules can also be written as an ensemble of if ... then rules

$$\bigcup_{i=1}^{N} \text{ If x is } A_i, \text{ then y is } B_i$$

where x and y are linguistic variables, and A_i and B_i are fuzzy sets over a universe of discourse X and Y.

To implement the above decision rules, an implication function is required. If the fuzzy relation between A_i and B_i is represented by $R_{A_i \to B_i}$ on the universe of discourse $X \times Y$, then its membership function is given in terms of T-norms as follows:

$$\mu_{R_{A_i \to B_i}}(x, y) = T(\mu_{A_i}(x), \mu_{B_i}(y)) \; x \in X, y \in Y \tag{22}$$

This is in fact the generalized Mamdani's implication function. If Zadeh's implication methods are used, the following conclusions can be drawn:

(1) $$R_{A_i \to B_i} = (A_i \times B_i) \cup (\bar{A}_i \times Y) \tag{23.a}$$

$$\mu_{R_{A_i \to B_i}}(x, y) = T^*(T(\mu_{A_i}(x), \mu_{B_i}(y)), N(\mu_{A_i}(x))) \tag{23.b}$$

(2) $$R_{A_i \to B_i} = (X \times B_i) \cup (\bar{A}_i \times Y) \tag{24.a}$$

$$\mu_{R_{A_i \to B_i}}(x, y) = T^*(\mu_{B_i}(y), N(\mu_{A_i}(x))) \tag{24.b}$$

Similar extensions can be made to other implication methods which may be found in Mizumoto et al (1979). It is up to the user to choose a particular implication method for a given decision process. A general representation of implication functions is defined by $f_{\to}(\cdot, \cdot)$. We have then,

$$\mu_{A_i \to B_i}(x, y) = f_{\to}(\mu_{A_i}(x), \mu_{B_i}(y)). \tag{25}$$

The overall fuzzy relation R is then given by

$$\mu_R(x, y) = \mathop{T^*}_{i=1}^{N} (\mu_{RA_i \to B_i}(x, y)). \tag{26}$$

Given an antecedent A' (control condition) and the fuzzy relation R (expert's knowledge), the consequent B' (control action) is inferred through the generalized modus ponens which is shown in Fig. 2.

The consequent B' is calculated from the antecedent A' and the fuzzy relation R by the compositional rule of inference as follows:

$$B' = A' \circ R \tag{27.a}$$

$$\mu_{B'}(y) = \sup_x T(\mu_{A'}(x), \mu_{R_{A_i \to B_i}}(x, y)) \tag{27.b}$$

Based on the Equations (25), (26) and (27.b), a generalized fuzzy reasoning algorithm is given by,

$$\mu_{B'}(y) = \sup_x T(\mu_{A'}(x), \underset{i=1}{\overset{N}{T^*}}(f_{\to}(\mu_{A_i}(x), \mu_{B_i}(y)))) \tag{28}$$

if N = 1 and $f_{\to}(\cdot, \cdot)$ = (22), then (28) can be further simplified as

$$\mu_{B'}(y) = T(\alpha, \mu_B(y)) \tag{29}$$

where $\alpha = \sup_x T(\mu_{A'}(x), \mu_{A_1}(x))$

If A' and A_1 are finite fuzzy sets, then we have

$$\alpha = \bigvee_x T(\mu_{A'}(x), \mu_{A_1}(x)).$$

Suppose that A(= A_1), A', and B are triangular fuzzy numbers which are usually the cases for fuzzy logic controllers. Substituting T by T_1 to T_5 in (29), five different types of fuzzy reasoning methods are obtained which are illustrated in Fig. 3.

6. Conclusions

The T-operators presented in this paper are flexible tools for designing fuzzy logic controllers and expert systems. More generally, these T-operators can be used for modelling decision-making processes where Zadeh's MIN and MAX operators are commonly applied. The broad range of T-operators that are available will enable designers to select the best one for their particular applications. The general fuzzy reasoning method discussed above is only one of the many possible approaches. Other implication functions and other operators can also be employed to produce similar methods in fuzzy reasoning. At the present, further research is underway towards implementing this fuzzy reasoning method in control systems applications.

Appendix

In the following, two major methods of generating T-norms and T-conorms are given which may be found in Kaufmann (1988) and Weber (1983). The difference between the two methods is that the second method generates a new T-norm (or T-conorm) based on a given T-norm (or T-conorm). Some other methods may be found in Kaufmann (1988).

Method 1

Let T: [0, 1] × [0, 1] → [0, 1]. If there exists a decreasing and continuous function f: [0, 1] → [0, ∞] with f(1) = 0, then

$$T(x, y) = f^{(-1)}(f(x) + f(y)) \quad x, y \in [0, 1]$$

is a T-norm, and $f^{(-1)}$ is the pseudo-inverse of f, and is defined by

$$f^{(-1)}(x) = \begin{cases} f^{-1}(x) & \text{for } x \in [0, f(0)] \\ 0 & \text{for } x \in [f(0), \infty] \end{cases}$$

Note that T is an Archimedean T-norm and if f(0) → ∞, T is strict.

Let T^*: [0, 1] × [0, 1] → [0, 1]. If there exists an increasing and continuous function g: [0, 1] → [0, ∞] with g(0) = 0, then

$$T^*(x, y) = g^{(-1)}(g(x) + g(y)) \quad x, y \in [0, 1]$$

is a T-conorm, and where $g^{(-1)}$ is the pseudo inverse of g, and is defined by

$$g^{(-1)}(x) = \begin{cases} g^{-1}(x) & \text{for } x \in [0, g(1)] \\ 1 & \text{for } x \in [g(1), \infty] \end{cases}$$

Similarly, T^* is an Archimedean T-conorm and if g(1) → ∞, T^* is strict.

Two examples are given in the following:

Example 1

$$f(x) = (\frac{1}{x} - 1)^{\lambda}, \quad g(x) = (\frac{1}{x} - 1)^{-\lambda} \quad \lambda > 0 \text{ and } x \in [0, 1]$$

$$f^{(-1)}(x) = \frac{1}{1+x^{1\backslash\lambda}}, \quad g^{(-1)}(x) = \frac{1}{1+x^{-1\backslash\lambda}}$$

$$\begin{aligned} T(x, y) &= f^{(-1)}((\frac{1}{x} - 1)^{\lambda} + (\frac{1}{y} - 1)^{\lambda}) \\ &= \frac{1}{1+((\frac{1}{x} - 1)^{\lambda} + (\frac{1}{y} - 1)^{\lambda})^{-1/\lambda}} \end{aligned}$$

Similarly,

$$T^*(x, y) = \frac{1}{1+((\frac{1}{x} - 1)^{-\lambda} + (\frac{1}{y} - 1)^{-\lambda})^{-1/\lambda}}$$

They are T_8 and T^*_8 in Table 1. Because f(0) → ∞ and g(1) → ∞, they are strict Archimedean T-norm and T-conorm.

Example 2

$$f(x) = 1 - x, \quad g(x) = x, \quad x \in [0, 1]$$

$$f^{(-1)}(x) = \begin{cases} 1-x, & \text{for } x \in [0, 1] \\ 0, & \text{for } x \in [1, \infty] \end{cases}$$

$$g^{(-1)}(x) = \begin{cases} x, & \text{for } x \in [0, 1] \\ 1, & \text{for } x \in [1, \infty] \end{cases}$$

$$\begin{aligned} T(x, y) &= f^{(-1)}(f(x) + f(y)) \\ &= f^{(-1)}(2 - x - y) \\ &= \begin{cases} x+y-1, & x+y-1 \geq 0 \\ 0, & x+y-1 \leq 0 \end{cases} \\ &= \text{MAX}(x + y - 1, 0). \end{aligned}$$

Similarly,

$$T^*(x, y) = \text{MIN}(x + y, 0)$$

They are T_3 and T^*_3. Because f(0) = 1 and g(1) = 1, they are non-strict Archimedean T-norm and T-conorm.

Method 2

Let T: $[0, 1] \times [0, 1] \rightarrow [0, 1]$. If T' is a T-norm and f(x) is strictly monotonic in a segment of R with f(1) = 1, then

$$T(x, y) = f^{-1}(T'(f(x),\ f(y))$$

is a T-norm.

Let T*: $[0, 1] \times [0, 1] \rightarrow [0, 1]$. If T'^* is a T-conorm and g(x) is strictly monotonic in a segment of R with g(0) = 0, then

$$T^*(x, y) = g^{-1}(\, T'^*(g(x),\ g(y))$$

is a T-conorm.

Two examples are given:

Example 3

$$T'(x, y) = xy, \quad f(x) = \frac{1}{x}$$

$$f^{-1}(x) = \frac{1}{x}$$

$$T(x, y) = f^{-1}\left(\frac{1}{x} \cdot \frac{1}{y}\right) = \frac{1}{\frac{1}{x} \cdot \frac{1}{y}} = xy$$

This is T_2 and it generates itself.

Example 4

$$T'^* = x + y - xy, \quad g(x) = x^2, \quad x \in [0, 1]$$

$$g^{-1}(x) = x^{1/2}$$

$$\begin{aligned} T^*(x, y) &= g^{-1}(x^2 + y^2 - x^2 y^2) \\ &= (x^2 + y^2 - x^2 y^2)^{1/2} \end{aligned}$$

This is a T-conorm.

References

1. Alsina, C., Trillas, E. and Valverde, L. (1983) On some logical connectives for fuzzy set theory, *J. Math. Anal. Appl.* (93), 15-26.
2. Bandler, W. and Kohout, L. (1980) Fuzzy power sets and fuzzy implication operators, *Fuzzy Sets and Systems* (4), 13-30.
3. Dombi, J. (1982) A general class of fuzzy operators, the De Morgan class of fuzzy operators and fuzziness induced by fuzzy operators, *Fuzzy Sets and Systems* (8), 149-163.
4. Dubois, D. and Prade, H. (1986) New results about properties and semantics of fuzzy set-theoretic operators, *Fuzzy Sets,* Plenum Press.
5. Giles, R. (1976) Lukasiewicz logic and fuzzy set theory, *Internat. J. Man-Machine Stud.* (8), 313-327.
6. Hohle, U. (1978) Probabilistic uniformization of fuzzy topologies, *Fuzzy Sets and Systems* (1), 311-332.
7. Kaufmann, A. and Gupta, M.M. (1988) *Fuzzy Mathematics Models in Engineering and Management Science,* North-Holland, Amsterdam.
8. Menger, K. (1942) Statistical matrics, *Proc. Nat. Acad. Sci. U.S.A.* (28), 535-537.
9. Mizumoto, M., Fukami, S. and Tanaka, K. (1979) Some methods of fuzzy reasoning, *Advances in fuzzy Set Theory and Applications* (Gupta, M.M. et al, Eds.), North-Holland, Amsterdam.
10. Schweizer, B. and Sklar, A. (1983) *Probabilistic Metric Spaces,* North-Holland, Amsterdam.
11. Weber, S. (1983) A general concept of fuzzy connectives, negations and implications based on t-norms and t-conorms, *Fuzzy Sets and Systems* (11), 115-134.
12. Yager, R.R. (1983) On a general class of fuzzy connectives, *Fuzzy Sets and Systems* (4), 235-242.
13. Yu Yandong (1985) Triangular norms and TNF-sigma algebras, *Fuzzy Sets and Systems* (16), 251-264.
14. Zadeh, L.A. (1973) Outline of a new approach to the analysis of complex systems and decision processes, *IEEE Trans. Systems Man Cybernet.* (3), 28-44.

Table 1 T-Operators

N	$T_N(x, y)$	$T^*_N(x, y)$	$N_N(x)$	Comment
1.	MIN (x, y)	MAX (x, y)	1 - x	Zadeh (1973)
2.	$x \cdot y$	$x + y - xy$	1 - x	Weber (1983), Bandler et al (1980)
3.	MAX (x + y - 1, 0)	MIN (x + y , 1)	1 - x	Giles (1976)
4.	$\frac{xy}{x + y - xy}$	$\frac{x + y - 2xy}{1 - xy}$	1 - x	
5.	$\begin{cases} x, & \text{if } y=1 \\ y, & \text{if } x=1 \\ 0, & \text{otherwise} \end{cases}$	$\begin{cases} x, & \text{if } y=0 \\ y, & \text{if } x=0 \\ 1, & \text{otherwise} \end{cases}$	1 - x	Weber (1983), etc.
6.	$\frac{\lambda xy}{1 - (1 - \lambda)(x + y) - xy}$	$\frac{\lambda(x + y) + xy(1 - \lambda)}{\lambda + xy(1 - \lambda)}$	1 - x	Weber (1983) $\lambda \to 0, \to T_5$ and T^*_5 $\lambda = 1, \to T_2$ and T^*_2 $\lambda \to \infty, \to T_4$ and T^*_4
7.	$\text{MAX}(1 - ((1 - x)^p + (1 - y)^p)^{1/p}, 0)$	$\text{MIN}((x^p + y^p)^{1/p}, 1)$	1 - x	Yager (1983) $p = 1, \to T_3$ and T^*_3 $p \to \infty, \to T_1$ and T^*_1

Table 1 (continued)

8.	$\frac{1}{1+((\frac{1}{x}-1)^{\lambda}+(\frac{1}{y}-1)^{\lambda})^{1/\lambda}}$	$\frac{1}{1+((\frac{1}{x}-1)^{-\lambda}+(\frac{1}{y}-1)^{-\lambda})^{-1/\lambda}}$	$1 - x$	Dombi (1982) $\lambda \to 0, \to T_5$ and T^*_5 $\lambda = 1, \to T_4$ and T^*_4 $\lambda \to \infty, \to T_1$ and T^*_1
9.	$\frac{xy}{MAX\ (x, y, \lambda)}$	$1 - \frac{(1-x)(1-y)}{MAX\ y(1-x, 1-y, \lambda)}$	$1 - x$	Dubois et al (1986) $\lambda = 0, \to T_1$ and T^*_1 $\lambda = 1, \to T_2$ and T^*_2
10.	$MAX\ (\frac{x + y - 1 + \lambda x y}{1 + \lambda}, 0)$	$MIN\ (x + y + \lambda x y, 1)$	$\frac{1 - x}{1 + \lambda x}$	Weber (1983) $\lambda \to -1, \to T_5$ and T^*_2 $\lambda = 0, \to T_3$ and T^*_3 $\lambda \to \infty, \to T_2$ and T^*_5
11.	$MAX(1 + \lambda) (x + y - 1)$ $-\lambda x y, 0)$	$MIN(x + y + \lambda x y, 1)$	$1 - x$	Yu Yandong (1985) $\lambda \to -1, \to T_2$ and T^*_2 $\lambda = 0, \to T_3$ and T^*_3 $\lambda \to \infty, \to T_5$ and T^*_5

Table 2 Properties of Eleven Sets of T-Operators

T, T^*, N	Distributivity	Idempotency	The Excluded Middle Laws	Assorption	Associativity	Commutativity	De Morgan's Laws
T_1, T_1^*, N_1	√	√	x	√	√	√	√
T_2, T_2^*, N_2	x	x	x	x	√	√	√
T_3, T_3^*, N_3	x	x	√	x	√	√	√
T_4, T_4^*, N_4	x	x	x	x	√	√	√
T_5, T_5^*, N_5	x	x	√	x	√	√	√
T_6, T_6^*, N_6	x	x	x	x	√	√	√
T_7, T_7^*, N_7	x	x	x	x	√	√	√
$T_8, T_8^* N_8$	x	x	x	x	√	√	√
T_9, T_9^*, N_9	x	x	x	x	√	√	√
T_{10}, T_{10}^*, N_{10}	x	x	√	x	√	√	√*
T_{11}, T_{11}^*, N_{11}	x	x	√**	x	√	√	√

*Only when $x + y + \lambda x y \geq 1$ $(\lambda \neq 0)$

** Only when $\lambda > 0$

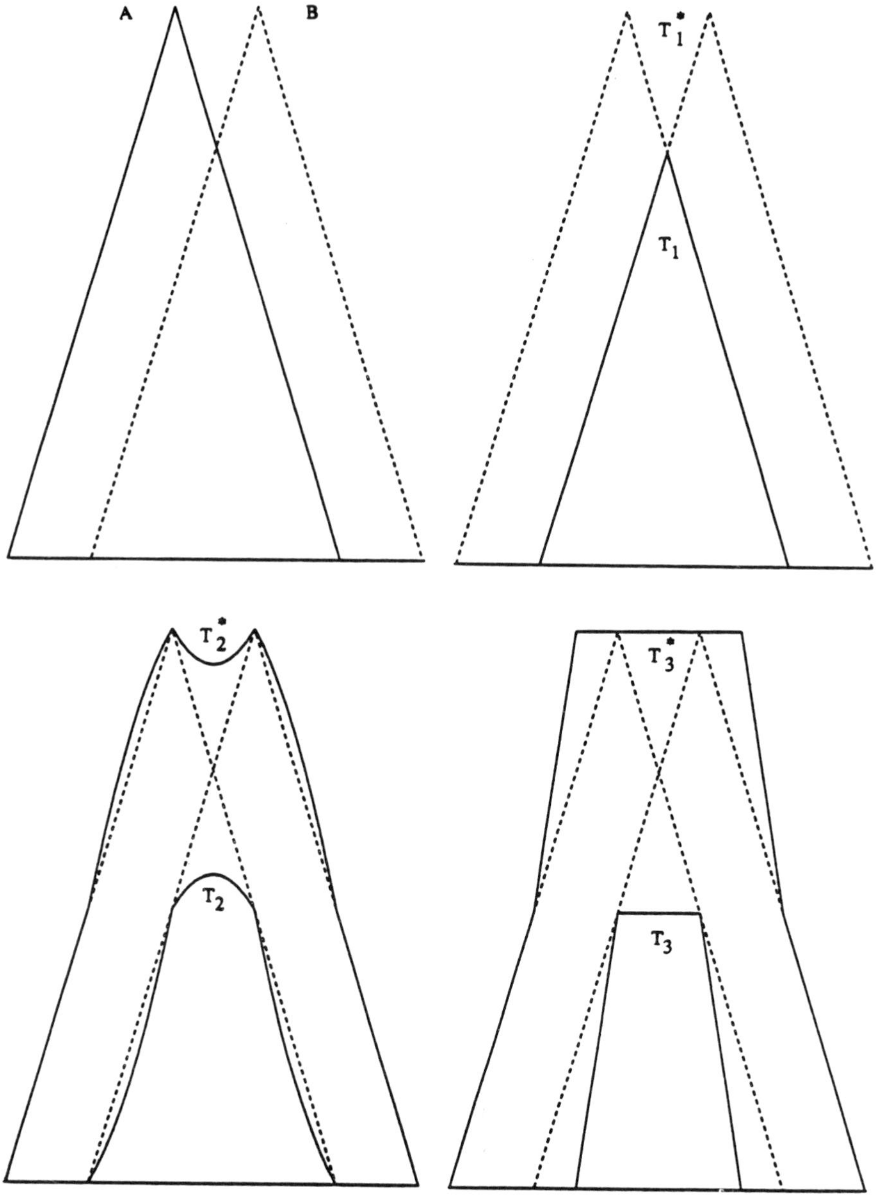

Figure 1 T-Norms and T-Conorms

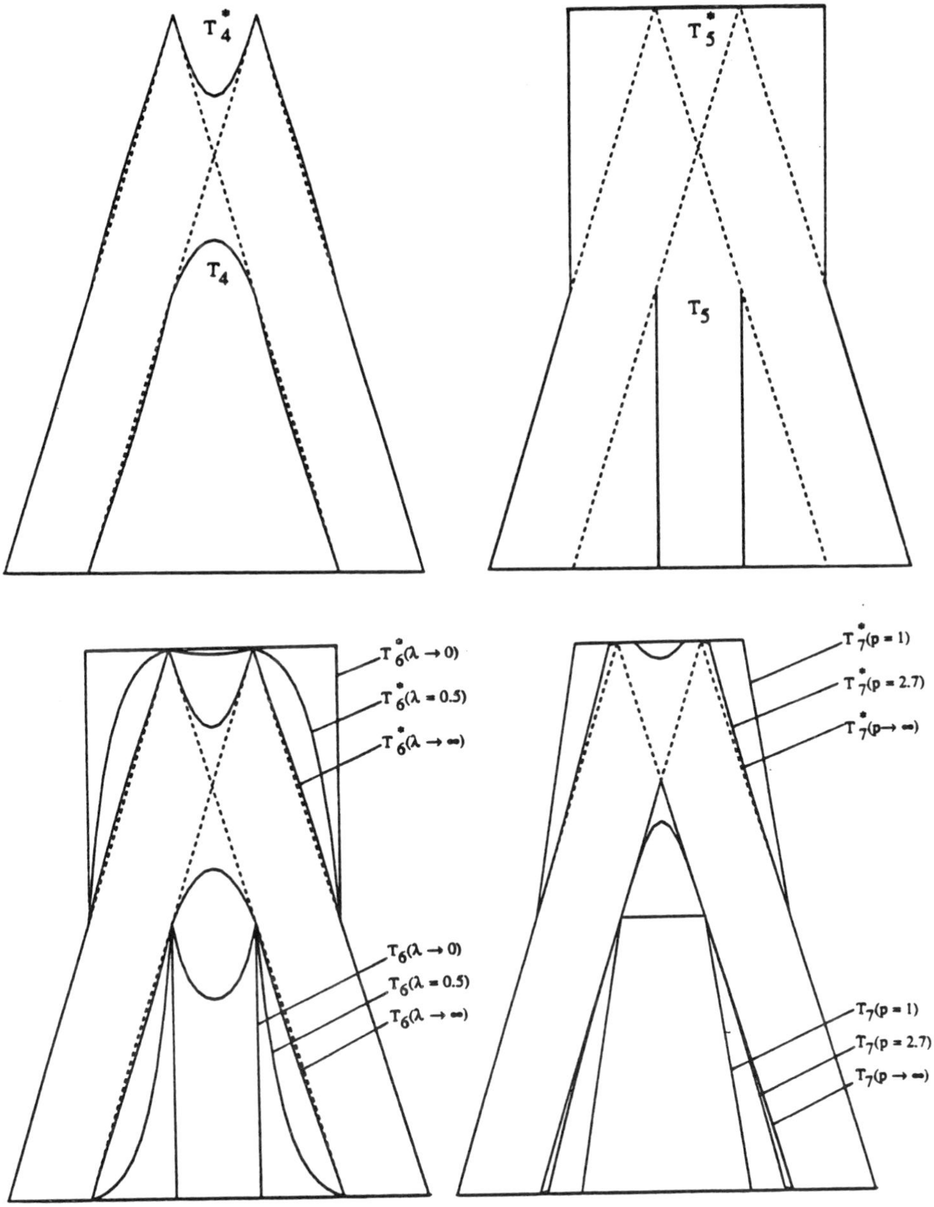

Figure 1 T-Norms and T-Conorms (continued)

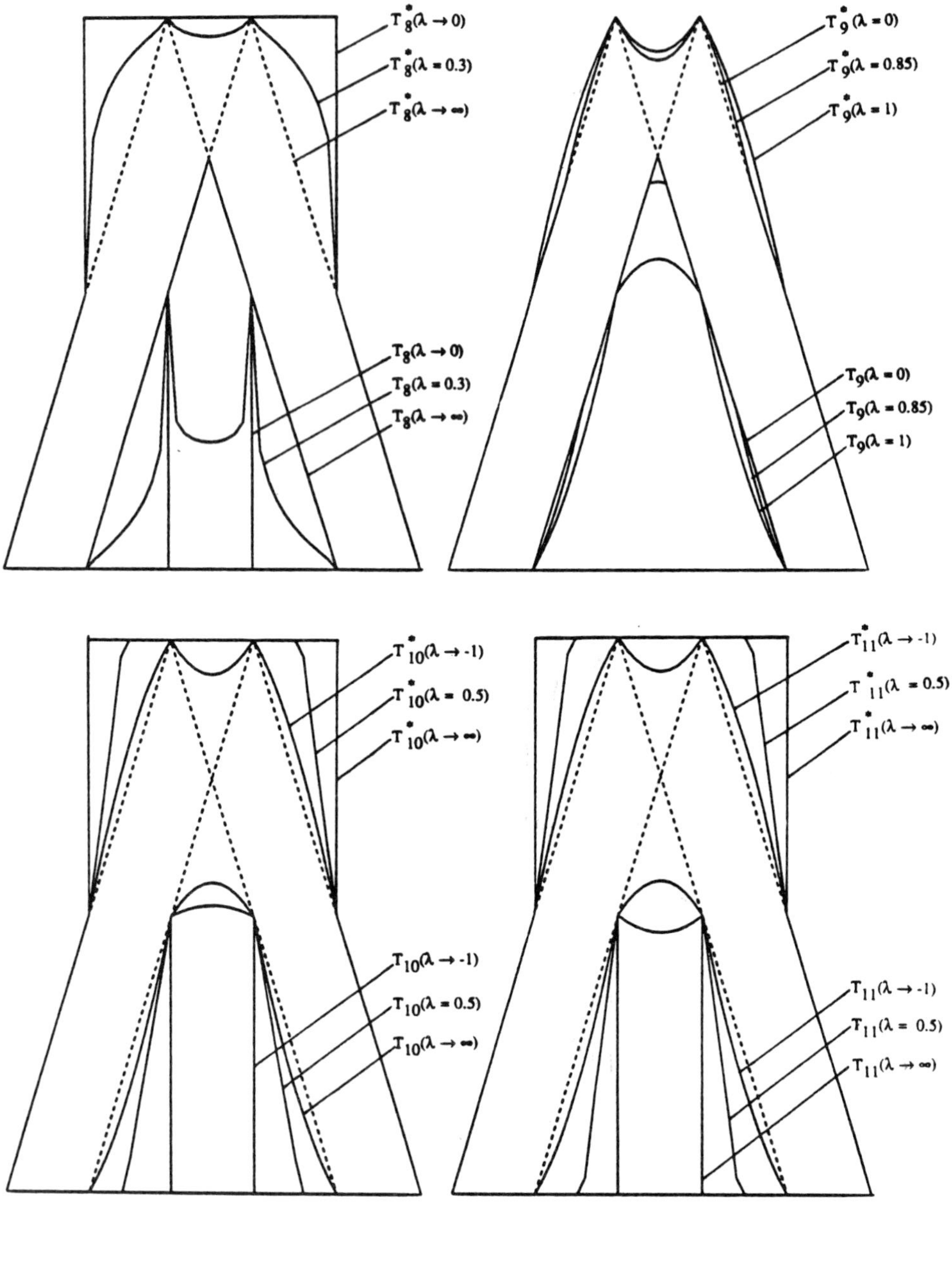

Figure 1 T-Norms and T-Conorms (continued)

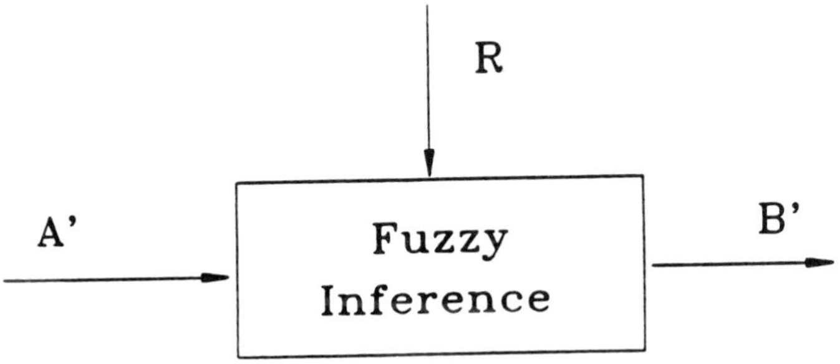

Figure 2 Fuzzy Inference

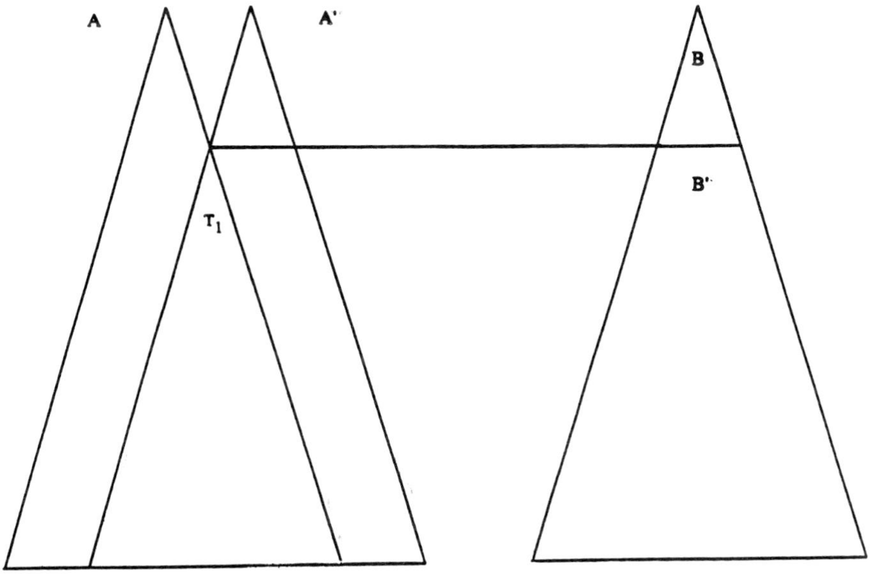

Figure 3 Fuzzy Inference Methods

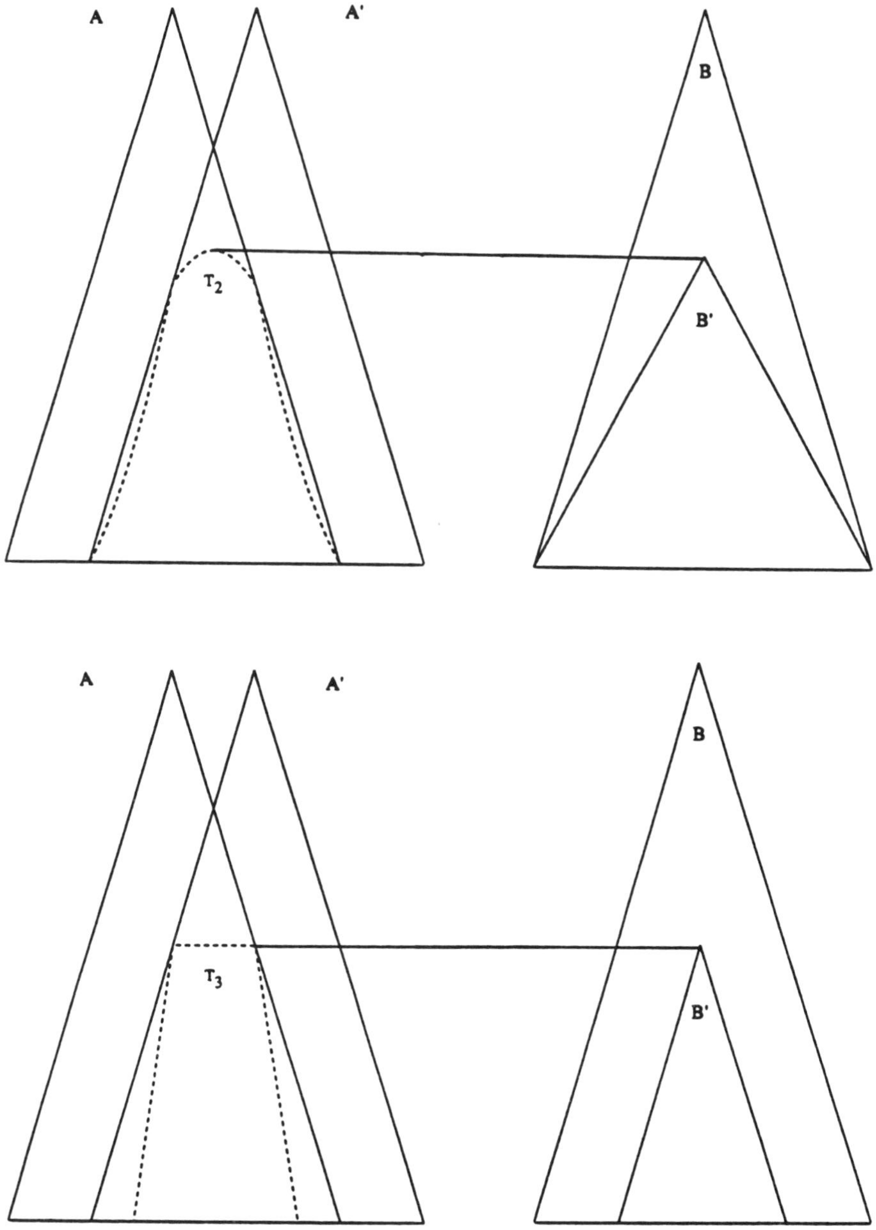

Figure 3 Fuzzy Inference Methods (continued)

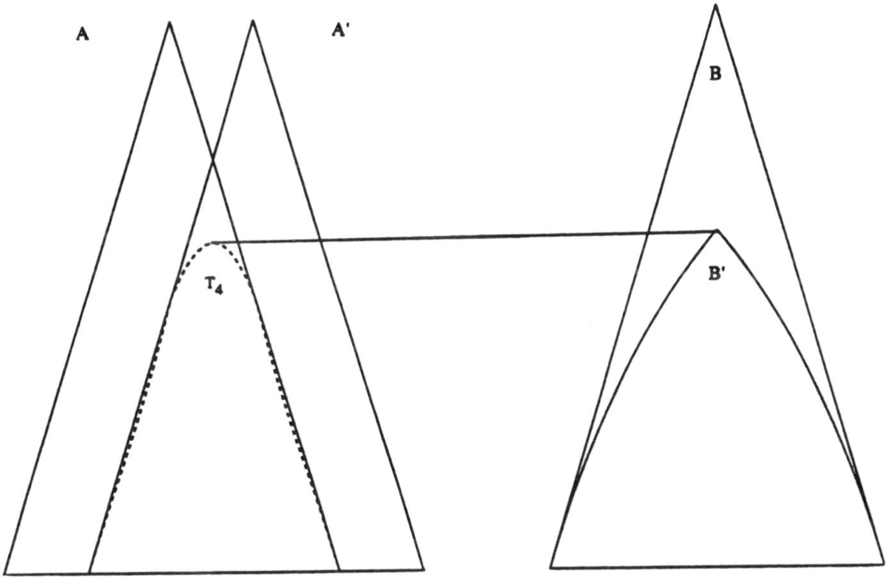

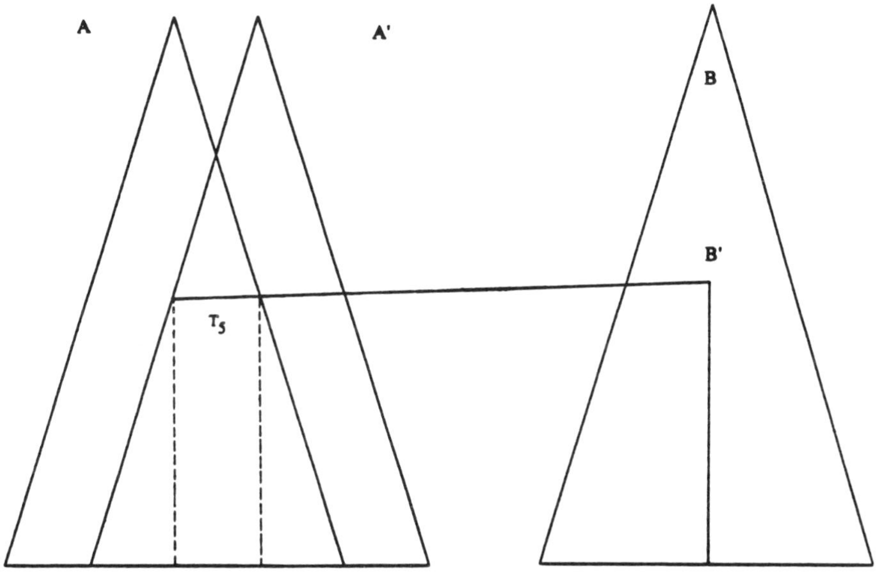

Figure 3 Fuzzy Inference Methods (continued)

Conditional Logic in Expert Systems
I.R. Goodman, M.M. Gupta, H.T. Nguyen and G.S. Rogers (editors)

IMPLICATION AND MODUS PONENS IN FUZZY LOGIC.

Philippe SMETS[1].
I.R.I.D.I.A.
Université Libre de Bruxelles
50 av Roosevelt, CP 194-6, 1050 Brussels, Belgium.

SUMMARY: A study of the representation of the implication in fuzzy logic: its meaning, its quantification and its use to define the meaning of a partly true proposition. Followed by a study of the modus ponens when propositions admit only partial degrees of necessity, possibility or truth.

1. Introduction.

This paper focuses on two related topics in fuzzy logic: the representation of the implication (conditional) and the modus ponens.

The first part focuses on 1) the meaning of the material implication (conditional) A→B (read "A implies B"), 2), the value of its truth status given the truth status of its components, and 3), the practical use of the conditionals to define the degree of truth of a fuzzy proposition and the degree of membership of the elements in a fuzzy set.

The second part focuses on the practical use of conditionals in approximate reasoning. The fuzzy modus ponens is defined when propositions admit only partial degrees of necessity or possibility or truth.

Part of this paper is based on the material published in Smets and Magrez (1987 for section 2 and 3, 1988 for section 4), Magrez (1985) and Magrez and Smets (1989a for section 5 to 8, 1989b for section 9).

1 The following text presents some research results of the Belgian National incentive-programme for fundamental research in artificial intelligence initiated by the Belgian State, Prime Minister's Office, Science Policy Programming. Scientific responsibility is assumed by the author. Research work has been partly supported by the ARCHON and DRUMS projects which are funded by grants from the Commission of the European Communities under the ESPRIT II-Program, P-2256 and Basic Research Project 3085.

Fuzzy logic is usually characterized by 2 components: the truth domain is the whole [0,1] interval, and the truth value can be a fuzzy subset of [0,1] (Mamdani and Gaines 1981, Turner 1984, Zadeh 1977). Only the first characteristic is considered here, reducing fuzzy logic to its multi-valued logic component.

In section 2, the semantic of the implication operator → is discussed. A definition of the meaning of the material implication is proposed when its components are fuzzy propositions. The implication considered is Russell's material implication or Reichenbach's adjunctive implication. The basic interpretation of the implication is that the formula 'A→B' is true when B is as true as A, and false when B is false and A is true. The full interpretation is that *the degree of truth of A→B quantifies to what extend B is at least as true as A.*

In section 3, the negation unary-operator ¬ and the implication binary-operator → and their axioms are introduced. The meaning of ¬P generalizes the classical interpretation 'P is false', and not 'P is refutable' or 'P is absurd' as in the Minimal Logic or the Intuitionistic Logic. (Grize, 1967, pg 210). We require that ¬¬P≡P whereas with the meanings 'P is refutable' or 'P is absurd' one has only P→¬¬P and ¬P→¬¬¬P but not ¬¬P→P.

Then, the mathematical representation of the material implication is deduced from the set of reasonable axioms for the ¬ and → operators presented e.g. in Weber (1983) and Trillas and Valverde (1985a). It is shown that:

1) there is a canonical scale on which the partial degree of truth of a proposition can be measured;
2) on that canonical scale, the truth of A→B reduces to the Lukasiewicz formula, i.e. truth(A→B) = 1 - truth(A) + truth(B);
3) the truth of ¬A satisfies the classical formula, i.e. truth(¬A) = 1 - truth(A).

The canonical scale and the implication representation can provide a meaning to the .7 value in the assertion 'the truth of P is .7' where P is some fuzzy proposition. Thanks to ideas introduced in Gaines (1976), a reference scale can be set up on which the truth of any fuzzy proposition can be constructed. This scale provides a tool to measure the degree of truth of any fuzzy proposition as well as the degree of membership of an element in a fuzzy set. (see section 4)

In the second part of this paper, we study the use of the conditionals in approximate reasoning. In common sense reasoning, two types of ignorance can be distinguished that lead to the use of different mathematical models. First, when information is certain but imprecise, one can use modalities (necessity and possibility) and multiple-valued truth. Second, when information is uncertain in that it conveys the idea that something may occur, that it is probable, that we can believe in it, ..., one can use classical theories of uncertainty such as probability theory, Shafer's theory of evidence (Shafer 1976, Smets 1988) and Sugeno's measures.

The first type of ignorance is qualified as an epistemic ignorance as it deals with the determination of the truth status of some proposition, given other propositions known to be true, even though they may be imprecise. Epistemic ignorance corresponds to the conformity obtained by a semantic matching between the meaning of a proposition and the reality as it is known. Imprecision - whether or not the result of vagueness - induces epistemic ignorance. When the truth status of a proposition is binary, either true or false, epistemic ignorance reduces itself to that part of classical logic in which one tries to deduce the truth status of a proposition given a set of true propositions, and to classical modal logic in which one tries to evaluate the necessity or the possibility of a proposition. The present paper generalizes this approach when it is accepted that the truth status, the necessity, and the possibility of propositions can admit degrees and can be defined on a bounded ordered interval like [0,1]. Partial truth is admitted and is essentially related to the use of vague predicates.

Example 1.1 A proposition such as 'Paul is young' will be qualified as true if we know that Paul's age is 15, but only possible if we know that Paul's age belongs to the interval 7 to 77 years of age.

The second type of ignorance is related to the uncertainty present in our opinion, our judgment about the truth status of a proposition. It fits the concepts of probability, credibility, plausibility, etc. When one speaks about the probability (credibility, plausibility, etc) of a proposition, one means the probability (credibility, plausibility, etc) that the truth status of the proposition is true. The probability (credibility, plausibility, etc) concerns our knowledge about the truth status of a proposition. It is part of a metalanguage constructed above the object language that deals with the propositions and their truth status. The object language may of course include some epistemic ignorance. But the probability (credibility, plausibility, etc) is build atop of the object language. Hence this type of ignorance is called supa-epistemic.

We will deal only with epistemic ignorance. We will find a link between the definition of imprecision in fuzzy set theory and the definition of ignorance in modal logic and multi-valued logic, a link which could bridge the gap between imprecision and epistemic ignorance in a general way. This link will be important in solving a variety of problems. For example, let an expert system reasoning process which contains the information: 'The truth that Paul is young is 0.8'. From this information, the expert system must be able to evaluate the truth of propositions like: 'Paul's age belongs to [25,35]', 'Paul is not very young' by some kind of approximate matching. The resolution of this problem will be possible once the initial proposition is transformed into a strictly true, but maybe fuzzier, proposition.

In section 5, we introduce the concepts of necessity and possibility. In section 6, we define a method for transforming a partly necessary (or possible) proposition into its parent proposition, i.e. a necessary, but possibly fuzzier and thus less precise, proposition. In other words, it becomes possible to remove any modal predicate and, therefore, to perform computations only in the imprecise environment. In section 7, we show that this transformation verifies the fundamental properties of necessity and possibility measures. In section 8, an interpretation of partial truth is proposed by reference to the two previous points. In the same way, we define how the partial truth predicate can be removed from a proposition to yield to a strictly true, but less precise, proposition. Classic properties of the truth measures are also shown to be satisfied.

Finally section 9 studies the fuzzy modus ponens, using the concepts of parent propositions.

2. The semantics of →.

The interpretation of the implication operator is hardly obvious. Intuition and common sense do not provide a clear answer. An interpretation is nevertheless required if the intention is to use this operator in Expert Systems to be able to deal with approximate reasonings and some non-standard logic. In classical binary logic, one can usually avoid the problem of the semantic of A→B as the Rule of Inference holds for all the interpretations of →. But as soon as an attempt is made to be a little more general, problems immediately appear. What is the meaning, for instance, in Probabilistic Logic (Reichenbach 1949) of the assertion 'the probability that A implies B is p'? Does it mean that $A \rightarrow (P_A(B)=p)$ with $P_A(B) = P(A\&B)/P(B)$ (conditional probability) or that $P(\neg A.OR.B) = p$ (probability of a conditional) (Lewis 1976).

For each truth-functional propositional operator, an adjunctive and a connective interpretation can be defined (Reichenbach, 1947, page 27 et seq.). Let * be any truth-functional propositional operator and consider the compound statement A*B. The adjunctive use of * corresponds to the evaluation of the truth status of the compound statement A*B given the truth status of its elementary propositions A and B. The connective use of * corresponds to the evaluation of the truth status of the elementary propositions A and B compatible with the truth status of the compound statement A*B.

Negation is mostly adjunctive. Knowing the truth status of A, the truth status of ¬A can be deduced. The equivalence and the exclusive OR are used mostly in the connective sense. Knowing A≡B is true, it can be deduced that either both A and B are true or both are false. Knowing A.OR.B is true, it can be deduced that either A or B is true, but not both. The inclusive OR is used in both interpretations. The AND is used mostly in the adjunctive interpretation. Knowing the truth status of A and of B, the truth status of A.AND.B can be deduced.

In conversational language, implication is usually used in its connective sense within an inference procedure. Knowing the truth status of A→B, what can be said about the truth status of A and of B, in particular when the truth status of A is known as in the Modus Ponens? The implication operator is used in sections 2 to 4 with its adjunctive (or extensional) interpretation: what is the truth status of A→B given the truth status of A and of B? The implication in its connective sense corresponds to Lewis's strict implication (it binds as a matter of necessity the consequent B to the antecedent A), whereas in its adjunctive sense it corresponds to Russell's material implication (it is a simple assertoric junction between two propositions A and B). The material implication "A implies B" means that in fact one does not simultaneously have A true and B false.The strict implication "A (strictly) implies B" means that one may not simultaneously have A true and B false, therefore if A is true, B is necessarily true (Blanché 1968, p. 88).

For any proposition A and B, the implication operator → in the formula A→B relates an antecedent A to a consequent B. The syntax of → within fuzzy logic has been widely studied (Baldwin and Pilsworth 1980, Bandler and Kohout 1980, Domingo, Trillas and Valverde 1981, Dubois and Prade 1980,1984, Mizumoto and Zimmermann 1982, Trillas and Valverde 1985a, Valverde 1982, Weber 1983). A semantic interpretation of → is required in order to choose an appropriate mathematical model for its representation. In Boolean Logic (BL), in Quantum Logic (QL) and in Intuitionistic Logic (IL), A→B is interpreted as being, respectively, equivalent to ¬A.OR.B (BL), equivalent to ¬A.OR.(A.AND.B) (QL) or obtained by residuation (IL) i.e. the truth of A→B is the largest value in [0,1] such that its AND combination with the truth of A is less or equal to the truth of B (Dubois and Prade 1984, Trillas and Valverde 1985a). These equivalences of A→B with other formulae might be acceptable in binary logic, essentially because the three representations happen to be identical. But there is no need for the definition of the implication in multi-valued logic to mimic these formulae, especially as the three representations are not necessarily equivalent in this context.

In this paper, we suggest that the semantic interpretation of the material implication in 'A→B is true' is that the consequent B is at least as true as the antecedent A. *The degree of truth of A→B quantifies to what extend B is at least as true as A.* This degree of truth is not a binary variable that is 1 when B is truer than A, and 0 otherwise. It will indeed be 1 whenever B is truer than A, but when A is somehow a little truer than B, the degree by which B is at least as true as A is an intermediate value between 0 and 1, where the 0 will be reserved for the extreme case where A is strictly true and B is strictly false. This idea is similar to the concept of a measure by which a fuzzy set contains another fuzzy set (Bandler and Kohout, 1980). As for any definition, this particular one is hard to justify, except by considering its consequences and its power to resolve problems encountered with other definitions.

This interpretation of → is consistent with the definition of A→B in each binary logic (BL, QL or IL). But it somehow clarifies the difference between the adjunctive (in which one constructs the truth of $A \rightarrow B$ as is the case here) and connective implications (in which one derives the truth status of A and of B). Furthermore, it may help to avoid some confusion between different forms of implications. To say 'B is at least as true as A' does not require any idea of causality (Hicks (1979) argues that 'A causes B' is true if '$\neg A$ implies $\neg B$' is true) or of relevance between A and B (as in the entailment concept of Anderson and Belnap (1975)), two properties often implicitly assumed in the use of the implication in conversational language.

The suggested interpretation of $\rightarrow$ also clarifies the concept of false implication, even within the context of binary logic. '$\neg(A \rightarrow B)$' means here 'B is less true than A', and the rule that allows $\neg B$ to be infered from A and $\neg(A \rightarrow B)$ is easy to understand (A is true and B is less true than A, so B is false, since there are only two truth values in binary logic). When $\rightarrow$ is interpreted as an implication in its connective sense, the concept of a false 'implication' and the deduction above are hard to understand. Most of the problems related to the implication operator come, of course, from the absence of a clear intuitive meaning of the concept it represents. It is reflected by the more or less arbitrary way with which the case where $\neg A$ applies is handled in the truth table. Some may feel that 'not(A implies B)', 'A does not imply B' and 'A implies $\neg B$' are equivalent. Others may feel that the negation of 'A implies B' should be 'nothing' (one claims either $A \rightarrow B$ or nothing, as is the case in PROLOG language) and not a proposition like A.AND.$\neg$B. These difficulties do not exist with the suggested adjunctive interpretation of $A \rightarrow B$.

This adjunctive interpretation is unrelated to the rule of modus ponens in which the truth of $A \rightarrow B$ is given as with the connective implications. Care should be taken here to restrict the meaning of the formula $A \rightarrow B$ merely to a proposition that can have a truth status. The modus ponens is the rule of inference by which one can assert that proposition B is true (to a certain degree) once proposition A is true (to a certain degree) *and* proposition $A \rightarrow B$ is true (to a certain degree) where the implication is used with its connective interpretation. The *and* is not the propositional operator AND encountered in propositions like A.AND.B. Furthermore, the truth of B derived from modus ponens is not necessarily a functional of the truth of A and of the truth of $A \rightarrow B$ (Magrez 1985), even if this truth-functionality is usually accepted (Trillas and Valverde 1985b). The rule of modus ponens is studied in section 9.

We distinguish between two forms of modus ponens. The difference is related to the position of the AND in the following two rules:

Meta-Level	*IF*			*THEN*	
Object-level		$A \rightarrow B$ AND A			B

Meta-Level	*IF*		*AND*		*THEN*	
Object-level		$A \rightarrow B$		A		B

In the first rule, the AND and the $\rightarrow$ operator are related because $A\rightarrow B \equiv \neg(A \text{ AND } \neg B)$. In the second rule, such a constraint is absent. The real modus ponens is the second rule. This is the only one we shall consider in this paper.

3. Implication and negation operators.

3.1. Implication.

Let $v(A)$ be the truth value of proposition A. Let $A\rightarrow B$ denote the "material implication", with A being the antecedent and B the consequent. We use the word 'proposition' for 'elementary proposition' and for a 'formula' obtained from propositions by some propositional operators.

In bi-valued logic, $v(A)\in\{\text{True}, \text{False}\}$. For the material implication, one has $v(A\rightarrow B)$ = False if $v(A)$ = True and $v(B)$ = False, and $v(A\rightarrow B)$ = True otherwise. It corresponds in essence to the idea that the implication is true whenever the consequent is at least as true as the antecedent (and True is at least as true as both True and False, and False is only as true as False).

In multi-valued logic, $v:\Pi\rightarrow\Delta$ is a mapping from the set Π of propositions to the truth domain Δ where Δ is a linear bounded set of cardinality $\aleph_1$ with maximal element True, minimal element False and the order relation "at least as true as" symbolized by $\geq$. Let $T\in\Pi$ be the tautology and $F\in\Pi$ be the contradiction with $v(T)$=True and $v(F)$=False. So for all $A,B\in\Pi$, one has $v(T)\geq v(A)\geq v(F)$ and $v(A)\geq v(B)$ or $v(B)\geq v(A)$. The operator = in $v(A)=v(B)$ means that both $v(A)\geq v(B)$ and $v(B)\geq v(A)$ hold.

For the material implication, $v(A\rightarrow B)$=True when $v(B)\geq v(A)$ and $v(A\rightarrow B)$=False when $v(B)$=False and $v(A)$=True. The cases not covered by these conditions are handled variously depending on the axioms added to the system. A classical postulate is the Lukasiewicz definition that we will be studied at length in this paper, but other formulae have been suggested (Dubois and Prade 1984)

As Δ is a bounded ordered set, there exists a strictly increasing relation w between Δ and the unit interval [0,1] such that: 1) $w\circ v(T)=1$; 2) $w\circ v(F)=0$; 3) $v(A)\geq v(B)$ is equivalent to $w\circ v(A)\geq w\circ v(B)$. To be strictly correct, the same symbol $\geq$ should not have been used for the order relation on Δ and the 'larger or equal' relation on [0,1], but the appropriate interpretation will be clear from the context. To simplify the notation, we define the function $v:\Pi\rightarrow[0,1]$ where v is $w\circ v$. In fuzzy logic, the whole unit interval is classically used as the domain of the truth value. The choice of such a domain is arbitrary but convenient. As there is no loss of generality, its adoption cannot be criticized. Furthermore we shall call $v(A)$ the truth value of A, thereby shortcutting the real statement that v(A) is the value obtained by the transformation on [0,1] of the truth value of A, the latter being defined in reality on Δ.

The meta-operator ≡ in A≡B means that the 2 propositions A and B are equivalent, in which case their truth values are equal: A≡B implies that v(A)=v(B) and v(A)=v(B).

3.2. Negation.

Let Π be the set of propositions with the tautology T and the contradiction F. Let $v : \Pi \rightarrow [0,1]$ with v(F)=0 and v(T)=1. For all A∈Π, v(A) is the truth value of A.

Let Π be such that for all A∈Π, there exists a negation ¬A∈Π. One postulates that the negation ¬A of a proposition A is a strong negation (Trillas 1979), i.e. it obeys the following axioms:

N1: v(¬A) is a function of v(A)
N2: v(¬A) > v(¬B) iff v(A) < v(B)
N3: ¬¬A ≡ A
N4: ¬T ≡ F

These axioms are those of all classical negations.

Given these axioms, there exists a strictly decreasing function $n : [0,1] \rightarrow [0,1]$ such that v(¬A) = n(v(A)), n(0)=1, n(1)=0, n(n(a))=a. If one further postulates that n is continuous, then n is a strong negation function.

Trillas (1979) has shown that for any strong negation function n, there exists a continuous strictly increasing function $t:[0,1] \rightarrow [0,\infty)$ such that t(0)=0, $t(1)<\infty$ and $n(a)=t^{-1}(t(1)-t(a))$. The often used negation function n(a)=1-a corresponds to t(a)=a.

To avoid cumbersome parenthesis, we use the notations nv(A) for n(v(A)) and na for n(a), the letter n being only used as the symbol for the strong negation function.

3.3. The Implication Axioms.

The following axioms are postulated for the implication operator →:

A1: v(A→B) depends only on v(A) and v(B)	truth-functionality
A2: v(A→B) = v(¬B→¬A)	contrapositive symmetry
A3: v(A→(B→C)) = v(B→(A→C))	exchange principle
A4: v(A→B) ≥ v(C→D) if v(A) ≤ v(C) and/or v(B) ≥ v(D)	monotonicity

A5: $v(A \to B) = 1$ iff $v(A) \le v(B)$ boundary condition
A6: $v(T \to A) = v(A)$ neutrality principle
A7: $v(A \to B)$ is continuous in its arguments continuity

This set of axioms are the properties considered in Trillas and Valverde (1985a) that lead to the pseudo-Lukasiewicz formula for the $\to$ operator. The following discussion includes an informal presentation of their meaning and consequences.

The truth-functionality axiom A1 is usually the least criticized axiom, more because without it hardly anything could be formalized than because it is natural. It implies that $v(A \to B)$ can be represented by a function of $v(A)$ and $v(B)$. To simplify notation, let $a=v(A)$, $b=v(B)$, $na=v(\neg A)$. Then A1 implies that $v(A \to B)=g(na,b)$ where $g:[0,1]x[0,1] \to [0,1]$. The use of na instead of a in the arguments of g simplifies later discussion: so defined g will be symmetrical.

The contrapositive symmetry axiom A2 mimics the interrelation postulated between the modus ponens and the modus tollens. It means that if A is less true than B than $\neg A$ is more true than $\neg B$ in agreement with N2, but also that the degree by which B is at least as true as A is equal to the degree by which $\neg A$ is at least as true as $\neg B$ when $v(A)>v(B)$. It implies that $g(na,b)=g(nnb,na)= g(b,na)$ as the negation is involutive. Therefore g is a symmetrical function.

The exchange principle A3 corresponds to the argument: 'if A then (if B then C)' is equivalent to 'if A&B then C' where the & is a symmetrical truth functional conjunction. Axiom A3 is used instead of some axioms based on the & operator, as otherwise it would have been necessary to define &. Axiom A3 implies that $g(na,g(nb,c))=g(nb,g(na,c))$; therefore g is associative.

The monotonicity axiom A4 is based on the idea that if the truth of the antecedent decreases and/or the truth of the consequent increases, then the truth of the implication does not decrease as the implication is essentially a measure of the fact that the consequent is truer than the antecedent. Axiom A4 implies that $g(a,b)$ is non decreasing in its arguments.

The boundary condition A5 claims that the implication is true iff the consequent is at least as true as the antecedent. It implies $g(na,b)=1$ iff $a \le b$. The if part corresponds to the fundamental property of the material implication as described in multi-valued logic (see section 2). The only if part rejects cases where an antecedent A somehow truer than a consequent B could nevertheless imply B strictly (i.e. with a truth value T). With the interpretation of $v(A \to B)$ as the degree by which B is at least as true as A, it seems natural to claim that this degree should be less than 1 whenever A is truer than B. The identity principle $v(A \to A)=1$ is a particular case of axiom A5 that covers the if part but not the only if part. The latter is necessary to prove that the implication and the negation share the same generator (see theorem 3.2).

The neutrality axiom A6 says that the degree by which the tautology implies A is nothing but the degree of truth of A. As n(1)=0, it implies g(0,a)=a. Given the contrapositive symmetry axiom A2, one has v(A→F)=v(¬A). One has also g(0,0)=0, thus the second case covered by the rule for material implication in multi-valued logic need not be explicitly postulated.

The continuity axiom A7 is justified by the fact that discontinuity seems unnatural. A small variation in the truth of an element of the implication should not lead to a large variation in the truth of the implication.

From axioms A1 to A7, it is deduced that g is a continuous Archimedian nilpotent S-conorm with g(a,b)=1 if na≤b (Theorems 3.1 and 3.2). Definitions and properties of the T-norms and S-conorms are given in appendix. Proofs of theorems 3.1 to 3.6 can be found in Smets and Magrez (1987).

Theorem 3.1: *Given A1 to A7, the function g:[0,1]x[0,1]→[0,1] that quantifies the truth value of the implication A→B is a continuous Archimedian S-conorm with g(na,b)=1 if a≤b.*

As g is an Archimedian continuous S-conorm, there exists an additive generator f of g with f a continuous strictly increasing function f:[0,1]→[0,∞] and $g(a,b) = f^{-}(f(a)+f(b))$ where f^{-} is the generalized inverse of f.

Theorem 3.2: *Under the conditions of theorem 3.1, the generator t of the strong negation n and the generator f of g are equal (up to a proportionality factor).*

This theorem implies that the g and n functions share the same generator. The negation being strong, t(0)=0 and t(1)<∞, therefore f(0)=0 and f(1)<∞ and g is thus nilpotent. Under those conditions,

$$na = f^{-1}(\ f(1) - f(a)\ ).$$

and

$$g(na,b) = f^{-1}(\ \{f(1) - f(a) + f(b)\} \wedge f(1)\ )$$

It might be argued that the set of axioms have been selected on an ad hoc basis in order to derive Lukasiewicz's operator so why not postulate Lukasiewicz's operator directly. We feel that this piecemeal axiomatic approach is useful in that it clarifies the requirements that lead to Lukasiewicz's operator. Their value can only be judged by examining their naturalness - a highly subjective criteria, of course. We feel that these axioms are sufficiently convincing to justify their acceptance. This approach also has the advantage that if one tries to use another operator for the →, at least one of the axioms will be unsatisfied. The knowledge of which axiom is rejected might lead to a re-examination of the foundations of the proposed operator and its appropriateness.

3.4. Further properties.

Theorem 3.3: *The transitivity of the implication is true:*

$$v((A \to B) \to ((B \to C) \to (A \to C))) = 1.$$

Theorem 3.4: $v(A \to (B \to A)) = 1$.

Such a theorem is usually considered paradoxical as it seems to mean that a true proposition is implied by any proposition. The paradox comes from the confusion between the adjunctive and the connective interpretations of the implication. The paradox disappears once the truth of an implication is interpreted in its adjunctive sense i.e. as a measure of the truth that 'the consequent is as true as the antecedent'. Theorem 3.4 only reflects that $v(B \to A) \geq v(A)$, a true property.

Theorem 3.5: $v((A \to (B \to C)) \to ((A \to B) \to (A \to C))) = 1$.

Theorem 3.6: $v((A \to B) \to B) = v((B \to A) \to A)$.

3.5. Canonical Scale.

Axioms A1 to A7 for the material implication operator have led to derivation of a pseudo-Lukasiewicz operator to be derived, i.e. there exists an arbitrary strictly monotone continuous transformation of the truth value of the propositions such that the $\to$ operator obeys the Lukasiewicz rule of implication.

Let $a = v(A)$ and $b = v(B)$. It has been proved that the implication and the negation operators can be generated by any member of the set of the bounded continuous monotone increasing functions $f:[0,1] \to [0,\infty)$ with $f(0) = 0$ and $f(1) < \infty$, such that

$$v(A \to B) = f^{-1}(\ \{f(1) - f(a) + f(b)\} \wedge f(1)\ )$$

and

$$v(\neg A) = f^{-1}(\ f(1) - f(a)\ ).$$

This f generator is defined up to a strictly monotone transformation. As the truth scale v(A) is also defined up to a strictly increasing monotone transformation, one can create a canonical scale for the truth value v(A) of a proposition such that $f(v(T)) = f(1) = 1$ and $f(v(A)) = f(a) = a$. In that case, one derives the Lukasiewicz operator for the material implication operator $v(A \to B) = (1 - v(A) + v(B)) \wedge 1$ and the classical negation operator $v(\neg A) = 1 - v(A)$.

In summary, we have successively considered that:

1: the truth domain is a bounded ordered set;

2: the implication $A \to B$ is a formula for which the degree of truth is equal to the degree by which B is at least as true as A;

3: the negation is represented by a strong negation;
4: axioms A1 to A7 for $\rightarrow$ imply that the truth of $A \rightarrow B$ is represented by a pseudo-Lukasiewicz function;
5: due to the arbitrariness of the numerical scale used to represent the truth value of a proposition, one can select a canonical scale such that the negation is represented by the classical 1-. operator and the $\rightarrow$ by the Lukasiewicz operator.

4. A reference scale for the truth value.

Fuzzy sets are sets such that for each element one can define its degree of membership μ in the set where $\mu \in [0,1]$. Fuzzy propositions are propositions that admit a degree of truth v where $v \in [0,1]$. Fuzzy sets and fuzzy propositions share the same relation as sets and and propositions. The relation between the two concepts degree of truth and degree of membership is given by the postulate that the degree of membership $\mu_A(x)$ of an element x in a fuzzy set A is numerically equal to the degree of truth v(x is A') that the fuzzy predicate A' describing the fuzzy set A applies to the element x.

$$\mu_A(x) = a \equiv v(x \text{ is } A') = a$$

For instance if A is the fuzzy set of tall man, the degree of membership μ_A(John) of John in the set A is numerically equal to the degree of truth of the proposition 'John is tall'.

What has been shown in section 3 is that once x and y are given with $\mu_A(x) = a$, $\mu_B(y) = b$, then $\mu_{\neg A}(x) = 1\text{-}a$ and $\mu_{A \rightarrow B}(x,y) = 1\text{-}a\text{-}b$, or equivalently with $v(x \in A') = a$, $v(y \in B') = b$, then $v(x \in \neg A') = 1\text{-}a$ and $v((x,y) \in A' \rightarrow B') = 1\text{-}a\text{-}b$.

In order to construct a logic with a multi-valued truth domain, a meaning has to be provided for each value in the domain, i.e. one must provide a set of propositions whose truth values are uniquely defined on the truth domain. Any new propositions would then be compared with those reference propositions and their truth is evaluated through comparison. This approach is identical to the one used by subjective probabilists who define the subjective probability of a proposition as p if one were indifferent to betting on the truth of the proposition or the fact that a ball randomly selected from an urn with a proportion p of white balls could be white. *The meaning of a subjective scale is in its measure.*

The canonical scale proposed in section 3 is convenient but does not explain what is meant by a truth value of .35. It means more than simply that it is between .34 and .36. A proposition must be formulated for which the .35 applies effectively and this must be done for each value in [0,1]. The existence of such reference propositions will provide a "meaning" to fuzzy logic. It resolves one of the usual criticisms of fuzzy logic, i.e. that it is only an intellectual game without "meaning".

In this section, a reference scale is constructed on which it will be possible to define the meaning of any truth value in [0,1]. This tool is constructed from ideas developed in Gaines (1976).

1. Let $A \equiv$ "Paul is tall" and $\neg A \equiv$ "Paul is not tall". The truth of A and of $\neg A$ depend on the height h of Paul. If h=110 cm, A is false and $\neg A$ is true. If h=190 cm, A is true and $\neg A$ is false (see table 1). Thus when h increases continuously from 110 to 190, a=v(A) increases continuously from 0=v(F) to 1=v(T) and na=v($\neg$A) decreases continuously from 1 to 0. There exists thus a value h' such that a=na. In such a case, $\neg A \rightarrow A$ is true; therefore $v(\neg A \rightarrow A)=1$ becomes $f^{-1}(f(1)-f(na)+f(a))=1$.

As $f(na) = f \circ f^{-1}(f(1)-f(a))=f(1)-f(a)$, one has

$$f^{-1}(2f(a))=1, \text{ thus } 2f(a)=f(1).$$

As $f(1)<\infty$, it is possible to use an f scale such that f(1)=1, in which case f(a)=0.5. (This result would have been directly obtained by considering the strong negation and the canonical scale as a=na is identical to a=1-a; thus a=.5. The lengthy justification is used to show its generality) .

2. Let $B \equiv$ "John is tall" and $\neg B \equiv$ "John is not tall". The truth of B and of $\neg B$ depend on the height k of John. Let us further postulate that $k \leq h'$, thus $b=v(B) \leq .5$. Consider then the proposition $\neg B \rightarrow B$ i.e. 'B is at least as true as $\neg$B'. Its truth value $c=v(\neg B \rightarrow B)$ depends on k. If k=h', c=1 as $v(B)=v(\neg B)$. If k=110 cm, B is false and $\neg B$ is true, therefore c=0. By increasing k from 110 cm to h', c increases from 0 to 1. There exists thus a k' such that $v(\neg B \rightarrow B)=v(A)$. In such a case, the relation $c=v(\neg B \rightarrow B) =v(A)=0.5$ implies f(1)-f(nb)+f(b) = 2f(b) = f(a) =.5, thus f(b)=.25.

3. Let P_0 › A, P_1 › B, h_0 = h', h_1 = k'. The procedure is iterated with propositions P_i › "X_i is tall" such that $v(\neg P_i \rightarrow P_i) = v(P_{i-1})$, i=1,2... and $v(P_i)<v(P_{i-1})$. The values of the heights h_i of X_i are derived as above. For such h_i and with $p_i=v(P_i)$, one obtains $f(p_i)=2^{-i-1}$.

height	110	k'	h'	190
v(A)	0		.5	1
v($\neg$A)	1		.5	0
v(B)	0	.25	.5	1
v($\neg$B)	1	.75	.5	1
v($\neg B \rightarrow B$)	0	.5	1	1

Table 1: Heights and truth values of A : "Paul is tall" and B : "John is tall".

4. As f(na)=f(1)-f(a), one obtains $f(np_i)=1-2^{-i-1}$.

5. Other values of f can be obtained from expressions based on the truth of $\neg P_i \rightarrow P_j$, as it corresponds to $f(p_i)+f(p_j)=2^{-i-1}+2^{-j-1}$.

6. Further values are obtained from expressions like $((\neg P_i \rightarrow P_j) \rightarrow P_k) \rightarrow P_l$ whose truth value is $f(p_i)+f(p_j)+f(p_k)+f(p_l)$ etc...

Appropriate sequences of implications based on propositions P_i can be constructed in order to obtain any f value. For instance let us construct the sequence to obtain f=0.65625. As 0.65625=0.50+0.125+0.03125, $0.65625=f(p_0)+f(p_2)+f(p_4)$, it corresponds to the truth value of the implication $(\neg P_0 \rightarrow P_2) \rightarrow P_4$ with P_i : "X_i is tall" and the height of X_i is h_i. Thus 0.65625 is the degree of truth of the proposition 'P_4 is at least as true as not "P_2 is at least as true as $\neg P_0$" ', or 'P_4 is at least as true as "P_2 is less true than $\neg P_0$" '.

The f function having be defined up to any strictly monotone transformation such that f(0)=0 and f(1)=1, one can state without loss of generality that f(x)=x, using thus the canonical scale of section 3.5. This solution is the most convenient from a computational point of view. Therefore $v(P_i)=2^{-i-1}$ and all other truth values can be equated to some sequence of implication based on propositions P_i. One has derived a reference scale for the truth value of any proposition Q by the use of the relation "Q is as true as P" where P is a sequence of implications based on propositions P_i. Thus P and Q share the same numerical truth value.

Any other scale could have been used for the truth value of a proposition as f was defined only up to a strictly monotone continuous transformation. The truth of P_i should thus be $f'(2^{-i-1})$. Computationally this would be a useless and cumbersome scale, as one should always go through the f' and f^{-1} transformations, and since there is no natural value for the truth value of P_i, the choice of f(x)=x seems best.

We have thus constructed a set of propositions for whose truth value is uniquely defined. We can give a meaning to the .7 in the statement "the truth value of A is 0.7". As has already been mentioned, what is said about fuzzy propositions applies directly to the degree of membership of an element in a fuzzy set. So our tool can also be used to define a reference scale for the degree of membership in fuzzy sets theory.

The reference scale is strictly personal as it is based on the determination of some height h such that for instance the 2 propositions "Paul is tall" and "Paul is not tall" are identically true. That h value is personal, and corresponds to our personal interpretation of the word "tall". One should not hope for some absolute, supra-human meaning of the word "tall" independent from the individuals; this would be an unrealistic requirement, if not a deleterious one as it would destroy every individualism and individual freedom.

We have constructed our reference scale on the word "tall" but it is obvious that we could use any other word whose meaning is based on some unidimensional continuous variable like weight (the box is heavy), money (IFSA is a wealthy association), temperature (this bath is hot), thickness (Fuzzy Sets and Systems is a thick journal), age (Mary is young)...

The operationality of the reference scale is not obvious. The suggested tool of measurement can indeed hardly be used in practice. This should not be taken as a criticism. A reference scale is required in order to define what is meant by the truth value of a proposition. It is not essential that such a scale could be used in practice. That such a tool could be used would be convenient but is not essential. The same difficulties were encountered for the evaluation of subjective probabilities. The exchangeable bet schema turned out to be hardly operational in evaluating someone's subjective probabilities. In order to use that schema, people have to be well trained in interpreting chances and probabilities, and even then the method is disappointing. These same difficulties will be encountered if one tries to apply our schema to assess the degree of truth of a proposition. One should first be trained to understand what is meant by a material implication i.e. by a rule that says that a fuzzy proposition is at least as true as another fuzzy proposition. This is not an obvious and easy task . Disappointments can be expected as a result of the weakness or imprecision of the method, if not its apparent incoherence.

5. Necessity and possibility.

Many propositions can be expressed under the form :' X is A' (Zadeh 1978, 1981a, 1981b), when the predicate 'A' restricts the possible values of the variable X in a universe of discourse Ω. This restriction is somehow related to the membership function of the subset of Ω represented by the meaning of 'A'. Let $\Pi(A|B)$ be the degree of possibility of a proposition A given the proposition B is true. Zadeh suggested that for any triple of propositions X, Y and Z, $\Pi(X \text{ Or } Y|Z) = \Pi(X|Z) \vee \Pi(Y|Z)$. Hence the definition of $\Pi(A|B)$ can be based on a possibility distribution $\pi_B(x)$ such that for all crisp A in Ω,

$$\Pi(A|B) = \sup_{x \in A} \pi_B(x) \qquad (5.1)$$

Its generalization for fuzzy subsets A on Ω is:

$$\Pi(A|B) = \sup_{x \in \Omega} T(\pi_B(x), \mu_A(x)) \qquad (5.2)$$

where T is a T-norm (usually one chooses the minimum operator, but the natural requirement that $\Pi(A|A) = 1$ leads to the selection of the T_∞ T-norm: see appendix).

Zadeh also suggested that the possibility distribution $\pi_B(x)$ that corresponds to the possibility $\Pi(x|B)$ of x in context B is numerically equal to the grade of membership of x to the set characterized by B:

$$\forall x \in \Omega \quad \pi_B(x) = \alpha \equiv \mu_B(x) = \alpha.$$

In section 4, we already suggested $\mu_A(x) = v(x \in A)$. One arrive at the following equalities:

$$\mu_{TALL}(h) = v(TALL|h) = \Pi(h|TALL)$$

where each term is read:

$\mu_{TALL}(h)$ = the degree of membership of somebody whose height is h in the set of tall men
$v(TALL|h)$ = the truth that somebody whose height is h is a tall man

$\Pi(h \mid TALL)$ = the possibility that the height of somebody is h given he is tall ($= \pi_{TALL}(h)$)
To avoid confusion, it must be underlined that in μ and ν, h is known precisely and with certainty, and the ambiguity lies in the meaning to be given to the word TALL. Instead in Π, TALL is known as true, and one evaluates the strength with which each h value satisfies the premiss TALL. If one tries to generalize these concepts by replacing h by some subset X of Ω (like X = [160, 170]) the possibility $\Pi(X|TALL)$ of X given TALL can be defined. But expressions like $\nu(TALL|X)$ and $\mu_{TALL}(X)$ are ill-defined. One knows the truth that somebody with height h is TALL, but what about somebody whose height is anything between 160 and 170. All that can be done in such a case is to consider that

$$\nu(TALL|X) = \{\nu(TALL|h) : h \in X\}$$

and to introduce the concepts of upper and lower truths:

$$\nu^*(TALL|X) = \sup_{h \in X} \nu(TALL|h)$$
$$\nu_*(TALL|X) = \inf_{h \in X} \nu(TALL|h)$$

The generalization with fuzzy X is:

$$\nu^*(TALL|X) = \sup_{h \in \Omega} T\,(\nu(TALL|h)\,,\,\mu_X(h)\,)$$
$$\nu_*(TALL|X) = \inf_{h \in \Omega} S\,(\nu(TALL|h)\,,\,1-\mu_X(h)\,)$$

where T is a T-norm and S its related co-norm.

As in modal logic, there is a dual relationship between necessity and possibility: the necessity is the complement of the possibility of the complement. Let N(A|B) be the degree of necessity that 'X is A' is true given that the proposition 'X is B' is true. The duality implies the following definition:

$$N(A|B) = 1 - \Pi(\neg A|B) \qquad (5.3)$$

Definition 5.2 Let A and B two predicates defined on an universe Ω. Knowing that 'X is B' is true, the necessity that the proposition 'X is A' is true, N(A|B), is given by:

$$\Pi(A|B) = \mathrm{Sup}_{x \in \Omega}\ T\,(\mu_A\,(x), \pi_B\,(x)) = \mathrm{Sup}_{x \in \Omega}\ T\,(\pi_A\,(x), \pi_B\,(x)) \qquad (5.4)$$

$$N(A|B) = \mathrm{Inf}_{x \in \Omega}\ S\,(\mu_A\,(x), 1-\pi_B\,(x)) = \mathrm{Inf}_{x \in \Omega}\ S\,(\pi_A\,(x), 1-\pi_B\,(x)) \qquad (5.5)$$

where T is a T-norm and S is the corresponding S-conorm (see appendix). $\mu_A\,(x)$ is the grade of membership of x to A and $\pi_B\,(x)$ is the possibility of x in the context B. Replacing μ by π reflects their interrelationship. To simplify the discussion, we use right hand side formalism.

6. Parent propositions.

We have defined how to compute the modalities (necessity N(A|B) and possibility $\Pi(A|B)$) of a proposition A from the knowledge of a strictly true proposition B. Now, the opposite must be considered: how to compute a proposition B strictly true from a proposition A qualified by a modality ? The problem is: given that N('X is A')=∂ (or that Π('X is A') = f) what is proposition B such as N('X is B') = Π('X is B') = 1.This kind of transformation will create a proposition B on which no uncertainty remains, a proposition B necessarily and possibly true, but possibly fuzzier than proposition A. This unknown proposition B will be called the *parent proposition.* (Such a problem has been alreday studied in Zadeh (1977), Sanchez (1978), Prade (1985), Dubois and Prade (1990).)

Definition 6.1. A parent proposition is a strictly true proposition induced by a set of propositions whose modalities are known, and from which these modalities would have been deduced if this parent proposition had been known initially.

Suppose proposition B is the parent proposition which was implied by proposition A such that N(A|B) = ∂. Suppose we want to compute the necessity of a proposition C on the basis of the partial information: 'there is a necessity ∂ that X is A':

$$N(C \mid N(A)=\partial) = ?$$

For example: what is the necessity that 'Paul's age is *young*' knowing that the necessity that 'Paul's age is around 25' equals .8 ? To do this, we should use the previous equation (5.5). But in that equation, the conditioning proposition B is strictly true, and not a partly necessarily true proposition. We have thus first to estimate such a strictly true, but unknown, B given that N(A) = ∂. Once we know B, then N(C|N(A)=∂) = N(C|N(A|B)=∂, N(B)=1) = N(C|B) and can be computed by (5.5).

6.1. Parent proposition based on a necessity measure.

From the information: 'the necessity of A equals ∂', two facts can be inferred:

1. The predicate A restricts the possible values of X, i.e. induces a possibility distribution $\pi_A(x)$ on Ω.
2. This distribution π_A may be partly necessary, as ∂ belongs to [0,1].

From equations 5.2 and 5.4, we have, for any B:

$$N(A|B) = 1-\Pi(\neg A|B) = 1 - \sup_{x \in \Omega} T(1-\pi_A(x), \pi_B(x)) \qquad (6.1)$$

where T is a T-norm.

We want a B such that N(A|B) = ∂. One obtains :

$$1 - \sup_{x \in \Omega} T(1-\pi_A(x), \pi_B(x)) = \partial$$

Thus
$$\sup_{x \in \Omega} T(1-\pi_A(x), \pi_B(x)) = 1-\partial \qquad (6.2)$$

The possibility distribution π_B must be such that the supremum of its intersection with the complement of the distribution π_A gives the scalar (1-∂). In general 6.1 does not yield to a unique solution for π_B, but to a family of acceptable distributions π_B. Let $\mathbb{B}$ be the family of acceptable predicates B such that π_B satisfies 6.1. $\mathbb{B}$ is a lattice with an order relation $\leq^*$. It is said that B $\leq^*$ B' if $\pi_B(x) \leq \pi_{B'}(x)$, $\forall x \in \Omega$. In that case, B' is not smaller than B, and reciprocally B is not larger than B'. The unique upper B* solution will be defined such that for all B $\in \mathbb{B}$, B $\leq^*$ B*.

Theorem 6.1 *The upper solution B* of (6.1) is given by:*

$$\pi_{B^*}(x) = Sup\ \{u: u \in [0, 1], T(1-\pi_A(x), u) \leq 1-\partial\} \qquad (6.3)$$

B* is the less specific, less informative solution because it least restricts the possible values on Ω.The degree of possibility of each singleton x defined by the predicate B* equals the greatest value u such that its conjunction (based on T) with 1-$\pi_A(x)$ remains less than or equal to 1-∂. In other words, B* corresponds to the largest predicate such that its conjunction with $\neg$A is always $\leq$ 1-∂.

For some classical T-norms, solutions are:

T = Min: $\quad \pi_{B^*}(x) = 1 \quad$, if $\pi_A(x) \geq \partial$ (6.4)
$\qquad = 1-\partial \quad$, if $\pi_A(x) < \partial$

T = Product: $\quad \pi_{B^*}(x) = [(1-\partial)/(1-\pi_A(x))] \wedge 1$ (6.5)
$\qquad = 1$, if $\pi_A(x)=1$

T = T_∞: $\quad \pi_{B^*}(x) = 1 \wedge [\pi_A(x) + 1-\partial] = \pi_A(x) \oplus (1-\partial)$ (6.6)

T = Tw: $\quad \pi_{B^*}(x) = 1-\partial \quad$, if $\pi_A(x)=0$ (6.7)
$\qquad = 1 \quad$, otherwise

The structure of B* depends on the T-norm used in 6.1. Whenever the proposition 'X is A' is in the knowledge base, the proposition is not only true, but necessarily true. It seems natural to further impose the requirement that if one focuses on the N(A), the inference engine should answer N(A) = 1. Therefore one needs N(A|A) = 1.

Axiom 6.1 . N(A|A) = 1 for all A.

Theorem 6.2. *The only continuous T-norm in the equation (6.1) verifying axiom 6.1 is the T_∞ T-norm (the $\oplus$ operator).*

Therefore by (6.6), one has $\quad \pi_{B^*}(x) = \pi_A(x) \oplus (1-\partial)$
which we shall also write as: $\quad B^* = A \oplus (1-\partial)$.

This estimation of B* is useful because it allows us to transform a partly uncertain proposition into a certain proposition - less specific of course. Moreover, one can now estimate the necessity (and the possibility) that a proposition is true given a partly uncertain proposition. Knowing that $N(A)=\partial$, we compute the largest B* such that $N(A|B^*)=\partial$. Then, we estimate $N(C|N(A)=\partial) = N(C|B^*) = f$, where $N(C|B^*)$ is computed by (5.5) with the S_∞-conorm. This ability to perform estimation of modalities from a knowledge base containing epistemically uncertain propositions is fundamental, especially for fuzzy expert systems whose working memory usually contains some partly necessary facts such as those inferred by fuzzy Modus Ponens.

6.2. Parent proposition induced by a possibility measure.

Sometimes, the proposition A is qualified by a possibility measure instead of a necessity measure. We would like to infer the parent proposition from the information $\Pi(A)=\partial$. The solution is straightforward thanks to the dual relation between the measures of necessity and possibility: $N(A) = 1-\Pi(\neg A)$. We only have to consider the solution for B induced by $N(\neg A)=1-\partial$.

Theorem 6.3. *The upper solution B* for the parent proposition obtained from the information '$\Pi(A)=\partial$' is given by:*

$$\pi_B^*(x) = 1 \wedge (1-\pi_A(x) + \partial) \qquad (6.8)$$

6.3. Parent proposition induced by a necessity and a possibility measure.

Suppose a proposition A qualified by a partial necessity and a partial possibility measure. We want to estimate the parent proposition B such that.

$$N(A|B) = \partial \text{ and } \Pi(A|B) = f, \ (\partial \leq f)$$

From the necessity requirement, one can compute the upper solution B_1^* and from the possibility requirement one can compute the upper solution B_2^*. One may postulate that, given both requirements, the general upper solution can be obtained by the conjunction of these two solutions. The conjunction will be performed by the use of the only idempotent T-norm, the minimum. Indeed, suppose that $B_1^* = B_2^*$; it seems natural to require that the conjunction should be equal to them.

Theorem 6.4. *The upper solution B* for the parent proposition obtained from the information '$N(A)=\partial$ and $\Pi(A)=f$' is given by:*

$$\forall x \in \Omega : \pi_B^*(x) = (\pi_A(x) + 1-\partial) \wedge (1-\pi_A(x) + f) \wedge 1 \qquad (6.9)$$

6.4. Necessity of a proposition given a partly necessary proposition.

In fuzzy modus ponens, we will need to compute the necessity of A given a proposition B whose necessity is ∂: $N(A|N(B)=\partial)$. Equation (6.1) does not apply, as it requires that B be strictly true (necessary, i.e. $\partial=1$). Nevertheless, the use of parent proposition permits the computation of the requested necessity. Given $N(B)=\partial$, one determines the parent proposition B' such that $N(B|B')=\partial$: $B'=B\oplus(1-\partial)$. One then computes $N(A|B')$ by (6.1) and axiom 6.1. B' is strictly necessary by construction. So

$$N(A|N(B)=\partial) = 1 - \sup\,(\neg A \otimes (B\oplus(1-\partial))\,) \qquad (6.10)$$

which is a convenient shorthand for

$$N(A|N(C)=\partial) = 1 - \sup_{x\in\Omega}\,(1-\pi_A(x)) \otimes (\pi_B(x) \oplus (1-\partial)\,)$$

7. Properties of necessity and possibilty measures.

This particular way of transforming an uncertain proposition into an imprecise proposition must keep the properties of the modalities intact. The fundamental property for necessity measures is:

$$N(P \,\&\, Q) = N(P) \wedge N(Q) \qquad (7.1)$$

where the & operator is represented by the minimum operator $\wedge$.

Let us first remember the definition of non-interactivity. Two variables X and Y which take their values on Ω_1 and Ω_2, respectively, and whose possibility distributions are π_X and π_Y, are said to be non-interactive if their joint possibility distribution $\pi_{X,Y}$ from $\Omega_1 x \Omega_2$ to [0,1] is defined by the Min operator:

$$\forall\, (x,y) \in \Omega_1 x \Omega_2 : \pi_{X,Y}(x,y) = \mathrm{Min}\,(\pi_X(x)\,,\, \pi_Y(y)) \qquad (7.2)$$

where π_X and π_Y are the marginal possibility distributions. As pointed by Zadeh (1975a, b, c), non-interactivity in possibility theory plays a role analogous to independence in probability theory.

Theorem 7.1. *Let X and Y be two non-interactive variables which take their values on Ω_1 and Ω_2, respectively. Let the two propositions P='X is P', and Q='Y is Q' have necessities: $N(P)=\partial$, $N(Q)=f$. Let P' and Q' be their corresponding parent propositions. Then, the necessity to have P&Q when we have P'&Q' equals the minimum of ∂ and f.*

$$N(P\&Q|P'\&Q') = \partial \wedge f \qquad (7.3)$$

This theorem (Prade 1982) means that:

$$N(P\&Q|P'\&Q') = N(P|P') \wedge N(Q|Q') \qquad (7.4)$$

Proof of theorem 7.1. $N(P\&Q|P'\&Q') = \mathrm{Inf}_{x,y}\,[\,(P\wedge Q) \oplus (\neg P' \vee \neg Q')]$
$= \mathrm{Inf}\{\, \mathrm{Inf}_{x,y}\,[P\oplus(\neg P'\vee\neg Q')]\,,\, \mathrm{Inf}_{x,y}\,[Q\oplus(\neg P'\vee\neg Q')]\,\}$.
$\mathrm{Inf}_{x,y}\,[P\oplus(\neg P'\vee\neg Q')]$ is obtained when P and $(\neg P'\vee\neg Q')$ are both minimal. The second

term is minimal when $\neg Q'$ is minimal, thus $Q' = 1$, which is achievable as Q' is normalized. Hence $\text{Inf}_{x,y}\ [P\oplus(\neg P'\vee\neg Q')] = \text{Inf}_x\ [P\oplus\neg P'] = N(P|P')$. The same holds for $\text{Inf}_{x,y}\ [Q\oplus(\neg P'\vee\neg Q')] = N(Q|Q')$. QED.

Similarly, we can prove that our transformation verifies the fundamental property of the possibility measures:

$$\Pi(P \text{ Or } Q) = \Pi(P) \vee \Pi(Q)$$

or equivalently:

$$\Pi(P \text{ Or } Q \mid P'\&Q') = \Pi(P|P') \vee \Pi(Q|Q')$$

Theorem 7.2 *Let X and Y be two non-interactive variables which take their values on Ω_1 and Ω_2, respectively. Let the two propositions P='X is P', and Q='Y is Q' have possibilities: $\Pi(P)=\partial$, $-\Pi(Q)=f$. Let P' and Q' be their corresponding parent propositions. Tten the necessity to have P Or Q when we have P'&Q' equals the maximum of ∂ and f.*

$$\Pi(P \text{ Or } Q|P'\&Q') = \partial \vee f$$

8. Multiple-valued truths.

The truth of a proposition may be understood as a measure of similarity between its meaning and what we know of the reality (Dubois and Prade 1982, Prade 1982). Since the conformity is not limited to a strict resemblance, or a strict dissemblance, some shades may appear. In these conditions, the truth value seems to be able to take different values between 0 and 1. Three-valued and multiple-valued logics are devoted to underlinying these concepts. But, whereas the axiomatics were well established, many problems emerged for the semantical interpretation of these partial truths (Rescher 1969). By using the concept of fuzzy sets (Zadeh 1965), and possibility (Zadeh 1981a), a very natural semantic interpolation can be suggested.

8.1 Semantic interpretation of partial truth.

We start with crisp predicate A for simplicity. Let v be a function from Ω to {0,1}, which estimates the degree of truth of an element of Ω where $v(A)=1$ means that proposition A is true, and $v(A)=0$ means that proposition A is false. Moreover, whenever A is true (in conformity to our knowledge base) we can say that A is necessarily and possibly true $\Pi(A)=1$ and $N(A)=1$. Reciprocally, if proposition A is false, we have $\Pi(A)=0$ and $N(A)=0$. A proposition is neutral when its truth-value is undetermined. We can say that its truth belongs to {0,1}: $v(A) \in \{0,1\}$. We have $\Pi(A) = 1$ and $\Pi(\neg A) = 1$, i.e. $N(A) = 0$. As seen, whenever the measure of possibility and necessity are equal, a single truth value is defined. On the contrary, an unique truth value can not be defined when modalities differ . A neutral proposition A only leads us to say that it is as possible that A is true as it is possible that A is false.

When propositions are fuzzy, Zadeh defines the truth value by the equality:

$$\mu_A(x) = v(x \in A) = v(A|x) \tag{8.1}$$

The degree of membership of a singleton x to the set A, $\mu_A(x)$ is numerically equal to the degree of truth of the proposition A at x. We can extend this definition by estimating the degree of truth of the proposition A, knowing that the proposition B is true. The information B does not necessarily induce an unique truth value for the proposition A. Nevertheless, upper and lower truth values can be estimated (Baldwin and Pillsworth (1980), Yager (1983)).

Theorem 8.1. *The upper truth value for $v^*(A/B)$ is given by:*

$$v^*(A/B) = Sup_{x\in\Omega} T\,(v(A/x),\, \mu_B\,(x)) \tag{8.2}$$

where T is a T-norm.

Definition 8.1 The upper solution for the truth of A equals the complement of the lower solution for the truth of ¬A.

$$v^*(A) = 1 - v_*(\neg A)$$

Corollary. The lower truth value for $v_*(A|B)$ is given by:

$$v_*(A|B) = 1 - Sup_{x\in\Omega}\, T\,(1-\pi_A\,(x),\, \mu_B\,(x)) \tag{8.3}$$

Given (5.4) and (5.5), it is obvious that:

$$v^*(A|B) = \Pi(A|B) \tag{8.4}$$

$$v_*(A|B) = N(A|B) \tag{8.5}$$

So, the upper solution is the possibility to have A true knowing that B is true. By duality, the lower solution is the corresponding necessity measure.

Theorem 8.2. *The degree of truth $v(A)$ of a proposition A knowing that a proposition B is true always belongs to the bounded interval $[N(A/B), \Pi(A/B)]$:*

$$v(A) \in [N(A/B)\,,\, \Pi(A/B)] \tag{8.6}$$

8.2 Parent proposition induced by a partial truth.

We would like to be able to infer the parent proposition B from a partial information based on a proposition qualified by a partial truth value:

$$v(A) = \partial$$

As was seen, a unique truth value can only be arrived at when necessity and possibility measures both equal that value; we can then state that: N [A|B] = ∂ and Π [A|B] = ∂. As a result to this close connection between the truth and the necessity and possibility measures, the upper solution for the unknown proposition B is given by Theorem 6.4 (with $\partial = f$).

Theorem 8.3. *The largest proposition B* for the parent proposition induced by* $v(A)=\partial$ *is:*

$$\forall x \in \Omega: \pi_B{}^*(x) = (\pi_A(x) + 1-\partial)) \wedge (1-\pi_A(x) + \partial) \qquad (8.7)$$

8.3. Properties of the truth measures.

Theorem 8.4 *Let X and Y be two non-interactive variables which take their values on* Ω_1 *and* Ω_2*, respectively. Let the two propositions P='X is P', and Q='Y is Q' have truth values '*$v(P)=\partial$*' and '*$v(Q)=f$*'. Let P' and Q' be their corresponding parent propositions.. Then, the following equalities hold for upper solution for the parent proposition:*

$$v(P \text{ Or } Q/P' \,\&\, Q') = Max(\partial, f)$$
$$v(P \,\&\, Q/P' \,\&\, Q') = Min(\partial, f)$$

Theorem 8.5. *The following equalities hold:*

(1a) $v_*(P \,\&\, Q) = v_*(P) \wedge v_*(Q)$, *which means:* $N(P \,\&\, Q) = N(P) \wedge N(Q)$

(1b) $v^*(P \,\&\, Q) = v^*(P) \wedge v^*(Q)$, *which means:* $\Pi(P \,\&\, Q) = \Pi(P) \wedge \Pi(Q)$

(2a) $v_*(P \text{ Or } Q) = v_*(P) \vee v_*(Q)$, *which means:* $N(P \text{ Or } Q) = N(P) \vee N(Q)$

(2b) $v^*(P \text{ Or } Q) = v^*(P) \vee v^*(Q)$, *which means:* $\Pi(P \text{ Or } Q) = \Pi(P) \vee \Pi(Q)$

9. Fuzzy Modus Ponens.

In binary logic, deduction process starts with a conditional A→B, a fact A to lead to a conclusion B. This rule, called the modus ponens, can be described as:

If x is A then x is B
x is A
____
x is B

or equivalently

A→B
A
____
B

We analyze the modus ponens when all propositions are fuzzy and when the conditional and the fact admit degrees of necessity, possibility or truth. The solution is very simple thanks to the concept of parent proposition. Let each proposition be weighted with one or several of $N=n$, $\Pi=\pi$, or $T=t$ where n is the degree of necessity, π is the degree of possibility and t is the degree of truth of the related proposition. One has $n, \pi, t \in [0,1]$, $n \le \pi$, and $n=\pi=t$ if t is given.

When applying the modus ponens, the problem is to define the deduced fuzzy proposition and its weights. The modus ponens is:

$$\begin{array}{ll} A\rightarrow B & N=1 \\ \underline{A \qquad} & \underline{N=1} \\ \quad B & N=1 \end{array}$$

This is nothing but the classical modus ponens applied to fuzzy propositions as in the following deduction

$$\begin{array}{ll} \text{if x is tall then x is heavy} & N=1 \\ \underline{\text{x is tall} \qquad\qquad\qquad\qquad} & \underline{N=1} \\ \qquad\qquad\text{x is heavy} & N=1 \end{array}$$

Both initial necessities being 1, the conclusion features the same degree of necessity.

In practice, the fact is not necessarily equal to the antecedent of the conditional, as in:

$$\begin{array}{ll} A\rightarrow B & N=1 \\ \underline{A^* \qquad} & \underline{N=1} \\ \quad B^* & N=1 \end{array} \qquad (9.1)$$

So we must derive B* given A*≠A. We will show that, in fact, it is necessary to determine the necessity of A given A*, and use that information in order to derive B*.

In classical logic, the Modus Ponens is a rule of inference which says: "IF A is true AND A->B is true, THEN B is true". In section 2, we distinguished between object-level implication (A→B) and meta-level implication (in capital itaalic letters). Table 2 presents the truth status of the meta-level implication given the struth status of the object-level propositions.

object-level truth status			meta-level truth status
A	A→B	B	IF A AND A→B THEN B
1	1	1	1
1	1	0	0
0	1	1	1
0	1	0	1
1	0	1	1
1	0	0	1
0	0	1	1
0	0	0	1

Table 2: Truth status of the meta-level implication given the object-level truth status.

The first row is the main point for the modus ponens: when A and A->B are true, so one can conclude that B is true, hence the meta-level proposition is true. The second line is false at the meta-level as one requires that B is true whenever A and A→B are true. This line is to be rejected once the meta-implication is accepted, i.e. once the modus ponens is accepted as an inference rule. When A is false and A->B is true (lines 3 and 4), nothing can be concluded about the truth of B (0, 1). Symmetrically, when A is true and A->B is false (lines 5 and 6), the truth status of B is undetermined. Finally, (-(lines 7 and 8), when A and A->B are false, the truth status of B is also undetermined.

To apply the modus ponens, we want to establish the truth status of B. The problem with the results of table 2 is that the truth status of B is not a function of the truth status of A and/or A→B. But it can be shown that the necessity of B is a function of the necessity of A and A→B when the meta-level implication is true (see table 3).

N(A)	N(A->B)	N(B)
1	1	1
0	1	0
1	0	0
0	0	0

Table 3: Relation between the necessity of B given the necessities of A and A→B.

So, the use of Modus Ponens entails a definition of the necessity of B as a function of the necessity of the two propositions A and A->B. We have:

$$N(B) = f(\ N(A), N(A\text{->}B)\ )$$

with f(1,1) = 1, f(1,0) = f(0,1) = f(0,0) = 0.

This relation is extended to propositions with partial degrees of necessity. It is easy to show that f is a T-norm, but we have no need for such a result here. We only postulate that f(a,1) = a, i.e. we postulate the following rule:

$$\begin{array}{ll} A\rightarrow B & N=1 \\ \underline{A\quad\ } & \underline{N=a} \\ \quad B & N=a \end{array}$$

A necessary implication transfers the necessity of the antecedent to the consequent. In the rule (9.1) we must therefore find what the necessity of antecedent A is given that we know the fact A* in order to compute the necessity of the consequent B:

$$N(B) = N(A|A^*)$$

The next problem is to solve the general case where:

$$\begin{array}{ll} A\rightarrow B & N=x \\ \underline{A^*\quad\ } & \underline{N=y} \\ \quad B^* & N=?? \end{array}$$

Its general solution is based on the parent proposition induced by the two premisses

$$\begin{array}{llll} A\rightarrow B & N=x & \text{is equivalent to} & A'\rightarrow B' \quad N=1 \\ A^* & N=y & \text{is equivalent to} & A^{*\prime} \quad\quad N=1 \end{array}$$

where A' and B' are defined below and A*' is the parent proposition of A*: $A^{*\prime} = A^*\oplus(1\text{-}y)$.
For simplicity's sake we write expressions like $A = B\oplus C$ to mean

$\forall x \in \Omega$: $\pi_A(x) = \pi_B(x) \oplus \pi_C(x)$

where A, B and C are three predicates on the same universe Ω.

Once A' and B' are known, compute $\alpha = N(A'|A^{*\prime}) = Inf(A' \oplus \neg A^{*\prime})$ by (6.10). One has:

$A' \rightarrow B'$	$N=1$
$\underline{A'}$	$\underline{N=\alpha}$
B'	$N=\alpha$

The remaining problem is to define A' and B' such that $N(A' \rightarrow B')=1$ and $N(A \rightarrow B | A' \rightarrow B')=x$.

As far as the implication is Lukaciewicz's implication (see section 3), one has $A \rightarrow B \equiv \neg A \oplus B$. So $x = N(\neg A \oplus B | \neg A' \oplus B')$.

The parent proposition of $\neg A \oplus B$ is $\neg A \oplus B \oplus (1-x)$. The problem is that $(1-x)$ could be arbitrarily split into a and b with $a, b \in [0,1]$, $a \oplus b = (1-x)$. In that case $\neg A' \oplus B' \equiv (\neg A \oplus a) \oplus (B \oplus b)$. Let $\neg A' \equiv \neg A \oplus a$ and $B' \equiv B \oplus b$. Usually, there is one degree of freedom in the choice of a (or b). But it turns out to be irrelevant when applying the modus ponens insofar as the conclusion will be the same whatever value is given to a.

***Theorem 9.1**: The largest solution of $A \rightarrow B$: $N=x$, A^*: $N=y$, is*

1) $B^* = B \oplus (1-x) \oplus (1-N(A/A^* \oplus (1-y)))$: $N=1$

2) B : $N = x \otimes N(A/A^* \oplus (1-y))$

Proof: 1) The parent proposition of A^* is $A^{*\prime} = A^* \oplus (1-y)$ (section 6.1).

2) The parent proposition of $A \rightarrow B$ is such that $N(A \rightarrow B | A' \rightarrow B') = x$. As $A \rightarrow B \equiv \neg A \oplus B$ (as shown in section 3), one has $x = N(\neg A \oplus B | \neg A' \oplus B')$ and $\neg A' \oplus B' \equiv \neg A \oplus B \oplus (1-x)$. Let $a \oplus b = 1-x$ where $a, b \in [0,1]$. So $\neg A' \oplus B' \equiv \neg A \oplus a \oplus B \oplus b$. Define $\neg A' \equiv \neg A \oplus a$ (equivalently $A' \equiv A \otimes (1-a)$) and $B' = B \oplus b$. The modus ponens becomes:

$A' \rightarrow B'$	$N=1$
$\underline{A^{*\prime}}$	$\underline{N=1}$
$B_a^{*\prime}$	$N=1$

where $B_a^{*\prime} = B' \oplus d_a$ with $d_a = 1-N(A'|A^{*\prime})$. Each $a \in [0,1]$ defines a solution for $B_a^{*\prime}$.

3) We must derive the largest solution $B^{*\prime}$, i.e. such that $B^{*\prime} \subseteq B_a^{*\prime}$ for all a.

Let $\varepsilon = \sup_v(A^{*\prime}(v) - A(v)) = 1-N(A|A^{*\prime})$ where $A^{*\prime}(v)$ and $A(v)$ are the grade of membership of v to the fuzzy sets $A^{*\prime}$ and A. One proves that $a \oplus \varepsilon \geq d_a$ for all a, i.e. one proves:

$$a + \sup_v (A^{*\prime}(v) - A(v)) \geq \sup_v (A^{*\prime}(v) - 1 + (1-A(v)+a) \wedge 1) \vee 0.$$

Let $V1 = \{v: a > A(v)\}$. The inequality is satisfied as

$$a + \sup_{v \in V1} (A^{*\prime}(v) - A(v)) = \sup_{v \in V1} (a + A^{*\prime}(v) - A(v)) \geq \sup_{v \in V1} A^{*\prime}(v)$$

Let $V2 = \{v: a \leq A(v)\}$. The inequality becomes

$$a + \sup_{v \in V2} (A^{*\prime}(v) - A(v)) = \sup_{v \in V2} (A^{*\prime}(v) - A(v) + a)$$

which is true as both terms are equal.
Since for all a, $a\oplus\varepsilon \geq d_a$, $B\oplus b\oplus a\oplus\varepsilon \geq B\oplus b\oplus d_a$.
So we have proved that

$$B^* = B\oplus(1-x)\oplus\varepsilon$$

is the largest solution . This B* solution is the parent proposition corresponding to B with $N=x\otimes N(A|A^{*\prime})$. QED

Generalization, when one receives degrees of possibility or degrees of truth, is handled identically by deriving the parent propositions.

A particular case of the theorem 9.1. is:

$$\frac{\begin{array}{ll} A\rightarrow B & N=x \\ A & N=y \end{array}}{B \quad N=x\otimes y}$$

One can also prove the transitivity property.

$$\frac{\begin{array}{ll} A\rightarrow B & N=x \\ B\rightarrow C & N=y \end{array}}{A\rightarrow C \quad N=x\otimes y}$$

Our modus ponens stands up to the sorites paradox as the necessity of A→C decreases toward 0 when a partly necessary conditional is applied iteratively (because $x\otimes y<x\wedge y$ when $x,y<1$).

Furthermore, the two following deduction schemes lead to the same results for C:

$$\begin{array}{ll} A^* & N=a \\ \underline{A\rightarrow B} & \underline{N=x} \\ \quad B & N=\ldots \\ \underline{B\rightarrow C} & \underline{N=y} \\ \quad C & N=\ldots \end{array} \qquad\qquad \begin{array}{ll} A\rightarrow B & N=x \\ \underline{B\rightarrow C} & \underline{N=y} \\ A\rightarrow C & N=\ldots \\ \underline{A} & \underline{N=a} \\ \quad C & N=\ldots \end{array}$$

In classical logic, each rule is related to a tautology at the object level. For the modus tollens, the tautology is A&(A→B)→B. We encounter the same tautology with our fuzzy modus ponens.

Theorem 9.2. *Suppose the rule*

$$\frac{\begin{array}{ll} A\rightarrow B & N=x \\ A^* & N=y \end{array}}{B\oplus(1-x)\oplus(1-N(A/A^*\oplus(1-y))) \quad N=1}$$

Then $(A^* \,\&\, (A\rightarrow B)) \rightarrow (B \text{ Or } (1-x) \text{ Or } (1 - N(A/A^*\oplus(1-y))))$ *is a tautology when the & is represented by the ⊗ operator, the Or by the ⊕, A→B ≡ ¬A Or B, and (1-x), (1-y) are fuzzy sets whose grades of membership are (1-x) or (1-y) on their whole domain.*

Proof.
Let $\varepsilon = \sup_v(A^{*\prime}(v) - A(v)) = 1\text{-}N(A|A^{*\prime})$ where $A^{*\prime} \equiv A^{*}\oplus(1\text{-}y)$, $A^{*\prime}(v)$ and $A(v)$ are the grade of membership of v to the fuzzy sets $A^{*\prime}$ and A. Let B(w) be the grade of membership of $w \in W$ to B. One must prove that for all v in V, all w in W, one has

$$(1\text{-}A^{*}(v)) \oplus (A(v) \otimes (1\text{-}B(w)) \oplus (B(w)\oplus\varepsilon\oplus(1\text{-}x)) = 1$$

i.e. $1\text{-}A^{*}(v) + (A(v) - B(w))\vee 0 + (B(w)+\varepsilon+(1\text{-}x))\wedge 1 \geq 1$

Suppose $A(v) > B(w)$, $B(w) + \varepsilon + (1\text{-}x) > 1$, the inequality becomes:

$$1 - A^{*}(v) + A(v) - B(w) + 1 \geq 1$$

i.e. $1 - A^{*}(v) + (A(v) - B(w)) \geq 0$

which is true as $A(v) - B(w) > 0$.

Suppose $A(v) > B(w)$, $B(w) + \varepsilon + (1\text{-}x) \leq 1$, the inequality becomes:

$$1\text{-}A^{*}(v) + A(v) - B(w) + B(w) + \varepsilon + (1\text{-}x) \geq 1$$

As $\varepsilon = \sup(A^{*}(v)\text{-}A(v))$, one has $1 - (A^{*}(v) - A(v)) \geq 1 - \varepsilon$ and hence, the inequality.

Suppose $A(v) \leq B(w)$, the inequality becomes:

$$1\text{-}A^{*}(v) + (B(w)+\varepsilon+(1\text{-}x))\wedge 1 \geq 1$$

which is always true. QED

10. Conclusions.

Throughout this paper, we have successively examined:

1) the difference between evaluating the degree of truth of the proposition A→B knowing the truth of A and of B (the adjunctive use) and evaluating the truth of B compatible with proposition A→B and B whose truth values are given (the connective use). (section 2);

2) the problem of the evaluation of the truth of an implication. It is shown that the truth of A→B is equal to $(1 - \text{truth}(A) + \text{truth}(B)) \wedge 1$. (section 3);

3) the use of the implication to provide a meaning to partial degrees of truth. (section 4);

4) the concept of parent distribution, i.e. the less specific strictly true proposition B such that $N(A|B) = \partial$ for given ∂;

5) the evaluation of the degree of necessity of a proposition in a context where the underlying propositions admit only partial degrees of necessity, possibility ,and/or truth;

6) the generalization of the modus ponens when the implication and the fact admit only partial degrees of necessity, possibility, and/or truth.

Appendix.

T-norms S-conorms.

The concept of T-norms and S-conorms are developed fully in Schweizer and Sklar (1961,1963,1983) and Weber (1983).

Definition 1. A T-norm is a function T from [0,1]x[0,1] to [0,1] such that for all a, b, c, d $\in$ [0,1], one has:

1. $T(a,b) = T(b,a)$	symmetry
2. $T(a,T(b,c)) = T(T(a,b),c)$	associativity
3. $T(a,b) \geq T(c,d)$ if $a \geq c$ and $b \geq d$	monotony
4. $T(a,1) = a$	boundary conditions

A T-norm is called Archimedian iff

5. T is continuous

6. $T(a,a) < a$

An Archimedian T-norm is called strict iff

7. T strictly increases in each of its places.

We see that 7 implies 6.

A S-conorm is a function $S:[0,1]x[0,1] \to [0,1]$ (Archimedian or strict) iff S has the same properties as a T-norm with the modifications:

4': $S(a,0) = a$

6': $S(a,a) > a$

Ling (1965) proved that for any Archimedian T-norm, there is a decreasing and continuous function $h:[0,1] \to [0,\infty]$ with $h(1)=0$ such that

$T(a,b) = h^{-}(h(a)+h(b))$

where h^{-} is the pseudo-inverse of h, defined by

$$h^{-}(y) = \begin{cases} h^{-1}(y) & \text{if } y \in [0,h(0)] \\ 0 & \text{if } y \in [h(0),\infty] \end{cases}$$

Moreover T is strict iff $h(0) = \infty$ in which case $h^{-} = h^{-1}$. When $h(0) < \infty$, T is said to be nilpotent. This h function is called the (additive) generator of T.

A similiar result holds for Archimedian S-conorms, except that the (additive) generator f of S increases with $f(0) = 0$ and with the pseudo-inverse f^{-} of f such that

$$f^{-}(y) = \begin{cases} f^{-1}(y) & \text{if } y \in [0,f(1)] \\ 1 & \text{if } y \in [f(1), \infty] \end{cases}$$

If S is strict, $f(1) = \infty$ and $f^{-} = f^{-1}$. If $f(1) < \infty$, S is said to be nilpotent.

Note that	$h^{-}(h(x)) = x$,	$h(h^{-}(y)) = \min(y,h(0))$
and	$f^{-}(f(x)) = x$,	$f(f^{-}(y)) = \min(y, f(1))$

For any T-norm T and S-conorm S, one has:

$T_W(a,b) \leq T(a,b) \leq T_\circ(a,b)$

$S_W(a,b) \geq S(a,b) \geq S_\circ(a,b)$

where T_W, T_0, S_W and S_0 are T-norms and S-conorms such that:

$$T_W(a,b) = \begin{cases} a & \text{if } b = 1 \\ b & \text{if } a = 1 \\ 0 & \text{otherwise} \end{cases} \qquad S_W(a,b) = \begin{cases} a & \text{if } b = 0 \\ b & \text{if } a = 0 \\ 1 & \text{otherwise} \end{cases}$$

$$T_0(a,b) = a \wedge b \qquad S_0(a,b) = a \vee b$$

where $\wedge$ ($\vee$) denotes the minimum (maximum) operator.

The T_∞-norm and S_∞-conorm are defined as:

$$T_\infty(a,b) = (a+b-1) \vee 0 \qquad S_\infty(a,b) = (a+b) \wedge 1$$

They are represented in this paper as $T_\infty(a,b) = a \otimes b$ and $S_\infty(a,b) = a \oplus b$.

Negation.

A function $n:[0,1] \rightarrow [0,1]$ is called a negation (function) iff

1. $n(0) = 1, \quad n(1) = 0$
2. $n(a) \leq n(b)$ if $a \geq b$ monotonicity

A negation is strong iff

3. $n(a) < n(b)$ if $a > b$ strict monotonicity
4. n is continuous

A strong negation is an involution iff

5. $n(n(a)) = a$ for all $a \in [0,1]$

For any negation, 5 implies 3, and $n^{-1} = n$.

Trillas (1979) proved that any strong negation function n can be generated from a continuous strictly increasing function k from $[0,1]$ to $[0,\infty)$ such that $k(0) = 0$ and $k(1) < \infty$ and $n(a) = k^{-1}(k(1) - k(a))$. In order to simplify the notations, we will write na for n(a) and drop the parenthesis whenever possible.

To any T-norm T and a strict negation n is associated a S-conorm defined as $S(a,b) = n(T(na, nb))$. S is called the n-dual of T. If T is Archimedian with generator h, then S is Archimedian with generator $f = h \circ n$.

Analogous results can be descibed when starting from Archimedian S-conorms S and deriving the Archimedian T-norms T n-dual of S from:

$T(a,b) = n(S(na,nb))$

References

Anderson A.R. and Belnap N.D. (1975) *Entailment: the logic of relevance and necessity.* Princeton University Press.

Baldwin J.F. and Pilswrth B.W. (1980) Axiomatix approach to implication for approxiamte reasoning with fuzzy logic. *Fuzzy Sets and Systems,* 3: 193-219.

Bandler W. and Kohout L.J. (1980) Semantics of implication operators and fuzzy relational products. *International Journal of Man-Machines Studies*, 12: 89-116.

Blanché R. (1968) *Introduction à la logique contemporaine.* Colin, Paris.

Domingo X., Trillas E. and Valverde E. (1981) Pushing Lukasiewicz-Tarski implication a little further. *Proceedings 11th IEEE Conference on Multiple-valued Logic*, Oklahoma City, 232-234.

Dubois D. and Prade H. (1980) *Fuzzy sets and systems; theory and applications.* Academic Press.

Dubois D. and Prade H. (1982) Degree of truth and truth-functionnality. *Proc. 2nd World Conf. on Maths. at the Service of Man*, Las Palmas, Spain. June 28-July 3, 262-265.

Dubois D. and Prade H. (1984) Fuzzy logics and the generalized Modus Ponens revisited. *Cybernetics and Systems*, 15: n°3-4.

Dubois D. and Prade H. (1990) Resolution principles in possibilistic logic. *Int. J. Approx. Reasoning* 4:1-22.

Gaines B.R. (1976) Foundations of fuzzy reasoning. *International Journal of Man-Machines Studies*, 8: 623-668.

Grize J.B. (1967) Logique. in Piaget J. ed., *Logique et connaissance scientifique.* Pléiade, Paris, 135-289.

Hicks J. (1979) *Causality in economics.* Blackwell, Oxford.

Lewis D. (1976) Probabilities of conditionals and conditional probabilities. *Philisophical Review* 85: 297-315.

Ling C.H. (1965) Representation of associative functions. *Pub. Math. Debrecen* 12: 182-212.

Magrez P. (1985) *Modèles de raisonnement approchés*. Thesis, Université Libre de Bruxelles.

Magrez P. and Smets Ph. (1989a) Epistemic necessity, possibility, and truth. Tools for dealing with imprecision and uncertaainty in fuzzy knowledge-based systems. *Int. J. Approximate Reasoning*, 3:35-57.

Magrez P. and Smets Ph. (1989b) Fuzzy modus ponens: a new model suitable for applications in knowledge-based systems. *Int. J. Intelligent Systems* 4:181-200.

Mamdani E.H. and Gaines B.R. (1981) *Fuzzy reasoning and its applications*. Academic Press.

Mizomuto M. and Zimmermann H.J. (1982) Comparison of fuzzy reasoning methods. *Fuzzy Sets and Systems*, 8: 253-283.

Prade H. (1982) Degree of truth: matching statement against reality. *BUSEFAL*, 9, 88-92.

Prade H. (1982) Modal semantics and fuzzy set theory. in *Fuzzy Set and Possibility Theory*, Yager ed. Pergamon Press, New York, pg. 232-246.

Reichenbach H. (1947) *Elements of symbolic logic*. McMillan.

Reichenbach H. (1949) *The theory of probability*. University of California Press.

Rescher N. (1969) *Many-Valued Logic*. McGraw-Hill, New-York.

Sanchez E. (1976) Resolution of composite fuzzy relation equations. *Information and Control*, 30, 38-48.

Sanchez E. (1978) On possibility qualification in natural language. *Inf. Sc.*15:45-76.

Schweizer B. and Sklar A. (1961) Associative functions and statistical triangle inequalities. *Publ. Math. Debrecen*, 8: 169-186.

Schweizer B. and Sklar A. (1963) Associative functions and abstract semi-groups. *Publ. Math. Debrecen*, 10: 69-81.

Schweizer B. and Sklar A. (1983) *Probabilistic metric spaces*. North Holland, New York.

Shafer G. (1976) *A mathematical theory of evidence*. Princeton Univ. Press.

Smets P. (1988a) Belief functions. in Smets Ph, Mamdani A., Dubois D. and Prade H. ed. *Non standard logics for automated reasoning*. Academic Press, London pg 253-286.

Smets P. and Magrez P. (1987) Implications in fuzzy logic. *Int. J. Approximate reasoning* 1:327-347.

Smets P. and Magrez P. (1988) The measure of the degree of truth and the grade of membership. *Fuzzy Sets and Systems* 25:67-72.

Trillas E. (1979) Sobre funciones de negacion en la teoria de conjuntos difusos. *Stochastica*, 3: 47-60.

Trillas E. and Valverde L. (1985a) On implication and indistinguishability in the setting of fuzzy logic. In Kacprzyk J. and Yager R.R. eds. *Management decision support systems using fuzzy sets and possibility theory*. Verlag TUV Rheinland, 198-212.

Trillas E. and Valverde L. (1985b) On mode and implication in approximate reasoning. In Gupta M.M. et al. eds. *Approximate reasoning in expert systems*. North Holland, Amsterdam 157-166.

Turner R. (1984) *Logics for Artificial Intelligence*. Ellis Horwood Ltd.

Valverde L. (1982) *Contribution a l'estudi dels models matematics per a logiques multivalents*. Ph.D.Thesis. Universitat Politecnica de Barcelona.

Weber S. (1983) A general concept of fuzzy connectives, negations and implications based on t-norms and t-conorms. *Fuzzy Sets and Systems*, 11: 115-134.

Yager R.R. (1983) Some relationships between possibility, truth and certainty. *Fuzzy Sets and Systems*, 11: 151-156.

Zadeh L. (1965) Fuzzy Sets. *Information and Control*, 8, 338-353.

Zadeh L. (1975a) The concept of a linguistic variable and its application to approximate reasoning: I. *Information Sciences*, 8, 199-249.

Zadeh L. (1975b) The concept of a linguistic variable and its application to approximate reasoning: II. *Information Sciences*, 8, 301-357 .

Zadeh L. (1975c) The concept of a linguistic variable and its application to approximate reasoning: III. *Information Sciences*, 9, 43-80 .

Zadeh L. (1977) A theory of approximate reasoning. Memorandum UCB/ERL M77/58.

Zadeh L. (1978) Fuzzy sets as a basis for a theory of possibility. *Fuzzy Sets ans Systems*, 1, 3-28

Zadeh L. (1981a) PRUF. A meaning representation language for natural languages. In *Fuzzy Reasoning and its Applications*, E.H. Mamdani and B.R. Gaines Eds, Academic Press.

Zadeh L. (1981b) Test-score semantics for natural languages and meaning representation via PRUF. Tech. note #247, SRI-International, Menlo Park, Calif. also and in *Empirical Semantics*. B.B. Rieger Ed. Brockmeyer Bochum, 281-349 (1982).

Conditional Logic in Expert Systems
I.R. Goodman, M.M. Gupta, H.T. Nguyen and G.S. Rogers (editors)

BELIEF FUNCTION COMPUTATIONS

H. Mathis Thoma

CIBA-GEIGY Corporation

556 Morris Avenue

Summit, NJ 07901

Abstract Two contributions are made that will make belief function computations applicable to larger problems than currently possible. First we introduce the fast Moebius transformation, an algorithm for efficiently converting among the different representations of a belief function. Secondly, we develop a scheme for storing belief functions, which generalizes graphical models. The storage scheme applies to belief functions that are not graphical and is more efficient than graphical models, but it still allows for local computations. In addition a brief overview of the belief function framework is given, and connections are drawn between aspects of our storage scheme and the theory of relational databases.

Keywords Belief functions, Moebius transformation, graphical models, local computations, factorization, relational databases.

1. Introduction

Belief functions have many appealing properties for encoding uncertain knowledge in automated reasoning systems. Their practical use, however, is limited by their extraordinary appetite for storage space. For example, situations considering as few as 32 different outcomes can reach the limits of ordinary computing equipment when handled naively. The article will present a fast algorithm for moving between the different set functions representing a belief function. It will also present a new way for efficiently storing arbitrary belief functions defined on multivariate spaces. Finally it will compare some aspects of our storage scheme with results from the theory of relational databases. Here is a brief summary of each of the four sections in this article:

Sections 2 and 3 give a brief overview of the mathematical aspects of belief functions. Belief functions are viewed equivalently as set functions characterized by intrinsic properties, as set functions induced by random set, and as lower and upper probabilities of a set of probability measures.

Section 4. A belief function can be represented by any of four equivalent set functions. The four representations are linked among each other by versions of the Moebius transformation. The fast Moebius transformation arranges the computational steps of the Moebius transformation such that a minimal number of operations is required. It is related to the fast Fourier transformation for real-valued functions.

Sections 5, 6, and 7. Kong (1986) introduced graphical belief functions defined on multivariate spaces as a class of functions that can be stored efficiently. Graphical belief functions are the combination of several component functions, each defined on a margin of the multivariate space. All components together require less storage space than does their combination. This holds because storage demand grows roughly exponentially with the size of the underlying outcome space. In addition, belief function computations can be performed based on the components alone, without ever having to reassemble the function they represent.

Section 8 shows that there is a much larger class of belief functions that can be stored efficiently, and for which we do not need to reassemble the function from its representation to do computations. To arrive at such representations we factor each focal element individually instead of factoring the overall belief function. An additional advantage of such representations is that it is easier to find factorizations of sets than factorizations of belief functions. Many of the computational principles discussed here have been implemented in a LISP-based program developed at the Harvard Statistics Department (Almond 1990).

Section 9 finally looks at how to find factorizations of sets and belief functions. The factorization of belief functions leads to an interesting new phenomenon not encountered in either the set or probability case.

Notation. The following symbols will be used throughout this article: $\mathbb{R}$ denotes the set of real number, $\emptyset$ is the empty set, and $\subset$ denotes set inclusion (including set equality). The set difference of a and b is written as $a \setminus b$, the set complement of a as $\bar{a}$. The symbol $:=$ is used to indicated that the symbol on the left is short for the expression on the right. If function f maps elements of A (domain of f) to elements of B (range or codomain of f), then we write this as $f : A \to B$.

2. The Belief Function Framework

In this section we will briefly explore the mathematical properties of belief functions. For the purpose of this article belief functions are viewed as set functions that can be interpreted simultaneously as distribution functions of random sets and as lower bounds of sets of probability measures. Like probabilities, belief functions can be used to model uncertain evidence, but unlike probabilities they offer a natural way for combining evidence (intersection of the corresponding random sets). Furthermore, belief functions can model uncertainty more flexibly than probabilities since they correspond to sets of measures.

Dempster introduced belief functions in a series of papers in the late sixties. In the seventies Dempster's theory was expanded by Shafer, who also coined the term 'belief function.' In the eighties the development of expert systems and the investigation into automated reasoning by the Artificial Intelligence community has stimulated the further development of belief functions.

Belief Functions and Random Sets Let $(\Omega, \mathcal{A}, \Pr)$ be a probability space, and let Θ be a finite outcome space, called a *frame*, relevant to some application. Consider a function

$$S : \Omega \rightarrow 2^{\Theta}$$

for which $\Pr\{S = \emptyset\} = 0$. The function S is a set-valued random variable, or *random set* for short. Such a random set provides a two stage model for selecting an outcome (element of Θ). First an element $\omega \in \Omega$ is chosen at random according to distribution Pr. Next an element is chosen from $S(\omega)$ in an unknown and not necessarily random manner. The case $S = \emptyset$ is excluded since we assume that frame Θ is *exhaustive*; whatever happens is described by an element of Θ. Hence S cannot be empty.

For convenience let $\mathcal{S}$ denote the power set 2^{Θ} of Θ. The random set S induces on the measurable space $(\mathcal{S}, 2^{\mathcal{S}})$ a probability measure $\mathrm{P}_S = \Pr \cdot S^{-1}$, which may be described by a probability mass function, and, since $\mathcal{S}$ is partially ordered, also by a (generalized) distribution function. There are four set functions commonly used to describe P_S: *belief* BEL_S, *plausibility* PL_S, *commonality* Q_S, and *basic assignment* m_S, They are defined as follows:

$$\begin{aligned}
\mathrm{BEL}_S(a) &:= \Pr\{S \subset a\}, \\
\mathrm{PL}_S(a) &:= \Pr\{S \cap a \neq \emptyset\}, \\
\mathrm{Q}_S(a) &:= \Pr\{S \supset a\}, \\
m_S(a) &:= \Pr\{S = a\}.
\end{aligned}$$

The basic assignment is the probability mass function, the belief the distribution function of P_S. The commonality is the *dual* distribution function, since inclusion '$\subset$' is replaced in the definition by the dual relation '$\supset$.' Later we will see that the commonality also plays the role of Fourier transform or characteristic function of the distribution. The role of the plausibility will be come apparent below.

The distribution P_S is completely determined by any of the four functions, and given one function the remaining three can be computed. For example, belief BEL_S can be computed from m_S as follows:

$$BEL_S(a) = \Pr\{S \subset a\} = \sum_{s \subset a} \Pr\{S = s\} = \sum_{s \subset a} m_S(s).$$

The transformation can be inverted, and the inverse relation is

$$m_S(a) = \sum_{s \subset a} (-1)^{|a \setminus s|} \cdot BEL_S(s)$$

($|a \setminus s|$ is the cardinality of set difference $a \setminus s$). Basic assignment and commonality are connected in a similar fashion:

$$\begin{aligned} Q_S(a) &= \sum_{s \supset a} m_S(s), \\ m_S(a) &= \sum_{s \supset a} (-1)^{|s \setminus a|} \cdot Q_S(s). \end{aligned}$$

By combining the two relations we can move directly from belief to commonality and back:

$$\begin{aligned} BEL_S(a) &= \sum_{s \subset \bar{a}} (-1)^{|s|} \cdot Q_S(s), \\ Q_S(a) &= \sum_{s \subset a} (-1)^{|s|} \cdot BEL_S(\bar{s}). \end{aligned}$$

Finally, belief and plausibility form a pair of *conjugate* functions, in the sense that $BEL_S(a) + PL_S(\bar{a}) = 1$.

Belief Functions as Lower Probabilities Let $\mathcal{M}$ be the set of probability measures on Θ. Associated with any belief function BEL is the set $\mathcal{Q}$ of *compatible* measures:

$$\mathcal{Q} := \{P \in \mathcal{M} \mid BEL(a) \leq P(a), \quad \text{for all } a \subset \Theta\}.$$

Dempster (1967) proves that the lower bound of $\mathcal{Q}$ is equal to BEL, and its upper bound equal to the plausibility, i.e. the function PL conjugate to BEL:

$$BEL(a) = \inf_{P \in \mathcal{Q}} P(a), \quad PL(a) = \sup_{P \in \mathcal{Q}} P(a), \quad \text{for all } a \subset \Theta.$$

Dempster's result turns out to be a special case of a theorem by Choquet (1954), which asserts that essentially the same result holds for a continuous Θ.

For a given set of probability measures $\mathcal{P} \subset \mathcal{M}$ the two bounds are also referred to as *lower* and *upper probabilities* induced by $\mathcal{P}$. The two bounds are always conjugate set functions, and hence it is enough to deal with one of them.

Set $\mathcal{Q}$ and function BEL mutually induce each other. Not every set of probabilities can be represented in this way, which shows that belief functions and their induced sets of probabilities are rather special. Huber (1981) analyzes in detail the circumstances in which lower bounds and sets of probabilities mutually induce each other.

Boolean and Bayesian Belief Functions A *focal element* of a belief function is any subset of Θ for which the basic assignment is different from 0. *Bayesian* belief functions arise from random sets that assign probability 0 to all subsets except those with exactly one element. Such random sets are equivalent to ordinary random variables if we ignore the distinction between elements of the frame and singleton subsets. The set of compatible measures of a Bayesian belief function contains only one element, the probability induced by the equivalent random variable.

By contrast a *Boolean* belief function arises from a random set that assigns probability 1 to exactly one subset of the frame. The set of compatible measures of a Boolean belief function consists of all probabilities whose support is contained in the designated subset. This set is equivalent to the set of all probability measures on that subset. The Boolean belief function for set Θ serves as a convenient representation of total ignorance, since it corresponds to the set of all probability measures.

Belief functions provide a bridge between probabilistic and categorical inference by including ordinary probabilities and categorical constraints in the same framework.

Combination of Evidence The *combination* of two random sets S_1 and S_2 is the random set

$$S_1 \oplus S_2 := S_1 \cap S_2 | S_1 \cap S_2 \neq \emptyset.$$

The intersection $S_1 \cap S_2$ will again induce a distribution function. But the induced function will only be a belief function if we condition $S_1 \cap S_2$ on $S_1 \cap S_2 \neq \emptyset$. Let m_1 and m_2 be the basic assignments of S_1 and S_2, respectively. Assuming that the two random sets S_1 and S_2 are *independent* (i.e., $\Pr\{S_1 = a, S_2 = b\} = \Pr\{S_1 = a\} \cdot \Pr\{S_2 = b\}$), we can compute the probability mass function of $S_1 \cap S_2$ as

$$m_S(a) = \Pr\{S_1 \cap S_2 = a\} = \Pr\{S_1 = s_1, S_2 = s_2, s_1 \cap s_2 = a\} = \sum_{s_1 \cap s_2 = a} m_1(s_1) \cdot m_2(s_2).$$

If we call

$$m_1 * m_2(a) := \sum_{s_1 \cap s_2 = a} m_1(s_1) \cdot m_2(s_2),$$

the *convolution* of m_1 and m_2, we can express the basic assignment of $S = S_1 \oplus S_2$ as

$$m_S(s) := \begin{cases} 0 & s = \emptyset \\ \frac{m_1 * m_2(s)}{1 - m_1 * m_2(\emptyset)} & s \neq \emptyset. \end{cases}$$

The other induced set functions can now be computed from m_S. The commonalities exhibit an interesting behavior. Let Q_1 and Q_2 be the commonalities induced by S_1 and S_2. The commonality of S is

$$\mathrm{Q}_S(a) = k \cdot \mathrm{Q}_1(a) \cdot \mathrm{Q}_2(a),$$

where $k = (1 - m_1 * m_2(\emptyset))^{-1}$ (there is no easy way to express k based on the commonalities alone). Except for renormalization, the two given commonalities multiply point-wise. This is reminiscent of Fourier transformation, which also replaces convolution by multiplication (the addition of random variables leads to a convolution of their densities, but their characteristic functions multiply point-wise). Thoma (1989) shows that we can interpret the commonalities as Fourier transforms or characteristic functions of the basic assignment in mathematically precise sense. The Fourier transformation is based on the semigroup $(\mathcal{S}, \cap)$, rather than the usual group $(\mathbb{R}, +)$.

In application one usually starts with beliefs or basic assignment rather than random sets. The random sets are essentially a mathematical tool to express the combination in a simple fashion and to define an interpretation for the belief functions. Whether two pieces of evidence are independent is therefore a subjective judgement and cannot be assessed by any formal method.

Conditioning An interesting property of belief functions is that conditioning can be expressed as combination of evidence. Assume we are given a random set S which we want to condition on $a \subset \Theta$. The conditioned belief function is $S \oplus a$. If S is a Bayesian belief function the result is as expected. If S is Boolean the result will be the Boolean belief function corresponding to the intersection of the two sets.

Set Functions Induced by Random Sets The starting point for our definition of belief functions was the random set. A random set induces a probability distribution on 2^S, which can be described by any of four derrived set functions. Alternatively we can start with either of the four set functions since each can be characterized by intrinsic properties. Below we will give properties that are necessary and sufficient for a set function to be the belief, plausibility, commonality, or basic assignment associated with a random set. Given one of the four function we know the distribution on 2^S, and it is always possible to construct a probability space and a corresponding random set that will induce this distribution. In fact, we may start with an arbitrary number of distributions and construct corresponding random sets that are independent, each inducing one of the given distributions.

The basic assignments is the easiest set function to characterize. A basic assignment is a probability mass function and therefore has to be *positive* and *sum to 1*. Furthermore it has to assign probability 0 to the empty set.

Belief Functions and Capacities A set function f on Θ is a *capacity* if $f(\emptyset) = 0$ and f is monotone (i.e., $f(a) \leq f(b)$ whenever $a \subset b$). It is a *normalized* capacity if in addition $f(\Theta) = 1$. Clearly every belief function is a normalized capacity. The reverse however is not true. The problem is that we can start with a basic assignment that is not positive and still get a monotone function after conversion.

Capacities can be classified further according to how they behave under successive differencing. The difference operator is defined as follows: $\nabla_s f(a) := f(a \cap s) - f(a)$, for any subset $s \subset \Theta$. Clearly, function f is monotone exactly if $\nabla_s f(a) \geq 0$ for all s and all a. It is *monotone of order k* if

$$\nabla_{s_1} \cdots \nabla_{s_k} f(a) \geq 0$$

for all a and all $s_1, \ldots, s_k \subset \Theta$, and is *alternating of order k* if

$$\nabla_{s_1} \cdots \nabla_{s_k} f(a) \leq 0.$$

A function is *completely* monotone (alternating) if it is monotone (alternating) of any order. Completely monotone capacities can also be characterized as follows. The function f is completely monotone, if for any subset I of $\mathcal{S}$ it holds that

$$f(\bigcup_{a \in I} a) \geq \sum_{\emptyset \neq J \subset I} (-1)^{|J|+1} f(\bigcap_{a \in J} a).$$

Dempster (1967) shows that the belief induced by a random set is a normalized, completely monotone capacity and that any such capacity can be viewed as the belief induced by some random set. Since the conjugate of a monotone function is alternating (of the same order), it follows that a set function is a plausibility exactly if it is a normalized, completely alternating capacity.

To define commonalities we take advantage of the fact that commonality and belief are dual distribution functions. A set of conditions dual to those that define beliefs can be developed using the difference operator $\Delta_s f(a) := f(a) - f(a \cup s)$ instead of ∇_s. A set function f is a commonality if it is positive, completely monotone (with respect to Δ_s), and if $f(\emptyset) = 1$. Thoma (1989) shows that commonalities can also be characterized as *positive definite functions* using ideas from Fourier theory on semigroups.

3. Basic Belief Function Computations

In this section we will focus on how to compute with belief functions. The goal of belief function computations is usually to report belief and plausibility values for certain events. It is possible to perform all computations using only beliefs (and/or plausibilities), but it is much more convenient to internally use basic assignments and convert them to beliefs and plausibilities only when necessary.

There are three types of basic computational procedures for belief functions: conversions, combination, and transformations.

Conversions are needed to compute belief and plausibility given a basic assignment, or more generally, to convert among the four induced set functions. We will deal with conversions in section 3 of this article.

Combination refers to the computations needed when independent belief functions are combined. We will deal with combination in this section.

Transformations arise when belief functions on product spaces are considered. Some general properties of transformations will be discussed in this section. Belief functions on product spaces are the subject of section 5.

These computational procedures will be defined for arbitrary set functions, rather than the more restricted basic assignments, since intermediate results of the computations may not be basic assignments. In addition, we will have reason to consider belief function computations on a class of set functions that contains basic assignments as a proper subset.

Notation for the Vector Space of Set Functions The real-valued set functions over Θ form a finite-dimensional vector space, denoted $\mathbb{R}^S$, when equipped with the usual addition and scalar multiplication of functions (i.e., $(f_1 + f_2)(s) = f_1(s) + f_2(s)$, and $(\alpha \cdot f)(s) = \alpha \cdot f(s))$. If Θ has n elements, then $\mathbb{R}^{\mathcal{S}}$ will have 2^n dimensions. A function $f \in \mathbb{R}^{\mathcal{S}}$ assigns to each $s \in \mathcal{S}$ a value $f(s)$, the *weight* of s. The family $(\delta_a)_{a\in\mathcal{S}}$ of functions, where

$$\delta_a(s) := \begin{cases} 1 & s = a \\ 0 & s \neq a, \end{cases}$$

forms a basis of $\mathbb{R}^{\mathcal{S}}$, and whence every function $f \in \mathbb{R}^{\mathcal{S}}$ can be written as $f = \sum_{s\in\mathcal{S}} f(s) \cdot \delta_s$.

The *size* of a set function f is the number $|f| := \sum_{s\in\mathcal{S}} f(s)$, the sum of its weights. The size is a linear functional on $\mathbb{R}^{\mathcal{S}}$ since $|\alpha \cdot f| = \alpha \cdot |f|$ for any $\alpha \in \mathbb{R}$, and since $|f_1 + f_2| = |f_1| + |f_2|$. The *normalization* of a function f is the function

$$\|f\| := \frac{f - f(\emptyset) \cdot \delta_\emptyset}{|f| - f(\emptyset)}.$$

Normalization is defined only if $|f| \neq f(\emptyset)$. A set function f is *normalized* if $\|f\| = f$, or equivalently, if $|f| = 1$ and $f(\emptyset) = 0$. Note that $\|\alpha \cdot f\| = \|f\|$ for all $\alpha \neq 0$, given the normalizations exist.

Convolution and Combination The *convolution* of two set-functions f and g is the function $f * g$, defined as

$$f * g(a) := \sum_{s_f \cap s_g = a} f(s_f) \cdot g(s_g).$$

The operation is associative, commutative, and bilinear, and it holds that $f * \delta_\Theta = f$ and $f * \delta_\emptyset = |f| \cdot \delta_\emptyset$. The size of a convolution is given by $|f * g| = |f| \cdot |g|$.

The *combination* of f and g is the function $f \oplus g := \|f * g\|$, which is the normalization of the convolution of f and g. If f and g are the basic assignments of two independent random sets, then $f \oplus g$ is the basic assignment of their combination.

Like convolution combination is commutative. It is also associative as the following computation shows. If f_1, f_2, and f_3 are three set functions, then

$$(f_1 \oplus f_2) \oplus f_3 = \|(\|f_1 * f_2\|) * f_3\|$$

$$\begin{aligned}
&= \|\frac{f_1 * f_2 - \kappa' \cdot \delta_\emptyset}{|f_1 * f_2| - \kappa'} * f_3\| \\
&= \|f_1 * f_2 * f_3 - \kappa' \cdot |f_3| \cdot \delta_\emptyset\| \\
&= \frac{f_1 * f_2 * f_3 - \kappa' \cdot |f_3| \cdot \delta_\emptyset - \kappa'' \cdot \delta_\emptyset}{|f_1 * f_2 * f_3 - \kappa \cdot |f_3| \cdot \delta_\emptyset| - \kappa'} \\
&= \frac{f_1 * f_2 * f_3 - (\kappa \cdot |f_3| + \kappa') \cdot \delta_\emptyset}{|f_1 * f_2 * f_3| - (\kappa \cdot |f_3| + \kappa')}.
\end{aligned}$$

Here $\kappa := (f_1 * f_2)(\emptyset)$ and $\kappa' := (f_1 * f_2 * f_3 - \kappa \cdot |f_3| \cdot \delta_\emptyset)(\emptyset)$, which is equal to $f_1 * f_2 * f_3(\emptyset) - \kappa \cdot |f_3|$. Hence $(\kappa \cdot |f_3| + \kappa')$ is equal to $f_1 * f_2 * f_3(\emptyset)$ and $(f_1 \oplus f_2) \oplus f_3 = \|f_1 * f_2 * f_3\|$. A similar computation yields $f_1 \oplus (f_2 \oplus f_3) = \|f_1 * f_2 * f_3\|$, which shows that combination is associative. For an arbitrary number of set functions it holds that

$$f_1 \oplus \cdots \oplus f_k = \|f_1 * \cdots * f_k\|.$$

This allows us to postpone normalization until the end, if many set functions must be combined, and to normalize the result in one step.

Transformations Consider an arbitrary mapping ϕ from frame Θ to frame Θ'. In section 3 of this chapter, Θ will be a product space, Θ' one of its margins, and ϕ the projection from Θ onto the margin Θ'. Any mapping ϕ induces a linear mapping $\tilde{\phi}$ from $\mathbb{R}^{\mathcal{S}}$ to $\mathbb{R}^{\mathcal{S}'}$ as follows. First extend ϕ to subsets in the usual fashion by mapping the set $s \in \mathcal{S}$ to $\phi(s) := \{\phi(\vartheta) \mid \vartheta \in s\}$, an element of $\mathcal{S}'$. As we have seen earlier, the elements of $\mathcal{S}$ and $\mathcal{S}'$ correspond to basis vectors for $\mathbb{R}^{\mathcal{S}}$ and $\mathbb{R}^{\mathcal{S}'}$, respectively. Furthermore, any mapping defined on the basis vectors of $\mathbb{R}^{\mathcal{S}}$ and $\mathbb{R}^{\mathcal{S}'}$ can be extended to a linear mapping for all set functions. Hence we may extend the function ϕ defined on the elements of Θ to a linear mapping $\tilde{\phi}$ from $\mathbb{R}^{\mathcal{S}}$ to $\mathbb{R}^{\mathcal{S}'}$. The image of $f \in \mathbb{R}^{\mathcal{S}}$ is

$$\tilde{\phi}(f) := \tilde{\phi}(\sum_{s \in \mathcal{S}} f(s) \cdot \delta_s) = \sum_{s \in \mathcal{S}} f(s) \cdot \tilde{\phi}(\delta_s) = \sum_{s \in \mathcal{S}} f(s) \cdot \delta_{\phi(s)},$$

and if $g := \tilde{\phi}(f)$, then

$$g(s') = \sum_{s \in \mathcal{S}} f(s) \cdot \delta_{\phi(s)}(s') = \sum_{\phi(s) = s'} f(s).$$

Note that $|\tilde{\phi}(f)| = |f|$ and $\|\tilde{\phi}(f)\| = \tilde{\phi}(\|f\|)$.

The same extension process can be applied to mappings defined for sets directly (for example 'set complement'), or for mappings with more than one argument. Many properties of a point or set mapping will carry over to the extension. For example, convolution is the bilinear extension of set intersection, and it is commutative and associative simply because set intersection is. This simple observation will shorten many arguments later on.

The transformation ϕ will map a random set S on Θ to a random set $S' := \phi(S)$ on Θ' with the basic assignment

$$m_{S'}(s') = \Pr\{\phi(S) = s'\} = \sum_{\phi(s)=s'} \Pr\{S = s\} = \sum_{\phi(s)=s'} m_S(s).$$

The basic assignment of S' is simply $m_{S'} = \tilde{\phi}(m_S)$. The effect of a transformation on either belief, plausibility, or commonality is much more difficult to compute.

Quasi-Belief Functions Strictly speaking belief functions are normalized completely monotone capacities, i.e., set functions that are beliefs for some random set. However, for the purpose of this article it is more convenient to use the term belief function for the probability distribution induced by such a capacity. Belief, plausibility, commonality, and basic assignment are then four different, but equivalent representations of the belief function. For later use it is convenient to introduce the class of quasi-belief functions defined as follows: A set function $m \in I\!R^{S}$ is the basic assignment of a *quasi-belief function*, if it is normalized, and if its commonality is positive: $Q(a) = \sum_{s \supset a} m(s) \geq 0$ for all $a \subset \Theta$. Like a belief function a quasi-belief functions induced a measure on 2^S, but there is no guarantee that the measure is positive, nor is it certain that its basic assignment is positive. Like a belief function a quasi-belief function has four equivalent representations, which we still call belief, plausibility, commonality, and basic assignment. Clearly ordinary belief functions are special quasi-belief functions, but the reverse is not true.

4. Fast Moebius Transformation

In this section we develop an algorithm, the fast Moebius transformation, for efficiently converting among the different representations of a belief function.

Moebius Transformation As in the previous section, Θ is a finite set, $\mathcal{S} := 2^\Theta$ is its power set, and $m \in \mathbb{R}^\mathcal{S}$ a set function over Θ. The function $f \in \mathbb{R}^\mathcal{S}$ is the *Moebius transform* of m if

$$f(a) = \sum_{s \subset a} m(s),$$

for all $a \subset \Theta$. The *Moebius transformation* assigns to each element of $\mathbb{R}^\mathcal{S}$ its Moebius transform. This transformation is a linear mapping of the vector space $\mathbb{R}^\mathcal{S}$ onto itself, and its inverse is given by

$$m(a) = \sum_{s \subset a} (-1)^{|a \setminus s|} \cdot f(s).$$

The Fast Algorithm Assume that Θ has n elements, $\vartheta_1, \vartheta_2, \ldots, \vartheta_n$. Our algorithm transforms m into f by applying to m a sequence of n elementary steps, each associated with exactly one of Θ's elements. The steps can be executed in an order.

Let m_{i-1} be the state of function m after steps associated with $\vartheta_1, \vartheta_2, \ldots, \vartheta_{i-2}$ and ϑ_{i-1} have been executed (for convenience set $m_0(a) := m(a)$). The i-th step (associated with ϑ_i) will change only values of m_{i-1} whose arguments contain ϑ_i. If $a_{-i} := a \setminus \{\vartheta_i\}$, the i-th step is defined as follows:

$$m_i(a) := \begin{cases} m_{i-1}(a) + m_{i-1}(a_{-i}) & \vartheta_i \in a \\ m_{i-1}(a) & \vartheta_i \notin a, \end{cases} \qquad (1)$$

We claim that m_n is equal to f, the Moebius transform of m.

Lemma *Let $\Theta_0 = \emptyset$, and for all $i = 1, \ldots, n$ let Θ_i be the subset $\{\vartheta_1, \vartheta_2, \ldots, \vartheta_i\}$ of Θ. After the i-th step of the algorithm defined by formula (1) it holds that*

$$m_i(a) = \sum \{m(s) \mid s \subset a,\ a \setminus s \subset \Theta_i\}.$$

PROOF. Let $\mathcal{S}_i(a) := \{s \in \mathcal{S} \mid s \subset a, a \backslash s \subset \Theta_i\}$. It is easy to show that $\mathcal{S}_i(a) = \mathcal{S}_{i-1}(a)$ if ϑ_i is not an element of a. If $\vartheta_i \in a$, then $\mathcal{S}_i(a) = \mathcal{S}_{i-1}(a) \cup \mathcal{S}_{i-1}(a_{-i})$, and $\mathcal{S}_{i-1}(a)$ and $\mathcal{S}_{i-1}(a_{-i})$ are disjoint. For $i = 0$ the lemma is trivially satisfied. To use induction assume the lemma is satisfied for all $j < i$, and prove that is is also satisfied for $j = i$: If $\vartheta_i \notin a$, then $m_i(a) = m_{i-1}(a) = \sum\{m(s) \mid s \in \mathcal{S}_{i-1}(a)\} = \sum\{m(s) \mid s \in \mathcal{S}_i(a)\}$. If $\vartheta_i \in a$, then

$$\begin{aligned} m_i(a) &= m_{i-1}(a) + m_{i-1}(a_{-i}) \\ &= \sum\{m(s) \mid s \in \mathcal{S}_{i-1}(a)\} + \sum\{m(s) \mid s \in \mathcal{S}_{i-1}(a_{-i})\} \\ &= \sum\{m(s) \mid s \in \mathcal{S}_i(a)\}. \end{aligned}$$

This completes the proof. □

The lemma implies that $m_n(a) = \sum\{m(s) \mid s \subset a, a \setminus s \subset \Theta_n\}$, and therefore $m_n(a) = \sum_{s \subset a} m(s)$ since $\Theta_n = \Theta$.

The Inverse Algorithm A closer look at formula (1) reveals that we can solve for m_{i-1}. If ϑ_i is not in a, then $m_{i-1}(a) = m_i(a)$. On the other hand, if ϑ_i belongs to a, it follows that $m_{i-1}(a_{-i}) = m_i(a_{-i})$, and therefore that $m_{i-1}(a) = m_i(a) - m_i(a_{-i})$. Together we get

$$m_{i-1}(a) = \begin{cases} m_i(a) - m_i(a_{-i}) & \vartheta_i \in a \\ m_i(a) & \vartheta_i \notin a. \end{cases}$$

Since each step in the fast algorithm can be inverted, stringing the inverted steps together will result in a fast version of the inverse transformation.

An Example For a three-element subset, $\Theta = \{\vartheta_1, \vartheta_2, \vartheta_3\}$, we can explain graphically how the algorithm works. The power set 2^Θ may be represented as a three-dimensional cube. Each corner of the cube corresponds to a subset of Θ, each edge connects two subsets that differ in exactly one element. Each dimension of the cube corresponds to one of the three elements of Θ, and to each subset we assign a number, based on the subset's bit string:

number	bit string	subset
0	000	$\emptyset$
1	001	$\{\vartheta_1\}$
2	010	$\{\vartheta_2\}$
3	011	$\{\vartheta_2, \vartheta_1\}$
4	100	$\{\vartheta_3\}$
5	101	$\{\vartheta_3, \vartheta_1\}$
6	110	$\{\vartheta_3, \vartheta_2\}$
7	111	$\{\vartheta_3, \vartheta_2, \vartheta_1\}$

At the i-th step of the algorithm the cube is partitioned into two hyperplanes. The function values for subsets in the 'lower' plane (the subsets that do not contain ϑ_i) are added to the values of the corresponding subsets in the 'upper' plane (the subsets that do contain ϑ_i). Subsets correspond to one other if they differ only in the presence or absence of ϑ_i. The procedure is repeated three times, once for each dimension of the cube (see Figures 1 and 2). The inverse algorithm subtracts the values in the lower plane from those in the upper plane.

Extensions The Moebius transformation is a linear transformation on $\mathbb{R}^S$, and, given a particular ordering of the elements of S, the transformation can be described by a corresponding matrix. For example, if Θ contains only one element ϑ_1, the transformation is

$$\begin{pmatrix} f(\{\vartheta_1\}) \\ f(\emptyset) \end{pmatrix} = \begin{pmatrix} 1 & 1 \\ 0 & 1 \end{pmatrix} \begin{pmatrix} m(\{\vartheta_1\}) \\ m(\emptyset) \end{pmatrix} \tag{2}$$

and its inverse is

$$\begin{pmatrix} f(\{\vartheta_1\}) \\ f(\emptyset) \end{pmatrix} = \begin{pmatrix} 1 & -1 \\ 0 & 1 \end{pmatrix} \begin{pmatrix} m(\{\vartheta_1\}) \\ m(\emptyset) \end{pmatrix}.$$

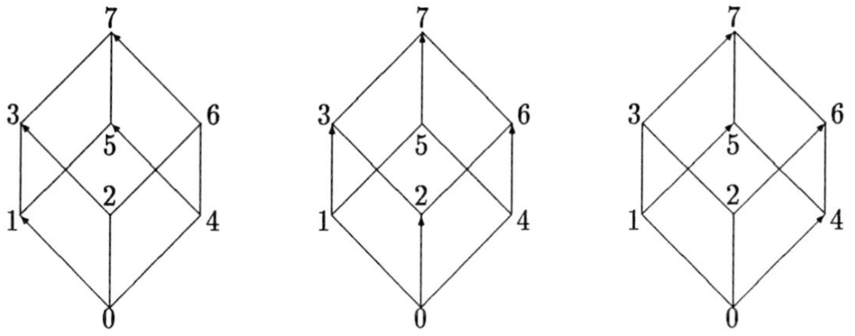

Figure 1: Stages of the fast Moebius transformation

a	$f_1(a)$	$f_2(a)$	$f_3(a)$
0	0	0	0
1	0+1	0+1	0+1
2	2	0+2	0+2
3	2+3	0+1+2+3	0+1+2+3
4	4	4	0+4
5	4+5	4+5	0+1+4+5
6	6	4+6	0+2+4+6
7	6+7	4+5+6+7	0+1+2+3+4+5+6+7

Figure 2: Intermediate values ($0 + 1$ is short for $m(0) + m(1)$)

For a two-element set, $\Theta = \{\vartheta_1, \vartheta_2\}$, and a corresponding ordering of the elements of 2^Θ we have matrices

$$\begin{pmatrix} 1 & 1 & 1 & 1 \\ 0 & 1 & 0 & 1 \\ 0 & 0 & 1 & 1 \\ 0 & 0 & 0 & 1 \end{pmatrix} \quad \text{and} \quad \begin{pmatrix} 1 & -1 & -1 & 1 \\ 0 & 1 & 0 & -1 \\ 0 & 0 & 1 & -1 \\ 0 & 0 & 0 & 1 \end{pmatrix}.$$

The two 4x4 matrices are each Kronecker products of their one-element analog. For example:

$$\begin{pmatrix} 1 & 1 & 1 & 1 \\ 0 & 1 & 0 & 1 \\ 0 & 0 & 1 & 1 \\ 0 & 0 & 0 & 1 \end{pmatrix} = \begin{pmatrix} 1 & 1 \\ 0 & 1 \end{pmatrix} \otimes \begin{pmatrix} 1 & 1 \\ 0 & 1 \end{pmatrix}.$$

Now consider the fast algorithm. Each step can be represented as

$$\begin{pmatrix} f_i(a \cup \{\vartheta_i\}) \\ f_i(a) \end{pmatrix} = \begin{pmatrix} 1 & 1 \\ 0 & 1 \end{pmatrix} \begin{pmatrix} f_{i-1}(a \cup \{\vartheta_i\}) \\ f_{i-1}(a) \end{pmatrix}, \tag{3}$$

where a is any subset of Θ that does not contain ϑ_i. It is no accident that the fast algorithm has the same matrix as the one-element transformation. Since 2^Θ is isomorphic to $\prod_1^n 2^{\{\vartheta_i\}}$, it follows that $I\!R^{\mathcal{S}}$ is isomorphic to the tensor product $I\!R^{\mathcal{S}_1} \otimes \cdots \otimes I\!R^{\mathcal{S}_n}$, where $\mathcal{S}_i := 2^{\{\vartheta_i\}}$. Consequently, the Moebius transformation is a tensor product

$$M_1 \otimes M_2 \otimes \cdots \otimes M_n$$

of simple transformations $M_i : I\!R^{\mathcal{S}_i} \to I\!R^{\mathcal{S}_i}$, each defined as in formula (3). A tensor product of mappings is inverted or transposed by inverting or transposing each factor. Hence the matrices for the dual transformation and its inverse are

$$\begin{pmatrix} 1 & 0 \\ 1 & 1 \end{pmatrix} \quad \text{and} \quad \begin{pmatrix} 1 & 0 \\ -1 & 1 \end{pmatrix} \quad \text{respectively.}$$

Using these results we can devise fast algorithms directly linking any of the four representations of a belief function. For example, the following 2x2 matrix specifies the algorithm for computing the commonality from a belief:

$$\begin{pmatrix} 1 & -1 \\ 1 & 0 \end{pmatrix} = \begin{pmatrix} 1 & 0 \\ 1 & 1 \end{pmatrix} \cdot \begin{pmatrix} 1 & -1 \\ 0 & 1 \end{pmatrix}.$$

The conjugation operation, $f'(a) := |f| - f(\overline{a})$, which links belief and plausibility, cannot be expressed directly in this scheme. However, we can write

$$f'(a) - |f| = -f(\overline{a}),$$

and the transformation from $f(a)$ to $-f(\overline{a})$ again factors and leads to the matrix

$$\begin{pmatrix} 0 & -1 \\ -1 & 0 \end{pmatrix}.$$

Now combine this transformation with ordinary Moebius transformation to convert from basic assignment to plausibility:

$$\begin{pmatrix} 0 & -1 \\ -1 & -1 \end{pmatrix} = \begin{pmatrix} 0 & -1 \\ -1 & 0 \end{pmatrix} \cdot \begin{pmatrix} 1 & 1 \\ 0 & 1 \end{pmatrix}.$$

After executing this transformation we simply subtract $|f|$ from the value at each subset to obtain the plausibilities.

Related Algorithms The fast Moebius transformation is related to Yates' algorithm. Yates (1937) (see also Snedecor and Cochran (1980)) has given simple rules for finding the factorial totals in a 2^n factorial experiment when given the totals for the individual treatment combinations. His algorithm exploits the structure of a Boolean algebra in the same way as our algorithm. Good (1958) extends Yates' algorithm to factors with more than 2 levels and relates the algorithm to Fourier transformation.

In probability theory the inversion formula for the Moebius transformation is also known as the inclusion/exclusion principle. Rota (1964) generalized the underlying principles beyond Boolean algebras of subsets to arbitrary locally finite partially ordered sets, and Barnabei, Brini, and Rota (1986) present a systematic account of this theory, which has become an important instrument of algebraic combinatorics.

5. Basic Strategies for Storing Belief Functions

Complete Tables of Function Values Consider storing an arbitrary set function $f \in I\!R^S$. The simplest scheme is a *complete table of function values*, where we store all function values in a (possibly) large table of numbers:

$$\Theta: \boxed{\begin{array}{c} f(s_0) \\ f(s_1) \\ f(s_2) \\ \vdots \\ f(s_m) \end{array}}$$

(If Θ has n elements, then $m = 2^n - 1$.) Each subset is determined by the elements it contains, and this information can be described by a bit string of length n. Each bit string in turn can be read as the binary representation of a number between 0 and m, the subset's *subset number.* If the table entries are arranged according to subset numbers, it will be easy to find a function value. However, as the size of the underlying frame increases, the table will quickly become larger and larger. The following numbers illustrate this:

$\lvert\Theta\rvert$	$\lvert 2^\Theta \rvert$
2	4
4	16
8	256
16	65,536
32	4,294,967,296

A set function on a frame with only 32 elements will fill the direct access memory of most current computers (usually 16 Megabytes or less) and will reach the limits of their addressing mechanism (typically an address cannot have more than 32 bits). Clearly, complete tables of function values are viable only in very simple situations.

Partial Tables of Function Values Functions that assign the same value (their *main value*) to many arguments can be stored efficiently in a *partial table of function values.* Each entry in such a table consists of two parts: a description of the argument subset and the corresponding function value. However, a partial table contains only those arguments that do not evaluate to the function's main value. For example, if function f differs from its main value on sets $s_1, \ldots, s_k$, we may illustrate its partial table as follows (the main value must be stored separately, and this is not shown here):

$$\Theta: \quad \begin{array}{|cc|} s_1 & f(s_1) \\ s_2 & f(s_2) \\ s_3 & f(s_3) \\ \vdots & \vdots \\ s_k & f(s_k) \end{array}$$

A function may have several main values, in which case we choose one at will. To determine the value of f at subset s the table is searched. If s is found, the table will also contain the function value. If s is not found, the function must evaluate to its main value. If we arrange the table according to subset numbers, we can use bisection to speed up the search.

Since we cannot change the number of subsets that need to be stored, the space required will depend on how compact we can store subset information. There are at least two approaches:

- *Subsets as Lists of Elements.* A subset can described by a list of its elements. If Θ has n elements we need at least $k := \lceil \log_2 n \rceil$ bits to identify one of them ($\lceil \log_2 n \rceil$ is the smallest integer larger than $\log_2 n$). To store a subset $a \subset \Theta$ will require $|a| \cdot k$ bits. We can list either the elements of a, or those of its complement $\bar{a}$, depending on which has fewer elements. However, an additional bit will be required to record our choice.

- *Subsets as Bit Strings.* Alternatively we can use a bit string of length n to describe a subset. The bit string representation is more efficient than the list of elements as soon as either a or $\overline{a}$ has more than $\lceil n/k \rceil$ elements.

If we choose the method of representation according to the number of elements in a subset, we will never need more than n bits to represent a subset. In addition, the empty set and the full frame should not be entered into the table. Both are readily recognized in either the bit string or list of elements representation, and it is not necessary to search the table. Furthermore, when either set is intersected with another set the result is predictable ($a \cap \emptyset = \emptyset$, and $a \cap \Theta = a$).

A partial table is more efficient than a complete table if the function to be stored differs from its main value on fewer than $(2^n - 1) \cdot \alpha/(n + \alpha)$ arguments. Here α is the number of bits required to store a function value. A single-precision floating-point number typically requires 32 bits.

Basic assignments often have few focal elements (i.e. their main value is 0), and are conveniently stored in partial tables. This is one of the reasons why internal computations should use basic assignments rather than beliefs, plausibilities, or commonalities. Another reason is that certain transformations are easier for basic assignments than for the other belief function representations.

Despite these tricks the space required to store a belief function is essentially determined by the size of the underlying frame. To reduce storage further we need to reduce the frame, and clearly this may not always be possible.

6. Multivariate Belief Functions

When modeling aspects of the real world we almost always deal with multivariate situations, where the frame is a product space. The product space bundles several individual frames together and provides a mechanism to study how evidence concerning a small set of variables impacts the whole model and, indirectly, the other variables.

Product Frames, Margins, and Projections Let $(\Theta_t)_{t\in T}$ be a (finite, non-empty) family of frames, and, to avoid trivialities, assume that each Θ_t has at least two elements. For any subset A of T there is a corresponding *product frame* $\Theta_A := \prod_{t\in A}\Theta_t$. The product frame Θ_T is the *common frame* (we will write Θ instead of Θ_T), all others are *marginal frames* or *margins* (it is convenient and consistent to set $\Theta_\emptyset = \{\emptyset\}$). For any product frame Θ_A there exists a corresponding projection p_A, which maps elements of Θ to elements of Θ_A.

A convenient way to visualize product frames and projections is to view an element ϑ of Θ as a tuple $(\vartheta_{t_1}, \vartheta_{t_2}, \ldots, \vartheta_{t_n})$ (assuming that T has elements $t_1, \ldots, t_n$). Projection p_A selects from tuple ϑ those components ϑ_{t_i} for which t_i belongs to A, and forms a new (shorter) tuple, which corresponds to an element of Θ_A.

Marginal Power Sets For every marginal frame Θ_A there is a corresponding *marginal power set* $\mathcal{S}_A := 2^{\Theta_A}$. The marginal power set of $\Theta_\emptyset$ is $\mathcal{S}_\emptyset := \{\emptyset, \{\emptyset\}\}$. The marginal power set of Θ is $\mathcal{S}_T$. As we did for the frame, we will drop the suffix T and write $\mathcal{S}$ instead of $\mathcal{S}_T$. Projections can be extended to power sets in the usual fashion. For example, the projection p_A maps set $s \in \mathcal{S}$ to $p_A(s) := \{p_A(\vartheta) \mid \vartheta \in s\}$, an element of $\mathcal{S}_A$.

To every projection p_A there is also an *embedding* $p_A^{-1} : \mathcal{S}_A \to \mathcal{S}$, which maps the subset $s_A \in \mathcal{S}_A$ to set $p_A^{-1}(s_A) := \bigcup\{s \in \mathcal{S} \mid p_A(s) = s_A\}$, an element of $\mathcal{S}$. Note that $p_A^{-1}(s_A)$ is the largest element of $\mathcal{S}$ that projects to s_A, and that $p_A \cdot p_A^{-1}(s_A) = s_A$, for all $s_A \in \mathcal{S}_A$.

The set $a_A^{\uparrow} := p_A^{-1}(a_A)$ is the *cylinder* associated with $a_A \in \mathcal{S}_A$. The elements of $\mathcal{S}_A$ are in one-to-one correspondence with their cylinders, and the set of all cylinders forms the *embedded marginal power set*

$$\mathcal{S}_A^{\uparrow} := \{a_A^{\uparrow} \mid a_A \in \mathcal{S}_A\}.$$

For formal derivations it is often convenient to assume that all marginal elements are embedded in the common frame. Projection can then be considered as an operation internal to the common frame, and any combination of projection can always be executed. Correspondingly, we define for any $A \subset T$ a mapping called *propagation*:

$$\pi_A : \mathcal{S} \to \mathcal{S}, \quad \pi_A(a) := p_A^{-1} \cdot p_A(a), \quad \text{for } a \in \mathcal{S}.$$

Two propagations combine in the following manner: $\pi_A \cdot \pi_B(a) = \pi_{A \cap B}(a)$. If a subset of Θ belongs to $\mathcal{S}_A^{\uparrow}$, we say it is *carried by margin* Θ_A. If $a \in \mathcal{S}$ is carried by Θ_A it is also carried by Θ_B, whenever $A \subset B$. Furthermore, if a is carried by Θ_A and Θ_B it is also carried by $\Theta_{A \cap B}$. Consequently, there is for any a a smallest set $A \subset T$ such that Θ_A carries a. If this is the case we call Θ_A the subset's *carrier margin.*

Set Functions on Product Frames Using the principles developed in section 2, it is now easy to extend projection, extension, and propagation to set functions defined on the common frame or one of its margins.

Let f be a set function on Θ. Its *projection* onto margin Θ_A is $f_A^{\downarrow} := \widetilde{p_A}(f)$, and it holds that

$$f_A^{\downarrow}(s_A) = \sum_{p_A(s)=s_A} f(s),$$

for all $s_A \in \mathcal{S}_A$. The *extension* of a set function f_A over Θ_A is the function $f_A^{\uparrow} := \widetilde{p_A^{-1}}(f_A)$ on Θ, for which

$$f_A^{\uparrow}(a) = \sum_{p_A^{-1}(s_A)=a} f_A(s_A) = \begin{cases} f_A(s_A) & \text{if } a = p_A^{-1}(s_A) \\ 0 & \text{else,} \end{cases}$$

for all $a \in \mathcal{S}$. The extension $f_A^{\uparrow}$ of f_A simply replaces all elements of $\mathcal{S}_A$ by those of $\mathcal{S}_A^{\uparrow}$, but does not change any of the weights. Given the extension we may consider $I\!R^{\mathcal{S}_A^{\uparrow}}$ as a linear subspace of $I\!R^{\mathcal{S}}$.

The *propagation* of $f \in I\!R^{\mathcal{S}}$ to margin A is the function $f_A := \widetilde{\pi_A}(f)$. It follows that

$$f_A(a) = \sum_{\pi_A(s)=a} f(s)$$

for all $a \in \mathcal{S}$. We will say that $f \in I\!R^{\mathcal{S}}$ is *carried by margin* Θ_A if all focal elements of f belong to $\mathcal{S}_A^{\uparrow}$. Margin Θ_A is the *carrier margin* of f if A is the smallest subset of T such that all of f's focal elements belong to $\mathcal{S}_A^{\uparrow}$. If the focal elements of f have carriers $\Theta_{A_1}, \ldots, \Theta_{A_k}$ then $A = \bigcup_{i=1}^{k} A_i$.

Finally, note that $|\widetilde{\pi_A}(f)| = |f|$ and $\|\widetilde{\pi_A}(f)\| = \widetilde{\pi_A}(\|f\|)$. The same is true if we replace $\widetilde{\pi_A}$ by either $\widetilde{p_A}$ or $\widetilde{p_A^{-1}}$.

Let S be a random set and m_S its basic assignment. From section 2 we know that $m_{\pi_A(S)}$, the basic assignment of the projection of S, is equal to $\widetilde{\pi_A}(m_S)$, the projection of the basic assignment. The same is true if we replace propagation by extension and projection.

One advantage of belief functions over probabilities is the ease with which they extend from a marginal frame to the common frame and then project to other marginal frames. Of course, we can extend a marginal probability in the same way, but the result will be a belief function rather than a probability. The maximum entropy principle is needed to select one element from the set of compatible measures induced by the belief function extension.

7. Graphical Belief Functions

Graphical belief functions are multivariate belief functions that are combinations of several marginal belief functions. Graphical belief functions are interesting because they can be stored efficiently.

The basic assignment m of a graphical belief function can be written as

$$m = m_1 \oplus \cdots \oplus m_k,$$

where the m_is are basic assignments carried by margins $\Theta_{A_1}, \ldots, \Theta_{A_k}$. The family $\mathbf{A} := (A_1, \ldots, A_k)$ is called the *graphical structure* of m. Graphical belief functions arise when several independent marginal pieces of evidence accumulate, or when it is possible to factor a given overall belief function. Graphical belief functions can be stored more efficiently than non-graphical ones, since each component can be stored as an element of its carrier margin. The sum of the components will require less space than the overall belief function. This is true because the space required to store a belief function grows roughly exponentially with the size of the underlying frame. At any time we can recreate the overall belief function from its pieces should that be necessary.

Often the graphical structure can be simplified. For example, the family **A** may contain the same subset several times. In such a case we should combine the corresponding basic assignments since their combination will be carried by the same margin or possibly by a smaller one. The same argument applies when one element of **A** is contained in another one. Combining the two will produce a belief function carried by the larger margin, which will usually require less space then the initial components.

A graphical structure **A** that does not contain superfluous elements will be called a *scheme* (this term is borrowed from the theory of relation databases). A scheme then is simply a set of incomparable subsets of T.

Local Computations Essentially we are able to disassemble a graphical belief function into smaller pieces that can be stored more efficiently. However, it seems that each time we want to compute we need to pull out the pieces, assemble them into the original belief function and then go about computing. Hence we can store a function efficiently only as long as we do not use it. However, it turns out that the usual belief function computations can be done on the pieces alone, without having to recreate the overall function first. This is usually referred to as the ability to do computations *locally.*

All belief function computations can be broken down into a sequence of the basic operations: combination (made up of convolution and normalization), projection, extension, and conversion. To combine two graphical belief functions simply collect all their components and then reduce the resulting graphical structure to a scheme by combining

components on comparable frames. Conversion and normalization can usually wait until the very end. The critical operation is therefore projection. Projection can be performed locally because the sequence of projection and convolution operations can be interchanged under certain circumstances. The following lemma describes these circumstances.

Exchange Lemma *Let R, A, and B be subsets of T, and let f_A and f_B be two set functions carried by Θ_A and Θ_B, respectively. If and only if $A \cap B \subset R$ is a subset of R does it hold that $\widetilde{\pi_R}(f_A * f_B) = \widetilde{\pi_R}(f_A) * \widetilde{\pi_R}(f_B)$.*

PROOF. We need to prove the result only for sets. Using the argument of section 2, the set result easily extends to the linear transformations induced.

Consider set a carried by Θ_A and set b carried by Θ_B. Without loss of generality we can assume that $R = A \cap B$. Any other situation reduces to this one by setting $A' := A \cup R$ and $B' := B \cup R$. It follows that $A' \cap B' = R$, that a is carried by $\Theta_{A'}$ and b by $\Theta_{B'}$.

Since $a \cap b$ is a subset of a as well as b, the projection $\pi_{A \cap B}(a \cap b)$ is a subset of $\pi_{A \cap B}(a)$ and of $\pi_{A \cap B}(b)$, and therefore a subset of $\pi_{A \cap B}(a) \cap \pi_{A \cap B}(b)$.

To prove that $\pi_{A \cap B}(a) \cap \pi_{A \cap B}(b)$ is a subset of $\pi_{A \cap B}(a \cap b)$ assume ϑ is an element of $\pi_{A \cap B}(a) \cap \pi_{A \cap B}(b)$, and show that ϑ is also in $\pi_{A \cap B}(a \cap b)$. There exist elements $\vartheta_a \in a$ and $\vartheta_b \in b$ such that $p_B(\vartheta) = p_B(\vartheta_a)$ and $p_A(\vartheta) = p_A(\vartheta_b)$. Based on $\vartheta, \vartheta_a, \vartheta_b$ define

$$\vartheta'(t) := \begin{cases} \vartheta_a(t) & t \in A \\ \vartheta_b(t) & t \in B \\ \vartheta(t) & \text{else.} \end{cases}$$

This is possible because ϑ, ϑ_a, and ϑ_b coincide on margin $\Theta_{A \cap B}$. Element ϑ' is in a, because $p_A(\vartheta') = p_A(\vartheta_a)$. Similarly, $\vartheta' \in b$, and therefore $\vartheta' \in a \cap b$. Since $p_{A \cap B}(\vartheta) = p_{A \cap B}(\vartheta')$, it follows that $\vartheta \in \pi_{A \cap B}(a \cap b)$, which completes the proof. □

The lemma extends to schemes with more than two elements. We will not dwell on the

details of local computations. Kong (1986) worked out the details for the belief function case. Almond (1990) and several papers in Shafer and Pearl (1990) give detailed descriptions too. The graphical structure is most conveniently described by schemes or *hypergraphs*, but several of the algorithms work with equivalent graph-based representations.

8. Storing Multivariate Belief Functions

Graphical belief functions can be stored efficiently because each factor is stored on a smaller marginal frame, and together the marginal factors require less space than the overall belief function would. Graphical belief functions have two drawbacks: (1) Not all multivariate belief functions are graphical, and (2) they do not exploit all the possibilities for factorization. For a belief function to be graphical each focal element has to factor, all focal elements have to factor simultaneously according to the same scheme, and the associated weights have to factor in the same way as the focal elements. However, we need not insist that the entire belief function factor. Efficient storage is possible if each focal element factors individually. We will also consider techniques for saving storage space based on decompositions rather than factorizations of belief functions and their focal elements.

8.1. Representations Based on Factorization of Focal Elements

When storing belief functions most of the space is used to store subset information. The amount of space used depends on the size of the underlying frame. The space requirements increase roughly exponentially with the size of the frame. Due to this explosive growth, it takes less space to store the components of a graphical belief function (each on its own frame) than to store the overall function.

Consider the graphical belief function $m = m_A \oplus m_B$ with graphical structure $\{A, B\}$, where $m_A = \alpha_1 \cdot \delta_{a_1} + \alpha_2 \cdot \delta_{a_2}$ is carried by margin Θ_A, and $m_B = \beta_1 \cdot \delta_{b_1} + \beta_2 \cdot \delta_{b_2}$ is

carried by Θ_B. It now holds that

$$\begin{aligned} m_A \oplus m_B &= \| (\alpha_1\beta_1) \cdot \delta_{a_1 \cap b_1} + (\alpha_1\beta_2) \cdot \delta_{a_1 \cap b_2} + (\alpha_2\beta_1) \cdot \delta_{a_2 \cap b_1} + (\alpha_2\beta_2) \cdot \delta_{a_2 \cap b_2} \| \\ &=: m_1 \cdot \delta_{s_1} + m_2 \cdot \delta_{s_2} + m_3 \cdot \delta_{s_1} + m_4 \cdot \delta_{s_4}. \end{aligned}$$

To store m we can use two partial tables of function values, one over frame Θ_A and one over frame Θ_B:

Θ_A:

a_1	α_1
a_2	α_2

Θ_B:

b_1	β_1
b_2	β_2

The two tables together form a *representation* of m. At any given time we can reconstitute m based on this representation. The representation was based on the fact that the belief function was graphical. However, there are convenient representations also for belief functions that are not graphical.

Imagine that two of m's focal weights are exchanged (for example exchange $(\alpha_1\beta_2)$ and $(\alpha_2\beta_1)$). Except in very special circumstances the new m will no longer factor, and the function is no longer graphical. However, the subset information has not changed, and can be stored as before. Our representation simply has to separate weights from subset information:

m:

m_1:	(A,1), (B,1)
m_2:	(A,1), (B,2)
m_3:	(A,2), (B,1)
m_4:	(A,2), (B,2)

Θ_A:	a_1, a_2
Θ_B:	b_1, b_2

The table on the left lists all focal elements. Each entry consists of the focal element's weight and a list of 'pointers' to marginal sets that form a factorization of the focal element. On the right there are two tables, each associated with a marginal frame. Each table contains descriptions of subsets carried by that margin. A pointer like $(A, 1)$ in the table on the left points to the first subset description in the table for margin Θ_A.

The storage scheme just introduced is called a *graphical representation* of a belief function. Every graphical belief function has a graphical representation, but not ever belief function with a graphical representation is graphical. In a graphical representation it is difficult to determine whether two sets are equal or not, and consequently it will not be easy to look up the function value for a given argument. However, only seldomly do we need to look up a specific function value.

The situation above is not the most general case, since the focal elements still factor jointly (all focal elements can be formed from sets of marginal subsets, and all intersections of the as and bs appear as focal elements). We now consider each focal element individually and try to find its best factorization. For example our belief functions may have the following representations

$$m = m_1 \cdot \delta_{a_1 \cap b_1} + m_2 \cdot \delta_{a_1 \cap c \cap d} + m_3 \cdot \delta_{a_2 \cap b_1} + m_4 \cdot \delta_{a_2 \cap c \cap d}$$

(b_2 can be factored into c and d). We may than use the following representation:

m:	m_1:	(A,1), (B,1)	Θ_A:	a_1, a_2
	m_2:	(A,1), (C,1), (D,1)	Θ_B:	b_1
	m_3:	(A,2), (B,1)	Θ_C:	c
	m_4:	(A,2), (C,1), (D,1)	Θ_D:	d

Since we were able to factor some of the focal elements further we have saved even more space. Clearly we want to factor each focal element as much as possible and we will store each subset factor on the smallest margin that can represent it, i.e., its carrier margin. In this new representation each focal element as opposed to the entire belief function has a graphical structure.

8.2. Representations Based on Decomposition

Decomposition can be used alone or in combination with factorization. Most often decomposition will be used when all factorization possibilities are exhausted. Like

factorization decomposition can be applied to a belief function as a whole or individually to each focal element.

Decomposition of Focal Elements A set $a \subset \Theta$ might not factor, but it may be the union of subsets that do. If this is the case we can simply factor each component. Or we can split the subset into a large component that factors, and store the remaining elements in whatever form is most convenient (as a list of elements or as a bit string). Or we can try to find the largest subset that factors, and then repeat the process for the remaining elements over and over until no further storage space can be saved.

Alternatively we can try to augment the set a with a few elements to a set that can be factored:

$$a'' = a \cup a',$$

where $a \cap a' = \emptyset$. Again, a' itself may factor too. Of course, we need to remember whether a component needs to be added or subtracted.

Decomposition of Belief Functions The same idea can be extended to belief functions, where we either decompose m as $m = m' + m''$ and factor one or both terms, or we write $m = m' - m''$ and then factor $m + m''$, and possibly m' independently of $m + m''$.

Local Computations Local computations for graphical belief functions are possible because the sequence of projection and convolution operations can be interchanged. However, this interchange depends only on the factorization of focal elements (think of belief functions as random subsets). It is therefore immediately clear that computations can still be done locally for our abstract representations. However, the algorithm and the tracking of the computational elements become more involved, and the components of the representation can no longer be interpreted.

Computations can be done locally for decompositions since projection or propagation are linear operations, $\widetilde{\pi_R}(m_1 + m_2) = \widetilde{\pi_R}(m_1) + \widetilde{\pi_R}(m_2)$, and because $\pi_R(a \cup b) = \pi_R(a) \cup \pi_R(b)$. However, subtractive decomposition of focal elements has do be treated special since $\pi_R(a \setminus b) \neq \pi_R(a) \setminus \pi_R(b)$.

9. Factorization of Sets and Belief Functions

Clearly, factorization of the focal elements is at the heart of the storage scheme we developed in the previous section. Factorization properties of sets are also studied in the theory of relational databases, from a different point of view though. In relational database theory subsets of product spaces are used to model relationships that hold in the real world (employee data, bank accounts, inventory data, etc.). Since the relationships modelled may change over time, it is necessary to consider classes of subsets rather than individual sets. Factorization properties, the ways in which all elements of the class factor, capture certain time-invariant structures in the data and can be used to optimize storage of the relations. Relational database theory offers rules for deducing from an initial set of factorizations new factorizations. These rules are such that any set that satisfies the initial factorizations will also satisfy the new ones.

There is an analogous situation in probability theory. Conditional independence among sets of random variables leads to a factorization of the induced density into two factors. Such independence statements can be used to specify the structural aspects of probability models (models specified in this manner are called graphical models). As in the set case one is interested in deducing from an initial set of independence relations new ones that are also satisfied by all models of the original ones. The same point of view can also be applied to belief functions. Shafer and Pearl (1990) contains several papers developing this idea for probability as well as belief function models.

Our approach here is simpler. We need to be able to determine for a given focal element whether it factors, and if it does, what the factors are. This is the topic of the first half of this section. In the second half we consider the same question for belief functions as a whole. There is a surprising twist to considering this question for whole belief functions. While belief functions in many ways behave like probabilities, this is one of the instances where they exhibit new properties.

9.1. Factorization of Sets

Below we will consider (1) how to *test* whether a set factors according to a given scheme, and (2) how to *search* for possible factorizations.

Searching for factorizations turns out to be tricky, since many potential factorizations may need to be tested. However, factorizations are not independent of each other, and we can exploit their interdependence. Such dependencies among factorizations have been investigated in the theory of relational databases, and we will be able to make use of these results.

Testing for Factorization with a Given Scheme Subset $s \in \Theta$ *factors over* $\{A, B\}$) if there exist two sets, $s_A \subset \Theta_A$ and $s_B \subset \Theta_B$, such that $s = s_A^{\uparrow} \cap s_B^{\uparrow}$. The factors s_A and s_B need not be unique, but each factor will contain the corresponding projection of s, i.e., $p_A(s) \subset s_A$ and $p_B(s) \subset s_B$, or equivalently, $\pi_A(s) \subset s_A^{\uparrow}$ and $\pi_B(s) \subset s_B^{\uparrow}$. In fact, the projections themselves are factors. Since $s \subset \pi_A(s)$ and $s \subset \pi_B(s)$ it follows that s is a subset of $\pi_A(s) \cap \pi_B(s)$. Furthermore, each factor contains the projection, and hence $\pi_A(s) \cap \pi_B(s)$ is a subset of s. The projections are the smallest factors, and it is therefore convenient to select the projections as *the* factors. The *factorization test* then amounts to checking whether $s = \pi_A(s) \cap \pi_B(s)$. Clearly, the test generalizes to any number of factors.

We say that two elements ϑ and ξ of Θ *coincide on margin* Θ_A if their projections on Θ_A agree, i.e., $p_A(\vartheta) = p_A(\xi)$. A second and equivalent way to express factorization into two factors is given by the following lemma.

Alternate Factorization Test *A subset s of Θ factors over $\{A, B\}$ exactly if for any two elements ϑ and ξ of s that coincide on $\Theta_{A\cap B}$, the set $\pi_A(\vartheta) \cap \pi_B(\xi)$ is a subset of s.*

PROOF. First consider the special case where $A \cup B = T$ and $A \cap B = \emptyset$. In this situation any two elements coincide on $\Theta_\emptyset$.

Assume that s factors and that ϑ and ξ are two distinct elements of s; then show that $\pi_A(\vartheta) \cap \pi_B(\xi) \subset s$. The set $\pi_A(\vartheta) \cap \pi_B(\xi)$ cannot be empty since $A \cap B = \emptyset$. Furthermore, since $\pi_A(\vartheta) \subset \pi_A(s)$ and $\pi_B(\xi) \subset \pi_B(s)$, it follows that $\pi_A(\vartheta) \cap \pi_B(\xi)$ is a subset of $\pi_A(s) \cap \pi_B(s)$, and therefore a subset of s. This proves one direction of the equivalence.

Now assume that for any two elements, $\vartheta, \xi \in s$, set $\pi_A(\vartheta) \cap \pi_B(\xi)$ is a subset of s, and prove that $s = \pi_A(s) \cap \pi_B(s)$. Clearly, $\pi_A(s) \cap \pi_B(s)$ can be written as $\pi_A(\bigcup_{\vartheta\in s}\{\vartheta\}) \cap \pi_B(\bigcup_{\xi\in s}\{\xi\})$, which is equal to $\bigcup_{\vartheta\in s}\bigcup_{\xi\in s}(\pi_A(\vartheta) \cap \pi_B(\xi))$ and is a subset of s. Hence, $\pi_A(s) \cap \pi_B(s) \subset s$. Since $s \subset \pi_A(s)$ and $s \subset \pi_B(s)$, it follows that s is also a subset of $\pi_A(s) \cap \pi_B(s)$, and hence $s = \pi_A(s) \cap \pi_B(s)$. This proves that s factors.

The general case is reduced to the special one in two steps, each independent of the other. First deal with the situation $A \cup B \neq T$. Set s will factor exactly if s is carried by $\Theta_{A\cup B}$ and if $p_{A\cup B}(s)$ factors over $\{A, B\}$. Since A and B cover $A \cup B$ we are back in a situation where $A \cup B = T$.

If $A \cap B \neq \emptyset$, consider for each $\nu \in \Theta_{A\cap B}$ the corresponding cylinder $\nu^\dagger$. The collection of these cylinders partitions frame Θ and 'slices up s.' Clearly, if s factors, so will any slice $s \cap \nu^\dagger$. Vice versa, if every slice of s factors, so will s. Furthermore, each cylinder $\nu^\dagger$ is really a copy of margin $\Theta_{A\triangle B}$ (the dimensions that belong to either A or B, but not to both), and within each cylinder a slice $s \cap \nu^\dagger$ is asked to factor over $\{A \setminus B, B \setminus A\}$. Since $A \setminus B$ and $B \setminus A$ are disjoint, we are back to the special case. This completes the proof. □

This second criterion is known in the theory of relational databases as *multivalued dependency* (Maier 1983). In the context of relational databases one would say that the dimensions (or attributes) in $A \cap B$ *multidetermine* those in $A \setminus B$ (or equivalently those in $B \setminus A$).

The slicing idea also points to an algorithm for finding decompositions. By separating the slices that factor from those that do not, we can create a decomposition of the given set into a part that factors and one that does not. The latter may be stored since it is smaller than the original set or may be treated further.

Searching for Factorizations Using one of the two factorization criterion we can now search for factorizations. A basic heuristic algorithm consists of the following two steps:

1. *Reduce the set under consideration to its carrier margin.* The reduction is achieved by eliminating superfluous dimensions. Whenever $\pi_{T\setminus t}(s) = s$ for some $t \in T$, we continue to work with $p_{T\setminus t}(s)$ instead of s. If T has n elements, we need no more than n steps to reach the carrier margin.

2. *Find two dimensions $t_1, t_2 \in T$ such that s factors over $\{T \setminus t_1, T \setminus t_2\}$.* If T has n elements, there are $n \cdot (n-1)/2$ cases to be considered. If s factors at all (into two factors), this step will find a factorization.

If step 2 finds a factorization the algorithm is run again on each factor separately, and again on factors of factors, and so on. The algorithm stops if no factor can be factored further.

This algorithm will find only *acyclic* factorizations. However, some cyclic factorizations can still be dealt with. A cyclic factorization is either *conformal* or *non-conformal* (for a definition of cyclic, acyclic, and conformal factorizations see Maier, 1983). Thoma (1989) shows that conformal factorizations can be described by graphs and equivalently by binary factorizations (factorizations with two factors). Any conformal, cyclic factorization induces several binary factorizations. A set may factor according to all induced schemes, but still may not factor according to the underlying cyclic one. To be sure we need to test using the first criterion (the second is not applicable since there are more than two factors). The underlying cyclic scheme can be determined from the induced binary factorizations. However, the effort required can be justified only in very special circumstances. Instead of searching for possible cyclical factorization it may be more efficient to consider decompositions instead.

9.2. Factorization of Belief Functions

Belief functions (or set functions in general) do not behave as simply as sets. For example, a belief function m that factors over $\{A, B\}$ does not satisfy the equation $m = \widetilde{\pi_A}(m) * \widetilde{\pi_B}(m)$, which would be the generalization of the corresponding set result. Below we will derive corresponding ways of dealing with factorization. We consider factorization in terms of convolution rather than combination. But all results can be extended to combination simply by normalizing all equations.

Binary Factorization Assume that f_1 and f_2 are two set functions on Θ carried by margins Θ_A and Θ_B, respectively. The function $f = f_1 * f_2$ factors over $\{A, B\}$ and is therefore carried by $\Theta_{A\cup B}$. Since $A \cap B$ is a subset of A, $\widetilde{\pi_A}(f_1) = f_1$, $\widetilde{\pi_B}(f_2) = f_2$, and using the exchange lemma it follows that $\widetilde{\pi_A}(f) = f_1 * \widetilde{\pi_{A\cap B}}(f_2)$, and $\widetilde{\pi_B}(f) = \widetilde{\pi_{A\cap B}}(f_1) * f_2$. Putting both results together, we find that f satisfies the equation $\widetilde{\pi_A}(f) * \widetilde{\pi_B}(f) = \widetilde{\pi_{A\cap B}}(f) * \widetilde{\pi_{A\cup B}}(f)$.

Definition A set function $f \in I\!R^S$ is said to be *modular with respect to scheme* $\{A, B\}$ if $\widetilde{\pi_A}(f) * \widetilde{\pi_B}(f) = \widetilde{\pi_{A\cap B}}(f) * \widetilde{\pi_{A\cup B}}(f)$.

If a set function admits a binary factorization, it will be modular with respect to the same scheme. For belief functions the reverse is true too, but there is a little surprise.

Lemma *Let $\{A, B\}$ be a binary scheme over T. If belief function $m \in I\!R^S$ is modular with respect to $\{A, B\}$ and is carried by $\Theta_{A\cup B}$, then there exist two set functions m_1 and m_2 carried by Θ_A and Θ_B, respectively, such that $m = m_1 * m_2$.*

PROOF. Assume m is carried by $\Theta_{A\cup B}$ and is modular with respect to $\{A, B\}$. Let Q_A, Q_B, $Q_{A\cap B}$, and $Q_{A\cup B}$ be the commonalities of $\widetilde{\pi_A}(m)$, $\widetilde{\pi_B}(m)$, $\widetilde{\pi_{A\cap B}}(m)$, and $\widetilde{\pi_{A\cup B}}(m)$, respectively. It follows that $Q_{A\cup B} \cdot Q_{A\cap B} = Q_A \cdot Q_B$. For every $a \subset \Theta$ define

$$Q_1(a) := Q_A(a), \quad \text{and}$$

$$Q_2(a) := \begin{cases} Q_B(a)/Q_{A\cap B}(a), & \text{if } Q_{A\cap B}(a) \neq 0 \\ 0, & \text{if } Q_{A\cap B}(a) = 0. \end{cases}$$

It follows that $Q_1(a) \cdot Q_2(a) = Q_{A\cup B}(a)$, whenever $Q_{A\cap B}(a) \neq 0$. The same is true if $Q_{A\cap B}(a) = 0$, since $Q_{A\cap B}(a) = 0$ implies $Q_{A\cup B}(a) = 0$. This in turn holds because $Q_{A\cap B}(a) = \sum_{\pi_{A\cap B}(s)\supset a} m(s)$ and therefore $Q_{A\cap B}(a) \geq Q_{A\cup B}(a)$, for all $a \subset \Theta$.

The commonalities Q_1 and Q_2 define two 'basic assignments' m_1 and m_2, such that $m = m_1 * m_2$. The factors m_1 and m_2 are certainly quasi-belief functions, but we cannot be be sure that they are belief functions, i.e., that they are positive. This completes the proof. □

It comes as a surprise that the factors we construct may not be belief functions. One could argue that this is simply a shortcoming of our construction and that there may exist other factors that are positive. However, the following example, due to Kong (personal communication), specifies a belief function that factors only into quasi-belief functions.

EXAMPLE. Let $T := \{1, 2, 3\}$, and let $\Theta_1 := \{0, 1\}$, $\Theta_2 := \{0, 1, 2\}$, and $\Theta_3 := \{0, 1\}$. Furthermore, let m_{12} be a belief function on $\Theta_1 \times \Theta_2$, and m_{23} a quasi-belief function on $\Theta_2 \times \Theta_3$. The two functions are defined as follows:

$s \in \Theta_{12}$	$m_{12}(s)$
$\{00, 01, 11\}$	1/6
$\{10, 01\}$	1/6
$\{10, 12\}$	1/6
$\{00, 02\}$	1/6
$\{01, 02\}$	1/6
$\{01, 11, 12\}$	1/6

$s \in \Theta_{23}$	$m_{23}(s)$
$\{01, 10, 11, 21\}$	1/2
$\{00, 10, 11, 20\}$	1/2
$\{01, 10, 20\}$	1/2
$\{01, 10, 11, 20\}$	-1/2

The function $m_{12}^{\uparrow} * m_{23}^{\uparrow}$ is positive and factors, but there is no factorization into belief functions.

Functions like the one just defined belong to the class of *generalized graphical belief functions.* A multivariate belief function is generalized graphical if it factors into quasi-belief functions carried by marginal frames. Clearly, any graphical belief function is also generalized graphical, since any belief function is a quasi-belief function. However, it is not known what additional condition a generalized graphical belief function has to satisfy to be graphical.

Graphical belief functions usually arise when several marginal belief functions are combined. Generalized graphical belief functions, in contrast, arise when we try to factor a given multivariate belief function to store it more efficiently. Using the test for binary factorization developed above and the method for constructing factors indicated in the lemma, we can find factorization using essentially the same strategy as in the set case. However, factoring focal elements is clearly faster and more efficient.

Acknowledgements

This article is based on the author's dissertation, written at Harvard under the guidance of Prof. Arthur Dempster. The author also profited from discussions with Prof. Hung Nguyen and with his colleagues Augustine Kong and Russell Almond. Joe Hill helped focusing some of the ideas, and Charles Matthews made suggestions on improving the writing of this article. Research for this article has been partially supported by ONR contract N00014-85-K-0745, ARO Contract DAAL03-86-K-0042, and NSF Grants DMS-85-03362 and DMS-85-04332.

References

1. Almond, R. (1990) Fusion and propagation of graphical belief models, Ph.D. thesis, Harvard Univ., Dept. of Statistics.

2. Barnabei, M., Brini, A. and Rota, G-C. (1986) The theory of Moebius functions, *Russian Mathematical Surveys* (41), 135–188.

3. Choquet, G. (1953) Theory of capacities, *Annales de l'Institut Fourier* (5), 131–292.

4. Dempster, A. P. (1967) Upper and lower probabilities induced by a multivalued mapping, *Ann. Math. Statist.* (38), 325–339.

5. Good, I. J. (1958) The interaction algorithm and practical Fourier analysis, *JRSS B* (20), 361–372.

6. Huber, P. J. (1981) *Robust Statistics*, Wiley, New York.

7. Kong, A. (1986) Multivariate belief functions and graphical models, Ph.D. thesis, Harvard Univ., Dept. of Statistics.

8. Maier, D. (1983) *The Theory of Relational Databases*, Computer Science Press, Rockville, MD.

9. Rota, G-C. (1964) On the foundation of combinatorial theory: I. theory of Moebius functions, *Z. Wahrsch. Theorie* (2), 340–368.

10. Shafer, G. (1976) *A Mathematical Theory of Evidence*, Princeton Univ. Press.

11. Shafer, G. and Pearl, J., eds. (1990) *Readings in Uncertain Reasoning*, Morgan Kaufmann, San Mateo, CA.

12. Snedecor, G. W. and Cochran, W. G. (1980) *Statistical Methods*, Iowa State Univ. Press, Ames, IA.

13. Thoma, H. M. (1989) Factorization of belief functions, Ph.D. thesis, Harvard Univ., Dept. of Statistics.

14. Yates, F. (1937) The design and analysis of factorial experiments, *Commonw. Bur. Soil Sci. Tech. Commun.* 35.

Conditional Logic in Expert Systems
I.R. Goodman, M.M. Gupta, H.T. Nguyen and G.S. Rogers (editors)

A RANDOM SET FORMALISM FOR EVIDENTIAL REASONING

Kevin Hestir, Hung T. Nguyen, Gerald S. Rogers

Department of Mathematical Sciences
New Mexico State University
Las Cruces NM, 88003

Abstract: This tutorial article addresses two themes:
i) the theory of random sets as a corner-stone of inferential techniques in evidential reasoning and
ii) random sets as a formal connection between popular approaches to modeling and manipulation of uncertainty in artificial intelligence. The emphasis is on using random sets as a mathematical language for the theory of belief functions. Foundations, knowledge representation, and inference are investigated in this spirit.

Keywords: artificial intelligence, evidence, uncertainty, belief functions, random sets.

1. Introduction

Debates about various approaches to modeling and manipulation of uncertainty in artificial intelligence (AI) are a sign of the healthy and vigorous activity in this field. Such real world problems always involve knowledge from different fields and very often mathematics is invoked not only as a means of communication but also as a referee. Moreover, modeling, as it progresses from dynamical physical laws to laws of random phenomena to laws of thought, is an increasingly complex task and the theories proposed in the AI literature for the latter cases have been justified mostly on an empirical basis. In this article we focus attention on "belief functions" which have received much attention in AI recently. We will show that it is possible to lay down a probabilistic basis for the "conditioning problem" which has been considered one of the drawbacks of the theory.

In our presentation, we have two specific audiences in mind:
i) AI researchers and computer scientists, for whom we present basic explanations of the mathematics involved and call attention to existing techniques and methodologies in statistics;
ii) probabilists and statisticians, to whom we extend the invitation to examine this field of application where their expertise will be a powerful weapon.

The mathematical material is based on a synthesis of various sources, in particular, Matheron (1975). In section 2, we give our interpretation of "evidential reasoning" in AI. Section 3 contains an elementary developement of random sets. This is needed in section 4 to examine the extent to which random sets can be used to model incomplete information and in section 5 to discuss the conditioning problem in inference procedures.

In preparing this paper, we have benefitted from discussions with the attendees of our seminar in 1989 and from a preprint of J. Pearl (1990).

2. The concept of evidence

Expert systems or intelligent machines in AI are computer programs which mimic some processes in human reasoning. The main goal of these systems is to provide support for decision making. The input to an AI program is what we call "evidence" and the output is created by the inference engine and "knowledge base". We discuss these concepts below.

Given evidence, the reasoning of a human expert involves at least two components, "his/her knowledge" and "his/her way of thinking" ; analogues for machines are the inference engine and the knowledge base. The inference engine is some reasoning procedure based on a logical consequence relation $\Rightarrow$. When reasoning with (conditional) uncertain information, some form of multi-valued logic is used instead of classical two-valued logic. Moreover, when the uncertainty involved is treated in a quantitative way, such as in conditional probability logic, the semantic of the logical consequence relation depends on the type of uncertainty measure used. This fact is expressed roughly as "reasoning with belief functions, fuzzy reasoning, probabilistic reasoning, etc." In this paper we will not deal with the problem of "reasoning with random sets," but simply present an elementary mathematical theory of random sets. Pragmatic aspects of random set theory are another matter. This is similar to the distinction between probability theory and applied statistics!

The knowledge base contains information which is uncertain, incomplete, and imprecise:

i) *uncertainty* As an example, we note that some medical knowledge can be represented by "If$\cdots$, then$\cdots$" rules with associated "degrees of belief" . This is the information obtained from the experts; it is interpretation of "degrees of belief" which leads to different concepts of uncertainty in AI. When these rules are viewed in terms of conditional probabilities, uncertainty is probability but not all experts do their reasoning in terms of probability theory.

ii) *incompleteness* If we have a model in which the uncertainty is probability and the probability law governing the model is completely known (specificied), then the reasoning task involves simply the calculus of probability. Unfortunately, real world problems are generally incomplete in that the probability law is only partially specified. Then the calculus of probability might be used to obtain approximations of those probabilities which are not known. A simple example is to approximate $P(a|bc)$ from $P(a|b)$ and $P(a|c)$. Different kinds of approximations generate different inference engines; this is, after all, decision theory with incomplete information. And, the term "probabilistic reasoning" means the computation of probabilities in a way that humans might reason.

iii) *imprecision* Although the information given by experts is to be stored in the data-base of the machine, it might be given in linguistic terms, adding still another facet to the encoding. How does one represent the ambiguity and imprecision in, for example, "If this person's blood pressure is high, then she has terrible disease T with belief .7" ? In general, these questions involve not only the assignment of probability to such fuzzy propositions but also their representation to begin with; thus, fuzzy logic (Zadeh, 1984) becomes a viable tool.

We would like to give precise definitions of all these terms but because of the generality of the problems, there is a reliance on natural language so that a strictly mathematical formulation would be too restrictive. Indeed, we really need to discuss "evidence" first.

Example 1: Suppose that we toss a coin (one or more times) and obtain the outcome "e" . We conclude either that the coin is biased or that it is unbiased. The matters referred to in these two sentences are "connected" in the sense that we would not toss a die to conclude something about the coin and we would not toss the coin to say something about the weather. Such associativity is at a metaphysical level and is assumed in all models; people do know what they are talking about!

More generally, then, with each observation e , we have a conclusion $\theta(e)$; or, with each piece of evidence e , we have a state $\theta(e)$. But now, continuing to generalize, "evidence" is not restricted to that of random experiments but may include any kind of observation. Similarly, a "state" might be a single point but could be a set of points not even very precisely delineated. The following descriptions illustrate the variety in the pairs of "evidence spaces E " and "state spaces Θ " .

Θ	E
i) a real parameter space in a statistical model	the sample space (with a σ-field and probabilities P_θ , $\theta \in \Theta$)
ii) the collection of all possible populations	some measurable characteristics
iii) the collection of all possible patterns	some observable characteristics
iv) the collection of all possible causes of a problem	facts pertaining to causes
v) a collection of probability measures on a space	values of $P_0(a)$, $P_1(b)$, etc.

Example 2: This is a completely artificial, but pointed, model in medical diagnosis. There are only three symptoms which can be either present (1), or absent (-1) or unobserved (0). The evidence E is the collection of all possible arrays of the symptom stati; here E can be represented by the set of 27 triples:

$$(1,1,1), (1,1,0), (1,1,-1), \cdots, (-1,-1,-1) .$$

Now the experts (doctors) provide a *knowledge base* by giving some probability distributions, complete or partial, on the power set $P(\Theta)$ of the state space Θ of all relevant diseases. Let the obtainable "distributions" be denoted as:

$\pi_{(1,1,1)}, \pi_{(1,1,0)}, \pi_{(1,0,0)}, \pi_{(1,-1,-1)}, \pi_{(0,1,1)}, \pi_{(-1,0,-1)}$

For example, $\pi_{(1,1,1)}(\theta_1) = 1/3$, $\pi_{(1,1,1)}(\theta_1,\theta_2) = 1/2$, and other values of $\pi_{(1,1,1)}$ are not given. Then the task reduces to prescribing an *inference engine* which can be used to obtain some knowledge, perhaps only lower and upper bounds, of, not only the missing values of $\pi_{(1,1,1)}$, etc., but also those of the 21 other distributions. One would have a somewhat different evidence space if the experts were not in agreement. Then the knowledge base may have $\pi_{(1,1,1;x_1)}$ for the expert x_1 , $\pi_{(1,1,1;x_2)}$ for expert x_2 , and so on.

In many applications, the evidence E and hypotheses (state) Θ would be expressed in terms of propositions (statements in some natural language) and, in the spirit of the Bayesians, degrees of belief or reliability would be expressed in terms of subjective probabilities. It can also happen that such values are interwoven with the evidence as in:

expert x_i says "If e_j then θ_k with probability α_{ijk} ."

Then one is immediately confronted with the problem of the *combination* of evidence; a simple case was noted before: "compute" $P(\theta_1 | e_1, e_2)$ from values $P(\theta_1 | e_2)$ and $P(\theta_1 | e_2)$. In MYCIN-like systems (Lauritzen and Speigelhalter, 1988), α_{ijk} is called a certainty factor and various ad hoc rules for combination have been considered. Dalkey (1985) studied simple problems as non-parametric estimation. For example, if K(e) is the set of "possible probability measures" in the knowledge set for evidence e , then the size of K(e) is some measure of uncertainty about the "true P_o" ; the weaker the e , the larger the K(e) .

All this suggests that "evidence" is understood and not defined, as, in many other mathematical discussions, "set" is an undefined primitive. The important ingredients are the knowledge base used in the representation and the "inference engine". The basic task is to combine these so as to "come up with a degree of belief" just as human experts "always" do. Probabilists and statisticians will recognize analogies with and differences from stochastic systems, in particular, that the lack of data eliminates the potential of using statistical estimation and hypothesis testing. For probabilistic reasoning in intelligent systems, see Pearl (1988), Neapolitan (1990).

In order to study connections between Bayesian, Dempster-Shafer, and Zadeh notions, it is necessary to have an understanding of random sets and so we now pursue this.

3. Random sets

Loosely speaking, a random set is merely a set-valued function defined on a probability space; expressed differently, a subset is chosen "at random" from the superset Θ . Perhaps the most familiar example is the confidence interval for parametric estimation wherein the evidence is a random observation X associated with a hypothesis θ in the state $\Theta \subset R$. The "random set" is the interval [L(X), U(X)] with, say,

$$P(L(X) \leq \theta \leq U(X) |\ \theta \text{ is true}) \geq .99 .$$

Robbins (1944) referred to such a closed interval as a closed random set.

In expert systems and some statistical models, random sets can arise as a result of the fact that outcomes of experiments cannot be observed precisely (see e.g, Henkind and

Harrison, 1988). Another example of this is the generalized gross error model discussed in Huber (1981); see also Wasserman (1987). Statisticians may recognize the concept of a random set on a finite set in the sampling design for sampling from a finite population (see Hajek, 1981). Although for most applications, results for finite Θ would be sufficient, whenever possible, we present a general case to include the possibly infinite sets. Other approaches which emphasize the topological aspects of random sets have been discussed in Debreu (1967), Kendall (1974), Matheron (1975), Norberg (1984), and Wasserman (1987).

We will be dealing with two power sets. The collection of all subsets of a given Θ is its power set, $P(\Theta)$; the collection of all subsets of $P(\Theta)$ is its power set $P(P(\Theta))$. To help keep the differences in mind, we include a simple example to illustrate the operations

union, intersection, complement, and inclusion:

$\cup, \cap, ', \leq$, in the power set $P(\Theta)$ and,

$\vee, \wedge, {}^{c}, \subseteq$, in its power set $P(P(\Theta))$.

Example 3: Let $\Theta = \{1, 2, 3, 4\}$. The power set $P(\Theta)$ contains 16 "points" including:

$$\text{a null set } \phi = \Theta' \text{ , } \{1,2\} = \{3,4\}' \text{ ,}$$

$$\{1,2,3\} \cap \{2,3,4\} = \{2,3\} \text{ , } \{1,2\} \cup \{2,3\} = \{1,2,3\} \text{ .}$$

Then $P(P(\Theta))$ has 2^{16} "points" including:

$$\text{a null set } \varphi = P(\Theta)^{c} \text{ ,}$$

$$\{ \{\phi\},\{1,2\},\{4\} \} \vee \{ \{1\},\{1,2\} \} = \{ \{\phi\},\{1\},\{1,2\},\{4\} \} \text{ ,}$$

$$\{ \{\phi\},\{1,2\},\{3\} \} \wedge \{ \{\phi\},\{1\},\{1,2\} \} = \{ \{\phi\},\{1,2\} \} \text{ ;}$$

$$\{\phi\}^{c} \text{ contains the other 15 points of } P(\Theta) \text{ .}$$

Note the cardinalities: $|\phi| = 0 = |\varphi|$ but $|\{\phi\}| = 1$.

After stating our definition of a random set, we will give some examples.

Definition: Let Θ be an arbitrary set with at least two points. Let $\sigma(\mathscr{C})$ be a σ-field on $\mathscr{C} \subseteq P(\Theta)$ and note that $\sigma(\mathscr{C}) \subseteq P(P(\theta))$; let $[\Omega, A, P]$ be a fixed probability space. A random set S is an A-$\sigma(\mathscr{C})$ measurable function on Ω . Briefly, a random set for Θ is the triple $[\mathscr{C}, \sigma(\mathscr{C}), Q]$ where $Q = PS^{-1}$.

Example 4: a) Suppose that we are given the structure $[\mathscr{C}, \sigma(\mathscr{C}), Q]$. To fit the above definition we have to find a map S to $\mathscr{C}$. In this case we can take $\Omega = \mathscr{C}$, $\mathscr{A} =$

$\sigma(\mathscr{C})$, Q = P , and $S(\omega) = \omega$ for all $\omega \in \mathscr{C}$. So, S is the identity map when Q is given.

b) If Θ is finite with $\mathscr{C} = P(\Theta)$, $\sigma(\mathscr{C}) = P(P(\Theta))$, then Q can be identified with a "density" $\tilde{Q} : P(\Theta) \to [0,1]$ such that $\sum_{x \le \Theta} \tilde{Q}(x) = 1$.

There are two ways to construct random sets which we will call canonical constructions. Heuristically, the first canonical construction describes random sets according to which of a number of finite points they contain or do not contain. The second canonical construction uses the topological structure of θ.

3.1 First canonical construction. If Θ is arbitrary and $\mathscr{C} = P(\Theta)$, then $\sigma(\mathscr{C})$ is constructed as follows. Let $\mathscr{I}$ be the collection of finite subsets of Θ. Let the closed intervals in $P(P(\Theta))$ be $[i,j] = \{ x \in P(\Theta): i \le x \le j\}$. Let $\mathscr{M} = \{[i,j'] : i, j \in \mathscr{I}, j' = \Theta\text{-}j\}$; here, $[i,j']$ is the set of subsets containing i and "missing" j . Then $\sigma(\mathscr{C})$ is the σ-field generated by $\mathscr{M}$, say, $\sigma(\mathscr{M})$. (The reader might note that this σ-field is, in fact, the Borel σ-field on the compact space $P(\Theta) = \{0,1\}^{\Theta}$.) Each probability measure Q on $\sigma(\mathscr{C})$ (= $\sigma(\mathscr{M})$) determines one random set.

3.2 Second canonical construction. Consider $\Theta = \mathscr{R}$, the real line (or, more generally, a locally compact space). Let $\mathscr{C} = \mathscr{F}$ be the class of closed subsets of $\mathscr{R}$; let $\mathscr{K}$ be the class of compact subsets of $\mathscr{R}$; let $\mathscr{G}$ be the class of open subsets of $\mathscr{R}$. The space $\mathscr{F}$ can be given a topology $\mathscr{T}$ using the open subbase $\{F \in \mathscr{F}: F \cap K = \phi$ for $K \in \mathscr{K}\}$ and

$$\{F \in \mathscr{F}: F \cap G \ne \phi \text{ for } G \in \mathscr{G}\} .$$

Then $\sigma(\mathscr{C}) = \sigma(\mathscr{T})$ is the Borel σ-field of $\mathscr{F}$ in this topology. Each probability measure Q on $[\mathscr{F}, \sigma(\mathscr{T})]$ determines a random set.

3.3 Belief Functions (*Generalized Distribution for a Random Set*). Associated with each random set $S : \Omega \to \mathscr{C}$, there is a generalized distribution function as in the following:

Definition: A function F is a generalized distribution function (GDF) if there exists a random set

$$S : [\Omega, \mathscr{A}, P] \to [P(\Theta), P(P(\Theta))] \text{ with}$$
$$F(a) = P(S \le a) \text{ for all } a \in P(\Theta) \text{ such that } [\phi,a] \in \sigma(\mathscr{C}) .$$

Now compare this definition to:

Definition (Belief Function): Let $B : P(\theta) \to [0, 1]$. Then B is a belief function on $P(\theta)$ if and only if there exists a probability m on $P(\theta)$ (called the probability allocation of B) with $m(\emptyset) = 0$ and

$$B(A) = \sum_{C \subseteq A} m(C) \quad \text{for all } A \in P(\theta) .$$

Remark: It is now generally accepted that the belief function of Shafer (Shafer et al, 1987; Nguyen, 1978) is a GDF of a random set S with the added condition $P(S = \phi) = 0$. Below, we illustrate the connection between belief functions and random sets in the two canonical constructions.

3.4 GDF (*Belief Function*) for the first canonical construction of random sets. Recall that Θ is arbitrary, $\mathcal{J}$ is the set of all finite subsets of Θ and $\mathcal{M} = \{[i,j'] : i, j \in \mathcal{J}\}$. Let $\mathcal{J}$ be the the collection of subsets whose complements are in $\mathcal{J}$, say, $\mathcal{J} = P(\Theta) - \mathcal{J}$. The GDF of a random set S is, by definition, the function $F : \mathcal{J} \to [0,1]$ given by

$$F(j') = P(S \le j') = Q([\phi,j'])$$

so that a random set S uniquely determins a GDF. Likewise we will show below that a function F on $\mathcal{J}$ which looks like a GDF uniquely determines a random set S. To find $Q([i,j'])$ from F with i and $j \in \mathcal{J}$, we can use the following.

Corollary 1: For the GDF defined above,

i) $F(\Theta) = F(\phi') = Q([\phi,\phi']) = Q(P(\Theta)) = 1$;

ii) for $i, j \in \mathcal{J}$, $Q([i,j']) = \sum_{\alpha=0}^{|i|} \sum_{t \in i_\alpha} (-1)^\alpha F((i \cup t)')$ where $i_\alpha = \{t \le i : |t| = \alpha\}$.

Proof: i) is obvious. ii) For $|i| = 0$, $Q([\phi,j']) = F(j')$. Make the induction hypothesis that $Q([i,j'])$ has the form ii) for $|i| = n$ and all j. Since

$$[i,j'] = [i,(j \cup \{x\})'] \vee [i \cup \{x\},j']$$

is a union of disjoint sets,

$$Q([i,j']) = Q([i,\{j \cup \{x\})']) + Q([i \cup \{x\},j']) \quad \text{and}$$
$$Q([i \cup \{x\},j']) = Q([i,j']) - Q([i,(j \cup \{x\})']) .$$

Substitution of the ii) form for each Q on the right-hand side yields the same form for Q on the left with cardinality $|i \cup \{x\}| = n+1$. This completes the induction and the proof.

Corollary 1 shows that for all i and j $\in \mathcal{J}$, the sum on the right of ii) is non-negative. This is equivalent to the condition that the set-function F be montone increasing of infinite order in Choquet's sense (Shafer, 1979): for all $n \geq 1$, and $j', i_1' \leq j'$, $i_2' \leq j', \cdots, i_n' \leq j'$ in $E = J' \cup \{\phi\}$, $F(j') \geq \sum (-1)^{|I|+1} F(\cap_{k \in I} i_k')$ where the summation is over the nonempty subsets I of $\{1,2,\cdots,n\}$.

This leads to the following theorem.

Theorem: A function F on $\mathcal{J}$ such that $F(\Theta) = 1$ uniquely determines a GDF for the first canonical construction iff

$$\text{for all } i, j \in \mathcal{J}, \sum_{\alpha=0}^{|i|} (-1)^{\alpha} \sum_{t \in i_\alpha} F((i \cup t)') \geq 0 . \quad (*)$$

Proof: If F is a GDF, then corollary 1 shows that (*) is true. For the converse, suppose that (*) is true; we need to find a unique measure Q for $[P(\Theta), \sigma(\mathcal{M})]$ such that

$$F(j') = Q([\phi, j']) .$$

In the appendix it is shown that $\mathcal{M}$ is a semi-algebra and a compact class of sets, and that the map $Q : \mathcal{M} \to [0,1]$ with $Q([i,j'])$ given by the double sum in (*) is a finitely additive probability measure on $\mathcal{M}$. From a general theorem of Neveu (1965, pp 25-28), Q can be extended (uniquely) to a probability measure on $\sigma(\mathcal{M})$. Finally, it is then clear that $F(j') = Q([\phi, j'])$.

The following are some applications of this theorem.

Example 6: a) Taking the special case that Θ is finite in the previous discussion makes $\mathcal{J} = \mathcal{J} = P(\Theta)$. Here F maps $P(\Theta)$ into $[0,1]$ with $F(\phi) = 0$, $F(\Theta) = 1$, and

$$f(a) = \sum_{b \leq a} (-1)^{|a-b|} F(b) \geq 0 \text{ for all } a \text{ and } b .$$

Then, by the Moebius inversion formula (in the appendix A.1),

$$F(a) = \sum_{b \leq a} f(b)$$

so that f is a density function on $P(\Theta)$. Define a measure on $P(P(\Theta))$ by $Q(\{a_1, \cdots, a_n\}) = \sum_{i=1}^{n} f(a_i)$ where the $\{a_i\}$ are "points" in $P(\Theta)$. Then if S is the identity function on $P(\Theta)$, the probability space

$$[\Omega = P(\Theta), A = P(P\Theta)), Q]$$

can be taken as the random set S .

b) The following situation in robust statistics is from Huber (1981). Let Θ be finite ; let $\mathcal{P}$ be the collection of all probability measures on $P(\Theta)$. Fix P_o in $\mathcal{P}$, ε in (0,1) ; let $\tilde{P} = \{Q = (1 - \varepsilon)P_o + \varepsilon P : P \in \mathcal{P}\}$. Define F mapping $P(\Theta)$ into [0,1] by

$$F(a) = \inf\{P(a) : P \in \tilde{P}\} = \inf\{(1-\varepsilon)P_o(a) + \varepsilon P(a) : P \in \mathcal{P}\}$$

$$= (1-\varepsilon)P_o(a) + \varepsilon\inf\{P(a) : P \in \mathcal{P}\}$$

$$= \begin{cases} 1 & \text{for } a = \Theta \\ (1-\varepsilon)P_o(a) & \text{for } a \neq \Theta \end{cases} .$$

Let $f(a) = P(S = a) = \sum_{b \le a} (-1)^{|a-b|}F(b)$. Then $f \ge 0$ since

$$(1-\varepsilon)\sum_{b \le a} (-1)^{|a-b|}P_o(b) \ge 0 .$$

Hence, $F(a) = \sum_{b \le a} f(b) = P(S \le a) \le P_o(a) \le 1 - F(a')$.

c) Let Θ be arbitrary; let $f : \Theta \to [0,1]$ with $\max_{\phi} f(\theta) = 0$. For $j' \in \mathcal{J}$, let

$$F(j') = 1 - \max\{f(\theta) : \theta \in j\} .$$

Here, the details involved in using the theorem have been relegated to the appendix, A.4.

d) Take Θ to be the nodes of a finite graph. Each node represents a Bernoulli zero-one random variable with its own "p" (as in Lauritzen and Speigelhalter, (1988)). A random set for Θ , i.e.,

a probability measure Q on $[P(\Theta), P(P(\Theta)]$,

represents a joint distribution of the random field or a distribution of the configurations of the system. Since the power set is finite, Q can be identified with its density (using the same symbol)

$$Q : P(\Theta) \to [0,1] \text{ such that } \sum_{a \le \Theta} Q(a) = 1 .$$

The GDF has values

$F(a) = Q([\phi,a])$ for each $a \in P(\Theta)$ and

$$Q(a) = \sum_{b \le a} (-1)^{|a-b|}F(b) .$$

If $Q(a) > 0$ for all $a \in P(\Theta)$, and

$$\sum_{b \leq a} (-1)^{|b-a|} \log[Q(b)/Q(\phi)] \neq 0$$

only when a is a complete subset of the graph, then Q is a *Markov random field* (Preston, 1974).

3.5 GDF for the second canonical construction (*Belief functions on locally compact separable spaces*). To be concrete, let $\Theta = \mathcal{R}$; let $\mathcal{B}$ be its Borel σ-field. Then the base measurable space is $[\mathcal{R}, \mathcal{B}]$. We now consider random sets whose range is in the class of closed sets $\mathcal{F}$ of $\mathcal{R}$. This is motivated by the fact that the theory of random closed sets is sufficiently developed in the literature of probability (Matheron, 1975) to be useful here. Thus, the range measurable space is $[\mathcal{F}, \sigma(\mathcal{F})]$ where $\sigma(\mathcal{F})$ is the Borel σ-field with respect to the topology defined by the open subbase consisting of the families

$$\{[\phi,K'] : K \in \mathcal{K}\} \text{ and } \{[\phi,G']^c : G \in \mathcal{G}\}$$

where $\mathcal{K}$, ($\mathcal{G}$) is the class of compact (open) sets of $\mathcal{R}$; K' is the complement of K in $P(\mathcal{R})$; $(\cdot)^c$ is the complement in $\mathcal{F}$; all the intervals are in $\mathcal{F}$ as

$$[\phi,K'] = \{F \in \mathcal{F} : \phi \leq F \leq K'\} .$$

The range space $[\mathcal{F}, \sigma(\mathcal{F})]$ being fixed, each probability measure Q on $\sigma(\mathcal{F})$ will determine one random closed set.

A characterization of a GDF for a random closed set begins with the definition of a function F on a domain similar to $\mathcal{J}$ in the first canonical construction. Since this procedure is actually an application of the theory of Choquet capacity, it is convenient to consider the "dual" of F, namely, $T(a) = 1 - F(a')$.

Theorem: A function F on $\mathcal{K}'$ uniquely determines a GDF in the second canonical construction iff

i) the dual $T(\phi) = 0$;

ii) when a sequence K_n in $\mathcal{K}$ decreases to K in $\mathcal{K}$,

$$T(K_n) \downarrow T(K) ;$$

iii) for all $n \geq 1$, all $K, K_1, \cdots, K_n \in \mathcal{K}$, the following functions are all non-negative:

$$\varphi_1(K;K_1) = T(K \vee K_1) - T(K)$$
$$\varphi_2(K;K_1,K_2) = \varphi_1(K;K_1) - \varphi_1(K \vee K_2;K_1)$$
$$\ldots$$
$$\varphi_n(K;K_1,\cdots,K_n) = \varphi_{n-1}(K;K_1,\cdots,K_{n-1})$$
$$- \varphi_{n-1}(K \vee K_n;K_1,\cdots,K_{n-1}) .$$

Proof: The fact that a GDF on $\mathcal{K}$ uniquely determines a probabiltiy Q on $[\mathcal{F}, \sigma(\mathcal{F})]$ such that for all $K' \in \mathcal{K}'$, $F(K') = Q([\phi,K'])$ is called Choquet's Theorem. A probabilistic proof can be found in Matheron (1975, pp 30-35).

To use these results in a Bayesian frame, we would like to have $[\phi,b] \in \sigma(\mathcal{F})$ for all $b \in \mathcal{B}$; technically, this is not true in the construction so far but can be attained as follows. Instead of taking the random set

$$S : [\Omega, \mathcal{A}, P] \to [\mathcal{F}, \sigma(\mathcal{F}), Q] ,$$

we take the image to be $[\mathcal{F}, \tilde{\sigma}(\mathcal{F}), \tilde{Q}]$ which is the completion of $[\mathcal{F}, \sigma(\mathcal{F}), Q]$. Then, we define

$$T(b) = \sup\{T(k) : k \in \mathcal{K}, k \leq b\} \text{ and}$$
$$F(b) = 1 - T(b') \text{ for all } b \in \mathcal{B}.$$

For convenience, we present the following summary with details given in the appendix A.5. For $[\mathcal{R}, \mathcal{B}]$, the random set

$$[\mathcal{F}, \tilde{\sigma}(\mathcal{F}), \tilde{Q}]$$

satisfies the conditions for a Bayesian analysis, namely,

i) F is defined on $\mathcal{K}'$ and T is defined on $\mathcal{K}$ by

$$T(K) = 1 - F(K') ;$$

ii) T is defined on $\mathcal{B}$ by $T(b) = \sup\{T(K) : K \in \mathcal{K}, K \leq b\}$ and F is defined on $\mathcal{B}$ by $F(b') = 1 - T(b)$;

iii) for all $b \in \mathcal{B}$, $[\phi,b] \in \tilde{\sigma}(\mathcal{F})$ and

$$F(b) = \tilde{Q}([\phi,b]) = P(S \leq b) .$$

4. Knowledge representation

In this section, we illustrate the use of random sets to represent incomplete or partial information or knowledge. We take the following view of knowledge representation providing a probabilistic foundation and beginning for inference.

Definition: A state of knowledge supplied by some evidence concerning the true value θ_o in Θ is represented by a probability measure Q on a measurable space $[\mathscr{C}, \sigma(\mathscr{C})]$ where $\mathscr{C} \subseteq P(\Theta)$.

When $\mathscr{C} \equiv \Theta$, Q will be a probability measure on $[\Theta, \mathscr{B}]$ with $\mathscr{B}$ some σ-field of Θ . For example, in classical Bayesian methods, Θ is a parameter space and a priori information about the true θ_o is a probability measure on $[\Theta, \mathscr{B}]$ given by experts, or statisticians, or empirical Bayes estimation (see Press, 1989). In medical contexts, it often happens that $\mathscr{C}$ contains only subsets of Θ , not "singletons" (Henkind and Harrison, 1988) and, as noted before in the generalized gross error model (Huber, 1981), each observation $\omega \in \Omega$ does not lead to a "singleton" in Θ , but to a subset $\Gamma(\omega) \leq \Theta$. This approach, also considered by Dempster (1967), focuses on the multi-valued mappings but is easily seen to be equivalent to an approach thru random sets as in the following.

Example 7: The state of knowledge is given by a random set Γ for $[\mathscr{C}, \sigma(\mathscr{C}), Q]$; let F be its GDF. Let Π be the "true" prior, i.e., the probability law associated with the (unobservable) random variable $X : [\Omega, \mathscr{A}, P] \to [\Theta, \mathscr{B}, \Pi]$, $X(\omega) \in \Gamma(\omega)$ for all $\omega \in \Omega$. Of course, "observed sets" cannot be empty; that is, $\Gamma(\omega) \neq \phi$ for all $\omega \in \Omega$. Then,

$$\{\omega : \Gamma(\omega) \leq b\} \subseteq \{\omega : X(\omega) \leq b\} \text{ for all } b \in \mathscr{B} \text{ implies}$$
$$F(b) \leq \Pi(b) \text{ for all } b \in \mathscr{B}.$$

This shows that F is a lower bound for the unknown Π ; from $F(b') \leq \Pi(b') = 1 - \Pi(b)$, we get $\Pi(b) \leq 1 - F(b')$ making this an upper bound for Π (Dempster, 1967, Wasserman, 1987, Kyburg, 1987).

For given F with $F(\phi) = 0$, the class of *compatible probability measures* is the non-empty collection, say $\mathscr{P}_F$, of all probability measures Π on $[\Theta, \mathscr{B}]$ such that $\Pi \geq F$. Then when $F(b) = \inf\{\Pi(b) : \Pi \in \mathscr{P}_F\}$,

$\mathscr{P}_F$ is *representable* by F .

It follows that

$$F(\phi) = 0 \text{ , } F(\Theta) = 1 \text{ , and } a \leq b \text{ implies } F(a) \leq F(b) .$$

The corresponding random set is said to be *non-empty*.

Example 8: The expert may provide knowledge in the form "$\theta_o \in A$" where A is a fuzzy subset of Θ. This is characterized by a map $\mu_A : \Theta \to [0,1]$ where $\mu_A(\theta)$ is the "degree of membership" of θ in A. (A reference for fuzzy sets and logic is Klir and Folger, 1988; for imprecision in statistical observations, see Gil, 1988, and Kruse and Meyer, 1987.) Of course, "imprecise evidence" should be dealt with in the theory of fuzzy sets and logic. Here we merely point out that μ_A determines a GDF. Recall from section 3.2 that $F : \mathcal{J} \to [0,1]$ such that $F(j') = 1 - \max_{\theta \in j'} \mu_A(\theta)$ is a random set with the probability space $[P(\Theta), \sigma(M), Q]$. When Θ is finite, F is actually a belief function; when $\Theta = \mathcal{R}$, it is necessary to assume that μ_A is upper semi-continuous. Then there is a random set S such that

$$F(a) = P(S \le a) \text{ or, equivalently,}$$
$$P((S \cap a) \ne \phi) = \max_{\theta \le a} \mu_A(\theta) .$$

Example 9: (Kyburg, 1987). This example shows that $\mathcal{P}_F$ is not empty. Let a finite Θ have fixed indexing $\theta_1, \theta_2, \cdots, \theta_K$. Let the "density" associated with F be given by

$$m(a) = \sum_{b \le a} (-1)^{|a-b|} F(b) \quad \text{for } a \in P(\Theta) .$$

Let $T(\theta_j)$ be the collection of subsets

$$\phi, \{\theta_j\}, \{\theta_j, \theta_{j+1}\}, \{\theta_j, \theta_{j+2}\}, \cdots, \{\theta_j, \theta_{j+1}, \theta_{j+2}\},$$
$$\cdots, \{\theta_j, \theta_{j+1}, \cdots, \theta_K\} .$$

Convert m to $f : \Theta \to [0,1]$ by

$$f(\theta_j) = \sum_{a \in T(\theta_j)} m(a) .$$

Since $P(\Theta) = \vee_{j=1}^{K} T(\theta_j)$, it follows that $\sum_{j=1}^{K} f(\theta_j) = 1$. Now let Π be the probability measure for $[\Theta, \mathcal{B}]$ with density f; that is,

$$\Pi(a) = \sum_{\theta \in a} f(\theta) .$$

Since $F(a) = \sum_{b \le a} m(b) \le \sum_{\theta \in a} f(\theta) = \Pi(a)$, $\Pi \in \mathcal{P}_F$.

When Θ is finite and $F(\phi) = 0$, it turns out that

$$F(\cdot) = \inf_{\Pi \in \mathcal{P}_F} \Pi(\cdot) \text{ on } P(\Theta) \qquad (****)$$

Note that the use of the symbol min in both Dempster (1967) and Kyburg (1987) is misleading since $\mathcal{P}_F$ is still uncountable. In the case of $[\mathcal{R}, \mathcal{B}]$ or, more generally, Polish spaces, (****) also holds on $\mathcal{B}$ (Wasserman, 1987). This raises a question in incomplete Bayesian models and robust statistics (Huber and Strassen 1973, Huber, 1981): what conditions on $\mathcal{P}$, a class of probability measures on $[\Theta, \mathcal{B}]$, are required to guarantee that the map of $\mathcal{B}$ into [0,1] defined by $F(a) = \inf_{\Pi \in \mathcal{P}} \Pi(a)$ is a GDF ?

Example 10: The example of Huber (1981) outlined in section 3.2 can be viewed as using a GDF in a hypothesis testing problem. The fixed P_0 is the hypothetical distribution and the probabilities $Q = (1-\varepsilon)P_0 + P$ for arbitrary P make up the parameter space.

Example 11: This model involving partial information was also included in Nguyen and Rogers (1990). The information given is only that the probability for one $b \leq \Theta$ is α. The random set S can be taken to have density

$$P(S = b = b_1) = m(b_1) = \alpha ,$$

$$P(S = b' = b_2) = m(b_2) = 1 - \alpha .$$

The GDF is $F_S(a) = P(S \leq a)$

$$= \sum_{b_i \leq a} m(b_i) = \begin{cases} 1 & \text{if } b_1 \cup b_2 \leq a \\ \alpha & \text{if only } b_1 \leq a \\ 1 - \alpha & \text{if only } b_2 \leq a \\ 0 & \text{otherwise} \end{cases} .$$

Then $F_S(a) \leq P_0(a) \leq 1 - F_S(a')$ as above and so $\mathcal{P}_a$ is the set of all probability measures assigning value α to the set a . Note that $F_S(a) = \inf\{\Pi(a) : \Pi \in \mathcal{P}_a\}$.

It is not to be expected that all incomplete Bayesian models can be represented by random sets. Moreover, because of the very nature of expert systems, one cannot consider the luxury of imposing a prior on $\mathcal{P}$ (as in Ferguson, 1973). On the other hand, it is possible that a maximum entropy principle could be used to provide a probabilistic prior, given the evidence. Now, it should be obvious that the design of an expert systyem is going to involve art as well as science and alternative approaches, that is to say alternative models, should be viewed as complementary rather than competitive. Some analyses, trials, repititions, $\cdots$ should be carried out to select the more appropriate one. The next example illustrates this possibility.

Example 12: This example has been discussed in Wasserman (1987), Chapter 3, as an application of belief functions. Suppose we have a box which contains two types of coins, type A and type B. Let p_A $[q_A]$ denote the probability of obtaining heads [tails] when tossing a coin of type A. Similarly, let p_B and q_B be the probabilities for a type B coin. We assume that type A favors heads more than type B, that is, $p_A > p_B$. Consider the experiment:

"Choose a coin at random from the box then toss the coin."

Based on the outcome of this experiment, we want to decide if we have a coin of type A or of type B. The following are two different "inference machines" which can be used to decide on A or B based on evidence given by the tosses.

i) **Belief function approach**

Let $\Theta = \{A,B\}$ and define the support function

$$m(A|X_k) = X_k s_A ,$$

$$m(B|X_k) = (1-X_k)s_B ,$$

$$m(\Theta|X_k) = 1 - [X_k s_A + (1-X_k)s_B]$$

where $0 < s_A < 1$ and $0 < s_B < 1$, and

$$X_k = 1 \text{ if the } k^{th} \text{ toss is Heads}$$

$= 0$ otherwise.

Such an m is called a simple support function because for a fixed value of X_k it assigns mass to two sets, Θ and a subset of Θ. Note also that because $\Theta = \{A,B\}$,

$$\text{Bel}(A) = m(A) .$$

To choose between A and B after k tosses, the standard belief function technique is to choose the subset of Θ with the largest belief. Thus, using Dempster's rule for combination of evidence (also discussed in section 5 below), we analyze changes in

$\text{Bel}(A|X_1,\cdots,X_k) = m(A|X_1,\cdots,X_k)$ as a function of k. Let

$$m_k(A) = m(A|X_1,\cdots,X_k) ;$$

similarly define $m_k(B)$ and $m_k(\Theta)$. Then,

$$m_{k+1}(A) = \frac{m_k(A)[X_{k+1}s_A + X_{k+1}s_B + (1-X_{k+1})(1-s_B)]+m_k(\Theta)X_{k+1}s_A}{1 - [m_k(A)(1-X_{k+1})s_B + m_k(B)X_{k+1}s_A]}$$

with a similar expression for $m_{k+1}(B)$. Also,

$$m_{k+1}(\Theta) = \frac{m_k(\Theta)[X_{k+1}(1-s_A) + (1-X_{k+1})(1-s_B)]}{1 - [m_k(A)(1-X_{k+1})s_B + m_k(B)X_{k+1}s_A]} .$$

With a little thought, it is easy to see that

$$m_{k+1}(\Theta) < c \cdot m_k(\Theta) \text{ for some constant } 0 < c < 1 .$$

This implies that $m_k(\Theta)$ is decreasing in k and comes as no surprise since our "ignorance" about coin type certainly decreases as the number of tosses increases. The interesting quantity in this analysis is $m_k(A)$. Let us look at its increments.

$$m_{k+1}(A) - m_k(A) = \begin{cases} \dfrac{-s_B m_k(A)[1 - m_k(A)]}{1 - s_B m_k(A)} & \text{when } X_{k+1} = 0 \\ \dfrac{s_A[m_k(\Theta) + m_k(A)m_k(B)}{1 - s_A m_k(B)} & \text{when } X_{k+1} = 1 \end{cases} .$$

This shows that $m_k(A)$ [similarly, $m_k(\Theta)$ and $m_k(B)$] are Markov processes. Thus the belief function inference rule in this example can then be stated

"Decide on type A when $m_k(A) > m_k(B)$."

Figure 1 on the next page contains plots of $m_k(A)$, $m_k(B)$ and $m_k(\Theta)$ for a coin tossing experiment with $p_A = 0.51$, $p_B = 0.49$, and $s_A = 1-p_A/p_B$, $s_B = 1-q_A/q_B$.

ii) **Hypothesis testing procedure**

As shown below, the approach in (i) is not the best for this problem but we include it as a simple example application of random sets with Dempster's Rule for combination. Wasserman (1987) and others have pointed out that a method superior to (i), using Belief Functions, should be based on a function of p_A, p_B and $X_1, \cdots, X_k$ in simpler way. Now recall that if we allow ourselves a decision based on p_A, p_B, $X, \cdots, X_n$ then the classical Neyman-Pearson Lemma tells us that a rule of the form:

choose type A when $L(X_1, ..., X_k|A)/L(X_1, ..., X_k|B) > d$

optimizes misclassification probabilities. Clearly this beats any belief function technique that could be applied to this problem. The reason for this is that the probability structure is so well specified that classical statistics is applicable. This shows that we must be wary of using simple examples to judge belief function procedures.

Concerning example (i), one can see that in any such setting with independent random variables, we would find that $m_k(A)$ is a Markov process for any $A \subsetneq \Theta$ and that the

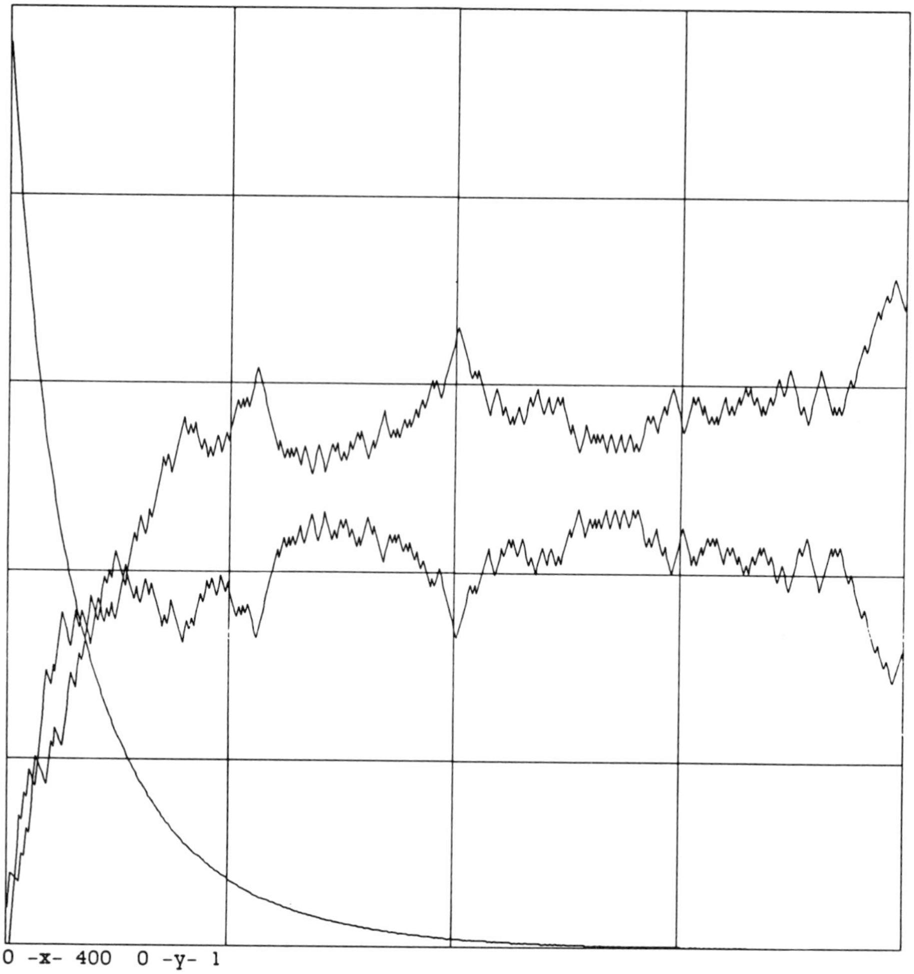
0 -x- 400 0 -y- 1

belief function procedure makes a decision based on the relative positions of the different Markov processes $\{m_k(A \subseteq \Theta)\}$. This leads to the following questions which seem difficult to answer: a) What is the probability of misclassification?

b) Is the procedure consistent? In other words, is $\lim_{k\to\infty} m_k(A) = 1$ or is $m_k(A)$ a recurrent process?

c) How does the choice of s_A (or other parameters), $A \subseteq \Theta$, affect the answers to these questions and how would one find optimal choices for the values of the s_A ?

The other way around, there appear to be three main problems with the belief function methodology. The first is the lack of understanding of the mathematical behavior and this leads to the second problem which is the arbitrary, probably nonoptimal, choice of some parameters used in the procedure, like the s_A above. Fianlly, as shown in (ii) above, there is the specious advantage that belief function methodology is easy to implement and widely applicable; it may be used in place of more classic procedures that are harder to implement or understand but are really more appropriate for a given problem. (See also Walley, 1987.)

5. Combination and conditioning

As explained earlier, the term *evidence* is to be "universally understood" and not defined "mathematically". This attitude contrasts with that of taking *events* as subsets of a sample space and is similar to modeling of "fuzzy" concepts. For example, everybody agrees that "tall" is a fuzzy concept and also that any attempt to define it "mathematically" can be only subjective. It follows that any "Mathematical Theory of Evidence" is really a "Mathematical Theory of *Representation* of Evidence". Each expert is to be cajoled into assigning one mathematical representation to given evidence, that is, one random set or its equivalent GDF.

While the concept of independent evidences can be formulated in a general way by considering joint random sets and product measures as in ordinary probability theory, the complexity of integration with the multi-valued maps needed later obscures the usefulness of the concept; hence we will limit our rigor to the case of finite Θ .

Definition: Let Θ be a finite set. Let S_1 and S_2 be two random sets mapping Ω

from the probability space $[\Omega, \mathcal{A}, P]$ into $P(\Theta)$. i) For all $a \in P(\Theta)$ and $i = 1$ and 2, the density and distribution functions are given by, respectively,

$$P(S_i = a) = m_i(a)\ ,\ F(a) = P(S_i \le a) = \Sigma_{b \le a}\, m_i(b)\ .$$

ii) S_1 and S_2 are *independent* iff

$$\text{for all } a, b \le \Theta\ ,\ P(S_1 = a, S_2 = b) = P(S_1 = a) \cdot P(S_2 = b)\ .$$

iii) $S_1 \cap S_2$ is the map with values

$$(S_1 \cap S_2)(\omega) = S_1(\omega) \cap S_2(\omega)\ .$$

Given two representations of knowledge, evidence e_1 and e_2 , with the corresponding random sets S_1 and S_2 , one "natural" representation of the "combination of evidence e_1 and e_2" is the set intersection of S_1 and S_2 . Taking independence of evidence to be independence of random sets, a GDF can be derived.

Corollary: Let $S = S_1 \cap S_2$ where S_1 , S_2 are independent as in the definiton. For each $b \in P(\Theta)$, let Θ_b be the set of pairs (x, y) such that

$$x \in S_1(\Omega),\ y \in S_2(\Omega) \ \text{ and } \ x \cap y = b\ .$$

Then $P(S \le a) = \sum_{b \le a} m(b)$ where $m(b) = \sum_{\Theta_b} m_1(x) \cdot m_2(y)$.

Proof: $P(\ S \le a) = P(\{\omega : S_1(\omega) \cap S_2(\omega) \le a\})$

$$= \sum_{b \le a} P(S_1 \cap S_2 = b)$$

$$= \sum_{b \le a} \sum_{\Theta_b} P(S_1 = x,\ S_2 = y)$$

$$= \sum_{b \le a} \sum_{\Theta_b} m_1(x) \cdot m_2(y) = \sum_{b \le a} m(b)\ .$$

This result can be related to the logical form $b \to a$, which is equivalent to $b' \vee a$, since

$$\Theta_b^a = \{\ y \in P(\Theta) : by \le a\}$$

$$= \{y \in P(\Theta) : y \le b' \vee a\} = P(\{b \to a\})$$

and then, $P(S \le a) = \sum_{b \le a} \sum_{\Theta_b} m_1(x) \cdot m_2(y)$

$$= \sum_{b \in P(\Theta)} m_1(b) \sum_{\Theta_b^a} m_2(y) .$$

With $P(S_1 = b) = m_1(b) = dF_1(b)$, this can be taken as a definition of a "convolution":

$$F(a) = F_1{*}F_2(a) = \sum_{b \le \Theta} F_2(b \to a)\, dF_1(b) .$$

In particular, if S_1 is the constant (degenerate) random set b , $P(S_1 = b) = 1$ and $F_1(x) = F_b(x) = \begin{cases} 1 & \text{when } x \ge b \\ 0 & \text{otherwise} \end{cases}$. Then, $F(a) = F_b{*}F_2(a) = F_2(b \to a)$ is the GDF of $b \cap S_2$. It is well-known that when F_2 is additive, that is, a probability measure on $P(\Theta)$, $F_2(b \to a) \neq F_2(a|b)$. One way to avoid such a "conflict of interest" in representation of evidence is to make the restriction that a random set is never empty, taking the Dempster-Shafer view that $P(S = \phi) = 0$. This is consistent with the idea that a random variable is never "empty"; moreover, one is reluctant to assign a positive degree of belief to the impossible.

Of course, when S_1 and S_2 are non-empty, it does not follow that $S_1 \cap S_2$ is non-empty and, at the other extreme, it can happen that $P(S_1 \cap S_2 = \phi) = 1$. This indicates a *conflict* between e_1 and e_2 and no "combination of evidence" should be considered.

Now suppose that for the non-empty independent random sets S_1 and S_2 , $0 < P(S_1 \cap S_2 = \phi) < 1$. (The magnitude of this probability might be used as a measure of the *degree of compatibility* of e_1 and e_2 .) Here the range of $S = S_1 \cap S_2$ contains ϕ as well as non-empty elements of the form

$$\alpha = xy \text{ , } x \in S_1(\Omega),\ y \in S_2(\Omega) .$$

Hence, the restriction of the mathematical representation of evidence to non-empty values, requires the definition of a non-empty $\tilde{S}$ which preserves the non-empty sets of S . Let the density of S be denoted by f ; let the range of S be $\{\alpha_1, \alpha_2, \cdots, \alpha_k, \phi\}$. Then, $\sum_{i=1}^{k} f(\alpha_i) = 1 - f(\phi) > 0$. Let $\tilde{S}$ have range $\{\alpha_1, \cdots, \alpha_k\}$ with density

$$\tilde{f}(\alpha_i) = \gamma_i\, f(\alpha_i)$$

where the γ_i are chosen so that

$$\tilde{f}(\alpha_i) > 0 \text{ , and } \sum_{i=1}^{k} \gamma_i f(\alpha_i) = 1 \quad (\text{whence } \tilde{f}(\phi) = 0) .$$

The canonical choice is $\gamma_i = 1/(1 - f(\phi))$ for $i = 1(1)k$ so that $\tilde{f}(\alpha_i) = f(\alpha_i)/(1 - f(\phi))$ but this is not the only form that these constants of proportionality can assume; most importantly, we note that different choices lead to different "rules" of combination.

For the canonical choice of weights, the corresponding GDF is

$$\tilde{F}(a) = P(S \le a \mid S \ne \phi) = \begin{cases} 0 & \text{for } a = \phi \\ P(\phi \ne S \le a)/P(S \ne \phi) & \text{for } a \ne \phi \end{cases} .$$

As $\tilde{F}(\phi) = 0$, $\tilde{F}$ is the GDF of the non-empty random set $\tilde{S}$ which, in the Dempster-Shafer spirit, is the combination $S_1 \oplus S_2$. Then when $a \ne \phi$,

$$F_1 \oplus F_2(a) \text{ is defined to be } \tilde{F}(a) = \frac{F(a) - F(\phi)}{1 - F(\phi)} .$$

As above, this can be related to "If$\cdots$, then$\cdots$" as

$$F_1 \oplus F_2(a) = \frac{\sum_{b \le \Theta} F_2(b \to a) dF_1(b) - \sum_{b \le \Theta} F_2(b') dF_1(b)}{1 - \sum_{b \le \Theta} F_2(b') dF_1(b)} .$$

In particular for $F_1 = F_b$ with $F_b(\phi) = 0$ and $F_2(b') < 1$,

$$\tilde{F}(a) = \frac{F_2(b \to a) - F_2(b')}{1 - F_2(b')} \text{ is the conditional } F_2(a|b) . \quad (*)$$

Of course, when F_2 is additive, $F_2(a|b)$ is the conditional probability.

With this choice of non-empty random set $\tilde{S}$, the GDF $\tilde{F}$ is called Dempster's Rule of Combination (see example 12) and combination with a constant random set is taken as *conditional belief*. This conditioning operator is *commutative* in the sense that for all non-empty b, c and all S with $F_S(\phi) = 0$,

$$(F_S \oplus F_b) \oplus F_c = (F_S \oplus F_c) \oplus F_b .$$

However, Diaconis (1978) pointed out that, when F_S is non-additive, conditioning does not satisfy the "common sense sandwich principle":

$$F_S(a) \ge \min\{F(a|b), F(a|b')\} .$$

In the following example, we follow Diaconis (1978) but in general terms.

Example 13: Let $\Omega = \{\omega_1, \omega_2, \omega_3\}$, $\mathcal{A} = P(\Omega)$, with probabilities $f(\omega_1) = f(\omega_2) =$

$f(\omega_3) = 1/3$ and for $x \in P(\Omega)$, $P(x) = \sum_{\omega_i \in x} f(\omega_i)$. Let the random set S map $[\Omega, \mathcal{A}, P]$ into $P(\Theta)$ where $\Theta = \{(\omega_1,\omega_2), (\omega_1,\omega_3), (\omega_2,\omega_3), (\omega_3,\omega_2)\}$:

$$S(\omega_1) = \{(\omega_1,\omega_2), (\omega_1,\omega_3)\}$$

$$S(\omega_2) = \{(\omega_2,\omega_3)\}$$

$$S(\omega_3) = \{(\omega_3,\omega_2)\} .$$

Let $F(a) = P(S \le a)$ for $a \in P(\Theta)$. For

$$a = \{(\omega_1,\omega_2), (\omega_1,\omega_3)\} \text{ and } b = \{(\omega_1,\omega_2), (\omega_3,\omega_2)\} ,$$

$$F(a) = P(\{\omega : S(\omega) \le a\}) = P(S(\omega_1) = a) = P(\omega_1) = 1/3 ;$$

the conditional (*) becomes

$$F(a|b) = \frac{F(b' \vee a) - F(b')}{1 - F(b')} = \frac{2/3 - 1/3}{1 - 1/3} = 1/2 = F(a|b') .$$

Of course, 1/3 < 1/2 .

Whether or not the "sandwich principle" should be a required property of an inferential conditioning operator has not been decided as yet; it remains "a common sense property". Various conditioning operators have been proposed to replace this operator of Dempster (see, for example Planchet, 1989). We note that Goodman, et al. (1989) defined a conditioning operator to study admissibility of belief functions in the Lindley framework, while Fagin and Halpern (1989) focused on the sandwich property. These conditioning operators seem to arise in an effort to extend probabilistic conditioning to non-additive set functions. The following are properties currently looked for in a conditioning operator with values $F_b(a) = F(a|b)$:

α) for each b , with $F(b') < 1$, $F(\cdot|b)$ is a belief function;

β) $F(\cdot|\Theta) \equiv F(\cdot)$ since $F(\phi) = 0$;

γ) for b , c with $F(b')$, $F(c') < 1$, $\left[F_b\right]_c(\cdot) = \left[F_c\right]_b(\cdot)$;

δ) for a , b with $F(b)$, $F(b') < 1$,

$$F(a) \ge \min\{F(a|b), F(a|b')\} .$$

Here we will briefly examine four of these operators:

$$F_1(a|b) = \frac{F(b \to a) - F(b')}{1 - F(b')} \text{ with } F(b') < 1 ;$$

$$F_2(a|b) = \frac{F(ab)}{F(b)} \text{ with } F(b) > 0 ;$$

$$F_3(a|b) = \frac{F(a) - F(ab')}{1 - F(b')} \quad \text{with } F(b') < 1 ;$$

$$F_4(a|b) = \frac{F(ab)}{F(ab) + 1 - F(b \to a)} \quad \text{with } F(b) > 0 .$$

It can be checked that all four of these operators are extensions of probabilistic conditioning; that is, when F is additive, all reduce to probabilistic conditioning. Also, they all satisfy α) and β) . While F_1 , F_2, F_3 satisfy γ) but not δ) , F_4 satisfies δ) but not γ) .

From the interpretation $F(a) = P(S \le a)$, it is reasonable to consider $F(a|b) = P(S \le a \mid S \le b) = F(ab)/F(b)$. By considering the correspondence $b \to [0,b]$, it is seen that

$$P(S \le a) \ge \min \{P(S \le a \mid S \le b), P(S \le a \mid (S \le b)^c)$$

is equivalent to

$$F([\phi,a]) \ge \min \{F([\phi,a] \,|\, [\phi,b]) , F([\phi,a] \,|\, [\phi,b]^c)\} .$$

However, this correspondence is not a homomorphism since b' does not correspond to $[\phi,b]^c$; thus δ) fails.

Example 16: A specific example of this can be constructed in the last example. Take

$$a = \{(\omega_1,\omega_2),(\omega_2,\omega_3),(\omega_3,\omega_2)\} , b = \{(\omega_1,\omega_3),(\omega_2,\omega_3)\}.$$

Then,

$$F(a) = P(\{\omega_2, \omega_3\}) = 2/3 ;$$

$$F(ab) = P(S \le ab) = P(S = (\omega_2,\omega_3)) = P(\omega_2) = 1/3 ;$$

$$F(ab') = P(S \le ab') = P(S = (\omega_3,\omega_2)) = P(\omega_3) = 1/3 ;$$

$$F(b) = P(\omega_2) = 1/3 ; F(b') = P(\omega_3) = 1/3 .$$

It follows that $F(a|b) = \dfrac{1/3}{1/3} = 1 - F(a|b') < 2/3$.

This discussion brings out the fact that conditioning involves two pieces of evidence represented by F and $b \ne \phi$. If one has "θ_o is in b", then it is reasonable to condition S on b and view belief in a as belief in ab . For this, consider a GDF $\hat{F}$ proportional to F(ab) , say

$$\hat{F}(a) = F(ab)/\alpha(a,b) \text{ with } \alpha(\Theta,b) = F(b) \text{ so } \hat{F}(\Theta) = 1 .$$

The simplest choice of $\alpha(a,b)$ is F(b) for all a ; another is $\alpha(a,b) = F(ab) + 1 - F(b \to a)$. (Planchet, 1989, discusses several conditioning operators.)

The conditioning problem in belief function theory has not been settled. When F is additive, all the conditioning operators are probabilistic so that (γ) and (δ) hold. Is there a conditioning so that (γ) and (δ) hold when F is not additive? The following is a non-trivial example for which this is true. In fact, as a belief function, it is even admissible (Goodman, et al., 1989). (The details of this example were worked out by C. Yu in our seminar.)

Example 17: Let Π be a probability measure on $P(\Theta)$, Θ finite. Let $F(a) = (\Pi(a))^2$ (or, more generally, $(\Pi(a))^n$, n a positive integer). The proof that F is a non-additive belief function follows from a more general result to be given below. Consider, for simplicity $n = 2$,

$$F(a|b) = \frac{F(ab)}{F(b)} = \frac{(\Pi(ab))^2}{(\Pi(b))^2}.$$

This F yields the following.

i) For each b , the function with values $F(a|b) = (\Pi(a|b))^2$ at a in $P(\Theta)$ is a belief function. The first two conditions are

$$F(\phi|b) = (\Pi(\phi|b))^2 = 0 \text{ and } F(\Theta|b) = (\Pi(\Theta|b))^2 = 1 .$$

Now define a mass function m_b on $P(\Theta)$ by

$$m_b(a) = \begin{cases} (\Pi(x|b))^2 & \text{when } a = \{x\} \\ 2 \cdot \Pi(x|b) \cdot \Pi(y|b) & \text{when } a = \{x,y\} \\ 0 & \text{when } a = \phi \text{ or } |a| \geq 3 \end{cases}.$$

Then $F(a|b) = (\Pi(a|b))^2 = \left[\sum_{x \in a} \Pi(x|b)\right]^2$

$$= \sum_{x \in a} (\Pi(x|b))^2 + \sum_{x \neq y} \Pi(x|b) \cdot \Pi(y|b)$$

$$= \sum_{c \leq a} m_b(c) .$$

ii) For $F(a|b) = (\Pi(a|b))^2 = F_b(a) = (\Pi_b(a))^2$, conditioning is commutative:

$$\left[F_b\right]_c(a) = \left[\left[\Pi_b\right]_c(a)\right]^2 = \left[\Pi_b(a|c)\right]^2 = \left[\Pi_{bc}(a)\right]^2$$

$$= \left[\Pi_{cb}(a)\right]^2 = \left[\Pi_c(a|b)\right]^2 = \left[\left[\Pi_c\right]_b(a)\right]^2 = \left[F_c\right]_b(a) .$$

iii) The sandwich principle holds. Indeed, if

$$F(a) < F(a|b) \text{ or } (\Pi(a))^2 < (\Pi(a|b))^2 .$$

But then, $\Pi(a) = \Pi(ab') + \Pi(ab)$

$$= \Pi(ab') + \Pi(a|b)\Pi(b) \geq \Pi(ab') + \Pi(a) \cdot \Pi(b)$$

from which it follows that

$$\Pi(a)[1 - \Pi(b)\} \geq \Pi(ab') ,$$

$$\Pi(a) \geq \Pi(ab')/\Pi(b') = \Pi(a \mid b'),$$

$$(\Pi(a))^2 \geq (\Pi(a \mid b))^2 \text{ or } F(a) \geq F(a \mid b').$$

Thus, $F(a) \geq \min\{F(a \mid b), F(a \mid b')\}$.

The conditioning operator $F(a \mid b) = (\Pi(a \mid b))^2$ can be defined in the context of measure-free conditioning (Goodman, et al., 1990) as follows. The space of measure free conditional events is

$$\mathcal{P}(\Theta) = \{(a \mid b) : a, b \in P(\Theta)\}$$

where the coset $(a \mid b) = a + P(\Theta)b'$ is in the quotient ring $P(\Theta)/P(\Theta)b'$. It is known that Π can be extended to $\mathcal{P}(\Theta)$ so that $\tilde{\Pi}((a \mid b)) = \Pi(a \mid b)$; then Π^2 extends to $\tilde{\Pi}^2$. It follows that F on $P(\Theta)$ extends to $\mathcal{P}(\Theta)$ with values

$$F((a \mid b)) = \Pi^2(a \mid b) = (\Pi(a \mid b))^2.$$

In view of this latter work, we point out two avenues for further research. Look for conditioning operators as solutions of certain functional equations. In fact, this is basically an extension problem and the situation might be similar to that in fuzzy logics (Bonissone and Decker, 1985) or conditional logics (Dubois and Prade, 1989). Or, a general approach to conditioning might be carried out as Rényi (1970) did for conditional probability spaces.

Appendices

A.1 Moebius Inversion

Theorem 1: Let Θ be a finite set; let f and g be real valued functions on $P(\Theta)$. Then,

$$f(a) = \sum_{b \leq a} g(b) \text{ iff } g(b) = \sum_{a \leq b} (-1)^{|b-a|} f(a).$$

A.2. **$\mathcal{M}$ is a semi-algebra and a compact class of sets.** The following elementary properties of the intervals in $\mathcal{M}$ are immediate:

i) $[i,j'] = \phi$ iff (if and only if) $i \cap j \neq \phi$;

ii) $\phi \neq [u,v'] \subseteq [i,j']$ iff $i \leq u$ and $j \leq v$;

iii) $[u,v'] = [i,j'] \neq \phi$ iff $u = i$ and $j = v$;

iv) if $[u,v']$ and $[i,j']$ are non-empty, then,

$[u,v'] \wedge [i,j'] = \phi$ iff $u \cap j \neq \phi$ or $v \cap i \neq \phi$;

v) for the singleton $\{x\}$,

$[\{x\},\phi']^c = [\phi,\{x\}']$ and $[\phi,\{x\}']^c = [\{x\},\phi']$;

vi) $\phi^c = [\phi,\phi']$.

Lemma 1: M is a semi-algebra in $P(P(\Theta))$; that is,

a) ϕ and $P(\Theta) \in M$;

b) M is closed under finite intersections in $P(P(\Theta))$;

c) If $M \in M$, M^c is a finite union of disjoint elements of M.

Proof: a) Let $i = \{\theta_1\}$ and $j = \{\theta_1, \theta_2\}$. Then,

$$[i,j'] = \phi \in M, \text{ and } P(\Theta) = [\phi,\phi'] \in M .$$

b) For $k = 1(1)m$, let $[i_k , j_k'] \in M$. Then,

$$i_k \leq x \leq j_k' \text{ for all } k \text{ if and only if } \cup i_k \leq x \leq \cap j_k'$$

so that $\bigwedge_{k=1}^{m} [i_k,j_k'] = [\cup i_k , \cap j_k'] = [\cup i_k , (\cup j_k)']$.

c) Now let $i = \{x_1, \cdots, x_n\}$ and $j = \{y_1, \cdots, y_m\}$ be finite sets of distinct elements in Θ . Then, by (ii) above, it is easy to see that

$$[i,j'] = \wedge_{\alpha=1}^{n}[\{x_\alpha\},\phi'] \wedge \wedge_{\beta=1}^{m}[\phi,\{y_\beta\}']$$

so that $[i,j']^c = \vee_\alpha[\phi,\{x_\alpha\}'] \vee \vee_\beta[\{y_\beta\},\phi']$

$= [\phi,\{x_1\}'] \vee [\{x_1\},\{x_2\}'] \vee [\{x_1,x_2\},\{x_3\}'] \vee \cdots$

$\vee [\{x_1,\cdots,x_{n-1}\},\{x_n\}'] \vee [i \cup \{y_1\},\phi'] \vee [i \cup \{y_2\},\{y_1\}']$

$\vee \cdots \vee [i \cup \{y_n\},\{y_1,\cdots,y_{m-1}\}']$.

Lemma 2: M is a compact class of sets; that is, for any sequence $\{M_n\}$ in M such that $\wedge_{n=1}^{\infty} M_n = \phi$, there is an N such that $\wedge_{n=1}^{N} M_n = \phi$.

Proof: Let $M_k = [i_k,j_k']$; then

$$\wedge_{k=1}^{n}[i_k,j_k'] = [\cup_{k-1}^{n} i_k, \cap_{k=1}^{n} j_k'] \text{ and}$$

$$\wedge_{k=1}^{\infty}[i_k,j_k'] = [\cup_{k=1}^{\infty} i_k,(\cup_{k=1}^{\infty} j_k)'] .$$

If $i_k = \phi$ for all k, then

$$\cup_k i_k = \phi \text{ and } \{\phi\} =[\phi,(U_k j_k)'] \neq \phi .$$

If $j_k = \phi$ for all k, then

$$(U_k j_k)' = \Theta \text{ and so } [\cup_k i_k, \Theta] \neq \phi .$$

Therefore, when $\wedge_k [i_k, j_k'] \neq \phi$,

$$\cup_k i_k \text{ and } \cup j_k \text{ are both non-empty.}$$

Also, $[\cup_k i_k, (\cup j_k)'] = \phi$ implies $\cup_k i_k \cap (U_k j_k) \neq \phi$ so that there is at least one θ in some $i_n \cap j_m$. Then, with $N = \max\{n, m\}$,

$$[\cup_{k=1}^{N} i_k, (\cup_{k=1}^{N} j_k)'] = \phi .$$

A.3. **Q defined in Theorem 1 is a finitely additive probability measure on $\mathcal{M}$.**

i) Let $Q([i,j']) = \sum_{\alpha=0}^{|i|} (-1)^{\alpha} \sum_{t \in i_{\alpha}} F((j \cup t)')$. (*)

This sum is non-negative by hypothesis. Since the representation of $[i,j'] \neq \phi$ noted earlier is unique, Q is well-defined for such $[i,j']$.

ii) If $[i,j'] = \phi$, let $x \in [i,j']$. Then $Q([i,j'])$ can be written as

$$\sum_{\alpha=0}^{|i|} (-1)^{\alpha} \sum_{\{t \in i_{\alpha} : x \in t\}} F((j \cup t)') + \sum_{\alpha=0}^{|i|} (-1)^{\alpha} \sum_{\{t \in i_{\alpha} : x \notin t\}} F((j \cup t)') .$$

Now in the first sum, $x \in t$ implies $|t| \geq 1$ and in the second sum, $x \notin t$ implies $|t| < i$. Hence the second sum reduces to $\sum_{\alpha=0}^{|i|-1} (-1)^{\alpha} \sum_{\{t \in i_{\alpha} : x \notin t\}} F((j \cup t)')$ (**)

Also, in the first sum, each t contains x so that

$$t = s \cup \{x\} \text{ with } |s| = |t| - 1 .$$

Then this first sum reduces to

$$\sum_{\alpha=1}^{|i|} (-1)^{\alpha} \sum_{\{s \in i_{\alpha-1} : x \in s\}} F((j \cup s)')$$

$$= \sum_{\beta=0}^{|i|-1} (-1)^{\beta+1} \sum_{\{t \in i_{\beta} : x \notin t\}} F((j \cup t)')$$

which is just the negative of that in (**) so that

$$Q([i,j']) = Q(\phi) = 0 .$$

ii) Q will be additive on $\mathcal{M}$ if for all $n \geq 2$,

$$\text{when } I_1, \cdots, I_n \in \mathcal{M}, I_i \cap I_j = \phi \text{ for } i \neq j$$

$$\text{and } \vee_{i=1}^{n} I_i \in \mathcal{M}, \text{ then } Q(\vee_{i=1}^{n} I_i) = \Sigma_{i=1}^{n} Q(I_i) .$$

Now $[i,j'] = [i,(j \cup \{x\})'] \vee [i \cup \{x\}, j']$ is a disjoint union so that, assuming the additivity,

$$Q([i,j']) = Q([i,(j \cup \{x\})']) + Q([i \cup \{x\},j']) .$$

This implies that

$$Q([i,j']) \geq \text{max of the two terms on the right.}$$

It follows that Q is increasing:

$$[i,j'] \subsetneq [u,v'] \text{ implies } Q([i,j']) \leq Q([u,v']) .$$

Hence, $Q([i,j]) \leq Q([\phi,\phi']) = F(\Theta) = 1$.

iii) The proof that Q is a finitely additive probability measure on $\mathcal{M}$ will be completed by the following development of the additivity.

Definition: Let $[i,j']$ be non-empty. Let K be a non-empty finite subset of $(i \cup j)'$. Then

$$\underline{P} = \{[i \cup u,(j \cup (K\text{-}u))'] : u \in P(K)\}$$

is called a canonical partition of $[i,j']$ with respect to K.

Lemma 1: The canonical partition of $[i,j']$ with respect to K is a true partition of $[i,j']$.

Proof: i) Let $u \in P(K)$; then by the second elementary property, (A.2 (ii)),

$$[i \cup u,(j \cup (K\text{-}u))'] \subsetneq [i,j']$$

so that all the intervals in $\underline{P}$ are contained in $[i,j']$.

ii) Let $a \in [i,j']$ and $u = a \cap K$. Then,

$$i \leq a \text{ implies } i \cup u \leq a \cup u = a .$$

Since $a = u \cup (K' \cap a)$, $a \leq K' \cup u$; then $a \leq j'$ implies

$$a \leq j' \cap (K' \cup u) = j' \cap (K \cap u')' = (j \cup (K\text{-}u))' .$$

Thus, $a \in [i \cup u,(j \cup (K\text{-}u)']$ and every set in $[i,j']$ is in some interval of $\underline{P}$.

iii) Let u_1 and u_2 be distinct elements of $P(K)$. Then,

$$(i \cup u_1) \cap (j \cup (K - u_2)) \geq u_1 \cap (K - u_2) \neq \phi$$

so that, by the fourth elementary property, (A.2 (iv)),

$$[i \cup u_1, (j \in (K\text{-}u_1))'] \wedge [i \cup u_2, (J \in (K\text{-}u_2)'] = \phi .$$

This says that the intervals in $\underline{P}$ are disjoint and completes the proof of the lemma.

Theorem 1: Let the non-empty intervals

$$[i_1,j_1'] , \cdots , [i_n,j_n']$$

be a partition of the non-empty interval $[i,j']$. Let

$$K = (\cup_{k=1}^{n}(i_k \cup j_k)) \cap i' \cap j' .$$

Let $\underline{P}_k$ be the canonical partition of $[i_k, j_k']$ with respect to $K \cap i_k' \cup j_k'$. Then $\cup_{k=1}^{n} \underline{P}_k$ is the canonical partition of $[i,j']$ with respect to K.

Proof: Now $[i,j'] = \cup_{k=1}^{n}[i_k, j_k']$ implies

$$i \leq \cap_{k=1}^{n} i_k \text{ and } j \leq \cap_{k=1}^{n} j_k$$

so that for each $k = 1(1)n$, there are subsets u_k and v_k of K such that $v_k \leq K\text{-}u_k$ and $i_k = i \cup u_k$ and $j_k = j \cup v_k$. Let $\underline{P}$ denote the canonical partition of $[i,j']$ with respect to K.

i) Let $I \in \underline{P}_k$. Since $K \cap i_k' \cap j_k' = K \cap u_k' \cap v_K'$, there is some $u \leq K \cap u_k' \cap v_k'$ such that

$$I = [i \cup u_k \cup u, (j \cup v_k \cup ((K \cap u_k' \cap v_k')\text{-}u))'] .$$

Since $v_k \cup ((K \cap u_k' \cap v_k')\text{-}u) = v_k \cup K\text{-}(u_k \cup v_k \cup u)$

$$= K\text{-}(u_k \cup u) ,$$

it follows that $I \in \underline{P}$ and $\cup_{k=1}^{n} \underline{P}_k \subseteq \underline{P}$.

ii) Let $I \in \underline{P}$ and $I = [i \cup u, (j \cup u)']$ for some $u \in P(K)$. Because $i \leq i \cup u \leq j'$, $i \cup u \in [i,j']$ and so there is a unique k such that $i \cup u \in [i_k, j_k']$. Write $i_k = i \in u_k$ and $j_k = i \in v_k$ with u_k and $v_k \leq K$ as above. Now $i \cup u_k \leq i \in u$ implies $u_k \leq u$ and so

$$u = u_k \in u_o \text{ with } u_o \leq K \cap u_k' .$$

Also, $i \cup u \leq (j \text{ U } v_k)' = j' \cup v_k'$ implies

$$u \leq v_k' \text{ with } v_k \leq K \cup u' = K \cup (u_k \cup u_o)' .$$

Then, $j \cup (K\text{-}u) = j \cup v_k \cup (K\text{-}u)$

$$= (j \cup v_k) \cup (K \cap u_o' \cap u_k' \cap v_k')$$

yields $I = [i \cup u, (j \cup (K\text{-}u))']$

$$= [i \cup u_k \text{ U } u_o, ((j \in v_k) \cup (K \cap u_k' \cap v_k')\text{-}u_o)']$$

$$= [i_k \cup u_o, (j_k \in (K \cap i_k' \cap j_k')\text{-}u_o))'] .$$

It follows that $i \in \underline{P}_k$ and so $\underline{P} \subseteq \cup_{i=1}^{k} \underline{P}_k$.

Lemma 2: Q is additive on canonical partitions; that is, if $\underline{P}$ is a conical partition of

$[i,j']$ with respect to some finite K, then $Q([i,j']) = \sum_{I \in \underline{P}} Q(I)$ where $Q(I)$ is defined by (*).

Proof: $\sum_{I \in \underline{P}} Q(I)$

$$= \sum_{u \in P(K)} \sum_{\alpha=0}^{|i|+|u|} \sum_{t \in (i \cup u)_\alpha} (-1)^\alpha F(j \cup (K-u) \cup t) .$$

Fix $j \cup (K-u) \cup t$ as $j \cup i_o \cup u_o$, $i_o \leq i$, $u \leq K$. Consider all occurrences of the term $(-1)^\alpha F(j \cup (K-u) \cup t)$.

i) For $u \in P(K)$ and $t \in (i \cup u)_\alpha$,

$$j \in (K-u) \in t = j \cup i_o \cup u_o \text{ iff}$$
$$u_o \geq K-u \;\&\; t = i_o \cup (u_o \cap u) \text{ iff}$$
$$K-u_o \leq u \;\&\; t = i_o \cup (u_o \cap u) .$$

Hence the sum of terms of the form $(-1)^\alpha F(j \cup i_o \cup u_o)$ is

$$\sum_{\{u \in P(K) \,:\, K-u_o \leq u\}} (-1)^{|i_o|+|u_o \cap u|} F(j \cup i_o \cup u_o)$$

$$= (-1)^{|i_o|} F(j \in i_o \cup u_o) \cdot \sum_{\{u \in P(K) \,:\, K-u_o \leq u\}} (-1)^{|u_o \cap u|} .$$

ii) Now consider $\sum_{\{u \in P(K):\, K-u_o \leq u\}} (-1)^{|u_o \cap u|}$. For $|u_o \cap u| = m$, there are $\begin{bmatrix} |u_o| \\ m \end{bmatrix}$ subsets of K such that $K-u_o \leq u$. Hence, this last sum is $\sum_{m=0}^{|u_o|} \begin{bmatrix} |u_o| \\ m \end{bmatrix} (-1)^m = 0$ if $|u_o| \geq 1$. This means that all terms of the form $(-1)^\alpha F(j \cup i_o \cup u_o)$ will vanish unless $u_o = \phi$.

iii) Hence consider terms with $u_o = \phi$. Then,

$$j \cup (K-u) \cup t = j \cup i_o$$

when $t = i_o$ and $K-u = \phi$, i.e., $u = K$. It follows that all non-zero terms are contained in

$$\sum_{\alpha=0}^{|i|+|K|} \sum_{t \in i_\alpha} (-1)^\alpha F(j \cup (K-K) \in t)$$

$$= \sum_{\alpha=0}^{|i|} \sum_{t \in i_\alpha} (-1)^{\alpha} F(j \cup t) = Q([i,j']) .$$

Corollary 1: Q is finitely additive on M .

Proof: Let $[i,j'] = \cup_{k=1}^{n} [i_k,j_k']$ be a disjoint union and without loss of generality, assume that none of these intervals is empty. Consider the canonical partitions $\underline{P}_k$ and $\underline{P}$ .Then, $\sum_{k=1}^{n} Q(i_k,j_k'] = \sum_{k=1}^{n} Q(\cup_{I \in \underline{P}_k} I)$

$$= \sum_{k=1}^{n} \sum_{I \in \underline{P}_k} Q(I) = \sum_{i \in \underline{P}} Q(I) = Q([i,j']) .$$

A.4. **Proof that F defined in example 6 c) is a GDF** . Take note that

$$\sum_{\alpha=0}^{|i|} (-1)^{\alpha} \sum_{t \in i_\alpha} 1 = \sum_{\alpha=0}^{|i|} (-1)^{\alpha} \begin{bmatrix} |i| \\ \alpha \end{bmatrix} = 0 \text{ for } |i| \geq 1 .$$

Then, $Q([i,j']) = \sum_{\alpha=0}^{|i|} (-1)^{\alpha} \sum_{t \in i_\alpha} F((t \cup j)')$

$$= \sum_{\alpha=0}^{|i|} (-1)^{\alpha} \sum_{t \in i_\alpha} (1 - \max \{f(\theta) : \theta \in t \cup j\}$$

$$= \sum_{\alpha=0}^{|i|} (-1)^{\alpha+1} \sum_{t \in i_\alpha} \max \{f(\theta) : \theta \in t \cup j\} .$$

Since $Q([\phi,j']) = 1 - \max_j f \geq 0$ and

$$Q([\{x\},j']) = - \max_j f + \max_{j \cup \{x\}} f \geq 0 ,$$

the proof that $Q([i,j'])$ is non-negative can be completed by induction on the cardinality of i . Thus suppose that

$$Q([i,j']) \geq 0 \text{ for } |i| \leq n \text{ and all } j .$$

As above, for $x \in I' \cap j'$,

$$Q([i \cup \{x\},j']) = Q([i,j']) - Q([i,(j \cup \{x\})']) .$$

Using F makes this equal

$$\sum_{\alpha=0}^{|i|} (-1)^{\alpha} \sum_{t \in i_\alpha} \{\max_{t \cup j \cup \{x\}} f - \max_{t \in j} f\} . \quad (***)$$

i) If $f(y) \geq f(x)$ for some $y \in j$,

$$\max_{t \cup j \in \{x\}} f - \max_{t \cup j} f = 0 \text{ for all } t$$

and so also the sums in (***).

ii) Otherwise, $f(y) < f(x)$ for all $y \in j$. Now take

$$A = \{a \in I : f(a) \geq f(x)\} ;$$

let A_h be its subsets of size h. If $A = i$, the sum in (***) is zero; otherwise, $|i - A| \geq 1$. Then the sum in (***) becomes

$$\sum_{\alpha=0}^{|i|} (-1)^{\alpha} \sum_{h=0}^{\alpha} \sum_{t \in (i-A)_{\alpha-h}} \sum_{s \in A_h} \{\max_{t \cup j \cup s \cup \{x\}} f - \max_{t \cup j \cup s} f\} .$$

If any s is not empty, $\max_{t \cup j \cup s \cup \{x\}} f - \max_{t \cup j \cup s} f = 0$ and so also the sums in (***).

Otherwise, the last sum reduces to

$$\sum_{\alpha=0}^{|i|-|A|} (-1)^{\alpha} \sum_{t \in (i-A)_{\alpha}} \{f(x) - \max_{t \cup j} f\}$$

$$= \sum_{\alpha=0}^{|i|-|A|} (-1)^{\alpha+1} \sum_{t \in (i-A)_{\alpha}} \max_{t} f = Q([(i\_a),j']) \geq 0 .$$

A.5. **Comments about Choquet capacities in the Bayesian frame.**

The domain $\mathcal{K}$ of T (that is, $\mathcal{K}'$ of F) is extended to $P(\mathcal{R})$ as follows:

$$\text{if } a \in \mathcal{G}, T^*(a) = \sup\{T(k) : K \in \mathcal{K}, K \leq a\} ;$$

$$\text{if } b \in P(\mathcal{R}), T^*(b) = \inf\{T^*(a) : a \in \mathcal{G}, a \geq b\} .$$

It can be shown that T^* on $P(\mathcal{R})$ is a Choquet capacity, alternating, of infinite order; that is,

i) for all $a, b \in P(\mathcal{R})$, if $a \leq b$, then $T^*(a) \leq T^*(b)$;

ii) if the sequence $a_n \in P(\mathcal{R})$ increases to a in $P(\mathcal{R})$, then $T^*(a_n) \uparrow T^*(a)$;

iii) if the sequence $K_n \in P(\mathcal{R})$ decreases to $K \in P(\mathcal{R})$, then $T^*(K_n) \downarrow T^*(K)$;

iv) if in the "φ" functions in the Theorem of section 3.5 above, K's are replaced by a's $\in P(\mathcal{R})$ and T is replaced by T^*, then for all $n \geq 1$, the new $\varphi_n \geq 0$.

To show that F(b) can be defined for $b \in \mathcal{B}$, we use the concept of "T^*-capacitable", ala' Meyer (1966), and similar to the concept of regular Radon measures on $[\mathcal{R}, \mathcal{B}]$.

Then, $\cup_n[\phi,a_n'] \leq [\phi,b'] \leq [\phi,\wedge_n K_n'] = \cap_n[\phi,K_n'] \in \sigma(\mathcal{F})$.

Also, since $Q([\phi,a_n']) = 1 - T^*(a_n)$,

$$Q([\phi,\wedge_n K_n']) = \lim_{n\to\infty} Q([\phi,K_n']) = 1 - T^*(b),$$

$$Q(\cup_n[\phi,a_n']) = \lim_{n\to\infty} Q([\phi,a_n']) = 1 - T^*(b).$$

Thus, when $\sigma(\mathcal{F})$ is completed to $\tilde{\sigma}(\mathcal{F})$ which is the set of

$$A \in P(\mathcal{F}) \text{ such that for some } A_1, A_2 \in \sigma(\mathcal{F}),$$

$$A_1 \leq A \leq A_2 \text{ and } Q(A_2 - A_1) = 0,$$

it follows that $[\phi,b] \in \tilde{\sigma}(\mathcal{F})$ for all $b \in \mathcal{B}$.

The measure Q on $\sigma(\mathcal{F})$ is extended to $\tilde{Q}$ on $\tilde{\sigma}(F)$ as usual by setting $\tilde{Q}(A) = Q(A_1)$ since the latter value is independent of the choice of A_1.

References

1. Bonissone, P. and Decker, K.S. (1985) Selecting uncertainty calculi and granularity: an experiment in trading off precision and complexity, *UCLA Workshop on Uncertainty and Probability in Artificial Intelligence*, 57-66.

2. Dalkey, N.C. (1985) Inductive inference and the representation of uncertainty, *UCLA Workshop in Uncertainty and Probability in Artificial Intelligence*, 109-116.

3. Debreu, G. (1967) Integration of correspondences, *Fifth Berkeley Symposium Math. Statist. and Prob.* (2), Univ. Cal. 351-372.

4. Dubois, D. and Prade, H. (1989) Measure-free conditioning, probability, and non-monotonic reasoning, *Proceedings Eleventh Inter. Joint Conference in Artificial Intelligence*, Detroit, 126-158.

5. Dempster, A.P. (1967) Upper and lower probabilities induced by a multi-valued mapping, *Ann. Math. Statist.* 325-339.

6. Fagin, R. and Halpern, J.Y. (1989) Updating beliefs versus conditioning beliefs, Unpublished report.

7. Ferguson, T.S. (1973) A Bayesian analysis of some nonparametric problems, *Ann. Statist.* (1), 209-230.

8. Gil, M.A. (1988) On the loss of information due to fuzziness in experimental observations, *Ann. Inst. Statist. Math.* (40), 627-639.

9. Goodman, I.R. and Nguyen, H.T. (1985). *Uncertainty models for Knowledge-based Systems*, North-Holland, Amsterdam.

10. Goodman, I.R., Nguyen, H.T. and E.A. Walker (1990) *Conditional Inference and Logic for Intelligent Systems: A theory of measure-free conditioning*, North-Holland, to appear.

11. Goodman, I.R., Nguyen, H.T. and Rogers, G.S. (1989) On the scoring approach to admissibility of uncertainty measures in expert systems, *J. Math. Anal. and Appl.*, to appear.

12. Hajek, J. (1981) *Sampling from a finite population*. Marcel Dekker, New York.

13. Henkind, S.J. and Harrison, M.C. (1988) An analysis of four uncertainty calculi, *IEEE Trans. Syst. Man. and Cybern.* (18), 700-714.

14. Huber, P.J. and Strassen, V. (1973) Minimax tests and the Neyman-Pearson lemma for capacities, *Ann. Statist.* (1) 251-263.

15. Huber, P.J. (1981) *Robust Statistics*, Wiley and Sons, New York.

16. Kendall, D.G. (1974) Foundations of a theory of random sets, in *Stochastic Geometry*, E.F. Harding and D.G. Kendall eds., Wiley and Sons, New York, 322-376.

17. Khr, G.J. and Folger, T.A. (1988) *Fuzzy Sets, Uncertainty and Information*, Prentice Hall, New Jersey.

18. Kruse, R. and Meyer, K.D. (1987) *Statistics with Vague Data*, D. Reidel, Dordrecht.

19. Kyburg, H.E. (1987) Bayesian and Non-Bayesian updating, *Art. Intell.* (31), 271-2293.

20. Lauritzen, S.L. and Spiegelhalter, D.J. (1988) Local computations with probabilities on graphical structures and their applications to expert systems, *J. Roy. Statist. Soc. B* (50), 157-224.

21. Matheron, G. (1975) *Random Sets and Integral Geometry*, Wiley and Sons, New York.

22. Meyer, P.A. (1966) *Probability and Potentials*, Blaisdell, Waltham.

23. Neapolitan, R.E. (1990) *Probabilistic Reasoning in Expert Systems*, J. Wiley.

24. Neveu, J. (1965) *Mathematical Foundations of the Calculus of Probability*, Holden-Day, San Francisco.

25. Nguyen, H.T. (1978) On random sets and belief functions, *J. Math. Anal. and Appl.*, pp 531-542.

26. Nguyen, H.T. and Rogers, G.S. (1991) (This Volume) Conditioning operators in a logic of conditionals.

27. Nober, T. (1984) Convergence and existence of random set distributions, *Ann. Probab.* (12), 726-732.

28. Pearl, J. (1988) *Probability Reasoning in Intelligent Systems*, Morgan Kaufman, San Mateo.

29. Pearl, J. (1990) Reasoning with Belief Functions: An Analysis of Compatibility, to appear in *International Journal of Approx. Reasoning*.

30. Planchet, B. (1989) Credibility and conditioning, *J. Theory Probab.* (2), 289-299.

31. Press, S.J. (1989) *Bayesian Statistics: Principles, Models, and Applications*, Wiley and Sons, New York.

32. Preston, C.J. (1974) *Gibbs States on Countable Sets*, Cambridge University Press, London.

33. Rényi, A. (1970) *Foundations of Probability*, Holden-Day, San Francisco.

34. Robbins, H.E. (1944) On the measure of a random set, *Ann. Math. Statist.* (15), 70-74.

35. Shafer, G. (1976) *A Mathematical Theory of Evidence*, Princeton University Press, New Jersey.

36. Shafer, G. (1979) Allocations of probability, *Ann. Probab.* (17), 827-839.

37. Shafer, G., Shenoy, P.P. and Mellouli, K. (1987) Propogating belief functions in qualitative Markov trees, *J. Approx. Reasoning* (1), 349-400.

38. Walley, P. (1987) Belief functtion representations of statistical evidence, *Ann. Statist.* (15), 1439-1465.

39. Wasserman, L.A. (1987) *Some applications of belief functions to statistical inference*, PhD Thesis, University of Toronto.

40. Wasserman, L.A. (1989) A robust Bayesian interpretation of likelihood regions, *Ann. Statist.* (17), 1387-1393.

41. Zadeh, L.A. (1984) The role of fuzzy logic in the management of uncertainty in expert systems, *J. Fuzzy Sets and Syst.* (11), 199-227.